FORTUNES
FIDDLES &
FRIED CHICKEN

Bill Carey
December 2001

FORTUNES
FIDDLES &
FRIED CHICKEN
A Nashville Business History

BILL CAREY

HILLSBORO PRESS
Franklin, Tennessee

TENNESSEE HERITAGE LIBRARY

Printed in the United States of America

0 4   0 3   0 2   0 1   2   3   4   5

Library of Congress Catalog Card Number: 00-105740

ISBN: 1-57736-178-4

Cover design by Gary Bozeman
Cover photo of Nashville cityscape courtesy of Ed Fulcher.
Credits for other cover photos appear with the photos in the text
Author photo courtesy of Visual Impact Photography.

HILLSBORO PRESS
PROVIDENCE HOUSE PUBLISHERS
238 Seaboard Lane • Franklin, Tennessee 37067
800-321-5692
www.providencehouse.com

To
LOUISE DEMPSEY CAREY

CONTENTS

The study of history is a curious thing. If you were to read every history book ever written, you might come away with images of a world dominated by politicians, wars, and natural disasters. The most important people in the lives of millions of Americans, however, are neither presidents nor generals. They are the people who determine when they work, how much money they make, what they spend most of their time doing, and in many cases where they live. They are employers.

It is almost impossible to overstate the role business has played on Nashville's landscape since the Civil War. In the late nineteenth century, the city had two main identities: a distribution hub (thanks to the Louisville & Nashville Railroad) and a center of refined culture (thanks in part to several religious publishing houses). In the early part of the twentieth century, Nashville became the Wall Street of the South because of a municipal bond house called Caldwell & Co. In the middle of the century, Nashville became an insurance town, a center for country music, and a major tourist destination, largely on the back of the National Life & Accident Insurance Co. At the end of the century, Nashville became a center of for-profit health care because of Hospital Corporation of America.

This is the story of how some of Nashville's citizens started and ran their own businesses. However, the purpose of this book is not just to recount entertaining anecdotes about people like Joel Cheek, Cornelius Craig, Horace Hill, Richard Boyd, and Silliman Evans. It is to remind people how they started with little and took big chances along the way. It is to explain how they beat the competition and how they lost to the competition. It is to talk about the wise decisions they made, the mistakes they almost made, and the mistakes they did make. It is to examine the role that idiosyncrasy, nepotism, friendship, and religious faith played in their decisions.

The Massey Foundation became involved in this project two years ago when I asked it to help me research a book on Nashville business history. Although the Massey Foundation was the largest supporter of my work, other contributors included the Shayne Foundation and Nelson Capital Corp. Under the terms of all three contributions, the donors agreed not to interfere with the contents of my book—which meant I was free to write what I thought was appropriate. After securing funds, I spent fifteen months working on this project at an office provided by the Massey School of Business at Belmont University. My work produced three things: a source list that will aid other historians, a collection of about 150 recorded interviews that will eventually become the property of Belmont, and the book you hold in your hands.

I hope this book adds to Nashville's sense of community and sense of identity. I hope that as people read the stories of entities such as Genesco, the United Methodist Publishing House, and the Nashville Bridge Co. they will become more proud of their hometown. I hope that this book will encourage businesses to hold on to their old documents and photographs rather than throw them away, as has been done too often before. But most importantly, I hope that this book helps the entrepreneurs and executives of the twenty-first century to avoid the mistakes of the past.

This book is the product of fifteen months of research and writing. I could not have done it without the support of several institutions and friends.

First of all, I could not have written this book without financial support from three organizations whose principals were broad-minded enough to see that the book and the oral history collection would be good for the community and courageous enough to give me creative freedom. Those three entities were as follows:

The Massey Foundation. Special thanks to the four trustees of the Massey Foundation: Alyne Queener Massey, Barbara Massey Rogers, Clarence Edmonds, and J. Bradbury Reed.

The Shayne Foundation. Special thanks to Herb Shayne and Jon Shayne.

Nelson Capital. Special thanks to Edward G. Nelson.

For other forms of support, I thank:

The Massey School of Business at Belmont University, which gave me a place to work, a computer, and a phone. Special thanks to James Clapper, Richard Lutz, Jennie Bowman, Linda Jenkins, Byron Hunter, Ashley McAnulty, and Robert Dillingham.

The *Tennessean*, which allowed me to use its library during my research and paid most of the cost of my health care during my leave of absence. Special thanks to Frank Sutherland, Annette Morrison, Nancy St. Cyr, Glynda Washam, Perry Baggs, Evelyn Atzlinger, Chantay Steptoe, and Jonathan Dees.

The Nashville Room of the downtown public library. Special credit goes to Mary Glenn Hearne, Carol Kaplan, Louise Cox, and Debbie May.

The Metro Archives. Special thanks to Ken Fieth, Debbie Cox, and Virginia Lyle.

The Tennessee State Library and Archives. Special thanks to Karina McDaniel, Wayne Moore, and Ann Alley.

Vanderbilt University, whose libraries I used extensively.

Several people whom I interviewed loaned me books, photographs, annual reports, and other materials to help me research the book. Among them were Ashley Levi, Joy Young, Amon Carter Evans, Claire McCall, A. J. Dyer III, Wilbur Creighton Jr., Lemuel Stevens Jr., Bill Wire, Barry Walker, Bill Farris, Julian Kottler, Victor Johnson Jr., Ashley McAnulty, Bert Mathews, Barbara Massey Rogers, Richard LaRoche Jr., and Andrew Miller.

Several fellow historians (professional and otherwise) helped me with ideas of how to research the book. They included Don Doyle, Ridley Wills II, John Hardcastle, Wilbur Creighton Jr., John Egerton, David Carlton, John Seigenthaler, Edward G. Nelson, and Tony Martin.

Several other people helped me by proofreading chapters as I went along. Among them were J. Bradbury Reed, E. Thomas Wood, Nicki Pendleton Wood, Stephen F. Wood Sr., Richard L. Fulton, Paula Lovell, Jon Shayne, Keith Jordan, Donna Perrett, Emme Nelson Baxter, Rick Locker, Tom Humphrey, and Terry Clements.

I thank friends who supported me during the endeavor: David A. Fox, E. Thomas Wood, Nicki Pendleton Wood, Adrienne Outlaw, Emme Nelson Baxter, and Ross Edwards.

I thank several people for helping me to become a better writer: David Lowe, Sandra Shipman, Avis Satterfield, and Mary Sedenquist.

Finally, special thanks go to my wife, Andrea Perrett Carey, for her continuing support and encouragement through many months of research and writing this book.

CHAPTER 1

Tradition vs. Progress

Nashville, Tennessee—which would invent country music and for-profit health care, play a major role in the development of publishing, fast food, and advertising, and dominate the South's banking and insurance industries—began the twentieth century with an inferiority complex.

In 1900, business leaders were not content with Nashville's economy and were trying hard to turn the city into a major manufacturing center. They also wanted Nashville to be big and keep pace with Atlanta. When the census showed that Nashville had only grown from about seventy-five thousand people in 1890 to about eighty-one thousand just ten years later, city leaders were indignant. The Chamber of Commerce demanded a recount.

The reason for this discontentment was that by standards of the time, Nashville's economy appeared to be falling behind. While places like Atlanta and Birmingham were luring huge amounts of heavy industry, Nashville had only the most basic manufacturers that sawed trees into lumber, ground wheat into flour, heated mud into bricks, and melted iron into stoves. Factories that required skilled labor were few. Entrepreneurs who tried to make something besides the most basic products had to overcome the fact that the city had a reputation—even among its residents—for making junk. When the Nashville Manufacturers Association had its first meeting in 1895, several local companies complained about this. Henry Buttorff, who owned the city's largest iron foundry, said he once tried to sell lamps made by his company to customers in Nashville. After he failed, he hired a salesman

from out of town who went to the exact same stores with the exact same lamps. Under the mistaken impression that the lamps were made elsewhere, merchants started buying them.

One thing that Nashville's business leaders didn't think was helping their city was Old South sentimentality—something very prevalent in a city that in many ways hadn't changed much since the Civil War. With neighborhoods such as Edgefield, religious structures such as the Vine Street Temple, historic mansions such as Polk Place, Belmont, and The Hermitage, and a state capitol that by many accounts was the nation's finest, Nashville had nearly as much to offer architecturally as New Orleans, Charleston, or Savannah. Nashville still had the charming feel of a town where everyone knew everyone else. Hundreds of households still publicized the evenings that they "received" guests into their homes. If an out-of-town guest visited a friend or relative, the newspaper would mention it in its gossip columns. It was possible to walk from the western edge of the city at Vanderbilt University to the eastern edge of the populated area in Edgefield. The tallest structures on the Nashville skyline were the state capitol, church steeples, and water towers. Davidson County still had over three thousand farms.

One way to tell whether a person was a business progressive or an Old South sentimentalist was to find out what nickname for Nashville they used. For as long as anyone could remember, Nashville had gone by the nickname Rock City (in honor of the rocky soil in what eventually became Nashville's downtown). At the turn of the century, most traditionalists referred to Nashville as the Athens of the South (in honor of Nashville's many colleges). Many businessmen preferred Minneapolis of the South (in honor of Nashville's number one export—flour). It would be decades before the phrase Music City U.S.A. appeared in the local vocabulary.

The struggle between traditional and progressive Nashville was perhaps best symbolized by two debates that took place at the turn of the century.

In 1900, the home of former president James K. Polk stood at the corner of Seventh Avenue and Church Street. After the death of Mrs. Polk in 1891, no one knew what to do with Polk Place. It was located in an area where mansions were quickly giving way to stores and offices, but the building and the property were considered sacred by Nashville's older citizens. During her four decades as a widow, Mrs. Polk had frequently entertained dignitaries at her home. When the Union army invaded Nashville in 1862, one of the first things Gen. Ulysses S. Grant did was pay his respects to Mrs. Polk. When President Grover Cleveland came to town in 1887, he visited Mrs. Polk and laid a wreath at the grave of her late husband.

Polk, who died in 1849, made it clear what he wanted done. In his will, Polk said he wanted his mansion and the grounds surrounding it to become the property of the state of Tennessee and specified that it never be sold to strangers. He also specifically wrote that the state "shall not permit the tomb to be moved . . . nor shall any building or other improvements be placed or erected over the spot."[1]

Unfortunately, Polk did not have a lawyer look over his will before he wrote it. Tennessee law did not allow wills to create a trust that reached into the infinite future. After the death of Mrs. Polk, her many nieces and nephews—hoping to inherit something from their famous uncle—successfully challenged President Polk's will on the grounds that it was invalid.

Since Tennessee's governor had no place to live at that time, many citizens advocated turning Polk Place into the governor's mansion. "Men who are elected to hold the office of Chief Executive should not have to live in hotels or boarding houses," the *Chattanooga News* opined.[2] The state, however, made a different choice. The legislature passed a resolution authorizing Polk Place to be sold and the bodies of President and Mrs. Polk to be dug up and buried on the capitol grounds.

In 1893, the president who specifically said he never wanted to be dug up and moved was dug up and moved. A few years later, after a long legal battle, the court sold Polk Place to a real estate developer named Dan Buntin and a Louisville & Nashville Railroad executive named Craig McLanahan. The pair tore down Polk Place and built an apartment building there in 1904. McLanahan later donated part of the Polk Place property to the city for use as a public library. The city was so grateful that it placed a plaque in his honor on the library wall.

The other symbolic downtown debate had to do with street names. In 1900, roads oriented north/south in Nashville had names like Front, Market, Cherry, and Vine. A councilman named Ed Wrenne thought this was too old-fashioned and proposed a bill to change the street names to numbered avenues. "The size of the city and its future growth demand this change," Wrenne said. "The present names are meaningless, and the reform will facilitate the citizen and stranger in finding their way."[3] Wrenne's bill was passed with three dissenting votes in December 1904. It did not receive much media attention because the council was also considering a bill that would have required separate streetcars for African Americans. Four years later, a women's civic group called the Centennial Club tried to have the street names changed back, but the attempt failed.

In their attempts to bring more industry to Nashville, the city's business leaders had five major points to boast about. The first was the presence of religious book publishing. Founded in 1854, the Southern Methodist Publishing House brought to Nashville well-educated writers and skilled craftsmen. It produced a university called Vanderbilt and helped recruit other religious publishers to town such as the Baptist Sunday School Board and the National Baptist Publishing Board. Thanks to the Southern Methodist Publishing House, people from all over the South read not only Sunday school publications that were made in Nashville, but also a highly influential regional newspaper called the *Christian Advocate* that had a circulation of seventy thousand in 1890.

The second feature that distinguished Nashville was its designation as the state capital. In addition to providing the city with an architectural gem, state government brought many people to town who stayed and became important. One example of this phenomenon was a young man from Giles County named Cornelius Abernathy Craig. After spending a couple of years learning about the insurance industry as an employee in the Department of Commerce and Insurance, C. A. Craig bought a small insurance company at auction and renamed it. That business, the National Life & Accident Insurance Co., became the most important firm in Nashville history. Not only did it become one of the city's largest and most reliable employers, it would eventually produce a bank (Third National), a radio station (WSM), a regional art form (country music), and a tourism industry (centered on Opryland).

The third benefit of the city was a thriving grocery wholesaling business. Grocery wholesalers—and there were dozens of them in Nashville between 1870 and 1920—turned Nashville into the traveling salesman capital of the South. An amiable young man with some education could land a job as a traveling salesman for a grocery wholesaler, a profession known as "drummer" because it was their business to "drum up" business from mom-and-pop grocers. The downside to being a drummer was that one had to take a train or steamboat out of town Monday morning and did not come back until Friday. The good side was that it was interesting and gave one a chance to learn a business and meet people. James Caldwell, Oscar Noel, Charles Nelson, and Joel Cheek—who would make their fortunes in telecommunications, flour, whiskey, and coffee, respectively—all started as grocery drummers. Another man who got his start as a wholesale drummer for a Nashville company was Luther Turner, who would one day help his son Cal Turner start a business in Scottsville, Kentucky, called Dollar General. By 1910, a Chamber-of-Commerce-sponsored book estimated that there were fourteen hundred traveling salesmen in Nashville.

The Nashville skyline, around 1910 (A. J. Dyer III).

The presence of several colleges and universities was also a great benefit to the city. Out West End Avenue was Vanderbilt University, founded by the Southern Methodist Church in 1874. Adjacent to Vanderbilt was Roger Williams University, a school for African

Americans that had been started after the Civil War by the northern wing of the Baptist church. In North Nashville, there were two more schools for blacks—Fisk University, which was built on what was once a Union army camp, and Walden University/Meharry Medical College. East Nashville, which narrowly missed getting Vanderbilt University, had an institution called Boscobel College. There were also several schools for well-bred young ladies, including Ward's Seminary (downtown), St. Cecilia (North Nashville), and Belmont Collegiate and Preparatory School.

No part of town had more of a concentration of schools than the hill just south of downtown, called College Hill. At the top of College Hill were Vanderbilt Medical School, Peabody Normal College, and a secondary school for young men called Montgomery Bell Academy. All three would move shortly after the turn of the century.

Probably the most important thing Nashville had was the railroad hub. In 1900, it was almost impossible to get from midwestern cities like Chicago and Cincinnati to Birmingham and Chattanooga without going through Nashville—the hub of the Louisville & Nashville (L&N) Railroad. It is almost impossible to overstate the power that L&N once had in Nashville. Later in the twentieth century, goods would come and go on trucks, and people would come and go by means of car or airplane. But between 1880 and 1930, trucks, cars, and airplanes were not a factor as far as commerce and regular passenger movement was concerned. Trains ruled. And in Nashville, that meant L&N.

L&N, as its name implies, started as a single line connecting Louisville and Nashville in 1858. In its early years, L&N was one of several railroads serving Nashville. Among the more important competitors were the Nashville & Chattanooga and the Nashville & Decatur.

Nashville's first experience as a railroad hub came during the Civil War, when the Union army used Nashville as a staging area, equipment warehouse, and place to care for sick and injured soldiers. After the Civil War, many southern railroads were in financial trouble because there wasn't much freight to carry to or from the South immediately following the war. However, L&N was healthier than some of its competitors because its north/south route had been so profitable during the war (thanks to the Union army) and because its tracks had emerged from the war in relatively good physical condition. During the decades following the war, L&N acquired every other railroad that served Nashville. The first of those takeovers took place in 1872, when L&N took over the Nashville & Decatur. The most important was in 1880, when L&N bought controlling stock in the Nashville, Chattanooga & St. Louis.

By 1884, L&N had 2,348 miles of track. The only railroad that could even be compared to L&N in terms of power was the Southern Railway, which had a similar network east of the Appalachians with Atlanta as its hub. Rather than compete against each other, L&N and Southern respected each other's territory.

Many Nashville residents grew to detest the powerful L&N. The "octopus," as it became known, had a monopoly on the city's commerce and could get whatever it wanted from the city council and the state legislature. It controlled both the *Banner* and the *American* newspapers and got nothing but favorable coverage from both. But the most important reason that some Nashville residents disliked L&N was because of its rate structure. Simply stated, it cost more money to ship goods in and out of Nashville than it did to ship the same goods in and out of northern railroad hubs.

Despite this perception, Nashville's business community benefited greatly from L&N Railroad. Nashville's freight rates may have been higher than those experienced in northern hubs like Chicago and Cleveland due to the fact that northern train systems were more congested than the more rural southern routes. But Nashville's rates were lower than the freight rates to places like Murfreesboro, Jackson, and Columbia since, unlike those cities, Nashville was the hub. Because of the hub, Nashville was the place to take products off the train in bulk, repackage them in smaller quantities, and put them back on the train. And it was because of these lower freight rates that Nashville became a logical place for activities like flour milling, coffee distribution, and meat packing.

At the turn of the century, L&N could also point to two concrete examples of its benevolence to the community. One was the construction, started in 1897, of a marvelous and ornate structure called Union Station. The other was its financial support of the Centennial Exposition, an event that an entire generation of Nashville residents would remember with fondness.

Expositions would eventually lose their luster, as airline travel and television made the world a smaller place. But in the late nineteenth century expositions were enormous events that could best be described as part theme park, part science fair, and part museum. For many Americans, a trip to the Philadelphia Exposition of 1876 or the Chicago Exposition of 1893 was the most wonderful experience of their lives. At expositions, many people were first exposed to inventions such as the telephone and the automobile.

Since Tennessee had become a state in 1796, the Centennial Exposition was supposed to be held in 1896. But a combination of hard economic times and statewide sectional jealousies left the plans for the event in tatters in 1895. The exposition might not have happened at all had a young lawyer named Tully Brown not made a dramatic speech at public meeting at the Ryman Auditorium in favor of the event. Two weeks after Brown's speech, the Centennial Company was organized and fund-raising was in full gear. By the end of the summer, the company selected a horse track called West Side Park as the site.

The Chicago Exposition of 1893 had featured a utopian White City, complete with neoclassical architecture and radial boulevards. Planners of Nashville's Centennial Exposition decided to do something similar. The Tennessee centennial featured thirty-four classical buildings filled with exhibits. Among those structures were the Machinery Building, the Agriculture Building, the Negro Building, the Woman's Building, and the Fine Arts Building, which was built as an exact replica of the Greek Parthenon. The exposition also featured shows, rides, and exotic animals. At night, it was lit by ten thousand lights, which must have been a stunning sight in an era when many people did not have electricity. "To us, the exposition was a fairyland," one visitor said later.[4] This was the first exposition occasion on which outsiders had visited Nashville in large numbers since the Civil War, and it brought 1.8 million people to Nashville at a time when the city's population was less than one hundred thousand.

Regardless of L&N's influence, some of Nashville's business leaders struggled against the company. The most dramatic effort in this regard was the ill-fated Tennessee Central Railroad. The Tennessee Central was the brainchild of zealous real estate promoter Jere Baxter, who in 1893 began raising money for a new railroad to link Nashville with Memphis and Knoxville.

Baxter had to overcome a number of obstacles. The financial panic of 1893 temporarily bankrupted his venture, forcing him to look for investors as far away as St. Louis. Nevertheless, the Tennessee Central began laying track in 1895. Baxter then turned his attention from the financial side of the equation to the political side. As L&N began construction of its ornate Union Station, he began lobbying the state legislature and the city council for the right to share it with L&N.

Baxter failed to get access to Union Station, in part because L&N had allegedly bribed state legislators with free passenger passes. But in 1901, he convinced Nashville's residents to vote by referendum to contribute $1 million in tax revenue to Tennessee Central stock.

The next year, the Tennessee Central's eastern leg was completed. With fifteen thousand Nashville residents lining the tracks or waiting at the terminal, Baxter gloriously rode into town. By that time, he was talking about building a huge train station for the Tennessee Central near where Broad Street met the Cumberland River. The Tennessee Central had also started on its western leg, which the company was forced by court order to build in a circuitous route around the city.

However, L&N was already making a countermove to solidify its train gulch as Nashville's commercial center—constructing an enormous warehouse complex south of Union Station called Cummins Station.

No one will ever know if Baxter could have defeated L&N because in 1904 he died of kidney disease at the age of fifty-four. Nevertheless, the Tennessee Central Railroad and its riverfront station eventually became reality. From the 1920s until the 1960s, the Tennessee Central operated out of Nashville primarily as a passenger line linking Nashville with other points in the state. After the decline of railroads, the awkward route that the courts had made the Tennessee Central Railroad use would be turned into Interstate 440.

L&N freight rates were the main reason—in fact, the only reason—Nashville became a major flour milling city. Because of L&N's freight rate structure, it made financial sense to ship grain to Nashville from the Midwest, grind it and package it in Nashville, and then distribute it throughout the South.

One of Nashville's earliest flour mills was built in 1868 at the corner of Market and Elm and given the name Jackson Mills because Andrew Jackson once had a home there. As the mills got larger, they concentrated in two areas: the industrial area north of the courthouse and the area that years later became the fairgrounds. The largest of these in the late nineteenth century were the Noel Mill and Elevator Co. and the American Mill Company, which were owned by brothers Oscar and Edwin Noel. At the turn of the century, flour was Nashville's number one export.

During Nashville's tenure as a milling city, it made one major innovation that gave it a step-up on Atlanta. Self-rising flour had appeared in the Northeast about the time of the Civil War. But at the end of the century, most southerners were still buying flour in its pure form and blending it with yeast and baking soda at home. In 1895, a Nashville firm called the Owsley Milling Company began to mass-produce self-rising flour. Three years later, Owsley was bought by a competitor called Ford Flour Company, which soon began to sell self-rising flour in small packages. Aggressive advertising and tireless efforts by traveling salesmen soon put Owsley Self-Rising Flour on grocery store shelves throughout the South; in 1908 alone, its sale increased by 1,000 percent. Soon, Nashville's grocery wholesalers were producing other brands, including Leonte (made by Hooper Grocery Co.), Pan-Dandy (made by Phillips-Trawick), and Martha White (made by Royal Mills).

Flour milling and blending indirectly created another industry. Nashville's many mills and blending plants needed bags in which to package their products. This demand for bags led to a firm called the Werthan Bag Company.

Nashville's railroad rate advantage was eventually challenged in the courts by a group of other southern cities and was altered. As a result, Nashville's flour milling industry began to disperse in the 1930s. However, the flour blending business remained in the Nashville area for the rest of the twentieth century in the form of a well-known company called Martha White Mills.

An inland city that was at first dependent upon homemade goods, Nashville has a long history of foundries, which heated iron ore into liquid form and shaped it into everything from kitchen utensils to farming equipment. As early as 1830, the city's foundries were producing boilers, bells, waffle irons, and gun mountings. When the Civil War broke out, a foundry called the Claiborne Machine Works, then located just south of the riverfront, was making twenty-five cannons a day for the Rebel army.

The Phillips & Buttorff Manufacturing Co. was founded shortly after the Civil War. At first it specialized in things like pans, buckets, and stove trimmings. In 1881, Phillips & Buttorff moved to a location adjacent to the train tracks in North Nashville—a sign that Buttorff understood the significance of railroads years before some of his competitors. By 1890 Phillips & Buttorff employed four hundred people and made about fifty thousand ranges, stoves, and furnaces per year. By that time, the firm was so important in the community that company president Henry Buttorff was elected the first president of the Nashville Manufacturers Association.

Phillips & Buttorff's foundry eventually grew to one hundred thousand square feet and was considered one of the most modern foundries in the United States. In 1930 alone, the company produced one hundred thousand ranges, stoves, and furnaces, many under the Enterprise brand name. Children knew Phillips & Buttorff's for its showroom that sold everything from wagons to doll trunks.

Gray & Dudley was another foundry with origins just after the Civil War. Around 1880, two well-established hardware retailers named John Gray and Robert Dudley combined their businesses to form what was by the standards of the time a hardware superstore. In 1895, Gray & Dudley sold shares to the public. By the turn of the century, the company was the largest hardware dealer in Middle Tennessee and sold tools, utensils, guns, toys, ornaments, and fishing tackle through a twelve-hundred-page catalog. Its founders did so well that Robert Dudley became mayor of Nashville in the 1890s. Dudley also had several affluent younger siblings, one of whom (Guilford) made a major investment in a start-up insurance company called Life & Casualty in 1903.

Gray & Dudley must have decided that national catalog retailers like Sears would be hard to compete with in the long run, and it chose to switch over to the production side of the business. In 1904, Gray & Dudley built a large foundry at the intersection of Clifton Road and Twenty-third Avenue, across Charlotte Pike from what eventually became Centennial Hospital. About three years later, Gray & Dudley won a contract with the state to build a second foundry in the state penitentiary in West Nashville, a contract that may have been made possible by Mayor Dudley's political connections. Soon, Gray & Dudley was manufacturing stoves under the name Washington in direct competition with Phillips & Buttorff. Gray & Dudley would operate a foundry at the penitentiary until 1937, and according to its records, paid convicts less than half what it paid free laborers.

Work at the Phillips & Buttorff Iron Foundry, around 1900 (A. J. Dyer III).

By the mid-1930s, Gray & Dudley was making more stoves and furnaces than Phillips & Buttorff and shipping two-thirds of them to markets outside of the Southeast. "They were shipped to so many faraway places that my grandfather used to say that the sun never sets on a Washington Stove," said Wilbur Creighton Jr., grandson of Robert Dudley. In 1936, Gray & Dudley's revenues were about $1.9 million.

Although there were several other Nashville foundries, including Allen Manufacturing, Liberty Range Works, and Jake's Foundry, probably the largest was the Kerrigan Iron Works. In the 1940s and 1950s,

Kerrigan was one of the largest manufacturers of steel flooring for bridges and factories in the United States. Years later, Kerrigan's fabricating shed would be converted into a development called the Riverfront Apartments.

Foundries were hot, dirty places to work. In summer, the temperature inside would reach unbearable levels. Most foundry jobs were unskilled, monotonous, and strenuous tasks such as shoveling coal and pouring iron ore into molds. Nevertheless, foundries gave many newcomers to Nashville a way to make a living. They were also the largest employers of African Americans in Nashville. In 1930, about 90 percent of the employees at Jake's Foundry in West Nashville were black.

Eventually, many of Nashville's iron foundries began making other kinds of products such as steel stoves. The complicated nature of the steel stove business led to the creation of several component suppliers. One of the largest of these was the Tennessee Enamel Manufacturing Co., which sold porcelain and enamel parts for Phillips & Buttorff and Gray & Dudley's stove lines in the 1940s and 1950s. Another was an oven shelf factory called the Nashville Wire Products Co., started in 1933 by former Phillips & Buttorff superintendent Clark Rollins.

All one had to do to get a tree from a hardwood forest on the Cumberland Plateau to Nashville was chop it down, lop off its branches, toss it in the Cumberland River, tie it to a raft, and guide it downstream. This time-honored method of transport, combined with Nashville's direct train line to Cincinnati, Chicago, and Detroit, made Nashville a major hardwood market.

From about 1880 until about 1930, Nashville was one of the world's leading producers of hardwood materials. During this era, someone standing near the river downtown could almost always hear the screech of sawmills and smell freshly cut lumber. They could also see two-hundred-foot log rafts lined up for miles on the river, waiting to be taken apart and made into lumber. "I remember logs lined up all the way from downtown to Shelby Park," said Wilbur Creighton Jr., who was born and raised in East Nashville. "We used to walk out onto them and go swimming."

The business of getting wood down the river created the rough and adventuresome occupation of raft rider. It took about six skilled riders five days to bring a raft down from Celina to Nashville. By day, they guided the rafts with several oars and rudders. By night, they slept in lean-to sheds built in the middle of the raft and cooked over a fire that they built on a pile of dirt. It was relaxing work but could be challenging at times. "A raft pilot had to know this old river and know

how she'd be actin' at every stage of water, at every bend and shoal,"
a riverman named Captain Lue Plumlee once said. "And every bend in
the river was a shade different than every other bend."[5]

Raft crews would celebrate their arrival in Nashville much like a
steamboat crew, with a night in places like the Silver Dollar Saloon.
Occasionally, one of the raft men would make it to a more fashionable
address, often causing amusing scenes. One time, an unkempt, smelly
man wandered into the exclusive Maxwell House Hotel. The hotel
staff was about to throw him out when a judge named Cordell Hull
suddenly put his arm around the man and began introducing his
friends to his father.

Many of Nashville's woodworking businesses were simply lumberyards. But others made products, including:

- Prewitt, Spur and Co., which was organized immediately after the
  Civil War. It turned cedar logs into wood buckets and served as a
  major lumberyard for northern factories. By 1890, it had three
  hundred employees.

  Wayne Lumber and Manufacturing Co., which made carriages and
  later automobile parts. It employed four hundred people in 1930.

  The Edgefield & Nashville Manufacturing Co, which was organized
  in 1874 and at its peak employed about two hundred men. It
  produced office furniture and school desks.

  The Nashville Casket Co., which produced so many coffins that in
  1907 the *Banner* proudly reported that "The coffins made in
  Tennessee every year would take care of the demand of all the
  Southeastern states, with enough left to care for most of the dead of
  the Southwest."[6]

  The Nashville Hardwood Flooring Co., founded in 1895 as the first
  factory in the world to specialize in the manufacture of hardwood
  flooring.

Most of the large hardwood companies were located along the river-
bank in Edgefield.

Not much has been written about the working conditions in these
large sawmills and woodworking plants. But in an era before safety
regulations and workers' compensation insurance, workers had to have
a healthy respect for sawblades. One hint of the danger in working at a
lumber plant was given in a 1928 advertisement for Life & Casualty
Insurance Co. For only five dollars per year, L&C would insure someone
for $1,250 for the loss of one hand and $2,500 for the loss of both.

After 1930, Nashville's lumber business declined because many of the products Nashville's factories were making out of wood (carriages, buckets, beer kegs, coffins, and golf clubs) were either no longer in demand or being made out of something else. The city's large wood-working factories were almost all gone by the end of World War II, and most of the structures that housed them were eventually torn down to make way for interstate highways or public housing. One notable exception to this was the Nashville Hardwood Flooring Co. After changing ownership twice, the plant was still in operation in 1998 under the name Bruce Hardwood.

In its attempt to secede from the Union, the Confederacy tried to prove that cotton was king. However, the antebellum South did not make its own clothes but rather shipped cotton in bales to the North by train and to Europe by boat. After the war ended, one of the first actions business leaders in the South took was to develop textile plants in their region to remedy this situation.

In 1869, a dry goods merchant named Samuel Morgan organized Nashville's first large textile business and called it the Tennessee Manufacturing Company. It started with a four-story factory in North Nashville that employed about two hundred women and fifty men. By 1890, it had grown to be one of the largest employers in the city with about eight hundred people.

The success of Tennessee Manufacturing resulted in the formation of other textile plants. Among them were the Nashville Cotton Mills, the Phoenix Cotton Mills, and the National Manufacturing Co. The latter was organized by a young man named Edward Stahlman, who would later become the owner of the *Nashville Banner*. In 1914, a handkerchief factory called Dodd-Comer opened in West Nashville. Years later, it would change its name to Washington Manufacturing and become one of the nation's largest apparel companies.

Like Nashville's foundries, lumberyards, and flour mills, the city's textile plants were enormous facilities surrounded by cheap rental housing. One visitor to the Phoenix Cotton Mills in 1898 was almost mesmerized by his first exposure to the world of manufacturing:

> Passing into the factory, I found myself in a great room with what seemed to me to be acres of machines, whirring and thud-thudding looms, canopies of cotton gossamer in patterns of vivid reds and greens and blues, and, among all these machines and finding their way in the maze of millions of threads, a few men and women who at first sight hardly became any part of the picture itself. . . . Almost at once I was come to the realization that the price of its existence was inseparably linked with the exploitation of the people who

swarmed in the maze of two-room houses that lines the muddy unpaved streets of the slums that surrounded the mill.[7]

In the plants, black workers were often segregated and did some of the more unpleasant jobs, such as drying the socks after they came out of a pit of hot dye.

One of Nashville's largest textile businesses started with an advertisement for prison labor. Jacob May was a German immigrant living in New Hampshire in 1896 when he read in a trade publication that the state of Tennessee was looking for someone to organize a sock factory inside its main penitentiary. May and a man named Leo Kaufman won the contract, moved to Nashville, and built the hosiery mill, becoming one of the first Nashville businesses to learn how to make a profit from prisons.

Eventually May Hosiery moved to Chestnut Street in South Nashville. In 1915, May Hosiery had over one thousand employees and was being run by Jacob's son Dan. In its early years, May Hosiery's main customers were Nashville's dry goods wholesalers. Later the company made socks for retailers such as Montgomery Ward, Woolworth, and K Mart. It also knitted socks for the Boy Scouts and the Girl Scouts. The business was especially profitable during the world wars because of huge orders of socks and metal fuses from the military and because of high apparel prices caused by the shortage of raw materials.

Like many other manufacturers, some of the apparel plants made their homes in the industrial suburb of West Nashville. One of the most important of these was the yarn factory Thomas Henry and Sons. In the 1920s, a wealthy young man from Minnesota bought a majority interest in the Henry yarn factory and moved to Nashville to run it. That man, O. H. Ingram, would later sell the factory and get into the oil business.

Nashville also developed a number of niche products, some of which left nothing behind but an interesting story, but others had a long-term impact. Among them:

Meat—Several of the more successful entrepreneurs in late-nineteenth-century Nashville were German immigrants who came to Nashville by way of Cincinnati. One of them was Henry Neuhoff, who in 1902 opened a slaughterhouse and packing company that soon became famous for producing boneless hams. For an entire generation, the Neuhoff Packing Company was the largest of several meat preparation companies in the area just north of what later became the Bicentennial Mall. In 1930, the business was sold to an Atlanta firm called Swift & Co. for $3.2 million.

Whiskey—In December 1850, fifteen-year-old Charles Nelson was immigrating to America from Germany with his family when the ship on which they were traveling capsized off the coast of New Jersey. Nelson's father drowned, taking with him to the bottom of the sea the family's entire net worth in gold that he carried in a money belt. A few years later, when the Union army occupied Nashville, Charles Nelson moved to Nashville from Cincinnati and went into the grocery wholesaling business. After the war, he built a distillery in the Greenbrier community of Robertson County. Greenbrier Whiskey became enormously successful and operated a distribution warehouse on Market Street.

Beer—Yet another German immigrant with Cincinnati connections was William Gerst. Gerst was the brew master of the Christian-Moerlein Brewers of Cincinnati in 1890 when he bought the old Nashville Breweries and renamed it for himself. Under Gerst's management, the brewery thrived and became the largest brewery in the Southeast—a four-acre building located in South Nashville that made 100,000 barrels of beer per year. Gerst made many types of beer, including Nashville Lager, Old Jug Lager, and Pilsener. During Prohibition, he changed the brewery into a soft-drink manufacturer.

Bricks—A Confederate veteran named William G. Bush founded a brick company along the Cumberland River in Edgefield in 1866. Later, Bush's son-in-law Thomas L. Herbert came into the business and started another brickyard directly across the river. In 1909, the business changed its name to T. L. Herbert and Sons, by which time it had branched off into general contracting. Eventually, Herbert had three brick plants in North Nashville, one in West Tennessee, and a barge line that dredged sand and gravel out of the Tennessee River.

For every business that made money, several failed. Perhaps the most fascinating business failure in Nashville history was the Marathon Motor Works.

Marathon started as a division of a Jackson, Tennessee, company called the Southern Engine & Boiler Works. At the turn of the century, Southern Engine's executives were becoming intrigued with the new horseless carriages that had made appearances at world's fairs and centennial expositions. Sometime around 1905, the company asked one of its engineers, thirty-one-year-old William Collier, to design a car. It wasn't easy. Collier's first gas-operated vehicle "should move, but don't," a company newsletter reported.[8] By 1907, Collier had designed a car that he and the company said was reliable. Backed by new investors, the company set up a car manufacturing division named Marathon in honor of the 1904 Olympic Games.

In 1909, Southern Engine produced about four hundred cars in two different models. At fifteen hundred dollars each, the cars were wildly expensive. But thanks to aggressive advertising, the company was able to sell the cars as they produced them. The next year, Marathon Motor Works split off from Southern Engine and moved to Nashville to be closer to the railroad hub and to wealthy investors. Among the Nashville businessmen who invested in the car factory were Phillips & Buttorff president Henry Buttorff, real estate promoter Johnson Bransford, and lumber magnate John Ransom.

Marathon cars were rolling off the assembly line at the old Phoenix Cotton Mills Building by October 1910. Among the first purchasers of a Marathon were the Nashville Fire Department, Bush Brick Company, and Prewitt, Spur & Co.

A few months later, officials from the state highway department drove three Marathons all the way to Bristol—taking dirt roads the whole way—to start planning a route for Tennessee's new east/west highway (later known as Highway 70).

For the next four years, Nashville's newspapers frequently reported the accomplishments of Marathon Motor Works. In 1911, the company sent a team of cars to the Glidden Tour, a promotional tour of various car types that began in New York and ended in Jacksonville. The next year, investment in the company jumped from $400,000 to $1 million and the company's network of dealerships reached every major city in the country. The company began producing several models, priced between $875 and $1,800. Advertisements for the Marathon appeared in national publications such as the *Saturday Evening Post*.

Nevertheless, the Marathon Motor Works went bankrupt in 1914, when several of the company's creditors sued it for unpaid bills. The reasons for the company's failure were not reported in the newspaper. But it goes without saying that a start-up car company with an enormous advertising budget was a risky venture.

Despite all its efforts, Nashville never developed a manufacturing base as strong as those of Atlanta or Birmingham. The reasons for this were numerous. First, Nashville's leaders were not aggressive in pursuing a manufacturing base until about 1895 and therefore missed the boat. One theory about why this happened is that Nashville survived intact through the Civil War and its citizens were therefore not as anxious to abandon tradition and pursue industry. Atlanta, on the other hand, was laid waste in 1865, and it was clear to everyone there that the city had to rebuild and take on a new image.

Geography also played a role in the growth rate of manufacturing. In the era of the steamboat and the train, the Appalachian Mountains were still a formidable boundary, at least as far as trade was concerned. In the era of the steamboat, Nashville had strong trade with St. Louis and New Orleans. In the era of the train, it also had a direct line to Chicago and St. Louis. But once trains eclipsed steamboats, Atlanta had a linkup with the eastern seaboard and to larger cities like New York and Philadelphia. In 1900, the combined population of New York and Philadelphia was 4.7 million, over twice the combined population of Chicago and St. Louis.

The third factor was availability of raw materials. Central Alabama had better iron ore resources than Middle Tennessee. Grain grew better in the Midwest than in the South. Cotton grew better in Mississippi and Alabama than in Middle Tennessee.

Nevertheless, Nashville's failure to become a huge manufacturing city eventually became a blessing in disguise. Nashville's leaders once envied High Point, North Carolina, for its thirty furniture factories and Birmingham and Chattanooga for their huge iron foundries. However, the residents of High Point never developed anything besides woodworking factories. The air pollution in Birmingham and Chattanooga was so bad that years after the steel industries dried up, those cities had to work hard to shake their image as dirty, grimy places. Rock City, on the other hand, would be comparatively unfettered.

CHAPTER 2

Bishops, Bibles, & Door-to-Door Religion

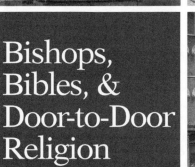

I t is impossible to talk about the business of Nashville without discussing religious publishing. And in order to talk about religious publishing, one has to go back to long before 1900. It all started when a woman died and left a young female slave to the Rev. James Andrew of Oxford, Georgia.

Andrew wasn't just an ordinary country preacher. He was a bishop in the Methodist Episcopal Church. Andrew did not believe in slavery, but the laws of the state of Georgia would not let him free the girl. He offered to send her to Liberia, but she did not want to go. He considered selling her to someone else but did not do it out of a fear that she would end up with an inhumane owner. So he kept her and let her come and go as she pleased.

Because it had many abolitionists in its flock, the Methodist national convention of 1840 considered forcing Andrew to resign his position but chose not to do so. By 1844, two things had changed. One was that Andrew had married a woman who had inherited a slave from her mother, making him the owner of two slaves. The other was that slavery had become a hot national issue because of the possibility of American expansion into Texas and the question of whether to allow slavery there.

On June 1, 1844, the General Conference of the Methodist Episcopal Church voted 110 to 70 to force Bishop Andrew to resign. Within days, Methodist leaders from the South decided they had to form their own separate denomination rather than allow an abolitionist church to minister to thousands of slaves.

It took ten years for the courts to decide how to divide up the money from the Methodist publishing concern, then located in New York and Cincinnati. In 1854, the settlement was finalized in a ruling by the U.S. Supreme Court giving the Southern Methodists the capital to start a new operation.

The Bishops

Had it not been for the Rev. John McFerrin, the Methodists probably wouldn't have chosen Nashville. McFerrin was the editor of a regional Methodist newspaper published in Nashville and a close friend of President James K. Polk. As the denomination considered where to put its publishing arm, McFerrin used his newspaper to argue in favor of Nashville. McFerrin pointed out that New Orleans had "broken levees, deluged streets, deserted mansions, and epidemic diseases." Louisville, he claimed, was a "border town," and "there is not a place in the South or West for which nature has done so much and man so little as the city of Louisville." But in Nashville, "Methodism is decidedly in the ascendant, and Tennessee is a commonwealth of primitive, real camp-meeting Methodists."[1]

Nashville had other things going for it as well. In the three decades prior to 1854, the city had sent two presidents to Washington and was therefore considered the political center of the South. Civic spirit was high because a beautiful new state capitol designed by the renowned Philadelphia architect William Strickland was under construction. The city's economy had also received a boost because of the new Louisville & Nashville Railroad, the first leg of which was then under construction.

Nevertheless, when the General Conference of the new Methodist Episcopal Church, South, considered the question in 1854, Nashville was hardly the unanimous choice. Eight cities petitioned the conference for consideration. On the first ballot, leading vote-getters were Memphis, Louisville, and an industrial suburb of Montgomery called Prattville. One by one, cities were eliminated from the list. On the sixth ballot, Nashville beat out Louisville sixty to fifty-seven.

Nashville's citizens were thrilled. The United States was predominantly a Protestant nation, and the Methodists were the largest Protestant denomination. In a burst of civic enthusiasm, the public raised seventeen thousand dollars toward the publishing house and the local government agreed to exempt it from taxes. Within a few months, a committee of business leaders found a good place for the business: a warehouse situated between the courthouse and the Cumberland River.

The Publishing House of the Methodist Episcopal Church, South, (better known as the Southern Methodist Publishing House) quickly began work producing books and other denominational literature. By the end of its first year in operation, the book concern had 123 employees. In 1855 alone, it published over twenty different books, ranging from a current events book called *Australia and Its Settlements* to a sermon book called *The First Day of the Week*. The concern also published hundreds of small religious tracts and numerous periodicals. The newspaper *Nashville Christian Advocate* was one of the most important publications in the antebellum South. Incredibly, the organization printed every single publication on one- and two-cylinder presses located in the Public Square Building.

As war loomed on the horizon, the Southern Methodist Publishing House was clearly aligned with the Confederacy. After rebels fired on Ft. Sumter, *Nashville Christian Advocate* editor Holland McTyeire advised his readers to "Get ready, for the worst. Our enemies (for so they have defined themselves) are unscrupulous in the means they will resort to, and in the means they aim at."[2] A few months later, the publishing entity came out with the *Confederate States Almanac* for soldiers. The *Almanac* included information about the Confederate government, including the chain of command from President Jefferson Davis on down. It also contained a catalog of books published by the Southern Methodists.

The Union army did not forget this when it marched into Nashville on February 25, 1862. One of the first things the army did was close the publishing concern down. Later, the army used it as a government printing office.

After the war, McFerrin went to Washington and made a personal appeal to President Andrew Johnson to restore the property of the Southern Methodist Publishing House to the church. Johnson granted his request. But when Methodist officials returned to the Public Square Building in June 1866, they found machinery damaged and the stereotype foundry destroyed.

Nevertheless, thousands of books that had been left behind years before were almost all still there, so it took only days to reopen the bookstore. Within months, the Methodist Publishing House was renovated, its presses back at work, and its officers losing sleep about how to pay its seventy-one thousand dollar debt incurred during the war. Although it had toned down its warmongering tendencies, the publishing house was still sectionalist enough to come out with books such as *Lee and His Generals* and *Life of Stonewall Jackson*.

In 1872, a fire damaged the concern's main two buildings. In order to help rebuild the structure, Nashville residents raised thirty-two thousand dollars. There were also donations from elsewhere in the country; McTyeire's wife had a rich cousin named Cornelius Vanderbilt who gave one thousand dollars to the cause.

Throughout Nashville history are examples of large businesses creating other industries, sometimes on purpose, often by accident. When the Louisville & Nashville Railroad made Nashville its southern hub, it created the city's flour and coffee business. When the National Life & Accident Insurance Co. started a radio station, it inadvertently started country music.

Perhaps no event had as much impact on Nashville's economy as the decision by the Southern Methodist Church to create a university in Nashville. Without Vanderbilt University, many of the people who started Nashville companies in the twentieth century might not have come to the city in the first place.

The notion of a Methodist university in Nashville was being discussed as early as the Southern Methodist General Conference of 1854. In the late 1850s, the idea of a central educational institution was mentioned repeatedly in Southern Methodist periodicals. Since those periodicals were written by Nashville residents, Nashville was always mentioned as the best potential location.

There were several schools of thought within the church as to what form the institution should take. Some Southern Methodist leaders favored a theological seminary. Others wanted a central university. In 1872, a commission met in Memphis and adopted a broad resolution calling for an institution in which young men could study theology, literature, and science. Under the resolution, the university needed five hundred thousand dollars to open.

One of the members of that commission was McTyeire, who had been elected to bishop of the Methodist Episcopal Church, South, in 1866. McTyeire was a strong advocate of the university and argued fervently for it in Methodist periodicals. One sign of the openness of the Southern Methodist Church to a healthy debate was the *Nashville Christian Advocate's* many articles by both McTyeire and opponents of establishing a Methodist college.

In February 1873, McTyeire went to New York for two reasons: to have a back operation and to spend time with his wife's relative Cornelius Vanderbilt. McTyeire was in luck. According to one historian, Vanderbilt "was seeking a suitable beneficiary for some of his money, a belated claim to a type of immortality. Sheer emulation of other wealthy men, if nothing else, led him in this direction."[3] Within a few weeks, Vanderbilt had pledged the five hundred thousand dollars, an amount he later increased to about $1 million.

Back in Nashville, McTyeire considered several sites for the university, one of which was in Edgefield. He eventually settled on a hill just off West End Avenue.

Two generations later, Vanderbilt University and the Southern Methodist Church split over the issue of whether the Vanderbilt board of trustees or the church ran the school.

The leaders of the Southern Methodist Publishing House did not revel much in the glory of their new university. By the time Vanderbilt opened, the church had serious financial problems. When the publishing concern rebuilt its Public Square Building after the 1872 fire, the new structure was far larger than the original. Instead of costing $50,000, as had been originally estimated, it cost $176,000. This extravagance was exacerbated by the fact that about half the money had been borrowed at 10 percent interest.

The publishing house had just moved into its new building when an economic depression hit the nation and a yellow fever epidemic hit the South. Real estate values and rental rates plummeted. The book concern found it could only get about half of what it had projected for renting extra space.

The Southern Methodist Publishing House survived the 1870s by soliciting donations from its flock, selling bonds to its members, and cutting its employees' salaries. Because of its economic problems, it also had to drastically reduce the number of books it printed. Despite its troubles, the publishing house's periodicals and newspapers were still widely read, and it even managed to increase the amount of Sunday school publications. Southern Methodists also took some consolation from the fact that at least they did not have a national scandal on their hands. (An investigation in 1870 revealed that the leaders of the Methodist Episcopal Church in New York were involved in all sorts of financial improprieties, the most embarrassing of which had to do with church money going to a house of prostitution.)

Despite financial troubles, the late nineteenth century was in many ways an apex for the Southern Methodist Publishing House and its denomination. At a time when society still adhered to strict Victorian principles, the influence ministers had cannot be overstated. But sometimes, the Methodist Church's strict rules backfired. On October 9, 1887, the influential Rev. Warren Candler, pastor of the McKendree Methodist Church and editor of the *Nashville Christian Advocate*, preached a sermon about the evils of the theater. Emma Abbott, star of a visiting opera company, stood up in the congregation and defended her profession with zeal. The secular *Nashville American* reported the next day that her remarks were followed by "deafening applause." At various times between 1870 and 1930, the Methodist publishing concern also took stands against everything from roller skating to bicycle riding.

It took until 1890 for the Southern Methodist Publishing House to dig its way out of debt. By then, it had grown into a much larger organization than it had been in antebellum Nashville. Thanks in part to the hymnbook of 1889, sales between 1886 and 1890 were $1.2 million, a 25 percent increase from the previous four-year period. The organization actually prospered in the economic depression of the mid-1890s.

Southern Methodist Publishing House finances took an even better turn in 1898. At the end of the Civil War, the publishing concern had filed

The Southern Methodist Publishing House's Public Square headquarters, around 1890 (Tennessee State Library and Archives).

a claim with the federal government for war damages. For years, it did not look as if anything would come of this claim. In 1895, the publishing house hired *Nashville Banner* publisher Edward Stahlman to lobby on its behalf and agreed to pay him 35 percent of whatever sum he could collect. Three years later, Congress voted to give the Southern Methodist Publishing House $288,000 in damages, $100,000 of which went to Stahlman. Several senators criticized Stahlman and the Southern Methodist Publishing House after the settlement, saying they had been led to believe that the entire settlement was going to the church.

In 1899, the publishing house opened its first branch office in Dallas. Seven years later, it moved its Nashville office to 810 Broadway.

At the turn of the century, the Southern Methodist Publishing House was one of the most important organizations in Nashville. Its office had about 120 employees, including pressroom workers, composers, printers, and clerks. Its many periodicals and newspapers—some of which were widely read—frequently spoke out on relevant issues such as woman's suffrage, temperance, organized labor, and evolution.

Relations between the southern and northern arms of the Methodist Church thawed quite a bit during the last few decades of the nineteenth century. In 1905, the publishing arms of the two churches took a major step toward reunion with the publication of a joint hymnal, the production of which proved to be an exercise in compromise. When the hymnbook was released, it was heavily criticized in the rural South because of its exclusion of such old-time classics as "When the Roll Is Called Up Yonder" and "Shall We Gather at the River." Many rural Methodist churches came out with their own hymn booklets as a supplement. But the joint hymnal was a bestseller for both northern and southern publishing arms for two full years and was used by fifteen million people.

American imperialist sentiment was at its height between 1895 and 1910 as made clear by the overwhelming popularity of the

Spanish-American War. At the Southern Methodist Publishing House, this mindset resulted in an emphasis on overseas operations and foreign language texts. The publishing house spent part of its Civil War settlement on a publishing branch in Shanghai, China, which survived until the 1920s. It also printed thousands of books and tracts in Spanish for distribution in Mexico and Cuba.

Another trend that affected the publishing concern was the renewed emphasis on educating children at the turn of the century. The popularity of Sunday school grew enormously during the first few decades of the twentieth century. Mainly because of Sunday school tracts, the revenue of the publishing house rose from $600,000 in 1906 to $2 million in 1920.

At the other end of the spectrum were Methodist newspapers such as the various regional *Christian Advocate* editons. The rising popularity of secular magazines took its toll on the readership of denominational newspapers. Circulation of the *Advocate* fell from about seventy thousand in 1890 to fourteen thousand in 1918. Revenues also were not helped by the fact that the church forbade such publications from accepting advertisements for liquor, beer, and cure-all medicines.

Despite running a small deficit in 1932, the publishing house did quite well during the Great Depression, thanks to the conservative business practices of the 1910s and 1920s and the strength of the Methodist Church in the South. According to Andrew Miller, who worked in the manufacturing division in the 1980s and did considerable research into the history of the Methodist Publishing House, no plant employees were laid off during the depression.

Meanwhile, the northern Methodist Book Concern in New York had its problems, one of them being a new printing plant on the banks of the Hudson River that turned out to be financially disastrous. These financial problems would later turn out to be quite significant for the Southern Methodist publishing concern. During the 1940s, after the denominations merged and combined their printing operations into one organization, the financial strength and stable management of the Southern Methodist Publishing House was one of the reasons Nashville was chosen as the site for the merged Methodist Publishing House.

The Preachers

Like the leaders in the Southern Methodist Church, many Southern Baptists did not care for the national Baptist organization, headquartered in Philadelphia under the name American Baptist Convention. And, like the Methodist Episcopal Church, the national Baptist Church split over the issue of slavery.

However, when the Southern Baptist Convention was organized in the 1840s, it was not nearly as dramatic and clear-cut a split as there had been in the Methodist Episcopal Church. Since the rift had to do with whether missionaries could own slaves, the Southern Baptist Convention was at first organized only for the purpose of domestic and foreign missions. Most Baptist preachers saw no reason to stop buying the literature produced by the American Baptist Publishing Society. After all, Baptist Church literature was more Bible-centered and dwelt less on secular issues than Methodist literature.

Nevertheless, one wing of Southern Baptists wanted to see Baptist literature produced in the South. In 1847, a group of Baptist leaders formed a publication society in Charleston, Virginia, that survived for sixteen years but was wiped out by the Civil War. A few months after its demise, Southern Baptists formed another publication arm in Greenville, South Carolina, that was wiped out by the national economic depression of 1873.

Because of the failure of the two publication societies, it took almost twenty years for Southern Baptists to form another. The key person in this formation was a fiery Baptist preacher named I. T. Tichenor, who resigned as president of Auburn University in 1882 to become head of the Southern Baptist's Home Mission Board. When it came to the idea of a Southern Baptist publishing arm, Tichenor was not above invoking military images in his many speeches. "Shall we attempt it or shall we surrender it to others?"[4] Tichenor once asked about the idea of forming a publishing concern.

Unlike the Methodists, who met quadrennially, the Southern Baptist Convention met annually. At every convention between 1885 and 1890 (none of which were held in Nashville), the idea of a publishing arm was debated and rejected. Finally, the Southern Baptist Convention voted to form a publishing arm called the Baptist Sunday School Board in 1891. Under the proposal, the board's location would be chosen by one of its principal advocates, a man named James Frost.

Frost, the leader of the Sunday School Board from 1891 until his death in 1916, later gave two reasons for his choice of Nashville. One was its central location. The other was the fact that Nashville already had a large printing industry, thanks to the Southern Methodist Publishing House.

The Baptist Sunday School Board wasn't an impressive operation in its early years. It had no money to begin operations and had to borrow five thousand dollars from the First National Bank to get started. During its first two years of existence, its office moved three times, and it only survived because many businesses offered it free office space or equipment. Foremost among these organizations was the Methodist Publishing House, which gave the Baptist Sunday School Board a free office from 1893 until 1897.

Despite the formation of the southern publishing entity, many Southern Baptists were still loyal to the Philadelphia concern. That would change after 1897 when the American Baptist Publication Society sent several of its representatives to the Southern Baptist Convention. One of them attacked the Sunday School Board from the podium. A speech given by one Sunday School Board supporter indicates just how divisive the issue of a separate southern publisher was. "We have our way of doing things," delegate William Hatcher of Virginia stated. "Woe betide the man who crosses our path."[5] Within three years, 80 percent of all Baptist churches in the South were getting their literature from the Baptist Sunday School Board in Nashville.

Baptist Sunday School Board founder James Frost with his secretary, around 1900 (LifeWay Christian Resources).

A few months later, the board bought its first real home, a residence located on Fourth Avenue. The next year it published its first book, a manuscript the American Baptist Publication Society had rejected. During the next few years, the bulk of the Baptist publications were Sunday school tracts, devotional books, periodicals, hymnbooks, and Bibles. The flagship publication of the Baptist Sunday School Board was a Sunday school primer called *Kind Words*.

The Sunday School Board could have set up its own printing operation rather than continuing to hire it out. However, the board chose to use vendors to do its printing—a decision that would remain firm throughout its history. The organization's largest vendor during its first four decades was Nashville printer Marshall & Bruce.

By 1911, the board's revenue had risen to $280,000. It then learned the financial benefits of owning Nashville real estate in a boom time, selling its Church Street office—which it bought in 1903 for $60,000—for $200,000. That sale enabled the board to build a Corinthian-style building, later named for Frost, on Eighth Avenue. A Nashville architect named Russell Hart designed that building. For the rest of the twentieth century, Hart's architectural and engineering firm, which eventually became known as Hart-Freeland-Roberts, designed every major building constructed by the Sunday School Board in Nashville.

Not everyone was thrilled when the Sunday School Board chose longtime board official Isaac Van Ness to succeed Frost in 1917. For one thing, Van Ness was from New Jersey. For another, he did not have the outgoing personality of his predecessor. "Van Ness was most comfortable sitting at his desk editing a transcript," a company history said.[6]

However, Van Ness was a competent administrator at a time when the Baptist Sunday School Board needed one. When Van Ness took over the board, he realized that it wasn't as much a business as it was a collection of 150 employees who were completely dependent on three or four dynamos at the top to tell them what to do every day. During his two decades as head of the Sunday School Board, Van Ness would change that. He standardized the production of Sunday school literature. He began opening Baptist bookstores. He reorganized the book publishing department and gave it the name Broadman Press. He built a much needed six-story shipping building on Ninth Avenue.

Van Ness tried to avoid confrontation. During his tenure, the Sunday School Board adopted an editorial policy that directed its writers to avoid issues that were the cause of divisiveness. Decades later, the board would use this policy to justify its position against books that discussed everything from Darwinism to race relations.

When Van Ness retired, the board elected Thomas Holcomb to replace him. Holcomb, a diminutive, dynamic man from rural Mississippi who paid careful attention to his personal appearance, looked and acted like a country preacher. "He brought to the board the art of promotion under inspirational leadership," the board history says. "He was not a scholar; nor did he possess the editorial or writing abilities of his predecessors."[7]

Holcomb's goal was to spread the gospel by making the resources of the Baptist Sunday School Board available to every church. At a time when Soviet Premier Joseph Stalin had made the phrase common, Holcomb set the board on "Five-Year Plans" to expand the number of Baptist churches and the programs each had. Between 1935 and 1940, for example, the number of Vacation Bible Schools at Southern Baptist Churches increased from about one thousand to almost six thousand.

In 1936, the Sunday School Board switched its printing contract from Marshall & Bruce to Baird-Ward. Since Baird-Ward could not print hardback books, the Sunday School Board continued to use Kingsport Press in East Tennessee for its hardback contracts such as *The Broadman Hymnal* in 1940.

When hundreds of thousands of GIs came home from World War II, the Baptist Sunday School Board experienced the biggest boom in its history. Between 1945 and 1953, Sunday school enrollment almost doubled. Meanwhile the board's revenue tripled, from $4.2 to $12.7 million.

The Entrepreneur

Richard Henry Boyd was born as the property of a Mississippi slave-holding family named Gray. For the first twenty-two years of his life, he went by their last name and the first name Dick given to him by his mother. As a child, Dick Gray was sold to a Texas slaveholder for twelve hundred dollars and sent away from his mother and three sisters.

When the Civil War broke out, Dick Gray followed his master and his three sons to the front. In November 1863, Master Gray and two of his sons were killed in the battle of Chattanooga. Dick Gray helped bury them and later escorted the youngest son back to their Texas home.

After emancipation, Dick Gray changed his name to Richard Henry Boyd for reasons that are unclear. He then got a job as a cowboy on a ranch in West Texas and later worked for a mill in southeast Texas, where a white girl helped teach him to read.

Reading made Boyd realize how much he needed to learn. In the late 1860s, he began taking courses at Bishop College, with the financial support of his second wife. Boyd's experiences at Bishop convinced him to enter the ministry.

As he began raising a family, Boyd found that his talent lay not so much in preaching but in organizing churches. In 1879, he became a moderator for the Central Baptist Association of Texas. Shortly thereafter, he became a leader in the movement of black churches to break away from northern white religious organizations such as the American Baptist Convention in Philadelphia.

Around 1895, Boyd went to Philadelphia to meet with the head of the American Baptist Publication Society. "The Negroes want representation," Boyd told him. "They want their writings published in your papers, and their pictures printed in your columns." The manager told him there was no way his organization could do that. "The time has not come when the American people will read after a Negro," the American Baptist official said.[8]

After Boyd got back to Texas, he began having friendly correspondences with James Frost, the founding president of the Baptist Sunday School Board in Nashville. Since the Baptist Sunday School Board was founded by a pro-slavery wing of the Baptist Church, this tight relationship was ironic in a way. But in many ways, Boyd and Frost were much alike. Both were proud, energetic, and incurable optimists. Both were great organizers. Both did not like the American Baptist Convention. And both would succeed in organizing publishing arms even though they had many detractors within their own denominations. In Boyd's case, that denomination was the National Baptist Convention, which by this time had emerged as the largest organization of African-American Baptist churches in the United States.

The National Baptist Publishing Board was hardly formed by unanimous vote. At the 1896 National Baptist Convention, Boyd was able to pass a motion authorizing a printing committee to prepare and publish a series of Sunday school tracts. However, the convention did not appropriate any money to do this. Making the most of his minor parliamentary maneuver, Boyd built support with a series of influential black Baptist ministers and then moved to Nashville.

From the beginning, the National Baptist Publishing Board was organized and entirely funded by Boyd. The decision to locate in Nashville was entirely his. Boyd probably chose Nashville because of Nashville's large printing industry, the city's several black colleges, and his relationship with Frost. When Boyd got to Nashville, Frost took him around town and introduced him to several of the most important people in the printing business, a move that no doubt helped the black entrepreneur immensely. Frost also agreed to lend the National Baptists his organization's printing plates, which meant that at first, his literature was identical to the Southern Baptist literature.

Since the National Baptist Convention gave Boyd no money, he mortgaged his wife's property in Texas to finance his publishing entity. He set up a one-room office at 408 Charlotte (where he slept on a cot for several months). At first, he spent fifty dollars on stamps and sent five thousand letters to every black preacher and church superintendent he could think of. Before long, orders began to trickle in. Within three months, the publishing arm had sent out sixty thousand lesson leaflets and seventy-eight thousand picture lesson cards. First quarter receipts were seventeen hundred dollars; expenses were fifteen hundred dollars.

Compared to business communities in other southern cities, Nashville was relatively receptive to Boyd and his publishing company. For the first several years of its existence, most of its actual printing was done by white-owned print shops. But also during the early years of its existence, there were frequent reminders that not everyone wanted to do business with a black-owned company. When the publishing board grew large enough to buy its own equipment, Boyd reasoned that bankruptcy auctions were the best place to find bargains. However, he soon learned he wasn't allowed to bid because he was black. Undaunted, Boyd got a white friend (whose identity is no longer known) to act on his behalf. Through this method, the National Baptist Publishing Board bought most of its early equipment.

The National Baptist Publishing Board made ends meet because black congregations were thrilled to get books of children's stories with black children in them. In 1899, Boyd bought a residential house three blocks north of the courthouse and began buying printing equipment to put in it. Soon the National Baptist Publishing Board (NBPB) was publishing sermon books, hymnals, and a flagship newspaper for African-American church leaders called *Union Review*. When a *Nashville American* reporter visited the publishing operation,

he was astounded by what he saw. "Dr. Boyd carried the reporter through his house, which is located on North Market Street," the *American* story said. "There are 107 employees on the place, and every one is a negro. Everything from the boiler-room to the counting-room is modern. . . . Every employee is governed by a set of printed rules, and all business is dispatched according to method."[9]

Richard H. Boyd (right) with son Henry Allen Boyd, around 1910 (National Baptist Publishing Board).

During the next few years, the publishing entity continued to grow. By 1915, the NBPB had 150 employees and revenues of over two hundred thousand dollars and was doing most of its printing in-house. It had also organized its own missionary effort, a Sunday School Congress, and an annual convention of church leaders and choirs. It had also branched off into sales of pulpits, organs, and even black dolls.

As the National Baptist Publishing Board grew, Boyd came under intense criticism from within his denomination that he was getting rich off the publishing business. While this certainly bothered Boyd, it is important to remember that the National Baptist Convention did not have any authority over the publishing board, since Boyd—not the convention—had established and incorporated it. Unlike the Southern Methodist Publishing House and the Baptist Sunday School Board, the National Baptist Publishing Board was an independent not-for-profit corporation, run by a board of directors chosen by Boyd. "The National Baptist Publishing Board was not started by the convention,"

A group of National Baptist Church members pose in front of the National Baptist Publishing Board head-quarters during the NBPB's annual convention, around 1920 (National Baptist Publishing Board).

Boyd's great-grandson T. B. Boyd III would explain a century later. "It was started for the convention."

Boyd also had two strong allies who repeatedly came to his defense. One was the Rev. E. C. Morris, head of the National Baptist Convention. The other was James Frost of the Baptist Sunday School Board. On several key occasions, Frost spoke to key officials in the black Baptist denomination and told them that, to the best of his knowledge, Boyd had run his publishing arm properly.

However, the relationship between the National Baptist Convention and Boyd's publishing entity came to a head in 1915. At the National Baptist Convention that year, Boyd was accused of mismanagement, nepotism, and using the publishing arm for his personal gain. Because of such attacks, the National Baptist Convention voted to incorporate and to take over the operation of the National Baptist Publishing Board. However, after they officially notified the board of this decision, Boyd told the convention that they had no authority to do so. After all, the publishing firm was incorporated and under the control of his board of directors. The National Baptist Convention sued. However, the Davidson County Chancery Court sided with Boyd, ruling that the convention had no authority over the NBPB.

Because of that decision, most of the churches in the National Baptist Convention decided to incorporate as the National Baptist Convention U.S.A. and form their own publishing entity that would be run without Boyd. The convention chose Nashville as the location for its publishing entity and opened its own publishing arm at 409 Gay Street. By 1921, it was producing Sunday school literature and newspapers and had thirty-two employees. At that point, it came under the leadership of Arthur Townsend, former president of Nashville's Roger Williams University. In 1924, the National Baptist Convention built a new headquarters at 400 Charlotte Avenue.

Meanwhile, Boyd's supporters formed a separate church organization called the National Baptist Convention of America, which officially aligned with Boyd's National Baptist Publishing Board.

Boyd lost some business because of the formation of the rival publishing arm; revenues were down 25 percent during the first year. But it got by nonetheless, because of the growth in the number of Baptists and because many Baptists were loyal to Boyd.

There were several attempts to merge the two church organizations during the next five years. None, however, came to fruition. Eventually, both organizations would grow into large, separate entities. Townsend would remain in charge of the National Baptist Convention U.S.A.'s Sunday School Publishing Board until 1960. He would become such an integral part of that organization that many would eventually refer to it as the "Townsend Group."

Meanwhile, Richard Boyd left little doubt whom he wanted to succeed him. In 1902, he brought his son Henry Allen into the publishing entity, a move for which he was heavily criticized at the time. When Richard Boyd died in August 1922, Henry Allen succeeded him.

Henry Allen Boyd would remain head of the publishing board until 1959. During that period, the board, and the Boyd name with it, became well-known throughout the United States. "Henry Allen was more educated and more charismatic [than his father]," T. B. Boyd III said. "He wasn't the businessman that his father was, but he had a personality that people just loved. . . . When people who knew Henry Allen remember him, a smile comes over their faces."

As many blacks left the South and migrated to places like Detroit and Chicago, the publishing board's materials found new markets. In the 1950s, budding African-American ministers in Texas were still affiliated with the Boyd name. "I came from Texas, and when I moved to Nashville in the 1960s, I was called a 'Boyd baby,'" the Rev. James Thomas, pastor of the Jefferson Street Baptist Church, said in 1998.

In 1950, the National Baptist Publishing Board's sales surpassed half a million dollars. Henry Allen Boyd had several children, but none of his sons survived. As he grew older, he chose his nephew Theophilus Bartholomew Boyd Jr. to be his understudy.

The Industry

Religious publishing wasn't the only reason Nashville's printing houses consumed a train carload of paper a day by 1900. Nashville—the railroad hub, the state capital, and the headquarters for insurance companies, banks, and bond houses—had plenty of things besides Sunday school literature for printers to work on.

A former Methodist bookbinder named Andrew Marshall and a former newspaper editor named James Bruce started one of Nashville's earliest printing businesses in 1865. In its early years, Marshall & Bruce specialized in the production of blank record books used by local and county governments. The company also printed the *Nashville City Directory*, an important historical document containing the name, address, and occupation of every adult Nashville resident. When the Baptist Sunday School Board came along, Marshall & Bruce became its largest vendor. In 1900, it employed about ninety people.

Another early printing company was started in 1865 under the name American Book and Office Supply. In 1880, a former state legislator named H. A. Hasslock and a former Louisville & Nashville Railroad clerk named Joshua Ambrose bought the business and changed its name. For years, Hasslock & Ambrose's main business was making logbooks for L&N, which had an enormous appetite for paper. Around 1900, Ambrose bought out his partner and began doing work for religious publishers, especially the Baptist Sunday School Board.

When Baptist Sunday School Board secretary James Frost took National Baptist Publishing Board founder Richard Boyd around town to introduce him to key people in the publishing business, one of the first people he took Boyd to see was Charles Brandon. Brandon, a former employee of the Southern Methodist Publishing House, had started a business called Brandon Printing in the 1870s. By the turn of the century, it was the largest printing business in Nashville. Besides the work it did for religious publishers, Brandon Printing specialized in the production of official bank documents, such as deeds, stocks, and bonds. The company's plant was located in a majestic building at 228 North Market Street (later Second Avenue). Out of that store, Brandon Printing operated Nashville's first office supply superstore— selling everything from typewriters to desks to stationery.

At the turn of the century, Brandon Printing had about 125 employees. But in 1936, the business became a casualty of the Great Depression, and its equipment was liquidated at public auction. At that point, Washington Manufacturing bought Brandon's building on Second Avenue and turned it into an apparel factory.

In 1912, three Brandon Printing employees, Adolph Brandau, W. E. Craig, and C. S. Dickerson, bought a business called Standard Printing Co. and gave it their names. Like Brandon Printing, Brandau Craig Dickerson found a successful niche in engraving and printing official documents for banks and trust companies. In 1933, when Nashville's banks decided to stay open despite a national panic, Brandau Craig Dickerson was one of the companies given the delicate task of printing scrip money that businesses temporarily accepted. By that time, the printing operation was housed in a four-story building across Tenth Avenue from Cummins Station.

In addition to the Southern Methodists, Southern Baptists, and National Baptists, Nashville had a few smaller religious publishing houses that helped create new businesses. One was the Gospel Advocate Publishing Co., which was loosely affiliated with the Church of Christ. In 1884, Gospel Advocate editor David Lipscomb hired a minister named J. Clayton McQuiddy as his office manager. About fifteen years later, McQuiddy started a printing business separate from (although co-located with) the publishing company. In addition to Church of Christ newspapers, Sunday school materials, and hymn-books, McQuiddy printed large numbers of envelopes, letterheads, and county record books. McQuiddy also developed a niche in corporate newsletters; one of its most reliable accounts was *Our Shield*, the weekly newsletter for the National Life & Accident Insurance Co.

After moving several times early in the century, McQuiddy built a six-story building on Seventh Avenue next to the Masonic Lodge in 1924. About that time, the founder died and the business was turned over to his son Leon McQuiddy. McQuiddy Printing and the Gospel

Advocate Publishing Co. would remain on that site and under family ownership for almost fifty years.

Baird-Ward Printing Co. was an offshoot of yet another religious publishing house. Between 1850 and 1917, the Cumberland Presbyterian denomination operated its publishing arm in Nashville, eventually out of a nine-story structure on Church Street known as the Presbyterian Building. The Presbyterians produced not only hymnals and Sunday school literature, but also influential trade publications such as the *Southern Lumberman*. In 1910, editors James Baird and William Ward left the Cumberland Presbyterian house and started their own printing business. Seven years later, the Cumberland Presbyterians merged with another denomination and moved their printing operation to Louisville.

For the first few years of its existence, Baird-Ward's main client was Southern Bell Telephone Co., for which it printed the telephone directories for Nashville and several other cities in the Southeast. In 1936, Baird-Ward underbid Marshall & Bruce to become the major contractor for the Baptist Sunday School Board. By World War II, Baird-Ward had about four hundred employees.

The Bible Salesmen

For generations, Nashville was known for its religious books and its traveling salesmen. No company better symbolized the mix than Southwestern.

J. R. Graves was the minister of Nashville's First Baptist Church before the Civil War. In the 1850s, he wrote and distributed a newspaper called *The Tennessee Baptist*. Since the populated part of the United States did not go much further west than Tennessee in those days, Graves named the company that published the newspaper the Southwestern Company.

Graves was a staunch advocate of the Confederacy. When the Union army took over Nashville, he and his family fled south. A few months later, he found out that there wasn't a single Bible printer in the South. Graves then smuggled printing plates to the South and began publishing pocket-sized Bibles for the Confederate army. He delivered one to Confederate President Jefferson Davis, who wrote Graves and thanked him for it.

After the war, Graves moved back to Nashville and continued to publish Bibles. He then expanded his business and started using college students to sell those Bibles door-to-door.

Graves died in 1871. During the fifty years following his death, Southwestern had a series of owners. Each ran the company much as Graves had done, bringing several hundred college students to Nashville every summer for a week of training, then sending them to remote corners of the South and Midwest to sell Bibles, Bible storybooks, and dictionaries door-to-door. The business changed hands several times until J. B. Henderson took it over in 1921.

No one will ever know how much impact Southwestern's annual army of salesmen had on Nashville's image. But it is safe to say that when many people in remote parts of the country thought of Nashville, they thought about Bible salesmen and the Grand Ole Opry. In an era when many parts of the South had no bookstores, Southwestern helped bring a bit of culture to a lot of farms. The experience of selling door-to-door also had a dramatic impact on thousands of young people, all of whom ended up with dozens of stories about strange experiences on the road. "He [the Southwestern salesman] is prepared to meet every type of humanity under the sun, especially female humanity, listen to arguments on the Bible's defense of foot washing as a congregational practice, help with the haying, sleep in a farmer's barn or a tobacco warehouse, take potluck with hill families as down payments on his sales and learn something about life in general," a *Tennessean* reporter wrote.[10]

The way a young man named Dortch Oldham first heard about Southwestern was probably quite typical. In 1935, Oldham was in a store near his home in Hartsville, Tennessee, when someone told him he could save one hundred dollars during a summer selling Bibles. Since one hundred dollars was a lot of money during the Great Depression—especially for a high school senior—Oldham signed up and paid his own way to Nashville. After the week of classes at the War Memorial Building in Nashville, Oldham hitchhiked to his assigned post in Vidalia, Georgia. "I had one nickel when I got to Vidalia and I bought some stale donuts with that," Oldham said.

Oldham's routine that summer was always the same. Wake up early. Hitchhike to a part of the county. Knock on doors all day. Walk from farm to farm. Then, after a day of selling, ask a farmer if he could spare a bed for the night.

"I never had any trouble getting a place to stay," Oldham said. "If anything, you had trouble getting any sleep because they would like for you to entertain them, since you were from out of state and they hadn't seen too many people from out of state."

Oldham saved $225 that summer. The next five summers, Southwestern sent him to Maryland, Pennsylvania, Louisiana, Ohio, and then Ohio again. During his sixth summer, Oldham saved $950.

After a stint in the Army Air Corps, Oldham decided he wanted to go to Vanderbilt Law School. But after he registered for classes, he got a call from his old boss at Southwestern. J. B. Henderson admitted to Oldham that Southwestern was in sorry financial shape and that he hadn't invested any money in the company since the late 1920s. But he promised Oldham that if he would help him build a sales force, he would one day sell him the company. Oldham called Vanderbilt and told them he wouldn't be coming after all.

CHAPTER 3

Horace the Upstart; Joel the Spin Doctor

Before the Civil War, many parts of the South had little use for wholesale food companies, grocery store chains, and food brands. After all, it was an agrarian culture where farmers grew enough of everything to make each region self-sufficient.

The Civil War and the Reconstruction era that followed it changed all that. Various parts of the South began to specialize in particular crops such as cotton, tobacco, soybeans, and peanuts. Meanwhile, high property taxes forced many farmers out of business. Some moved to cities like Atlanta, Nashville, and Birmingham to work in factories. Others left for Texas and California, abandoning their farms overnight and leaving property assessors to deal with what they left behind.

As the old agrarian system of self-sufficiency broke down, a new system of food distribution, which actually got started during the Civil War, took its place. While the Union army occupied Nashville, many wholesale food distributors from Cincinnati opened branch offices in Nashville to make money by feeding the troops. When the war ended, many of those distributors remained in Nashville.

Dozens of companies were in the wholesale food business. Two of the largest were Cheek-Neal Coffee Co. and H. G. Hill Stores Co.

Sometime around 1870, a newspaper advertisement for cheap land caught the eye of a Millford, Ohio, grocer named Amos Hill. Hill apparently thought the Reconstruction South was a place of great opportunity—at least for his children. He bought about one thousand acres in Van Buren County, sight unseen, and gave it to his oldest daughter Lectra and her new husband Albert Lowe.

According to family legend, the newlyweds soon found that their new home was not exactly the land of milk and honey. For one thing, it was inaccessible. For another, it was mountainous, rocky, and hardly conducive to farming. After a couple of years of struggling, Albert and Lectra made it very clear in letters home that they were not doing well.

Amos then sent his son George to help out. But George Hill did not fare any better at mountaintop farming than his brother-in-law. "They damn near starved to death up there," George Hill's great-grandson Wentworth Caldwell Jr. said 120 years later. "And it's a good thing that they did, because they left." About the only thing good that happened to George Hill when he lived in Van Buren County was that he met and courted Hulda Rogers, the daughter of a nearby farmer. After Hill and Rogers were married, George Hill decided he had to find a more stable way to make a living.

At the turn of the century, virtually all grocery stores in Nashville were owned and operated independently. Most grocers lived above their stores, and with the help of their wives and children, kept their businesses open from very early to very late. In an era before brand names took over the shopping business, grocers generally sold the same thing as their competitors. They also bought their food from the same places: staples from grocery wholesalers on Market Street (later Second Avenue) and produce directly from farmers at the farmers' market next to the courthouse. Most stores regularly delivered groceries.

The nature of the grocery business was also dictated by the methods of transportation available to the average person: walking and riding the streetcar. Few people had the luxury of being able to choose between one store and another.

Most people also ran a tab with the grocer closest to their homes. "No well-to-do person ever thought of paying cash for his groceries," Arch Trawick, a turn-of the-century grocery salesman and wholesaler, said in 1938. "Folks who paid cash were the poor folks, cooks, laborers, factory workers, and such."[1] By 1895, this practice—once a necessity under the South's agrarian economy—was being continued more out of tradition and courtesy than any real economic need.

Because of this lack of mobility and mom-and-pop ownership structure, there was little direct competition between grocery stores. Pricing, though it obviously varied somewhat from store to store, wasn't commonly used as a way to take business away from competitors. Most grocery retailers did not advertise because they could not afford to do so.

George Hill's store was located in South Nashville, near where the interstate later passed over Third Avenue South. Since that area would have been on the border between an affluent white area (Rutledge Hill) and a black area (Trimble Bottom), it can be assumed that George Hill had both white and black customers. Hill was a lot better at selling groceries than at farming. By the time his son Horace Greeley was growing up, George was doing so well that he could afford to send Horace to Montgomery Bell Academy (MBA), then located south of downtown in an area later known as Rutledge Hill.

As was customary for children of merchants, Horace Hill spent most of his spare time helping his parents run the family business. But by the time the younger Hill was out of high school, it was obvious that he had his own ideas about things. "Horace was not particularly interested in waiting on customers or getting his clothes soiled by helping arrange the stock," Trawick said.[2]

But Trawick, who would eventually sell his wholesale grocery business to Hill, said Horace was often deep in thought when others thought he was being lazy. "Horace Hill had no idea of time," Trawick said. "If he saw an excavation being made and it presented a different angle from any he had seen, he stood on the spot 'til he got the hang of what was going on."[3]

After graduating from MBA, Horace talked his father into sending him on a trip to California. Years later, Hill would say that he spent a lot of time on this trip giving himself a business education.

There were of course still mom-and-pop grocery stores in California when H. G. Hill went there. But chain stores such as the Great Atlantic and Pacific Tea Company were also emerging. And it was this new development that intrigued Hill the most.

Unlike the grocery stores in Nashville, chain stores were geared to lure customers by selling at lower prices. One way they did this was by finding ways around wholesalers. Another was to stop delivering groceries, thus saving the company the money and hassle of having to employ delivery boys. A third was to stop selling groceries on credit and use the new cash influx to invest back in the business.

But perhaps the biggest difference between the chain stores out west and mom-and-pop stores in Nashville was advertising. Once they had found ways to cut their prices, stores in the West would boldly circulate their prices in the newspapers.

After getting his fill, young Horace Hill wired home and said he needed money. "You got out there, you get back," George Hill told his son, according to family legend. If it hadn't been for the fact that Horace's mother wired him sixty dollars, he might never have come back to Nashville.

Back home, Horace Hill decided that he too would get into the grocery business. He leased a grocery store at Eighteenth Avenue and State Street in 1895 (one hundred years later, the company owned this property and referred to it as "Lot Number One"). Since a well-known hat store on Union Street was already called Hill's, H. G. gave the store his first two initials.

Whether Hill's store made money or not is unclear. But by the next year, young Horace had closed his store on State Street and had a new store at 700 Broadway. A story about how Hill acquired this store shows how aggressive he was. In an era when shopkeepers were in a constant state of debt with wholesalers, it was quite common for a store to go bankrupt and its entire inventory sold at auction to another retailer. Hill attended an auction of one such store, knowing quite well that the published rules of the auction called for cash only. After Hill made the winning bid of six hundred dollars, he told the auctioneer that he did not have the money. The auctioneer was no doubt furious, but since the crowd had dispersed, there was nothing he could do but give Hill the opportunity to pay him later. Hill had a successful closeout sale the next day and paid the court officer in full.

Hill's taking over the 700 Broadway store proved he had guts. But he certainly couldn't afford to make his mark on the world with only one store, especially one at Seventh and Broadway. In order to do that, he knew where he had to go.

In the latter part of the nineteenth century, Nashville's prime retail marketplace for clothes and supplies was located on what was then called the Public Square, a piece of land south of the courthouse that was eventually turned into a parking lot during the 1960s. Starting about 1910, many of these stores would be relocated in the direction of Church Street, Union Street, and Fourth Avenue. But in the 1890s, the Public Square was still the crossroads of Nashville and still the only place to reach large numbers of shoppers. And while H. G. Hill was running his small store on Broadway, the Public Square turned into a place to buy groceries.

In 1895, a grocer named William Leahy closed his store at 600 Main Street in Edgefield and opened a new one on the east side of the Public Square. Like other grocery stores of the era, it was a family business run by Leahy, his wife, and his three sons. But by standards of the time, Leahy's was a superstore. And unlike any grocery retailer in Nashville at the time, it advertised its prices in the newspaper—first in small classified advertisements, and by the fall of 1896, in bold quarter-page advertisements that described it as the "People's Cash Grocery."

By 1897, a grocery store called Crone & Jackson had also moved to the Public Square. Like Leahy's, it too ran advertisements in the newspaper that detailed its low prices.

For two years, Hill watched closely while Leahy's and Crone & Jackson became successful. Then, in January 1899, he closed his Broadway store and opened a new store on the Public Square. "New

Store! New Goods! New Prices!" read the newspaper advertisement the week it opened.[4] Like Leahy's store, it operated on a cash-only basis, calling itself the "Spot Cash Grocers." Among the items advertised were lard (twenty pounds for $1), flour ($3.85 per barrel), and tomatoes (twelve cans for 85¢).

During the next three years, the three stores dueled it out. Each store ran large, detailed advertisements in the *Banner* and *American*, usually on Thursday. The advertisements promoted private labels, such as Hill's Golden Gate Coffee or Leahy's Fit for a King Coffee. Sometimes it was not easy for an unsophisticated customer to tell whose prices were lower; Leahy might advertise eight cans of corn for forty-eight cents, while Hill might advertise two cans for fifteen cents.

In 1901, Hill made a move that he knew would either give him a leg up or spell his doom. At a time when his cash flow must have been precarious, Hill opened a branch store near the site of his father's old store (which by now no longer existed). Now, Hill could order more goods than Leahy's and Crone & Jackson's, and therefore get a slightly better deal from wholesalers. He could also get a double boost from his advertisements.

Nevertheless, many people, including his father, told young Horace Hill that he wouldn't succeed with a chain. "My grandfather told Uncle Horace that he never would make a living in the chain business," Horace Hill's niece Jane Hill Head said a century later.

Hill must have been quite satisfied when he picked up the *Banner* on March 7, 1902. "Going to California," read the Leahy's advertisement. "Our immense stock of $20,000 worth of groceries, produce, and feed must be sold regardless of cost before March 22nd."

Many retailers would have celebrated. Hill knew better. Just because Leahy was moving did not mean the end of competition. He still had Crone & Jackson to worry about. More importantly, the powerful Atlantic and Pacific Tea Company (A&P) had opened a store on Union Street. The chances were good that another grocer might buy Leahy's store.

Hill bought Leahy's stock and property. During the first week of April, Hill advertised heavily and sold the remainder of Leahy's stock. He also changed the name of his private coffee label from Golden Gate to Fit for a King, which it would remain for the next century.

Invigorated by the departure of his closest competitor, Hill decided it was time to take a big step. Knowing that the best way to reduce prices was to eliminate the wholesaler, Hill turned Leahy's old store into a wholesale business that sold to his retail store.

Since there was no newspaper coverage of retail in that era, it is difficult to know why this venture into wholesaling failed. But it is easy to understand why Hill's experiment would have alarmed Nashville's powerful wholesalers. Trawick said some wholesalers actually organized against Hill and saw to it that his distribution channels were cut off. Within two months, Hill had closed his wholesaling business.

In 1903 and 1904, Hill added stores on Jefferson Street, Church Street, Foster Avenue, Lafayette Street, and Fatherland Street (a store located in the front yard of Hill's new home). By 1906, Hill's chain had grown to a dozen stores, making him far and away the city's top grocery retailer. Unlike many retailers of that era, Hill even catered to African Americans, with large advertisements in the black-owned *Nashville Globe* that promised that Hill's "wagons deliver all over the city."[5]

In 1907, Hill leased a five-story building across from his Public Square store, putting a store on the bottom floor and filling the top four with a coffee roasting plant, a bakery, and offices. To help run his business, Hill hired the man who had been the manager at the A&P store. With the Nashville business firmly established, he acquired five stores in St. Louis and moved there.

One of the greatest fortunes ever made in Nashville was made in coffee by a man who rarely drank the stuff.

Joel Owsley Cheek was born in Burkesville, Kentucky, in 1852, and was, therefore, too young to fight in the Civil War. It may have been because of a postwar shortage of young men that Cheek was teaching school at seventeen. But after he married, Cheek decided he needed to find a more lucrative career. In 1873, Cheek took a boat to Nashville and got a fifty-dollar-per-month job as a traveling salesman, or drummer, for a wholesale grocery firm called Webb and Scoggins.

The profession of drummers would vanish quickly at the turn of the century, as people migrated to the city and as channels of communication improved. But at that time, people still made their living traveling from town to town by horse carrying everything from molasses to coffee to oranges, with samples on one side of their saddle and a change of clothes on the other.

It was difficult work, since roads were rough and since most hotels in rural areas did not have heating. Joel Cheek was apparently quite good at it; in only two years he became a partner in the firm.

After a few years in the grocery business, Cheek had done well enough to buy a large house at 513 Woodland Street and fill it with no less than nine children. He had done so well, in fact, that he convinced his cousin Christopher Tompkins (C. T.) Cheek to move down from Kentucky and go to work for his firm. C. T. had fought for the Union during the Civil War, which must have caused quite a stir since some of his brothers fought for the Confederacy. By 1890 he had money and social standing, having once been a sheriff and having married the daughter of former Kentucky governor Preston Leslie.

Between 1873 and 1895, Joel Cheek saw a lot of changes in the grocery wholesaling business. In the decades following the Civil War, many small grocers in the rural South still bought green coffee beans, roasted them in an oven, ground them up, and mixed them on their own. By the 1890s, wholesalers were beginning to carry packaged coffee. But since brand names had not taken over the southern coffee business yet, grocers had no choice but to carry whatever the wholesaler happened to bring that week. It wasn't always a good blend.

Cheek began staying up late in the kitchen of his Woodland Street house mixing various blends of coffee. And he became obsessed with his work.

"At that time, I had no assurance that my work would not be wasted, for it was truly an experiment, a departure from the coffee customs of the day, and it is hard to change the habits of people," Joel Cheek said years later. "But I kept on. This work had to be sandwiched into my regular duties as a salesman, for I was on the road. I would get home from my trips and dive right into different sorts and grades of coffee. Often it would be long after midnight before I would retire, and I went to bed dreaming of that 'perfect blend' that beckoned somewhere out there in the dim future.

"No astronomer ever searched the heavens for a new planet with more real enthusiasm than I did for the right combination of coffee beans."[6]

Finally, Cheek came up with what he thought was a tasty, affordable mix. In 1898, he and his partner John Norton began to manufacture and package coffee out of their wholesale grocery business at 210 Second Avenue. At first, they gave it the name Eagle Coffee. "If you use Package Coffee, ask your grocer for Eagle, the cleanest, best packaged coffee on the market," newspaper ads claimed.[7]

Cheek & Norton was by no means Nashville's only coffee maker. Much as it had in flour milling, Nashville's privileged status as the hub of L&N railroad gave Nashville a thriving coffee industry. Other coffee companies included Orr-Mizell (Statue Blend), Phillips-Trawick (Capital Blend), Holland (Blackstone), and Fletch-Wilson (which packaged University Club coffee in a structure that in later years became known as The Cannery).

In 1901, Cheek and Norton took on a new business partner named James Neal and renamed their business the Nashville Coffee and Manufacturing Co. In 1901, the company had several blends, including a low-grade blend called Porto Rico, two middle-grade blends called Banquet and Tennessee Club, and Eagle, the top-of-the-line grade. Business was so good that the company couldn't meet its orders and had to run advertisements apologizing for it. The company borrowed money and increased the output of the manufacturing plant to two hundred cases per day, making it the largest coffee plant in the South.

At this time, the Maxwell House Hotel, located at the corner of Fourth and Church, was Nashville's most elegant hotel. At some point (the date of which is unknown), Cheek asked hotel manager Billy Black if he could name his top-grade coffee after the hotel. After

serving it on a trial basis, Black agreed. By November 1901, the Nashville Coffee and Manufacturing Co. was advertising Maxwell House Blend.

The fact that Maxwell House tasted good did not hurt. But creative and ubiquitous advertisements were what drove its sales and made it stand out against its local competitors. "Common horse sense will teach you that coffee sold in airtight sealed tin cans is purer, cleaner, and fresher than coffee kept in open bins," said one ad, illustrated with a bespectacled horse.[8] Another advertisement featured Uncle Sam extending a cup of piping hot Maxwell House Coffee.

In 1902, Norton moved to Louisville and the business was renamed Cheek-Neal. The next year, Cheek-Neal sold fifty thousand dollars in stock, increasing its capitalization to two hundred thousand dollars. With its new capital, the company built a three-story plant in Houston that produced even more coffee than the one in Nashville. Neal moved to Houston to run the plant. Within a couple of years, Maxwell House Coffee was being sold on the West Coast and the company had about thirty traveling salesmen.

Perhaps there is no greater evidence of Joel Cheek's salesmanship than his ability to put words—not to mention coffee—in Teddy Roosevelt's mouth. One of the most famous advertising slogans in American history was the one for Maxwell House Coffee. "Good to the last drop" was such a good catchphrase, in fact, that it had a history, told time and time again in articles, books, and television shows for the rest of the century. According to the story, Roosevelt coined the phrase on a visit to Nashville in 1907.

In fact, there is little evidence that Roosevelt ever made the comment, and considerable evidence that he did not. And the only cup of coffee Roosevelt drank on his visit to Nashville might not have even been Maxwell House blend.

October 21, 1907, was the only time Roosevelt visited Nashville as president. It was a short stop, lasting only four hours. But it was the first time a president had visited Nashville since the Centennial Exposition ten years earlier. Nashville, anxious to show the world it was a progressive city, gave Roosevelt a warm reception.

Roosevelt made a speech at the Ryman Auditorium. He made a brief statement from his car at George Peabody College. Then the president visited The Hermitage and pledged federal money to help restore it, to the delight of the Ladies' Hermitage Association.

OPPOSITE PAGE: This picture, taken around 1901, shows the Nashville Coffee and Manufacturing Co. plant on Market Street (later Second Avenue). According to advertisements, the company named its flagship blend after the Maxwell House Hotel about the time this picture was taken (Metro Nashville Archives).

While touring The Hermitage, Roosevelt said he was impressed at everything he saw. Right after the president saw Jackson's bedroom, and as he was entering the dining room, he asked for a cup of coffee. "You know I must have the privilege of saying that I have eaten at General Jackson's table," the October 22 *American* quoted the president saying. Roosevelt apparently enjoyed his cup. "I like this coffee," the October 22 *Banner* quoted him saying. "This is the kind of stuff I like, by George, when I hunt bears." According to the *American*, Roosevelt then bowed to Mrs. John Gray and Mrs. Rachel Jackson Lawrence, who had served it to him. "I am honored at receiving the hospitality of this house at your hands, Madame."

Neither paper reported that Roosevelt said anything even close to "Good to the last drop." For that matter, neither paper said what kind of coffee the president was drinking.[9]

Nevertheless, the president had apparently complimented the cup of joe, and at least two Nashville coffee manufacturers took credit for it. Three days after his visit, H. G. Hill ran a quarter-page advertisement in the *Banner* that implied that it was the Fit for a King brand that Roosevelt liked so much. "The president, at The Hermitage, told the ladies he had often taken lunch at other places than the White House, but he had never tasted such good coffee," the advertisement said. "Of course the ladies were pleased. So that's what everybody says when they have a cup of Fit for a King coffee."

The next day, Cheek-Neal Coffee Co. came out with their version of the story. "This was Maxwell House Blend Coffee and was served from the famous old Jackson urn," an advertisement in the October 26 *Banner* claimed. "Maxwell House Blend Coffee pleased the palate of the head of the Nation, and will please all who desire the best in the cup."

In any case, that appeared to be the end of the Roosevelt coffee controversy, at least as far as newspaper advertisements were concerned. Cheek-Neal would continue to advertise aggressively for the next several years, but the advertisements made no reference to Roosevelt until after his death. "He leaned to the aroma; And, somehow, caught her lips; And then and there this happy pair; Enjoyed, in fragrant sips: Maxwell House Coffee," a 1915 *Tennessean* advertisement said, indicative of the kind of advertisements Cheek-Neal ran in that period.

In 1917, Cheek-Neal began using the "Good to the last drop" slogans in advertisements and Maxwell House Coffee menu booklets, but made no mention of the claim that Roosevelt had coined the phrase. A few years later, in the midst of an ambitious advertising campaign to break into the New York market, Cheek-Neal began running advertisements in national magazines featuring Roosevelt, a New York native. One advertisement claimed that Roosevelt stayed at the Maxwell House on his visit to Nashville "to gather material for his book on pioneer days," obviously referring to a trip the future president made to Nashville in 1888. "The coffee served at this fine, old hotel had spread its fame most widely," the advertisement said. "A special blend was used there, so rich and mellow that those who tasted it, never forgot it."[10]

There is no evidence that Cheek was even manufacturing coffee as early as 1888—let alone providing it for the city's most important hotel.

Nevertheless, the advertisements, combined with Cheek's spin on what happened at The Hermitage in 1907, eventually merged into a tale about how Roosevelt coined the "Good to the last drop" slogan on a visit to Nashville. When Joel Cheek died in 1935, the story of how Roosevelt coined his coffee's slogan was repeated in obituaries across the country. By 1946, full-page advertisements in the *Saturday Evening Post* were telling the story of how Roosevelt visited the Maxwell House Hotel in 1907 and how he had a cup of Maxwell House Coffee at The Hermitage later that day. "During this visit he enjoyed his first cup of Maxwell House Coffee, and when offered another cup, the president exclaimed, 'Delighted! It's good to the last drop!'"[11]

By the time the Houston plant was on solid ground, Cheek's personal wealth had begun to build. Following a migration of Nashville's elite, he and his family left Edgefield and moved into a house on Louise Avenue (next door to National Life executive Ridley Wills). Cheek ate lunch in that house at exactly noon every day, eschewing the growing practice among the wealthy of eating out. As he was a creature of habit, the menu was always chicken. When one of his children suggested that they occasionally vary the menu, he told them that if they were tired of it that they could eat somewhere else.

In 1909, Cheek moved the Nashville plant from Second Avenue to the new Cummins Station warehouse. Cheek-Neal then built a plant in Jacksonville, Florida, in 1910, a facility that enabled Maxwell House to become the dominant blend in the Southeast. A plant in Richmond, Virginia, followed in 1915. By World War I, Maxwell House Coffee was so big that American troops drank it in Europe. But it was still a regional brand, shut out of most large markets outside of Dixie. And it was New York—then at the height of its economic domination of the United States—that enticed Cheek the most.

How Cheek was able to come up with the capital to expand so aggressively is not entirely known. But at some point his cousin Leslie made a major investment in Cheek-Neal. Leslie's investment may have come about 1915—after his father C. T. died and after he sold a small chain of grocery stores to H. G. Hill.

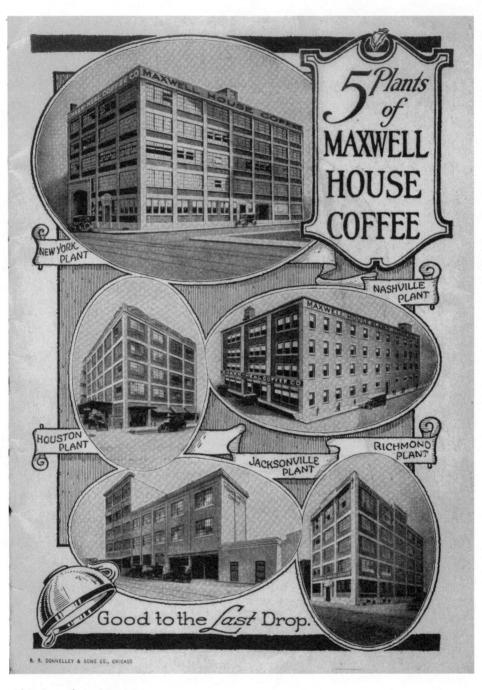

This page, from a promotional booklet put out by Cheek-Neal around 1925, shows drawings of the company's several plants.

In 1921, Cheek built a plant in Brooklyn. At first, the company had a terrible time getting the coffee produced there into stores. Many of Cheek's friends advised him to close the plant, saying there was no way that a southern coffee maker could break into a city dominated by Arbuckle and Chase & Sanborn. Cheek, by now a widower and not interested in playing it conservatively, would not relent. "The harder a market is to get, the easier it is to hold," became his slogan. At about the same time, he added Maxwell House Tea to his line.

Maxwell House advertisements were so quaint that they almost seemed as if Joel Cheek himself were making them up. But in fact, Cheek-Neal succeeded because it hired professional firms such as the J. Walter Thompson Co. of Chicago to handle its advertising and sales strategy. Thompson turned the sale of Maxwell House Coffee into a science, systematically dividing the nation into 625 sales districts, researching the demographics of each, and closely following the success of various advertising strategies in each district. "The Cheek-Neal company operates a system of sales analyses which could and should be used by any type of business," an official with J. Walter Thompson said in 1927.[12]

After moving into New York, Cheek-Neal also started spending far more money on advertising, increasing its magazine advertising budget from twenty thousand dollars in 1921 to five hundred thousand dollars in 1926. The company bought eighteen billboards on a thirty-seven-block stretch of Broadway. At a time when there were only a handful of radio stations nationally, there were even Maxwell House commercials on the airwaves.

Cheek-Neal's timing couldn't have been better. After Prohibition was imposed in 1920, consumption of coffee went way up. Sometime around 1924, the company started making a profit in New York. In 1927, sales of Maxwell House totaled $28 million—four times what it had been only four years earlier—and profits were $2.7 million. The company that once had a handful of coffee grinders on Market Street now had 680 employees. By 1927, Cheek-Neal was being cited across the country as an example of the power of advertising.

As the Cheek-Neal empire grew, it remained a family business. Cheek had eight sons, and all of them worked in the company to some degree. His oldest son Leon ran the Jacksonville plant. Son Robert Cheek headed up advertising and by that time could have made a very strong case for being the most important executive at the company. Frank Cheek ran the New York plant. Jim Cheek ran the Richmond plant and later the plant in Los Angeles that was opened in 1925.

By the time Joel Cheek was seventy-six years old, he faced a difficult decision. Cheek's sons were strongly in favor of keeping the company in the family. But rather than have to name one of his sons his successor, Cheek decided to sell his company.

At the time, Postum Co. of Battle Creek, Michigan, was buying everything from Log Cabin Syrup to Jell-O in an attempt to put together a complete line of food products. In 1928, Postum agreed to buy Maxwell House Coffee for $45 million in cash and stock—the largest sum ever paid for a food product at that time. The purchase was somewhat ironic since Postum had once waged an advertising campaign based on the idea that coffee was an unsafe breakfast alternative to its wholesome cereals and beverages. In fact, a Postum advertisement that ran in the *Banner* in 1915 compared caffeine to whiskey, morphine, and cocaine. Another advertisement said "coffee IS HARMFUL to many, even in moderate quantity . . . and that it is dangerous when used to excess has also been time and time again proven."[13] Because of this propaganda crusade, Marjorie Merriweather Post, daughter of Postum founder Charles Post, later admitted that the Maxwell House acquisition "nearly finished me off" because "I had been raised with the idea that coffee was just like taking dope."[14]

Not long after the purchase, Postum was bought by General Foods. In 1933, General Foods closed down Cheek-Neal's Cummins Station plant and moved it to Mobile, Alabama. General Foods later sold Cheek-Neal's roasting and grinding equipment to Nashville grocery wholesaler Robert Orr, which used it in the manufacture of Hermitage Coffee for several decades.

The sale of Cheek-Neal made Joel and Leslie Cheek rich (along with all their descendants). But it still left the C. T. Cheek & Sons wholesaling business (now run by Leslie) intact. As late as November 1928, C. T. Cheek and Sons still had thirty-five salesmen. But Cheek's wholesaling business was still operating the old-fashioned way—by essentially loaning large inventories of groceries to individual retailers, who would only pay the wholesaler after the items were bought. When the Great Depression hit, Leslie was investing enormous amounts of money in a grand mansion west of town called Cheekwood. "It wasn't such a good time for him to be showing up and taking thousands of dollars out of the company, but that is exactly what was going on," Leslie's nephew, Will T. Cheek Jr., said seventy years later. In 1935, C. T. Cheek and Sons declared bankruptcy.

That same year, Joel Cheek died. He had lived in the Louise Avenue house until his death even though he obviously could have afforded a much larger one.

None of the descendants of Joel and C. T. Cheek would start a major company in Nashville during the rest of the century. But their fortune ensured that Cheek family members would prosper for the rest of the century. Many of them worked in various capacities in Nashville; some in real estate, some in finance, and some in academia. One branch of the family tree even ventured into politics. Will Cheek Sr.

unsuccessfully ran for Congress in 1936 after running newspaper advertisements that claimed that he was "A Grocerman—Not a Politician." Half a century later, his son Will Cheek Jr. served as head of the Tennessee Democratic Party during the term of Gov. Ned McWherter.

At the end of the twentieth century, Maxwell House still claimed about 20 percent of the American coffee market.

Little is known about why grocer Horace Greeley Hill's venture into the St. Louis market failed. But within a couple of years, he sold his St. Louis stores and moved back to Nashville.

By this time, things had changed quite a bit since Hill had lost out to wholesalers in 1902. Hill had grown from a chain of two to a chain of about fifteen stores. He had built up a lot of capital. He was becoming accepted among Nashville's other business leaders—one of the first retailers to have that privilege.

Hill knew his chain would grow enormously fast if he could eliminate the wholesaler. But he had not forgotten his failed attempt at wholesaling.

In 1910, wholesaler Phillips-Trawick had just moved into Cummins Station when it went bankrupt. Hill bought the business, then announced the purchase in a half-page advertisement in the *Banner*. A few days later, H. G. Hill's advertisements made references to wholesalers for the first time. "To buy from first hands and save the middleman's profit should be your motto," the advertisement stated.[15] Unlike his previous effort, Hill withstood pressure from wholesalers who resisted his attempt to break the retailer-wholesaler system in place at the time.

His wholesaling problem solved, Hill refocused his efforts on new stores in and near Nashville. By 1913, his chain had ballooned to thirty-five stores. Then, Hill began putting stores in places like Franklin, Lebanon, and Columbia.

During this time, Hill also started separate chains in other parts of the Southeast. In 1912, Hill bought six small grocery stores in Birmingham and sent his younger brother James to run them. After two years, Horace wasn't happy with the way James was running the stores. Horace replaced James with an even younger brother named Nelson, but only after working out a deal where the three Hill brothers each owned one-third of the Birmingham chain. Under Nelson Hill's leadership, the Birmingham Hill chain began to grow even faster than the Nashville Hill chain and eventually expanded to have stores in Montgomery, Mobile, and Decatur.

In a similar manner, Hill helped his sister Elizabeth and her husband Bill Penick start a Hill grocery chain based in New Orleans.

He also helped an employee named Grady Parrell start a grocery chain called Red Front in Chattanooga.

Horace Hill knew shopping patterns, and he knew real estate. During the first three decades of his company's existence, streetcars dominated Nashville, taking people from the heart of downtown and dropping them off within four or five blocks of home. Hill knew that people wanted to buy their groceries after getting off the streetcar and before they walked home. He tried to build a store at every streetcar stop, and on the right side whenever possible so it would be in front of them when they disembarked. "He was a very dynamic and decisive individual," his grandson Wentworth Caldwell Jr. said. "He was the kind of person who would get off a streetcar, turn to his employee and say, 'We are going to build a store here! Get everybody out here! We are going to have that thing opened by Monday and by God that is what we are going to do.'"

Not all of Hill's stores were new, however. In 1913, he added eight stores to his chain. One, at Tenth and Woodland, was previously owned by a man named Chas Reol. Another, at 501 Twenty-sixth Avenue North, was bought from a grocer named Jesse Bradley. Several others—which included one on Lower Broad—were formerly part of a competing chain called United Grocers (previously owned by Leslie Cheek).

Hill probably made these takeovers by offering both a carrot and a stick. He almost certainly told grocers that if they sold him their business they would be able to stay on as store manager. Many grocers, still running under the old-fashioned method of borrowing from wholesalers and loaning to the public, might have seen it as an enticing way to simplify their lives and protect themselves from bankruptcy. Others probably figured it was better to sell to Hill than have him open a store across the street from them.

After all, there was no way that a small store selling groceries on credit could match the prices that Hill was advertising. A chain such as Hill's could use its employees more efficiently. It could arrange its stock better. It could advertise.

In 1917, Hill discontinued grocery delivery, giving the chain yet another way to cut costs and transfer that to lower prices. Five years later, the company outgrew Cummins Station and built a larger warehouse on Second Avenue South.

Of course, H. G. Hill Food Stores was by no means the only grocery store chain taking off at this time. At the exact same time Hill was putting stores all over Nashville, other chains such as Piggly Wiggly in Memphis, Winn-Dixie in Jacksonville, and Kroger in Cincinnati were doing much the same thing. Many of these chains were following in the footsteps of A&P, which had over fifteen thousand stores by 1928. "The time may arrive, almost before we know it, when it will be difficult to buy anything of importance without patronizing the chains," bemoaned a national article in 1928.[16]

Nevertheless, Hill's domination of the Nashville market must have been extreme, even in the era of emerging chains. By 1930, when Davidson County's entire population was only about 220,000, H. G. Hill had 102 locations in Nashville. The next largest chain in town was Piggly Wiggly, which had entered the Nashville market in 1920 and had sixteen stores by 1930. Most of Hill's stores were small, often sixty feet deep and twenty feet wide. But they seemed to be on every commercial corner in Nashville. There were six Hill stores on Gallatin Road, six on Twelfth Avenue South, four on Jefferson Street, and even three on Fatherland Street.

Horace G. Hill Sr. (far right) with his father George Hill (center) and Nelson Hill (far left) at the family's property in Van Buren County (H. G. Hill Stores Co.).

Hill also bought property as it came available next to his stores. An early believer in the concept of "one-stop shopping," Hill would often lease the acquired property to a drugstore or some other kind of retailer. Before long, Nashville was seeing its first suburban shopping centers in places like Hillsboro, Five Points, and Elliston Place. H. G. Hill stores were not only the anchor tenant but also the landlord.

By this time, Hill had taken leadership positions in other organizations and business ventures. In 1920, he was one of several investors in the Nashville Industrial Corp., which bought the abandoned Old Hickory powder plant from the federal government and tried to develop it as an industrial park. About that time, Hill and two riverboat captains formed an upper Cumberland trade company called the Nashville Navigation Co. The firm bought a paddleboat at a receiver's sale and had another one built (christened the *H. G. Hill*). The Nashville Navigation Co. did not make any money because of the difficulties of navigating the Cumberland River upstream from Nashville in the era before large dams. The *H. G. Hill* was later converted to a pleasure boat, used by companies and church groups for day outings.

Hill had more success with the Young Men's Christian Association. In 1921, he became YMCA president at a time of great financial difficulty for the organization. After Hill instituted cost savings at every level of the entity, its financial crisis abated.

In 1928, Hill followed the success of Kroger's initial public offering very closely. At about the same time, he called Merrill Lynch and had them explore the idea of merging his stores in Tennessee, his brother's stores in Alabama, and his sister's stores in Louisiana into one big public company.

All that changed with a phone call.

As one of Nashville's business leaders, it was logical that H. G. Hill would have some involvement in banking. Years before, Hill had served on the board of directors of the Fourth and First National Bank. As that institution became closely affiliated with financier Rogers Caldwell, Hill resigned from that board.

On November 14, 1930, Caldwell and Co. declared bankruptcy. A few weeks later, Paul Davis's American National Bank took over many of Caldwell's assets and the former assets of the Fourth and First National Bank, which by that time included the Nashville Trust Co. As the depression worsened, the trust company needed some new investors.

At that time, Hill was vacationing at the Pelican Hotel in Stuart, Florida, where he spent his winters after about 1920. Davis called Hill and told him that the bank needed his help. Without a major infusion of capital, Davis said the trust company would fail.

Hill, who by that time had gotten into the habit of traveling with a lot of luggage, got on the next train to Nashville with nothing in his pocket but a toothbrush.

Back in town, Hill met with Davis, other members of the bank board, and Robert and Newman Cheek, two of the sons of Joel Cheek. Hill sold his interest in the Birmingham and New Orleans Hill chains and used the money to buy 80 percent of the stock in the Nashville Trust Co. for $1 million. He then moved his office into the trust company, a move that was as much symbolic as anything else.

"It wasn't just the money," said John Hardcastle, who worked for the Nashville Trust Co. before becoming president of H. G. Hill Realty Co. "Mr. Hill was a Calvinist Presbyterian, who had a reputation in the community of being a straight-shooter. So much of the depression was not just economic but emotional and mental. People just did not have confidence in institutions. But Hill was a credible figure whose standing in the community meant a whole lot of credence to the Nashville Trust Co."

The trust company survived, which almost certainly kept the depression from hitting as hard in Nashville as it would have otherwise.

Joel Cheek and H. G. Hill were not the only people in the Nashville business community who made a fortune off food. During the depths of the depression, a Nashville man started a business that would eventually make his name one of the most recognized in the food industry.

In 1932, a South Carolina native named Herman Lay became a Nashville delivery man for an Atlanta-based potato chip company called Barrett Food Products. Lay delivered chips from a Nashville plant to restaurants and grocery stores all over Tennessee and Kentucky. After seven years of delivering, Lay purchased the Barrett dealership and named his new business the H. W. Lay Distribution Co. Although few details are known about this transaction, Lay later credited Third National Bank with helping him expand his business during the 1930s. "I have been associated with the bank since the difficult days of the last depression and have always appreciated the fairness Third National has shown the little man," Lay said in 1968.[17]

Since gas was being rationed during World War II, it was difficult to successfully operate a potato chip distribution company during the early 1940s. Lay managed, in part because of the help of Ed and Bernice Johnson, owners of the Belmont Boulevard Esso station across the street from the Lay's distributorship.

In 1947, Lay raised forty thousand dollars in a stock sale and bought Barrett, which then had potato chip factories in Atlanta, Memphis, and Nashville. To the dismay of Bernice Johnson, Ed Johnson was one of Lay's largest investors. "She [Bernice] cried for more than a day," said Peggy Grow, the Johnsons' niece. "This was their life savings and she was not a risk-taker."[18] Lay moved to Georgia, changed Barrett's name to Lay's, and began to expand into new markets. Within two years, business was going so well that he almost sold it. "I just felt it was too good to be true," Lay said years later. "I couldn't see how people could eat more snacks than they were already eating."[19]

Instead, Lay held onto the business and acquired five more plants throughout the Southeast. By 1956, when the company went public, it had a fleet of three hundred trucks and total sales of $11 million (a lot of money when a bag of chips sold for between five and nine cents). Five years later, Herman Lay merged his business with Frito

Co. of Dallas, which then became Frito-Lay. Five years later, Pepsi-Cola Co. bought Frito-Lay, and Lay became PepsiCo chairman.

Because Lay's was based in Nashville for a very short time, the company left few legacies behind. By far the most notable was a series of stock donations that the Johnson family made to Belmont University, estimated to be worth about $25 million in 1999.

The day Horace Greeley Hill moved his office into the Nashville Trust Co. was the day the Hill chain hit its zenith of dominance. There was no more talk about consolidating all the Hill-family stores in Nashville, Chattanooga, and Birmingham into one public company. By the end of the decade, competing chains were not as likely to concede the Nashville market to H. G. Hill. In 1937, A&P reentered the Nashville market after a twenty-year absence. And in 1939, a Cincinnati-based chain called Kroger opened its first Nashville store at 700 Nineteenth Avenue North.

There were three reasons that the Hill chain did not grow in the 1930s. One was economic. The depression brought residential and commercial growth to a standstill. There was no way that the Hill's chain could have grown very fast in the 1930s, especially after its president made a million-dollar capital infusion into the trust company.

The second was demographic. When the automobile replaced the streetcar, there was no longer a need for a store on every street corner. If anything, the public wanted fewer stores that carried more. As people began to demand more unusual food items and as competing brand labels took over the market, the Hill chain began to consolidate stores. By the mid-1930s, many Hill stores had increased from about twelve hundred square feet to between three and five thousand square feet.

But a third reason was personal. Beginning in 1930, Hill simply became preoccupied with other things, such as running the Nashville Trust Co., and public service projects such as the YMCA.

As Hill grew older, it became obvious that the reins of the company were reserved for Hill's only son, H. G. Hill Jr., who had worked for the company since graduating from Vanderbilt in 1921. Although the Hills did everything possible to keep the business out of the public eye, everyone who knew of the family knew about the differences between H. G. Hill Jr. and his father.

If H. G. Hill Sr. was decisive, then H. G. Hill Jr. was deliberate. If Senior liked to experiment with new business ventures, Junior preferred to avoid anything that wasn't a sure bet. If Senior did not mind the occasional confrontation, Junior preferred to do everything he could to avoid conflict.

Horace Sr. and Horace Jr. also had major differences when it came to lifestyle. Senior believed in being prompt and showed up for work early every day, if for nothing else than to make sure everyone else was getting to work on time. Junior often slept until 11:00 A.M. and made it a habit to always be late to everything.

"One time, one of his girlfriends was having a dinner party for Horace on his birthday," said Horace Jr.'s cousin Jane Hill Head. "She told him to wear a black tie and come at seven. They waited and waited and Horace never came, and they finally had dinner. "The next night he arrived at seven o'clock, twenty-four hours late."

Another indication of H. G. Hill Jr.'s personality is that he remained single and lived with his mother from the time of his father's death until he married in 1960—at the age of fifty-nine. Not surprisingly, H. G. Hill Jr. married someone already in the family—his brother-in-law's cousin Edith Caldwell.

When the United States declared war on Germany and Japan in 1941, H. G. Hill Jr. enlisted and was sent to Ft. Oglethorpe, Georgia. But the younger Hill would never see the war. In 1942, H. G. Hill Sr. died of a heart attack. H. G. Hill Jr., as the only son, was let out of the army, came home, and became president of the grocery store chain.

When he got back to Nashville, H. G. Hill Jr. moved into his father's office at the Nashville Trust Co. Between then and 1964, when he sold his family's share of the trust company, Hill would spend most of his time there. During that period, the grocery chain's day-to-day operations were run by L. P. Thweatt.

After World War II, the United States went through a period of enormous residential and commercial growth, as millions of soldiers came home, got married, and bought houses with the help of the new GI Bill program. In Nashville, residential neighborhoods in places like Green Hills, Oak Hill, and Inglewood popped up overnight.

Hill knew all about this building boom because he played a major part in it. Back in 1910, H. G. Hill Sr. had purchased some farmland adjacent to his home off Harding Road, thinking it might one day be turned into a planned residential area like Belle Meade. In the 1930s, Hill started developing it.

Hillwood, as it became known, proved that H. G. Hill Jr. had inherited his father's good sense, at least when it came to real estate. In an era when most residential developers were still building straight roads, Hillwood had curving and meandering roads (something that would become common decades later). In an era when developers usually tried to utilize every acre for homes, Hill donated land for two schools to be built in the neighborhood, thus ensuring that families with children would live there.

The interior of a newly opened Hill Store, around 1940 (H. G. Hill Stores Co.).

While he was supervising the development of Hillwood, H. G. Hill Jr. announced his chain would be adding several new supermarkets in Nashville during the next few years. But between 1942 and 1960, the H. G. Hill chain actually shrunk from about eighty stores to about twenty-five. Hill enlarged its existing stores, as increased merchandising after World War II caused each store to dramatically increase its shelf space. But the chain did not build a single new store during this period. Meanwhile, Kroger was building stores all over Nashville. "The truth is that he let the grocery business get away from him in Nashville," Wentworth Caldwell Jr. said of H. G. Hill Jr. in 1998. "Other stores, such as Kroger, came into Nashville with a very aggressive building program and he did not react quickly enough to their moves and he lost it."

There was some irony in the fact that Horace Jr. would not upgrade or expand the Hill grocery chain. While his father was alive, Horace Jr. and Horace Sr. were as different from one another as two people could be. "I think young Horace thought that his father was ruthless in many ways, and I think old Horace thought that his son was too much of a playboy," Head said. Nonetheless, Hill Jr. treated the business that he had inherited from his father as if it were almost too sacred to change.

It wasn't that Hill did not know what his competitors were doing. But Hill wasn't the type of businessman who would have borrowed a lot of money or mortgaged a lot of the company's property to finance a massive building effort. "He spent a lot of time observing Kroger and A&P when they came here with their bigger stores," Caldwell said. "He was very conscious of what they were doing. But he was not quite ready, or did not feel like the organization was ready.

"His standard answer was 'they have their programs. We have ours.'"

In 1964, Hill sold his interest in the Nashville Trust Co. and moved his office back to the grocery office. About that time, the company began to build supermarkets for the first time, jumping up to about fifteen thousand square feet while it closed many smaller stores. New locations went up in Nashville on Nolensville Road, in Donelson, in Green Hills, on Charlotte Avenue, and on Dickerson Road. Elsewhere in Middle Tennessee, the company built stores in Clarksville, Gallatin, Winchester, and Fayetteville. However, this growth paled in comparison to the new stores Kroger was building at the same time.

By 1975, the Hill chain had developed a reputation as a retailer that was slow to change with the times. Hill eventually started building much larger grocery stores, but long after its competitors were doing so. Once it built those stores, it was reluctant to change them. When Caldwell tried to remodel a Murfreesboro store at one point, Hill angrily ordered him to change it back to the way it was. Hill generally focused its product mix on an older clientele, sending many younger shoppers to other stores in search of ingredients. Most notably of all, H. G. Hill Jr. never opened his stores on Sunday, nor did he allow his stores to sell beer.

Hill was suspicious of new technology, which is why his grocery chain and trust company were slow to automate. A year after Third National took over the Nashville Trust Co., Third National president Sam Fleming said that the trust company had become very outmoded. H. G. Hill stores were years behind their competitors when it came to developing more modern distribution and pricing systems. Years after copiers became standard equipment, for example, the H. G. Hill Co. was still using carbon paper.

Hill was also legendarily reclusive, something that often encouraged speculation about his health and the company's future. Hill ventured out so rarely that he grew out of touch with changes in American society. Once, he went into a fast food restaurant and sat down, expecting someone to come and ask him his order. Another time, he had his realty company brick up the glass wall fronting the Belle Meade Barber Shop so no one would see him sitting in a barber's chair with a sheet over him. Hill is also believed to have never granted an interview to a reporter. When he died, the only photo the *Tennessean* had of him was at least forty years old.

By the mid-1970s, H. G. Hill had developed such a reputation of stagnancy that there were constant rumors of it being bought by competitors. Winn-Dixie, which had bought the Hill chains in Birmingham and New Orleans in the 1950s, was the company cited most often in news reports. But there were others.

However, Hill had no intention of selling, and since his company had no debt, he had no need to do so. Since he never retired, it gave him something to do. "Sell it?" John Hardcastle said in 1998. "Hell, he wouldn't even retire from it!"

In the late 1970s, Hill built sixty thousand-square-foot stores in Brentwood, Hermitage, Belle Meade, and on Eastland Avenue. But by that time, Kroger had been joined in Nashville by Bruno's and a chain called Mega Market. In the late 1980s, H. G. closed a wave of old stores. By 1993, the chain had only fourteen stores.

On September 5, 1993, Horace Greeley Hill Jr. died at the age of ninety-three. A few days after his funeral, the board of directors of the company (which H. G. had dominated while he was alive) met and elected Wentworth Caldwell Jr. president.

Caldwell's first major step as president was to grant an interview to the *Tennessean* in which he stated that his company was not for sale. He funded a massive advertising campaign—starring his daughter Ashley Caldwell—that said there was "a new spirit in an old friend" at Hill's.

But Caldwell's most controversial moves, taken only a few months after Hill's death, were to open the company's stores on Sunday and to sell beer in them.

"What are those subterranean rumblings coming from the cemetery?" *Tennessean* reporter E. Thomas Wood asked after Caldwell made these announcements.[20] But Caldwell said that his company had no choice but to sell beer and be open on Sunday if it wanted to stay in business. "The fact is that if you are in the retail business today, you have to be open on Sunday and you have to sell beer in order to attract the younger people into your stores," he said.

Caldwell also said that the founder of the Hill chain might have agreed with his move. "I knew enough about him that I think he was kind of a person who would jump on a market trend in a heartbeat," Caldwell said. "If there was a market trend that people would be open on Sunday, he would do that I think."

CHAPTER 4

Burial Insurance & Hillbilly Music

B efore Nashville became an insurance city, before insurance beget radio, before radio beget country music, and before country music beget tourism, a streetcar frightened a horse and caused a buggy accident.

Robert Hutchinson broke his leg in that incident. According to the one-paragraph account of the event in the *Nashville Banner*, Hutchinson was taken to Eve's Infirmary, where his condition at first appeared to be improving.

But there was no such thing as a minor injury in those days. After Hutchinson's leg was set, it developed an infection and had to be amputated. For a few days, his condition improved. Then, on Friday night, November 1, 1901, Hutchinson was sitting up in his bed, when he suddenly "threw up his hands, gasped and was gone," said witnesses.[1]

During the next few weeks, Hutchinson's widow had to decide what to do with her husband's business—the National Sick and Accident Insurance Co.

The growth of the insurance business around the turn of the century was one of the economic offshoots of the Civil War. Before Reconstruction, the South was dominated by an agrarian economy in which salaried jobs were the exception, and many people stayed close to their place of birth their whole lives. When something went wrong, they often had family members to take care of them. But after about 1870, thousands of southerners fled the farm and migrated to manufacturing plants in cities like Birmingham, Atlanta, and Nashville.

There was no such thing as Medicaid, paid sick leave, or manda-
tory disability insurance. If a man got sick or injured and couldn't
work for a week, he did not get paid. It did not matter whether he had
ten kids. It did not matter whether he was living from paycheck to
paycheck. And it did not matter if he had no family living nearby that
could bail him out.

It was in this more mobile society that hundreds of thousands of
southerners bought something called industrial insurance. Such policies, which cost a nickel or a dime per week, would pay your
salary—or a close approximation of it—if you were sick or injured and
couldn't go to work. They would also give your family a larger sum if
you died. But it was usually only enough money to pay the cost of
burial.

At the turn of the century, there were two types of entities from
which southerners would buy industrial insurance. Fraternal organizations, with secret rituals and familiar customs, were one. They
offered a sense of community, if not always solvency. The other
consisted of northern insurance companies such as Prudential
Insurance Co. of New York (which started the industrial insurance
industry in America in 1875) and its main competitor, Metropolitan
Life. Tennessee-based insurance companies had less than 5 percent of
the state's market at the turn of the century.

The National Sick and Accident Insurance Co. had a tumultuous
history. It was founded in Huntsville, Alabama, in 1897 by a
seafaring man named Captain Robert Pengilly. Pengilly knew little
about the insurance business. But he was "fine looking, wore a silk
hat, a long-tailed coat, and carried a gold-headed cane," according
to National Life cofounder Ridley Wills. Pengilly could also sell
anything to anybody.[2]

National Sick and Accident was organized as a fraternal order, in
all likelihood because Pengilly was hoping to avoid paying taxes.
About a year after it was founded, Pengilly moved the business to
Chattanooga because of disputes with his business partners. Not long
afterward, he came to Nashville and talked Hutchinson, then an
agent with Metropolitan Life, into coming on as a partner. A couple
of years later, Pengilly sold his interest to Hutchinson and moved
away.

At the time of Hutchinson's death, National Sick and Accident had
about fifty salesmen and collected fifteen hundred dollars in
premiums per week. It was licensed to operate in Tennessee, Alabama,
and Kentucky.

National Sick and Accident's customers had one thing in
common: they were all black. Since National Sick left few records,
one can only speculate as to why this was the case. Most likely,
African Americans were a market Metropolitan Life and Prudential

ignored. In any case, it is easy to understand why after failing in Huntsville and Chattanooga, Hutchinson's company did so well in Nashville. A stable community is absolutely necessary for insurance sales. With black colleges and a black publishing industry, Nashville had what was by the standards of the day an affluent African-American community.

Hutchinson's widow, who had five children, decided to sell her husband's business.

National Sick and Accident did not exactly have a stable past, and it sold insurance to customers that many white businessmen looked down upon. No one knew this better than Cornelius Abernathy Craig, deputy insurance commissioner for the state of Tennessee. After all, Craig had ordered National Sick and Accident to reorganize itself as an association and pay its taxes in 1901. But he knew an opportunity when he saw one.

At the time National Sick and Accident went on the auction block, C. A. Craig was less well known than his older brother Edward Burr Craig, who had recently resigned as state treasurer to accept a job with the Virginia Iron, Coal, and Coke Company in Bristol. As C. A. considered quitting his job to buy an insurance company, he went to Bristol to talk his brother into joining him. E. B. told his brother it sounded like a good opportunity but said he wasn't interested in switching jobs. But a man named Ridley Wills, who worked for E. B. both at the state and in Bristol, told C. A. Craig he would not only invest but also work for the company. Wills had an exceptional aptitude for mathematics, something Craig knew would come in handy at an insurance company.

The founders of the National Life & Accident Insurance Co. in 1930. From left to right are W. R. Wills, C. R. Clements, Dr. Rufus Fort, Thomas Tyne, and C. A. Craig (Metro Nashville Archives).

Back in Nashville, Craig was able to get two more people on board—an insurance agent named C. J. Hebert and a lawyer named Thomas Tyne. There is no way of knowing how many people turned Craig down, but one of them was his brother Robert, a Methodist minister who thought stock ownership was the moral equivalent of gambling.

Despite the fact that Craig had several partners, banks would not loan him enough money to make a bid because he had insufficient collateral. Craig then went to his native Giles County to see a wealthy farmer named Newton White. White agreed to cosign a loan in exchange for stock.

On December 27, 1901, at an auction held at the courthouse, two men bid against each other for the right to own the National Sick and Accident Insurance Co. One was Charles Sykes, who was acting on behalf of Craig's group. The other was a man named C. R. Clements, who had worked for National Sick and Accident under Hutchinson.

According to newspaper accounts, "a large crowd was present and the bidding was at times spirited."[3] Sykes's final bid was $150 a share—twenty-five cents higher than Clements's. For $17,250, Craig's group had bought the company.

Immediately after the auction, Craig approached Clements and convinced him to jump on board as an investor. A few days later, Hebert sold his stock to a physician named Rufus Fort.

Within weeks, the new owners changed the name of the company to the National Life and Accident Insurance Co.

Andrew Mizell Burton did not exactly make a grand entrance to Nashville.

Burton was a farm boy from the Sumner County town of Castalian Springs, Tennessee. His mother died when he was a boy, leaving his two unmarried aunts to raise him. The two women gave him all they could—love, a work ethic, and a sense of right and wrong. They couldn't give him money or a formal education, which is why Burton did not attend high school.

When he was eighteen, Burton decided it was time to seek his fortune and go to Nashville. His aunts did not have any money, but they gave him a milk cow that he could sell when he got to town. Family legend has it that Burton and the cow walked to Nashville together.

Luck, it turns out, was on Burton's side. He arrived in Nashville while the city was preparing for the Centennial Exposition, and jobs were easy to come by. After he sold his cow, Burton found work as a day laborer, building the exposition buildings.

After the centennial, Burton got a job as an insurance salesman for the Nashville office of the Traders Mutual Insurance Company of Illinois. Not wanting to disappoint his aunts, he worked hard and excelled at the business. Within five years, he had been promoted to manager of the Nashville office.

However, in 1902, the state of Tennessee revoked Traders Mutual's license, leaving the company's Tennessee staff of about fifty jobless. With a policy infrastructure and sales force already in place, Burton thought it wouldn't be hard to convince another insurance company to jump into the Nashville market. So it was with all confidence that he went to Cincinnati to ask W. J. Williams, president of the Western and Southern Insurance Company, if it would buy Traders Mutual's policies and staff. However, the company president had other things on his mind and advised Burton to start his own insurance company.

On the train back to Nashville, the twenty-four-year-old Burton decided to follow the man's advice. Whether he was inspired by the example shown by C. A. Craig and the other National Life founders two years earlier is not known. But like Craig, he needed money; his entire savings amounted to one thousand dollars. According to Tennessee law, an insurance company had to have at least twenty-five thousand dollars in assets to go into business. So upon his return to Nashville, Burton started approaching people he knew. Within a few weeks, he had solicited investments from an independent insurance agent named Guilford Dudley, an attorney named P. M. Estes, a druggist named J. C. Franklin, and Burton's secretary Lena Haralson. Haralson, by coincidence, had worked as Robert Hutchinson's secretary at National Sick and Accident.

Burton called his company The Life & Casualty Insurance Co. Like the other insurance company in town, it started off with nothing more than an industrial insurance policy. At first, L&C's home office had two employees—Burton, who worked as president, claim inspector, sales manager, and janitor, and Haralson, who was secretary, policy writer, and clerk. Although he had not played a major role in rearing his son, Burton's father J. Booker Burton showed his support for his son by taking out L&C's first policy.

Not long after he started his company, Burton attended a revival at which a traveling Church of Christ preacher, who was also from Castalian Springs, converted him. "He was thoroughly convinced that was his life from then on," A. M. Burton's son Nelson said over eight decades later. "He promised God at that time that if He blessed him in his business, he would give Him back every dime he made."

Like National Life, Life & Casualty sold a lot of insurance to African Americans. But because of Burton's religious affiliations, it also had an inroad with members of the Church of Christ. Burton also had a tendency to hire agents who were in the Church of Christ.

Burton preached industriousness and austerity. But he also had public-relations savvy. The first policy L&C ever paid out was to an African-American woman in North Nashville whose hand had become infected from a snag on a washboard. Burton sent his entire Nashville sales force to the neighborhood to deliver the $2.25 claim check. After the ceremonious delivery, L&C agents canvassed the neighborhood and sold $7.50 worth of weekly premiums.

L&C lost money in 1904 and 1905. But in 1906, the company made a profit of $6,600. About that time, it made its first real estate loan on a house near the corner of Fourth Avenue North and Jefferson Street. One year later, L&C began running small advertisements in the black-owned *Nashville Globe*.

After five years in operation, L&C had almost twenty-five thousand policies in force, all in Tennessee. But Burton knew his company had to expand beyond the state's borders. In 1909, L&C sold five hundred shares of stock for three hundred dollars per share. After the successful offering, L&C embarked on a major expansion effort, opening sales offices in Mississippi, Louisiana, Arkansas, and South Carolina. It was the presence of a large black population in these states that motivated L&C's growth strategy. "The state of Mississippi with its big plantations and its large negro population was the first state chosen by the Life and Casualty to extend its field of operations," a company history reports.[4]

Meanwhile, National Life and Accident was growing even faster. In the years following the auction, Craig and Wills spent most of their time on the road, hiring, training, and encouraging agents. Clement and Tyne spent most of their time running the home office. There wasn't a large amount of technical training to be done because the only policy sold by National Life during this time was an industrial insurance policy that cost five cents per week. It paid $1.25 per week in case of sickness, $2 for a disabling work-related injury, and $12.50 in case of death.

Like Mr. Hutchinson before them, National Life's new owners found a lot of black southerners willing to buy industrial insurance. National Life had expanded into Georgia, Louisiana, Kansas, Arkansas, and Indiana by 1911. The fact that the company ventured north of the Ohio River was some indication of how bold its founders were; in that era, southern companies usually confined themselves to southern markets.

Soon, both National Life and L&C had so many agents that each started a newsletter. Upper management at both companies would use those publications to encourage competitiveness and reward top salesmen. But both would use it as a stick as well as a carrot. "Place your eyes squarely on the allotments fixed for you as your year's-end goal," National Life vice president Ridley Wills wrote in 1922. "Then have a feeling so intense on the subject that it is very nearly a matter of life and death to reach this goal."[5]

At Life & Casualty, Burton bombarded his agents with tips on how to sell insurance, such as "visit ten new homes each week" and "spend thirty minutes each night planning the next day's work."[6] But his religious beliefs frequently mixed with company doctrine. "There is no question that Mr. Burton was a very staunch Church of Christ

member and that his basic philosophies were based on that teaching," said Sydney Keeble Jr., a longtime L&C executive whose father was L&C's general counsel in the 1940s and 1950s. "Besides, if you live clean, you live longer and have fewer claims."

The sales force of the Life & Casualty Insurance Co. pose in front of the company's downtown office, around 1910 (Metro Nashville Archives).

It is difficult to imagine what life was like for National Life and L&C's salesmen. They were paid solely on commission, so if they did not sell, they did not last. Most of them had no college education. But the ones who succeeded soon found they were accepted in the neighborhoods, or debits, in which they sold. One book about insurance agents describes the plight of industrial salesmen:

Agents ran into much ignorance and many prejudices, were often
met with sneers, had doors slammed in their faces, and were
ridiculed by regular agents—"How many kids did you insure today?";
"How is the peanut insurance company?" Their work was a combination of insurance business and social work; the agent who was
qualified for it and who liked it became family advisor and general
consultant on many matters not strictly in the line of business.[7]

Meanwhile, people in the home office were busy reviewing claims,
processing applications, investing assets, figuring how much everyone
got paid, and writing up the company newsletter. Most of those
people, except the ones making decisions, were women.

According to company photographs from the 1920s through the
1960s, about four-fifths of the people who worked for National Life
and Life & Casualty's home office were young women. Most of them
had graduated from high school in rural parts of Middle Tennessee
and southern Kentucky and had come to Nashville looking for better
opportunities.

It wasn't always easy for these women to find a place to stay. Most
would end up in boarding houses or in the YWCA. Around 1918, Life
& Casualty set aside two floors in its headquarters for small apartments for its female employees. The usual career pattern for female
employees was to work for National Life or L&C for three or four
years and then get married (married women were generally not
allowed to work for either company for the first part of the century).
Even though both National Life and L&C "loosened up" and allowed
married women to work there after World War II, both companies
were still extremely traditional employers. "It was a very conservative
place to work with a strict dress code," said Virginia Lyle, who worked
as a secretary at L&C in the late 1940s. "I remember one time a girl
came in to apply for a job wearing a backless sundress. We just
laughed and laughed about her chances of getting a job."

L&C did, however, have at least one woman who was far more
than a clerk. Lena Haralson, who had been one of L&C's original
investors, resigned her job with the company in 1908 when she
married a man named Thurston Johnson. But Mrs. Johnson later
came back and worked as manager of L&C's policy department until
1935.[8]

Later in the century, it would be impossible for a company to get
away with having all-white management, an all-white sales force, and
an all-white clerical staff when its customers were predominantly
black. But even though neither National Life nor Life & Casualty
hired their first black agents until the late 1950s, neither found that to
be a problem in black neighborhoods. "The black customers would
buy a small policy from a black-owned insurance company just to

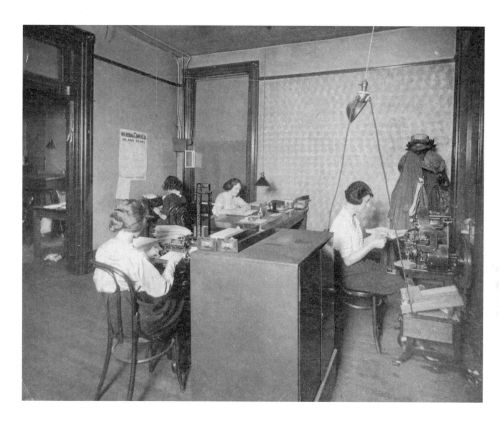

support the race, but they did all their big business
with us," said C. A. (Neil) Craig II, who went to work
as a National Life agent in the 1950s.

*Clerical workers at the Life
& Casualty Insurance Co.,
around 1910 (Metro
Nashville Archives).*

One indication of how fast both National Life
and Life & Casualty grew was how frequently each
moved its home office. National Life started on the second floor of a
residence at 421 Union Street. The company moved three more times
in the next five years before ending up in a mansion at the northeast
corner of Seventh Avenue and Union Street. After World War I, the
mansion was torn down to make way for the state's War Memorial
Office Building. National Life then built a classical-style, five-story
office building across Seventh Avenue, which would remain its home
for over forty years.

Life & Casualty started in a one-room office on Fourth Avenue. It
later bought what had once been the Chamber of Commerce Building
at 307 Church Street and moved there before building a six-story
office building at 159 Fourth Avenue North in 1925.

Emblems were a tradition in the insurance business; Prudential,
for example, displayed the Rock of Gibraltar in newspaper and magazine advertisements. In 1922, National Life decided to start using a

shield as its emblem. "The National will be known as The Great Shield Company," its newsletter *Our Shield* stated. "Its mission is to shield humanity in its fight with sickness, accidents, and death. . . . What nobler goal could a great business have?"[9]

L&C didn't have an emblem, but it did have a slogan. Keeping with Burton's philosophy of austerity, the words "Thrift—the Cornerstone" were cast into the cornerstone of the company's headquarters on Fourth Avenue. The word "thrift" also frequently appeared in L&C literature and, in the 1920s, even on the jerseys of a company-sponsored girls' basketball team.

Industrial insurance was a profitable market for both National Life and L&C to develop during those early years. But after World War I, both companies expanded from industrial into ordinary life insurance, defined as insurance whose face value was one thousand dollars or more and with premiums paid either annually or semi-annually. As Americans became more affluent, ordinary insurance was growing faster than industrial insurance. It had a lower lapse rate than industrial insurance, meaning the policyholder was less likely to stop paying. The influenza epidemic, which crippled industrial insurance companies all over the United States, also encouraged National Life and L&C to move into ordinary insurance.

Between 1915 and 1920, both National Life and L&C tripled in size in virtually every category, a remarkable record considering neither company made a major acquisition. By 1920, the two companies had combined assets of $7 million and were considered major players in Nashville's economy.

In 1923, National Life's board of directors made a decision that would have an enormous impact on Nashville's future. From all accounts, it did so to please C. A. Craig's son.

As a young boy growing up in Nashville, Edwin Craig was a HAM radio enthusiast. Using the directions found in magazines, Edwin built his own receiver at home. After graduating from Vanderbilt, Edwin went to work for National Life and was first sent to work as an agent in Dallas. But he never forgot his childhood hobby, and he followed very closely the early development of radio stations that started nationally after World War I.

At some point, Edwin became convinced National Life should have its own radio station. After all, the company had money to invest in bonds and real estate, and a radio station appeared to be a good investment. Since the airwaves were far less cluttered then, an AM radio station in Nashville could, on a clear night, reach the entire country. It would be good for Nashville. A radio station also offered the company the ability to keep in touch with its agents—and intracompany communication was a challenge for a sales company that by 1925 had twenty-five hundred agents.

Most importantly, National Life could use the station to advertise among white customers. As an added touch, Edwin Craig decided the station's call letters could even spread National Life's logo, not to mention exaggerate its customer base. The station could be called WSM, an acronym for "We Shield Millions."

The first time Edwin approached the National Life board with the WSM idea, they turned him down flat. But showing the same persistence his father had shown twenty years earlier when he started the company, Edwin eventually convinced them it was a good idea. Even after the board agreed, there was still some feeling among upper management that this was something the company was doing simply because Edwin Craig was the founder's son. Years after it went on the air, WSM was still known within the company as "Edwin's toy."

By 1925, radio station WSB in Atlanta was playing a type of music known then as southern folk. Not long after its debut, WSM would quickly became affiliated with this kind of music and Nashville with it. But when WSM first went on the air, National Life executives had no idea this would take place. When it announced the new radio station in *Our Shield*, WSM's executives told their employees there would be many different kinds of programs on the station, including lectures, sermons, sports, and music. But the only kind of music it mentioned was the only kind Nashville was affiliated with at the time—Negro spirituals sung by the Fisk Jubilee Singers.

The company did make it clear that the station would be wholesome. In an article in the company newsletter shortly before WSM's debut, the company made a case for radio being pro-family:

> The radio is in direct competition with every crosscurrent that would harm the home. Pictures that poison the mind, shows that speed up sensuality, and the many other endangerments that eventually engulf our boys and girls find a very powerful and very successful competitor in radio.[10]

Obviously, National Life did not repeat these arguments twenty-five years later when it started a television station.

Once National Life's board decided to get into radio, it spared no expense. The studio for the new station, located on the fifth floor of the headquarters building, was lavish and opulent. The station started with one thousand watts of power; wattage increased to five thousand a couple of years after it went on the air.

When Craig first came up with the idea for his radio station, he hoped National Life's would be the first in town. But in September 1925, WDAD was started by L. N. Smith, the owner of Dad's Radio

Supply Store at 184 Eighth Avenue North. Like WSM, WDAD was started to sell something, in this case radio equipment. And like WSM, it quickly found that listeners loved to hear hillbilly music.

Nevertheless, National Life had far deeper pockets than Smith, and it was probably for this reason that the general public and the newspapers got very excited about WSM's debut. When the station went on the air on October 5, 1925, crowds surrounded the five-story National Life Building to listen to the broadcast on speakers set up in the windows. That night several dignitaries made comments on the air including Gov. Austin Peay and Mayor Hilary Howse. Among the performers that night were a vocal quintet from Fisk University, Beasley Smith's orchestra, and Francis Craig's orchestra from the Hermitage Hotel.

One person who noticed the attention and excitement generated by WSM was A. M. Burton. Not long after WSM went on the air, Life & Casualty began to make plans for its own station. WLAC debuted about a year after WSM.

Throughout most of the twentieth century, Nashville society revolved around two poles on opposite sides of the cultural world—country music and Vanderbilt University. Nevertheless, the first person who probably ever played old-time or hillbilly music on WSM was a Vandy man.

Dr. Humphrey Bate, who got his medical degree from Vanderbilt in 1895, was a practicing physician who lived in Castalian Springs (the same town that produced Life & Casualty founder A. M. Burton). In his spare time, Bate enjoyed playing harmonica with a band he called the Castalian Springs Barn Dance Orchestra.

Bate and his band probably first appeared on the radio on station WDAD. According to printed schedules (which were not always accurate), Bate and his band first appeared on WSM on October 18, 1925. Like everyone else who appeared on WSM during those first few months, Bate and his band wore suits.

The notion of turning hillbilly music into a regular show was apparently the idea of George Hay. Hay, who was born in Attica, Indiana, and grew up in Chicago, once worked as a court reporter for the *Memphis Commercial Appeal*. "Memphis had the world record in murders then," Hay later said with pride. "I covered 137 murders in one year."[11]

As a reporter in Memphis, Hay's popular articles that ridiculed the way unsophisticated African Americans behaved in court earned him the nickname "the Judge." When the *Commercial Appeal* started radio station WMC, it put Hay to work as a part-time announcer, where his nickname evolved into "The Solemn Old Judge." It was while working as a reporter and moonlighting as an announcer that he attended a hoedown in the Ozark Mountains—the first time he had ever been exposed to the enthusiasm generated by hillbilly music.

Hay eventually made such a name for himself over the airwaves that Sears and Roebuck in Chicago hired him to work for radio station WLS (which stood for World's Largest Store). Just before he arrived, WLS had started a weekly show of hillbilly music called the Barn Dance, and Hay became its host. In 1924, Hay won an award for being the most popular radio announcer in the country. In November 1925, WSM hired him to be its director.

Almost all of the music WSM played in its first weeks was classical, big band, or opera (with occasional appearances by Bate and his band being the exception). But within weeks of his arrival, Hay started experimenting with country folk music.

About three weeks after Hay's arrival, a seventy-seven-year old champion fiddle player from Wilson County named Uncle Jimmy Thompson made an unscheduled two-hour appearance on WSM. The response from the public in the way of telegrams, letters, and phone calls was overwhelming, even more than it had ever been for Bate. A week later, Hay brought Thompson in to play again, and again, listeners loved it. For a few weeks, Hay wrestled with National Life about what to do. Then, around Christmas, WSM announced it would be devoting a regular Saturday night show to "old familiar tunes."[12] The show, which for two years was simply called the Barn Dance, featured performers like Thompson, Bate (whose band Hay later renamed The Possum Hunters), a black harmonica player named Deford Bailey, and a well-known vaudeville performer named Uncle Dave Macon.

The content of the letters that came in from places as far away as Newcastle, Texas, and Rochester, New York, gives some indication of just how excited people were when they heard the Barn Dance. Mr. V. E. Fraker from Noti, Oregon, wrote:

> Ain't radio wonderful? Last night an old Tennessee hillbilly out in Western Oregon was giving the dial a final twist about 10:15 Pacific Time when he hit banjos like they never have. The wife dropped her knitting and moved over closer to the old set, and out popped something about life insurance.[13]

What Hay and WSM had discovered was something about American culture and demographics on which Nashville would capitalize for the rest of the century. Even though millions of Americans had migrated from the country to the city, and millions of other Americans had migrated from east to west, they still retained an attachment to the culture they had left behind. For a lot of them, the music they had played and heard in their childhood—whether it be hillbilly, folk, or blues music, was a major part of that culture. But almost none of this music was being played on the radio in the 1920s, an era when classical music, the opera, and big bands dominated the airwaves. When people heard more earthy sounds on WSM, many people got very excited or very sentimental. "The music was the best I have got [sic] on the air for some time," Gertrude Bellringer of Atlantic City, New Jersey, wrote to Our Shield. "Your city must be wonderful to produce such old time music. It is so different than what we folks in the East hear."[14]

Soon, Hay began devoting an entire four-hour time slot to the Barn Dance. Some listeners wrote and said they liked the show so much that they wanted a souvenir from Nashville. Others said they wanted to come to Nashville to hear such music, the first hints that country music would eventually sprout its own tourist industry. "[The music] makes me think of my boyhood days back in Tennessee," wrote George Harrison of Fullerton, Nebraska. "I would like to visit your studio sometime."[15]

A station known for hillbilly music hadn't exactly been what National Life executives had intended. The kind of music they had in mind when they started WSM was more along the lines of the orchestra music played by Edwin Craig's cousin Francis.

As WSM and Nashville became affiliated with country music, many Nashville residents became embarrassed about the station's impact on Nashville's image. The criticism from the community got so bad that in May 1926, WSM announced it would stop having the Barn Dance. "WSM will continue the barn dances through the month of May, but beginning June 1 will probably discontinue the old-time music for the summer, unless the public indicates the desire to have it continued throughout the hot weather," a column in the Nashville Banner said.[16] A couple of weeks later, National Life executives reversed that decision after Barn Dance fan letters came in from as far away as California. "The proportion is about fifty to one," the Banner wrote, although the article implied that most of the letters against the Barn Dance were written locally.[17]

About a year later, Hay started calling the show The Grand Ole Opry, a name he came up with spontaneously when he compared the type of music featured on the Barn Dance to another popular radio show at the time called the Grand Opera. "For the last hour, we have been listening to music taken largely from grand opera and the classics," Hay said. "We now present our own Grand Ole Opry!" It took a while for the new name to settle in. The first few times the show was listed under its new name in the National Life newsletter, it was called "The Grand Old Op'ry." And as late as 1935, National Life was still giving away a calendar advertising the Saturday night show that showed barn animals playing musical instruments.

In the early days of radio, everything was live. But even after other stations began to use a lot of taped programming, Hay made sure WSM did not. This approach gave the Opry a spontaneity that the performers felt, the listeners picked up on, and that eventually became a sacred tradition. "We were so committed to being live that if Procter & Gamble or some other major advertiser wanted us to play a transcribed commercial, we wouldn't do it," said Irving Waugh, who started working for WSM after World War II. "We would instead take the transcription and convert it to live copy and read it. In fact, we were arrogant, without really realizing it, in our attitude toward anything that wasn't live."

The cast of the Grand Ole Opry, around 1927. Dr. Humphrey Bate is on the second row from the bottom, third from left. George Hay is standing on the far right (Country Music Foundation).

Within a few years, the Grand Ole Opry was getting sixty thousand fan letters per week and people were cramming into the fifth floor of the National Life Building on Saturday night to watch the show. WSM even started having to pay their performers to keep them from going to WLAC. When the National Life Building added a new wing, it built a room to accommodate more spectators, which by 1930 numbered into the hundreds.

By then, the Opry had gotten so big that Hay was having to remind people that WSM had other shows. And Nashville residents were learning to live with their city's new image. "The Nashville citizenry, though not reconciled to the point of listening to the program in any large numbers, are beginning to be proud of the fame it has brought the city," a *Tennessean* article said in 1937. "Maybe hillbilly capital is not such a bad tag for Nashville after all."[18]

The 1920s were good for the insurance industry in general but even better for Nashville's two insurance companies. Between 1920 and 1930, the amount of insurance sold by Life & Casualty tripled, from $46 million to $155 million. National Life's insurance in force more than quadrupled, from $77 million to $315 million. Not only did this growth far exceed that of national companies such as Metropolitan Life and Prudential, it came in the face of increasing competition in the South from companies such as Southern Life & Health of Birmingham and Industrial Life & Health of Atlanta. Top insurance companies were so impressed with National Life that the top national life insurance trade organization elected C. A. Craig as its national president.

After National Life and Life & Casualty got their radio stations off the ground, both companies began to have much higher profiles in Nashville. By 1928, both were regular advertisers in the local newspapers. National Life's advertisements frequently showed families gathered together, the father assuring his loved ones "You are shielded." National Life also used advertisements to boast about its balance sheet, promote an endowment plan, or encourage people to donate to the Community Chest.

L&C often used its advertisements to explain the way its ordinary policies worked. For $5 per year, a policyholder would get $2,500 in the case of death, blindness, or the loss of two limbs (loss of one limb only paid $1,250). On other occasions, Burton would use advertisements as a pulpit to preach the virtues of thrift and to explain its relationship to life insurance. "Beware of drifting," one advertisement warned in bold text. "Success is largely a matter of determination, or unalterable purpose. You can attain what you desire if you so will. But the path is not easy. It is not adorned with inconsequential pleasures purchased for seemingly trifling sums. But it is, nevertheless, a plain and well-trodden path. . . . One of the best ways to begin saving is by investing in a Life Insurance Contract."[19]

The newspapers inevitably returned this goodwill with articles promoting insurance. "He who sells a life insurance policy sells a certificate of character, an evidence of good citizenship, an unimpeachable title to the right of self-government," a story in the February 5, 1918, *Tennessean* reported.

In 1929, an American National banker named Richard Shillinglaw convinced National Life's executives it was time for National Life to sell some of its stock to the public. Like L&C's leaders twenty years earlier, National Life's management was no doubt anxious to raise capital to expand the company. But estate planning was also on their minds. By the late 1920s, many of National Life's founders were getting old. Shillinglaw pointed out to them that a public offering would set a legitimate price for the company and help their descendants avoid disputes with the government over inheritance amounts. On December 28, 1928, American National sold 6,250 National Life shares for $840 each to the public.

With the public offering, many of National Life's founders took their place among the city's wealthiest people. Ridley Wills, who at the time of the initial public offering lived near Elliston Place (in a home eventually turned into Jimmy Kelly's restaurant), built a mansion in Oak Hill. The family eventually sold that mansion to the state of Tennessee, which used it as a governor's residence.

A development at National Life that took place more gradually was the turning over of the company's management to the children of the founders. C. A. Craig had two children: son Edwin, who started WSM and became president of National Life in 1943; and daughter Kathryn, whose husband Douglas Henry became National Life's chief legal counsel. Edwin Craig subsequently had three children; son C. A. II (Neil), who would grow up to be a National Life executive; and daughters Elizabeth and Margaret Ann, whose respective husbands, Bill Weaver and Walter Robinson, would one day head the company. Douglas Henry's son Douglas Jr. would also be an attorney for National Life and a longtime state senator.

C. R. Clements's son C. R. Clements Jr. would become National Life's president in 1967. C. R. Sr.'s son-in-law Dan Brooks would also become company president.

Ridley Wills's son Jesse at first did not appear to be insurance material. While at Vanderbilt, Jesse made a name for himself as a poet with the literary group known as the Fugitives. But when his father started having health problems, Jesse decided to go to work for National Life. Jesse Wills started in 1922 and became president in 1963. Jesse's younger son, Ridley II, would also grow up to be a National Life executive.

Thomas Tyne's son Thomas Jr. went to work for National Life after graduating from Vanderbilt but died prematurely in 1936.

Rufus Fort's son Rufus Jr. would become a National Life executive and his son Garth became the company's chief medical officer.

Since National Life's executives wanted their sons to learn the company from the ground up, the company instituted an unwritten policy. Children of executives had to start as agents in places far away from Nashville before they were allowed to come home and become a home office executive. Because of this rule, C. A. (Neil) Craig II started at National Life as an agent in Dallas, and later went to San Antonio and Beaumont, Texas. Ridley Wills II started in north Georgia and then went to Akron, Ohio. "It started snowing when I crossed the Ohio River and it never quit," Wills said.

Nevertheless, National Life's management had such a reputation for being void of foreign bloodlines that it got a nickname in the business community: "Snow White."

The Great Depression hit Nashville's two insurers hard. Stock in both companies plummeted to a fraction of their pre-1930 values. As layoffs and bank closures swept through the country, many people could no longer afford to continue to pay their weekly premiums. The normal practices of both home offices often went out the window. "If LaGrange, Georgia, was doing well, but a lot of people were sick in Akron, Ohio, the company would tell the chief in LaGrange to send his money straight to Akron," C. A. (Neil) Craig Jr. said. The depression also had an impact on the investment side of the insurance business. In 1935 alone, National Life foreclosed on $3.75 million worth of property. The company also lost about $40,000 because of bank closures.

Meanwhile, Life & Casualty found there was a price to be paid for its close affiliation with the Church of Christ. In addition to selling a lot of insurance to church members, L&C had backed a lot of mortgages for church buildings. During the depression, a lot of churches defaulted on these loans, leaving L&C with assets that, unlike home or commercial mortgages, couldn't be resold. As a result of its investment problems, state regulators advised Burton to invite J. C. Bradford Sr. onto the Life & Casualty board, where he remained until 1951 "Mr. Burton was a genius at selling life insurance, but he was a sucker at investing," said J. C. (Jimmy) Bradford Jr., the son of the J. C. Bradford & Co. founder.

One of the things L&C divested during this period was its radio station, which it sold to one of its executives named Truman Ward.

WSM lost money for the first ten years of its existence, so there were almost certainly people at National Life ready to sell it as well. But rather than get out of radio, National Life decided to use it to sell insurance. In 1932, National Life upgraded WSM from five thousand to fifty thousand watts, making it one of the most powerful stations in the United States. About that time, it started openly advertising National Life's insurance products on WSM for the first time.

The Grand Ole Opry had been almost an instant success with WSM's listeners. But National Life's executives had been reluctant to embrace it or treat it as something permanent. The financial crisis of the early 1930s resolved that ambiguity. Traditionally, door-to-door insurance agents would hand out trinkets to policyholders such as needle kits, calendars, and booklets. In 1933, National Life produced a brochure called "Fiddles and Life Insurance" for its agents to give away. At first glance, it appeared to be nothing more than a little booklet about country music with pictures of Opry stars on it. But throughout the brochure were advertisements for insurance.

Soon, as the Opry became more popular, the company's fleet of agents started reporting that WSM and the Opry were quite a "door opener." In 1931, when the Opry outgrew the downtown office building and moved to the Hillsboro Theater, management came up with another way to use the Opry to sell insurance: tickets to the Opry could only be obtained from National Life agents.

Country music proved to be a perfect partner for National Life. The Grand Ole Opry became enormously popular with working class whites all over the country—the demographic that the company was trying to reach. "We used to listen to it every Saturday night," said Waylon Jennings, who grew up in Littlefield, Texas, in the 1940s and went on to become a country music star. "Since we couldn't afford new radio batteries and had no electricity, we used to pull the truck up beside the house and run jumper cables through the window into our old Philco radio."

Agents soon found that the easiest way to get their foot in the door of a prospective client was to mention that their company was the one that owned WSM. "Our agents were trained to walk through neighborhoods on Saturday night with pen and paper in their hands," said Neil Craig II. "In those days, there was no air conditioning, and it was very easy to tell who was listening to WSM. They were trained—I was trained—to go back to that house a few days later and say 'I couldn't help but notice, ma'am, that you were listening to WSM.'" E. W. (Bud) Wendell, who started as a door-to-door salesman for National Life in Hamilton, Ohio, in 1950, said the Grand Ole Opry was a tremendous help when it came to selling insurance. "My sales experience was in the Midwest, in places like southern Ohio, West Virginia, Detroit, and Indiana," Wendell said. "Many of those people had migrated from the South, where the Opry and country music was so strong, during the second World War. . . . Because you were from the Grand Ole Opry, people accepted you and would invite you in."

There is no way to statistically prove how much WSM and the Opry helped National Life's agents during this time. But between 1929 and 1934—a time when insurance sales declined nationally—National Life's sales increased 28 percent.

As the nation's economy began to recover, National Life and L&C began to grow even faster. Between 1935 and 1940, L&C and National Life more than doubled the amount of insurance both had in force. Meanwhile, national giants such as Metropolitan Life and Prudential grew at about half that rate.

By the eve of World War II, National Life was ranked sixth among national insurance companies in the sale of industrial policies. L&C ranked ninth.

CHAPTER 5

Kings Caldwell

L ike so many people who made a fortune in Nashville, James E. Caldwell never invented anything, nor was he necessarily the first person to go into a particular industry. But he put capital with the right idea and the right business plan at the right time.

Caldwell came to Nashville after the Civil War and went to work for a wholesale grocer. Right away, he began to act like someone who knew how to make a lot of money. One time, he cornered the city's market on millet seed. The next day he sold the seed for twice what he paid for it.

Caldwell later left wholesaling and prospered as a fire insurance salesman. In the early 1880s, he became intrigued by the phone business, then in the incubation stage in Nashville.

The first man to start a telephone company in Nashville was James W. Braid. In 1876, Braid attended the Centennial Exposition in Philadelphia and saw a telephone for the first time (it had only been invented a year earlier). When he got back to Nashville, Braid sought the advice of one of his friends, a dentist named James Ross. Braid and Ross quit their jobs, obtained the necessary franchise from American Bell and formed a phone company that eventually became known as Cumberland Telephone & Telegraph.

Braid and Ross knew the value of a good public relations stunt. In May 1877, the duo put together a crude phone system, strung the line between the Polk Place mansion and another downtown residence, and notified the newspapers. When Mrs. Polk heard a voice coming from the machine, she thought it was some sort of a trick. Only when she heard a piano tune that she had requested being played at the other end of the line did the grand dame of Nashville society believe her voice was being carried by the phone wire.

A few months later came public relations stunt number two. Ross took a train to Bowling Green, Kentucky, and Braid stationed himself at the Western Union station in Nashville. On a Sunday in the fall of 1877, Braid and Ross had Nashville's first long distance conversation. One of the men on the Nashville end of the line—a man named William Stockell—was so thrilled that he sang "Meet Me Alone by Moonlight" on the telephone. Stockell thus became the first person in Nashville to have his singing voice transmitted, something Nashville would became famous for fifty years later.

Within five years, Cumberland Telephone & Telegraph (CT&T) had sold a few hundred "talk boxes" for the enormously high price of five dollars per month. But Braid and Ross realized it was going to require far more capital and years of work before they could earn a profit. They began looking for buyers.

James E. Caldwell, who by this time had gotten into the streetcar business, knew this was his chance. In 1889, Caldwell and flour mill owner Oscar Noel bought Braid and Ross's franchise for

James E. Caldwell (pictured with bow tie and cane) walks down Fourth Avenue, circa 1915 (Tennessee State Library and Archives).

thirty thousand dollars. Caldwell then sold one hundred thousand dollars in CT&T stock to the public, reduced its rates dramatically, and spent far more money on advertising than his predecessors. He also secretly set up a separate entity to buy and sell CT&T stock in order to popularize its sale, something for which Caldwell was prosecuted years later.

As the state's largest and best-capitalized phone company, Cumberland Telephone & Telegraph improved its service and began taking over smaller phone companies throughout the region. By 1900, CT&T dominated the phone business from Louisville to Memphis to New Orleans to Knoxville, and Caldwell was one of the wealthiest and most revered men in Nashville. "Mr. Caldwell was a dignified aristocrat and never let anyone forget it," Nashville construction company owner Wilbur Creighton Sr. wrote. "He wore a cutaway coat, standing collar, white vest, and striped pants. He carried a gold-headed ebony cane, and when walking the streets of Nashville, which was seldom, he never looked to the right or the left."[1]

In 1911, Caldwell sold CT&T to American Telephone and Telegraph in one of the first takeovers ever of a large Nashville company by an out-of-town entity. Many people in the Nashville community did not like it. "The community of Nashville gazed on the event, first with surprise and then with resentment," Caldwell later wrote. "For the community took great pride in having the headquarters of so respectable and successful and extensive a business located in its midst. . . . Yes, a great commercial tragedy had taken place."[2]

About the same time Caldwell sold CT&T, Nashville's two largest banks went through a leadership vacuum when Samuel Keith of the Fourth National Bank died and F. O. Watts of the First National Bank was hired by a bank in St. Louis. Caldwell was asked by the directors of both banks to help execute a merger of the two institutions and to become the merged entities' president. The merger took place in July 1912, creating the largest bank in the South. At the end of World War I, the Fourth and First National Bank controlled about 40 percent of Nashville's bank deposits. Members of its board included Caldwell, printer John Ambrose, iron foundry owner Henry Buttorff, grocer H. G. Hill, whiskey distiller Victor Shwab, and flour mill owner and former Nashville mayor William Litterer. It had branches on Church Street and Lower Broad, in North Nashville, West Nashville, and Madison. In other words, it had every economic and geographic corner of Nashville covered.

In 1916, the Fourth and First built a glorious six-story bank building at the northeast corner of Fourth and Union. One indicator of Caldwell's brashness was the way he reacted when he realized that the bottom floor of his building was not perfectly even with the sidewalk. Convinced that people in wheelchairs make good customers, Caldwell

asked the city to fix the sidewalk to match his building. When the city refused, Caldwell had workers tear up the sidewalk and repave it so it was even with the entrance to the bank. Because of what he had done to the sidewalk, Caldwell was summoned to court and ordered to pay a fine. But in the process he created the first handicapped entrance to a business in Nashville history.

The interior of the Fourth and First National Bank, around 1920 (First American National Bank).

If ordinary Nashville residents had an account at the Fourth and First, wealthy people had assets with the Nashville Trust Co. The Nashville Trust Co. was started in 1889 by a promoter named Herman Justi, primarily through the financial backing of whiskey distiller Charles Nelson. Although the Nashville Trust Co. actually had savings and checking accounts after 1904, its primary business was handling estates, trust accounts, and wills. "If you were old money, you were likely to be dealing with the Nashville Trust Co.," said John Hardcastle, who went to work for the trust company in 1958 and later researched its history.

The closest thing that the Fourth and First National Bank and the Nashville Trust Co. had to competition was American National Bank. American National was organized in 1883 by railroad magnate Edmund "King" Cole and nineteen other investors. In October 1918, American National came under the control of two men. One was a Stanford graduate, insurance agent, and real estate developer named Paul Davis. The other was a banker and a descendant of former Texas and Tennessee governor Sam Houston named P. D. Houston. Both Houston and Davis had money because of family connections to Tullahoma's Dickel Distillery.

There were many other banks in Nashville before 1920, but only one of them would emerge healthy and strong after the Great Depression. The Commerce Union Bank was first organized by a twenty-year-old upstart named Ed Potter Jr., who left his father's employ at the Broadway National Bank because his daddy wouldn't promote him fast enough. Potter called his bank the German American Bank, knowing that the name would inspire many first and second generation German Americans—such as meat packer Henry Neuhoff, bag maker Joe Werthan, and retailer Lee Loventhal—to jump in as initial investors. The German American had sixty-seven initial stockholders, none of whom owned more than 4 percent of the stock. It opened its doors in January 1917 at 310 Third Avenue North—a space previously occupied by a barbershop.

Anti-German sentiment during World War I caused Potter to change the name of the bank to Farmers and Merchants Bank, a name that would later be changed to Commerce Union Bank. Even so, within three years of its organization, Mr. Potter's Bank—as many called it—had deposits close to one million dollars. It had also outgrown the barbershop and moved into the Stahlman Building.

One thing Nashville's larger banks had in common early in the twentieth century was that they did not make many loans to African Americans. "There was no ready credit source for the average poor negro," James C. Napier, one of the first black attorneys in Nashville, said in the 1930s. "Negro workmen often had difficulty finding a creditor for even as small a loan as five or ten dollars."[3]

Because of this, a group of about twenty African Americans led by Napier, National Baptist Publishing Board president Richard Boyd, and Greenwood Park and Cemetery owner Preston Taylor formed the One-Cent Savings Bank & Trust Co. The bank opened in January 1904 and at first operated out of Napier's law office at 411 North Cherry Street (later Fourth Avenue). In the 1920s, after the bank changed its name to Citizen's Savings Bank & Trust, it moved to a former hotel at the corner of Fourth and Charlotte.

Compared to the large white-owned banks in Nashville, Citizen's was small and would remain so throughout the century.

But like the city's leading white-owned banks, Citizen's was accused by many of its potential customers of being too conservative. In 1909, the People's Savings Bank & Trust Co. opened across the street from Citizen's. Among the individuals who founded People's were physician Robert Boyd—a physician and former Meharry professor who was not related to Richard Boyd—and Arthur Townsend, the former president of Nashville's Roger Williams University and one of Richard Boyd's chief rivals in the National Baptist Convention.

There was more to the rivalry between Citizen's and People's than bank philosophy. During the 1910s and 1920s, many members of Nashville's black community had an allegiance to either Boyd, who many considered an elitist, or Townsend. These allegiances bled over not just into banking and church affiliation but even to which park a person went to (Boyd's Greenwood Park or Townsend's Olympic Park). Richard Boyd, however, had a weapon that Robert Boyd and Arthur Townsend did not have—the newspaper *Nashville Globe*, which promoted Citizen's Bank, Greenwood Park, and the National Baptist Publishing Board in its articles and editorials.

The 1920s were an exciting time to be a Nashville banker. As a financial center, Nashville was in many ways superior to Atlanta, Birmingham, and New Orleans. Mergers and acquisitions were so frequent that total deposits in Nashville almost tripled during the decade. Had good business journalism existed at that time, newspapers would have been replete with stories about proposed takeovers, intense competition, and new ways to get around the few banking laws that existed at the time.

The 1920s were also a time when fortunes were made overnight, and when a good tip was considered to be the difference between earning a million and losing a million. "There was no research as we know it today," said J. C. (Jimmy) Bradford Jr., whose father founded J. C. Bradford & Co. in the 1920s. "The best information anyone could get was inside information. You might hear someone say, 'My brother-in-law works in the treasury department at General Motors and he says so and so.' The feeling at the time was that if you could get into the charmed circle, you could make a lot of money."

During the 1920s, banks often reflected the personalities of the people who controlled them. At American National Bank, that person was Paul Davis. Largely due to Davis's aggressiveness, American National rapidly became popular with "new money" in the 1910s and 1920s, meaning fortunes made after the turn of the century. Among the prominent businesses that became affiliated with American National during this period were Cheek-Neal Coffee, Bransford Realty, and J. W. Carter Shoe Co.

Davis's biggest coup came in northeast Davidson County. After the federal government abandoned its $67 million gunpowder plant in Old Hickory, Davis put together a group of Nashville and out-of-town investors called the Nashville Industrial Corp. The group then launched a national publicity campaign to find a new industrial tenant and sell unused equipment left over from the powder plant. In 1923, DuPont, which had built the plant and operated it under contract with the federal government, agreed to come back, buy the entire five thousand-acre complex, and convert the factory to a rayon plant.

The Nashville Industrial Corp. raised a few eyebrows in town, especially after some of Davis's fellow investors in the U.S. War Department were indicted for improper bidding processes. But as a result of Davis's involvement in the Nashville Industrial Corp., American National Bank got a new customer. When the plant started producing rayon, American National was the only bank authorized to open a branch in the company-owned town of Old Hickory, giving it a monopoly in a town of thirty thousand people.

Davis was also causing his competitors a few headaches in town. In 1920, American National Bank started an affiliated trust company in its headquarters, located right next door to the Nashville Trust Co. This move broke with tradition in a city where banks historically stayed out of the trust business and trust companies stayed out of banking. Nashville Trust president William Nelson, the son of Nashville Trust cofounder Charles Nelson, wasn't about to lose a game of one-upmanship with Paul Davis.

In 1926, the Nashville Trust Co. built a new headquarters building adjacent to the old one, creating an L-shaped structure that surrounded American National Bank. At fourteen stories tall, the new Nashville Trust Building was the largest structure in the Southeast. Not to be outdone, Davis added eleven stories to his building, making his building one story taller. Davis also made certain his floors did not match up with those next door in order to discourage the future merger of the two organizations. As soon as Davis's eleven-story addition was completed, Nashville Trust added one more story to ensure that it remained the tallest building in town. Davis and Nelson might have kept going had the depression not turned their minds to more serious matters.

American National also made a noteworthy acquisition in the early 1920s: the 1921 purchase of a small Nashville institution called the Cumberland Valley National Bank & Trust Co. An American National lawyer named Frank Berry and two Cumberland Valley attorneys named Frank Bass and Cecil Sims handled the legal work on that merger. The trio got along so well that they formed a new law firm shortly thereafter that became known as Bass, Berry, & Sims.

"We've represented the bank ever since," Bass, Berry, & Sims partner James Bass Sr. said in 1998. After the merger with Cumberland Valley, American National moved into the Stahlman Building.

Meanwhile, young Ed Potter was also making a name for himself. Unlike many of the bankers of his day, Potter did not have a background in a related field such as insurance or real estate. Since he started his bank at such a young age, no one had ever shown him how it was done. But Potter made up for his lack of experience with an intense obsession with his work. "He lives with it, eats with it and sleeps with it," a company history stated. "The bank comes first. All else is secondary. At this stage he has no hobbies, no distractions."[4]

Potter's main distraction during the 1920s was expanding his bank outside of Nashville. Since Commerce Union was chartered by the state rather than the federal government, it was legal for it to buy banks in other counties, something federally licensed banks such as the Fourth and First and American National could not do. Between 1923 and 1924, Commerce Union took over close to a dozen banks in outlying areas such as Springfield, Murfreesboro, Gallatin, and Lebanon. This expansion alarmed other banks in small towns across Tennessee, leading them to lobby the legislature for a new law in 1925 that outlawed branch banks in counties except the county where the head office was located. However, Commerce Union was allowed to keep its network of banks under the new law's grandfather clause, something that would prove to be of great significance in future decades.

Commerce Union was also rising in stature within Nashville's boundaries. In 1923, a time when most banks considered it beneath themselves to try to steal customers from each other, Mr. Potter's bank was boasting in newspaper advertisements that its savings accounts yielded four percent interest. The next year, Potter's bank bought the State Bank and Trust Co., a small financial institution with $1.5 million in deposits. Five years later, Commerce Union merged with the Broadway National Bank, which must have been especially satisfying to Ed Potter since his father was Broadway National's president.

However, all the developments in the Nashville banking community paled in comparison to the story of Caldwell & Co.

Rogers Caldwell, the seventh of James E. Caldwell's ten children, grew up on his father's fifteen hundred-acre estate on Franklin Pike and rode a horse to Montgomery Bell Academy every day. Like his father, Rogers Caldwell took to capitalism like a fish to water; at the age of thirteen he was caught selling water to thirsty railroad workers who were working on his father's property. Rogers later attended Vanderbilt, but, like many young men of his generation, left school early to make his fortune.

Rogers Caldwell's first job was with his father's insurance company. But instead of sticking to the insurance business, Rogers started sidelining in the municipal bond business, helping local governments that were trying to raise money to build schools and roads find northern investors who would buy their bonds. Young Caldwell learned the hard way that northern investors were not very enthusiastic about buying southern municipal bonds because many local governments had defaulted on their bonds during the Reconstruction era. In May 1915, Caldwell thought he had worked out a deal to sell Hickman County bonds to the Harris Trust and Savings Bank of Chicago. When the deal was nearly completed, a German submarine sunk the British ship *Lusitania*, causing a national financial panic. The bank then sent Caldwell a telegram telling him they were not interested anymore. "I decided on the spot to get in shape so nobody else could ever withdraw a bid on me," he told a reporter half a century later.[5]

In 1917, Rogers Caldwell started his own company. At first, Caldwell & Company's main business was buying municipal bonds from small counties in Tennessee and selling them to institutional investors. Caldwell & Co.'s first bond issue came from Robertson County and was sold to the Fourth and First National Bank (the bank over which Caldwell's father presided). The younger Caldwell took the profit from that sale and invested the money in advertisements in the *New York Times* and *Wall Street Journal*.

Within two years of its formation, Caldwell & Co. took two huge steps. One was the purchase of an old Nashville security house owned by brothers Goulding and Frank Marr, a purchase that brought with it many of Nashville's wealthiest customers. The other was the formation of a subsidiary organization called the Bank of Tennessee.

The Bank of Tennessee wasn't a real bank in that it had no individual depositors, no tellers' windows, and little cash on hand. The bank's sole purpose was to hold proceeds from the sale of bonds until the money was needed for actual construction of the projects being financed (a role historically carried out by a third party bank). In later years, numerous state and federal laws would regulate what could be done with such money. But there were few such laws in the 1920s. Since the Bank of Tennessee was owned and controlled by Rogers Caldwell, the bank gave Caldwell access to enormous amounts of money that otherwise would be sitting in an account doing nothing.

Starting about 1919, the bond market in the South began to grow rapidly because of increased urbanization, high agricultural prices, and a land boom in Florida. As communities grew and built schools, paved roads, and dug levees, they increasingly called on Caldwell & Co. to help them finance their projects. "We Bank on the South" became the firm's proud slogan, stated in newspaper advertisements from New Orleans to Boston.

Caldwell & Co. soon outgrew its original home and in 1924 built an eight-story headquarters at 400 Union Street. By that time, Caldwell & Co. had nine branch offices, including New York and St. Louis.

Rogers Caldwell is frequently remembered as the man who built a financial house of cards, but it is important to note how vital his bond business was to the South. "In many ways, he was the first pioneer to bring northern capital in this area," said Sam Fleming, who went to work for Nashville's Third National Bank in 1931. "All of the investment houses that came later were based on the foundation that Rogers Caldwell laid." In 1931, a *Time* magazine article stated that "Rogers Caldwell had a dream of economic empire in the South. . . . Self-confident, ambitious, no financial scheme was too big for him to tackle. He believed in the economic destiny of the South, sought to force its maturity."[6] The trade journal *Manufacturer's Record* thought so much of the municipal bond trader that it headlined an August 1929 article "The Business Romance of Rogers Caldwell."

The Caldwell & Co. Building at 400 Union Street, around 1925 (Metro Nashville Archives).

As far as the South's economic development was concerned, perhaps the most important things Rogers Caldwell did were help manufacturers finance new factories and help developers finance new real estate ventures. The 1920s were a time of enormous industrial growth for the South, as hundreds of manufacturers invested in new factories and hundreds of thousands of people left their farms to work in them. Caldwell & Co. played a major role in the financings of dozens of such factories. One Caldwell & Co. bond issue, for example, paid for five hundred thousand dollars worth of upgrades to the Werthan-Morgan-Hamilton Co. bag plant in North Nashville. The way such arrangements would often work is that Caldwell & Co. would buy the bonds from a

manufacturing company in exchange for stock. Caldwell & Co. would then sell the bonds to the general public or institutional investors at denominations of one hundred or five hundred dollars and at a yield of either 6 or 7 percent.

Caldwell & Co. sometimes found buyers for the stock and sometimes would keep it. In this way, the firm acquired considerable ownership in many companies, among them a cotton mill builder called Alabama Mills, a St. Louis apparel manufacturer called Alligator Raincoat Co., a mining business called Kentucky Rock Asphalt, and a retail chain called Southern Department Stores (which operated a Nashville store called Lebeck's).

On the real estate side, Caldwell & Co. sold bonds that built hotels, churches, and apartment buildings. Among the real estate projects underwritten by Caldwell & Co.: the 425-room Kentucky Hotel in Louisville; the twelve-story, 231-room Noel Hotel in Nashville; and the eight-story National Garage in Memphis.

Meanwhile, Caldwell & Co. began using its Bank of Tennessee assets to acquire other things. According to a doctoral thesis written at the University of North Carolina in 1938—later published as John Berry McFerrin's *Caldwell and Company: A Southern Financial Empire*— Rogers Caldwell did not make much money from bond commissions. The real business of Caldwell & Co. was what it did with the proceeds from the sales of bonds while they sat in the Bank of Tennessee.

Caldwell & Company's early investments would be relatively safe ones. First, the business bought a big chunk of Fourth and First National Bank stock, making it easier for Rogers to get loans from his dad's bank. Caldwell & Co. also bought two small insurance companies, the Cotton States Life Insurance Co. and North American National Life Insurance Co.

In the late 1920s, Caldwell became adept at leveraging insurance companies, banks, and manufacturers to buy even more insurance companies, banks, and manufacturers. Starting in about 1927, Caldwell went on one of the most remarkable buying binges in American history. Among the larger assets purchased: eight insurance companies, led by the Missouri State Life Insurance Co. of St. Louis; large blocks of stock in the Holston National Bank of Knoxville and Union Planters Bank of Memphis; two newspapers, the *Memphis Commercial Appeal* and *Knoxville Journal*; and even the Nashville Volunteers minor league baseball team.

In 1929, Caldwell & Co. had 250 employees and assets of $38 million. However, Caldwell had leveraged so much that the assets of the companies controlled by Caldwell & Co. were almost $500 million. Many Nashville residents viewed Caldwell & Co. with pride. After all, the business was a major force in helping the South and the main reason that by the 1920s Nashville had earned the nickname "Wall Street of the South."

The South by electrifying industry is creating new investment values

The South is favored with cheap electricity in unlimited quantities. Stream and steam power vie with one another to pare American manufacturing costs.

Swiftly and surely industry is coming South . . . to lower costs and larger dividends. From hydro and steam plants, Southern utilities are already producing annually nearly 3,000,000,000 KWH of electric current.

In a single section of the South, new industries are now locating at the rate of one every four days. The whole South is gaining wealth and building investment values at a fast rate.

Caldwell & Company is a Southern investment organization, underwriting and distributing sound Southern securities. "Shares in The South, Inc." is an investment trust which will interest investors desiring to share in the South's diversified and steady progress. Write for details.

✦ ✦   We Bank on the South   ✦ ✦

CALDWELL & COMPANY

400 Union Street
Nashville · Tenn.

Chicago . Detroit . Cincinnati
Kansas City . St. Louis . Jackson
Louisville . Knoxville . Tampa
Memphis . Chattanooga . Dallas
Greensboro . New Orleans
Birmingham . Jacksonville

Rogers Caldwell & Co., Inc.
. 150 Broadway, New York

This advertisement for Caldwell & Co. appeared in many business publications between 1925 and 1929.

Caldwell had no greater fan than *Nashville Tennessean* publisher Luke Lea. Lea had one of the most remarkable careers in Tennessee history, developing Belle Meade, serving in the U.S. Senate, and leading an unsuccessful mission to kidnap the German Kaiser all before he was forty. In 1925, Lea helped organize a Nashville financial institution called the Liberty Bank and Trust. A few months later, he began a series of business partnerships with Caldwell. The first was the purchase of the *Knoxville Journal* and *Memphis Commercial Appeal*, which Lea hoped to use as the basis of a large chain of newspapers. Later, Lea and Caldwell would purchase partial ownership of more banks, including an Asheville, North Carolina, institution called the Central Bank & Trust.

Lea's control of so many newspapers no doubt helped keep reporters from writing negative stories about his friend Rogers Caldwell. But many in the Nashville business community—especially those who had insight into the way Caldwell & Co. did business—were concerned about the solvency of Rogers Caldwell's financial empire by around 1927. For one thing, the firm's accounting practices were deplorable. "The accounting department was by far the weakest spot in the organization," McFerrin wrote. "The affairs of the department were handled in a very haphazard manner, each employee making whatever entries he thought should be made and the department more or less running itself."[7] Since Rogers Caldwell owned almost all the stock, there were no board meetings and no stockholder meetings.

Rogers Caldwell's lifestyle also bothered many people who knew him. In the midst of his buying binge, Caldwell loaned himself enough money through the Bank of Tennessee to build a $350,000 mansion called Brentwood Hall. He also developed a taste for lavish entertaining, fox hunting, early American silver and furniture, and anything related to his hero Andrew Jackson. Years later, Commerce Union Bank founder Ed Potter would recount a conversation between Caldwell and himself. "Rogers, some of those s.o.b.'s that hunted with you and hung around with you paid more for their pink coats than they paid for their horses," Potter said. "And you hadn't the sense but to listen to them because they told you what you wanted to hear."[8]

Caldwell also had at least one employee who warned him that his business was on a course toward disaster. In May 1930, DeWitt Carter, an executive vice president at Caldwell & Co. wrote a long letter of resignation to Rogers Caldwell. In the letter, Carter accused Caldwell of running the firm like a dictatorship and of attributing constructive criticism to "hardheadedness, prejudice, unfairness and so forth which is very wrong for it makes further discussion on merits of a proposition impossible." Carter also wrote that as best he could tell, Caldwell & Co. was "more of a trading vehicle for your [Caldwell's] activities than an institution."[9]

No one had a better seat to view Rogers Caldwell's buying binge than the board of the Fourth and First National Bank. And although Fourth and First president James Caldwell was no doubt proud of his son, not all the other board members were amused. The most important dissenter was Cornelius Craig, president and founder of the National Life & Accident Insurance Co. Craig was conservative and did not like the idea of loaning money to someone who leveraged that loan to buy something else. He was especially disturbed when the Fourth and First began loaning Caldwell & Co. money so that Rogers Caldwell could buy insurance companies that competed with National Life.

There were other reasons people at the Fourth and First should have been concerned about their bank's relationship with Caldwell & Co. Between 1926 and 1929, the bank made several loans to Caldwell totaling $1.7 million. Even though this amount far exceeded the amount that the bank could actually loan to one entity, the Fourth and First would use many affiliated companies, such as the Nashville Trust Co., to filter money to Caldwell. The Fourth and First also did at least one stock offering through Caldwell & Co. that later audits would show as poorly organized and even set up to insure that Caldwell & Co. received ridiculously high commissions.

About the same time, two American National bankers were looking to branch out on their own. Frank Farris and Walter Diehl were dissatisfied with American National and had even fought an unsuccessful proxy battle to take over the bank. In addition to knowing how to run a bank, Farris had a small fortune of his own to invest—his share of the insurance settlement left over from the death of his father Willis Farris in a 1918 train accident.

Farris and Diehl convinced National Life's Cornelius Craig and several other Nashville businessmen—including Watkins Crockett, flour mill owner Oscar Noel, and department store merchant John Cain—to become major shareholders in a new bank called The Third National Bank. Word spread quickly through the Wall Street of the South, and over four hundred citizens bought stock before the bank went into business in the Independent Life Building at Fourth and Church. On opening day in July 1927, the bank received about $1 million in deposits. Third National showed an innovative streak by starting Nashville's first night depository, something that helped the bank generate accounts from retailers and theaters.

Craig wasn't the only director who left the Fourth and First for another bank. Sometime in the late 1920s, longtime Fourth and First director H. G. Hill Sr. resigned to become a director of American National Bank. Like Craig, Hill was nervous about the Fourth and First relationship with Caldwell & Co. Hill's departure from the board was made awkward by the fact that his daughter Frances had married Rogers Caldwell's nephew Wentworth Caldwell Sr.

The staff and investors of Third National Bank on opening day 1927. On the left side of the front row, wearing a dark suit, is bank cofounder Frank Farris Sr. To his left is C. A. Craig, board member and head of the National Life & Accident Insurance Co., Third National president Watkins Crockett, and Third National cofounder Walter Diehl (William Farris).

After the stock market crash of October 29, 1929, Nashville braced for the worst. But to everyone's surprise, the local economy did not collapse during the first part of 1930. As summer turned to fall, it appeared as if the financial institutions in the "Wall Street of the South" were somehow insulated from the terrible events in New York. "Financial condition of city's banks show Nashville to be sound as a rock," a *Nashville Banner*-sponsored advertisement proclaimed, on November 2, 1930. The next day, the *Tennessean* published an article authored by Caldwell & Co. headlined "Business Turn for Better Seen."

In fact, Caldwell & Co. was in serious trouble, and Nashville's largest bank with it. Between 1927 and 1929, Rogers Caldwell lost almost seven hundred thousand dollars by incorrectly predicting stock market crashes. When the market did crash in late 1929, it set into motion a series of events that would eventually bankrupt his teetering empire. Some of the industrial companies owned by Caldwell & Co. lost huge amounts of money or went bankrupt. The bond issues that Caldwell & Co. had bought, but not yet sold to the public, became impossible to sell. A plan to publicly sell a sort of mutual fund comprising Caldwell & Co.'s insurance companies became no more than a pipe dream.

Rogers Caldwell spent the twelve months following the stock market crash in a mad scramble to find cash to shore up his troubled operation. To this end, Caldwell & Co. obtained control of BancoKentucky, a troubled holding company that owned the National Bank of Kentucky, through a stock swap. "It seems as if it were a case of one drowning man calling for the aid of another,"[10] stated an account of the deal written several years later. Nevertheless, Caldwell & Co. got more from the Bank of Kentucky than the Bank of Kentucky got from it. Throughout 1930, Caldwell & Co. borrowed $2.4 million from the Kentucky bank, enabling Rogers Caldwell to hold off his creditors for several months.

Caldwell's second source of funds in 1930 was the one that would drag him and his business partner Luke Lea into a federal investigation. For years, the standard practice at Caldwell & Co. was to deposit bond monies into the internally controlled Bank of Tennessee, then use that money to buy something else. In 1930, Tennessee governor Henry Horton, a political ally of Lea's, pushed through $29 million in new bond monies for roads and bridges and steered all the bond business to Rogers Caldwell. By October 1930, the state had more than $3.4 million on deposit at the Bank of Tennessee. As his debts mounted, Rogers Caldwell began to withdraw money from the Bank of Tennessee, pulling out over $2.6 million from the bank between October 1 and November 12, 1930.

At least one person understood how much trouble Caldwell & Co. was in, that being the comptroller of the currency in Washington,

Preston Delano. Sometime in October, Delano called Paul Davis, knowing that the only person in Nashville who could possibly save the city's largest bank was the president of the second largest bank. Delano told Davis that Caldwell & Co. was insolvent and would probably take down the Fourth and First National Bank unless something was done. When Delano first proposed to Davis that American National take over the Fourth and First, Davis's initial response was that his bank had enough problems.

"You may be, but you aren't as broke as the Fourth and First," Delano replied. "And if you don't take over it, you are going to emasculate that whole area down there."[11]

However, at least one banker from that era says it was perception and not reality that drove the end of the Fourth and First. "People just assumed that the bank must be tied in with Rogers Caldwell—which they really were not—and so they put a run on the bank," Sam Fleming said. "The loans from the Fourth and First to Caldwell were not enough to make any particular difference, but people thought the two were connected so they lined up to take their money out. And in those days you did not have to be an insolvent bank. The question was whether you had the cash on hand to handle a bank run."

Whether the Fourth and First's demise was because of perception or reality, Delano convinced Paul Davis that his bank needed to merge with it. Delano talked to Jesse Holman Jones, head of the Reconstruction Finance Corporation and a native of Springfield. The RFC bought $4 million in preferred stock from American National Bank, an infusion that made it possible for the bank to orchestrate a takeover of the Fourth and First. "Without Jones, we would not have been able to do it because we had borrowed all the money we could borrow at that point," said Andrew Benedict, who went to work for First American in 1935 and later became its president.

In the fall of 1930, Rogers Caldwell was hosting *Chicago Tribune* publisher Col. Robert McCormick at a hunting club in Gallatin. During dinner, an aide discreetly told Caldwell that he had lost $2 million in the market that day. Caldwell did not let his guests know that anything was wrong. "I just did not see what good could come of crying about it at dinner," he said decades later.[12] But the losses made him realize that there was no way he could keep shoring up his flailing financial empire.

Caldwell somehow kept his firm afloat until after Gov. Henry Horton was reelected to a third term on November 4 (years later, Caldwell would admit that he and Luke Lea did so to ensure Horton's victory). On Election Day, many Nashville residents began withdrawing money from Caldwell-affiliated banks en masse. Because of this, the Nashville Clearinghouse—the cooperative organization consisting of Nashville's top bankers—met and appointed a committee to "deal" with the situation. "Rumors about Caldwell & Company are branded as false," read the headline in Luke Lea's *Tennessean*.[13]

Within days, however, the worst rumors would prove to be true. On November 7, the state superintendent of banks took over the Bank of Tennessee, cutting Rogers Caldwell off from one of his main sources of funds. A week later, a bankruptcy judge placed Caldwell & Co. in the hands of a receiver. The next week, the receiver effectively shut down Caldwell & Co., laying off 215 of the firm's 250 employees and leaving only the accounting department to sort out the mess. By early December, auditors were reporting that several million dollars of state money that had been deposited in Caldwell-controlled banks was gone.

Caldwell & Company's failure did away with any illusion that the South would escape the depression. By this time, the financial affairs of Caldwell & Co. and its Bank of Tennessee were so intertwined with so many other banks that a domino effect inevitably followed. During the two weeks after Caldwell & Co.'s failure, depositors formed lines a block long around virtually every bank in Nashville, Knoxville, Asheville, and Little Rock. Knoxville's Holston-Union National Bank and Holston Trust Co. closed their doors for several days. Nashville's Tennessee-Hermitage National Bank withstood a long run and was on the verge of collapse when Ed Potter's Commerce Union Bank agreed to take it over. Shares of BancoKentucky plummeted from the fifteen-dollar range to less than fifteen cents. No state was hurt worse than Arkansas, where seventy banks failed in two weeks.

One of Nashville's more dramatic failures was the Liberty Bank & Trust. Lea was a major shareholder in both Nashville's Liberty Bank and Asheville's Central Bank & Trust Co. When the panic hit Asheville, Lea raised cash for Central by selling Central certificates of deposit to Liberty. A few days later, when panic hit Nashville, Liberty president R. E. Donnell was unable to find anyone to buy the certificates. When Lea saw that no one would buy the CDs, he deposited twenty thousand dollars of his own money into Liberty, money that was withdrawn in less than fifteen minutes. Liberty failed on November 13. Two weeks later, after trying fruitlessly to find new financial backers to help him reopen his bank, Donnell strangled himself. Neither the *Tennessean* nor the *Banner's* account of his suicide mentioned *Tennessean* owner Luke Lea's connection to the Liberty Bank.

The same day Liberty folded, Paul Davis announced the merger of American National and the Fourth and First. The merger saved the Fourth and First's depositors, who lost none of their deposits despite the situation. But under the terms of the merger, shares in the Fourth

R. E. DONNELL, HEAD OF LIBERTY BANK, KILLS SELF

Spirit Believed Broken by Effort to Reopen Institution

FOUND IN HOTEL

Search Reveals Him with Shoestring About Neck

(Nashville Tennessean; Nov. 28, 1930). R. E. Donnell, 63, founder and president of the Liberty Bank and Trust company until it closed its doors Thursday Nov. 13, was found dead in a room in a local hotel at 12:30 o'clock this morning.

The banker had strangled himself with a shoestring removed from his left shoe which he had noosed about his neck after carefully placing a handkerchief under it.

The body, fully clothed, was found by M. D. Johnson, assistant cashier of the bank and close friend of Mr. Donnell, who had been seeking him throughout the afternoon and night. Still warm with life at 12:30 o'clock, the body gave mute testimony that had Mr. Johnson found him only a few minutes earlier that his life might have been saved.

No notes giving reasons for his act had been found in the room or about Mr. Donnell's clothing early this morning, except an envelope in which he had carefully placed his watch in its regular vest pocket at the end of its chain. This envelope bore in his handwriting the words "To Ridley E. Donnell Jr., from Daddy." At the desk a few feet away a blotter bore the same words as they had been made in reverse as the father made his last gift to his young son.

The body, clad in a brown business suit with white linen and brown shoes, was lying on top of the single bed with none of its covers disturbed. Mr. Donnell was lying on his side with his hands still clutching tightly the shoestring from his left shoe. His knees were drawn up closely to his body. Otherwise he was in a normal comfortable position.

Since the closing of the bank to which he had given many years of his life, friends of Mr. Donnell had feared that he might let the matter prey too closely on his mind. He firmly believed, and expressed this belief to the newspapers, in announcing the bank's closing, that the institution was solvent, but rumors as to the bank's strength grew so persistently that the daily withdrawals were more than it could stand.

With the hope of reopening the institution, for days and nights, Mr. Donnell had personally supervised the work at the bank, and friends believed that this overwork and nervous strain had broken his resistance. In announcing the closing of the bank he had built up, Mr. Donnell spoke of the institution as a lost friend, taking its financial difficulties as a personal grief.

and First became almost worthless. Under the *Tennessean's* front-page story about the merger was a story about the retirement of Fourth and First president James E. Caldwell. "I feel that I have a right to retire," Caldwell was quoted as saying in the article, which did not mention his son Rogers.[14]

As part of the merger, Davis moved American National's offices into the Fourth and First National Bank Building, where they would remain for forty-two years. He also combined the Nashville Trust Company's business with his American Trust Co., creating an organization called the Nashville and American Trust Co. Within a year, however, it became obvious that this had to be a temporary arrangement. As Congress began debate on new banking regulations—a debate that would eventually produce the landmark Glass-Steagall Act of 1933—Davis had to spin off the trust business into a separate organization. Needing a businessman with a lot of capital, Davis convinced H. G. Hill to buy 80 percent of the stock in the trust company. Hill moved his office from his grocery headquarters to the trust company and installed Charles Nelson, grandson of Nashville Trust's founder, as its president. Hill and Nelson stabilized the trust company and reset it on the course of conservatism it had been known for prior to 1927.

The national banking collapse was extremely hard on African-American institutions. In Tennessee, three of the four black-owned banks closed in 1930, including the People's Savings Bank & Trust in Nashville. The only one that survived was Citizen's Bank & Trust. It did so mainly because of its conservative philosophy and the solvency of its primary shareholder—National Baptist Publishing Board president Henry Allen Boyd.

After Caldwell & Co. failed, there was no more absurd talk about the South escaping the Great Depression. When over 120 southern banks closed in November and December of 1930, thousands of depositors lost their life savings. When the crash came, manufacturers across the South began to lay people off in droves.

Although there were many reasons for the bank failures, many of the affected shareholders and depositors blamed Rogers Caldwell, Luke Lea, and Gov. Henry Horton. "When banks closed and mills were shut down and workers' children went hungry, there was talk of Rogers Caldwell," a *Tennessean* story said years later.[15]

In December 1930, Caldwell, Lea, and Horton were condemned at mass meetings across the state organized by Horton's political opponents. The next month, the legislature formed a committee to investigate the relationship between the Caldwell empire and the state government.

The committee heard testimony from Caldwell & Co. officials and state government officials. It heard evidence that the Horton administration gave bond business to Caldwell & Co. without taking bids from other firms. It also uncovered the fact that Caldwell & Co. had successfully lobbied for laws raising limits on the amount of money that the state could deposit in any one bank. Three current and former highway commissioners testified that Luke Lea had tried to use his influence to get the state to use the Caldwell & Co.-owned Kentucky Rock Asphalt Co. as its sole road contractor.

As opposition newspapers such as the *Nashville Banner* and *Chattanooga Times* reported the scandal and as "Boss" Ed Crump of Memphis began to come out in opposition to Caldwell, a picture of an evil trio began to emerge. "Most people considered Horton to be a misguided weakling," McFerrin wrote in 1938. "Rogers Caldwell was considered to be the scheming financier who had laid most of the plans and received most of the financial rewards. Luke Lea was looked upon as the middleman between Caldwell and Horton, the skillful politician who had seen that Caldwell's plans had been carried out by the governor and who had reaped political rewards as well as financial returns."[16]

As public opinion turned nasty toward Horton, Crump became more aggressive in his attacks upon the governor, which turned out to be positive for Horton. By the time several Republican legislators drew up articles of impeachment against the governor, the public perceived the battle at the legislature as one between Horton and Crump. Many newspapers, although they were critical of Rogers Caldwell, were worried that if Horton were removed from office, Crump would become state dictator. The articles of impeachment were voted down, with about a dozen Republican House members voting against the proposal. Horton was allowed to serve out the rest of his term.

While the legislative committee was hearing damning testimony about the affairs of Caldwell & Co., legal action against Caldwell and Lea had begun all over the South. In Kentucky, Caldwell was indicted by a federal grand jury on charges related to Caldwell & Co.'s merger with the Bank of Kentucky. In Asheville, North Carolina, Lea was indicted on charges related to the collapse of the Central Bank & Trust Co. In Knoxville, Lea was indicted on charges related to the Holston-Union National Bank.

Since Lea and Caldwell had well-placed friends all over Nashville, getting indictments returned against them wasn't an easy task locally. At first, Davidson County attorney general R. M. Atkinson—a political ally of Lea's—simply refused to bring charges. This infuriated the *Banner*, which called for Atkinson's impeachment. Eventually, Lea and several other men (not including Caldwell) were indicted on charges of defrauding the Liberty Bank and Trust Co. However, the indictments only involved a misdemeanor charge.

Luke Lea lost virtually all of his assets in the Caldwell & Company debacle. Chief among those were his three large newspapers in Tennessee, which were all placed in receivership. After changing hands two times, Scripps-Howard bought the *Memphis Commercial Appeal* in 1936. That same year, a Knoxville businessman named Roy Lotspeich bought the *Journal* from the Canal Bank and Trust Co.

Lea kept possession of the *Tennessean* until March 1933, when to his consternation, the paper was placed in the hands of a receiver. A Roosevelt crony and Maryland Casualty Insurance Company executive named Silliman Evans bought the paper out of receivership in 1937.

Eventually, Lea was convicted of fraud in North Carolina in a case that concerned Caldwell & Company's 1929 takeover of Asheville's Central Bank and Trust Co. After several months of wrangling over extradition, Lea was imprisoned in Raleigh. The former U.S. senator, Belle Meade developer, army colonel, and *Tennessean* publisher served a two-year sentence. The man who once donated 868 acres of Belle Meade property for use as the Warner Parks died in 1945, with little money to his name.

Rogers Caldwell was never convicted on any felony counts and never served a day in prison. Although the reasons for this vary with each particular jurisdiction, the main one was that even though it may have been irresponsible to run a bond house the way he did, no one could prove that it was illegal under the laws of the time. After 1935, Caldwell retired to a life of lazy days and weekly lunches with some of the leading personalities in town. "You would find on any given Saturday at his house a couple of CEOs, a couple of powerhouse lawyers, some bankers, even a Congressman," said longtime *Tennessean* editor John Seigenthaler, a regular at Caldwell's lunches after 1962. "He presided with great charm and great wit, and no one ever spoke seriously ill of anyone else at that table." Caldwell would frequently make amusing philosophical comments at the lunches. One of his more famous sayings was, "A very wise man once told me I would always get along if I did not pay too much attention to a woman's hips and I voted the straight Democratic ticket. I think that's good advice." In 1963, Caldwell told a reporter, "I should have had more schooling and a better understanding of economics."[17]

The state filed a claim against Rogers Caldwell almost immediately after the collapse of Caldwell & Co. but never recovered most of the $6.5 million it had deposited in Caldwell-controlled banks. However, through means that only he knew, Rogers Caldwell was able to live a comfortable life until his death in 1963. "He lived in the finest house in Tennessee for twenty years and owed more money than anyone else in Tennessee, so he must have had a magic wand," said James Bass Sr., a partner in Bass, Berry, & Sims.

One of Caldwell's assets was Brentwood Hall, which became the subject of one of the longest-running legal battles in Tennessee history. When the state tried to take possession of Brentwood Hall in the late 1930s, it discovered that Rogers Caldwell had built the house on his father's property. Because of this, the case dragged on for almost two decades. It wasn't until 1957 that the state took over Brentwood Hall and converted it to the Ellington Agricultural Center.

Anyone who worked in the financial industry during the depression will tell you that several times the economy appeared to be improving when the stock market crashed again. Those businesses that did survive probably did about as well as a small brokerage firm that had been started in 1927 by a young man named James C. Bradford. "He hung grimly on," his son J. C. Bradford Jr. said many years later. "It was bad."

On March 1, 1933, while Franklin Roosevelt was preparing to be sworn in, economic panic became so vast that—as *Time* magazine put it—"the banking heart of the country, New York, stopped beating momentarily."[18] As depositors swarmed banks, almost every governor in America declared a "banking holiday," which authorized banks to close until the panic died away. The next day, Nashville's banks opened, but imposed stringent limits on how much an individual depositor could withdraw.

Merchants were severely hurt by the bank holiday and met with the Nashville Clearinghouse at a 1:00 A.M. meeting on March 3. At that meeting, bankers decided to do what many banks had done in previous times of panic: issue special "scrip" as a means of exchange. For the next twenty-four hours, several printers, including Brandon Printing and Brandau Craig Dickerson, worked round the clock printing 275,000 sheets of scrip in one, five, ten, and twenty dollar denominations. Virtually every large retailer in town—from H. G. Hill to Castner-Knott to Harley-Holt Furniture Co.—ran advertisements in the newspaper that day, ensuring people it would accept the scrip. The next day—payday for thousands of Nashville residents—the scrip went into circulation.

On March 15, the national bank holiday ended. Banks and merchants tried to get back to business as usual, with help from the newspapers. "Nashvillians trooped to their banks this morning and deposited millions of dollars," a *Tennessean* story read. "There were no 'fraidy cats' wanting to withdraw entire deposits, according to reports from all the banks."[19]

However, by that time the city had another crisis to deal with. The night before the banking holiday ended, a tornado had hit East Nashville, killing seven people and damaging about five hundred homes.

CHAPTER 6

We Built the South

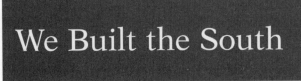

B y the year 2000, it seemed like everyone in Nashville pushed paper for a living. But there was a time when Nashville built things. No two companies exemplified this more than two family-owned businesses, Foster & Creighton and the Nashville Bridge Co.

Through most of the twentieth century, it was virtually impossible to stand in Nashville, Birmingham, Lexington, or Knoxville and not see a skyscraper, factory, bridge, road, dormitory, football stadium, or barge built by one of these two Nashville firms. If Caldwell & Co. banked on the South, Foster & Creighton and the Nashville Bridge Co. built the South—from Miami's Dade County Courthouse to Birmingham's Legion Field to the barges and towboats that brought products down the South's rivers. When World War II came, Foster & Creighton built army bases and Nashville Bridge built small ships for the U.S. Navy. Both companies thrived during the postwar boom of the 1950s and 1960s. But neither made it past 1985, as competition from larger firms and the limitations of family ownership took their toll.

Wilbur Foster was a rarity—a Confederate soldier who after the war was able to pick up his promising business career where he had left off.

In the 1850s, Foster surveyed or supervised the construction of virtually every train track that led to Nashville. He was also the engineer in charge of the city's first bridge across the Cumberland River. After the war broke out, Foster enlisted in the Confederacy and rose to senior engineer in the Army of Tennessee. He found himself back in Nashville in 1873, working on the landscape for the new state capitol.

While doing engineering work on the state capitol, Foster hired a young man named Bob Creighton to be his apprentice. After the capitol project was completed, the two worked on the foundation of the first buildings at both Vanderbilt University (Kirkland Hall) and Fisk University (Jubilee Hall). They also surveyed the Woodland Street Bridge, which must have been easy for Foster since it was located on the same site as the bridge he had surveyed thirty years earlier.

In 1885, the fifty-year-old Foster and the twenty-nine-year-old Creighton pooled fifteen hundred dollars and created a partnership. At first it confined itself to small projects such as stone walls and foundations for residences. That changed in 1888, when the Louisville & Nashville Railroad hired Foster & Creighton to build a twenty-mile spur from Glasgow, Kentucky, to Mammoth Cave. From that point on, the firm maintained a strong business building tracks for L&N and locks along the Cumberland River.

The Centennial Exposition of 1897 was a godsend for Nashville's construction companies. In two years, Nashville transformed a horse track called West Side Park into a glorious pseudo-city with over a dozen large buildings, each of which posed architectural and engineering challenges. It was quite a coup, therefore, for Bob Creighton to land the job as director of public works for the event. It was also an honor for Foster & Creighton to lay the foundation for the replica of the Parthenon, the structure that was the exposition's centerpiece.

Foster did not have any children who followed him into the company. But Creighton's son Wilbur started spending summers working with his dad's company when he was six. In those days, crews worked from sunrise to sunset and spent the night at camps adjacent to the job site. Wilbur Creighton never forgot the experience. "Handmade bunks, ticks filled with straw for mattresses, no cover except a blanket and no thought of hygiene except the cook weekly sweeping the chinches out of the corners with a whisk broom into a pan of hot water," were the living conditions under which Wilbur Creighton and his coworkers spent their summers.[1]

After graduating from Vanderbilt, Wilbur Creighton went to work full-time for F&C. In 1905, he married Julia Dudley, daughter of Gray & Dudley foundry president Robert M. Dudley. The next year, Wilbur Creighton took over F&C's construction work. By that time, F&C had purchased limestone quarries near Columbia, Tennessee, and Sheffield, Alabama. The quarries made F&C's operation more profitable since it kept the company from having to buy as much of its raw material.

Throughout the twentieth century, the list of Foster & Creighton's projects reflects what was happening in Nashville and the South. Between 1895 and 1910, when Nashville was going through a growth spurt and residents left the inner city for new streetcar suburbs, F&C's main projects were subdivisions and bridges. F&C surveyed, laid sewer lines, and paved roads for several new neighborhoods, including Belmont and Richland. In 1907, the city decided to build two bridges across the Cumberland River—the Sparkman (later Shelby) Street Bridge and the Jefferson Street Bridge. Too small to bid on either project alone, F&C formed a joint venture with two other contractors. The combined companies built both bridges.

With two successful bridges under its belt, F&C started bidding on bridges and viaducts all over the South at a time when most parts of the South were building steel bridges to replace wooden ones. Between 1909 and 1914, F&C built no less than forty-three bridges, one of the larger being a long railroad bridge that crossed Shelby Park and the Cumberland River in Nashville.

F&C shifted its focus from bridges to buildings around 1915, just in time to build several important structures in Nashville. Between 1915 and 1917, the company built the Doctor's Building, a dormitory at Ward-Belmont College, and the Peabody College Library. The most prestigious contract during this period was the new headquarters for James E. Caldwell's Fourth and First National Bank. Part of the reason that F&C won the bid for the six-story bank building was because of Caldwell's insistence that the bank lobby have no columns. (Columns, he believed, would encourage bank robbers.) "I think we were the only bidder because of that," said Wilbur Creighton Jr., who went to work for Foster & Creighton around 1920.

Business came to a halt in 1918, not so much because of a shortage of materials but a shortage of manpower brought on by World War I and the construction of the DuPont gunpowder plant in Old Hickory. DuPont did not hire a Nashville general contractor when it built the $100 million plant in 1918 but brought with it an outside contractor. About the only thing that generated cash flow for F&C during the war was its quarry in Sheffield, Alabama, which was replete with an element called air nitrate that was essential in the making of explosives.

Times got so bad that in 1919 the firm nearly went bankrupt. On one occasion, the Fourth and First National Bank ordered F&C to pay an outstanding loan, which it could not afford to do. Wilbur Creighton Sr. had a long talk with Fourth and First president James E. Caldwell, and the bank instead refinanced the firm's outstanding loans.

OPPOSITE PAGE: The Foster & Creighton Co. begins work on the Fourth and First National Bank Building, 1916 (First American National Bank).

Caldwell wouldn't regret his generosity. During the 1920s, while Nashville's manufacturing sector grew at an astounding rate, F&C managed to build almost every factory of note (other than the DuPont rayon plant). The first large facility was built in West Nashville for Chicago's Victor Chemical Co., a firm so secretive about its production process that it operated with partial building plans. Other large industrial contracts included the Gray & Dudley foundry on Clifton

Road (1921), the Neuhoff Packing Co. on Cowan Street (1922), and the Washington hosiery mill on Charlotte Pike (1925). When flood waters ruined the Jarman Shoe factory at Fifth Street and Shelby, J. F. Jarman hired F&C to build a new factory at Fifth Street and Main.

Meanwhile, F&C also managed to build just about every noteworthy new structure in the central business district during the 1920s. One of the first was the Tennessee Central Railroad terminal at the foot of Broadway. Others included the National Life & Accident headquarters (1923), the Caldwell & Co. Building (1924), the Bennie Dillon Building (1926), the Life & Casualty Building (1926), and the second Nashville Trust Building (1926). The Nashville Trust contract was unusual because the entire project was done by verbal agreement between Wilbur Creighton Sr. and Nashville Trust president William Nelson.

In 1929, when Nashville decided to rebuild the Parthenon replica, this time using materials that were meant to last, the city hired F&C to do the job. Of all the projects that the company did during the first half of the century, this one meant the most to its image. In the 1950s, F&C was still using the Parthenon in its advertisements.

Of course, with all the demand for new buildings in Nashville, someone in the construction business had to be doing well. But what is so remarkable about F&C is that in addition to all its projects in Nashville, the firm did enormous amounts of work elsewhere.

Nowhere was F&C's regional presence as noteworthy as in Birmingham, which grew so fast during the first part of the century that it became known as Magic City. It must have been a constant source of frustration to Birmingham's general contractors that a Nashville company built the Birmingham Library (1925), the nineteen-story Thomas Jefferson Hotel (1927), and the Protective Life Insurance Building (1928). F&C also built the Birmingham-National Parking Garage, a facility whose bonds were underwritten by Caldwell & Co. That same year, F&C built a stadium for Birmingham that later became virtually a house of worship for Alabama football fans. Its eventual name: Legion Field. Seven decades later, Wilbur Creighton Jr. remembered the Legion Field project well. "It was so muddy that we had to use mules to pull the concrete forms," he said.

The depression hit F&C hard. The Birmingham branch almost shut down entirely. In Nashville, the company had to get by on residential and small retail projects. Total revenues slumped from $3.5 million in 1929 to $600,000 in 1932.

When business finally picked up, all the big projects were government-related. In the 1930s, F&C built three prisons in Kentucky, courthouses in Jackson and Shelbyville, and the Cheatham Place housing project in Nashville. Its highest profile project during this period, however, was the State Office Building across Sixth Avenue from the state capitol (later called the John Sevier Building). Meanwhile, the company paved hundreds of miles of roads in Kentucky, Tennessee, and Alabama.

F&C had two major defeats in the late 1930s. One was the Tennessee Valley Authority's decision not to use general contractors to build its dams. Wilbur Creighton Sr. lobbied TVA hard not to make that decision, going so far as to try to organize a company consisting of several contractors to build dams. But TVA chose instead to be its own general contractor, a policy that remained in place until the 1950s. It was one of only many aspects about the New Deal that irked Creighton. "One alphabet agency followed another with such amazing rapidity, so fast, in fact, that that they sometimes overlapped," he wrote, stating an opinion shared by many Nashville business leaders of that era. "Never since the beginning of time had such crack-pots, such glassy-eyed zealots been able to spend billions of dollars experimenting on human welfare and never was there a greater failure."[2]

The second bitter pill was the company's failure to get the contract to build the new Davidson County Courthouse. That project, which was bid publicly, went to Charlotte, North Carolina-based contractor J. A. Jones.

The million people who visited the Tennessee Centennial Exposition in 1897 loved the wonderful architecture, were amazed at exhibits such as the Moorish Palace, and were dazzled by fireworks every night. However, nothing thrilled them more than a seesaw ride that lifted visitors to two hundred feet above the ground. In an era before skyscrapers and amusement parks, the ride was nationally famous. A ride identical to it was later built at New York's Coney Island.

The man who designed that ride was a young employee of the Youngstown Bridge Company's Nashville office named Arthur J. Dyer. But it wasn't amusement park rides that fascinated Dyer so much as bridges. Dyer loved bridges, thought about them all the time, and designed them in his sleep. In 1891, while a senior at Vanderbilt's engineering school, Dyer wrote his thesis on a plan for a new bridge across the Cumberland at the foot of Broad Street. A few years later, when city planners started talking about the need for such a bridge, they pulled out Dyer's thesis and began using it to build support for such a project. A version of the bridge was later built four blocks south of Broadway at Sparkman Street (later Shelby Street).

There wasn't much work for an engineer in Nashville during the economic depression of the early 1890s, so Dyer took a job with Pennsylvania's Phoenix Iron Company after he graduated. He later found work in Washington, D.C., and New York, but 1895 found him unemployed and back at his parents' home in Chattanooga. He was then offered a job with Youngstown's Nashville office. The pay was scant (one hundred dollars per month), but Dyer needed the work. He moved to Nashville in 1895 and found a room in a boardinghouse near Main Street in East Nashville.

Dyer knew the technical side of designing a bridge, but until then, he did not know the ins and outs of public bidding. He soon learned them from his new boss. The first time Dyer successfully bid on a public project was 1896, when he bid on a bridge across the Duck River in Waverly. A few months later, Dyer made a name for himself by designing the seesaw ride.

Youngstown was a big company with projects all over the South. Among Dyer's assignments was constructing a line of beacons along the reef between Miami and Key West. The job required Dyer and a fellow worker to dive into the water and drive steel piles into the coral rock, something Dyer never forgot because of his fear of sharks.

Meanwhile, Arthur Dyer found time to marry well. Like Bob Creighton, Dyer married a girl whose family owned a big iron foundry—in this case, Henry Buttorff's daughter Elizabeth.

In 1899, the Youngstown Bridge Company was one of twenty-seven small firms folded into a new company called the American Bridge Co. After the merger, Dyer found that he did not like working for a company as large as American Bridge and decided to form his own business. In a city where two of the largest financial institutions were the American National Bank and the Nashville Trust Co., the former American Bridge Co. employee decided to call his new business the Nashville Bridge Co. At first, his only full-time employee was a black man named Reuben Stout.

The Nashville Bridge Co. had plenty of work its first year. In 1902, flood destroyed or damaged almost every bridge in Middle Tennessee. That year, Dyer built or repaired about thirty bridges on the Elk, Buffalo, and Harpeth Rivers. Jobs such as these would have required Dyer to recruit several strong laborers; in an era before torch cutting and heavy machinery, a large part of building or repairing bridges involved cutting steel with a hacksaw and using mules to drag it into place.

Dyer then turned his attention to building the steel framework for buildings in Nashville. The Nashville Bridge Co. fabricated steel for the Arcade (1904), the first Nashville Trust Building (1904), and the Hermitage Hotel (1909). Meanwhile, Nashville Bridge got plenty of business elsewhere. One of the most interesting projects was a series of observation towers for the Vicksburg National Memorial in Mississippi.

In 1908, Dyer decided he needed a much larger building on his company's property at the foot of Shelby Avenue in East Nashville. Dyer drew up plans for a two-story building. But before he started building it, the city began work on a new bridge across the river right next to it, loosely based upon the design he created at Vanderbilt seventeen years earlier. (Dyer's former employer, the American Bridge Co., fabricated the steel for that bridge.) Dyer revised the plans and made his building five stories, with the main entrance on the top story, level with the bridge.

The steel shortage during World War I forced Nashville Bridge to change its strategic direction. When the federal government began reserving most of the nation's steel for military use, Dyer went to New York, learned shipbuilding, and obtained a contract to build eight two-hundred-foot oil tankers. He then converted much of his Nashville operation to marine construction and set to work building the tankers. A few months later, the war ended, and the government cut its order in half. After it finished the four tankers, Nashville Bridge converted the shipyard to the construction of barges, towboats, and steamers.

The steel industry thrived in the 1920s and Nashville Bridge along with it. As new bridges and buildings went up all over the South, Nashville Bridge was often the subcontractor hired by general contractors such as Foster & Creighton to do the steel work. In 1923, Nashville Bridge built a steel fabricating plant in Bessemer, Alabama, next door to the Tennessee Coal & Iron Co. (later U.S. Steel). Eventually, the company fabricated bridges and buildings in Bessemer and barges and towboats in Nashville. By the late 1920s, Nashville Bridge had about five hundred employees at its two locations.

After World War I, Dyer took his place as one of the leaders in the Nashville business community. In 1918, he became the president of the Chamber of Commerce. Two years later, he was one of several business leaders who formed the Nashville Industrial Corp., the entity that bought the Old Hickory powder plant from the federal government and sold it to DuPont. About that time, he became a director of the American National Bank. And in 1932, when the city of Nashville formed its first Planning Commission, Dyer became its chairman, a position he retained until 1955. In that forum, he spent many hours working on what eventually became the Capitol Hill Redevelopment Plan, and he became one of the early advocates of metropolitan government in Nashville.

The founder of the Nashville Bridge Co. also became a benefactor of his alma mater. In 1946, an astronomer spoke at a Rotary Club luncheon at which Dyer was present. A few years later, Dyer spearheaded a fund-raising effort to build an observatory for Vanderbilt, later named in his honor.

Dyer also had quirks that made him memorable. An avid hunter, he sometimes brought large quantities of wild game to the plant so he could feed his workers animals that he had killed on his expeditions.

"One time I went to one of those dinners and ate opossum and squirrel and a lot of other things that I never want to eat again," said Littleton Anderson Jr., who worked for the company when he was a college student in the late 1930s. Dyer also had a dislike for riding elevators and chose instead to walk up and down the five stories of stairs every day at the office. "Good place for thinking, climbing stairs," he would say.[3]

It had been Dyer's intention all along to turn the reigns of the company over to his oldest son, A. J. (Jimmy) Dyer Jr. However, Jimmy Dyer was killed at the age of twenty-five while working on a bridge in Panama City, Florida. Jimmy's younger brother Harry graduated from Lehigh about the same time Jimmy was killed. Harry's interest was not bridges but boats, and when he went to work for his father's company, Harry worked on the shipyard side of the business. "Harry Dyer was a boat man," said Howard Pruett, who began work for Nashville Bridge in 1936 and worked his way up from machinist helper to superintendent, "and he was one of the best."

The offshoot into barges and towboats paid off in the 1930s. During the Great Depression, building construction dropped off precipitously. However, the marine business actually picked up, especially after the New Deal provided money to improve inland waterways.

In 1940, Harry Dyer became president of the firm his father had started four decades earlier. The company had a healthy marine business, with towboats under construction on the south side of Shelby Avenue and barges on the north side. Meanwhile, the structural department in Bessemer was building far more bridges than buildings. But it still bid on the occasional large contract, such as the Dade County Courthouse in Miami, Florida.

No two Nashville-based companies were affected more by World War II than Foster & Creighton and Nashville Bridge.

In March 1941, the U.S. Navy announced contracts to build eighteen minesweepers and thirty-six submarine chasers. Only two of those fifty-four ships were assigned to inland locations—two minesweepers assigned to the Nashville Bridge Co.

Immediately, the Bridge Company became a bustling center of activity like it had never been before and would never be again. In less than a month, the company completed $150,000 worth of upgrades, transforming the barge plant into a site that could produce deep-sea vessels. Employment at the Nashville site jumped from five hundred to thirteen hundred and included women welders for the first time. The plant went to twenty-four-hour operation.

OPPOSITE PAGE:
Workers at the Nashville Bridge Co. work on a boat-launching dock, 1919 (A. J. Dyer III).

The minesweepers were christened the U.S.S. *Fidelity* and the U.S.S. *Fierce* and delivered in March 1942. As soon as they were completed, the company started working on submarine chasers, which were in great demand at a time when Germany was winning the naval war in the North Atlantic.

Nashville's vessels were tiny compared to the ships being produced in places like Philadelphia and constituted a minuscule fraction of the nearly twenty thousand vessels built in America. Nevertheless, the sight of deepwater vessels on the Cumberland was a source of immense pride for Nashville residents during World War II. Unlike the Vultee aircraft plant located near the airport, Nashville Bridge was right in the middle of downtown for everyone to see. In July 1943, there were six sub chasers—each at a different stage of development—lined up across downtown. Each had a sign attached to it that could be seen from the other side of the river. "To make a hobo out of Tojo," read one. "A Razz in der Fuehrer's face," read another.[4]

Meanwhile, Foster & Creighton also had its hands full. As war became imminent, the U.S. Army Quartermaster Corps decided to build a classification and training area for the army's 33rd Infantry Division near Tullahoma to house up to thirty thousand people. Most of the construction work on what later became known as Camp Forrest fell to two companies: Foster & Creighton of Nashville and Hardaway Contracting of Columbus, Georgia.[5]

The joint venture (called Hardaway-Creighton) signed the contract in July 1940. Within months, Hardaway-Creighton had twenty thousand men and women building 472 barracks, 198 mess halls, sixty-eight administrative buildings, a fifteen hundred-bed hospital, and fifty-three miles of roads. The trick was not to build beautiful or long-lasting buildings, but to build them quickly. To that end, every phase of the project was organized like an assembly line. By November, building materials were coming in at the rate of five hundred railroad cars per day, most of which was being used as fast as it arrived. "It was such a fantastic thing that you just wouldn't have believed it," said Wilbur Creighton Jr., who was in charge of the estimating section for Camp Forrest. "Anyone who had a hammer could get a job as a carpenter." Sixty million feet of lumber and four months later, the army took over its base.

Camp Forrest, it turned out, was only the beginning. After Pearl Harbor, F&C built an engine test building for the army near Mobile, Alabama. Next came the Army Classification Center off Murfreesboro Road in Nashville, Seward Air Base in Smyrna, Camp Campbell (later Fort Campbell) near Clarksville, and several other war-related projects. One of the most unusual, and a sign that the war was going well for the Allies, was a camp for German prisoners of war near Crossville.

Race relations were always an issue in the labor-intensive construction business, and the Crossville POW camp was an example of just how strange such situations could get. F&C had many black laborers, and one of the requirements of the federal contract was that there be no discrimination in hiring on the basis of race. However, in an era where racially motivated lynchings sometimes occurred, Wilbur Creighton Sr. was worried about bringing African Americans to a work site in Crossville. "The race feeling there was very strong; so strong, in fact, that a negro was not allowed to stay in the mountains after nightfall," he later wrote.[6] Creighton offered to bring black workers to the site, but to require them to sign an agreement releasing them from any liability if they were injured off site. None came.

After the war, the government needed more bridges and dams, the private sector needed more factories, and colleges needed more dormitories to make way for students on the GI Bill.

Foster & Creighton could hardly keep up with all the contracts. The company built plants for Washington Manufacturing in Nashville in 1946, Victor Chemical in Tarpon Springs, Florida, in 1947, and Wolverine Copper Tubing in Decatur, Alabama, in 1948. It also built new buildings at Vanderbilt, Tennessee A&I (later Tennessee State University), and the University of Tennessee in Knoxville. At UT-Knoxville, F&C built new dormitories, a new student activities building, and an addition to the football stadium (later called Neyland Stadium). A few years later, F&C developed a huge presence at the University of Kentucky, building a hospital, several dorms, and yet another football stadium.

In the 1950s, F&C continued to take on huge projects. One was the $8 million Cordell Hull federal office building at Seventh and Broadway. Another was a new terminal and barge dock for the Tennessee Iron and Coal Company's Mobile operation. A third was a $9 million structure for Trans World Airlines in Kansas City, Missouri, which F&C constructed in joint venture with McDonald Construction Co. of St. Louis. Unfortunately, the TWA project was a bust, with delays due to strikes and bad weather. TWA sued when the structure wasn't completed on time, causing F&C to lose money on the project.

In 1958, Wilbur Creighton Jr. succeeded his father as company president. That same year, the company moved its headquarters from the First American Bank Building to a new site on Sidco Drive.

Nashville Bridge also flourished after the war. After a strike in 1947 interrupted production for several months, demand for bridges became so great that the company stopped fabricating steel for buildings. One of Nashville Bridge's highest-profile contracts after World War II was the superstructure of the Victory Memorial Bridge over the Cumberland River, done for general contractor Marion Construction Co. Other large bridges included two that crossed the Watauga River in northeast Tennessee—one in Johnson County and the other in Carter County.

However, barges and towboats were the even bigger growth items after World War II. Between 1945 and 1948, rail freights rose about 40 percent nationally, causing many companies to switch from rail to barges. Americans began buying cars and traveling as never before, causing an enormous demand for gasoline. Regional oil companies such as Murphy, Spur, Humble, and Ingram began ordering barges and towboats in huge quantities. Nashville Bridge had about one thousand employees and $20 million in annual sales by 1960.

By this time Nashville's construction industry had changed quite a bit since the 1920s. There were new competitors in the city Foster & Creighton had once dominated. This was best demonstrated by the fact that there were three very large projects in Nashville in the 1950s that F&C did not build: the Aladdin Industries plant (built by R. C. Mathews of Nashville), the Life & Casualty Tower (J. A. Jones of Charlotte) and the Ford Glass Plant (McDevitt & Street of Charlotte). Meanwhile, Nashville Bridge had become in many ways a second-tier steel company compared to other regional competitors such as Ingalls Industries, Bethlehem Steel, and Virginia Bridge.

Nevertheless, the 1960s were still busy years for both F&C and Nashville Bridge. President Dwight Eisenhower's interstate highway system meant that between 1960 and 1967, F&C was constantly paving part of I-59, I-65, or I-40. Meanwhile, Nashville Bridge had so much business building bridge overpasses that it soon only bid on large projects. One of these was the Roosevelt Bridge across the Potomac River in Washington, D.C.

Other major contracts for the two companies during the 1960s and early 1970s were as follows:

Dams. In the early 1960s, Nashville Bridge built the superstructures for Wheeler Dam in Alabama and Barkley Dam in Kentucky.

Federal government. In 1960, Nashville Bridge was hired by NASA to fabricate steel for the three-hundred-foot service tower that was used to piece together the Saturn missiles. Meanwhile, the federal government hired F&C to build several defense-related structures in Oak Ridge, Tennessee.

Genesco. Foster & Creighton's long-standing relationship with Genesco paid off in 1962, when the apparel company hired F&C to build its new headquarters, factory, and retail store complex on Murfreesboro Road.

Metro. In 1972, Foster & Creighton built a Thermal Transfer Plant just south of downtown that burned solid waste to provide power for buildings downtown.

Foster & Creighton always took great pride in its ability to retain large customers, such as Washington Manufacturing and Vanderbilt University. It was therefore with great pride that the company landed the contract to build the First American Center in 1972. The building opened on time and on schedule. But the project generated some unexpected excitement when F&C workers, digging the foundation, discovered the prehistoric remains of a saber-toothed tiger. Years later, Nashville's NHL hockey team named itself the Predators in honor of the discovery.

The big moneymakers for F&C in the 1970s were hospitals and universities. The company built over a dozen hospitals in the first half of the decade, most of them designed by architect Earl Swensson and owned by Humana of Louisville. Meanwhile, the company built several dormitories at Vanderbilt, a new athletic center at Tennessee State, and an addition to the Vanderbilt football stadium. The company also built a bridge across the New River George in West Virginia that was the largest in company history. And in 1978, F&C completed the first of several projects in the Middle East by building a power plant in Riyadh, Saudi Arabia.

However, in 1984—one year before the company would have celebrated its one hundredth anniversary—Foster & Creighton liquidated. Wilbur Creighton III said that the business was still profitable at that time and was still able to successfully bid on and complete projects. But he said that large companies were taking over the construction industry so fast that it was obvious that it would be much harder to compete into the indefinite future.

"The timing seemed right," Creighton III said. "I had several senior managers who were retiring, and profits were at an all-time high. There were several firms that wanted to acquire us, but quick liquidation was the best answer."

Some of F&C's equipment and many of its employees went to a start-up construction business called the Parent Co., headed up by former F&C executive Roy Slaymaker. Other parts of it, including out-of-state branches, were sold to competitors in those regions.

In 1969, Nashville Bridge was granted the largest bridge contract in its history: the $11.4 million superstructure of a mile-long interstate bridge across the Ohio River at Paducah, Kentucky. But by that time, it had started a series of ownership changes that transformed Nashville Bridge into a company that did not make bridges and wasn't owned in Nashville.

*The Nashville Bridge
Co. dominates the east
bank of the Cumberland
River in downtown
Nashville, around 1960
(Tennessee State Library
and Archives).*

By this time, Harry Dyer was past retirement age and had no sons, daughters, nephews, or nieces interested and old enough to run the company. The business was still making a profit; it still had plenty of contracts to build barges and bridges and grossed over $30 million in 1968 alone. But the steel industry had begun to decline and was also getting more competitive as large companies and conglomerates bought up family-owned companies.

In 1968, Henry Hooker called Harry Dyer and offered to buy Nashville Bridge in exchange for stock in a Minnie Pearl's Fried Chicken offshoot called Whale Inc. Dyer, skeptical of the long-term value of Whale stock, said he would accept only $15 million in cash. A few weeks later, Hooker called back and said he could get the money.

As it turns out, Dyer had good reason to be skeptical about the future of Whale stock. Within months of its takeover of Nashville Bridge, Whale and its sister fried chicken company (which by this time had changed its name to Performance Systems Inc.) were in serious financial trouble. Whale stock plummeted from over fifty dollars a share to less than one dollar in months. Desperately needing cash, Whale sold Nashville Bridge to the American Ship Building Co.—the same company Arthur Dyer had left seven decades earlier to start his own business. American Ship Building had several shipyards on the Great Lakes and was by this time run by an industrialist named George Steinbrenner.

Steinbrenner bought Nashville Bridge because of its barge and towboat manufacturing capability and never intended to get into the bridge business. In 1972, American Ship Building sold the bridge division, which included the Bessemer plant, to Bristol Iron and Steel Co.

Nashville Bridge employees later said that working for American Ship Building wasn't the same as working for Harry Dyer. "With Harry Dyer, it was more family-like," said longtime employee Howard Pruett. "After he sold it, I felt like I was just a number on the computer." Despite the loss of local ownership and the sales of the bridge division, some of the Nashville shipyard's busiest days were still ahead. The backlog of barge and towboat orders was so extensive that in 1973, American Ship Building built a $1 million plant in Ashland City. "We could use seventy more welders and fitters right now," Nashville Bridge president William Barton said about that time.[7] In 1974, Ingram Barge signed a $40 million contract for four large towboats and forty-eight large barges, an order not unusual for that era. Laws encouraging investors to build barges as tax shelters contributed to the demand.

In 1981, the barge business went bust because of overproduction and changes in tax law. Although the company occasionally increased its employment to meet a contract, by 1990 Nashville Bridge was down to about 200 workers in Nashville and 150 in Ashland City. At that point, American Ship Building was sold to Trinity Industries of Dallas, Texas.

By the mid-1990s, industrial companies such as the old Nashville Bridge Co. no longer fit in a downtown dominated by high-rise office buildings and tourist attractions. Although some locals and tourists still loved to watch the occasional barge launching, few people defended the need to have heavy industry in the middle of the city anymore. The need to "clean up" the east bank of the Cumberland became a favorite topic for urban planners and politicians. Master plans often called for replacing the area with office buildings, residences, or some type of sports facility.

In 1995, when Nashville mayor Phil Bredesen began selling Nashville on the idea of luring the Houston Oilers to town, the east bank industrial area became the obvious site for the new stadium. In May 1996, Nashville voters authorized the government to buy the one hundred acres between Shelby Avenue and Woodland Street and move all the industrial tenants off the land. There was very little sentiment expressed for the Nashville Bridge Co., at least not in public forums. The next year, Trinity Industries left Nashville and moved everything to its expanded facility in Ashland City.

CHAPTER 7

Gunpowder & Fighter Planes

T he war fraud scandal over the construction of the Old Hickory powder plant and its subsequent sale to DuPont was embarrassing to the U.S. War Department, the Justice Department, and the world's largest chemical company. It was also the first time a business in Nashville made national news. But in the end, DuPont and the Calvin Coolidge administration survived the fiasco. The American National Bank scored one of the greatest coups in its history. And several prominent Nashville business leaders made a lot of money.

Middle Tennessee had never seen anything like it.

As war neared in 1914, the U.S. government commissioned the DuPont chemical company to build a gunpowder factory in Hopewell, Virginia. After an explosion at the Hopewell Plant demonstrated how vulnerable a single factory can be, the government told DuPont to build two more: one in West Virginia and another on a bend in the Cumberland River. The bend, then known as Jacksonville and later as Old Hickory, was chosen because it was centrally located, close to a railroad hub, and in an area that contained a lot of cotton, sulphur, and coal (all necessary in the manufacture of gunpowder). It was also chosen because it was surrounded on three sides by water—security being a huge issue at a factory that can go up in flames with only one match.

Under the arrangement that was set up, the government agreed to pay DuPont five hundred thousand dollars up front, plus 5 percent of construction cost. Once the factory was completed, the government would own it and DuPont would operate it.

The construction of the Old Hickory plant was a Herculean undertaking. It took two thousand men, five hundred mules, and twenty-nine days to build a railroad spur from Hermitage to the site. After that came men, bricks, lumber, steel, concrete, and more men, more lumber, more steel, and more concrete. Some of the men worked on the factory itself—a massive structure with sixty-eight boilers and nine two-hundred-foot smokestacks. Others built houses for the estimated thirty thousand people who would be working there.

At the height of the construction phase, about fifty thousand men—carpenters, laborers, machinists, mechanics, welders, architects, and engineers—were working around the clock on Old Hickory's powder factory. Many of the workers slept in shifts, ten to a room, in tiny shacks called tar babies. Others stayed in hotels and boardinghouses in Nashville or Gallatin and commuted by train every day. Not all the workers survived the experience. Over five hundred died during the flu epidemic of 1918, many of them Mexican immigrants who lived in horrible conditions.

On July 2, 1918—less than six months after the project had been announced—Old Hickory began producing powder. By November, it was producing a million pounds of gunpowder a day. In building the powder plant and its surrounding village, the government spent $85 million, about $3 million of which went straight to DuPont.

The problem was, the army did not need it anymore. In the fall of 1918, the Allies broke through on European's Western front. On November 11, 1918, the war ended.

The army abandoned its Old Hickory plant and the surrounding village. Middle Tennessee had a ghost town on its hands.

The scandal involving the subsequent sale of the Old Hickory powder plant to DuPont is one of the most forgotten episodes in Nashville business history.

In 1919, a group of Nashville businessmen formed an entity called the Nashville Industrial Corporation (NIC). The list of NIC's Nashville investors reads like a roll call of the wealthy and ambitious business leaders of that time and included American National Bank president Paul Davis, grocers H. G. Hill and Edgar Derryberry, developer George Bennie, Nashville Bridge president Art Dyer, and Bush Brick president Thomas Herbert. According to its charter, the NIC was formed to purchase the Old Hickory plant and develop it as an industrial park.

Sometime after NIC was formed, the organization developed a business relationship with Ernest Morse, sales director for the U.S. War Department during World War I, and Alexander Phillips, the owner of a chemical company in New York. In 1922, the NIC offered to buy the Old Hickory plant and the surrounding village from the government for $3.5 million (considerably less than the $85 million that the federal government had paid to build it a few years earlier). According to an indictment returned against Morse a few months later, there were two other bids, one of which was for $4.7 million. Nevertheless, Morse's former colleagues at the War Department sold Old Hickory to NIC.

The NIC then began a two-pronged national publicity campaign. One was to sell off all the machinery inside the powder plant—a yard sale of everything from boilers to belts to blowers. The other was to find a company to take over the plant.

In a twenty-page brochure, Nashville Industrial Corp. boasted that Old Hickory had everything an industrial company needed to make a profit—an empty factory building, a coal-fueled power plant, a water treatment plant, a train spur, and union-free labor. "Old Hickory has no labor problem," the brochure boasted. "The industries now in the territory operate on the open shop plan and labor statistics over a long period of years show this territory to be free from strikes and strike menaces." The brochure also assured northerners that in Tennessee, "all heavy unskilled labor is done by the negro, who is especially qualified physically for such work."[1]

In the middle of this sales campaign, Morse and Phillips were indicted for conspiring to sell the Old Hickory plant to an entity (NIC) that was not the highest bidder. But none of this seemed to matter. In July 1923, DuPont announced that as long as the city built a bridge connecting Old Hickory to Madison, it would buy Old Hickory from NIC and convert the facility into a plant that produced rayon. Paul Davis was regarded as a hero. "Fortune has surely smiled graciously on Nashville," a front-page *Banner* story said. "We can scarcely realize what this great industry is going to do for us."[2] Nashville attorney Thomas Tyne, who represented DuPont in the transaction, went as far as to speculate that General Motors would build a plant in Old Hickory next.

Neither paper paid much attention to the fact that NIC's purchase of the Old Hickory plant may have been fraudulent in the first place. The next February, Attorney General Harry Daughtrey allowed the DuPont purchase to go forward so long as the Nashville Industrial Corporation paid the government an additional $1.7 million.

That wasn't the end of the Old Hickory controversy, however. In the spring of 1924, Congress began a series of inquiries into accusations of war fraud. The construction of the Old Hickory powder plant was at the center of the investigation.

In retrospect, it is hard to imagine how naive the federal government was to hire DuPont to build a massive powder plant with no oversight and agree to pay DuPont a percentage of the cost. Nevertheless, the accusations about what happened at Old Hickory during the massive construction project of 1918 were disturbing because they also revealed possible corruption at the Justice Department. A. V. McLane, the U.S. district attorney in Nashville, testified that he had found several cases in which DuPont overcharged the government for everything from cotton to building supplies to medical bills. He couldn't get his superiors to prosecute the case even though he made nineteen trips to Washington asking that the government do so.

The most disturbing testimony had to do with the handling of corpses, which became big business during the deadly influenza epidemic of 1918. McLane said he had found evidence that DuPont was buying coffins for $23 and selling them to the government for $250. A Department of Justice accountant named George Storck testified that DuPont paid a Nashville undertaking firm called Well Brothers the outrageous sum of $75 per body to dispose of the dead, plus $20 per body to haul corpses from Old Hickory to Nashville. "[DuPont] piled them in, six, seven, or ten in the ambulance, and charged them $20 for each body," Storck testified.[3]

The war fraud scandal hurt DuPont's image, cost a few Republican appointees their jobs, and gave several congressmen a chance to be in the spotlight. But in the end, DuPont got to keep Old Hickory. Paul Davis's American National Bank got a new customer. And the Nashville area got its largest industrial employer in its history.

DuPont wasn't lured back to Tennessee by the factory building but by the company town. The production of rayon was so different than the production of powder that in 1924 DuPont ignored the old powder plant and built a new rayon plant next to it at a cost of $4 million.

The new rayon factory opened on January 23, 1925, with about two thousand employees. That number would triple by the end of the decade, by which time DuPont added a cellophane plant (the key element in both cellophane and rayon being nitrocellulose). Even though business tapered off a bit in the 1930s, demand for rayon (used in women's clothes and tires) was so high that relatively few people lost their jobs at Old Hickory during the Great Depression.

Old Hickory's transformation from gunpowder factory to rayon factory reflected what DuPont did to its factories all over the United States. By 1930, DuPont had changed from gunpowder company to inventor and mass-producer of chemicals and fabrics that became the building blocks of the modern age. In the middle of the century, some viewed DuPont as a miracle of the business world; others viewed it as a dangerous monopoly with almost unlimited power. Perhaps the best indicator of DuPont's size is the fact that the main competition for rayon did not come from other companies but from the experimental division of DuPont, which began to make rayon obsolete when one of its scientists invented nylon in 1938.

The Old Hickory operation was only a small part of this huge international company which for most of the century had between eighty and one hundred plants in the United States. Nevertheless, the DuPont facility at Old Hickory was plenty large to the people who worked for the company or whose parents worked there. In fact, DuPont played a much larger role in the lives of its employees than did most Nashville companies. DuPont was the only employer in the Nashville area that operated as a pseudo-government. Since the plant owned the community of Old Hickory, it served as landlord, city planner, and police officer. If a child got into trouble, he wasn't taken to the police station but to the plant's main gate. If a person wanted to open a store, barber shop, funeral home, or church near the plant, he had to go see the DuPont plant manager. If there was a dispute between two people who lived in Old Hickory, DuPont got to decide who was right and who was wrong. The company newsletter *Rayon Yarn* was the closest thing to a newspaper that Old Hickory had for many years. The service superintendent of the DuPont plant was referred to—even in the *Nashville Tennessean*—as Old Hickory's "unofficial mayor."[4]

There were many parallels between DuPont's Old Hickory community and a military base. Much like a military base, Old Hickory was segregated on the basis of rank. Common laborers were assigned small houses in one part of town, skilled workers in a second, upper management in a third. The higher up you were in the hierarchy, the closer to the river you lived. The plant manager lived in a house on Riverside Drive, a residence nicknamed the "Colonel's House."

Since there were tight controls on who came and went, crime was almost nonexistent. "All the houses looked alike, and everyone left their doors wide open," said Jim Fyke, who grew up in Old Hickory and whose father worked at DuPont for thirty years. "One person's daddy might have been a supervisor, and another person's daddy might have been a common laborer. But everyone had the same lifestyle. The only difference was where your house was located. We went to school together, church together, played baseball together, shopped together. It was like a huge family with the last name DuPont."

Fyke, who later became director of Metro Parks, said he did not realize how wonderful the fringe benefits of DuPont were until he was older. "You couldn't find a better place to grow up," Fyke said. "Everything I wanted to do and everything I loved to do was free or so inexpensive that it might as well have been free, such as the gym, the swimming pool, the ball fields, the golf course." The other thing that was free was attendance at company baseball games between DuPont and rivals such as the Nashville Bridge Co., the equivalent of the major leagues in the forties and fifties in Old Hickory.

The emphasis on conformity in Old Hickory, combined with DuPont's insistence that its plant managers stay out of local politics, had an impact on Nashville's politics for decades. Early in the twentieth century, a man named Warrick Gale Robinson married into the Hadley family, the largest property owner on what was then called Hadley's Bend. After the DuPont plant opened, the Robinson family owned the first grocery store in the area. Eventually, the Robinsons became one of the best-known families in the area, putting them in a position to take advantage of the political vacuum left by DuPont. In 1946, Warrick's son Garner Robinson was elected sheriff of Davidson County. Robinson eventually put together a political machine that remained influential for the rest of the century. In 1999, one of Garner's daughters (Muriel) and one of his grandsons (Gale) were judges.

Unlike many other large manufacturers in the Nashville area, DuPont's Old Hickory plant did not change what it made during the Second World War. The only difference was that most of the rayon that was being made in Old Hickory would be turned into parachutes after it was shipped to apparel factories.

Nevertheless, the culture of the DuPont factory changed in the early 1940s. The *Rayon Yarn* was almost entirely devoted to news about DuPont's male employees who were away at the war and the female workers who had taken their place as machinists and mill-wrights. Since many copies of the *Rayon Yarn* were being sent overseas, the company even had a monthly pinup girl pictured in each issue (modestly dressed by later standards). "During the war, it was a different climate," said Earl Swensson, whose father became plant manager in 1944. "Everyone worked hard and felt like they were involved in the war because everyone had a relative at the war."

After World War II, DuPont came under national criticism because of its size and power. The company's domination of the chemical industry wasn't the only reason for this—DuPont was also the largest single shareholder of General Motors stock.

With enough problems on a national level, DuPont decided to scale down its domination of its environs on a local level. In 1948, the Old Hickory plant announced it would sell the town that surrounded it. DuPont then upgraded every home in the village and brought each up to codes, replacing tarpaper shingles with clapboard. When the homes went on the market, most were bought by the people who were living in them at the time. DuPont's employees were grateful. "Everyone said my dad was responsible for turning the village from a plant rental into a pure village," said Swensson, who later became a prominent architect in Nashville. DuPont sold the houses for so little—between eleven hundred dollars and forty-five hundred dollars—that some people actually bought houses in Old Hickory and

The DuPont plant at Old Hickory, around 1940 (Tennessee State Library and Archives).

moved them across the Cumberland River to Madison.

The late 1950s were bad years for the Old Hickory DuPont plant. Rayon—still the main product being made at Old Hickory—was almost entirely obsolete by this time because of nylon. By 1960, the plant was down to about twenty-two hundred employees. During this period, getting a job at the plant was difficult if not impossible, unless you had a political connection. "To even be considered for a job at DuPont in those days, someone in your immediate family had to have worked here," said Paul Hall, a DuPont worker who eventually became the plant's unofficial historian.

However, DuPont had no intention of abandoning its investment in Middle Tennessee. Starting in 1958, DuPont made a series of upgrades to the factory under plant manager Murray Acker. Once the upgrades were completed, the main products of the plant included:

Dacron polyester, a synthetic fiber used in clothes and carpets.

Reemay, a spun-bonded material used for carpet backing.

DMT, a chemical used in car dashboards, cassette tapes, and wire insulation.

Corfam, a shiny leather substitute that had a particularly strong market in the military.

By 1965, employment had risen back to five thousand, and the company had completely shut down the old rayon and cellophane plants.

After the sale of the company town in the early 1950s, many DuPont managers began moving to places such as Hendersonville. After the upgrades to the plant in the early 1960s, many plant workers began living in Madison. Soon, Old Hickory no longer felt like a picturesque military base. As the company village declined, residents began to get sentimental about the old days. "Back when DuPont owned the town, if they had some undesirable, they had them move out," said Maria Tootle, a schoolteacher who lived in DuPont from 1945 through the end of the century and who wrote a history of Old Hickory.

In the 1980s and 1990s, DuPont continued to make changes to its products at Old Hickory. Like rayon, Dacron eventually became outmoded. Meanwhile, Corfam production was moved overseas. In its place, the plant began producing Crystar, a refined DMT used for the production of film, and Santara, a product used in the production of throwaway rags and disposable diapers. However, the size of the DuPont facility gradually declined toward the end of the century. The company's 1995 decision to build a new Santara factory in Spain rather than expand in Old Hickory was a major blow to its Nashville area operation. At the end of the twentieth century, the DuPont plant had about 950 workers.

The coming of the Aviation Corporation's factory was in many ways a watershed in Nashville business history. Prior to its arrival in 1940, Nashville's biggest manufacturers were textile factories (General Shoe, Washington Manufacturing, Ingram Manufacturing, Werthan Bag, May Hosiery) and iron foundries (Phillips & Buttorff, Gray & Dudley, Kerrigan). For the most part, these employers required few skills, did not pay well, and had few benefits. These employers had also successfully kept unions and labor strife out of Nashville, the exception being the summer of 1937.

Avco, as Aviation Corp. became known after World War II, was Nashville's first manufacturing facility that required skilled laborers. Unlike Nashville's other factories, it made complex products such as airplanes, televisions, washing machines, and buses. Avco plant workers were organized almost from the beginning, its employees being members of the United Association of Machinists (later the International Association of Machinists and Aerospace Workers). The company paid far better than many other Nashville employers. "You couldn't beat the pay and benefits we had," said Richard Elliott, who went to work for Avco in 1950 and whose brother worked for Washington Manufacturing. "To compare working for a company like Washington to working for Avco is like comparing hamburger to sirloin."

Avco's very presence in Nashville may have been because of one person. In 1930, a young American Airways executive named Silliman Evans became friends with a financier named Victor Emanuel. Eight years later, when Evans was the owner of the *Tennessean* and Emanuel was president of Aviation Corp., Emanuel visited Evans at his home in Nashville. Evans knew that Emanuel was looking for a place to build a new factory, so he asked his friend to build it in Nashville. At first, Emanuel dismissed the idea since there wasn't a single airplane factory south of Baltimore at that time. But Evans spent the next several months lobbying his friend. Evans argued that Nashville had three things going for it: the availability of cheap power from the Tennessee Valley Authority, the close proximity of East Tennessee's Alcoa plant (from which Aviation Corp. plant got most of its sheet metal), and the fact that Nashville was an inland city and therefore secure. "We finally gave him the factory in self-defense," Emanuel said later.[5] On October 4, 1939, Aviation Corp. announced it would be building a factory adjacent to the Nashville airport.

At the time Aviation Corp. announced it was coming to Nashville, the world of airlines and airline companies was a new one. Aviation Corp. was originally formed in the late 1920s, when airline routes and airplane factories were being put together into publicly owned holding companies. During the depression, when many of these holding companies were merging with each other, Aviation Corp. got out of the crowded passenger airline business and turned its attention to manufacturing and research. By 1937, Aviation Corp. had several divisions, two of which were known as Stinson and Vultee. Both were controlled by Emanuel.

Under the initial plans, the Nashville facility would cost $1 million, employ about one thousand people, and make small civilian airplanes for the company's Stinson division. It would be located adjacent to Berry Field Airport on a thirty-six-acre plot leased for five hundred dollars a year from the city of Nashville. As a part of the agreement between the city and the company, Nashville agreed to level the site to the elevation of the airport, extend the runway to the factory, build two new hangars on the site, and run roads, water, and power lines to the factory. But the city gave no tax incentives.

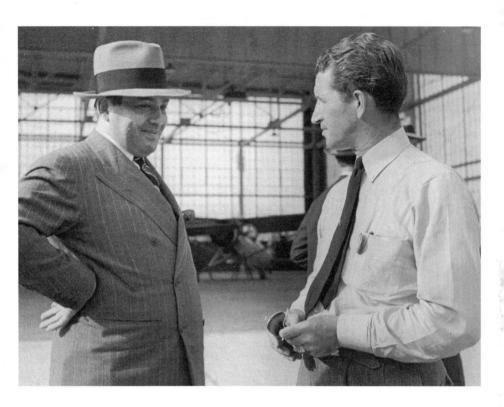

Victor Emanuel, left, with unidentified man, 1942 (Metro Nashville Archives).

By the time the Avco factory opened in the spring of 1940, much had changed since the announcement. The American government had begun preparing for World War II and had ordered thousands of planes from facilities such as the Douglas plant in Chicago, the Bell plant in Atlanta, the Boeing plant in Seattle, and the Pratt & Whitney plant near Kansas City. As a part of that build up, the government ordered a huge shipment of O-49 observation planes that were being made by Avco's Vultee factory. By the official grand opening in May 1941, the $1 million plant for Avco's Stinson division had become a $9 million plant for Avco's Vultee division. Rather than one thousand people, it needed seven thousand workers.

During the war, the Nashville Vultee plant basically made three kinds of aircraft. The first was the O-49. Next came the A-35 Vengeance dive bomber, of which the Nashville factory produced 1,531 between 1942 and 1944 (most of which went to Australia). Toward the end of the war, Vultee merged with another aircraft manufacturer called Consolidated Aircraft. Nashville's Consolidated Vultee plant then shifted its production to make the P-38 Lightning fighter plane.

At a time when thousands of men in Nashville were being drafted into the armed forces, many of the people who worked at Vultee were

women. Many of Vultee's employees lived in houses that were located across from the plant.

Long before the end of the war, aircraft companies such as Avco were thinking about what they would do after the war. In May 1945 the government cut back on P-38 orders and Victor Emanuel began shifting his company toward the production of consumer durable goods. His main steps in this direction were the purchase of two consumer products companies called Crosley and Bendix. These plans for diversification were still only in the early stages when Japan surrendered and World War II ended in August 1945. That fall, about 6,900 of the 7,000 employees at the Nashville plant were issued pink slips. "It was traumatic, but it wasn't a big shocker to anybody," said A. V. Wallace, who worked for the Vultee plant during the war. "Everyone knew that the whole country would have to get on a peacetime basis." Nevertheless, the layoff created a temporary recession in Nashville.

In late 1945, Avco's remaining Nashville employees designed and rebuilt the Nashville factory for the production of Crosley gas and electric stoves. As the factory began to reopen and hire people in 1946, Avco added two major products to the line: Crosley refrigerators and Bendix washing machines. Next came passenger buses, a production line Avco acquired with its takeover of a Philadelphia company called Brill. Soon, the company also started making television sets in Nashville. By 1951, Avco had fifteen hundred people at its Nashville factory, a facility that must have been one of the most versatile manufacturing plants in the United States.

Avco's venture into the consumer products area failed, however. The main reason for this was that the company was trying to compete with giants such as General Electric and Westinghouse while producing on a relatively small scale. "Too many makers turning out too many appliances," *Business Week* succinctly explained.[6] In the late 1950s, Avco shut down its Crosley line and sold the Bendix line to Philco, a larger player in the home appliance business.

Philco continued to make washing machines at the Nashville plant until 1960. At that point, Philco shut down the Nashville line and laid off about one thousand workers. "I remember it very well because at one point, I was the next to go," said Elliott. "You could hear a pin drop in that factory back in 1958." As was often the case at Avco, lean times coincided with labor troubles. The company had a month-long strike in 1960—its second since its workers voted to unionize in the 1940s.

What saved Nashville's Avco factory, appropriately enough, was its role as a maker of airplane structures. But Avco's return to the airplane business did not seem like a big deal at the time.

In 1949, despite its production of stoves, refrigerators, and buses, the Avco plant still had some unused space. One Friday afternoon, chief industrial engineer John Mihalic Jr. surprised several of his key officials by telling them that the company would bid on the assembly of an aircraft part (a flap for the B-36 bomber) being bid out by General Dynamics. "We worked our tails off that weekend," said Julian Kottler, an engineer at Avco from the late 1940s until the 1980s. Avco turned in its bid the next week. A few days later, Avco's executives were almost surprised to learn that they had been the low bidder. The company quickly got to work on the B-36 flap, but it did so quietly because the Defense Department wanted the project treated with secrecy.

The B-36 project wasn't a big moneymaker because the aircraft was discontinued after only a couple of years in production. However, the B-36 got the Nashville factory back into the aircraft business and put it in a good position to bid on projects that came during the Korean War.

In 1953, Avco successfully bid on a contract to build tail assemblies for a new cargo plane called the C-130. The initial order was for only seven planes, but it ended up being the most important contract in the history of the Nashville plant. During the next forty years, the Lockheed C-130, because of its durability, long legs, and ability to land on a short runway, would become one of the most enduring aircraft in American military history. It would not only be used by the army, air force, and coast guard, but also by the navy, which used it to transport supplies to and from aircraft carriers. By the end of the century, the Nashville facility would manufacture over twenty-one hundred C-130 empennages for the United States and its allies.

In addition to the C-130, other major projects at Avco included:

Convair 880—Beginning in 1957, Avco built wing sections for the Convair 880, which was at the time the fastest commercial airliner and the first commercial airliner for which the factory had built parts.

Lockheed C-141—The C-141 was one of the most tangible results of President Kennedy's buildup of American conventional forces. When Avco received the contract to build C-141 wings, it was by far the largest military contract the company had received since World War II.

Lockheed C-5—The enormous C-5 was the successor to the C-141 and was the airplane that took hundreds of thousands of military personnel and their equipment to hot spots around the world for a generation. Between 1968 and 1983, Avco produced 420 C-5 wings.

Lockheed 1011—Avco produced 250 sets of wings for the L-1011 TriStar jetliner between 1968 and 1983.

Bell UH-1—In 1964, Avco began producing tail booms for Bell helicopters, the most common of which was the UH-1 Huey. During the Vietnam War, Huey helicopters would be used to carry troops and transport patients. In future years, Bell helicopters would be used heavily in the oil, construction, and logging industries.

Gulfstream GII, GIII, and GIV—In 1965, Avco began making wings for small Gulfstream jets. Many of these aircraft were eventually put in use as corporate planes.

Richard Elliott's career path was typical of those of many people who worked for Avco. When Elliott joined the factory in 1950, he worked on the short-lived Crosley television assembly line. In later years, he built C-130 wings, C-141 wings, and Huey tail assemblies before he was promoted to the managerial level.

The number and extent of projects performed by Nashville's Avco plant almost gives the impression that employment there was constant. In fact, just the opposite was true. In the late 1950s, employment at the factory dwindled. It then grew to over four thousand in the 1960s because of the military's appetite for cargo planes during the Vietnam War and the Cold War. In the early 1970s, employment fell to about two thousand when the C-5 and L-1011 projects began to wind down.

The most extreme case of feast and famine at Avco concerned the B-1 bomber. When the federal government ordered Rockwell to begin producing the B-1 in 1976, Avco got the contract to build its wings and hired five hundred people in Nashville for the job. (Very few people outside the plant knew this, however, because the B-1 was surrounded by secrecy.) Two years later, Carter cancelled the B-1 program and Avco laid off its B-1 workers.

When President Reagan took office, he brought the B-1 back and ordered a new shipment of C-5s. Avco's Nashville operation was so busy that the company leased another plant on Lebanon Road. Avco employment jumped from twenty-five hundred in 1980 to forty-five hundred in 1984, and to seventy-two hundred in 1986. As soon as the B-1 and C-5 orders were filled, the plant laid off about thirty-five hundred people in 1987.

Because the employment at Avco was so dependent on the federal government, politicians frequently tried to take credit for Avco's contracts. When Avco received a contract to build B-1 wings in 1976, U.S. Senator Jim Sasser announced the contract as if it were something he had arranged. When Carter cancelled the B-1 for cost-cutting reasons a couple of years later, Sasser broke ranks with other Democrats and heavily criticized the president for doing so. Sasser later praised Reagan for bringing the B-1 back.

Kottler, who was involved in contract bidding during his entire career at Avco, said politics had nothing to do with Avco's contract. "Politicians often took credit for a contract, but they had nothing to do with whether we got a job or not, at least as far as I know," Kottler said. "If we were the lowest bidder, we got the contract."

In 1984, the Rhode Island firm Textron purchased Avco. The change in ownership had very little impact on the Nashville operation, which was then in the middle of large projects to build B-1 and C-5 wings.

Even though Textron secured several large contracts in the 1990s— the empennage for the V-22 Osprey being the largest of those—Textron was a smaller economic player in Nashville than it had been in previous decades. With the end of the Cold War, the U.S. military had a much smaller appetite for military aircraft.

In 1996, a group of investors led by former Secretary of Defense Frank Carlucci bought Textron's aerostructures division, which included the Nashville plant. At the end of the twentieth century, it was known as The Aerostructures Corporation and employed about two thousand people in Nashville.

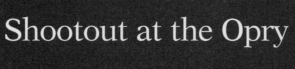

CHAPTER 8

Shootout at the Opry

Through the 1930s, the Grand Ole Opry gained listeners and helped its parent company get through the Great Depression. But for most people at the National Life & Accident Insurance Co., WSM was a tool to sell insurance. It wasn't a new industry or an alternative way of making money. So for several years, the home of the Grand Ole Opry had no recording studios, no record publishers, no music industry of any kind.

The breakthrough years were between 1939 and 1941, during which four important events changed country music and Nashville forever. The first was when the William Esty advertising agency of Chicago convinced Prince Albert Tobacco to sponsor a thirty-minute segment of the Grand Ole Opry on NBC every week. At a time when there were many other country music radio shows—Chicago's WLS, Atlanta's WSB, and Ft. Worth's WBAP had similar shows—the sponsorship solidified WSM's show as the best known in the country.

The second was when Esty convinced the R. J. Reynolds Tobacco Co. to sponsor a traveling group of Grand Ole Opry entertainers called the Camel Caravan. The group, which included Minnie Pearl and Eddy Arnold, put on 175 shows. As they performed in front of town squares and military units, the Camel Caravan helped the Opry's popularity and demonstrated the cash potential of country music as an advertising medium.

The third was the resolution of a dispute over music licensing rights. Songwriters and musicians are entitled to royalties every

Shootout at the Opry   141

time a song is played on the radio. Before World War II, an organization called ASCAP (American Society of Composers, Authors, and Publishers) had almost a monopoly in the royalty business and generally refused to deal with country music. In 1940, ASCAP demanded twice as much money from the nation's broadcasters in licensing fees as it had been getting. In response, the broadcasters formed their own licensing organization called Broadcast Music Inc. and refused to use any songs held by ASCAP. Because BMI had so few songs in its domain, the new organization was far more open to the so-called "hillbilly" music that ASCAP had been reluctant to license. For the first time, country music songwriters could make a living at their trade.

The fourth event that affected country music was the American entry into World War II and the massive mobilization that followed. Millions of Americans were relocated by the war, some to faraway military bases and foreign countries and others to cities in the United States, where they were put to work at aircraft and munitions factories. "During World War II, hundreds of thousands of young men were sent to training camps in the South, where they were exposed to country music," said Irving Waugh, who later became manager of WSM. "Meanwhile, hundreds of thousands of Southerners went into war plants that were located in the North and the Midwest and took their love of country music with them."

Nonetheless, Nashville's status as home of country music was by no means established by the end of World War II. So why did Nashville become the home of country music? One reason was that the Grand Ole Opry was by many accounts the best of the country music radio shows, thanks to the creativity of its founder George Hay. Another was WSM's status as a clear-channel station—the only station legally allowed to broadcast on or near 650 megahertz. Because of this, WSM and the Grand Ole Opry could be heard as far north as Maine and as far west as Hawaii. Another possible reason is that Nashville is directly at the center of the antebellum South and halfway between the hillbilly music of the Appalachian Mountains and the folk and blues music of the Mississippi Delta.

But the real reason may have been that a few entrepreneurs were astute enough to know moneymaking opportunities when they stumbled across them and gutsy enough to risk everything if they thought the prize was worth it.

The most important of these entrepreneurs was Jim Denny, a fourth-grade graduate who couldn't play an instrument or carry a tune. Denny came from a poor background; at one point in his youth, he slept on the *Tennessean's* press room floor while employed as a

The Grand Ole Opry is performed at the War Memorial Auditorium. Roy Acuff stands on the right, while George Hay sits at the back of the stage wearing a tie (Country Music Foundation).

messenger boy there. But in 1929, he got what turned out to be the biggest break of his life when a family friend serving in the state legislature spoke to National Life & Accident president C. A. Craig on his behalf. Denny, then eighteen, was thus hired to work in National Life's mailroom.

Denny worked a number of odd jobs at National Life, from the mailroom to the filing room to the accounting department to the actuarial department. But his real love was the Grand Ole Opry, at that time still being performed on the fifth floor of the National Life Building at Seventh and Union. National Life executives viewed the Opry as a way to sell insurance. Denny thought it was much more than that. The first time Denny made money off the Opry was by scalping tickets. In 1936, he got a part-time job as a bouncer at the Opry. A few years later, during the Opry's short stint at the War Memorial Auditorium, National Life authorized him to run a concession and souvenir stand during the Opry and keep all the profits from it. Many of the Opry's early ashtrays, seat cushions, and hand fans were made in Denny's garage.

Despite all this moonlighting, Denny still managed to perform his desk job in National Life's tabulating room. But it must have been an enormous relief to Denny when in 1946 the company picked him to run the Grand Ole Opry's artist bureau, which coordinated public appearances by WSM stars. Denny quickly transformed the bureau from a small-time operation into a much more professional enterprise. "Where WSM acts once played schoolhouses and tiny halls, Denny soon had Opry package shows in auditoriums, arenas, and fairs."[1] Denny did this by identifying a handful of concert and show promoters and working almost exclusively with them. Those promoters, which included Connie B. Gay, Tom Parker, Opry comedian Whitey Ford, and many others, all became powerful as the music industry evolved in the 1950s.

Meanwhile, Denny continued his ownership of the Opry's concessions and souvenir stands (National Life did not buy it from him until 1951). He started a concert promotion business of his own on the side. After Hank Williams made his spectacular debut on the Opry in June 1949, Denny managed the star's career—not an easy task because Williams was almost always drunk or stoned. Denny matched up a lot of Opry stars with Third National banker Sam Hunt to help some of them save money. And when Grand Ole Opry founder George Hay wrote a history of the show called *Story of the Grand Ole Opry*, Denny underwrote the book's printing and made almost as much money off the book as Hay did.

Denny had power over Opry stars, and many of them resented his influence. In 1954, Hank Snow was one of the biggest stars in country music. But when Denny fired one of Snow's band members from the Opry for getting into an argument with an Opry usher, Snow was powerless to do anything about it. The band member, Joe Talbot III, went on to run a record pressing company called Precision Record Pressing and to serve on Third National Bank's board of directors. But he never forgave Jim Denny. "Jim Denny was a hard-hearted person," Talbot said years later.

In an era before competing talent agencies and a well-established music industry, Denny became the boss of country music. And there were two things about Denny's style of doing business that helped him and the Opry. One was that although Denny knew how to look out for himself, he was not a swindler in an industry that had its share of them. The other was that he was a tough negotiator. "In business negotiations he had a favorite gimmick he used when he was in someone else's office and the talk wasn't going his way on a deal: he'd snap his briefcase shut and stand up, ready to walk out," said Gay, the promoter credited with discovering Patsy Cline. "A lot of times the other person would tell him to sit down, and they'd start talking more along his terms."[2]

Although the impact of stars such as Williams cannot be over-stated, Denny's success in promoting Opry stars was also an important reason the business of the Grand Ole Opry took off so dramatically after World War II. By 1949, WSM's artist bureau had about two hundred employees and generated $640,000 in booking fees for its parent company. Denny's impact had not gone unnoticed. In 1951, National Life promoted him to manager of the Opry, a position that had not existed before.

While Jim Denny was building a financial machine right under National Life's nose, several Nashville businesses were being formed that would have a dramatic impact on both the city and country music. All three were started by people who either worked at WSM or had a close affiliation with it.

Roy Acuff grew up in the foothills of East Tennessee with dreams of playing professional baseball. But after a near-death experience with sunstroke ended his athletic career, Acuff learned how to play the fiddle. In 1938, Acuff and his band the Smoky Mountain Boys graduated from the Knoxville radio circuit to the Grand Ole Opry. Almost instantly, Acuff became the Opry's biggest star. By the time NBC began its thirty-minute Opry shows in 1939, the East Tennessee fiddler and gospel singer was the host of the show. During World War II, Acuff became a superstar, playing to sold-out audiences in the United States and abroad. Perhaps the best indication of his popularity was the fact that in 1945, during the American invasion of Okinawa, Japanese troops attacked a Marine position while crying out "To hell with Roosevelt! To hell with Babe Ruth! To hell with Roy Acuff!"[3]

Unlike many Opry stars, Acuff lived a fairly clean life and managed to save money on the side. Eventually, he had twenty-five thousand dollars in his savings account and was looking for a way to invest it. At that point, he got together with Fred Rose, a successful pop and country songwriter from the Midwest who moved to Nashville in 1936, and started talking about the idea of forming a country music publishing company. (Years later, there would be conflicting stories about whether Rose approached Acuff or Acuff approached Rose.) In 1943, the duo formed the first exclusively country music publishing house, calling it Acuff-Rose. "We had only one real agreement," Acuff said years later. "Our company would be honest. The writers would always be taken care of, and no one would ever act in a shady way."[4] Even though the public always associated Roy Acuff with the company, Acuff's wife Mildred was actually the person who wrote checks and was Rose's legal partner.

In the late 1940s and early 1950s, Acuff-Rose was an important and at times helpful organization to people trying to make a living in country music. "Fred (Rose) was one of the most important people in my life because he showed confidence in me when a lot of others didn't," Chet Atkins said in his autobiography. "If a guy came in broke or down on his luck, Fred would write him a song, teach him how to sing it, cut a record and make the guy some money. He paid hospital bills for people who couldn't afford it and sent money to people who had misfortune, even if he had only read about it in the newspaper. And he did it all anonymously."[5]

Not long after Acuff-Rose was formed, Fred Rose asked his son Wesley to come down from Chicago and leave his job as an accountant with Standard Oil to run the music publishing business. Wesley objected, saying he knew nothing about music. "My father said not to mind that, the music industry was full of people who knew nothing about the business," Wesley Rose said years later.[6]

Since there wasn't much overhead in a music publishing company, Acuff-Rose started making money from its inception. The fact that Nashville had almost no studios and record companies was a nuisance at first. But since Acuff-Rose was the only country music publisher in town, the company had a monopoly on whatever or whomever walked through its door. In September 1946, Fred and Wesley Rose were playing ping-pong during their lunch break when a skinny kid from Alabama named Hank Williams, accompanied by his wife, came up and asked them to listen to his songs. Father and son finished the game, listened to the songs, and bought several of them. A few months later, Acuff-Rose helped Williams get his first record contract with an independent New York firm called Sterling Records. During the next few years, Hank Williams had one of the most sensational—and short-lived—careers in country music history. "Hank gave us [the country music industry] the strength to crack the popular music field," Wesley Rose said years later.[7]

Wesley's business acumen was the main reason for the overwhelming success of Acuff-Rose and the main reason that the younger Rose became one of country music's most powerful people. Like Jim Denny, Wesley Rose eventually learned the value of owning businesses that operated in different aspects of the industry. In the 1950s, Rose started a record label called Hickory Records that put him at odds with Nashville's other record label executives.

In 1945, three WSM engineers named Carl Jenkins, George Reynolds, and Aaron Shelton began using WSM's equipment to do professional recordings in their spare time. They called their business Castle Recording Laboratory, taking the name from WSM's claim to be the "Air Castle of the South." After a few months, WSM insisted that Castle get its own place of business. The trio then borrowed one thousand dollars from the Third National Bank, rented a second-floor suite of the Tulane Hotel at the corner of Seventh and Church, and turned it into a studio. "It was close to WSM," Shelton said fifty-four years later. "We could sneak out the back door and go do a recording session and slip back in."

Although there had been small, limited-capability studios in Nashville before this time, Castle was Nashville's first professional recording studio. Thanks to their connections at WSM, it did not take Jenkins, Reynolds, and Shelton long to spread the word that Opry singers did not have to go to Chicago or New York anymore. After national record companies such as Decca and Capitol began using Castle regularly, the Tulane Hotel's studio remained busy. Among the stars who recorded at Castle were Red Foley, Ernest Tubb, and a former employee of the Washington Manufacturing Co. named Kitty Wells.

About the same time Castle was going into business, three other Nashville men started a record company and small record pressing plant at 423 Broadway. In 1946, former WSM announcer Jim Bulleit, Opry star Wally Fowler, and record store owner J. V. Hitchcock borrowed one thousand dollars from the American National Bank and started Bullet Recording. Although Bullet produced some records for Opry stars such as Pee Wee King, Zeb Turner, and Chet Atkins, its main success stories were in jazz (black pianist and singer Cecil Gant) and pop (Nashville big-band musician Francis Craig).

Bullet's first big hit, Craig's "Near You," sold more than a million copies—so many that the company built a separate pressing plant on nearby Franklin Street. Bullet ran out of hits shortly thereafter, and the business folded in the mid-1950s. But its temporary success in the record pressing business inspired other Nashville entrepreneurs to start three other record pressing companies: Sound of Nashville (Second Avenue and Demonbreun), Southern Plastics (Chestnut Street), and Precision Record Pressing (Fesslers Lane).

The people who started Nashville's record pressing companies had high hopes of getting big New York record companies as clients. But Nashville's record pressing companies were mostly used by small independent labels throughout the South.

Starting about 1948, national record companies began sending representatives to Nashville such as Decca's Paul Cohen, RCA's Steve Sholes, Mercury's Murray Nash, Columbia's Don Law, and Capitol's Ken Nelson. At first, these executives saw no reason to establish a full-time presence in the South. For years, their usual practice was to come to Nashville for a few days, do business out of a hotel room, and then move onto another city like Dallas or Atlanta to tape some songs there. Many of these executives found that it wasn't easy to convince their companies that country music had a bright future. "I remember sitting through meetings every week where the producers would present the records that they were going to release," said Nelson. "Each of them would play the pop records all the way through. But when it came my turn, they would just listen to a few bars and say 'that's enough' and they would start laughing. They had no idea of the potential of country music, and they looked down on country music."

Since these record executives were outsiders, they needed to find someone in Nashville to identify talent, put together backup bands, and run recording sessions. Through this process, an East Nashville piano player named Owen Bradley and an East Tennessee guitar player named Chet Atkins got their big breaks.

Owen Bradley's main instrument was the piano, but his first instrument was a Hawaiian steel guitar that he got for buying ten cans of salve from a traveling salesman. Bradley's first gigs were in pop music bands that played at walkathons and illegal gambling joints in the late 1930s. Later, he found a job as a studio musician for WSM, playing for programs such as "Noon Town Neighbors" and "Sunday Down South."

After a stint in the U.S. Navy during World War II, Owen Bradley became one of WSM's three orchestra leaders. Like many other people at WSM, he watched closely while fellow WSM employees Jim Denny and Aaron Shelton started successful music-related businesses.

In 1947, Cohen began using Owen Bradley to lead recording sessions for Decca artists, which would soon include such stars as Kitty Wells and Webb Pierce. Three years later, the sessions had become so regular that Owen Bradley talked his brother Harold into helping him start a small studio at the corner of Second Avenue and Lindsley. After the landlord tripled their rent, the Bradley brothers built a new studio on Twenty-first Avenue. In addition to Decca's business, Bradley used the studio to produce demo tapes and corporate jingles (some of which were sent to him by WSM's Jim Denny).

However, the Twenty-first Avenue studio was still too small. After Cohen told Bradley that he was going to have to start recording in Dallas because they had better studios there, Bradley gathered his courage and borrowed fifteen thousand dollars on his life insurance policy. He then found a house between his existing studio and downtown for only seventy-five hundred dollars. "Owen thought it was convenient to downtown, and it was reasonably priced," Harold Bradley said half a century later.

At first, the Bradley brothers built the studio inside the house. Later, they hired a contractor to build a new structure in the backyard that was similar in design to Quonset huts that both brothers had seen on Pacific islands during World War II. Soon, the hut became famous in country music, not just because of its acoustics but because of Owen Bradley's skill. "Owen Bradley was the greatest country producer because he had fantastic musical ability and he had the feeling of country," said Nelson.

Chet Atkins was one of the first country artists signed by RCA in 1947. The main strength of Atkins was not his voice but his marvelous skill at playing guitar, and because of this, his career as country superstar did not take off at first. A couple of years after RCA signed him, Atkins was living in Knoxville and playing backup for the Carter Sisters when a representative of Opry sponsor Martha White decided to bring the Carter Sisters to the Opry. Atkins thus moved to Nashville and started playing recording sessions in his spare time.

By the time RCA executive Steve Sholes started a permanent office in Nashville in 1955, Atkins had become his advisor and producer. Atkins had also made it clear to WSM's Artists Bureau that he did not like to travel, which put him in the doghouse with Jim Denny. Because of this, Atkins was delighted in 1952 when Sholes asked him to run the RCA studio. Atkins quit the Carter Sisters and became a full-time studio man. Like Bradley, Atkins soon began to show an innate ability to match a song with the style and musicians that could turn it into a hit.

Country music would change a lot after the 1950s. The industry would get more crowded, the pay higher, the music more complex, the decisions about which artists to sign and which songs to play on the radio far more deliberate. People who lived long enough to see it all change never hesitated to point this out. "There was a camaraderie then that has been gone from the Nashville scene for a long time," Chet Atkins wrote in 1974. "We all saw each other a lot more often. . . . We may have been separated when we did all-star country shows on the road, but we were always back together again in Nashville on Saturday night for the Opry."[8]

During the early 1950s, there were very few music companies and no established Music Row. That left the WSM office on the fifth floor of the National Life Building as the heart of Nashville's budding music industry. Despite National Life's ambivalence about its ownership of country music, WSM did not discourage Opry musicians from hanging out at WSM. "All of the stars would meet up there and hang out with each other and the mail came there," said Buddy Killen, a bass player at WSM who later left to work for a music publishing company called Tree. "It was just a big family affair."

In the 1950s, there was also a personal relationship between country singers and disc jockeys. One of the main reasons for country music's early success was that network radio crumbled after the emergence of television, leaving disc jockeys with enormous amounts of airtime and the freedom to play whatever they felt like playing. Since the powerful airwaves were in such subjective hands, country artists often stopped at radio stations, making friends with disc jockeys and leaving them plenty of records to play. The best example of this was Loretta Lynn, whose early songs became hits only after she had taken her records from one disc jockey to another in 1960. "Were she to try that approach in today's play-it-safe radio scene, she would be an old woman by the time she got past her first receptionist, and when she did, she would encounter a helpless disc jockey, working from a playlist harder to amend than the Constitution," a country music historian wrote in the 1980s.[9]

Another way in which the industry was simpler was in the area of recording. In the days before most record labels had a full-time presence in Nashville, executives such as Steve Sholes and Ken Nelson would stop in Nashville for only a few days at a time and do recording sessions as quickly as possible. "We might play a song two or three times, and that would be it," said Joe Talbot III, who played steel guitar for Hank Snow in the early 1950s. "Today, they'd have to play it nine thousand times." Since songs were recorded directly onto a disc in those days, there was no way to cut and paste a song as in much later years. If someone made a mistake, everyone had to start all over again.

Because the industry was still so small, the amount of money people made was relatively modest. Talbot said he remembered making ten dollars a day to tour with Snow, out of which he had to buy his food and clothes. "There was no money, but I just wanted to pick," Talbot said. "If I'd had an extra ten dollars a day, I'd have paid the little bastard to get to play with him. And that was the way we all felt back then." In country music's early days, a long road trip was the only way that a star could make money. "Back then, you were not supposed to make money from the record company," said Jerry Kennedy, who came to Nashville in 1961 to work for Mercury Records. "The record company was a vehicle to get your records on the radio so you could sell concert tickets." Perhaps there was no better indication of the relatively modest salaries in the country music industry than the residences of country artists. Patsy Cline, for example, lived in a small house on Nella Drive in Madison when she died in 1963.

In the small country music community of the 1950s, there were only a handful of people with the power to make a singer or band famous. The most powerful was Denny who, in addition to managing the Grand Ole Opry and the WSM Artists Bureau, had his own music publishing company after 1953 called Cedarwood. Others included Roy Acuff and Wesley Rose, who were constantly being sought out by aspiring songwriters and artists who wanted them to hear their songs. WSM program director Jack Stapp, who in 1951 started his own publishing company called Tree, was a fourth.

Stapp's original partner in Tree was Lou Cowan, a New York game show producer who had known Stapp when both were in the army. Tree started off slowly and did not really become a factor until the mid-1950s, when some of its songs became hits under the direction of bass player Buddy Killen. "We started off on a shoestring and stayed on a shoestring for many years," Killen said in 1999. "For years and years, I made a whole lot more as a musician than I ever made with Tree because Tree couldn't afford to pay me very much."

Killen was skilled at identifying good songs and good songwriters. Within a couple of years, he had signed songwriters such as Roger Miller and Jim Reeves and bought the rights to a piece by two obscure songwriters named Mae Axton and Tommy Durden called "Heartbreak Hotel." Killen found that the music publishing business required that he carry around a tape recorder, since he never knew when he would be approached by a self-proclaimed songwriter. He later said that networking was the real key to the music publishing business. "Virtually every writer who happened for me was brought by another writer or recommended by some other music professional," Killen later wrote. "Contrary to popular belief, most hit songs are not written by a housewife who stands at the kitchen sink feeling angry, lonely, or heartbroken."[10]

Killen's ascent from part-time WSM musician to full-time music industry executive was only one example of the wonderful business opportunities that existed at the station. But the most dramatic example was a WSM receptionist named Frances Preston. Like everyone else who worked at WSM, Preston knew the Opry stars and the politicians—such as U.S. Senators Al Gore Sr. and Estes Kefauver—who made appearances on WSM. Preston also traveled to New York to help promote WSM's annual disc jockey convention. In 1958, Preston's country music and political connections were the main reasons she was offered a job by Broadcast Music Inc. Shortly thereafter, she opened BMI's first full-time office in Nashville. For the rest of the century, Preston remained one of the only female executives in an industry dominated by men.

By the mid-1950s, country music and the Grand Ole Opry had gotten bigger than anyone at National Life & Accident could have predicted. Opry stars—once farmers and factory workers who played in their spare time—were now professionals. Many of them had managers, fan clubs, and big-time recording contracts. All of them had a busy booking schedule handled by WSM's Artist Bureau. Ironically, all this growth was about to force National Life to scale back its relationship with the country music industry it had accidentally created.

By the 1950s, several key WSM employees were spending increasing amounts of time moonlighting at companies such as Castle, Tree, and Cedarwood. All three of these companies were operated out of tiny offices close to the National Life Building to facilitate frequent trips back and forth from WSM. In addition to interfering with people's ability to do their job, these many side companies created numerous conflict-of-interest possibilities. Denny, for example, had the power as Opry manager, WSM Artists Bureau head, and Cedarwood president to pick an act for the Opry, buy the rights to all its songs, and make sure it got all the best public appearances.

Crowds gather outside the Ryman Auditorium (postcard).

Denny's case brought the situation at WSM to a head. As he rose in power at WSM, Denny developed several rivals, including station manager Jack DeWitt and Opry stars Roy Acuff and Ernest Tubb (who consistently complained that Denny never gave them good bookings). In 1954 and 1955, DeWitt had several conversations with National Life CEO Edwin Craig about Denny and the other WSM employees who were moonlighting. In August 1955, Craig issued a policy under which the business activities of all WSM employees had to be reviewed by WSM's board of directors. A month later, Denny was fired because of his failure to divest his interest in Cedarwood. "Jack DeWitt did not think it was ethical for a man to be in the broadcasting business and the songwriting business at the same time," Denny later said. "I, of course, disagreed. So they fired me."[11]

After leaving WSM, Denny announced on the grapevine that he was forming a new artist bureau. When WSM heard about this,

DeWitt let it be known that known that everyone who went with Denny would no longer be able to appear on the Opry.

What followed was the closest thing that the Grand Ole Opry has ever seen to a revolt. Many Opry stars credited Jim Denny with launching their careers and therefore wanted to be loyal to him. Others were uncertain of WSM's ability to schedule their public appearances without him. Within a few days, most Opry acts—including Minnie Pearl, Cowboy Copas, Kitty Wells, Marty Robbins, and George Jones—risked their relationship with the Opry by signing contracts with Denny's new artist bureau. And although Acuff and Tubb did not go over to Denny, it was clear that WSM could not carry out its threat to expel all the Opry artists who went with Denny. In the end, the Opry went on. But the WSM Artists Bureau was quietly disbanded in 1962.

Denny continued to play an important part in country music until his death in 1963. But the former WSM executive never mended fences with Ernest Tubb. About a year after Denny left the station, he and Tubb got into a disagreement that resulted in Tubb calling Denny on the phone and challenging Denny to a duel on the steps of the National Life Building. Tubb arrived in his cowboy suit. Denny did not show. Tubb walked into the front door of the National Life Building and fired a bullet from his pistol into the paneling over the back door of National Life's lobby.

There had always been a contrast between ultraconservative National Life and the wild antics at WSM, and many executives at National Life had little stomach for the Jim Denny controversy and the bizarre incident with Ernest Tubb that followed it. During the 1960s, the insurance company would continue to view WSM as a tool to sell insurance rather than the door to a new industry.

Perhaps there was no better indication of this than the 1963 decision to appoint a life insurance man named E. W. (Bud) Wendell—who had no experience in the music business—as assistant to WSM's Jack DeWitt. "I was told later that he [Edwin Craig] wanted to put somebody from the insurance company over at WSM to kind of tone it down a bit," Wendell said years later. When Wendell was promoted to manager of the Grand Ole Opry in 1963, some of the Opry stars thought it was a strange choice. "I know Ernest Tubb pitched a fit, saying that they were sending a damn bean counter down there to run the Grand Ole Opry," Wendell said. Wendell soon became friendly with most of the Opry stars, including Tubb. But the former door-to-door insurance salesman knew that the Opry had a role to play at National Life. "They [National Life] saw the Opry as a promotional vehicle. It was not something to make money with. . . . We were there to sell insurance. We were the broadcasting service to the National Life & Accident Insurance Co."

In the mid-1950s, country music seemed to be on the verge of a new threshold with the announcement that Ralston Purina had agreed to sponsor live broadcasts of Grand Ole Opry shows every fourth Saturday on ABC-TV. However, within months of that announcement, country music was in a steep decline because of the emergence of rock and roll. And even though rock eventually became quickly identified with other cities, such as New York and Los Angeles, it is interesting to note that Nashville also played an important role in its development. "I played with twelve people who are now in the Rock and Roll Hall of Fame," said country music guitarist Harold Bradley.

Theoretically, Nashville could have emerged as the home of rock music. After all, Nashville had record labels and talented musicians. But it is hard to imagine Nashville's conservative nature and country music fans coexisting with rock music culture. Nashville was limited to the music that the Opry fans liked and the music that Nashville's companies wanted to produce. There are probably no two better examples of this than what happened to Elvis Presley and Buddy Holly.

In July 1954, Presley signed a record contract with an independent record company in Memphis called Sun Records. His first single featured an old rhythm and blues tune called "That's All Right, Mama" on one side with Presley's version of Bill Monroe's "Blue Moon of Kentucky" on the other. A few months later, Presley appeared on the Grand Ole Opry. Accounts of Presley's appearance vary (there are no tapes of that night's performance). But many who were present that night said the Opry crowd was less enthusiastic about Presley than it was about other acts.

Presley never made another appearance on the Opry. But he came back to Nashville many times in the late 1950s and early 1960s for recording sessions. Among Presley's hits that were recorded in Nashville were "Heartbreak Hotel" and "I Forgot to Remember to Forget." And although Presley eventually became so popular that his recording sessions had to be conducted late at night, his demeanor impressed Nashville's studio musicians. "Elvis was a super nice guy in the studio," said Harold Bradley, who played several sessions with Presley. "He never embarrassed anybody and if the song wasn't working he never blamed anybody—he just stopped and [went] to another song. . . . Years later, one of the engineers told me about the drugs and I couldn't believe it."

Not all aspiring rock singers had success in Nashville's studios. In 1955, Jim Denny heard about a talented singer from Lubbock, Texas, named Buddy Holly. Through Cedarwood, Denny bought several of Holly's songs and put Holly in touch with RCA Victor. In 1956 Holly came to Nashville for three recording sessions that were supervised by

Denny and Owen Bradley. Those sessions were unsuccessful. "Buddy always told me that they did not have any intention of listening to what he was, but creating what they thought he should be," said Waylon Jennings, who later played in Holly's band. "He said that they wouldn't let him use his own musicians and that the arrangements that they did were awful."[12] The next year, Holly traveled to New Mexico and rerecorded several of his songs at a studio there. The New Mexico recordings were successful but resulted in a legal dispute between Cedarwood and Holly over the rights to the song "That'll Be the Day."

Many of the studio musicians working in Nashville at that time say that they would like to have recorded more rock and roll music. But they said that the record labels—most of which were controlled in New York and Los Angeles—wanted their Nashville offices to produce country. Harold Bradley recalled one day when he and Capitol Records executive Ken Nelson saw Gene Vincent, a rock singer who enjoyed considerable fame with the 1956 song called "Be-Bop-A-Lula." According to Harold Bradley, Nelson turned to him and said, "I'm supposed to be down here doing country music, and he is rock and roll. I'll probably get fired."

Another reason Nashville never emerged as the home of rock music was the city's reputation among disc jockeys. In the late 1950s, radio stations began becoming classified for a certain type of music, such as rock or country. Many rock station disc jockeys would make the assumption that a record with Nashville stamped on the cover was a country record. "It was frustrating," said Mercury's Jerry Kennedy. "Sometimes, I was tempted to leave my name as producer off the record so it wouldn't be automatically classified as country."

As rock and roll became defined as a separate type of music from pop and country, the national music industry began to shift its production elsewhere, leaving country music in a terrible slump. And it was during this retrenchment that the industry formed its first trade association. In the early 1950s, mindful of radio's enormous importance to country music, WSM put together an annual convention of disc jockeys in Nashville. In 1958, that convention grew into an organization called the Country Music Association. In its early years, the CMA had one main goal: to get country music played by as many radio stations as possible. "The purpose of the CMA was to get country music in places like Chicago, Detroit, and St. Louis," said BMI executive Frances Preston, one of the CMA's early leaders. This wasn't easy and required the CMA to resort to creative methods. "I remember coming to New York and giving away cases of Jack Daniel's to advertisers in order to get them to buy country music."

Eventually, country music did not assimilate with rock but changed because of it. In the late 1950s and early 1960s, the definition of country music went through a major transformation, taking on a more sophisticated and less hillbilly sound. The new style of country music—which became known as the Nashville Sound—evolved in Bradley's Quonset hut and Atkins's RCA studio. Much of its evolution can be traced to the skill and creativity of studio musicians such as guitarist Hank Garland, bassist Bob Moore, drummer Buddy Harmon, and pianist Floyd Cramer.

There were dozens of country acts that fall into the Nashville Sound genre, including RCA's Jim Reeves, Columbia's Marty Robbins, and Capitol/Mercury's Faron Young. Two of the best examples of its influence were Don Gibson and Patsy Cline. Gibson's early records, dominated by fiddles and steel guitars, failed. But after coming to RCA in 1955, Atkins got Gibson in his studio and did two recordings, "I Can't Stop Loving You" and "Oh, Lonesome Me" that were a completely different style. Both were smash hits.

Despite the following that her music retained decades after her death, Patsy Cline's career started very slowly. She got her first record contract in 1954 with a California company but did not get her first hit until two years later, when she recorded "Walkin' After Midnight" in Owen Bradley's Quonset hut. Cline (who was born Virginia Hensley) reportedly couldn't stand the song because she detested pop music and preferred to do songs that sounded more country. But it was Cline's gentle pop hits such as "Crazy" and "I Fall to Pieces"—all recorded under Bradley's influence—that sold the most.

At a time when music was beginning to be classified as rock, pop, and country for the first time, the Nashville Sound generated a debate about exactly what country music was and wasn't. "It was carefully formulated, inoffensive music designed to appeal to fans of pop music while still retaining enough of a country identity to make it on juke-boxes in the honky-tonks, even though the fiddles had been replaced by violins," *Billboard's* Chet Flippo once wrote.[13] Atkins had his own way of explaining it. When asked to define the Nashville Sound, Atkins put his hand in his pocket and gently jingled the change. "That," Atkins said, "is the Nashville Sound."[14]

The Nashville Sound provided the city with a lot more than pocket change. The emergence of country could be seen everywhere in 1962; in the fact that Ray Charles released two country albums; the fact that Mercury Records created two new additional country labels called Smash and Phillip; the fact that ASCAP finally opened a Nashville office; and in the fact that a group of Opry stars sold out Carnegie Hall. By 1963, music had become a $40 million industry in Nashville that employed about two thousand people. Trade publications were reporting that half of U.S. recordings originated in Nashville.

The upsurge in country music changed the industry from a local embarrassment to something that was being accepted in Nashville.

Starting around 1962, the city's affluent residents were beginning to look more favorably at the music industry. Perhaps the best example of this change was the fund-raising drive for a Country Music Hall of Fame, headed by First American Bank president Andrew Benedict. "When I first got here, I was such an outcast that I couldn't borrow fifty-five cents," said Jerry Kennedy. "But everything changed in the middle of 1962. All of a sudden, people were falling all over themselves to cater to us."

Such explosive growth turned country music into an industry that could no longer be contained in small offices surrounding the National Life Building. Starting in the early 1960s, music companies began moving to the residential neighborhood near Bradley's studio. Among the first businesses to join Bradley's were Atkins's RCA studio and Tree Publishing. Before long, the once-declining neighborhood was beginning to take on a unique feel, with people like Elvis Presley and Roy Orbison showing up for occasional studio sessions. It also took a unique name—Music Row.

CHAPTER 9

Brokers for Belle Meade

W hen Caldwell & Co. collapsed in November 1930, it created an economic vacuum in Nashville and in small communities throughout the South. It did not take long for new businesses to fill it.

In the late 1920s, the head of the Fourth and First National Bank's bond department was Brownlee O. Currey, a great-grandson of a Nashville mayor in the 1840s. When the Fourth and First became merged into the American National Bank, Currey and several of his colleagues found themselves with connections and knowledge of the municipal bond business but no jobs. Currey, his brother-in-law Ralph Owen, George Bullard, Laird Smith, and Cale Haun pooled $47,262 in capital and started a new bond business called Equitable Securities. One of the first things Equitable did was spend $2,500 to buy Caldwell & Company's old customer list from the state of Tennessee, which had already begun selling Caldwell's assets to the highest bidder.

Equitable started off much the way Caldwell & Co. had fifteen years earlier: matching big investors with communities and companies throughout the South that needed money for new capital projects. Much as Caldwell had discovered years earlier, many northern investors were very skeptical about buying southern municipal bonds. Ewing Bradford, who sold bonds for Equitable from 1931 until the 1980s, often told a story about the lengths to which he had to go to sell Louisiana highway bonds when Huey Long was governor. On one occasion, Bradford was having such a hard time with a hesitant buyer that he said if the bonds did not mature, he'd personally buy them back with interest.

Nevertheless, there were two very important ways in which Equitable was different than Caldwell & Co. One was that Equitable made all of its employees shareholders in the company. The other was that Equitable had to be more conservative and deliberate about its business practices than Caldwell & Co. had been. New laws passed in 1933 placed far more restrictions on how bonds made it to the open marketplace and how bond money must be handled.

In 1935, Equitable took a major step by starting a New York office headed by a man who had previously been in charge of Chemical Bank's bond department. Equitable's New York branch made it much easier to sell bonds to northern investors. It also allowed Equitable to start a corporate bond department and to begin underwriting common stocks. That same year, Equitable purchased a four-story building at 322 Union Street. The firm moved into that building in 1940, about the same time it branched off and became a brokerage house.

Eventually, Equitable's two offices developed completely different styles. "In its building at 322 Union Street in Nashville, there is no high-speed ticker, and the atmosphere is quiet, if not leisurely," an article once said. "Equitable's New York operations seem faster, and the office is manned mostly by northerners who are commuters and apartment dwellers more attuned to the swift-moving over-the-counter bond trading market."[1]

By 1941, Equitable had offices in New York, Memphis, Knoxville, Chattanooga, Hartford, Birmingham, Greensboro, Atlanta, and New Orleans. During the next two decades, Equitable was the dominant bond house in the South and the main reason that, according to trade publication *Manufacturer's Record*, Nashville was considered the "investment banking center of the South" in 1949.[2] "Brownlee Currey's idea was to create branches all over the Southeast, each headed by a mature, first-class gentleman," said Bill Cammack, who went to work for Equitable in 1955. "Each of those men had working for them one or two ambitious people. Those branches were expected to get as much business out of the state employment fund as they could, as much business as they could from every insurance company headquartered in the state, and as much business as they could out of the twelve or fifteen largest banks in the state. They were also supposed to be on the lookout for promising companies that needed capital."

Perhaps there is no better indicator of Equitable's importance than the list of the companies it helped take public in the postwar years, including:

Georgia Hardwood Lumber of Augusta, Georgia, which Equitable took to the stock market in 1948. Georgia Hardwood later bought hardwood mills in Washington and Oregon, became the nation's leading producer of plywood, and changed its name to Georgia-Pacific.

Gulf Life Insurance of Jacksonville, Florida, which Equitable took public with a Charlotte investment banker called R. S. Dickson & Co. in 1953.

Daniel Construction of Greenville, South Carolina, which later became a part of engineering giant Fluor Corp.

Martha White Mills. After the flour milling industry in Tennessee declined in the 1930s, an entrepreneur named Cohen Williams bought a Nashville business previously known as Royal Mills and named it Martha White, after a brand of flour that Royal sold. In 1950, Martha White Mills began sponsoring the Grand Ole Opry, and a few years later, it hired the country music band Lester Flatt, Earl Scruggs, and the Foggy Mountain Boys to tour the South as spokesmen for the company. The country music sponsorships paid enormous dividends at Martha White and were among the earliest indications of how powerful the regional art form had become. In February 1965, Equitable Securities took Martha White public.

Holiday Inn. In 1951, a Memphis developer named Kemmons Wilson took his family on a vacation to Washington, D.C., staying at fleabag hotels along the way. After he got back home, Wilson built a clean and moderately priced motor hotel, naming it Holiday Inn after a Bing Crosby movie. Starting in 1953, Wilson began franchising the name and concept to other developers. After the appearance of the interstate highway system and the inevitable shift of hotels to new sites, Wilson could no longer finance his chain's growth without publicly owned stock. In 1957, when Holiday Inn sold 120,000 shares for $9.75 a share, Equitable Securities served as its lead underwriter.

Of all the companies Equitable took public, none had a stranger history than Spur Oil Co.

A man named Mason Houghland started Spur as a single gas station in Old Hickory in 1928. In the mid-1930s, he convinced Wilhelm von Opel, one of the founders of Germany's Opel Motor Works, to invest in his business. By 1940, Spur had grown into a chain of service stations backed by a formidable distribution network.

During World War II, the American government seized all assets owned by Germans in the United States. Those properties included stock in about five hundred companies, one of the most valuable pieces being 55 percent of the stock in Spur Oil Co. owned by the Opel family.

After the war, it took the government several years to decide what to do with the Spur Oil stock. Fritz von Opel, son of Wilhelm von Opel, appealed to the Office of Alien Property to have his property returned, claiming he was a citizen of neutral Liechtenstein during the war. Meanwhile, Americans were buying cars in record numbers, and Spur was building gas stations to meet their fuel needs. By 1958, Spur had 306 stations in twenty states.

In 1957, the U.S. Court of Appeals ruled that Opel had been an agent for his father when he took ownership of the Spur stock during World War II. A few months later, the U.S. Justice Department put up for bid the seventy-three thousand shares of Spur stock previously owned by Opel. Houghland's $5 million bid was the only one submitted.

No sooner had Houghland obtained complete control of Spur than he decided to take it public. In February 1959, in the first size-able public offering of a Nashville company since the 1930s, Equitable sold a million shares of Spur stock for $11.25 per share.

Despite the public offering, Spur Oil did not have a huge presence or many employees in Nashville. The company's headquarters were located on Franklin Road in Berry Hill, where it had a warehouse for items such as cheap dishes that it gave to frequent customers.

Spur wasn't a stand-alone public company for long. Only months after the public offering, Mason Houghland died, leaving the presidency of the company to a man named Henry Hines. A few months later, Equitable put together a merger between Spur and Murphy Oil of El Dorado, Arkansas. Through the deal, the Houghland family retained a gasoline and oil distribution company that later became known as Fleet Transport Co.

The next year, Equitable helped put together a deal under which Murphy bought a privately held Nashville-based fuel company called Ingram Oil & Refining.

In addition to underwriting and selling stocks and bonds, Equitable kept a few in order to build up its balance sheet. And as the years went by, the small Nashville bond business began to build up quite a portfolio.

Some of the municipal bonds that Equitable underwrote were used to start or improve public transportation systems, especially bus lines. As the company became one of the primary underwriters of public transport bonds, Currey and Owen became more and more convinced that bus lines were a great investment. About 1940, Equitable obtained majority control over the Nashville Bus Company. Around that time, fuel shortages brought on by World War II forced almost everyone to ride the bus. The conservative investment in the bus company suddenly became a cash cow, leading Equitable to buy other bus companies in other cities: Knoxville; Chattanooga; Akron,

Ohio; Springfield, Illinois; and Richmond and Norfolk, Virginia. As well as earning profits, Equitable's expertise in the municipal bus business helped it win a reputation as an expert in the field. After World War II, Equitable put together a merger between three southwestern bus systems—Continental, Dixie, and Santa Fe—into a bus line called Transcontinental.

Equitable divested from bus companies shortly after World War II. Soon, word got out in the national investing community that a municipal bond house in Nashville was looking for a good, large, long-term investment. Equitable then became a major player with a financial services company called American Express.

In 1929, American Express was controlled by Chase National Bank, which later became Chase Manhattan Bank. A few years later, the chairman of Chase Manhattan, a man named Albert Wiggin, became the target of a U.S. government investigation into stock market manipulation. The scandal cost Wiggin his job at Chase Manhattan, but when he was forced out at the bank, he kept a 26 percent chunk of American Express's outstanding stock. When Wiggin died in the late 1940s, there was considerable speculation that the sale of that stock would eventually lead to American Express being broken up.

At this point, American Express president Ralph Reed approached Brownlee Currey and a man named Joe King, the president of a New York investment banking firm called Union Securities. (The first meeting of the three took place at the Augusta National Country Club.) Reed convinced Currey and King that American Express was a wonderful brand name with enormous earning potential. Shortly thereafter, Equitable Securities and Union Securities each purchased half of Wiggin's stock. "No changes are contemplated in its [American Express] management or policies," stated the short account of the event in the *Wall Street Journal*.[3]

Reed, it turned out, was right. In the 1950s, as passenger airplanes, interstate highways, and added leisure time made international tourism big business, many Americans preferred to travel with American Express Travelers Cheques rather than cash. Since American Express is essentially in the business of taking interest-free loans from the general public, the more travelers cheques the company sold, the more money it made. American Express also made a lot of money from travelers cheques that people never cashed in. During the twelve years after the war, American Express grew so fast that its total employment rose from one thousand to nearly nine thousand.

Brownlee Currey died in 1952, leaving Owen in charge of the business. Owen, a quiet, shy man, eventually took on dual roles as Equitable president and American Express chairman. Despite constant offers from New York investment firms, he tenaciously held on to his American Express stock. "Peck Owen was a very careful cautious guy," J. C. (Jimmy) Bradford Jr. said in 1998. "He was the kind of guy who would walk around, kick the tires, and do nothing. When you are sitting on 13 percent of American Express at that time, that's the most brilliant investment decision you could make."

As Equitable became wealthy on American Express stock, the investment had a favorable impact on Equitable's bond business. Under post-depression law, investment firms could not at any time owe more than twenty times their capital, a rule that during times of high bond activity limited the amount of business a firm could do. By the time Lyndon Johnson's Great Society programs created a new wave of government investment in schools, libraries, and highways, Equitable Securities had the capital to back an enormous amount of bond activity. "The American Express investment helped us from the standpoint of participating in underwritings," said Gus Halliburton, who worked for Equitable from 1941 until 1967. "It also helped us that our president was chairman of the board of American Express."

By 1967, Equitable's ownership in American Express exceeded $70 million—the main reason the Nashville firm was ranked second nationally among all securities concerns by net worth (behind Merrill Lynch). But by that time, thirty-seven years of generational turnover and stock distribution to Equitable employees had turned Equitable into a company with about 120 shareholders, some of whom wanted to see their ownership converted to something more liquid. "Equitable did not have a history of paying large dividends, because we had always used the capital to grow," said Brownlee Currey Jr. "The ownership of the company was one hundred people who owned something worth a lot of money but were not really seeing it."

In November 1967, Equitable and American Express agreed to reorganize the relationship between the two firms. Under the arrangement, American Express bought Equitable, converting Equitable private shares into 190,000 shares of American Express, worth about $150 a share.

American Express then merged its Equitable division into its W. H. Morton & Co. operation and shifted its control to New York, effectively ending the history of the Nashville company known as Equitable for the time being.

However, this was not the end for the name Equitable Securities. In 1971, a group of eleven longtime Equitable executives led by William Cammack bought the Equitable Securities name, a Midwest Stock Exchange seat, and a lease on a downtown office building from American Express. "The company had gotten what it wanted, which was its block of stock that they distributed to a number of shareholders," said Cammack. "We saw an opportunity to have a nice Nashville business with a good name and a good reputation."

Cammack said American Express was "very accommodating" during the negotiating process. He also said he and most of his fellow executives borrowed money from First American National Bank to finance the deal and to meet the capital requirements to get back in business.

Too small to plunge back into the corporate securities, the new Equitable Securities began rebuilding its municipal bond business, becoming a notable player in the region by the end of the decade. In the mid-1980s, Equitable began getting back on the corporate side of the business and within a few years began participating in initial public offerings of public companies, developing a specialty in small health care firms such as Phycor, Healthcare Realty Trust, and American Retirement Corporation. "We became a recognized investment banking and research factor, particularly in emerging growth stocks," Cammack said. By 1997, Equitable had 185 employees in Nashville, Atlanta, and Houston. At that point, SunTrust Bank bought Equitable Securities in a $151 million stock deal.

As big as Equitable Securities was in 1950s and 1960s, it did not own a seat on the New York Stock Exchange. The only Nashville firm that did so was J. C. Bradford & Co.

Before he took over the American National Bank, Paul Davis developed a lot of real estate with a lawyer named James C. Bradford. One of their projects was a residential area called Belmont.

Developer Bradford had a nephew also named James C. Bradford whose father died when he was an infant. Bradford (the nephew) lived with his uncle for most of his childhood and, like so many finance sector workers of his generation, the younger Bradford left college early because he thought he was ready to make money.

The relationship between the Bradford family and Paul Davis became very important to the younger Bradford. Not long after he left college, the younger Bradford became a partner with a small insurance agency called Davis, Bradford & Co. The way Davis, Bradford & Co. worked was quite simple. Davis used his many banking contacts to get prospects. Bradford then went to see the prospects to sell them insurance.

In 1923, Piggly Wiggly founder Clarence Saunders asked Davis to participate in a takeover of the grocery chain, by now publicly owned and out of Saunders's control. Davis did so, but in the subsequent series of events, he and the other new owners of Piggly Wiggly decided they no longer wanted Saunders to run it. Davis then sent thirty-year-old James C. Bradford to Memphis to be president of the four-hundred-store chain. "He used to tell me that it was just common sense to run it," Bradford's son Jimmy Bradford Jr. said in 1998. "He'd go in and there would be forty stores in Missouri, and thirty-five of them were losing money and five were making money. He would go talk to the five managers who were making money and pick one of them and put them in charge of Missouri."

After two years, Bradford's short stint as head of Piggly Wiggly ended. Back in Nashville, Bradford got a job with Davis's American National Bank. But by now, Bradford had seen too much and had too many contacts to stay a small player at the bank. When a small brokerage firm called Joe Palmer Co. became available in 1927, Bradford bought it for ten thousand dollars. "I guess I was pretty brash then," Bradford Sr. said in 1977.[4]

The Great Depression wiped out several Nashville brokerage houses, and it almost knocked out J. C. Bradford as well. It was perhaps fortunate for Bradford that his investment firm was so small in the 1930s—consisting of little more than a couple of salesmen, a cashier, and a teletype operator.

In 1930, Gus Halliburton got a job at J. C. Bradford running the teletype machine (in those days, the firm communicated with New York by morse code). A few years later, at the height of the depression, Halliburton became a salesman. "It was just amazing what Mr. Bradford was able to do," said Halliburton, who left Bradford in 1941 to work for Equitable Securities. "We did a little business. Not anything big, of course, but we got through. I do remember that a man came in one day with a great big jar of pennies and he wanted to open a stock account, and we helped him."

Bradford Sr. frequently told his son that it got so bad during the depression that he sent the entire staff out to meet individually with each client. "He told all the salesmen that they were going to start building for the future, and that they were going to call on people and say to them 'Look, you may not be able to do any investing now, but I just wanted to come by and meet you and tell you that we are available if and when you ever want to do it,'" Jimmy Bradford Jr. said in 1999.

"When the market picked back up, they were overwhelmed with business. He always said that was the start of J. C. Bradford as a company."

Bradford wasn't the only brokerage house in Nashville at the end of the 1930s; another firm called Webster & Gibson sold shares in everything from National Life to Phillips & Buttorff. But because of its New York Stock Exchange seat, Bradford stood head and shoulders above the competition in Nashville. In 1943, the firm opened a branch in Knoxville. Three years later, it opened branches in Memphis, Jackson, and—most importantly—New York.

J. C. Bradford would eventually develop a national reputation as a firm with expertise in the insurance business. That affiliation began at the height of the depression. The Life & Casualty Insurance Co. had made many poor real estate loans in the 1920s. In 1935, federal regulators told L&C president Andrew Burton to get someone who knew something about investing money on his board. Burton then named Bradford Sr. his board chairman. "Mr. Bradford pretty much ran the [insurance] company's investments for several years in the late thirties," said Charles Trabue Jr., who began doing legal work for L&C in 1943 and later became a director for the insurance firm.

Bradford remained an L&C director for seventeen years, during which he learned the ins and outs of the life insurance business. That knowledge led Bradford to invest some of his business's money in Lincoln National Life Insurance Co. of Indiana just before the end of World War II. "That investment took off like a scalded dog," Jimmy Bradford Jr. said. "That gave him the capital that enabled J. C. Bradford and Co. to grow."

The insurance affiliation came up again in 1955, when Bradford started Life Insurance Investors Inc., the first mutual fund investing exclusively in life insurance stocks. The fund started with $21,000 in its original offering. By 1971 the fund was worth $90 million.

Bradford Sr.'s expertise in the insurance business also led to the largest takeover of the company's history. In 1962, a syndicate led by the Bradford company purchased 51 percent of Northwestern National Life of Minneapolis from Nationwide Corp. Two years later, Bradford sold stock in Northwestern National Life in a secondary offering to recoup its investments. The transaction netted the Bradford syndicate about $18 million, making it an investment that more than doubled in less that two years.

Although Bradford's main source of growth over the years was by acquiring one account at a time, the company also grew through buying other investment banking firms. Major acquisitions have included Elder & Co. of Chattanooga (1965), Jack M. Bass & Co. of Nashville (1966), Almstedt Bros. of Louisville (1979), and Frost, Johnson, Read & Smith of Charleston (1980).

By the mid-1960s, J. C. Bradford had six thousand accounts and 220 employees, half of them in Nashville. It had also begun taking part in public offerings. Two of the early companies that Bradford helped take public were a color developing plant in Athens, Tennessee, called Cherokee Photo Finishers and a shell home company called Leeds Homes.

The 1967 purchase of Equitable Securities by American Express had a dramatic impact on J. C. Bradford because so many clients preferred to do business with a locally owned company. "That left us as the only game in town, so to speak," Bradford Jr. said.

Like many other regional brokerage houses, a big part of doing business is identifying promising private companies near its home base and talking them into going public—a process that can require

The staff at J. C. Bradford & Co., around 1970. J. C. Bradford Jr. is standing on the left (J. C. Bradford Jr.).

persistence. However, it took time for Bradford to build a reputation as a company that could handle IPOs (initial public offerings). Perhaps there is no better indication of this than the fact that Bradford did not take part in two very important public offerings in late 1968—Hospital Corporation of America and Hospital Affiliates International.

In 1969, Bradford took public a small Nashville company called Danner Foods Inc., a small Big Boy and Kentucky Fried Chicken franchisee. Within a couple of years, Danner Foods bought its franchiser, came up with a fish-and-chips fast food chain called Captain D's, and changed its name to Shoney's. Years later Shoney's founder Ray Danner said he might never have gone public had it not been for the determination of the people at Bradford. "It wasn't particularly my idea to go public," Danner said.

Bradford's ascendancy after the sale of Equitable was so dramatic that in 1971, *Business Week* described it as one of the nation's best regional brokerage houses. "They know the executives of the companies in ways that a Wall Street analyst could not. They belong to the same clubs as the executives, eat at the same restaurants, and entertain them at their homes. They are in a good position to spot a situation or a company that has potential long before the fact becomes apparent on Wall Street."[5]

Between 1970 and the end of the century, Bradford took part in over fifty initial public offerings, including some of Nashville's most important companies. Among the more significant IPOs in which Bradford took part: Bruno's (1971), McDowell Enterprises (1972), Cracker Barrel (1981), O'Charley's (1990), Central Parking (1995), Ingram Micro (1996), and MindSpring (1996). One of the key people in executing these IPOs was Luke Simons, who became managing partner at Bradford in 1982.

By 1999, J. C. Bradford & Co. had nine hundred brokers, twenty-five hundred employees, and annual revenues of over $550 million. But it was hard to predict whether Bradford would continue to thrive as an independent organization into the twenty-first century because of the impact of online trading and because of mergers between banks and brokerage houses. In 1999, Bradford promoted forty-five-year-old Jeff Powell, previously the head of its retail brokerage operations, to CEO—marking the first time that the company had ever had someone other than a Bradford at the helm.

CHAPTER 10

King Maxey

G enesco's ascent from small shoe manufacturer to world's largest apparel company is one of the most amazing success stories in Nashville business history.

Its collapse may be the biggest failure.

From the mid-1930s, when it began getting national attention, until 1968, when it passed $1 billion in annual revenue, Genesco (earlier known as Jarman Shoe and General Shoe) could do no wrong. When Americans needed a less expensive dress shoe during the Great Depression, Jarman Shoe had manufacturing plants in the union-hostile South that could make a cheaper shoe than the union factories in New England. When hundreds of thousands of U.S. servicemen went to war, General Shoe made their combat boots. When shoe manufacturers got into the retail business, General Shoe led the way.

As a major corporate headquarters, General Shoe was important to Nashville. But the company was absolutely vital to the small towns in Middle Tennessee that were lucky enough to have a General Shoe plant. General Shoe helped Nashville's economy, but in places like Carthage, Cowan, Centerville, and McMinnville, General Shoe *was* the economy.

In the late 1950s, General Shoe changed its name to Genesco, to reflect its new image as a diverse apparel company. Between 1958 and 1968, it went on one of the most remarkable buying sprees in corporate history, acquiring over seventy-five companies that did everything from make perfume to run variety stores. In press releases and annual reports, the company emphasized how much stronger and larger all these new companies were making Genesco. But Genesco got a little more into debt with every acquisition it made. And with every new business it bought, Genesco acquired a unique set of problems.

By 1970, Genesco's retail side was poorly situated for the shift from downtown to suburban shopping, and its manufacturing side was terribly positioned for the era of the imported shoe. It would take Genesco decades to dig its way out of the administrative and structural mess caused by all its acquisitions. By that time, it would no longer be a dominant apparel company. In fact, Genesco would no longer even be a dominant shoe company.

Genesco also became a sad story about a family feud. Before it was all over, longtime Genesco chief executive officer Maxey Jarman would hire, promote, and fire his son. Son Franklin would come back and supplant his father.

"It is a tragic story," said Jim Cheek Jr., who headed Genesco's manufacturing operations from 1953 until his retirement in 1969.[1]

James Franklin Jarman was making thirty-five thousand dollars a year—big money for 1919—as vice president in charge of sales and manufacturing for Nashville's J. W. Carter Shoe Co. As such, he was an important employee with one of the first shoe factories in the South. The business started in the 1890s, when a shoe wholesaler named Joel Carter took a trip to New England to study shoe manufacturing. When Carter came home, he organized his own business, which had a capacity of five thousand pairs of shoes per day. When asked by a reporter why he thought he could produce a good shoe for 25 percent cheaper than a plant in the North, Carter answered by saying, "Cheap fuel. Cheap living. Intelligent, cheap American labor."[2]

After twenty years with Carter, Jarman thought he could do a better job running a shoe company. For one thing, he thought he could treat employees better than Carter did. For another, he thought he could improve the company's relations with its leather suppliers. "He was disgusted with the way that the shoe manufacturing industry treated the leather industry," said John Gifford, who went to work for Jarman in 1939. "In his opinion, the way the shoe industry bought leather and reneged on its contracts with the leather industry was very short-sighted."

One day Jarman, a Baptist deacon, drove to Franklin and checked into a hotel. Years later, he would say he spent an entire day in his room, reading his Bible, and praying for guidance. By the time Jarman checked out, he had decided to start his own company and run it differently.

Jarman convinced two Carter employees named William Weymss and J. H. Lawson to join him as partners. It took five years for the three to line up financing and find a location. In April 1924—with

$135,000 in cash and $65,000 in notes and real estate as backing— Jarman Shoe Company announced it was building a shoe plant at the northeast corner of Second Street and Shelby Avenue. Jarman was president of the company, with Weymss in charge of sales and Lawson in charge of manufacturing. When the factory opened in August 1924, it employed 120 people and made three hundred pairs of shoes per day. Jarman was so excited that he talked his son Maxey into skipping his senior year at Massachusetts Institute of Technology to come home and help him.

Three years later, J. F. Jarman must have felt like Job. In January 1927, the Cumberland River rose several feet over its banks, which it was apt to do in the era before the Tennessee Valley Authority. Jarman Shoe's employees worked all night, piling sandbags and moving equipment out of harm's way. The plant was soon under three feet of water and was out of commission for almost a month.

However, Jarman and his partners were not about to give up. After all, in only three years of operation, they had increased their production to three thousand pairs of shoes per day and were even making a profit. After the flood waters subsided, the company bought property at the corner of Fifth and Main (several feet higher than the previous site) and started work on a much larger factory. Jarman Shoe opened its new plant with six hundred employees in November 1928. The *Tennessean* was so impressed with Jarman's determination that it came out with a special advertising section to honor the occasion.

The key to Jarman Shoe Company's success in the early years was that it produced a breakthrough product. At that time, inexpensive dress shoes could not carry a shine because of the type of leather used to make them. Jarman, however, was able to produce a shoe that could carry a shine that retailed for only five dollars. The company called them "Friendly Fives." To ensure that retailers did not try to get more than five dollars for them, Jarman took the added step of stamping the price on the soles of each pair of shoes.

Jarman was a bold company. Only five years after it was founded, it began a national advertising campaign, running advertisements in the *Saturday Evening Post* in direct competition with much larger shoe companies. "The day of beating a path to the man who makes the better mouse trap is past," J. F. Jarman told the *Banner* about this time. "If the mouse trap maker wants to get any business, he has to advertise the fact that his mouse traps are better."[3] The next year, Jarman opened its first retail store in Louisville, Kentucky, a sign that the company had its eyes on other aspects of the shoe business.

Many years later, Genesco executives would rave about Maxey Jarman's energy level, but it is important to note that he inherited this trait from his father. According to company profiles, J. F. Jarman was constantly on the move, visiting leather wholesalers in the Midwest, banks in Chicago, and retail stores in New York to see what was going on in the shoe business. "As contrasted to the executive who spent most of his time at an office desk, Mr. Jarman was out in the field gathering manufacturing and merchandising ideas which he must have passed on in considerable volume to his associates," a business publication reported years later.[4]

The 1930s were dark years for most companies but growth years for Jarman Shoe. The reason for this is simple: Americans still had to buy shoes during the depression; they just were not buying expensive ones. "When the depression came and retailers threw out thousands of pairs of shoes because they couldn't sell them, Jarman shoes were the last ones to be thrown out," Gifford said. "Jarman made money in the depression because it was the identifiable product in cheap shoes." Perhaps the best indication of how Jarman Shoe did during the depression was the fact that its sales grew from $4.1 million in 1929 to $5 million in 1930. As economic times got hard, Jarman had over one thousand people working at its Main Street factory, making fifty-six hundred pairs of shoes every day.

In 1932, Jarman expanded its line with a $3.50 dress shoe and a $5 pair of riding boots. The boots, which Mr. Jarman conceived on a buying trip to Chicago, were especially successful because most boots at that time retailed for about $20. Breaking a practice common among large manufacturers at the time, Jarman gave each type of shoe a different sales forces. "We thought that our salesmen, trained to do a first class sales job with a $5 line, couldn't do full justice to a $3.50 line," Maxey Jarman later explained.[5] Business was so good that the same year Jarman opened a second plant in Gallatin. A couple of years later Jarman built a factory to make a boys' shoe in Tullahoma that the company named Belle Meade.

Jarman Shoe changed its name to General Shoe in 1933 and sold stock to the public shortly thereafter. The next year, it made its first acquisition, an Atlanta-based women's shoe manufacturer called J. K. Orr. By the time Jarman Shoe celebrated its tenth birthday, annual sales topped $5 million. Soon, General Shoe had a second factory in Gallatin and new factories in Lewisburg, Pulaski, Cowan, and Hohenwald.

On August 23, 1938, James Franklin Jarman died at the age of sixty-one. During the long illness preceding his death, Jarman spent long periods of time with his son Maxey, telling him how to run the company. After his father's death, Maxey took his father's old job.

Like many new company presidents, Maxey wanted to make his mark. He would do so with an aggressive advertising campaign built around its Jarman Shoe line. In the biggest advertisement deal ever signed by a men's manufacturer with *Esquire* magazine, General Shoe ran four-page color advertisements in every 1939 issue telling men

"Which shoes to wear with what." The advertisements showed drawings of men playing golf, attending a baseball game, and riding a ship, all wearing different styles and colors of suits. "Combining high style with cool comfort, this brilliant new Jarman model features tan natural calf in a woven leather pattern," the advertisement said. "It is ideal for informal shipboard or lounge wear with tweeds, flannels, gabardines, etc." For the first time since the Maxwell House Coffee advertisements of the 1920s, Madison Avenue took note of a Nashville company. "This is believed to be the first time a campaign built around the idea of matching suits with shoes has been widely used in the shoe industry," one trade publication noted.[6]

General Shoe supplemented the campaign by sending a representative to every retailer that carried its shoes, armed with a slide presentation and attractive window display material. The company also agreed to pay 50 percent of the cost of advertisements run in local newspapers, with the retailer paying the other 50 percent.

General Shoe's massive advertisement campaign was a success. By the fall, the company was also running advertisements in *Life*. Retailers were especially grateful, and put General Shoe's product in the most visible parts of their stores. "Our spring business this year is 22 percent ahead of last year, and we give the Jarman promotion credit for a large part of that increase," the advertising manager of a New Orleans apparel store said.[7]

On the eve of World War II, General Shoe had thirteen plants and four thousand employees, making it one of the largest employers in Tennessee.

When war came, Maxey Jarman saw an opportunity. All those sailors, all those soldiers, and all those aviators had at least one thing in common: they needed shoes.

As early as 1938, General Shoe had a full-time employee in Washington, D.C., whose job it was to coordinate contracts with the federal government. That person would end up being one of the busiest at General Shoe during the next seven years.

During World War II, General Shoe made more than five million pairs of shoes and boots for U.S. troops (a generation later, the same company would be the principal maker of combat boots during the Vietnam War). General Shoe excelled when it came to getting government contracts for two main reasons. For one thing, Jarman could underbid rivals such as U.S. Shoe of Massachusetts and Brown Shoe of St. Louis, which were unionized. For another, Jarman had a better relationship with the leather industry, and company executives were resourceful when it came to finding raw materials that were hard to come by during the war. Early in the war, a General Shoe executive named Noble Caudill flew to Cuba and bought a shipment of leather aprons. Caudill had them shipped to Tennessee, where they were cut to pieces and made into shoes. Later, General Shoe bought a leather tannery in Michigan and opened a polish and adhesive plant in Nashville to ensure an adequate supply of material.

When Gen. Douglas MacArthur accepted the surrender of the Japanese on board the battleship U.S.S. _Missouri,_ he wore a pair of shoes specially made for him by General Shoe Co. of Nashville, Tennessee.

Between 1940 and 1945, when most shoe companies suffered because of raw material shortages, General Shoe's revenue actually tripled. During that period, it also made its first international venture, buying two shoe factories in Mexico City.

Maxey Jarman's optimism also gave General Shoe a leg up on its competition during the war years. In 1944 Jarman was so convinced that the war would end soon and that the shoe business would be healthy afterward that General Shoe raised $5 million in a bond offering. The company would use that money to acquire or build nine plants in 1945 and 1946, making General Shoe a large employer in places like Danville, Kentucky; Carrollton, Georgia; and Huntsville, Alabama.

The years immediately following the war were a period of great activity for organized labor. In part because labor issues had been bottled up during the war and in part because 1945–1947 was a down time for the apparel industry, strikes were frequent. Several thousand shoe workers went on strike in New England in 1948 and again in 1951.

In this environment, General Shoe's status as a non-union employer was challenged. Dozens of times between 1945 and 1975, General Shoe plants in Tennessee voted on whether they wanted to be represented by the Boot and Shoe Workers Union.

Maxey Jarman hated unions, seeing their absence as one of the keys to his company's success. When Jarman bought union manufacturers in the North, he sometimes shut down the plants and moved the work to non-union plants down South, which is why Johnston & Murphy shoe production was moved from Massachusetts to Nashville in 1957. When union votes came up in Tennessee plants, Jarman would use several tactics to make the vote come out his way. One was to threaten to move work to other Genesco factories, a tactic that large apparel companies frequently used. "If there was talk of a union at one factory, they would switch all the work to other factories," said Cecil Branstetter, one of Nashville's premier labor attorneys. Another was to simply call the employees into his office in groups and tell them to vote no, a stunt that led the National Labor Relations Board to throw out a General Shoe plant vote in Pulaski in the 1950s. Jarman later adopted more subtle tactics, such as showing anti-union films or organizing a big party for plant workers on the eve of the vote, complete with free food, employee awards, and an appearance by Grand Ole Opry stars like Minnie Pearl.

James Fowlkes of the Boot and Shoe Workers Union tried to organize Genesco (General Shoe Company's name after 1956) plants in the south from 1961 to 1975, and his efforts were almost always fruitless. Fowlkes said Jarman would tell Genesco's employees—usually through plant management—that if a union vote was successful that he would shut down the plant. But Fowlkes said Genesco's workers treated him well, mainly because of how they were treated by Genesco whenever a vote was imminent.

"I remember getting a call late one night from a woman who worked at a Genesco plant," Fowlkes said. "She told me 'we don't want a union, but I wish y'all would stand out in the street and hand out literature. They're a lot better to us when y'all are passing out literature.'"

Rarely did one of Genesco's plants vote to unionize. The General Shoe plant in Cowan, Tennessee, voted for the union in 1955. But after a year of unsuccessful negotiations between the union and the company, the plant voted the union out. In 1964, Genesco opened a plant in Hobson City, Alabama, an entirely African-American community outside of Anniston. After Martin Luther King Jr. helped organize the workers there, Genesco sold the plant. A few years later, a Genesco warehouse in Chapel Hill, Tennessee, voted to unionize. Genesco shut it down.

One reason General Shoe was successful in keeping unions away is that in its early years, the company paid more than other manufacturing plants such as the woodworking factories near the General Shoe facility in East Nashville. But like many other employers of that era, General Shoe did not give men and women the same pay for the same work. "The disparity between the salaries of men and women at Genesco was deplorable," wrote a woman who grew up near the factory in East Nashville and who had several friends who worked there.[8]

Genesco got a lot of good press during its existence for doing nice things for its employees, such as setting up a company-matching savings account plan for them as early as the 1920s. But it is important to remember that working in a shoe factory was not easy and that Genesco's factory workers did not have a retirement system. "Shoe factory work was the hardest work that there ever was," said Nell Massey, a longtime worker at the Genesco plant in East Nashville whose husband also worked there. "My husband worked there for forty years, and when he retired all he got was about one hundred dollars."

Maxey Jarman never forgot his successful 1938 advertising campaign. With the war over, he decided that from now on his company wouldn't just make shoes—it would also expand into the business of selling shoes.

Starting around 1936, General Shoe built a handful of retail stores under the names Flagg Brothers, Hardy, Holiday, and Jarman. But it had been careful as it moved into retail. After all, it was first and foremost a shoe manufacturer that sold its goods to other retailers such as Sears and J. C. Penney. As General Shoe began to get into the retail business, it tried to ensure its large customers that it wasn't trying to compete with them.

Starting about 1950, however, Jarman made a change in strategy that would have a long-lasting effect on the company and the industry. In addition to opening new outlet stores, General Shoe began buying up existing shoe chains and converting them to stores that carried its brands. Jarman started with a Massachusetts-based chain of sixty-four stores called Douglas Shoes, a purchase that increased its retail division by almost 50 percent. During the next two years, General Shoe added the 46-unit Nisley chain, the 11-unit Innes Shoe chain, and the 102-unit Berland Shoe chain. About the same time, it added two important shoe manufacturers to its fold: Johnston & Murphy and I. Miller and Sons.

Other companies, such as Brown and International, were buying retailers during this period as well. (International bought Florsheim; Brown bought Regal.) But when it came to shoe manufacturers buying up retail chains, "General Shoe has set the pace," a financial publication reported in 1953.[9]

This trend of manufacturers buying up retailers terrified small shoe manufacturers, who lost a major customer every time General Shoe or Brown Shoe made an acquisition. "If the big ones buy the retail chains, who's going to buy our shoes?" an economist from the New England Shoe and Leather Association asked in 1951.[10]

The trend also worried small retailers. By the mid-1950s, chains had begun to take over every sector of retail. Meanwhile, stores of all kinds were being forced to expand, as brand names multiplied and as Americans became more mobile. This spelled trouble for the mom-and-pop retailer, which began to exert pressure on the federal government to do something about the unbridled power of big business.

In March 1955, General Shoe announced it was buying a New York retailer called Delman. A few weeks later, the federal government filed an antitrust suit against General Shoe, charging it with trying to substantially lessen competition in the shoe business through its acquisitions. In its defense, General Shoe pointed out that it was only one of about one thousand shoe manufacturers in the United States and that it made less than five percent of the shoes sold in America.

But by this time, General Shoe had a public relations problem of a new kind. While the antitrust lawsuit was pending, the Nashville firm became the subject of a steamy dime store novel. In Richard Marsten's *The Spiked Heel*, a Georgia firm called Titanic Shoe takes

over a shoe factory in New Jersey. After the takeover, a backstab-
bing man named Jeff McQuade becomes head of the factory.
McQuade runs the factory into the ground by overpromoting and
underpricing an alligator skin high-heeled shoe called Naked Flesh.
The author of the book denied any similarity with real life, as all
fictional novelists do. But readers who followed business news no
doubt drew parallels.

A year after the suit was filed, General Shoe signed an antitrust
settlement. According to the consent decree, General Shoe could not
make any shoe acquisitions for five years. It also had to partially stock
its stores with some of its competitors' brands.

By this time, General Shoe needed a new building. Back in 1946,
the company leased a seven-story building from the Baptist Sunday
School Board at the corner of Seventh Avenue and Commerce Street.
By 1955, General Shoe had six hundred people working there in
cramped and outdated offices.

Like Guilford Dudley Jr., whose thirty-one-story Life & Casualty
Tower was going up at the same time, Maxey Jarman was thinking
big. But unlike Dudley, Jarman wasn't thinking about downtown.

In the mid-1950s, Nashville mayor Ben West was trying to get
companies to relocate to the Capitol Mall Redevelopment Area,
which was being cleared as a part of an urban renewal project. West
called his former roommate at Vanderbilt, General Shoe executive
Ben Willingham, and asked him if his company would be interested
in moving its headquarters to the new James Robertson Parkway.
Willingham, after conferring with Jarman, told the mayor the answer
was probably no. He said that when it came time for General Shoe to
relocate, the company wanted to put its headquarters next to a
manufacturing plant and a large shoe store, creating a "General Shoe
Campus" of sorts. There wasn't nearly enough land to do that near
the capitol.

A couple of years later, West drove Willingham out to a site near
the municipal airport, then undergoing a major upgrade. West
explained how the sewer system and roads in the area near
Murfreesboro Road were being improved. He mentioned how cheap
the land was compared to downtown and said that it made sense to
put a company with as many distant assets as General Shoe near the
airport. "We're going to have the finest airport in the South before
long," West told Willingham. "We're also going to have a lot of land
out here that some smart industrialist is going to want to grab up for
a real showplace."[11]

In 1959, General Shoe announced it would build a $15 million
headquarters on a fifty-acre site on Murfreesboro Road. Under the
deal worked out with the city, General Shoe agreed to pay an annual

$12,000 "real estate tax" to Nashville, equivalent to what it would be paying in property taxes had it stayed downtown (at that time, the Murfreesboro Road site was outside of Nashville's city limits). The project was backed by industrial revenue bonds and built in phases, with the manufacturing plant going up first and the two hundred thousand-square-foot General Shoe headquarters building last. General Shoe made it clear that the new plant on Murfreesboro Road would not replace its East Nashville plant but would add new manufacturing jobs in Nashville.

Maxey Jarman (left) with Mayor Ben West (second from left) and Ben Willingham (far right) at the groundbreaking for Genesco's new headquarters, 1959. The two other men in the foreground are unidentified (Metro Nashville Archives).

The announcement marked the first time in Nashville history that local government had helped a company build a new headquarters building. West was delighted.

When the company's new headquarters building opened six years later, many were dazzled by its architecture and amenities. Every floor had garbage and mail chutes, to minimize the number of times that janitors and mail clerks had to walk up and down stairs. In order to cut down on the length of coffee breaks, there was a snack bar on every floor. In order to eliminate the need for outside window washers, the windows revolved on pivots. "From the engineering room penthouse to the ground floor computer room, the imposing glass and concrete structure is a monument to planning ahead," the *Tennessean* reported.[12]

Most of General Shoe's home office employees were women who did clerical or secretarial work. And when it came to female employees, General Shoe was looking for two things. One was experience, or a degree from a good secretarial school. The other was tiny feet. Since General Shoe made women's sample shoes in size five, the company liked to have females with that shoe size. Female employees of General Shoe with size five feet would get free pairs of sample shoes, as long as they wore them regularly and gave the company feedback on how they liked the shoes.

It was right about this time that two young Genesco executives left the company to start their own shoe factory in Franklin. The executives—Henry Keeling and Bill Watkins—teamed up with Nashville resident John Bransford and called their business Durango Boot. Within a few years, Durango had around seven hundred employees.

At first glance, the 1956 federal lawsuit appeared to put a damper on General Shoe's plans to grow through acquisition. But Maxey Jarman wasn't the kind of person who gave up easily. If he couldn't expand his company in shoes anymore, he would find another way. He would branch off into other areas of apparel. Not just shoes, not just socks, but suits, dresses, and jeans. The company would have a new slogan: "Anything you wear."

In retrospect, it may seem hard to believe that a man who spent his whole life making and selling shoes thought he could master any kind of apparel. But the late 1950s was the beginning of the age of the conglomerate, and the overriding feeling on Wall Street was that it made sense for large companies to diversify. General Electric would eventually buy mining companies, and ITT would buy hotels and food products. If General Foods could successfully make and sell coffee, Jell-O, and dog food, why couldn't General Shoe sell blue jeans, men's suits, and lingerie?

Jarman also did not think it was necessary to have a solid background in an area before buying into it. "Maxey had a theory that he expounded on a number of times that you did not have to be an expert on a particular thing to run a company," Jim Cheek Jr. said. "Anyone could run a company no matter what kind of company it was, as long as you were a good manager."

Once Jarman decided on his strategy, he wanted to get New York to notice. The best way to do that, Jarman thought, was to start with Bonwit Teller, a department store chain whose flagship store was across the street from General Shoe's New York office. In June 1956, General Shoe bought 65 percent of the stock in Hoving Corp., which owned controlling interest in Bonwit Teller. With the purchase, General Shoe also acquired ownership of another Hoving property— the world famous jewelry store Tiffany's. Years later, some former General Shoe executives said that Jarman did not know Hoving owned Tiffany's until after he bought it.

General Shoe sold Tiffany's a couple of years later. But the purchase gave General Shoe's executives a taste of what was about to come.

A month after the purchase, Maxey Jarman made a believer out of a *New York Times* reporter. "Like his father, Mr. Jarman has made prayer the guiding factor in his business operations and Christian principals his business policy," a *Times* article reported. "He opens his directors' meetings with prayers, gives recognition to the Deity in his annual reports, reads his Bible through once a year and when home holds daily devotions with his family."[13]

The next year, General Shoe bought a posh New York specialty shop called Henri Bendel. Bendel was losing a lot of money at the time, but Jarman was convinced it could be turned around.

In 1959, General Shoe changed its name to Genesco, since the name General Shoe no longer seemed appropriate. Although the company did not admit it at the time, the shift from General Shoe to Genesco was almost certainly an imitation of National Biscuit Company's new status as Nabisco.

About this time, there were three important events at Genesco's top level. In January 1956, Maxey's brother James Franklin Jarman Jr. was killed in a car accident in France. Jim Frank, as he was known, was much younger than Maxey and had served in the navy during World War II after graduating from Massachusetts Institute of Technology (MIT). At the time of the accident, Jim Frank Jarman was in charge of women's fashion for Genesco. Before his death, it was widely known that Jim Frank was being groomed to succeed Maxey.

With the death of Jim Frank, Maxey's likely successor became Genesco president Henry Boyd. But in February 1958, Boyd died of an aneurysm. Years later, several former Genesco executives would describe Boyd as the only person who could talk Maxey Jarman out of anything. "Our problems started when Henry Boyd died," Cheek said. "Henry and Maxey were opposites in the sense that Maxey was the visionary and Henry was the operating man." Bill Wire II, who went to work for Genesco in 1962 and became its CEO in the 1980s, said "After Henry Boyd died, Mr. Jarman was surrounded by people who in my view were unwilling to tell him anything in disagreement."

In 1957, Genesco hired Maxey's son Franklin to work in its retail division. Like his father, Franklin Jarman was a whiz at math and science and even built crude computers out of the instructions he found in magazines. After graduating from MIT, Franklin became a naval aviator. Later in his life, Franklin would say that if he had gotten orders to the navy's test pilot school, he would have stayed in the service.

Soon, Genesco's acquisitions began to come so fast and furious that the media could hardly document them. In September 1959, Genesco bought a Chicago-based woman's underwear manufacturer called Formfit Rogers. By the end of the year, it added a Chattanooga lingerie manufacturer called Kingsboro Mills and a Baltimore-based men's suit maker called L. Greif & Brothers. Since Greif's workers were organized under the United Amalgamated Apparel Workers, Genesco now had to regularly deal with a union for the first time.

Genesco's motive in making all these acquisitions was to build an apparel giant. As for the companies that were being acquired, they were often attracted by the idea of having a much larger entity take care of the administrative side of business. Genesco would frequently point out to privately owned apparel manufacturers that if they became a part of Genesco, it would be the Nashville company's job to deal with accounting, taxes, and legal problems. Selling to Genesco, in other words, would allow company management to concentrate on more important things.

In 1961, Jarman moved his office to New York. In March of that year, Genesco bought two French perfume companies called Parfum Givenchy and Parfum Millot. In June, it announced it was building five new manufacturing plants and thirty-five new retail stores. In July, it bought two Cincinnati retailers called Giddings and Jenny's. In September, it bought Agnew-Surpass, the largest shoe retailer in Canada with 150 stores. In October, it bought a New York pajama manufacturer called Rutledge.

How did Genesco afford all these acquisitions? One way is creative financing, such as the company's regular practice of sale–lease backs. Many of the manufacturers that Genesco bought in the 1950s and 1960s owned their own factories and stores. Whenever Genesco bought a new company, it would have all its real estate appraised. Genesco would then sell the real estate to a third party, such as its retirement fund, thus giving Genesco's earnings a one-time boost in the process.

Sale–lease backs eventually became common practice on Wall Street. But at this time, public company financial statements were not nearly as detailed as they later became. And while Genesco was expanding wildly between 1955 and 1968, this method of boosting its earnings via a one-time windfall was never discussed in newspapers or the company's annual report. When Genesco's buying binge ended

in the 1970s, the company would no longer be able to inflate its earnings with sale-lease backs.

The grand opening of the new Genesco shoe plant on Murfreesboro Road, around 1962 (Genesco).

Genesco also made a regular practice of offering generous preferred stock packages to the owners of the companies it was buying. The most common type of preferred stock in these arrangements was stock that guaranteed a certain dividend, no matter what the financial status of the company. By 1970, Genesco had an "alphabet soup" of preferred stock deals on the books, something that would become a financial nightmare for its chief executive officers through the end of the century.

One thing Jarman was concerned about was the possibility that he was buying companies that had inflated their earnings in recent years by neglecting long-term investments such as equipment maintenance. Because of this, Jarman would often offer a bonus to the owners of acquired companies if they met profit goals during the first three years after being acquired by Genesco.

However, this practice created yet another long-term financial problem that would begin to burn Genesco in the late 1960s. Owners of acquired companies would always somehow find a way to meet their profit goals for those first three years, often through creative accounting. Wire, Genesco's treasurer in the 1960s, said one division head tried to sign a deal with his landlord to get his rent dramatically reduced during the three-year period, then dramatically increased later. When the three-year window ended, profits inevitably sagged.

The long-term pitfalls of Genesco's balance sheet tricks would not become clear to anyone until about 1970. But by the mid-1960s, one thing was clear: Genesco was buying businesses so fast that even Jarman often knew little about the acquisitions. Bill Wills, who was Genesco's public relations man in the mid-1960s, once suggested to Jarman that as company spokesman, Wills should visit all the companies Genesco had bought. Jarman said it would be a waste of time, since there were many he himself hadn't visited.

Wills was amazed. "You mean you bought these companies without even seeing them?" he asked.

Jarman responded: "That's not the way you do it. You buy a business on paper based on earnings and things like that."

Once Jarman had decided he wanted to buy a company, executives and board members rarely tried to talk him out of it. "I was the only one who voted no on a couple of those deals," former Genesco board member Candler Butler told the *Tennessean* in 1994. "Maxey thought it was funny the first time. The second time, he did not appreciate it a damn bit."[14]

Wire said there was only one time that he could ever remember talking Maxey out of something.

"I had lunch with him one time in New York when he said he was thinking about buying a watch company. I almost fell out of the chair I was so stunned. You did not criticize Mr. Jarman, but I said 'Mr. Jarman, why would we do that? We don't know anything about it.'

"And he said, 'Well, you wear it. It is just something you wear, and we buy everything you wear. It is just like a piece of jewelry. People don't actually care what time it is, they just wear them to look good.'"

According to several former executives, Genesco also acquired a Belgian clothing manufacturer called Nadia even though no one in top management, including Jarman, intended to do so. "One of our salesmen told Nadia that Genesco would guarantee their payrolls if they would just keep making a certain kind of shoes," said Robert Hilton, then vice president in charge of Genesco's international operations. "The next thing we knew, we got a bill for $250,000 from a company we did not know anything about."

Genesco ended up taking over Nadia, which became a financial disaster. Five years later, after having to deal with enormous labor problems at the company, Genesco shut it down.

One reason Genesco's executives did not argue with Maxey about acquisitions was that no one outside of the company was arguing with him either. In addition to the local newspapers, Genesco was regularly written about in trade publications such as *Footwear News* and mainstream business publications such as the *Wall Street Journal* and *Business Week*. During the decade that Genesco was buying up apparel companies left and right, none of these publications ever quoted anyone saying that the company was getting in over its head.

Eventually, many Genesco executives became convinced that there was no grand logic to the company's acquisitions, except to get the company's revenue to the ten-figure mark. When Jarman bought L. Greif and Brothers, he told David Greif that Genesco would one day have a billion dollars a year in sales. "I'm afraid I sold this business to a nut," Greif said at the time.

By the mid-1960s, Genesco had a curious culture. At the top was Maxey Jarman, a dynamic optimist obsessed with his company's revenue but not worried about its profits. He spent most of his time in New York and slept only about four hours a night. Reporting to him were about a half-dozen executives in Nashville, most of whom were white male Protestants, most of whom grew up in the South, most of whom were intimidated by the boss, and most of whom knew little about anything but shoes. Those same executives made up the board of directors, which before 1969 did not have a single non-Genesco employee.

Meanwhile, Genesco was buying firms that did everything from making brassieres to marketing perfume to selling high-fashion jewelry. And many of the companies Genesco bought catered to female taste and were owned by northern Jewish families.

As Genesco acquired these firms, many executives found themselves in charge of companies they knew nothing about and working with people from a completely different world. "When you start getting into the Seventh Avenue type businesses in New York, the Nashville, Tennessee, mentality can't deal with that," said Wire.

However, one way in which Jarman was ahead of his time was in the hiring of women in executive positions. In 1956, Jarman named Geraldine Stutz, a twenty-six-year-old New Yorker who once worked as *Glamour's* shoe editor, to lead Genesco's I. Miller retail division. After Stutz turned it around, Jarman asked her to run the high-profile Henri Bendel store, which was losing over $1 million a year at the time. Stutz was reluctant at first and told Maxey that she would only do it on two conditions: one, that he give her five years, and two, that he "keep all those gumshoes from Nashville out of the store." Jarman agreed, and Stutz's new appointment made waves in New York. "Back then, there were no young presidents of national stores unless they were family kids, and there were no women in high executive positions except the ones who owned their own stores," Stutz said. "But Maxey thought it was absolutely right for women to be leaders in fashion business."

Stutz succeeded in turning Bendel around. Five years after her promotion, Maxey Jarman celebrated with the Bendel staff by having a glass of champagne—a rare deed for the teetotaling Jarman. "As far as I know, that is the only drink he ever took," Stutz said.

Like many former Genesco executives, Stutz said one thing that hurt Genesco was a lack of middle management. "The reason you are able to buy companies cheap is because they are in trouble and they lack good management," she said. "Most of the time, Genesco would stick to the proprietors who had sold them the businesses. But they would often just coast along on the dough they had made from selling the business and not do much.

"Maxey was a terrific captain. He needed a lot of first-rate first mates and he did not find them."

In 1964, Genesco made the largest acquisition in its history with the purchase of Kress, a retail chain with 350 stores in thirty states. The transaction cost Genesco about $60 million in stock and took six months to negotiate, since Kress management was averse to the sale at first. But Genesco was persistent, in part because the acquisition was the brainchild of Franklin Jarman, by now a top executive. Since Kress was a variety store chain like Woolworth's that did not specialize in apparel, the purchase confused some Genesco executives, who thought the company was trying to focus in the apparel business. "We were kind of surprised that we got into that because it was different than anything that we had done," said DeVaughn Woods, Genesco's comptroller in the 1960s.

Once the deal with Kress was signed, Genesco continued to acquire companies with speed. Later that same year, it bought a men's shirt manufacturer called Ainsbrooke, a work-clothes maker called J. M. Wood, a men's suit manufacturer called Phoenix, and an Italian apparel company called Confezioni San Remo. Next came a women's swimsuit manufacturer called Lee Beachwear and an apparel company called Salant and Salant. Then, Genesco bought a California-based speciality clothing chain called Roos Atkins and a Swiss apparel manufacturer called Interstyle, which owned ten manufacturing plants in Europe.

Genesco bought over fifty companies between 1964 and 1968—through acquisition, Genesco more than doubled in size. And in 1968, Jarman proudly announced to his board that he had reached his billion-dollar goal. He also told them he was going to retire. When asked by close friend Rev. James Sullivan why he wanted to retire, Jarman said, "We built the largest apparel company in the world. But now men are carrying purses, women are wearing pants, and kids are going barefoot. I've had it."

During Maxey Jarman's three decades as head of Genesco, the company had grown from a regional shoe manufacturer with $15 million in revenue to the world's largest apparel company, with over $1 billion in revenue. Jarman had made so many acquisitions that in 1968, footwear accounted for less than 40 percent of Genesco's revenue. It had sixty-five thousand employees, making it the largest employer in Nashville history. Genesco's stock was selling at an all-time high of $58 a share. It had paid dividends to its shareholders for thirty-six straight years.

Jarman selected Ben Willingham to be his replacement. And as Willingham took the helm, he let it be known that he saw no reason to change Genesco's course. Willingham even predicted that Genesco would reach $2 billion in sales by 1975 by acquiring more apparel companies. "When you have worked with a man for as long as I have with Mr. Jarman, you find that you think the same and function much the same," Willingham told the *New York Times*.[15]

Having taken over Fifth Avenue, Maxey Jarman set out to conquer the minds and hearts of Tennessee's voters. In the spring of 1970, he announced he was seeking the Republican nomination for governor of Tennessee. "I'm getting my running shoes well polished," he told the *Banner* on the day he made the announcement.[16]

The 1970 governor's race would go down as one of the most memorable in Tennessee history. During the eighteen years preceding the election, Democrats Frank Clement and Buford Ellington had taken turns occupying the governor's mansion, giving the Volunteer State two decades of what many observers dubbed "leapfrog government." Clement died in an automobile accident in 1969, and Ellington could not legally succeed himself after 1970.

When Jarman made his announcement, it had been five decades since Tennessee had a Republican governor. However, the GOP was making enormous advances in the South during this period because many southern voters were beginning to perceive the Democratic party as the party of northern liberals.

During the campaign, Jarman was considered the front-runner among several Republican candidates, including an East Tennessee legislator named Bill Jenkins, a Knoxville attorney named Claude Robertson, and a Memphis dentist named Winfield Dunn. The favorite on the Democratic side was John Jay Hooker Jr., who had run unsuccessfully in 1966 and since then had made (and lost) millions with a restaurant chain called Minnie Pearl's Fried Chicken.

Candidate Jarman emphasized his resume and said if the state government were run more like a business that it would be run more efficiently (he did not present many specifics on how he would do this, though). He generally tried to avoid controversy, the one exception to this being when he said that he did not think atheists should be allowed to teach public school.

In those days, most of the people who voted Republican in Tennessee came from the eastern third of the state, and Jarman knew that most people in Nashville would be voting in the Democratic primary. Nevertheless, Jarman's campaign was certainly not helped when the Republican *Nashville Banner* endorsed Democrat Stan Snodgrass. The *Banner* admitted that it endorsed Snodgrass only because it wanted to do everything it could to keep Hooker from getting elected. Nevertheless, Jarman was disgusted and even told a reporter that had he received the *Banner's* endorsement he might have repudiated it. Jarman's failure to get the *Banner's* endorsement destroyed the impression that he was the Republican candidate overwhelmingly favored in Nashville.

On election day, Jarman learned a lesson that other Nashville gubernatorial candidates such as Dortch Oldham, Clayton McWhorter, and Phil Bredesen would later learn. People from other parts of

Tennessee are not impressed by a successful track record in a Nashville boardroom. In fact, many resent the implication that they should be impressed. Boosted by an outstanding Republican turnout in Memphis, Dunn got 33 percent of the primary vote—three percent more than Jarman. The Memphis dentist would pull off one of the biggest upsets in Tennessee political history three months later by defeating Hooker.

Lee Smith, a Dunn staffer who later became the publisher of a statewide political newsletter, later said that had Jarman won the nomination, he almost certainly would have been governor.

"The Democratic Party was extremely polarized at that time," Smith said. "The conservative Democrats hated the *Tennessean* and John Jay Hooker, and the liberal Democrats hated the *Banner*, Clement, and Ellington.

"I'm sure that Jarman could have put together the same coalition of Republicans and conservative Democrats that Dunn put together."

Ben Willingham's tenure as Genesco chief executive officer was a short one. Four months after he took over as Genesco's CEO, he resigned because of what the company described as a "respiratory ailment." However, Genesco veterans attribute his abrupt departure to personal changes that took place in his life after he became CEO.

The board named Franklin Jarman chief executive officer and Owen Howell president. For the next three years, Genesco's employees and investors would be confused about who was actually running the company. In fact, it was Maxey Jarman who ran Genesco from the boardroom during the years immediately following his unsuccessful run for governor.

About this time, Genesco began to report lower earnings for the first time in its history. Part of the problem had to do with clothing lines and styles that failed. And although the late 1960s and early 1970s were unpredictable years for fashion, the direction in which Genesco's white, male, middle-aged, southern executives thought fashion was heading couldn't have been more inaccurate. "Clothing won't go out of style," Genesco's 1969 annual report predicted. "But sewing will. Seams will be joined with adhesive, not thread. New fibers and fabrics will maintain body temperature in all climates. Stretch materials will gain—even in men's suits, dress shirts, footwear—adding to comfort, reducing inventories. All clothing will be travel oriented—comfortable, wrinkle-resistant, packable, non-seasonable, easy to wear and change. Disposable apparel will enable people to travel light."

Some of Genesco's retail divisions also had a location problem. Between 1950 and 1970, millions of Americans moved to the suburbs. It would take years before all the long-term impacts of this migration were fully understood. But among the changes that it wrought in retail were a decline in downtown shopping, the construction of massive enclosed shopping malls, and the rise of huge discount stores.

In 1970, Genesco had dozens of retail divisions that accounted for about $400 million in sales. Some of them, such as Johnston & Murphy, would be able to adjust to the changes and eventually succeed in mall locations. But in many cases, Genesco had invested in retail concepts that would simply not survive. Kress was a variety store chain with most of its branches downtown. After shoppers discovered K Mart and Wal-Mart, Kress's sales plummeted. Bonwit Teller was a women's apparel chain that sold middle-level merchandise. Most of the items that were sold there would eventually migrate to department stores. Roos Atkins was also having hard times by 1970, unable to decide whether it wanted to sell top quality merchandise or be a small discounter.

Because of problems in the retail division and because Genesco had slowed its acquisitions and could no longer use them to artificially boost earnings, Genesco's profits continued to decline in 1971. Franklin Jarman—under the close supervision of the Genesco board—reacted by trying to cut costs. But after two years of poor earnings and weak stock performance, Maxey decided it wasn't enough. In May 1972, Maxey came back as chief executive officer of Genesco. National publications reported a rift between father and son. "Maxey is a publicity seeker, and he wasn't getting any of it when he retired," the *Times* quoted one unnamed observer as saying. "He's a domineering type, and he has hurt his son."[17]

However, Maxey Jarman soon found out—for the first time in his life—that his magic did not always work. During the next year, Genesco's revenue increased 6 percent, to an all-time high of $1.4 billion. But thirteen of the company's one hundred divisions lost money. Genesco's net income declined 45 percent.

Genesco's board of directors had changed since 1968. Under Maxey, the board had consisted entirely of Genesco employees, most of whom Maxey had hired to begin with. During Franklin's term as chairman from 1969 to 1971, several outsiders had been named to the board. Some of them were of the opinion that Maxey's domineering ways were to blame for many of the company's ills.

In February 1973, the board voted Maxey out and replaced him with Franklin. Later, Franklin Jarman would give a four-word explanation for what happened: "I outpoliticked my father."

The financial woes of a teetering company were obviously the main source of tension between Maxey and Franklin Jarman. But the situation was exacerbated by the fact that the two were so different. Throughout his life, Maxey Jarman was described as outgoing, energetic, flamboyant, and vain. "If Maxey came into a room with one hundred people, everyone would know he was there within thirty seconds," Wire said. Meanwhile, Franklin was introverted and was described by more than one reporter as frequently carrying a calculator and a slide rule around with him.

Unfortunately for Franklin, the slide rule doesn't exist that could have fixed the problems he would encounter as head of Genesco during the next four years. During Franklin Jarman's tenure, trade publications would closely monitor the various strategies that Genesco would try with its many retail and manufacturing divisions. They would also mention complaints about Franklin Jarman's micromanagerial leadership style, which sharply contrasted with his father's way of doing business. But given Genesco's position by 1972, it is hard to imagine how anyone could have continued to turn a profit as CEO. "I think it would have been extremely difficult for anyone to succeed at that time," longtime Genesco board member David K. (Pat) Wilson would say years later. "The company was carrying such a load."

Franklin Jarman may have suspected the same thing as he focused his attention on how to deal with poorly performing retail chains. But about this time, there were two enormous changes taking place in the shoe industry that Genesco—under Jarman and his successors—would completely miss.

One had to do with technology and lifestyle. The American shoe industry historically regarded athletic shoes as a niche business that catered to children. But in the 1960s, a track coach at the University of Oregon named Bill Bowerman began designing light athletic shoes that he thought would help his runners. One of Bowerman's athletes, a man named Phil Knight, later went on to the Stanford Business School. There, he came up with a plan to make money off Bowerman's shoes. By 1970, the two formed a company called Blue Ribbon Sports. In 1971, it changed its name to Nike.

Genesco was in the sneaker business; in the 1970s, it made athletic shoes for J. C. Penney at a plant on Charlotte Pike. But Genesco's athletic shoes were made out of canvas, and the technology that went into making them hadn't changed in decades. Meanwhile, Nike utilized the latest synthetic technology to make a leather shoe that was engineered with the human foot in mind.

After the 1968 Olympics, the sale of athletic shoes started to climb. Within a year or two, the media had begun to take note. "Track shoes take off as a fad in casual footwear," noted the *Wall Street Journal*.[18] But fitness was no fad. It was the beginning of a change in American lifestyle. None of the big American shoe companies recognized it as such and continued to produce formal shoes as if they would always be the bulk of the shoe market. By the mid-1980s, two of the top three shoe companies in the world (Nike, Brown, and Reebok) produced nothing but athletic shoes.

"American shoe companies had always been driven by what the factory made," Peter Mangione, president of the Footwear Distributors and Retailers of America, said in 1998. "Along comes Nike, and it was a design, development, and marketing enterprise. They were never in bricks in mortar, and they were never driven by what the factories made. The way Nike did things is that it came up with what it wanted, and then went and found someone to make it for them."

The factories Nike found were all in Asia. And as companies like Nike began to make their apparel in the Third World, they added to the second big factor that would hurt Genesco's shoe business. Historically, the shoes Americans wore were almost always made in America—first in New England and later in the Midwest and South. But starting in the 1960s, apparel manufacturers began to shift their production overseas. The problem was so bad that Genesco executives repeatedly lobbied Congress for higher tariffs on shoe imports between 1963 and 1975. Presidents Kennedy, Johnson, Nixon, Ford, and Carter refused to pass the tariffs. But by 1978, the federal government was giving millions of dollars in subsidies to shore up the hobbling American shoe business.

A manufacturer with almost all of its 250 plants in the United States and Europe, Genesco was terribly positioned for this shift in the world's economy. And it would take Genesco far too long to take action in this regard, in part because top executives couldn't bear the thought of moving plants overseas. "I remember the first time that I said we should close some plants," Wire said. "The room just erupted. . . . The company just did not want to recognize it. To me, it was like an ostrich with its head in the sand."

Genesco actually formed an import division in the early 1960s. But the company did not allow it to deal directly with Genesco's retail customers and it was required to work through a sales staff whose first priority was Genesco's manufacturing division. "The mindset of Genesco in the early 1970s was still slanted very much toward the domestic manufacturing and to protecting that manufacturing base," said Joe Russell, an executive in Genesco's import division who later cofounded a successful shoe import company called Elan Polo. "However, that was not unlike all the other major footwear manufacturing companies in the United States at that time."

On June 20, 1973, Genesco announced it was suspending dividends for its regular shareholders. The company said the main cause of its problems was Kress and labor problems at a manufacturing division in Italy. Howell resigned as president and was replaced by Ralph Bowles.

A few months later, Franklin Jarman announced a series of cost-cutting moves intended to restore earnings. The company laid off about ten thousand people, including one thousand managers. It closed over one thousand retail stores, including about one hundred Kress locations. It closed most of its manufacturing plants in Europe and in the United States (including the shoe plant on Centennial Boulevard in Nashville). With the announced cuts, Genesco began to withdraw from its major position in the shoe retailing business, a position that would soon be filled by competitors such as Kinney's Foot Locker chain.

Genesco also suspended dividend payments to preferred stockholders. Jarman let it be known that there was little love lost for some of them. "Many of them sold Genesco companies that never made money," Jarman told *Business Week*. "If it were not for us, most would be out of business. I really can't feel sorry for them."[19]

A few months later, Jarman announced that in order to write off all these reductions, the company would take a fiscal year loss of $53 million—this only one year after it reported a profit of about $12 million. The stock, which had sold for as high as $35 earlier that year, fell to about $10. A Genesco shareholder from Chattanooga ran a classified advertisement in both Nashville newspapers. "Please come back Maxey. Franklin can't run the store."[20]

The next year, Genesco reported $17 million in profits. But it lost $14 million in 1974, in large part because a national recession hurt its retail sales divisions. In 1975, Genesco made about $16 million, thanks to a strong year by its shoe division. By 1976, analysts began to talk confidently about a recovery at Genesco. But this was right at the time that imported shoes and athletic shoes began to rock the American shoe industry. By the end of 1976, it was obvious to Genesco's top management that the company was going to miss its earnings targets by a mile.

In December 1976, some of Genesco's board members began to have private discussions about firing Franklin Jarman. According to a later account by the *Wall Street Journal*, the instigators of those talks were Larry Shelton and Ralph Bowles, who told the board that Franklin Jarman was guilty of a series of management foul-ups. On January 4, 1977, during a ten-hour board meeting, Jarman was fired and replaced with longtime Genesco executive William Blackie. For the first time in the fifty-three-year history of the company, a member of the Jarman family was no longer in charge of Genesco.

Twenty years later, board members were still mum about exactly what was said during that marathon meeting. "The board had lost confidence in Franklin," director Wilson laconically said.

Two months after Genesco's board fired Jarman, Genesco board member and former Third National Bank president Sam Fleming teamed up with Hospital Corporation of America cofounder Jack Massey to buy about four hundred thousand shares of Genesco stock. In May, at the insistence of Massey and Fleming, the board named Jack Hanigan to be Genesco's new president. Hanigan had previously been the president of a bowling equipment company called Brunswick—the same firm to which Massey had sold his surgical supply business in 1961.

Hanigan was the first of four chief executive officers Genesco would go through in the next seventeen years. In their effort to make Genesco profitable, all four would lay off employees by the thousands and close manufacturing plants. All four would sell some of the companies Maxey Jarman had acquired. All four would try to focus the company on an area that seemed to have a bright future. And all four would find it wasn't enough.

The first thing Hanigan did was announce the worst financial news any chief executive officer in Nashville had ever delivered. In September 1977, Genesco said it would lose $136 million in its fiscal year in order to sell off losing divisions and focus the company on shoe retailing. Since Wall Street was braced for bad news, analysts praised Hanigan's action. "It's a very positive sign that he is getting rid of a lot of junk," *Business Week* quoted one analyst as saying.[21] Thousands of Genesco employees might have had a different point of view. During his three-year tenure, Hanigan reduced Genesco's employment from fifty thousand to about twenty-two thousand and laid off more workers than any other chief executive in Nashville history.

All totaled, Hanigan sold or closed about fifty companies in the greatest fire sale the apparel world has ever seen. On the manufacturing side, Hanigan got Genesco completely out of the business of making women's and children's clothing. On the retail side, Hanigan sold Whitehouse & Hardy, Baron's, Henri Bendel, and Bonwit Teller.

Finding buyers for some of the pieces wasn't hard. Genesco executive Geraldine Stutz bought Henri Bendel from the company that had put her in charge of the store twenty-two years earlier. An ambitious developer named Donald Trump bought Bonwit Teller, tore it down, and built Trump Towers there.

Selling white elephants such as Kress and Roos Atkins wasn't so easy. Genesco eventually closed both of those retail chains and sold off the real estate. Hanigan also started the long process of closing Genesco's shoe plants in Tennessee, including those in Smithville, Carthage, Cowan, and Gallatin. He also eliminated Genesco's import division, a move that made critics wonder if the company was interested in future growth or just cleaning up its balance sheet.

During Hanigan's term, there were frequent reports in the media about Genesco being a possible takeover target. In fact, no one in their right mind would have taken over Genesco because of its capital structure. By 1980, Genesco owed its preferred shareholders about $40 million in back dividends.

On September 9, 1980, Maxey Jarman died. During the last five years of his life, the man whose drive and enthusiasm had shaped Genesco withdrew to his home. Knowing that Genesco was a painful subject for him to discuss, friends rarely brought it up. One of the more important things Jarman did during his declining years was offer moral support and advice to Thomas Nelson, Inc. president Sam Moore regarding the New King James Version of the Bible, which Thomas Nelson undertook as a project from 1975 until 1982.

Hanigan's drastic actions stabilized the company, at least in the opinion of Wall Street analysts. But Genesco still had financial problems when he left in 1981. His replacement was Dick Hanselman, who had a successful track record as a turnaround artist at Samsonite. Like Hanigan, Hanselman believed Genesco's future was in shoe retailing. He too closed some Tennessee shoe plants, including those in Lewisburg, Pulaski, Tullahoma, and Centerville.

Hanselman had rough years in 1982 and 1983, but the company's performance dramatically improved in 1984. Then, in 1985, Genesco lost $34 million and Hanselman resigned. He later said that the stress of running Genesco was far worse than it had been at Samsonite.

"My blood pressure was two hundred over one hundred," Hanselman said. "The board had lost confidence in my leadership ability. My doctor said if you stick around you will be dead in a year."

Longtime Genesco executive Bill Wire II was next. When Wire took over, Genesco was on the verge of bankruptcy, and its stock was an all-time low of $2.75 per share. "We were going broke—there wasn't any question in my mind," Wire said. In order to keep the banks from closing in, Wire sold Genesco's three hundred Canadian shoe stores. By 1989, analysts were asserting that Genesco was finally on the course to consistent profitability. They were even happier two years later, when Genesco got the exclusive license to market Levi Strauss's Dockers shoe line.

By 1992, the apparel company that once had sixty-five thousand employees only had about one-tenth that number. Wire then retired and was replaced with Procter & Gamble veteran Douglas Grindstaff. Under Grindstaff's direction, Genesco made its first acquisitions in twenty-two years when it bought a producer of soccer equipment called Mitre UK, a children's shoe company called University Brands, and a men's suit manufacturer called LeMar Manufacturing. The company also invested heavily in Genesco's western boot brands, figuring that the upturn in country music would lead to a boom in boot sales. Wall Street began to get enthused about Genesco once again, and its stock price climbed back up to about $11.50.

However, 1993 was another disastrous year for Genesco. LeMar ended up being worth nowhere near what Genesco paid for it, and the boom in boot sales tapered off more quickly than expected. In February 1994, Genesco announced it had lost $52 million during the year. Another fourteen hundred Genesco workers got pink slips, and the stock fell to $4.25. Grindstaff was fired and replaced by David Chamberlain.

Like his five predecessors, Chamberlain liquidated major parts of Genesco, selling University Brands, Mitre, and Greif, getting the company entirely out of men's apparel. By 1998, Genesco was back to being a men's shoe company, and it was so small that focus was no longer a problem. The company had about 650 stores, made up of retail chains called Journey's, Jarman, and Johnston & Murphy. It had a license to design and oversee the production of shoes for the Levi's casual men's line called Dockers. And Genesco's only manufacturing plant left was the one adjacent to its Murfreesboro Road headquarters.

By the time Genesco celebrated its seventy-fifth anniversary in 1999, management professors were using Genesco to illustrate things companies shouldn't do. Genesco's retirees—and there were thousands of them in Nashville—would wonder about all the traveling that they would have been able to do in their old age if their Genesco stock had kept its value. "It really hurt me to see it go down like that," said Elizabeth Barrett, a fifty-year employee of the Genesco accounting department. "I would have made some money to retire on if it hadn't gone under like that." Nashville businessmen would also use Genesco as a target for one-liners such as, "Genesco has had more turnarounds than the Vanderbilt football team" and countless jokes. "One old man says to the other, 'I just got back from the doctor and he told me that I had gonorrhea,'" the joke went. "'Can you imagine: Gonorrhea at eighty-five!'

"The other one says, 'Hell, that's nothing. I had Genesco at fifty-eight!'"

However, the fall of Genesco was not a laughing matter to many Genesco executives. "What happened hurt us personally," said DeVaughn Woods, who worked for Genesco from 1938 until 1974. "It was like losing a child." Other former Genesco executives would ask themselves why they had ever gone to work for Genesco in the first place. "I often wonder where my career would be had I gone to work for General Electric or Procter & Gamble or IBM," said Robert Hilton.

One thing all former Genesco executives had in common was they would constantly wonder whether the company failed more because of bad acquisitions, bad decisions, or bad luck. "I think the right management team could have avoided some of this," Wire said. "I don't necessarily think all this had to happen."

CHAPTER 11

Banks, Sibling Rivalries

L ike three brothers constantly trying to one-up each other, Nashville's three largest banks duked it out. One frequently pointed out that it was the biggest and the oldest and therefore the best. Another claimed to be the friendliest and the hardest-working and therefore the best. The third claimed to be the toughest and most original. And, of course, the best.

The largest of the three was First American—the bank formed in the 1930 merger between Paul Davis's American National Bank and James Caldwell's Fourth and First National Bank. Steeped in tradition and with a board of directors dominated by old money, First American (which changed its name from American National in 1950) encouraged the perception that it was Nashville's only top-notch bank.

The second largest bank was Third National, which encouraged the perception that First American was old-fashioned and not amenable to change. This strategy often worked because of the energy and personality of Sam Fleming, who dominated Third National during the postwar years.

Meanwhile, Commerce Union Bank founder Ed Potter Jr. took pride in his ability to defy tradition and irritate the other two banks. That practice would continue in the 1960s, when Potter turned his bank over to a new generation of leaders.

Granted, it was a friendly game, often played out between distant relatives or former classmates. But it could get personal at times. "One time, First American president Andrew Benedict got so mad at me that he called me up and said to me, 'Ed, you are not your father's son,'" said Edward G. Nelson, Commerce Union president in the 1970s and a son of Nashville Trust Co. president Charles Nelson.

One thing that Nashville's banking and investment executives agreed on was that state law was hindering them. Tennessee had a long history of suspicion toward banks dating back to the days of Andrew Jackson. Throughout the middle part of the twentieth century, Tennessee had two laws that hampered the growth of banks. One limited all loans to 10 percent interest, a regulation that became troublesome for banks, savings and loans, auto dealerships, and department stores when interest rates soared in the 1970s. The other outlawed the ownership of bank branches across county lines.

Not every state had such laws. North Carolina, for example, allowed its banks to have statewide branches in the 1940s and 1950s. When federal restrictions on interstate banking were lifted in the 1970s, North Carolina's history of pro-banking laws would give its institutions a jump on the rest of the South.

Even though its merger with the Fourth and First National Bank left American National as Nashville's largest financial institution, the next ten years were hardly smooth sailing for Paul Davis's bank.

During the Great Depression, American National had a larger share of the local market than any bank in Nashville history. In 1935 it had 48 percent of all total bank deposits in Nashville and over three times as many deposits as its nearest rival. Thanks to the fact that the Fourth and First had aggressively expanded, American National also had ten branch locations.

But along with all those deposits came many bad loans. "Third National and Commerce Union did not have nearly as much bad paper as we did," said Andrew Benedict, who went to work for American National in 1935 and eventually became its chief executive. "It took us about twelve years to liquidate the Fourth and First after we took it over."

Davis is generally acknowledged to be the dominant figure at American National before 1950. But according to Benedict, it was Parkes Armistead who really kept the bank alive during the 1930s and 1940s. "Parkes Armistead was the best banker I have ever met," Benedict said. "He was the one who got us all those national accounts. He was the one who took the bookkeeper off the pen and ink ledger and put him on a machine. He was the first one who started a pension plan, group insurance, and a retirement plan. He did all of those things before the other banks did."

Of course, Third National and Commerce Union also had a rough time during the depression. But each had a strategic advantage that enabled them to stay alive in the 1930s. Third National was only three years old when the depression hit Nashville and was being run under the conservative influence of National Life founder C. A. Craig. Consequently, Third National would have very few defaulted loans during the depression, which would allow it to have a much more liberal loaning policy than the other banks in town.

Third National's health manifested itself several times between 1935 and 1937, otherwise terrible years for the Nashville economy. First, the bank offered four thousand additional shares in a successful secondary offering that raised five hundred thousand dollars. Then it purchased the Independent Life Building at Fourth and Church and changed its name to the Third National Building. In 1937, Third National announced it would spend almost half a million dollars to double the size of that building and install air-conditioning, then an unheard-of luxury for office buildings.

Commerce Union's big strength was the network of out-of-county bank branches it had built in the early 1920s (prior to the law that prohibited their development). Starting in 1937, the

Left to right: Paul Davis, Ed Potter Jr., and Warner McNeilly, around 1950 (Metro Nashville Archives).

U.S. Army began using Middle Tennessee as a maneuver area. Since Commerce Union had so many branches, army officials asked the bank to help take care of the logistical nightmare of paying troops. On one occasion, the bank carried over

$3 million to its Lebanon branch to fill payrolls of four divisions, sending tellers from downtown Nashville to Lebanon for the day.

Commerce Union's branches were a sore point not only for its Nashville competitors but also to small banks across rural Middle Tennessee. "The other banks in those outlying counties couldn't stand Commerce Union because we were so much bigger than they were and had much more lending capability than they did," said Ed Nelson, whom Ed Potter hired in 1961 and who later became president of the bank.

Potter's gruff way of doing business also proved to be a plus in an era when loan defaults were common. "He was good at calling up people and telling them to pay up," Nelson said. "He had an expression: 'Put the cold steel to 'em.' I never really knew what that meant." According to longtime Commerce Union director Charles Trabue Jr., a customer came to Potter with a complaint one day. "Why are you loaning me money at 6 percent interest when you are loaning money to someone else for 5 percent interest?" the customer asked Potter.

"Just how long will it take you to get your ass out of my bank?" snapped Potter, who kept a handgun on top of his desk.

Since Potter knew his bank was always a distant third in size to American National and Third National, he rarely hesitated to do anything it took to get business. In 1935, Potter recruited two long-time American National vice presidents to work at Commerce Union, something rarely done in an era where people remained loyal to their employer. The next year, Commerce Union made the bold move of starting an auto loan department. As soon as American National and Third National got used to that, Commerce Union started a personal loan department. While American National ran advertisements that played up its size, and the Third National ran advertisements that emphasized its helpfulness, Commerce Union ran advertisements for mortgages, car loans, and loans for stoves and refrigerators.

A few years later, when Potter married one of the daughters of National Life cofounder Thomas Tyne, his detractors accused him behind his back of doing it just to steal some of Nashville Trust Company's trust accounts. "I know I am not popular," Potter once said at an employee meeting. "In every wolf pack there is always a tough old wolf who is the leader, but if he falters, the pack will destroy him and another wolf will take his place."[1]

The persona of Ed Potter was made all the more dramatic by his brother. Justin "Jet" Potter went to work as a coal miner in 1920 and soon thereafter started his own mining and distribution company called Nashville Coal. At a time when coal mining was on the decline, Jet Potter managed to make lots of money in the business. Having a brother who owned a bank and who could secure loans for him did not hurt. But another important part of Jet Potter's financial success, he told his friends, was that he was probably the most anti-union man in Nashville. According to family legend, Jet Potter hired armed guards to run organizers away from his coal fields in western Kentucky. Potter also drove a bulletproof car just in case a union man ever took a shot at him. "One Christmas vacation when I was a little boy, my grandfather took me to a work site where people were picketing—I don't remember where," said Jet Potter's grandson Justin Wilson, who became a top aide to Govenor Don Sundquist in the 1990s. "He asked me to walk through the picket line and I did. Then we went down and walked across the Cumberland River, which was frozen solid. On the way home, he told me that I had done two things that day that I would be proud of for the rest of my life."

As World War II ended, American National was still head and shoulders above any other bank in town. Deposits in 1945 totaled $205 million at American National, $100 million at Third National, and $84 million at Commerce Union. During the next few decades, Third National and Commerce Union would close the gap—not so much by acquisition but by competing with their larger rival at every turn. And since no bank was allowed to build new branches outside Davidson County, each had to find ways to compete for Nashville's business.

One of the first ways in which this competition manifested itself was in the construction of bank branches. Third National had a lot of catching up to do since American National had inherited the Fourth and First National Bank's extensive network of branches. In 1948 and 1949, Third National built five branches, while Commerce Union built two.

Another salvo on Union Street took place on August 1, 1948, when Ed Potter's Commerce Union Bank broke with eighteen years of established practice and raised interest rates on savings accounts from one to two percent. This move infuriated Commerce Union's rivals, which called a meeting of the Nashville Clearinghouse to try to talk Commerce Union out of the move. Potter and Commerce Union executive vice president James Kellam attended the meeting and refused to yield. A few weeks later, American National and Third National raised their interest rates.

The scenario would be repeated in 1955, when Commerce Union raised rates to 2.5 percent; in 1957, when it raised rates to 3 percent; and in 1962, when it raised rates to 4 percent.

Another offshoot of the rivalry between the banks took place in the retail world. At the height of the depression, Church Street department store and Commerce Union customer Lebeck Brothers filed for bankruptcy, leaving Mr. Potter's bank with an expensive empty building. A few months later, a department store broker told Potter that he knew a man in Chicago who wanted to start his own

The interior of the American National Bank, around 1932 (First American National Bank).

department store in Nashville. That man was Fred Harvey, and the more Potter heard about him, the more he sounded like Potter's kind of guy. Commerce Union brought Harvey to Nashville and financed the opening of Harvey's Department Store. For the next twenty years, Potter got immense pleasure from the headaches that Harvey gave Third National customer Cain-Sloan and First American customer Castner Knott.

The real competition in the banking world was over large corporate customers. More than any other two people, Sam Fleming and Andrew Benedict dominated this area during the twenty years after the war.

When Andrew Benedict applied for a job at American National in 1935, the person that interviewed him was skeptical. "You Vanderbilt graduates just are not willing to do the menial jobs that everyone has to do who starts to work here," Benedict was told. However, the young man's persistence paid off, and American National hired him to go around town collecting on bad checks, a busy job during the height of

*The American National
Bank (a structure first
built for the Fourth and
First National Bank),
around 1950 (Metro
Nashville Archives).*

the depression. Over the next few years, Benedict worked as a book-keeper, cashier, and credit officer before he became an executive vice president in 1951.

Benedict eventually became one of the most well-known and respected bankers in the Southeast and would spend a year as the president of the Association of Reserve City Bankers. Benedict also took a lot of pride in his bank's relationships with many of Nashville's oldest and most successful companies, such as Phillips & Buttorff, Washington Manufacturing, Gray & Dudley, Genesco, Nashville Bridge, Spur Oil, DuPont, and Avco. "At one point, we had almost all the national accounts," Benedict said in 1998.

Like his colleague Guilford Dudley Jr., Sam Fleming's life and career seemed to last forever. Born in Franklin, Fleming's great grand-father Newton Cannon and great-uncle Aaron Brown were both Tennessee governors in the early nineteenth century. At the age of eight, Fleming started working as a runner for the Harpeth National Bank of Franklin, where his father was a director. After graduating from Vanderbilt a month after his twentieth birthday, Fleming went to work for the New York Trust Company.

The stock market crash and the massive layoffs that followed took the glamour off New York. In 1931, Fleming accepted an offer from Frank Farris to work for the Third National Bank's credit department. The four-year-old bank had about $6 million in deposits at that time.

During the depression, American National couldn't make many loans because it had to concentrate on trying to absorb the Fourth and First National Bank and deal with delinquent loans. Commerce Union was still a very small bank that also had its share of bad loans. Sam Fleming became the man to see if you wanted to get money in Nashville. He relished and excelled in this role. "Fleming has a lot of sense and a lot of personality and a lot of salesmanship," Ed Nelson said a few months before Mr. Fleming died in January 2000. "He was the perfect person to flourish in that type of environment, where he did not have to spend all his time collecting loans. I think he infuriated First American."

While American National/First American acted like it was above the practice of asking for business, Fleming turned it into an art. "If we wanted to go after the General Electric account, for example, we would start by trying to find something we could do for the local manager," Fleming said in 1979. "Then, with his recommendation, we'd go to New York and try to sell them on the idea that we were the ones who could do more for them down in Nashville.

"And it was the same with Metropolitan Life Insurance and others. We began to start breaking through and gain more and more accounts, mainly because we outworked our competition."[2]

Thanks to the leadership of Frank Farris and the other officials at the bank, Third National grew at an astounding rate during the depression.

Deposits at American National increased 57 percent between 1930 and 1940. Meanwhile, they grew by over 550 percent at Third National.

As Nashville's newest bank loaned money and made friends during the depression, it became known as the "The Friendly Third." And for the next thirty years, there would be no better ambassador for the Friendly Third than the energetic optimist named Sam Fleming.

One thing that made Sam Fleming so hard to compete with was his connections. Fleming was a member of the prestigious Augusta National Country Club, where he frequently played golf with Dwight Eisenhower. A few years later, Fleming became a supporter of Lyndon Johnson, something for which he took a lot of heat in the Nashville business community.

Two small business owners who became friends with Fleming during the depression made it very big. One was Jack Massey, who owned a struggling drugstore on Church Street in the 1930s and years later made a fortune with Kentucky Fried Chicken and Hospital Corporation of America. The other was Herman Lay, who started a small potato chip business in Nashville in 1939 and went on to be chairman of PepsiCo. People like Massey and Lay would remember Sam Fleming when they had a lot of money.

Perhaps the most important loan Third National ever made was in 1946, when the bank loaned one thousand dollars to three WSM engineers who were trying to start a recording studio in their spare time. That small business, Castle Recording, was enormously important to Nashville's eventual role as a music recording center. During the 1950s, thanks to an ambitious banker named Sam Hunt, Third National became the bank most closely affiliated with country music. Hunt found that country stars were not always wise when it came to handling money. "Daddy used to tell me the story of the time Hank [Williams] handed him a bag of money," Sam Hunt Jr. told a country music historian years later. "'How much money do you have there, Hank?' Daddy asked. Hank answered, 'Hell, I don't know, Sam—you're the banker!'" [3]

Another Third National legend concerns bluegrass star Bill Monroe. For years, Monroe would put proceeds from various shows in small paper bags under his bed. One day, Hunt talked Monroe into bringing all the bags down to Third National. Bank employees counted the money and deposited it in a savings account. A few weeks later, Monroe called the bank and said he needed to make a withdrawal. When a bank employee asked him how much, Monroe answered: "About three sack fulls."

Years later, other bankers developed a niche in country music. One was Commerce Union's Clarence Reynolds, who helped many country music artists finance their purchases of tour buses. Another was the Nashville Trust Company's John Hardcastle. In an era when many country music artists lived in Madison, many of them did business at

Nashville Trust's Dickerson Road branch, which Hardcastle once managed. "One of the things that helped me was that I would sometimes go to the Opry and hang out backstage," Hardcastle said. "In those days, security at the Opry was so lax that if you wore a coat and tie they let you backstage automatically because the security guard figured you worked at National Life." Hardcastle's interest in country music eventually led him to finance the production of a country music song called "Harper Valley PTA."

In Nashville, Fleming had an inside track with the National Life & Accident crowd, thanks to the fact that National Life had helped start Third National in the first place. Twice in the 1960s, Fleming used this connection to pull off coups that left his competitors shaking their heads.

In the 1950s, under the influence of new president W. S. Hackworth, Nashville Trust expanded its banking business and changed its name to Nashville Bank & Trust. With checking accounts and bank tellers, it was in many ways a real bank just like First American or Third National.

However, during the three decades since the depression, the Nashville Bank & Trust had remained under the independent ownership and control of grocer H. G. Hill, and later, his son H. G. Hill Jr. This affiliation with the well-respected Hill family gave Nashville Trust a loyal clientele in Belle Meade, not to mention among the city's grocery wholesalers. But Hill's conservative philosophy kept the trust company from investing in new technology and making changes that other banks were making. "In the early 1960s, we were still posting trust ledgers and general ledgers by hand," said Hardcastle, who went to work for the trust company in 1958. "We were still maintaining mortgage books the same as we had in 1889. We had no credit analysis department. It was very, very conservative."

While other banks had branches all over town, the Nashville Bank & Trust had few branches. While other banks had aggressive lending departments, the Nashville Bank & Trust was very conservative in the area of consumer loans. While other banks tried to pay well, the Nashville Bank & Trust paid so poorly that it became almost impossible for the business to hire and keep good young talent.

American National had spun off Nashville Trust during the depression because of the demand by federal regulators that Nashville have more independent financial organizations. But the world had changed a lot in thirty years. By the early 1960s, the general feeling in the banking community was that federal regulators would allow one of Nashville's banks to buy the trust company.

When Hackworth was diagnosed with cancer in 1963, Hill realized he would soon be left without someone who he knew and trusted to run Nashville Bank & Trust. As word spread that Hill might be looking to sell, bankers throughout town began dreaming about the idea of getting their hands on Nashville Trust's old-money trust accounts. "Checking accounts and savings accounts come and go," said James A. (Jimmy) Webb Jr., who went to work for Third National in 1957 and later became president of the Nashville Bank & Trust Co. "But when you have a customer in the trust department, those contacts and those accounts go on for years."

Had it been anyone else, the sale of the trust company would have simply been a matter of setting a price. But H. G. Hill Jr. was devoted to tradition and the memory of his father. If he had to sell the company, he would only sell it to a person his father would have trusted. Several prospective buyers approached Hill about buying his stock in the trust company in 1964. One was a partnership consisting of Bronson Ingram and Ed Nelson, who thought Hill would accept their offer since Nelson's great-grandfather had founded the trust company in 1889. Another was Ed Potter, who must have stayed up at night dreaming about how much a merger between Commerce Union and Nashville Trust would aggravate First American.

Hill declined both offers. He then accepted one for $3.43 million from a group of thirty-six investors led by National Life & Accident executive Bill Weaver and consisting largely of family members of National Life executives. "I was deflated," said Ed Nelson, who learned about the sale at the hospital the day his daughter Emme was born.

A few months after Hill sold his stock, Weaver—who borrowed $1.4 million from Third National in order to finance the purchase of Hill's stock in the first place—turned around and sold the trust company for $4.12 million to Third National Bank. Third National thus acquired an organization with deposits of about $40 million and deep ties to old Nashville money. "Hill passed it to Weaver, who then lateraled it right over to Fleming," Nelson said.

After Third National took over the trust company, Hill would say he had no idea that Weaver would sell the trust company to another bank. This naturally raised the question as to whether Bill Weaver had bought the business intending to flip it to Fleming. Weaver emphatically denied that at the time. But thirty-five years later, no one in Nashville seemed to be able to say for sure. "I don't know, and I don't believe Horace Hill Jr. ever knew either," said Hardcastle. "But it is important to point out that during the eight months that Mr. Weaver owned it, he acted like he was going to run the company, assessing the way the organization worked and interviewing possible successors to Mr. Hackworth."

Third National bought Nashville Trust confident that federal regulators would approve the takeover. But a few weeks after the merger was announced, the U.S. Justice Department filed an antitrust suit to block the merger. During the subsequent trial, Fleming— flanked by young attorneys Henry Hooker and John Jay Hooker Jr.—testified that his bank had already made immense improvements to the outmoded trust company. These included raising salaries, starting a new pension plan, and raising its loan limits. Fleming tried to prove that Third National was far from a monopoly in Nashville, especially since it was not even the city's largest bank.

The case between the U.S. government and Third National Bank dragged on for four years. Finally, in 1968, the U.S. Supreme Court sided with the Justice Department and ordered the bank to spin off the trust company, reasoning that it was unhealthy for Nashville to lose another financial institution. After a long series of negotiations, the federal government agreed to let Third National keep Nashville Trust's trust business, but sell its banking business. The divestiture was a complicated one, described by many who were involved as "unscrambling eggs." In the end, the old Nashville Bank & Trust Co. became an independent financial institution once again, though now under public ownership.

The Friendly Third's other short-lived merger of the 1960s also involved National Life & Accident Insurance Co. Since the depression, the federal government had not allowed banks to take over companies in other commercial fields. Gradually, however, it had begun to ease up on these rules. By the 1960s, the government had begun allowing banks to form a holding company that owned the bank, then use the holding company as an avenue to invest in other things. In the mid-1960s, these new entities were in vogue and became known as "one-bank holding companies." Like the name implies, they were only allowed to own one bank.

In 1967, Fleming suggested merging National Life and Third National into a one-bank holding company called NLT, which would stand for "National Life-Third." The new company would be dominated by National Life management, since the insurance company was about five times larger than the bank. It would have an asset base of more than $2 billion, making it the South's largest financial institution.

Given its conservative history, this did not seem like the kind of thing the National Life board would go for. But at the time, investing in other areas of commerce seemed like something that would impress Wall Street. Besides, National Life and Third National had such a close affiliation that it wasn't as if either the bank or the insurance company would be controlled by outsiders.

In December 1968, National Life and Third National formed NLT, with Dan Brooks as chairman and Fleming as president. NLT quickly got to business on new ventures, forming a separate real estate arm called Intereal (which soon owned shopping malls at Green Hills, Rivergate, and Hickory Hollow) and a new computer company called NLT Computer Services. It also began discussions with Ralston Purina about the idea of a merger (something that did not come to light for a couple of years).

However, the National Life/Third National merger was short-lived. By the time NLT was formed, members of both political parties had great concern about the rise of one-bank holding companies. "We appear to be drifting toward a repetition of serious errors that the banking industry fell into in the 1920s," James Robertson, vice chairman of the Federal Reserve Board, told Congress.[4] In 1969, President Nixon recommended legislation making it illegal for one-bank holding companies to buy controlling interest in companies not in the financial business. Several months later, Congress did what Nixon recommended, which required NLT to divest Third National. Nashville would never again be able to claim it was home of the South's largest financial institution.

In addition to using connections to acquire Nashville's oldest trust company and merge with Nashville's most important insurance company, Fleming also found a way to turn old friendships into profitable ones. In 1968, when Jack Massey put together a company called Hospital Corporation of America with Dr. Thomas Frist Sr., Dr. Thomas Frist Jr., and Henry Hooker, Third National was quick to extend HCA a line of credit. First American did the same at first, but later it refused to take part in a consortium of banks that was loaning HCA $35 million. Third National's affiliation with HCA gave the company the inside track with several subsequent HCA clones and spin-offs, including Hospital Affiliates International, General Care Corp., and Surgical Care Affiliates.

As busy as Fleming was running Third National, sitting on the National Life board, and participating in American Bankers Association events, he made time to own and operate a very interesting business on the side. In the 1950s, Fleming formed a venture capital company called Hillsboro Enterprises. Hillsboro, which Fleming would describe as a "holding company," was a private firm owned by Fleming and a Franklin businessman named Stewart Campbell. Hillsboro Enterprises bought and sold several businesses, from the Tennessee Tufting Co. (once the property of the Ingram family) to a building supply company called Breeko Industries. Hillsboro Enterprises had large holdings in a number of banks outside of Nashville. It also helped develop the Green Hills Mall, the Metro Industrial Park area on Elm Hill Pike, and a 170-home subdivision in Bellevue. Despite its very interesting and varied activities, Hillsboro Enterprises was rarely discussed in the media.

In 1960, Ed Potter Jr. named thirty-five-year-old West Point graduate Bill Earthman to succeed him. Many people at the bank were furious with this decision and attributed it to the fact that Earthman's wife was related to Potter's wife. "I think the feeling with Ed Potter and with [Commerce Union board member] Jet Potter was that it was time that they brought in some new blood," Earthman said.

It wasn't long before Earthman found a way to continue the tradition of being an upstart young bank. Ever since the depression, Nashville's banks had contributed to charities en masse through the Nashville Clearinghouse, which accepted solicitations on behalf of all the banks and had a committee that decided how to disperse donations. But in 1965, Commerce Union broke ranks with the other banks and took on the sponsorship of the Nashville Symphony. "I thought that the whole Clearinghouse situation was silly," Earthman said. "Dividing up charitable solicitations was the wrong thing for that association to take upon themselves. I thought each bank should just do what it wanted to do."

One of Earthman's most important contributions was bringing Ed Nelson into Commerce Union. Nelson, a native Nashvillian whose father, grandfather, and great-grandfather had all been bankers, focused his efforts on trying to get some of Nashville's larger commercial clients to shift at least some of their money to Commerce Union. "My approach was to go to everyone and say 'I'm not asking you to leave your current bank,'" Nelson said. "'I just want you to expand your opportunity. There is a lot that our bank can do for you and I just want to open an account [for you].' And before you knew it we were expanding and bringing in other people."

Much as Ed Potter once irked First American and Third National over interest rates on savings accounts, Earthman and Nelson took many steps to one-up the other banks when it came to customer service. In the mid-1960s, Commerce Union began experimenting with Saturday banking hours, a break with tradition that annoyed First American and Third National so much that they called Commerce Union to complain. In 1973, Commerce Union became the first Nashville bank to install automatic teller machines. "Everyone else was scoffing at ATMs and saying they did not want to put them in," Nelson said. "We could hardly wait."

Earthman also took the important step of starting an international business department in 1970. "Bill Earthman had a broader vision of things," said Dennis C. (Denny) Bottorff, who went to work for Commerce Union in 1968 and twenty-three years later became president of First American. "He did not think of the competition on a local basis. He thought more about it on a U.S. or global basis." Commerce Union's international division accounted for about 15 percent of its earnings by the mid-1970s. Among the larger loans

Commerce Union helped underwrite: a housing project in Venezuela, a dam in Yugoslavia, and the purchase of three airplanes by the government of Zaire.

Despite all this growth, all three large Nashville banks were still located in old buildings that had been built for other companies. First American had been headquartered in the Fourth and First National Bank Building at Fourth and Union since it took over that bank in 1930. Third National was two blocks away, in a turn-of-the-century structure built around 1910 for the Independent Life Insurance Co. Commerce Union was a tenant of the Stahlman Building before 1940 and then in the old Caldwell & Co. Building at the northwest corner of Fourth and Union.

Third National broke the long period of dormancy. On Christmas night 1961, the venerable Maxwell House Hotel at the corner of Fourth and Church burned to the ground. After about a year, it looked as though a convention center and hotel might be built on the site, but those ambitious plans fell through. For almost four years, the site was unoccupied to the dismay of property owner Life & Casualty Insurance Co. As the automobile began to drag residential, retail, and offices into the suburbs, some people began to wonder if anything would be built there besides a parking lot. But eventually, Life & Casualty Insurance Co. president Guilford Dudley Jr.—whose building dominated Nashville's skyline at the time—convinced Fleming that the site was a perfect place for a new bank headquarters. L&C financed the twenty-story structure and named it the Third National Center in honor of its main tenant.

The Third National Center was Nashville's first downtown office building that tried to incorporate trees and landscaping into its original design. Civic leaders and journalists could hardly restrain their enthusiasm. "From the gurgle-fountain majesty to its tip high above Nashville's soot-covered plain, the new Third National Bank Building is definitely one of the most beautifully built things to hit Nashville since Miss Universe came to town," *Nashville* magazine proclaimed in April 1968.[5] For the next five years, Nashville's skyline was dominated by the city's second largest insurance company and second largest bank.

First American wanted to build a new structure right away, but it wasn't that simple. After all, it isn't easy to acquire a square block of land in downtown Nashville. Through the legal help of the Nashville Housing Authority's Urban Renewal project—which allowed large commercial tenants to acquire entire city blocks to build large buildings—the bank acquired the block bordered by Union, Deadrick, Third, and Fourth Avenues in 1971. In the process, First American displaced the old Equitable Securities Building and a showroom store for Washington Manufacturing. First American remained in its old home while construction of its new twenty-eight-story office tower and adjacent bank building went on from 1972 to 1974.

Under the urban renewal guidelines, First American had to devote 25 percent of its property to open-air vista. Because of this require-ment, First American later tore down the old Fourth and First National Bank Building and replaced it with an open-air plaza. Years later, Andrew Benedict would regret tearing down the old Fourth and First, almost undoubtedly Nashville's most handsome bank building of the era. "I should have used that building and made an eclectic thing out of it," Benedict said.

Commerce Union first announced its intention to build a new office tower in 1967, and for a while it looked as if First American would have a race to see whose building would go up first. But it wasn't until 1974 that Commerce Union started the legal process of clearing its block for the new structure. Never one to do things the same as the other banks, Commerce Union built a twenty-story struc-ture which, viewed from above, had a triangular shape to it. Commerce Union moved into its new headquarters in 1977. Shortly thereafter, it razed the old Caldwell & Co. Building and signed a deal to develop a fourteen-story hotel on the site.

As Nashville entered the 1970s, the city's largest three banks were as close to each other in size as they had ever been. First American was still the largest, with $579 million in deposits and 1,090 employees. Third National, because of its forced divestiture of Nashville City Bank, was still in second place with $491 million in deposits and 980 employees. Meanwhile, Commerce Union had grown more in relative terms in the 1960s than any other bank, ending the decade with $352 million in deposits and 720 employees.

It was at this point that the nature of banking in Nashville changed.

In the late 1960s, major changes in banking law were in the works at both the state and national level. After Congress forced one-bank holding companies to divest their controlling interest in companies which were not closely related to banking, it agreed to ease the restrictions on where and how banks could have branches. Federal changes precipitated state changes, and in 1969, the legisla-ture passed a bill authorizing one-bank holding companies in Tennessee to own banks in different counties. Almost immediately, Nashville's banks formed holding companies and began to fan out across the state:

> Third National Corp. took over banks in Lawrenceburg, Cleveland, Pulaski, and Savannah. Third National also bought a mortgage

servicing company called John Murphee and two finance companies, the Mobilehome Guaranty Corp. and Friendly Finance Inc.

First American initially called its bank holding company First Amtenn. In addition to buying small banks in Tullahoma, Cleveland, Clinton, Milan, and Union City, First American acquired a commercial and mortgage servicing company called the Guaranty Mortgage Co. from Hershel Greer, a member of the bank's board of directors. First Amtenn also bought a Jacksonville, Florida, consumer finance business called Atlantic Discount Co.

Commerce Union Corp. purchased banks in Clarksville, Greeneville, and Johnson City, and established new Commerce Union Banks in Memphis and Chattanooga. It lost out to the First Tennessee Bank of Memphis, however, in its attempt to buy the failing Hamilton National Bank of Chattanooga. Commerce Union also bought a residential mortgage firm called the Noel Palmer Mortgage Co.[6]

While all this was going on, there was also an important merger between one of Nashville's oldest banks and one of its newest. In August 1969, Nashville Bank & Trust merged with Capital City Bank, a new institution controlled by Jack Massey and Fleet Transport president Calvin Houghland. The merged entity, called Nashville City Bank, bought small banks in Franklin, Hendersonville, and Gallatin. In 1973, former Third National officer Jimmy Webb became president of Nashville City Bank, whose offices were still located in the old Nashville Trust Building on Union Street. Before long, Nashville City Bank was developing a chain of branches and trying to compete with Nashville's larger banks in areas such as car loans.

Thus the early 1970s were a feast for Nashville's bank holding companies and the attorneys that handled their acquisitions. (The same could be said for large bank holding companies in Memphis, Knoxville, and Chattanooga.) But it was a nervous time for small independent banks in rural parts of the state, many of which lobbied the legislature to impose a moratorium on further expansion by the holding companies.

As it turned out, small banks would need no moratorium. When First American and Third National bought Guaranty Mortgage and John Murphee, both were basically residential mortgage companies. But both banks quickly moved their mortgage companies into the commercial field to expand them as quickly as possible. Commerce Union did not take this course and left Noel Palmer much the way it found it.

When the recession of 1974 hit, the commercial real estate market collapsed in parts of the Southeast. Both Murphee and Guaranty

Mortgage had serious problems, causing the holding companies that controlled both to make major personnel changes.

Guaranty's biggest problem had to do with its loans to a thirty-three-year-old California businessman named Allen Glick. In 1973, Guaranty—still under the management of Greer—made several loans totaling $22 million to Glick (despite the fact that the bank supposedly had a $7 million lending limit). In the case of one $5 million loan, the bank thought the money was being used to develop a shopping center in California, but it was actually being used to renovate the Hacienda Casino in Las Vegas. When the real estate market collapsed, Glick defaulted. The *Tennessean* got wind of Glick's loans when Glick and his Nevada gambling operation became the target of several federal and state investigations. "We made two mistakes that we wouldn't have made had we followed two rules," said Sam Bartholomew Jr., First American's general counsel from 1973 until 1977. "Don't loan money more than five hundred miles away from the bank, and don't loan money to people you don't know anything about other than a financial statement."

As the newspaper reported Glick's relationship to the bank in great detail, First American's loan department came under heavy criticism. There were even reports that First American was losing depositors over the matter (reports denied vehemently by Benedict).

The Glick loans were the best publicized of many real estate loans that went sour for First American during the mid-1970s. In fact, First American's foreclosures nearly tripled between 1974 and 1975. The low point for the bank came in 1975. In October, the Federal Reserve Board rejected First Amtenn's proposed takeover of a small bank in Sparta because the holding company did not have sufficient cash reserves. "It was their response to how we were managing the company," said Jack Fox, who had been hired as First American's financial officer in 1972. A few months later, First Amtenn announced it had lost $44 million in bad real estate loans and $3.8 million during the year—the first time the bank had lost money in its ninety-two-year history.

First American fired CEO Scott Fillebrown. Under the strong influence of First American board member David K. (Pat) Wilson, the bank hired as the new CEO Ken Roberts, a one-time Commerce Union Bank officer who had moved to Virginia years earlier. One of Roberts's first actions was to sign an agreement with the Comptroller of the Currency to essentially operate the bank under close federal supervision.

Third National, meanwhile, took the rather dramatic step of naming Charles Kane, an outsider, to be its new CEO in 1974. Kane, formerly with Citizen's Fidelity Bank & Trust in Louisville, brought with him several other outsiders in his attempt to upgrade the bank's marketing and systems. On a more urgent note, however, Kane learned immediately after taking his job that the bank had more problems with Murphee than he had realized. Unlike First American, Third National never reported a loss, although it only reported a profit of $150,000 during the fourth quarter 1975. "A lot of banks had to skip a dividend, but we never did," Kane said.

If the mid- and late 1970s were in some ways dark days for Nashville's banks, they at least scored a victory on Capitol Hill.

Tennessee's constitution contained a clause that limited all loans to 10 percent interest. When interest rates soared in the 1970s, banks, loan companies, department stores, and car dealers found ways around the state's usury law through creative financing or partnerships with out-of-state competitors. However, there was a fear that the courts might throw out such laws as unconstitutional. In 1975, the Tennessee Banking Association decided to launch an all-out effort to change the clause through a constitutional convention.

Changing the state constitution through the convention method is a difficult and tedious process that requires several legislative hurdles and two statewide referenda, not to mention the chaos of the convention itself. Banks, savings and loan associations, and finance companies united to change the law under an umbrella organization called the Tennessee Consumer Finance Association. Its chief lobbyist was former state treasurer Tommy Wiseman Jr.

Wiseman would eventually succeed when Tennessee's voters chose to strike the interest rate limit from the constitution in 1976. But the crusade to lift the so-called usury law was a tough one. As the convention neared, most of the large newspapers in Tennessee were opposed to changing the law. Wiseman and leading bankers (especially Benedict) traveled the state in support of the change and raised a lot of money to advertise in favor of the change. "Our polling found that necessity for bank profitability was the least salable argument and that the logical economic arguments were very little better," Wiseman said years later. The effort might have failed had it not been for the fact that in the middle of the debate, the Supreme Court ruled that the laws exempting various types of loans from the 10 percent limit were unconstitutional. Auto dealers, department stores, and credit card companies panicked and jumped headlong into the debate. Soon, many Tennessee residents began to see the existing usury law as something that kept honest hardworking citizens from being able to borrow money.

Wiseman and the banks were also lucky. The convention and referendum would never have taken place had the legislature not passed it. And in a story typical of the way the Tennessee legislature operates on its last day of session, three state senators walked out of the chamber in a last-ditch effort to kill the convention proposal. When they got on the elevator, one accidentally pushed the button that sent the elevator up instead of down. When the elevator door reopened in front of the Senate chamber, Lt. Gov. John Wilder was standing in front of it. The wily and colloquial Wilder talked the trio back into the Senate chamber.

Years later, Wilder recounted the episode. "I told them they broke my quorum, and they said 'we know, guvunuh.' I told them I could have them arrested and dragged back into the chamber, and they said 'we know, guvunuh.' I told them I wasn't going to do that and they said 'thank you, guvunuh.' Then I told them, 'I tell you what. You're gonna go back in there and give me my quorum back.' And they did."

CHAPTER 12

The Old Guard Sells

A s the jet lifted off, Walter Robinson Jr. may have had second thoughts. Only a few hours earlier, when he had attended Palm Sunday church services, Robinson had no idea he was going anywhere that afternoon. He did not have any luggage with him. He had never even met the "Oracle of Omaha" and had never heard of him before a few hours ago.

How would he even know Warren Buffett when he saw him?

But Robinson, whose company was in the middle of the biggest hostile takeover attempt in Nashville history, couldn't get the pep talk out of his mind that an attorney named Brad Reed had just given him. "This is like a fight between a little scrawny fella and a great big guy who has got a lot of power and a lot of assets and he isn't using them," Reed had said. "And you are the big guy who has got the power and the money. And you are not really fighting hard."

Robinson, the chief executive officer of NLT Corp., gritted his teeth just thinking about it. We won't lay down. We will fight hard, by God.

Between the end of World War II and 1980, insurance was the most important business of Nashville. National Life was by far the city's largest white-collar employer, with over fifteen hundred employees by the mid-1950s. Life & Casualty built the city's first skyscraper. A host of smaller insurance companies such as Cherokee Life and American Educational Life popped up.

As for the other businesses in town, they sometimes seemed like mere offshoots. National Life owned the Grand Ole Opry, country music's most revered institution, and WSM, its most influential radio station. It built Opryland, turning Nashville into a major tourist destination and starting it on the course toward being a major convention city. When it came time for the Third National Bank to finance a new office tower, it did so with the financial backing of Life & Casualty. When the television era arrived, National Life started Nashville's first station (WSMV) and Life & Casualty started the second (WLAC). And in 1961, National Life loaned money for a nursing home next to Centennial Park called Park Vista. That nursing home later became a hospital, the first in a chain called Hospital Corporation of America.

In many ways, it seemed like everyone worked for the insurance companies in one way or another. Banks and investment firms depended on the accumulating assets of the insurance companies. Real estate developers rarely got a major project off the ground without the backing of one of the insurance companies. Retailers on Church Street sold a lot of clothes to employees of Life & Casualty at one end of the shopping district and to employees of National Life at the other.

But Nashville's reign as "Hartford of the South" would not last forever. At the same time they reigned supreme, Nashville's insurance giants were becoming dinosaurs.

The world changed a lot in the half-century after Cornelius Abernathy Craig bought the National Sick and Accident Insurance Co. In 1901, the South was changing from an agrarian to an industrial economy. As people moved from the farm to the city to work low-paying factory jobs, many spent nickels and dimes on industrial life insurance because that was all they could afford. As long as this class of Americans remained poor, industrial life insurance had a solid base. And as long as the northern life insurance giants continued to ignore African-American customers, Nashville's insurance companies had a market all to themselves.

From the turn of the century until about 1940, the national demand for industrial life insurance remained steady. By World War II, Nashville's two big insurance companies had done so well that they were both ranked among America's top insurance companies when it came to selling industrial policies.

However, when thousands of soldiers returned home from the war, American society changed. As a result of the post-World War II economic boom, millions of men soon landed a better job than the one they had before they left. After they married, had children, bought a car, and moved into homes in the suburbs, they needed a lot more insurance than they once had. Instead of industrial insurance, they needed a more expensive policy that could pay their mortgage and take care of their wives and children. What they needed was ordinary life insurance paid semi-annually, not industrial life insurance paid weekly.

National Life and Life & Casualty sold ordinary life insurance, but neither was well-positioned for this demographic shift. At the end of World War II, over two-thirds of the insurance held by both Nashville insurers was of the industrial variety. Meanwhile, competitors such as Metropolitan Life and Prudential were already making more money from ordinary life insurance than they were from industrial insurance.

From the 1950s on, demand for industrial life insurance began to decline. National Life and Life & Casualty knew this and were making efforts to expand insurance sales of the ordinary variety. But making the change was not easy, since both companies had organizations centered around agents making calls in poor neighborhoods. As late as 1955, National Life and Life & Casualty were still getting over half of their insurance premiums through industrial policies. By this time, Met Life and Prudential had not only made the shift from industrial to ordinary, but they were also making enormous strides in the area of group insurance. It would be well into the 1960s until either National Life or Life & Casualty made any inroads in group insurance, an area that grew fast as employers began to improve their benefits after World War II.

National Life, which was much larger than L&C, was criticized heavily for staying with industrial insurance for so long. But the company was very frank about its decision to remain with industrial insurance. "There are certain segments of the market and areas of the country in which weekly premium insurance still has a place," a company history explained in 1975. "The company intends to fulfill its social responsibility to the weekly-premium market by continuing to serve it as long as the need exists, while redirecting its marketing efforts toward other needs and opportunities."[1]

As larger competitors abandoned industrial insurance, the two large Nashville insurers would be able to take over their business and show gains every year. But by the 1960s, Wall Street recognized that both National Life and L&C were in a shrinking market.

As the century passed the halfway point, people were beginning to wonder if anyone would ever build another building downtown.

It had been a quarter of a century since Paul Davis built the fifteen-story American Trust Building. Now, everyone was moving out to the suburbs, thanks to new roads, new neighborhoods, and new federal programs that made home ownership more accessible than ever. Downtown was considered dirty, unfashionable, and incompatible with the automobile.

In 1949, Life & Casualty founder A. M. Burton announced that his company would soon build another headquarters building downtown. However, the project was delayed because of steel shortages during the Korean War. The next year, Burton retired.

During his career, Burton had given away a lot of his voting stock to charities such as David Lipscomb College.[2] When he retired, L&C's voting shares were mostly in control of the families of the other founders, which had included Guilford Dudley Sr., J. C. Franklin, and P. M. Estes.

Upon Burton's retirement, one of Franklin's descendants, a Knoxville businessman named Paul Mountcastle, became a caretaker president. Two years later, he was replaced by forty-five-year-old Guilford Dudley Jr. By that time, many people in L&C's upper management were in favor of simply adding a few stories to the existing L&C Building. After all, it was a tradition at L&C to take the thrifty way out. Dudley would have none of that.

Boldness was a tradition in the Dudley family. Guilford Jr.'s uncle Richard Houston Dudley commanded a regiment of cavalry at the Battle of Nashville in 1864 and became mayor of Nashville from 1897 to 1899. His father eschewed a comfortable life in the family hardware business and went into insurance instead. His mother, Anne Dallas Dudley, was the first president of the Nashville Suffragette League. In 1914 she dressed young Guilford Jr. up and made him march at the head of a suffragette parade from the state capitol to Centennial Park.

When he was at Vanderbilt, Guilford Jr. played football even though he had neither the size nor the skill to do so. When he graduated, he got a job with Rogers Caldwell, a hunting buddy of his father's, even though Guilford Jr. knew almost nothing about banking.

After Caldwell's financial empire collapsed and almost all his employees were laid off, Dudley took a job as an L&C agent. At that time, the insurance company was almost entirely in the business of selling small industrial policies to poor people. With his family connections, Dudley thought it made more sense to sell life insurance to the rich. So he started trying to sell policies to the people he met in the banking business. On Christmas Eve 1931, he showed up at J. C. Bradford Sr.'s office and gave him a pitch. "Son, I'm going to buy what you are selling me, because you are the only person I know who is also working on Christmas Eve," said Bradford, a former insurance salesman. It wasn't long before Dudley became L&C's first-ever million-dollar salesman and was being sent all over the Southeast to train other agents on how to sell policies to a more affluent customer.

By the time Dudley returned from his stint in World War II as a navy fighter pilot, it was obvious he would one day be head of Life & Casualty. It was also obvious that he was a different kind of person than Burton. Burton was always working, going to church, or at home. Dudley played tennis or golf, rode steeplechases, and was once described by the *Washington Post* as a "debonair playboy."[3] Burton was so thrifty that he tried to conserve toilet paper. Dudley lived an extravagant life, hosting opulent parties at his one-hundred-acre Northumberland estate in Nashville and his fourteen-room home in Palm Beach, where visiting New Yorkers jokingly referred to him as their "Ashley Wilkes." Burton voted Democratic and his favorite charity was David Lipscomb College. Dudley gave money to Republican politicians.

Not surprisingly, Burton tried to convert Dudley. "He tried to talk me into joining the Church of Christ," Dudley said fifty years later. "I told him I'd been an Episcopalian all my life, and I'd prefer to keep it that way. He never mentioned it again after that."

Shortly after becoming L&C president, Dudley invited architect Edwin Keeble to his house and told him he wanted a much larger building than the one Burton had talked about. In a city where the largest building was fifteen stories, Dudley wanted to build a building twice as high. According to Dudley, Keeble sketched the first rendering of the building on a napkin.

Years later, Dudley explained why he wanted to build a skyscraper. "For one thing, I thought it would help us sell life insurance and help us grow. There was a tendency back then for people to move out, and to say that downtown was a thing of the past. I did not think it was. I thought downtown had a future. And I turned out to be right on that."

Dudley rarely admitted another reason he wanted to build a building so narrow that it was terribly inefficient and so large that his business would never fill it. That, of course, was ego. After the L&C Tower was built, it acquired a nickname—"Guilford's biggest erection"—that his rivals at National Life must have smiled at a hundred times. "When [former National Life CEO] Bill Weaver had his portrait made, he moved his chair by the window, and you can see the L&C Tower out of his office," National Life executive C. A. (Neil) Craig II said. "He had the painter make the L&C Tower considerably smaller than it really is. I thought Guilford was going to die when he saw it."

Dudley was right in thinking the L&C Tower would help sell insurance, at least to people who drove into Nashville looking for National Life. "We would frequently get people who would come into our building thinking they were visiting National Life," said L&C executive Sydney Keeble Jr. "But we'd often take care of their insurance needs without sending them to the competition."

The L&C Tower was the largest building in the South for several years, and its observation deck became a tourist attraction. But city officials and newspaper editorials were mistaken in their confidence that the L&C Tower would start the first new wave of new downtown construction since Franklin Roosevelt's New Deal funded a federal office building, two state office buildings, and a new courthouse. It

would be several years until Nashville got its second skyscraper.

The ceremonial opening of the L&C Tower in 1955. Guilford Dudley Jr. is at the podium. To his right are Gov. Frank Clement and Mayor Ben West (Metro Nashville Archives).

If Life & Casualty looked solid and independent on the Nashville skyline, it was an illusion.

One of L&C's original founders was a man named J. C. Franklin. In 1953, Franklin's only daughter Elizabeth Young died and left 24 percent of the company's stock and a majority of its voting stock in a trust. Young had stated in her will that she did not want the L&C stock to be sold. But Young's nephew (and L&C president) Paul Mountcastle was one of Young's many heirs who wanted the right to sell the stock. After a long court battle in which Mountcastle was represented by L&C attorney Charles Trabue Jr., the court ruled that the stock could in fact be sold. Years later, Trabue said that it was his success in this case that got him two other clients: Commerce Union Bank and Werthan Bag Co.

As existence of the block of stock became known, suitors began lining up. After all, L&C was a small insurance company and therefore easy for dozens of companies to swallow. It had a reliable flow of revenue. It had over $200 million in assets. And its stock price was very reasonable, in part because Wall Street did not look favorably on industrial insurance companies.

About this time, Dudley got a call from Texas oil magnate Clint Murchison. Murchison by then had an estimated wealth of over $600 million, which included everything from oil companies to chemical companies to part-ownership of the New York Central Railroad. (Murchison's role in founding the Dallas Cowboys NFL team came later.) Murchison told Dudley he wanted to build a national chain of small and medium-sized insurance companies and to make Nashville the base of the chain. In order to do so, Murchison offered to buy 1.2 million shares of L&C from Dudley, Mountcastle, and director P. M. Estes for about $33 a share—about $10 above the market price.

Murchison's offer was the only one on the table that gave L&C autonomy to continue running its own company. Dudley was also excited about the idea of working with Murchison. "At the time, there were an awful lot of people trying to buy the company or take it over that I did not want to be taken over by," Dudley said.

In August 1958, Murchison paid $40 million for 24 percent of the stock in Life & Casualty Insurance. The purchase was the largest transaction in Nashville involving a Nashville company since the 1928 purchase of Cheek-Neal Coffee by Postum.

During the next couple of years, it looked as though Clint Murchison might very well build his insurance empire. By 1960, L&C was talking about taking over three smaller insurance companies. But Murchison then suffered a debilitating stroke. For several years, Murchison's sons John and Clint Jr. kept their L&C stock and let executives in Nashville run the day-to-day operations. But in 1967, the Murchisons let it be known on Wall Street that they wanted to sell their stock to concentrate on other holdings. Again, Dudley was inundated with suitors.

Dudley then had a conversation with Third National Bank president Sam Fleming that nearly changed the course of Nashville business history. (Who initiated the conversation was a matter of friendly disagreement thirty years later.) Dudley asked Fleming, a longtime National Life board member, whether National Life would be interested in buying Murchison's stock and taking operational control of L&C.

In hindsight, it would have made a lot of sense for Nashville's two largest insurance companies to merge. The combined company would have been able to cut costs by eliminating overlapping staff. With its formidable assets, it might have scared off possible suitors. It could have made acquisitions and positioned itself better in ordinary and group life insurance. It could have even branched off into health insurance.

However, the National Life board, then led by Edwin Craig, was not interested. It saw no reason to merge and wasn't looking for ways

Life & Casualty founder A. M. Burton (left) with Paul Mountcastle and Guilford Dudley Jr., about 1960 (Metro Nashville Archives).

to cut costs, especially at the home office. "There was a little bit of jealousy on one part or both, I can't really remember," Sam Fleming said in 1998. "But they did not feel like they could work together."

With the National Life idea thwarted, Dudley turned his undivided attention toward one of the suitors. The chairman of a Houston firm called American General Insurance Co. was Benjamin Woodson, whom Dudley had known since he was managing director of the National Association of Life Underwriters. "I had known Woody forever," Dudley said. "We had been [in] on an awful lot of insurance meetings and we played poker together. Here was a man I trusted and I thought would do a fair job with us. The rest of them I did not trust."

American General also had a reputation for knowing how to execute takeovers. Four years earlier, the Houston company had doubled in size with the acquisition of Maryland Casualty Co., the firm once headed by *Tennessean* publisher Silliman Evans.

In September 1968, American General bought the Murchison's stock. Under the deal, American General took over working control of L&C, and Woodson was named L&C chairman.

L&C employees, who had seen little impact of the Murchison ownership, noticed a lot more under American General. "From the day American General acquired the company, there was more policy control from Houston, and maybe for the first time, policy was being impacted by outsiders," said Sydney Keeble Jr.

Not long after the purchase, American General moved the staff of its Life Insurance of Delaware subsidiary from Pittsburgh to Nashville. That move, which brought with it two hundred jobs, ensured that Tennessee would remain a major center of operations for American General.

About a year later, President Richard Nixon offered Dudley—who had donated fifty thousand dollars to his campaign—the ambassadorship to Denmark. American General replaced Dudley with Allen Steele, an L&C employee since 1946.

Nashville's largest insurer threatened to leave town again and again.

During the early 1950s, National Life was in a constant fight with Nashville and Davidson County over its tax bill. The dispute centered on the insurance company's personalty tax, a tax levied on a company's personal property and assets. Insurance companies—with enormously high asset bases—are tricky entities to tax. In the 1950s, Tennessee was one of the few states in the United States that allowed its counties to base their tax assessment of a life insurance company on the market value of the company's stock. Because of this, National Life was paying a higher percentage of tax than many of its competitors in other states.

National Life executives began making public statements in 1952 about what they perceived as an unfair tax structure. Then in 1956, the company announced it had purchased two hundred acres in Williamson County and that it would be moving its headquarters there. Under the deal that had been worked out with Williamson County officials, National Life would only have to pay $3,750 in personalty taxes per year for ten years—less than 1 percent of the $627,000 the company was paying in Nashville. "When we move to the Hillsboro Road site, we will simply be following a trend, which has been in progress in the life insurance industry for a number of years," National Life president Edwin Craig told reporters.[4] To get his message out, Craig hired public relations company Noble-Dury to lobby the media and civic leaders. In doing so, National Life became one of the first big Nashville businesses to hire a PR firm.

If National Life was looking for the city to pay attention to the matter, it succeeded. The day after the announcement, the Nashville Chamber of Commerce appointed a board to study the National Life tax situation. Meanwhile, the *Tennessean* sent a reporter to visit other insurance companies such as Connecticut General, Prudential, and Mutual Benefit to find out why they either chose to stay in downtown or to go to the suburbs.

In the months following National Life's announcement, some Nashville residents found it hard to believe that the city's largest company would actually move across the county line. The property National Life had bought was in a completely undeveloped area at that time. It had no water or sewer lines and a two-lane road leading to it. Virtually none of National Life's fifteen hundred Nashville employees lived near there.

Nevertheless, company officials insisted they were not bluffing. After city and county officials considered the impact of losing National Life on everything from the tax rolls to downtown shopping, they backed down. In May, the county reduced National Life's taxes by $167,000 a year. Shortly thereafter, the company began buying real estate adjacent to its home office, saying it was making plans to build a much larger building.

However, that still did not close the book on National Life's tax problems. In 1965, Metro raised National Life's personalty tax assessment from $10 million to $12.5 million. National Life hired an outside consultant, who recommended the company relocate to the suburbs. For the second time in a decade, National Life announced it might move, buying four hundred acres in Cheatham County to amplify the point.

Metro Davidson County and National Life went back into negotiations. This time, however, they worked out a longer-term deal. Due in a great part to the political efforts of Mayor Beverly Briley and Metro tax assessor Clifford Allen, the city agreed to limit National Life's personalty tax increase to five hundred thousand dollars per year until the year 1975. The two entities also worked out a deal, made possible by the legalities of the Capitol Hill Redevelopment Plan, under which the assessed cost of any new construction would be written off as a credit toward National Life's personalty tax.

The arrangements between National Life and its local government marked the first time a Nashville company had its tax bill altered through political negotiation. Many criticized the arrangement as corporate welfare. But in following decades, other companies such as Gaylord, Columbia/HCA, Thomas Nelson, and Ingram would also work out special deals with Metro government.

Once the deal was finalized, National Life started working on plans for a new headquarters building. Over the years, National Life had repeatedly bought adjacent tracts and added new wings to its headquarters. By the 1960s, National Life's seventeen hundred Nashville employees were spread out across half a dozen buildings, most of which occupied the square block bordered by Seventh and Eighth Avenues and Union and Charlotte Avenues.

In 1966, National Life purchased the remaining parcels of land on the block, which included the Young Men's Hebrew Association and the Masonic Lodge. It then started on its new thirty-one-story building. When it was completed in 1970, the company occupied the tallest building in Nashville for the first time.

In 1968, National Life and Third National Bank merged to form a one-bank holding company called NLT. A 1969 congressional mandate forced NLT to sell the bank. But the insurance company kept the name NLT and most of the conglomerate philosophy that led to its formation.

NLT then turned its attention to its country music properties. Ever since 1943, the Grand Ole Opry had been performed at the Ryman Auditorium, a decaying structure located in the middle of a fast-deteriorating neighborhood. By the late 1960s, NLT decided it was time to either sell the Opry or move it. After a long debate among top executives at the company, NLT went with the latter.

While the new Opry house was under construction, NLT also decided to build a theme park and motel next to it. By the time that theme park was opened in 1972, the motel had become a six-hundred-room convention hotel. National Life's plan to move the Ryman, therefore, evolved into an entertainment complex that almost single-handedly made Nashville a major tourist destination.[5]

Between the new building, the formation of NLT, and the development of Opryland, NLT had a lot of things on its plate between 1965 and 1975. But none of those things got Wall Street off its back.

Despite all the things NLT had done, industrial insurance was still its largest source of income. And by the late 1970s, industrial insurance was beginning to dry up for good. Between 1970 and 1979, NLT slid from being the twenty-first-largest life insurer in the United States to being the thirty-ninth. In 1980, NLT reported its first decline in profits in a decade.

Industrial insurance even had a public relations problem. Industrial premiums had always been higher than ordinary premiums because of higher death rates among the poor and the high cost of door-to-door collections. In the years following the Civil Rights Movement, industrial insurance was portrayed by consumer interest groups and the media as an industry that exploited the poor. A 1979 *60 Minutes* report on debit insurance (which focused on abuses by some NLT agents) painted a picture of an industry that abused poor, elderly policyholders. That report hurt the price of NLT's stock.

NLT was also hurt by a perception—which may have been accurate—that it was being run more like a paternal organization than a company constantly trying to maximize its profits. "Our answer administratively for a long time was when we had a problem, we just added a worker instead of finding a better way of doing it," said lifelong NLT employee George McIntosh.

By the late 1970s, analysts considered NLT's stock undervalued, its insurance business poorly positioned, and its management not amenable to change. "Wall Street perceived that management had tunnel vision," said Norris Nielsen, a researcher at J. C. Bradford and Co. in the 1970s. "Instead of worrying about shareholder value, management was just concerned about increasing its debit line by a little more year by year. Meanwhile, the company had a hoard of assets, but not much of an investment strategy, and a lot of companies wanted to get their hands on those assets."

The National Life Building, built in 1925, sits in front of the newly built National Life Tower, around 1973 (Metro Nashville Archives).

However, it is only fair to point out that NLT was still making a profit. In fact, neither National Life nor NLT ever lost money or failed to pay dividends to its shareholders.

In an environment replete with corporate mergers, speculation about an NLT takeover became frequent. In April 1978, those rumors grew loud when it became publicly known that American General had been buying NLT stock since 1972 and by that time owned five percent of NLT.

In contrast to NLT, American General was quite popular in the investment banking community. After its takeovers of Maryland

Casualty and Life & Casualty, the company bought Sacramento's
California-Western States Life Insurance Co. in 1970.

NLT executives knew they needed to make a move. Days after NLT
became aware of American General's stock ownership, NLT asked the
New York investment banking firm Morgan Stanley to come up with
a list of insurance companies NLT might acquire.

In August 1978, NLT announced its intention to buy Great
Southern Corp., a $900 million insurance company based in Houston.
The takeover made strategic sense for NLT, since the Houston firm
sold insurance to a more affluent market than did NLT. NLT's assets
totaled about $3.5 billion, making it a takeover the Nashville company
could easily afford.

Great Southern fought the takeover, saying NLT's offer at fifty
dollars a share was "inadequate." It asked the Texas Board of
Insurance to block the takeover and sued NLT in federal court in
Houston for stock manipulation, charges NLT vigorously denied.

Three months later, NLT raised its offer to fifty-eight dollars a
share and assured Great Southern management that they would allow
the company to run with some autonomy. Great Southern then agreed
to the merger, and NLT chalked up the biggest corporate takeover in
Nashville history. Company executives admitted that the whole thing
gave them a sense of invigoration. "You have to look at this as a chess
game," NLT chairman Rusty Wagner said.

If Wagner was hoping the Great Southern merger would scare off
suitors, he was wrong. Within two months, Ashland Oil Co. of
Ashland, Kentucky, had purchased from American General an option
to buy NLT's shares, sending NLT's stock price from the low $20s in
May to the mid $30s in June. But in September, Ashland Oil
announced it was no longer interested.

Soon, there were other rumored suitors, including Charter Oil
Company, Seagram, and even Nashville's own Hospital Corporation of
America. By late 1979, NLT was under siege and it had a dramatic
effect on the outlook of its executives. "I remember being at a meeting
when [NLT chairman] Rusty Wagner was very concerned about the
problem of the stock and the fact that the assets of the company were
so undervalued that it was obviously a prime target for a takeover,"
said E. W. (Bud) Wendell, then president of NLT's WSM division. "I
remember him saying that the company needed to hit a home run—
something that is really spectacular." Wagner's desire to improve
NLT's stock led the WSM staff to come up with the idea for a new
cable network called TNN (short for The Nashville Network).

In February 1980, state senator Douglas Henry Jr., a grandson of
C. A. Craig, proposed a bill in the legislature that would have made it
almost impossible for an insurance company in Tennessee to be taken
over by hostile means. The bill went nowhere. But Henry's action

showed how badly NLT management wanted to remain independent.

By this time, some of the old guard members were even getting physically ill at the thought of being taken over. "It was traumatic," said Ridley Wills II, an NLT executive and the grandson of National Life cofounder Ridley Wills. "I have an occasional constriction of my esophagus, and it bothered me a good deal during that period because of the stress that I was under."

Harold Hook, who was raised on a dairy farm near Kansas City, knew all about the trauma of seeing his company taken over. When American General took over California-Western States Life Insurance Co. in 1970, Hook was Cal-West's CEO. But by 1978, Hook had worked his way to the top of American General's corporate ladder. And by that time he was a firm believer in growth by acquisition. "Internal growth is not an option," he once told *Business Week*. "It takes too much capital, and you can't build an organization fast enough."[6]

NLT executives were determined to remain independent from American General, seeing it as a matter of personal survival. Proud of their company's long record of growth from within, they had little taste for a company and a CEO who put so much emphasis on acquisitions. "I knew about American General because I had seem them take over a lot of other companies, and I did not like them at all," said C. A. (Neil) Craig II.

"The Harvard business school has a harvest theory. You harvest everything but you never replant. I think Mr. Hook imitated that theory. It follows a pattern of companies that they took over before and after us."

In August 1981, American General asked the Securities and Exchange Commission and state regulators in Tennessee, Texas, and Iowa for permission to increase its ownership of NLT to 25 percent. Wall Street analysts and NLT executives immediately recognized this as American General's attempt to "test the waters" on a takeover attempt. However, American General said its only purpose in trying to buy the stock was accounting, since under federal law, it could count NLT's dividends as a part of its own earnings only if it owned at least 25 percent of NLT. "The acquisition of NLT is not American General's long-range goal," George Reed, vice chairman of the Texas firm, told Tennessee Commerce and Insurance Commissioner (and former HCA president) John Neff at hearings at Legislative Plaza.[7]

When NLT heard about American General's attempt to buy more of its stock, it made clear to its shareholders and to the general public that it would resist takeover attempts. The Nashville company filed suit in federal court, asking the court to prevent American General from increasing its stock ownership in NLT on antitrust grounds.

In December, NLT won this first round in the bout when Neff ruled that American General could not, according to Tennessee law, acquire any more NLT stock.

Four months later, American General came back with an open offer to take over NLT, saying it wanted to trade 0.8 of a share of American General stock for each NLT share. Under the offer, each NLT share would have been exchanged for about $35. Investors, figuring the deal would go through, started buying up NLT stock, sending its price from $23 to $28.87 the next day.

The NLT board called a special meeting. It then sent a letter to shareholders describing American General's offer as "a cheap price."[8]

Unfortunately for NLT's board, many years had passed since the days when a small group of Nashville families owned the company. By the time of the American General takeover, 80 percent of NLT's stock was owned outside of the cofounders' families. And by 1982, a lot of these shareholders had more faith in American General's ability to boost the stock price than NLT's.

It is also worth pointing out that the descendants of National Life's founders were hardly unanimous on how to handle takeover attempts. Bill Tyne, the grandson of founder Thomas Tyne, was a banker at Commerce Union Bank in 1982. Given NLT's financial situation and the trends in business at that time, Tyne was convinced that some company was going to take over NLT and that it was in the best interest of shareholders for NLT to be more amenable to suitors.

A few days after NLT's board voted not to allow its shareholders to consider American General's offer, Tyne submitted a proposal that NLT's board form an independent committee to evaluate merger offers. If the committee found a merger offer to be fair, the proposal would automatically be forwarded to shareholders.

The NLT board tried to keep Tyne's proposal from being considered. But after the Securities and Exchange Commission ruled in Tyne's favor, his proposal was put in a proxy statement and considered. NLT's shareholders rejected it. But Tyne's proposal got enough votes to convince Wall Street that there was significant shareholder dissent at NLT.

"Even if it hadn't been for American General, NLT would have been sold to someone else because of all that was happening in the 1980s," said Tyne, who eventually moved to England. "But my proposal was terribly significant at the time."

Meanwhile, NLT executives didn't know what to make of Harold Hook. During the height of the takeover battle, Hook called NLT chief executive Walter Robinson Jr. several times. "He would call and just talk," Robinson said years later. "But I couldn't tell what he was proposing or talking about."

It was in this environment that some of NLT's investment bankers and lawyers, which included Brad Reed, Robins Ledyard, and Bob Walker, began to present Robinson with an interesting strategy. Even if the board was able to resist American General's offer at thirty-five dollars a share, they would probably have to give in when the offer got higher. The only way to avoid the takeover, they told him, was to employ what was then known as a "Pacman" strategy: eat the other company before it eats you.

After all, NLT was a huge company in its own right, with $4.6 billion in assets. The company wasn't as big as American General, but it had less debt on its balance sheet than American General. It also had a lot of valuable assets to draw on, including WSM and Opryland.

Nevertheless, Robinson and the NLT board of directors were nervous about the idea of making a bid for another company, especially one with as much experience with mergers as American General. It was about then that Reed, who had worked with a Nebraska investor named Warren Buffett, suggested Robinson make a trip to Omaha.

Eventually, Buffett became one of the best-known investors in the United States. But in 1982, Buffett and his holding company, Berkshire Hathaway, were still known mostly by Wall Street insiders.

Under the plan, NLT would first announce its plan to buy American General. Then, Buffett would announce his intention to buy a sizeable percentage of the merged company to convince the investment community that Buffett was NLT's "white knight." Once the merger took place, Buffett would agree to vote his shares the way the NLT board wanted him to. In return, the company would turn over its investment portfolio to Berkshire Hathaway.

Reed encouraged Robinson to talk to Buffett about getting involved with NLT because Buffett had a long history of investing in insurance companies. A few years earlier, Berkshire Hathaway had purchased 33 percent of a struggling Texas insurer called Geico. Geico's insurance sales and profits increased consistently during the next ten years. Meanwhile, Geico's investments, now under Buffett's direction, outperformed the Standard and Poor's 500 Index by over 50 percent.

Robinson flew to Nebraska. Buffett picked Robinson up at the airport and drove him to downtown Omaha in an old Pontiac. For three hours, Robinson sat in Buffett's office and tried to convince him to buy part of NLT.

Buffett told Robinson that NLT should keep fighting. But he made it clear that he did not want to get involved in a hostile takeover. "His policy was not to acquire in hostile situations, and I was never able to budge him from that," Robinson said.

Despite Buffett's rejection, Robinson and the NLT board decided to fight back at American General. On May 19, NLT shocked Wall Street by announcing it was making a $1.3 billion turnaround offer for American General, or about $50 a share. American General was caught off guard, and its stock shot up from $33 to $37.50 amid speculation that NLT would pull it off. Many in Nashville cheered. "We admire your leadership, Walter Robinson Jr.," a *Banner* editorial said. "You have displayed an aggressiveness on the part of the management of NLT Corp. that commands the greatest respect and admiration."9

For the next few weeks, American General and NLT stared each other down like two western gunfighters. A few days after NLT's counteroffer, American General's board met and voted to reject NLT's offer, calling it "inadequate, unsound, and of questionable legality."10 The Houston firm then filed suit in federal court seeking to stop NLT from proceeding with its takeover.

About two weeks later, NLT raised its offer from fifty to fifty-five dollars a share. American General's board met and recommended rejection again.

American General then made two simultaneous offers that it knew would pit NLT's stockholders against its management. On the one hand, it offered thirty-eight dollars a share for each of the first fifteen million NLT shares tendered to it. On the other, it offered forty-six dollars a share if NLT ended its takeover opposition within the next ninety days.

During the next two days, Wall Street became so convinced American General would prevail that NLT's stock rose from twenty-nine to thirty-eight dollars.

American General did not stop there. On June 29, American General ran full-page advertisements in both the *Banner* and the *Tennessean*, appealing directly to NLT's shareholders and telling them this would be the final offer. Hook also appeared before both the *Banner* and *Tennessean* editorial boards.

By this time, Robinson had few alternatives left. He had tried to get a white knight, and that had failed. He had tried to scare American General's management out of the takeover by making an offer, and then by raising that offer, and that had failed. If he and the board continued to hold out against American General's offer, NLT's stock would tumble back to the twenty-five dollar range. If that happened, some shareholders might file a class-action lawsuit against the board. They might even overthrow it.

Sometime around July 1, Robinson met with Hook in New York and told him the NLT board would agree to the new offer. The merger war was over. By October, NLT was a part of American General, the fourth-largest shareholder-owned insurer in the nation.

During the next few months, American General made changes at NLT that some of the old founding families would look back on with some bitterness.

The first order of business was debt. It had been American General's intention all along to sell off a lot of NLT's assets. Since the Houston company had spent a lot more to acquire NLT than it had originally hoped, that became a necessity. As soon as the ink was dry, Hook announced that his company was selling NLT's computer services group and Great Southern Life Insurance. He also began hinting that he wanted to sell Opryland U.S.A., the Grand Ole Opry, the Ryman Auditorium, and other related assets (called WSM Inc.).

Marriott, U.S. Tobacco, Anheuser-Busch, and the New York capital investment firm of Kohlberg, Kravis and Roberts all showed interest in WSM. But after several months, the leading candidate to buy WSM appeared to be a group of Nashville investors consisting of Robinson, C. A. (Neil) Craig II, Ridley Wills II, and Ingram Industries president Bronson Ingram. As the bidding went higher, Robinson, Craig, and Wills dropped out, but Ingram stayed in. At one point, according to both Martha Ingram and one-time Ingram Book president Phil Pfeffer, Ingram thought he had settled a deal with Hook over a price.

About this time, Craig got a call at home from Sarah Cannon, the Opry performer known as Minnie Pearl.

"Neil, I understand you are trying to buy the Opryland complex," she said.

"Miss Minnie, we are sure trying but I am not sure whether we will be able to make it or not," Craig said.

"I have a good friend who would like to be a player."

"Who is that?"

"A man named Ed Gaylord."

At the time, Craig didn't know Gaylord, an Oklahoma City businessman who owned the *Hee Haw* television show. But he gave Minnie the phone number of the person at American General to call.

Within a few weeks, American General announced that it had sold WSM to Gaylord for $225 million. When he heard about the sale, Ingram was furious. "Bronson felt blindsided," Martha Ingram said in 1999. "But as it turns out, had we bought it, we never would have been able to develop Ingram Micro and do some of the other things that we did later."

Meanwhile, American General had started doing something that Sam Fleming and Guilford Dudley Jr. had discussed years earlier: combining National Life and L&C into one structure. The company did not admit it publicly at the time, but several hundred people were laid off in this consolidation.

American General then put the L&C Tower on the auction block. After over twenty entities made offers, Nashville's first skyscraper was sold to a group of Nashville investors including Guilford Dudley Jr., John Bransford, and developer Robert C. (Bobby) Mathews Jr.

By this time, it had become obvious that American General's culture was a lot different than NLT's. The Houston company required all employees to attend classes on "modelnetics," a collection of over one hundred maxims that Harold Hook wanted his employees to know. It decreased the amount of company money it would give to match employee contributions to charity. It told the NLT legal staff that virtually all decisions had to be made in Houston. "We were accustomed to doing everything," said E. M. Haywood, NLT's chief legal counsel, who quit three years after the American General takeover. "But I felt like a law clerk after they took over."

American General also started charging NLT's retirees for a percentage of their health benefits, something most other companies were already doing by that time. NLT's retirees tried to challenge this move in court, but the suit failed.

Not long after the merger, the descendants of National Life's founders began a mass exodus. First to leave was Robinson, who resigned almost immediately after the merger and went to the law firm of Bass, Berry, & Sims. Others, such as John Tipton Jr., Ted Lazenby, Ridley Wills II, and Bill Weaver III, would eventually follow.

Craig's departure was especially ugly. About a year after the takeover, Craig, then chief executive officer of the National Life and Accident division, was invited into the office of Jack Bremermann, head of American General's Nashville operations. According to Craig, Bremermann told him a decision had been made about National Life's new executive lineup. Craig was floored. "You guys have changed my executive lineup without even talking to me about it?" he asked. Within an hour, Craig, whose grandfather started National Life and whose father had been its most influential president, turned in his resignation letter and was on his way to his attorney's office. Craig then sued American General for breach of contract, a suit later settled out of court.

Years later, Craig would say it was American General's intention during those first years to "break the National Life spirit."

"I've been told by people since I left that there was hardly any increase in premiums during the first five or six years, that they were just milking the company for everything they could before they went out to buy another company. . . . Hell, when I was chief marketing officer, if I had one quarter per year where I did not show growth over the previous quarter, my self would have been out of there."

Craig was so upset about the American General takeover that he sold his stock in the process. Not every member of the founding families did the same, and many were glad about that later. By 1998, American General's stock was worth about twelve times what it had been worth at the time of the NLT takeover. When asked if that took away the pain of the NLT takeover, Ridley Wills II admitted, "It certainly mitigates it."

Many of American General's Nashville employees were saddened at the departure of the old guard. But some viewed it as an opportunity. "A lot of people told me that the change was great for them, because under NLT there had been a feeling that if you aren't family that there was a glass ceiling," said Jim Tuerff, a one-time Life & Casualty executive who eventually became American General's president.

Craig and other former NLT executives at least had the pleasure of seeing American General become the target of a hostile takeover. In part because of the expense of buying NLT, American General had to slow down its acquisition program after 1983. Hook then found it wasn't easy to make all the parts of his company fit into place. American General tried to raise its earnings by getting out of group and property and casualty insurance. But its earnings remained low through the late 1980s.

In 1990, a Birmingham insurance company called Torchmark made a $6.3 billion offer to take over American General. After American General rejected the offer, Torchmark began waging a proxy fight, recommending five new members to American General's board.

American General survived its battle with Torchmark but only after fighting the Birmingham firm in regulatory channels, newspaper advertisements, and on Wall Street. After the battle ended, American General began putting more emphasis on internal efficiency in order to improve its earnings and please shareholders. In 1991 and 1992, it consolidated its Jacksonville and Nashville offices, eliminating about six hundred jobs in Jacksonville and four hundred in Nashville. The next year, American General sold its downtown Nashville building to the state and moved its headquarters to a site just north of the Williamson/Davidson County line. The state at first renamed the building the Tennessee Tower. But in 1999, the legislature named it again, this time after longtime state comptroller William Snodgrass. Thus the National Life/NLT/American General/Tennessee Tower got its fifth name.

At the end of the twentieth century, Nashville no longer had an insurance company based in its downtown for the first time since the end of the nineteenth century. The original WSM studios were gone. Official Ryman Auditorium literature made little mention of the insurance company that once owned it or the historic preservationists who saved it. Opryland U.S.A. had been torn down to make way for a massive shopping mall. And few Nashville residents could even tell you how their city first became known for country music, how the Grand Ole Opry got started, or what the letters WSM stood for.

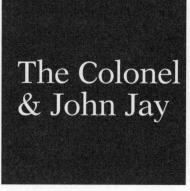

CHAPTER 13

The Colonel & John Jay

J ack Massey and John Y. Brown Jr. knew the old man was ticked off about something. For one thing, Harlan Sanders had been avoiding them lately, a sure sign he had some grievance. For another, he was wearing a black suit instead of his ubiquitous white one.

What Massey and Brown did not know was just how mad "Colonel" Sanders was. But the chairman and president of Kentucky Fried Chicken would soon find out. They would find out that night, when Sanders delivered his speech to the annual convention of franchisees—the hundreds of small business owners whom Sanders, Massey, and Brown had made rich. When it came to the restaurant chain that he had started ten years earlier, the Colonel did not mince words. And on this night, Sanders—who could cuss like a sailor when he had a mind to—had a few things to get off his chest.

Sanders spoke for about forty-five minutes. Brown never forgot it. "He chewed us out unmercifully," Brown said. "He told everyone that Jack and I did not know anything about the chicken business. He told everyone that we were out to get their money. He told them that we had brought some experts in that were going to change the recipe.

"The whole thing was really mean-spirited, and of course it wasn't true. But I remember a lot of wives around the room were crying. It seemed like the whole thing was over and that everyone's dreams were shattered."

Brown, who was thirty-one at the time and who had stayed up the night before drinking and playing cards, was scheduled to speak next.

"I did not know what to do. Here I was with eight pages of prepared notes, and obviously they were not any good. You could hear a pin drop."

Brown then gave what he later described as the most important speech of his life—strong words for the man who later became governor of Kentucky. Instead of blasting Sanders, from whom he and Massey had bought Kentucky Fried Chicken two years earlier, he praised him. "I said that the Colonel was an artist, and like all artists, he is a perfectionist," Brown said. "I said that what the Colonel has done is create a dream for all of us. And I said it was our responsibility to go out and reach and try as hard as we can to meet up with the Colonel's perfection."

Brown then asked the crowd of KFC franchisees if any one them had made a deal with the company in the previous two years that the company hadn't honored. Not one raised his hand. Brown then reminded everyone that they had made more money from the remarkable rise of KFC stock—made possible by Massey and Brown's management—than they had ever actually paid the company in franchise fees and payments.

"That was the moment, I think, when the company really came over to Jack and myself," Brown said thirty-three years later. "Up to then it was still the Colonel's deal."

How Nashville capitalist Jack Massey, Louisville lawyer John Y. Brown Jr., and Kentucky chicken king Harlan Sanders ever got together in the first place is a story in itself.

Jack Carroll Massey would eventually become the first man in American history to take three unrelated companies to the New York Stock Exchange. But he started his career with a little white lie. In 1923, after his freshman year at the University of Florida, Massey took the test to become a registered pharmacist in Georgia, a test that required the applicant to be twenty-one. Not only did Massey pass the test, he got the second-highest score of all the applicants. After he got his license in the mail, the nineteen-year-old Massey considered sending it back. But the prospect of paying another three years of tuition weighed heavily on the young man who had already set as his goal to own his own drugstore by the time he was twenty-five. Massey left school and got a job with a small drugstore in Columbus, Georgia. Two years later, after a dispute with his boss over pay, Massey left to work for the Liggett drugstore chain in Atlanta.

In 1929, Liggett sent him to Nashville to manage its store at 530 Church Street. Within a couple of years, Massey found a drugstore down the street that was for sale. After working out a handshake deal to buy the store, Massey walked down the street to explain to Third National Bank President Webb Johnston the arrangement that he and

Jack Massey, Colonel Harlan Sanders, and John Y. Brown Jr. (Barbara Massey Rogers).

the previous owner of the store had made. "He was completely frank with us," Johnston said years later. "I think it was his candor as much as his self-confidence that appealed to us."[1] It was the first of many transactions between Massey and Third National.

Like thousands of other Americans, Massey survived the 1930s by moving in with his in-laws and asking creditors for more time to pay off his debts. "Banks and everybody told me to take bankruptcy," Massey said years later. "But I said 'no, if you put me in bankruptcy then I'll lose everything. But if you leave me alone, I'll pay you off.'"

"I had companies like Johnson & Johnson on me all the time. I think I owed Johnson & Johnson twenty-five hundred dollars, so I sent them a check for five dollars and told them this is evidence of good faith. I can't pay you more than that now, but every month I will send you a check. Well, as time went on, I finally paid everyone off."[2]

In the era before chain drugstores and Wal-Mart, it was quite possible to make a healthy living as the owner of a small drugstore. Jack Massey did just that, mainly because of his location and hard work. After two years in operation at 718 Church Street, Massey moved the business to the bottom floor of the Bennie Dillon Building at 702 Church Street. In addition to walk-in customers shopping at downtown department stores, Massey Drug did good business filling prescriptions for patients as they came down from doctors' and dentists' offices in the building.

Although his career as a pharmacist would eventually be dwarfed by other achievements, Massey liked to talk about his years as an independent apothecary. He frequently repeated the story about how he frantically chased a customer two blocks down Church Street because he had given him the wrong prescription. Massey was less sentimental, but quite affected, by his memory of young women who came into his store needing medical attention because of botched abortions. Because of those experiences, Massey later became a benefactor of Planned Parenthood.

During his early years running the pharmacy on Church Street, Massey made several friends who would be extremely important years later. One was a young Third National Bank officer named Sam Fleming, whom Massey remembered as being patient when he had a hard time repaying his loan during the height of the Great Depression. Another was a recent Vanderbilt Medical School graduate named Thomas Frist, whose office was located on the second floor of the Doctor's Building, next door to the Bennie Dillon Building. A third friend was attorney Henry Goodpasture.

Some of Massey's most reliable customers were doctors such as Frist who sent staffers downstairs to get fresh supplies of bandages or sutures. Most of these doctors ran credit accounts at the store, an arrangement that naturally led to close ties between Massey and the more than one hundred independent physicians who had private practices on Church Street between Seventh and Eighth Avenues. Massey soon learned that many doctors had a tough time financing the purchase of medical equipment such as X-ray machines from existing medical supply companies. In 1936, convinced that lending money to doctors was a safe bet, Massey started a side business at the same location called Massey Surgical Supply.

One of Massey Surgical's first customers was a young doctor named Lawrence Jackson, then trying to set up a practice in Dickson. "I did not have anything but a family and a 1934 Plymouth," Jackson recalled years later. "I tried to borrow money at the bank and of course I had no collateral and they refused me. So I went to Nashville and met Jack Massey. He agreed to furnish all my office furniture, all the equipment and supplies and everything and have them in the office on July 1, and I wasn't to make the first payment until October. Jack was just a prince of a fellow to do this and I never deserted him."[3] A few years later, Jackson started a hospital in Dickson called

Goodlark, which bought almost all its equipment from Massey Surgical.

Massey also wasn't above making creative business deals with medical students. In the 1940s, a Vanderbilt student named Jeff Pennington noticed that the university's bookstore was selling microscopes for considerably more than Massey. Pennington, who had known Massey for years, worked out a deal with Massey whereby he bought twenty microscopes at wholesale prices and sold them to his classmates. Everything seemed to work out fine, until the bookstore found out about it and complained to the dean. "Would you like to get kicked out of school?" the dean asked Pennington when he found out about his side business. Massey was so amused with Pennington's spirit that years later, he offered Pennington the chance to buy insider stock in Kentucky Fried Chicken (which Pennington turned down).

As soon as World War II ended and credit became more readily available, Massey greatly expanded the surgical supply business and moved it to 2110 West End Avenue, taking out a huge loan from the Third National Bank to do so. "My mother stayed up all night, she was so scared about that loan," Massey's daughter, Barbara Massey Rogers, said in 1998.

Massey Surgical Supply nearly went out of business shortly after World War II. After lending about forty thousand dollars in medical equipment to Nashville's Protestant Hospital, Massey learned that the hospital was about to go bankrupt. To his good fortune, the Tennessee Baptist Convention took over Protestant Hospital and renamed it Baptist Hospital. "He told me at that time that he could not have stood the forty thousand dollars in loss because it would have thrown him in bankruptcy," said Rev. James Sullivan, a leader in the Tennessee Baptist Convention and Massey's pastor at Belmont Heights Baptist Church in the 1940s. "After that, he told me he was going to give a lot more to charity than he had in the past."

Years later, when Massey had a lot of money to give away, he would give much of it to organizations affiliated with the Baptist Church, most notably Belmont University.

As for Baptist Hospital, Massey became one of its trustees and remained so for twenty years. As such, Massey was heavily involved in finding a way to finance a two-hundred-bed, $3 million upgrade for the hospital in 1957. Much of what he learned on the Baptist Hospital board would come in handy in 1968, when he cofounded a for-profit hospital company called Hospital Corporation of America.

Massey did all his banking with Third National from the moment he got to town, and he referred to the bank many of the doctors who bought or leased their supplies from Massey Surgical. In 1946, the bank rewarded him with a seat on its board of directors, which brought with it prestige and business contacts. "That was a very big coup because it gave him a lot of liquidity and flexibility with capital that he never had before," Massey's daughter Barbara said.

Massey would make good use of this access to capital. After the surgical supply firm began to do well, Massey began to diversify so fast that it was hard for his friends to keep up. When he heard that a small pesticide factory called Rigo Chemical was up for sale, he, Goodpasture, and W. L. Bainbridge bought it. Convinced that his surgical supply company was paying too much money for braces and crutches, Massey started his own business called Massey Brace to make them in-house. When he noticed that the Vanderbilt Hospital had no florist, he opened a flower shop there. Massey's experience in surgical equipment loans also led him to form Commercial Investment Co., which lent money to other types of businesses such as restaurants.

By the mid-1950s, Massey owned and operated drugstores at 702 Church Street, 2026 West End Avenue, and 1211 Twenty-first Avenue; the surgical supply store at 2110 West End Avenue; a laboratory at 1926 Division Street; the brace shop at 1925 Broadway; a florist at 1211 Twenty-first Avenue; and the pesticide factory at 638 Benton Avenue.

Massey's business operations grew so fast that it is easy to visualize him as a wealthy man in the 1940s. In fact, he expanded his businesses so fast and took out loans so frequently that it was hard to tell. "It always seemed like he was always working on borrowed money," said Omega Sattler, who worked for Massey from 1948 until his death in 1990. Hunter Woods, who ran Rigo Chemical Company for Massey, said it seemed to him that Massey did not have much liquidity until about 1960. "But everyone knew that he would be rich one day," Woods said. "He was too good an operator. . . . He was not highly educated when it came to book learning, but he was the smartest man I have ever known when it came to business and finance. He was natively smart."

Of all the businesses, surgical equipment was by far the most profitable. By the late 1950s, Massey Surgical had branches in Knoxville, Chattanooga, and Kingsport. Most of its eighty employees were salesmen who covered an area from Virginia to Alabama.

In January 1961, fifty-six-year-old Jack Massey sold his surgical supply business to Brunswick Corp. of Chicago, a bowling equipment company that had gotten into the health care business two years earlier with the purchase of A. S. Aloe Co. Under terms of the purchase, Massey received 16,754 shares of Brunswick stock. In doing so, he learned an expensive lesson about not selling for cash. During the two months after the purchase was announced, the stock fell in price by almost 50 percent. Massey's friends were telling him it was time to retire.

Harlan Sanders was a peculiar fellow. He was a man who drifted from one low-paying profession to another but who saw hundreds of people become millionaires based on the work he did; a one-time enlisted man who went down in history as one of the most famous colonels in American history; a teetotaler who thought drinking coffee and playing cards were immoral but who cussed like a sailor. "He still has great difficulty calling a no-good, God-damned, lazy, incompetent, dishonest son of a bitch by any but his rightful name," a profile once explained.[4]

A seventh-grade dropout, Sanders changed jobs ten times by the time he was forty, doing everything from working on a streetcar to selling tires. Around 1930, he opened a service station in Corbin, Kentucky. There, Sanders found that he could make a little extra money selling southern-style vegetables, homemade biscuits, and fried chicken to road-weary travelers. When food became a bigger sell than gasoline, Sanders took the pumps down and set up a restaurant that he later expanded to seat 150 people. In his attempt to serve tasty chicken, Sanders came up with a blend of eleven herbs and spices. In order to serve it promptly, he came up with a method of cooking the chicken in a pressure cooker rather than a pan.

In 1955, Sanders's restaurant became one of many small businesses in America to be transformed by interstate highways. Interstate 75 missed Sanders's restaurant by several miles, forcing him to sell the building at auction. After a few months of trying to get by on Social Security, Sanders decided to franchise his chicken recipe to other restaurants. At first, Sanders traveled through the Midwest with his pressure cooker, using his "finger-lickin' good" drumsticks to sign up one restaurant owner at a time. Eventually word got out and prospective franchisees started coming to him.

One such person was Marvin Hopper, then working as a salesman for Alcoa in St. Louis. Around 1960, a college friend of Hopper's who lived in Louisville told him about Kentucky Fried Chicken. "He told me that there was a funny-looking guy running around in a white suit calling himself Colonel Sanders selling fried chicken," Hopper remembered almost forty years later.

That weekend, Hopper and his friend paid a visit to the Colonel's home. After a long talk with the Colonel and his nephew Lee Cummings and a visit to two franchised outlets, the two men negotiated the rights to the Nashville franchise (picking Nashville because it was centrally located to their parents and their wives' parents). Under the one-page contract, the pair obtained the exclusive right to serve the Colonel's secret recipe in Nashville free of charge. All they had to do in return was pay Sanders five cents for every chicken sold (not five cents per piece of chicken, but five cents per actual chicken).

Hopper and his partner then borrowed six thousand dollars from the bank and opened Nashville's first Kentucky Fried Chicken outlet in a small strip mall in Donelson. After three months, they thought they had made a terrible mistake. "Business was terrible," Hopper said. Things were so bad that they couldn't even afford to pay Sanders for paper boxes and supplies. Hopper's partner sold his half of the business to Hopper and got out of chicken altogether. Hopper held on and opened a freestanding location on Gallatin Road six months later. That location did much better, thanks in part to the fact that he put a drive-in window on the side of the small building.

By 1963, thanks to small franchise owners like Hopper, Sanders had over five hundred franchised outlets.

Harlan Sanders's search for a real estate lawyer led him to the two men who were about to change his life.

At this point, twenty-eight-year-old John Y. Brown Jr.'s main claim to fame was that he was the son of former U.S. Senator John Y. Brown of Kentucky. When Sanders heard that Senator Brown's son had graduated from law school and set up practice in Louisville, he gave him a call.

What Sanders did not know was that John Brown Jr. was having second thoughts about being an attorney. "It finally hit me that the only reason I became a lawyer was because my father was a lawyer," Brown said years later. Brown had of course heard of Colonel Sanders (just about everyone in Louisville had), but hardly took the goateed old man seriously. "We all thought he was a bit of an oddball, walking around in his white suit with a big mug picture on the side of his Cadillac," Brown later said. But after spending a day running around with Sanders, and after looking over some of the receipts from franchisees, Brown decided that Sanders was more genius than eccentric. When Sanders mentioned that he had always wanted to open a barbecue chain, Brown convinced him that he was the man to run it. Within a few weeks, the Colonel agreed to let Brown open his first barbecue restaurant.

All Brown needed was sixteen thousand dollars. But he did not have the money, and no bank would lend it to him because he had no collateral. In his search for the sixteen thousand dollars, Brown found out about Commercial Investment Co., Jack Massey's company that loaned money to restaurants to buy equipment.

By now, Massey had sold his surgical supply business and was thinking about retiring. But he still enjoyed business so much that he actually flew to Louisville to check out loan applicant John Y. Brown Jr. According to Brown, the two of them spent three hours negotiating the sixteen thousand dollar loan. "I did not know anything about finance, but I am a negotiator by nature, and so we sat and spent hours negotiating whether it would be six or six and a half percent interest." At the end of the day, Brown had his loan.

Massey's new relationship with Brown inevitably led to his learning all about Harlan Sanders and his chicken business. A few weeks later, Brown introduced Massey to Sanders, primarily to help Massey make loans to other prospective franchisees. Somehow, the Colonel sensed that more was at stake. "We go to lunch, and right off the bat, the Colonel says 'I just want you to know that no slick southern so and so is going to come in here and take over my company,'" Brown said. "It was the first time that very thought had even been thrown out there."

The very realization that Sanders was so adamantly opposed to turning over control of his company may have been what got Massey's attention. It wasn't long before he was encouraging Brown to talk to Sanders about selling. But buying Kentucky Fried Chicken away from Colonel Sanders was no easy task. Chicken was far more than just a business to Sanders; it was his life. Many times during the discussions about the sale of the company, Sanders would sound like he was ready to sign a deal and then suddenly change his mind.

In a story Massey told often during the last twenty years of his life, the three of them were in the Colonel's office trying to negotiate a price when suddenly Sanders turned away and said he still did not know whether he wanted to sell. He then opened his desk drawer and read his horoscope, which his secretary was required to put there every day. "Something good will happen to you today," it said. Sanders then decided to sell, unaware that Massey had timed the meeting to coincide with that very horoscope.

Massey then handwrote a contract on a yellow sheet of legal paper that he, Brown, and Sanders all signed. Under the terms of the deal, Massey and Brown paid $2 million for all Kentucky Fried Chicken franchise contracts, plus the title to all of Sanders's patents and trademarks and the rights to Sanders's image. Sanders agreed to remain with the company as a public relations ambassador, drawing a salary of forty thousand dollars. "Forty thousand dollars a year for life," Sanders told a reporter a few weeks later. "That's a pretty good incentive, too, isn't it?"[5]

According to Brown, the Colonel turned down ten thousand shares of stock. "It was hard for him to accept the possibility that the company could possibly be better off without him running it," Brown said. "And so he said 'I don't want any of your stock. It's not going to be worth toilet paper.'"

It was only after the Colonel agreed in principle to sign that Massey and Brown came to agreement with each other. Over a hand-shake, Massey, who put up almost all the money to finance the deal, agreed that he would own 60 percent and Brown 40 percent of the new company.

Massey thus became chief executive officer and Brown president of the new Kentucky Fried Chicken Corporation.

After setting up a corporate office on Sidco Drive in Nashville, Massey and Brown went to work organizing the business. Their first step was to figure out exactly what they had bought and put a moratorium on new franchise agreements for the time being. After about a year of looking over the books and studying the industry, they came to several conclusions.

One was that Kentucky Fried Chicken needed standardization. At that time, most KFC franchisees were full-service restaurants that offered the Colonel's recipe as one of many menu items. Other outlets were in strip mall locations (such as the one in Donelson) or in stand-alone buildings (such as the one on Gallatin Road). The stand-alone units—which had almost no place in the restaurant to sit—clearly made the most money. Since the long-term plan was to build Kentucky Fried Chicken into a national chain, it made a lot of sense to come up with a tried-and-true "takeout" building designed to operate at peak efficiency. Massey and Brown assigned Atlanta franchisee Ted Davis the task of coming up with this design.

The second necessity for Kentucky Fried Chicken was to get the word out. Up to now, the company had left advertising up to each individual franchisee, which meant that there were no Kentucky Fried Chicken advertisements on television. For the most part, the only people who knew about Kentucky Fried Chicken were the people who stumbled across a location.

The third change the company needed to make was in the pay arrangement between company and franchisees. A nickel per bird may have made sense to the Colonel, but accountants preferred a verifiable system where franchisees paid a percentage of revenues. They also needed to work into contracts a method whereby the company could audit a franchisee if need be.

It would be easy to work standardization, advertising, and a new pay arrangement into contracts with new franchisees, but that left the issue of the many and different existing contracts. In order to get existing franchisees on board, Massey and Brown used both the carrot and the stick. Under the proposed new program, existing franchisees had to agree to build standardized buildings, contribute twenty-five dollars per month per location toward a national advertising campaign, and pay 3 percent of revenues to the company if they wanted to build new outlets. Massey and Brown also came up with a program of stock options that allowed a franchisee to buy into Kentucky Fried Chicken Corp. as he or she opened new locations.

This new arrangement at first caused a rift between the company and its franchisees. But those franchisees that stayed with the company, signed new contracts, built new outlets, and acquired stock options would eventually have cause to be very happy about the new program. Franchisees who left the company were replaced quickly.

When the Louisville franchise came open, Massey called Shoney's Big Boy franchisee Ray Danner up and talked him into taking it over.

How the company handled the production and distribution of its secret recipe was important. In order to minimize the number of people who knew it, half the formula was made in one place and half in another before they were mixed together by a third group of employees. The mixture was then shipped to franchisees in bags, who mixed it with twenty-five bags of flour and five cups of salt.

In early 1966, KFC got back to the business of selling franchises. Under the new arrangement, new franchise holders had to pay a three thousand dollar fee, buy or lease sixteen thousand dollars worth of cooking equipment, and build or lease a store that cost about forty thousand dollars. They were also required to attend a company-owned school in Louisville where the cooking methods of Professor Emeritus Harlan Sanders were the required curriculum.

The new arrangements between company and franchisee would eventually put Kentucky Fried Chicken commercials on national television. But during the first couple of years after Massey and Brown bought the company, the advertising program hadn't really started to gel, leaving the company to make do with whatever free press it could muster. In this area, Massey and Brown were truly fortunate, because they had on board a one-man publicity machine named Harlan Sanders.

Years later, when the effect that free television publicity had on a brand became better understood, it would be quite difficult to get the front man for a fried chicken outfit on national television free of charge. But network television shows were easier to crack in the 1960s, and Colonel Harlan Sanders was a novelty. Shortly after Sanders sold his company to Massey and Brown, a public relations consultant for the company got the Colonel a slot on the television game show *What's My Line*. Shortly thereafter, Sanders appeared on *The Tonight Show*, *The Merv Griffin Show*, and several other national programs. The white-suited, goateed Colonel was a hit on TV for the same reason that businessmen such as Orville Redenbacher and Dave Thomas were hits in later years: he was quirky, original, and genuine.

Massey and Brown also encouraged the cult of Harlan Sanders by wearing—and requiring other Kentucky Fried Chicken executives to wear—string ties at work and in all company photographs.

After Kentucky Fried began generating advertising money, it hired the Nashville advertising firm Noble-Dury to devise a way to get the public's attention. Noble-Dury's first series of commercials were loosely based on the British movie *Tom Jones*, which had just come out. In the commercials, costumed men and women devoured chicken by candlelight while gazing lustily at each other. "I remember when they hit the air, because they just blew the roof off our business,"

Hopper said. Franchisees who had complained about paying for advertising piped down.

The *Tom Jones* commercials were effective but short-lived. The next year, KFC began producing television commercials featuring Colonel Sanders himself. Soon a majority of Americans recognized Sanders and had heard the company's two catch phrases: "Finger-lickin' good" and "Secret recipe of eleven herbs and spices." In 1968 alone, the company spent over $9 million on advertising.

Harlan Sanders turned out to be much more than just a spokesman. A cantankerous old man who viewed his recipes as his greatest achievements, Harlan Sanders wasn't about to let the company serve bad food in his name. During the last decade of his life, Sanders became a one-man quality control team that no one at KFC could—or wanted to—rein in. "During his travels on company business, he will occasionally pay an unexpected visit to a KFC outlet in order to inspect the kitchen and sample the gravy," the *New Yorker* once reported. "If the gravy meets his low expectations, he delivers one of his withering gravy critiques, sometimes emphasizing his points by banging his cane on whatever furniture is handy. Months or even years after these ordeals, franchisees winced at the memory of such a gravy judgment from the Colonel as 'How do you serve this God-damned slop? With a straw?'"[6]

Other franchisees grew to appreciate the Colonel because he gave them advice behind management's back. Dave Wachtel III, who worked for Louisville franchisee Ray Danner in the 1960s, remembered the time that Sanders tasted his chicken and announced that there was something wrong with it. "The Colonel came in and said, 'The ginger's wrong. They're using domestic ginger. They're not using imported Jamaican ginger.' So from then on, we added four ounces of Jamaican ginger to our spice pack. And next thing you know our sales went up."

Although Sanders frequently complained about the company making alterations to his chicken and gravy recipes, most people affiliated with KFC said that it devoted considerable attention to the food. "They were extremely meticulous about the quality of the chicken that came out of every store," said Ben Betty, owner of a Nashville machine shop that designed and produced cooking equipment for KFC in the late 1960s.

Kentucky Fried Chicken went public on March 18, 1966, with 425,000 shares of stock hitting the market at fifteen dollars per share. For the next three years, the company's sales growth, franchise growth, and stock growth were unparalleled in the history of restaurants. In 1966 and 1967, the company opened about three hundred new outlets. In 1968 it opened about six hundred. Soon the red and white striped chicken stores were more plentiful than the McDonald's arches.

Meanwhile, sales per unit soared, mainly because of a discovery made by the company about the nature of the chicken business. "The takeout arrangement worked wonderfully, because it turns out that chicken is an eat-at-home food anyway," Brown said.

During Massey and Brown's first two years running the company, they devoted all their attention to standardizing stores, selling franchises, and advertising. But after the initial public offering, they came up with another way of helping the stock, and that was to buy up the more profitable franchises. "Since the restaurants themselves were very profitable businesses, it made a lot of sense to buy them and make a 15 percent royalty rather than a 2 percent royalty," Brown said. Between 1968 and 1970, KFC bought over fifty of its franchisees and over five hundred restaurants, always by exchanging stock in the company for an amount equal to five to six times the franchise's earnings. In doing so, the company turned many franchisees into instant millionaires. One was Dave Thomas, who in 1974 started Wendy's Old Fashioned Hamburgers restaurant chain.

In 1965, Kentucky Fried Chicken earned $800,000 on a gross of $8.5 million. Four years later, it earned $12.1 million on a gross of $430 million. The young Louisville lawyer and the Nashville venture capitalist—neither of whom had taken a business course in his life—had revolutionized the restaurant business.

Harlan Sanders came to regret his decision not to take any KFC stock as a part of his sale. That regret would occasionally surface in the form of bitterness, as it did at the 1966 meeting of the franchisees. But Sanders got his $2 million and at least had the satisfaction of knowing that he had made many of his friends rich. Franchisees (and other friends of Sanders) who bought the stock in 1964 and 1965 became rich beyond their wildest dreams because of the stock's later performance. By 1970 Sanders's personal secretary was worth over $3 million and Pete Harman, a Utah man who was the Colonel's first franchisee in 1956, was worth over $15 million.

Sanders, the one-time jack-of-all-trades, also had the satisfaction of being warmly received in that most inhospitable of places: the New York Stock Exchange. In January 1969, when Kentucky Fried Chicken was listed on the big board, floor traders cheered Colonel Sanders while he handed out drumsticks.

By that time, however, Kentucky Fried Chicken was no longer the pride of Nashville. In October 1968, the company announced that it was moving its corporate headquarters to Louisville—an idea that Massey and Brown had discussed as early as 1964. "When Jack and I bought the business, we made a deal that we would only be based in Nashville for two years, but things got so hectic that that turned into four years," Brown said. "This was the only big thing that Jack and I disagreed on, and it strained our relationship and I regret that. But I felt almost patriotic about Kentucky Fried Chicken being in Kentucky."

By 1969, the franchise industry that Kentucky Fried Chicken had helped create was beginning to get a bad name. A couple of ventures started by KFC, such as a chain of fish-and-chip restaurants and a chain of roast beef restaurants, had failed. And Wall Street had become so adapted to enormous earnings growth that the stock price was being damaged by the fact that its growth was coming down to earth. "I remember going to Wall Street and telling them that we were only to grow 50 percent a year for the next five years," Brown said. "Our stock fell eight points the next day."

After Kentucky Fried moved its offices to Louisville, Massey continued to make six or eight trips a year to the company headquarters. But by this time, he had become more involved in other enterprises, such as Hospital Corporation of America and a new venture capital company called Massey Investment Corp. In March 1970, Massey resigned as KFC chairman.

Brown stayed with KFC for two more years but said he no longer enjoyed it nearly as much as he had before they bought out so many franchisees and brought them to the home office. "At one point, I had twenty-one millionaires reporting to me," Brown said. "Eventually, I realized that once they made a million dollars they were gone. They were into condominiums and depreciation and stuff like that. I remember my wife Elle telling me that I should fire them all, and she was probably right."

In 1972, Massey and Brown sold KFC to Heublein for $239 million, about $100 million of which went to Massey. The next year, Brown resigned from KFC to run for governor of Kentucky.

Kentucky Fried Chicken made so many people rich and made it look so easy, that it was inevitable that there would be imitators. None was more famous than Minnie Pearl's Fried Chicken—one of the most bizarre chapters in Nashville business, political, and journalism history.

Minnie Pearl's was the brainchild of John Jay Hooker Jr., a colorful, energetic, and well-connected Nashville attorney who narrowly lost the Democratic nomination for governor in 1966. As KFC grew and its franchisees and shareholders became wealthy, Hooker and his younger brother and law partner Henry became convinced there was room for a second fried chicken chain. According to several people with whom they discussed the idea, they built their case on two arguments. One was that the success of Kentucky Fried Chicken paved the way for such a business, much like Coke had paved the way for Pepsi. The other was that there were many medium-size markets into which KFC had not yet moved.

There was, however, one important difference between Minnie Pearl's Fried Chicken and Kentucky Fried Chicken. KFC had started small and grew under the watchful eye of Harlan Sanders, who spent years perfecting his recipe and cultivating his market before he sold the company. The Hooker brothers, on the other hand, had not run a single restaurant before.

Nevertheless, John Jay and Henry Hooker were thinking big. And both acknowledged that they were inspired by Rogers Caldwell, who forty years earlier had put together his financial empire in the same building that in the mid-1960s housed the law office of Hooker & Hooker. "I hope you make as much money as I did in this building," Caldwell told the Hooker brothers in the early 1960s. "But I hope you keep more of it than I did."[7]

During the next several months, John Jay and Henry Hooker sold stock in the new venture for fifty cents or one dollar per share to their friends, relatives, and political supporters, among them: U.S. Representative Richard H. Fulton, former Tennessee Secretary of State Eddie Friar, Federal Judges William Miller and Frank Gray Jr., attorney Bill Willis, *Tennessean* publisher Amon Carter Evans, *Tennessean* editor John Seigenthaler, *Banner* publisher Jimmy Stahlman, former state legislator (and later federal judge) Tommy Wiseman Jr., attorney Jim Neal, Democratic activist (and later Davidson County sheriff) Fate Thomas, former University of Tennessee football coach Doug Dickey, Commerce Union banker Bill Earthman, and Ingram Corp. president (and Henry Hooker's brother-in-law) Bronson Ingram. Several of those buyers borrowed money from Commerce Union Bank to buy the stock, the bank agreeing to lend money for the stock purchases.

Some early stockholders, such as Fulton, Seigenthaler, and Ingram, would later claim they were reluctant to buy the stock at first and did so after some arm-twisting by John Jay Hooker. "In Bronson's mind, it was money he had kissed goodbye forever," Martha Ingram said. But according to Jimmy Bradford Jr. of J. C. Bradford & Co., many people were begging John Jay to let them have a shot at it. "People just went hog-wild," said Bradford, who said he never bought any of the stock. "I remember going to a cocktail party where John Jay walked in and there were about ten people wanting to grab him because they wanted to get in."

Hooker's idea caught fire, thanks to his personal magnetism and the free publicity given to him by Nashville's newspapers. On Sunday, June 18, 1967, the *Nashville Tennessean* ran a front-page story announcing the "establishment" of Minnie Pearl's Fried Chicken. In the story, John Jay Hooker predicted that the firm—which had not yet sold a drumstick—

would have five hundred stores by the end of 1970. "It's going to be fun for me," Sarah Cannon (Minnie Pearl's real name) was quoted as saying. "I think it's about time I went into some sort of business."

Nashville architect Earl Swensson came up with a design for the Minnie Pearl's restaurants based loosely on the colors of Minnie Pearl's hat. In August, the company announced it had sold its first group of franchises to a group of Knoxville businessmen that included Dickey. On October 14, the *Tennessean* reported that the company had sold a block of thirty franchises "representing an eventual investment of $4 million" to a group of Shelbyville investors. Three days later, Minnie Pearl's was back on the front page, this time for having sold a block of ten franchises in Atlanta. The company made the front page again on December 31, when it sold thirty franchises in Florida and thirty in California. By this time, the company had opened its first restaurant, a stand-alone building in front of its headquarters at 2708 Franklin Road.

Minnie Pearl's Fried Chicken publicity shot (postcard).

The cost of franchises and the company's method of reporting franchise fees in its income statement would eventually come under fire from the Securities and Exchange Commission. During Minnie Pearl's first few months of existence, the company sold a single franchise (or the exclusive right to operate a Minnie Pearl's restaurant in a particular region) for twenty thousand dollars. The company preferred to sell a group of franchises rather than a single franchise in order to raise more money. Franchisees paid 10 percent of this amount up front and agreed to pay the other 90 percent later. But Minnie Pearl's Chicken Systems Inc.

reported the entire twenty thousand dollars as earnings at the time of the agreement. Not only was this accounting method unusual (Kentucky Fried Chicken did not report franchise fees in this manner), it also burdened Minnie Pearl's with extremely high nonrecurring earnings that it could never repeat. But company officials including Henry Hooker would later defend this practice, claiming that the company's accounting firm instructed them to do it this way.

By February 1968, Minnie Pearl's had sold the rights to almost three hundred franchised stores, only five of which were in operation. It was then that the company announced its intention to sell almost 300,000 shares to the public. According to documents filed with the SEC, the stock was already owned by about one hundred Tennessee residents. Leading shareholders were John Jay and Henry Hooker— who owned 650,000 shares between them—and Sarah Cannon, who owned 96,000 shares.

By the time the stock went public, its sale had been cleared in twelve states, including New York. But its registration was not approved by the Tennessee Department of Insurance and Banking because the commissioner viewed the offering price—"a maximum of $30 per share"—as too high.[8]

Fair or not, Minnie Pearl's stock was a hit on the initial public offering or IPO day, rising from $20 to $40.50 a share on May 2, 1968. The Hooker brothers had pulled it off, turning an idea into a company worth $64 million, at least on paper.

During the summer that followed, many Nashville residents began their day by checking the Minnie Pearl's stock price and shaking their heads in amazement. Only a few weeks after the IPO—apparently confident it had perfected one concept and was ready to move onto another—Minnie Pearl's announced it was starting a second chain named after black gospel singer Mahalia Jackson. Before news of Mahalia Jackson's had sunk in, the company announced it was starting a third chain called Minnie Pearl's Roast Beef (to imitate Arby's).

On August 3, 1968, the "grand opening" of Minnie Pearl's five Nashville outlets made the *Tennessean* front page. The next day, the morning paper gave front page coverage to yet another speculative venture by the company—the development of a chain of dry cleaning establishments. A week later, Minnie Pearl's announced it had earned $2.6 million on revenues of $6.2 million for the first six months of the year. Boosted by this news, the stock climbed to $56 a share. By September, the company had sold the rights to eight hundred restaurants, less than forty of which had actually opened.

In October 1968, *Fortune* magazine ran an article that sounded a skeptical note for the long-term success of Minnie Pearl's. "Profits from actual food sales are still very slim, but profits from franchise

Several friends gather to wish Minnie Pearl Fried Chicken the best. From left to right: Roy Acuff, John Jay Hooker Jr., Mrs. Richard H. Fulton, Congressman (and later Mayor) Richard H. Fulton, Sarah Cannon (a.k.a. Minnie Pearl), and Tex Ritter (Tennessean).

sales have been very strong," the story said. "If the food does not agree with the people who are supposed to patronize all these outlets, then Minnie Pearl's will find itself with a balance sheet full of deserted buildings."[9] The Nashville media, however, would have no such skepticism for another year.

At this point, the Hooker brothers hired long-time friend and Commerce Union executive Ed Nelson to be president of the company. Years later, Nelson said he became concerned about the direction that the business was headed almost immediately. Nelson knew they could sell franchises for only so long. Eventually, the focus had to be changed from selling franchises to approving sites, opening stores, and selling chicken. Minnie Pearl's simply did not have the organization—or the money—to do this. "Being president of the company was like being shackled to the train tracks when you know there is a train coming right at you," Nelson said.

John Jay and Henry Hooker also tried to strengthen the company's board of directors by appointing Life & Casualty president Guilford Dudley Jr. as a director. Years later, Dudley said he would never forget the first—and last—board meeting he attended. "They couldn't even have a board meeting. Neither Henry nor John Jay would come in because they were too busy on the telephone. . . . We were sitting there waiting for them and waited for an hour for one of them to come in so that we could have a quorum.

"After that, I decided I did not want any part of it and I got out. I wish I'd sold my stock then."

By the end of 1968, Minnie Pearl's still had fewer than forty restaurants open, almost none of which was making a profit. It also had over a hundred under construction and another three hundred in some stage of development. With all the construction plans, real estate acquisitions, equipment distribution, and franchise sales going on, Nelson said there was almost no way to actually figure out how much money was being spent. "It was like watching the Seabees build a new airbase in the Pacific," Nelson said.

A magnificent salesman with little interest in details, John Jay Hooker told Nelson to deal with the nuts and bolts of running the company while he spent all his time and energy coming up with new franchises to sell. In January 1969, Minnie Pearl's Chicken Systems Inc. changed its name to Performance Systems Inc. (PSI) in order to emphasize the idea that it planned to sell more than just fried chicken. Before long, the company announced it was branching off into three new concepts: a start-up day care chain, an automotive repair chain, and a chain of ice cream stands. Meanwhile, the company's stock price was still so strong that the firm made its first acquisition: a 180-unit hamburger chain based in Florida called Royal Castle.

As PSI announced and the daily newspapers reported these grandiose plans, it occurred to the Hooker brothers that there was one very obvious group of people to whom they could sell franchises. By this time, the two-year-old company had made many of the Hookers' friends rich. As many of them sold stock at an enormous gain, the Hookers convinced some of them to reinvest at least some of those gains in roast beef franchisees. Shareholder and U.S. Congressman Richard H. Fulton became a franchisee in California and Florida. Shareholder Tommy Wiseman Jr. became a franchisee in Michigan and in California. Shareholder Jim Neal became the part-owner of a company called West America that owned Minnie Pearl's franchises all over the western United States.

However, not everyone who sold stock bought franchises. Bronson Ingram bought four thousand shares of stock for fifty cents a share, sold it after it went public and built a swimming pool with the proceeds. "We called it the Minnie Pearl's Fried Chicken swimming pool," Martha Ingram said.

Thanks in part to this second wave of franchise sales, PSI continued to have a decent cash flow for the next several months. By March 1969, PSI had sold fourteen hundred franchises, the sale of which managed to offset the high cost of opening over two hundred chicken restaurants.

By this time, Minnie Pearl's had made it look so easy that it had created its own wave of copycats. Among the franchising companies founded in Nashville in 1968 and 1969: Tex Ritter's Chuckwagon, Hank Williams Jr. Barbeque Pits, Al Hirt's Sandwich Salons, Tennessee Ernie's Foods, and Eddy Arnold's Tennessee Fried Chicken. "I sure would hate to be a chicken in Middle Tennessee," Eddy Arnold president Dick Hall said.[10]

The first hint that something was wrong came when Minnie Pearl's restaurants began to open and customers began to taste the food. Its meteoric rise notwithstanding, almost no one at Performance Systems actually knew anything about cooking chicken. This was not a secret; the Hooker brothers admitted to prospective investors that they knew nothing about cooking. But they always downplayed that problem. "One time I told Henry Hooker that no one at the company knows a damn thing about cooking chicken," J. C. (Jimmy) Bradford Jr. said. "And Henry said to me, 'You're damn right. But the easiest thing to do is fix the chicken. We can just call up General Mills or any restaurant we want and they'll get us someone who knows that any time we want.' After the restaurants opened, everyone would go try the chicken and they wouldn't go back after that."

Richard L. Fulton, the son of then-U.S. Representative Fulton, got a job working at the Minnie Pearl's real estate department in 1968. The younger Fulton said the company was building new restaurants so fast that there was no way that the food could possibly have tasted the same. "No two Minnie Pearl's restaurants ever served the same chicken," said Fulton. "The company put out a recipe book that told all the cooks how to make chicken, gravy, rolls and everything, but no one followed it because many of the managers were retired cooks from the military and each wanted to use their own recipe."

Performance Systems had several other problems that had begun to affect its stock price. Convinced that he could leave the details of actually operating a chain of restaurants to others, John Jay Hooker had left fried chicken behind in his mind and had moved on to roast beef, day care centers, and transmission repair by the middle of 1968. As hundreds of franchisees borrowed money and built stores, they found it cost money. As they opened stores, few made a profit, which made the idea of building more stores problematic if not impossible.

Meanwhile, the home office in Nashville was doing little to help them in the way of providing technical expertise and assistance. The big national advertising program promised by the company never materialized. By late summer 1969, banks and Wall Street analysts began to realize that PSI was in real trouble, and the company's stock sank from forty dollars to about ten dollars.

John Jay Hooker's political ambitions also distracted the company's attention from the chicken business. From the beginning, Minnie Pearl's ownership and management had been dominated by the Hooker brothers and their political allies. By the summer of 1969 these workers were spending more time on John Jay's next gubernatorial campaign than helping PSI's franchisees.

Nevertheless, Nashville's local newspapers did not act as if anything were amiss, at least not yet. On August 21, when John Jay Hooker resigned his job with PSI , the *Tennessean* made it sound as if Hooker had built a solid company. "His very entry into the Minnie Pearl's Chicken System—which later became Performance Systems Inc.—was in large measure to answer the political criticism that he had no business experience. Well, he has it now."[11] The *Tennessean* even gave credibility to Hooker's grandiose talk about his next venture, a firm called Corporate Concepts Inc. that the paper explained "will buy franchises of all kinds from Performance Systems."

However, if reporters had dug they would have found a lot of interesting stories. The once high-flying firm had stopped selling franchises. Newly opened Minnie Pearl's chicken and roast beef restaurants were losing money fast. Some were closing within months of opening. Banks, concerned about Minnie Pearl's cash flow situation, were no longer lending money to its franchisees.

Perhaps the most potentially damaging story concerned a related company called Whale Inc. The Hooker brothers started Whale in 1967 in an attempt to form a "conglomerate" of sorts that might diversify their holdings. After buying a couple of small unrelated companies, Whale, which was primarily run by Henry Hooker, bought a group of California Minnie Pearl's franchises with money that the Hookers' had made from PSI stock sales. After going public, Whale's stock shot from two dollars to over fifty dollars a share, making it possible for the company to make several other purchases.

In April 1968, Whale bought Temco, a space heater, stove part, and explosive shell manufacturer on Charlotte Pike, for $4 million in Whale stock. The Hooker brothers later leveraged Temco's assets to buy other Nashville companies. One was the Nashville Bridge Co., which Whale bought from Harry Dyer in November 1968 for $15 million in cash (some of which Whale borrowed from Third National Bank). Others included a machine shop called Dolphin Tool, a steel fabricator called Cole Steel, a yearbook printer called Benson Printing and—in a deal that was signed but never transacted—a century-old brick manufacturer and building supply wholesaler called T. L. Herbert & Sons.

Years later, many Nashville residents remembered Minnie Pearl's in some detail, but few knew anything about Whale. One reason for this disparity is that in 1967 and 1968, while Whale was purchasing assets such as Temco and the Nashville Bridge Co., neither the *Banner* nor the *Tennessean* reported that John Jay and Henry Hooker had anything to do with it. Henry Hooker founded Whale and served as its first president. But the only official at Whale who was ever mentioned in the newspapers before 1970 was its president Albert Hill.

After a couple of years of acquiring assets at a remarkable rate, Whale began to have serious financial problems. For several months, John Jay and Henry Hooker managed to keep the company afloat by moving assets from one part of the company to another. But by the summer of 1969, Whale's stock was sliding fast.

In the fall of 1969, there were more hints that the Hookers' empire was about to come unglued. Ed Nelson, hired a year earlier to put Performance Systems on solid ground, resigned and went back to Commerce Union. Nashville advertising and public relations firm Noble-Dury announced it was dropping the PSI account.

On November 5, PSI made a grave announcement that, unlike most of its other press releases, did not make the front page of either newspaper. The company announced that its retail units had experienced an "unexpected decline" in sales that had caused the company to show "a substantial loss" for the first six months of 1969. Neither paper followed up with more detail. The *Banner* gave more play to an adjacent story about the early success of Hank Williams Jr.'s Barbecue Pits franchise sales.

The revelations about Performance Systems Inc. that surfaced in 1970 are too numerous to detail. But in general, the company had lost enormous amounts of money in its attempt to build a chain of fried chicken outlets overnight. Meanwhile, several divisions of Whale—some of which had long histories of making money—were now losing it.

In February, PSI stated it had lost $5.5 million during the first half of 1969. About that time, PSI came under investigation by the Securities and Exchange Commission for its accounting practices. Soon, *Business Week* dubbed the unwise practice of taking nonrecurring franchise fees and applying them immediately to earnings "Minnie Pearling."[12] The next month, *Fortune* said "the classic example of what can happen to an unsophisticated entrepreneur is provided by the trials and tribulations of Performance Systems Inc., once known as Minnie Pearl's Chicken System."[13]

By late summer, over half of the 250 stores the company had managed to open were closed. The corporate office, which only a year earlier had been coming out with new ventures almost every week, was now over its head trying to help franchisees get out of leases.

As revelations about PSI went from bad to worse, the *Banner* began to change its tone. After all, this was no longer just a business story. The PSI debacle centered on Democratic candidate John Jay Hooker Jr. The Republican *Banner* suddenly couldn't get enough of it. Front page press releases about new PSI franchising ideas disappeared, replaced by pieces about Minnie Pearl's stores that were closing down and Whale subsidiaries that were in financial trouble.

PSI's 1969 report was supposed to have been filed with the SEC in April 1970. In July, the SEC announced that the company still had not filed the report and had been given even more time. That extension may have helped Hooker win the Democratic nomination for governor on August 5, because when PSI came out with its 1969 report in September 1970, the numbers were far worse than anyone had imagined. Incredibly, the three-year-old company had lost almost $31 million in 1969. The annual report also stated that the company's revenues were insufficient to meet its day-to-day needs and that it no longer had the ability to borrow money. PSI stock, which once sold at $67 a share, now fell to 44¢.

About the same time, Whale declared bankruptcy, turning several Nashville employers over to the hands of a receiver. Some of Whale's assets, such as Benson Printing, Dolphin Tool, and Cole Steel, were later returned to the entities from which Whale had bought them. Temco, which once had over seven hundred employees, now had about one-tenth that number. Nashville Bridge, which had a seventy-year record of building bridges, barges, and buildings all over the South, was taken over by a bank that sold it to the American Ship Building Co. of Ohio. Whale stock that had been purchased by long-time Nashville Bridge employees was now worthless.

For the next eight weeks, Republican candidate Winfield Dunn hammered away at Hooker over his business record. Meanwhile, in what became one of the most personal crusades against a candidate by a newspaper in Tennessee history, the *Banner* ran story after story about the Minnie Pearl's debacle on the front page. It even made the unprecedented move of running front-page editorials opposing Hooker's candidacy, citing PSI as evidence of his incompetence. "While Mr. Hooker himself may not care about the misfortunes of those who have become the victims of his get-rich-quick business schemes, four million Tennesseans—already struggling to pay their mounting tax bills—should consider the risks of placing him and his associates in charge of the public treasury," stated one such piece.[14] Meanwhile, *Banner* cartoonist Jack Knox came up with several memorable depictions of a frazzled Hooker, a chicken and a whale nipping at his heels, being dragged down by his legal and financial debacle.

As the PSI fiasco became national news, however, both Nashville newspapers became part of the story. On January 27, 1970, the *New York Times* ran a front-page story in which it pointed out that

Tennessean editor John Seigenthaler, *Tennessean* publisher Amon Carter Evans, and *Banner* publisher Jimmy Stahlman were among the 106 initial investors who got Whale stock for fifty cents a share. Stahlman denied the charge at the top of the front page of his newspaper that day (under the pretext that the stock was in his wife's name). Eight months later, the *Wall Street Journal* ran a front-page story about the danger of newspaper executives sitting on corporate boards. One of the examples it cited was Evans and Seigenthaler serving on Minnie Pearl's board in 1967 and 1968. "As the Hooker fortune fades, critics charge, so did the *Tennessean's* coverage of his franchise company," the story charged.[15]

In a 1999 interview, Seigenthaler admitted that his involvement in the Minnie Pearl's venture was a bad move, even though he made a six-figure profit off his investment. "It was a mistake on my part to join the board," he said in 1999. Seigenthaler said he resigned from the company's board of directors as soon as he realized it was going to be heavily covered in the newspaper. Seigenthaler said he never discussed the coverage and play of the Minnie Pearl's story with then-*Tennessean* business editor Albert Cason. He said the heavy coverage of Minnie Pearl's had more to do with Hooker's political past and future than any grand scheme for profits by shareholding journalists. "It was more than just another company," Seigenthaler said. "Everyone knew that John Jay had just lost the governor's race in part because of his lack of business experience."

As Hooker fought off charges of mismanagement and incompetence, one person who came to his defense was Sam Fleming. "There has been nothing dishonest done," the Third National Bank president told *Business Week*. "A lot of people in Nashville made a lot of money. The only people to lose big were the funds."[16] Fleming was referring to a mutual fund called SMC Investment that bought 305,000 shares of Whale for $27.50 per share in December 1968 and then watched the stock spiral to less than a dollar a share. His defense of Hooker was made all the more remarkable by the fact that the now-bankrupt Whale owed Fleming's bank $3.7 million.

In November 1970, Winfield Dunn defeated Hooker, becoming Tennessee's first Republican governor since the 1920s.

It took years to sort out the legal mess left by PSI. After a year and a half, the SEC ruled that the company had filed financial statements that were false, rewriting the company's 1968 annual report to show that the company lost $1.2 million rather than earned $3.2 million.

That conclusion would eventually prove to be the basis of a class-action lawsuit by PSI's shareholders, who were able to recover a small part of the money lost through ownership of the company's stock. By 1974, the stock was going for less than a quarter a share.

In order to meet its debts, PSI had to sell its major assets, most notably the Royal Castle hamburger chain. That process took until 1975, after which the company became inactive for two years. Then, in 1977, the company actually made a comeback under a Nashville attorney named John Chambers, who converted it into a small computer company and changed its name to DSI Corp.

Many Nashville residents—especially those who invested in it—never forgot the Minnie Pearl's fiasco. "It is one of those experiences that I have to look back on and laugh, because I screwed it up," said Thomas Wiseman Jr., who watched his expensive roast beef franchise become worthless. "John Jay was a great idea man. But he did not follow through with a lot of implementation, and that was what happened to the company. The thing could have succeeded."

For former Congressman Richard H. Fulton, the Minnie Pearl's experience was one he would just as soon forget. "I never have been one to dwell on the past," Fulton said in 1998. Although Fulton claimed that the Minnie Pearl's investment brought him more headaches than profits because he too bought franchises with his capital gain, the experience changed his life in an unforeseen way. Fulton met his second wife Sandra Ford—then John Jay Hooker's secretary—on one of his trips to the Minnie Pearl's office.

For Fulton's son Richard, the experience was one he looked back on with a combination of amusement and cynicism. But years later, the younger Fulton said he probably learned more during his two years at Performance Systems Inc. than he would have learned anywhere else. "It led me to real estate," said Fulton, who later became chairman of a commercial real estate company called Grubb & Ellis/Centennial.

For Ed Nelson, who went on to be president of Commerce Union Bank, the Minnie Pearl's experience was a diversion that people never stopped kidding him about. "The day I left, I was extremely relieved and immediately felt that I had the best education of my life," Nelson said years later. "But I was very lucky to graduate from it."

For John Seigenthaler, who remained an executive with the *Tennessean* until 1991, the experience made him realize the danger of stock ownership and board membership. "It was a wonderful lesson and it taught me where I belonged, which was in that newsroom," he said. "And in the end, it made me a better editor." Seigenthaler said that about the same time as the Minnie Pearl's fiasco, he resigned from the Rotary Club because of its refusal to accept black members. The two experiences kept Seigenthaler from joining boards for the rest of his tenure at the *Tennessean*.

Like most everyone else who got Minnie Pearl's Fried Chicken stock before the company went public, Opry star Sarah Cannon made a lot of money off her investment. But Cannon, a Ward-Belmont graduate who managed to walk in both country music and Nashville society circles her whole life, was embarrassed about the failure of the company that carried her stage name. "She was very bothered by all the negativity and the fact that she was attached to something that had a stigma to it like that," said Tree Publishing executive Buddy Killen, a friend of Cannon's.

Although John Jay Hooker Jr. ran for public office again, he never came as close to winning an important post as he did in 1970. For the rest of his life, people wondered what might have happened had the Minnie Pearl's fiasco never happened and had Hooker won the governor's race in 1970. Some went as far as to speculate that Hooker—a more inspirational speaker than a Georgia governor named Jimmy Carter—would have been in line to take advantage of the political vacuum that followed the Watergate scandal.

Nevertheless, the rise and fall of Minnie Pearl's Chicken Systems by no means put Hooker on the outside for the rest of his life. Five years later, he would help engineer a transaction that would make him publisher of the *Nashville Banner*.

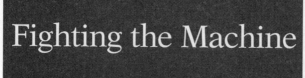

CHAPTER 14

Fighting the Machine

Karl Eller, John Seigenthaler, and John Jay Hooker Jr. walked out of Amon Carter Evans's office, their minds racing about what the deal meant to them. To Eller, it meant more money. To Seigenthaler, it meant he probably had to leave town. To Hooker, it meant a chance to get out of debt.

As the three men walked into the parking lot, Hooker reminded Eller that he was entitled to five hundred thousand dollars for having bartered the sale of the *Tennessean* to Gannett—not bad money for a few days' work. Eller told Hooker that he would give him the money the day the deal was finalized.

The next thing that took place was so surprising that Seigenthaler never forgot it. Hooker told Eller he could keep the five hundred thousand dollars. That is, Eller could keep the money if he gave Hooker the right to form a consortium to buy the *Nashville Banner*.

"Mr. Hooker," Eller said. "No one has ever given me half a million dollars before."

Eller and Hooker agreed. With their handshake, Hooker became part owner of the *Nashville Banner*, the newspaper that had crusaded against him in two previous gubernatorial races.

"I went back to my office sad but laughing," Seigenthaler said later.

The story of Nashville's newspapers in the twentieth century centers on two families named Stahlman and Evans.

Edward Bushrod Stahlman was born in Germany in 1843 and broke his leg as a boy, leaving him lame for life. His family emigrated to

Louisville when he was ten years old. A few years later during the Civil War, the teenage Stahlman had the good fortune of meeting a railroad engineer named Albert Fink. When Gen. John Morgan's Confederate raiders blew up a Louisville & Nashville Railroad tunnel near Gallatin, Stahlman was one of the workers who came south to fix it. Fink, by that time a young executive with L&N, recognized Stahlman and had his friend put in charge of the commissary. A few months later, Stahlman was arrested by the Union army for selling food to people who had family members in the Confederate army. Fink secured Stahlman's release.

After the war ended, Stahlman remained in Nashville, married, and went to work for L&N. Between 1870 and 1880, Stahlman held several executive jobs at L&N, including freight agent and traffic manager. His acquaintance with Fink, who eventually became president of the railroad, no doubt played some role in Stahlman's rapid rise at the company.

The *Nashville Banner* had been organized in 1876 but was on shaky financial ground during its first few years of existence. Twice in the 1880s, Stahlman stepped in and invested about fifty thousand dollars in the *Banner* to keep it from going into bankruptcy. In 1885, Stahlman bought out *Banner* owner A. L. Landis Jr. and became the paper's sole owner. "His friends advised vigorously against it," one *Banner* history states. "They suspected that he did it because he was very fond of newspaper editorials."[1]

Stahlman expanded the *Banner's* circulation by broadening the paper's coverage and setting up a network of state correspondents. He also showed right away he was not afraid to use the paper to help his former employer. One of the most contentious local debates in the 1890s was whether the city of Nashville should issue $1 million in bonds to help Jere Baxter build the Tennessee Central Railroad. The *Banner* consistently editorialized against Baxter and from that point on was a loyal ally of Nashville's dominant railroad.

In 1905, Stahlman and several investors, including Nashville Trust president Joseph Thompson, hardware merchant J. Horton Fall, Southern Soda Works executive William Cummins, Bon Air Coal Co. president Jesse Overton, and real estate developer Thomas Felder organized the Mecklenburg Real Estate Company. That firm developed the Stahlman Building, a $750,000, twelve-story structure that for years towered over Nashville's skyline and served as the home to Nashville's Fourth National Bank. Stahlman helped the property by regularly running a list of its tenants on page three of the *Banner*. Three years after the Stahlman Building was completed, the *Banner* editor made a major investment in the $350,000 Hermitage Hotel.

In addition to his local contacts, Stahlman had them in Washington and used them to his financial advantage at least once. At the end of the

Civil War, the Southern Methodist Publishing House sued the federal government for war damages. For decades, it did not look as if anything would come of this claim. But in 1895, the publishing entity hired Stahlman to lobby on its behalf and agreed to pay him 35 percent of whatever sum he could collect. Three years later, when Congress voted to give the Southern Methodist Publishing House $288,000 in damages, Stahlman collected a $100,000 fee. But in a subsequent Senate investigation, Stahlman admitted that he told several U.S. senators that the entire $288,000 was going to the church.

The founder of the *Nashville Tennessean* was Luke Lea, a descendant of one of Nashville's earliest mayors. In 1906, at the age of twenty-seven, Lea first made news when he presided over the state Democratic convention. By the next year, when Lea's father gave him fifteen thousand dollars to start a newspaper, he was known to be an advocate of Prohibition and an outspoken critic of the Louisville & Nashville Railroad. One of the reasons Lea thought Nashville needed another newspaper was that both the *Banner* and *American* were closely allied with L&N.

The *Tennessean* (as the *Nashville Tennessean* became known in 1972) lost a lot of money during its first few years and might not have survived had it not been for the most sensational murder in Nashville history. In the Democratic primary for governor in 1907, Malcolm Patterson defeated Edward Carmack after an especially ugly campaign. After the primary ended, Lea hired Carmack to be editor of the *Tennessean*. From that point on, the *Tennessean* became a harsh critic of Patterson, portraying him as a puppet of liquor forces. The newspaper's editorials also made many sarcastic references to a Patterson advisor named Duncan Cooper.

On November 9, 1908, Carmack ran into Cooper and his son Robin near the corner of Seventh and Union. Three shots were fired. Within seconds, the *Nashville Tennessean* editor lay dead in the street.

The trial of Duncan and Robin Cooper lasted two months. In the end, the Coopers were found guilty of second-degree murder and sentenced to twenty years each in prison. However, neither man served his term because Patterson pardoned Duncan Cooper and the state supreme court reversed Robin Cooper's conviction.

It is easy to understand why Edward Carmack became a martyr and why many Nashville residents were in an uproar over the fact that no one served jail time for his murder. Only months after Carmack's death, the state legislature passed Prohibition over Patterson's veto. Two years later, Tennessee voters rejected Patterson and elected Ben Hooper, Tennessee's first Republican governor since Reconstruction. Eventually, the state erected a statue of Carmack beside the capitol.

The entire Carmack-Patterson saga played out on the front page of the *Tennessean*, which became a must-read during that period.

High circulation numbers during the Carmack trial were one of the reasons Lea was able to buy controlling stock of the *American* in 1910 and merge the two papers together, creating a strong rival to the *Nashville Banner*.

The rivalry between Lea's *Tennessean* and Stahlman's *Banner* played itself out many times in the 1910s and 1920s. At times, the battle between the newspapers involved businesses, such as the time a *Tennessean* crusade led to Interstate Commerce Commission hearings on the power of L&N Railroad in 1922. At times, it got ugly, as when Lea questioned Stahlman's loyalty as an American citizen during the anti-German crusades of World War I. And at times things got a bit bizarre, such as the time Luke Lea—an army colonel during the war—tried to kidnap Kaiser Wilhelm of Germany.

Despite the newspapers' political differences, however, they had a lot in common. Early in the twentieth century, both the *Banner* and *Tennessean* got the lion's share of their revenue from five types of advertisers. The largest group was patent drugs, which constantly ran exaggerated claims about how their secret formula could cure any ailment. Example of these drugs included Drake's Palmetto Wine (for bladder problems), Dr. Thatcher's Worm Syrup (children's intestinal problems), and Dr. Bell's Pine Tar Honey (lungs). The next largest group was department stores, which between 1900 and 1915 included The Palace, Lebeck Brothers, Cain-Sloan, Castner-Knott, and the New York Store. Behind them were specialty retailers such as Hirshberg Brothers, Lowenheim Brothers, and Timothy's. Next in line were brand name food products, such as Postum, Maxwell House Coffee, and Lion Coffee. After the advent of a chain called H. G. Hill, grocery stores also became regular advertisers.

The *Banner* and *Tennessean* also had similar styles when it came to marketing themselves and had no problem with the idea of mixing absurd promotions with news. In 1901, the *Banner* gave away tickets to the opera to get new subscribers and published front-page stories on the promotion for a week. Other prizes the *Banner* gave away to new subscribers during this period included dictionaries, bikes, ponies, and handguns. Seven years later, the *Tennessean* gave away fourteen trips to Europe and publicized it on the top of its front page.

Another area in which the *Banner* and *Tennessean* were almost identical was in business coverage. During the first three decades of the twentieth century, both Nashville newspapers contained weekly pages devoted to business. The short articles in these sections were usually straight from companies and written by executives. The weekly business pages usually contained advertisements for large companies such as Gray & Dudley, Phillips & Buttorff, Colonial Milling Co., and Life & Casualty Insurance Co.

Also of interest were the *Tennessean* and *Banner's* special sections honoring a particular business when it hit a milestone or moved into a new building. The newspapers made money from such sections by selling advertisements to firms that did business with the company being honored. In November 1928, the *Tennessean* carried an entire section honoring Jarman Shoe Co. for the construction of its new factory in East Nashville. Two years later, the *Banner* came out with a special section to commemorate Watts Laundry's move into a new building. In that section, the *Banner* sold advertisements to Hippodrome Motor Co. (which sold trucks to Watts), St. Bernard Coal (which sold coal to Watts), and Clayton Paving (which did work on the new building).

Finally, each newspaper saw it as its duty to promote the city's commerce. When businesses were formed, there were usually glowing stories about them in the paper. When conventions came to town, they almost always made the front page. In 1903, the *Banner* listed twelve reasons real estate had increased in value in the city during the previous eight years. Reason number seven was, "Eight years ago, our people were despondent and timid, while now they are optimistic and aggressive."[2] Five years later, a *Tennessean* news story about Nashville's developing suburbs declared, without attribution, "She [Nashville] stands today as one of the most prosperous cities in the south, with prospects far brighter than they have ever been."[3]

Both newspapers were also alike in that they had no black reporters and generally did not cover the black community. This neglect gave four African-American entrepreneurs the impetus for a new publication. In 1906, Richard Boyd, Henry Allen Boyd, Joseph Battle, and Dock Hart started the weekly *Nashville Globe* to provide news and advertisements for the city's black community. The *Globe* used printing presses owned by Richard Boyd's National Baptist Publishing Board.

Although the *Globe's* circulation never rivaled that of the *Banner* or *Tennessean*, it played a vital role in the life of some of Nashville's most important black institutions, such as Fisk University, Citizens Bank, the National Baptist Publishing Board, and Greenwood Park. It also gave a completely different perspective on race-related issues, such as Jim Crow laws and public lynchings.

One reason the *Globe* made a good read was its sarcastic editorials. In April 1907, the *Globe* was infuriated with the fact that the city refused to shut down whorehouses near the capitol. "The deputy sheriffs of Davidson County can scent a Negro crap game twelve miles into the country but seemingly know and can find no evidence of bawdy houses run by Negro women for white men," an editorial stated.[4] The *Globe's* largest advertisers were black-owned businesses such as Greenwood Park and the National Baptist Publishing Board. But many white-owned businesses also advertised in the *Globe* during its early years, including H. G. Hill and Hirshberg Brothers.

In the 1940s and 1950s, Silliman Evans was arguably the most powerful man in Nashville. He would have been the first to tell you that the greatest sources of his power were his luck of being at the right place at the right time and his knack of making friends in high places.

Evans was born dirt poor, the son of a Methodist circuit rider in Joshua, Texas. After dropping out of high school and failing an army physical, he got a job covering rural parts of Texas for the *Ft. Worth Star-Telegram*. After he started covering the state legislature, Evans's relentless reporting style, his penchant for smoking cigars, and his extravagant expense accounts became legendary. "They [state legislators] were making only $5 a day, and Silliman would invite them up to his room to eat, drink and make their long distance telephone calls," Evans's editor explained years later. "He justified it on the grounds that they were all potential news sources. And we had a hard time arguing with him because he was getting the news."[5]

Evans went on to do just as well covering Congress as he had the legislature. After the *Star-Telegram* made him its Washington correspondent in 1924, he made friends and enemies among the nation's most powerful people. Among the former was Texas Senator John Garner, who would often sneak off and drink with Evans in the U.S. Capitol. Among the latter was Texas Senator Earle Mayfield, who once slugged Evans in an elevator.

In 1928, Evans left journalism to work as head of public relations for a start-up airline called Texas Air Transport, which at the time did nothing more than move mail. During the next few years, Evans traveled the country, securing leases and landing rights for his company. His circle of powerful friends grew wider and soon included an airline promoter named Victor Emanuel. In 1930, Texas Air Transport became one of the key parts of a new company called American Airways (which later changed its name to American Airlines). Evans later became an American Airlines board member.

In the spring of 1932, Evans took a leave of absence from the airline to head up Garner's presidential campaign. The Texas senator lost the Democratic nomination to Franklin Roosevelt but did so well in the race that Roosevelt selected Garner to be his running mate. (Years later, Garner reportedly decried that the vice presidency was "not worth a bucket of warm spit.") After Roosevelt defeated Herbert Hoover in the general election, Evans was appointed to the post of Fourth Assistant Postmaster. At first, Evans was disappointed with the position. But he soon found himself in charge of the largest building program in U.S. Post Office history.

Evans's next opportunity was unbelievably fortuitous. One of the many important people with whom he had become acquainted was Jesse Holman Jones, a Texas banker, Springfield, Tennessee, native, and the head of the Reconstruction Finance Corporation (RFC). The RFC's main job was to save bankrupt businesses by loaning them money and, in some cases, by changing their management. In the spring of 1934, Jones was on a train with Evans, Garner, and Texas Congressman Sam Rayburn when he mentioned that he needed to find someone to run a troubled insurance company called Maryland Casualty. Garner waved a cigar in Evans's direction and recommended the former reporter for the job. "But I don't know anything about the insurance business," Evans protested. "That's what we need," Jones told him. "Nobody who knows insurance would take this job."[6] Evans thus became president of an insurance company with about $20 million in premiums per year.

Silliman Evans turned Maryland Casualty around in only three years. His more important moves were bringing in new people to run the company's investment side and hiring a comptroller (which the company had never had before). Evans also made one very dramatic change to Maryland Casualty's culture by buying full-page advertisements in national publications such as *Fortune* and *Business Week*.

Nevertheless, Evans missed journalism. When Caldwell & Co. collapsed in November 1930, one of the assets tied to it was Luke Lea's *Nashville Tennessean*. Lea was able to keep the *Tennessean* out of bankruptcy for another two and a half years. But in March 1933, Nashville's morning newspaper fell into receivership and was placed in the control of a lawyer named Lit Pardue.

In 1937, Evans contacted American National Bank president Paul Davis (whose bank owned about half of the *Tennessean* through its 1930 takeover of the Fourth and First National Bank). Evans's next step was to borrow $290,000 from Victor Emanuel's Aviation Corporation. On January 7, 1937, Davis, acting on Evans's behalf, bid $850,000 for the *Tennessean* at an auction on the courthouse steps. No one bid against Davis, although J. C. Bradford Sr. had given serious consideration to making a play for the newspaper. "Father always told me that he was unable to buy the paper because the Reconstruction Finance Corp. wanted to keep it in Democratic hands," J. C. Bradford Jr. said in 1999.

Silliman Evans wasted little time in making two major changes to the *Tennessean*.

The first had to do with the newspaper's business relationship to its rival. Shortly before coming to Nashville, two newspapers in El Paso, Texas, had received the federal government's blessing to combine their business operations in order to save money. Within weeks of moving to Nashville, Evans approached Jimmy Stahlman, who had succeeded his grandfather as *Banner* publisher upon the elder Stahlman's death in 1930. Stahlman and Evans decided to do the same thing in Nashville.

Under the *Tennessean* and *Banner* Joint Operating Agreement (JOA), the two newspapers formed a single business entity called the Newspaper Printing Corporation (NPC) and agreed to split profits from that point on. NPC contained one circulation, advertisement, accounting, and printing department that worked for both newspapers. NPC's board, which included members of both newspapers, came up with editorial budgets for both newspapers. But the editorial functions and news-gathering operations of both newspapers remained separate.

The JOA set many important precedents. Under the agreement, the *Banner* could not produce a Sunday newspaper or a morning edition, a term that became vital when afternoon newspapers declined later in the century. The JOA also created a business relationship that few Nashville residents understood. There would be many times during the rest of the century when it seemed as if the two newspapers were at each other's throats. In fact, Nashville's two newspapers were business partners. If one paper did well and made money, they both made money. If one did poorly and lost money, they both suffered.

Evans's second move was an offspring of the JOA. In 1937, the *Tennessean's* office was in the Southern Turf Building on Fourth Avenue, a structure so inadequate that its staff was afraid that the building would collapse at any time. The *Banner* was printed a few blocks away, in a building at Third and Church that wasn't much better. Both newspapers needed a new building, but neither could afford one. Evans went to H. G. Hill Sr., who in addition to being the city's largest grocer and the head of the Nashville Trust Co. was the city's largest advertiser. Hill reluctantly agreed to build a $175,000 newspaper plant at 1100 Broadway, which he leased to the *Tennessean* and *Banner*.

The decision to merge their business operations and move into the same building was about the last thing the owners of the *Tennessean* and *Banner* would ever agree on. Evans was a New Dealer who believed government should correct society's wrongs. Stahlman believed that the government that governed least governed best.

In 1938, the *Tennessean* began listing several objectives for which it planned to crusade at the city and state level. Among them were the following: inclusion of the Cumberland River into TVA, smoke abatement, a better airport, a municipal auditorium, and what the paper called "honest elections." During the next several years, as the *Tennessean* crusaded for these goals, the *Banner* often crusaded against them.

The most dramatic of the *Tennessean's* crusades was not against the pro-Republican *Banner* but against an entrenched Democrat, "Boss" Ed Crump of Memphis. In 1891, the Tennessee legislature passed a law requiring citizens to have to pay a tax to vote. This poll tax severely reduced voter turnout and was by the 1920s the key to Crump's political power. Under Evans's leadership, the *Tennessean* fought the poll tax in a fifteen-year battle that involved three governors. The *Tennessean* would eventually win this battle when the constitutional convention of 1953 threw out the poll tax.

There are many interesting aspects to the *Tennessean's* battle with Boss Crump. From a business point of view, the long debate made good theater and helped circulation. Many times during the battle, Evans attacked Crump personally in bitter front-page editorials, calling the poll tax issue "a battle for sacred human rights and political decency." Many times, the *Tennessean* printed Crump's angry responses. "You [Evans] accidentally blew in Tennessee on a money-making scheme three or four years ago and you will probably blow out the same way," a Crump letter in January 1941 stated. "Only a puffed-up foreign frog who did not know the people of this state would assume such arrogance."[7] During the long war between Crump and the *Tennessean*, Crump often bought full-page advertisements in the *Tennessean* to express his contempt for Evans. In doing so, he of course helped the *Tennessean's* bottom line.

The poll tax was probably the most significant political change for which Silliman Evans successfully crusaded, but there were several economic developments in which he played a key role. In 1939, the *Tennessean* attained one of its loftiest goals when the Tennessee Valley Authority bought the Tennessee Electric Power Company's operation in Nashville. A few months later, Evans talked his friend Victor Emanuel into building an aircraft factory in Nashville. Emanuel's factory had seven thousand employees by 1941.

Evans also had a hand in creating one of Nashville's most enduring sports venues. In 1939, a local horseman told Evans about his dream of building a steeplechase course at Percy Warner Park. Evans asked Col. Harry Berry, state director for the Works Progress Administration, if the WPA could build the course. Berry said there was no way. A few weeks later, Evans used his connections to get an audience with Roosevelt. "Well, Silliman, the pink-coat crowd has been ridiculing the WPA so much I think it would be fun to make them the beneficiaries of one of its projects," Roosevelt reportedly told Evans. "We'll do it."[8]

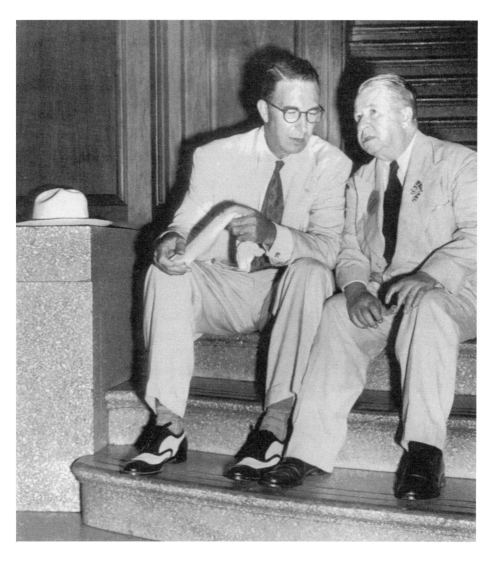

Silliman Evans died in 1955 while attending the funeral of his longtime friend and former boss Amon Carter. Control of the newspaper then fell to Evans's widow and to his oldest son, Silliman Evans Jr. By this time, the *Tennessean's* weekday circulation was 114,000 and had begun to pull away from the *Banner's* at 92,000.

U.S. Sen. Estes Kefauver (left) with Tennessean publisher Silliman Evans, around 1950 (Metro Nashville Archives).

The three decades after World War II would be very competitive years for the two Nashville newspapers. Although reporters from that era can ramble endlessly on this point, it is perhaps best illustrated with three examples.

In 1931, Thomas Buntin, a Belle Meade resident and father of three children, suddenly vanished. Two months later, his former secretary Betty McCuddy also disappeared. An exhaustive search for Buntin and McCuddy followed but turned up nothing. The Tennessee Supreme Court declared Buntin legally dead in 1942, forcing the New York Life Insurance Co. to pay a fifty thousand dollar policy on Buntin.

Eleven years later, the insurance company said it had found Buntin, and it obtained an injunction in Nashville Chancery Court tying up the money still left in Buntin's trust fund. But New York Life refused to say where Buntin was living.

Silliman Evans was determined to find Buntin, especially after one of New York Life's lawyers said Buntin was living in Evans's home state of Texas. Evans dispatched a reporter named John Seigenthaler and a photographer named Jimmy Holt and began using every Texas connection he could think of. After about two weeks, Seigenthaler and Holt located Buntin and McCuddy living together in Orange, Texas, as husband and wife under the name Palmer. The story that ran in the *Tennessean* the next day—November 26, 1953—gave the paper national acclaim.

In 1963, Frank Clement was reelected governor despite the *Tennessean's* opposition to him. The night after Clement's inauguration, *Banner* political reporter Neil Cunningham and *Tennessean* reporter Bill Kovach were drinking whiskey together. Cunningham told Kovach that the new governor wasn't going to give Kovach any stories because of the *Tennessean's* opposition to him. In fact, Cunningham told Kovach, Clement had already given the *Banner* ten stories about his cabinet appointments that were already written and sitting in his desk in the newsroom waiting to be published. "He told me that they were going to do the Chinese water torture to me and dribble them out one a day for the next ten days," said Kovach. "He just kept rubbing it in."

The idea of being tortured for ten days was too much for Kovach. When Cunningham went home, Kovach went to the newspaper office and borrowed a tire iron from fellow reporter Jerry Thompson. Using the iron, Kovach pried open the top of Cunningham's desk and stole the stories.

The next morning, Jimmy Stahlman reported to the police that someone had broken in and burglarized the *Banner*. Kovach came in and apologized to Stahlman. To his great relief, Stahlman dropped the charges and did not demand that the *Tennessean* fire him.

The *Tennessean* would not regret its decision to forgive its young reporter. A year later, Kovach refused to leave the State Senate

Chamber while the legislative body was present, saying he had a right to be present when the lawmaking body was discussing state business. Nashville's morning newspaper backed its reporter with a lawsuit in federal court. After the court backed Kovach, the legislature passed an open meetings law that theoretically required all governing bodies in Tennessee to allow the public to attend.

Kovach left the *Tennessean* for the *New York Times* in 1967 and many years later became curator of the Nieman Foundation. Ironically, the state's so-called "Sunshine Law" actually exempted the state legislature, which is why reporters were still being denied access to key legislative meetings in the late 1990s.

In November 1973, the country music industry was shocked when Grand Ole Opry star David "Stringbean" Akeman and his wife Estelle were murdered at their home. Eight months later one of the suspects in the case, a man named Doug Brown, granted an exclusive interview to *Banner* reporter Larry Brinton in which he confessed to his part in the murder. In that interview, Brown said that he and his brother John had tossed a bag of items from Stringbean's house into a pond in Robertson County. The bag contained several of Stringbean's personal possessions, including his stage costume.

After the interview, Brinton got homicide detective Sherman Nickens and *Banner* photographer Jack Gunter and went on a search for the bag. It didn't take them long to find it. By the time they did, it was at a time of day that if the story had been released at that instant, it would have been in the *Tennessean* before it had been in the *Banner*. To make matters worse, word was already beginning to leak that Brown had confessed and told Brinton the whereabouts of the bag.

Brinton wasn't about to give his biggest story to the competition, so he hid the bag in the trunk of his car and sat in it all day. "We watched them dive for the bag for several hours," Brinton said twenty-five years later. "But I couldn't tell them where it was, because if I had the *Tennessean* would have gotten the story." As soon as the *Tennessean's* deadline had passed, Brinton opened his trunk and turned it over to the police. The next day—July 23, 1974—the *Banner* devoted most of its front page to Brown's confession and Brinton's discovery of the bag.

Another thing that made the *Banner-Tennessean* rivalry intense was how each paper felt about the race issue.

After Silliman Evans's death in 1955, the reins of the *Tennessean* fell to his son Silliman Jr. However, Silliman Jr. died of a heart attack in 1961, leaving the family business to his younger brother, Amon Carter Evans. Not long after taking over, Amon Carter Evans called former *Tennessean* reporter John Seigenthaler—then working for Attorney General Robert Kennedy—and asked him to come back to Nashville to be his editor. "John Seigenthaler was made for the newspaper business," Evans said in 1999. "He is one of those people who gravitates to it and gets his whole insides churned up with it."

Evans and Seigenthaler were both strong advocates of racial integration, and during the 1960s the *Tennessean* became one of the most powerful voices for integration in the South. Jimmy Stahlman, on the other hand, was an old-fashioned southerner who viewed integration as a threat. "I had an old Negro mammy, lived among Negroes and worked with them all my life, and have a deep affection for a lot of them and a high regard for most, but I don't want any part of the NAACP," he told *U.S. News and World Report* in 1956. "People down here just don't believe in social mixing of the races. We want to give the Negro every opportunity to live as a free man in this country, as he is entitled to live under the law. . . . But there are a lot of us who don't want any social integration in any particular, and a lot of us are determined that it isn't going to happen so long as we can do anything about it legally."[9]

In 1960, Vanderbilt University expelled a divinity student named James Lawson for taking part in the sit-in movement downtown. The *Tennessean* blasted Vanderbilt, especially Chancellor Harvie Branscomb. The *Banner* praised Branscomb.

Seven years later, the *Banner* blasted Vanderbilt Chancellor Alexander Heard for his decision to allow black activist Stokely Carmichael to speak on campus.

Stahlman, who wrote a front-page editorial column called "From the Shoulder," frequently mixed his opinions on race relations with his views of international politics. A former navy captain who helped start the Navy ROTC program at Vanderbilt, Stahlman was a great admirer of J. Edgar Hoover and Richard Nixon. He was also such an extreme anti-communist that he occasionally put quotes from Vladimir Lenin over the *Banner's* masthead, just to remind readers about the ubiquitous Red Threat. "A lot of people thought Jimmy Stahlman was a patriot and a lot of people thought he was a racist," said *Banner* reporter Larry Brinton. "I'm not going to argue with either one."

Despite his political differences with Evans and Seigenthaler, Stahlman respected the men who ran the *Tennessean* and worked cordially with them as business partners under the JOA. "Jimmy Stahlman was like a second father to me," said Amon Evans. "He taught me the newspaper business." Stahlman also dreaded the day when he or Evans would have to sell one of Nashville's newspapers to an out-of-town company. "Newspaper ownership, Mr. Stahlman maintained, should not be 'reposed in those whose sole aim is the almighty dollar or who have little or no regard for the high obligations of such trust,'" Mr. Stahlman's obituary stated.[10]

In 1972, Jimmy Stahlman was seventy-nine years old and had no children interested in taking his place. "My sister and I did not want to run it and there was nobody else to leave it to," said his daughter Dr. Mildred Stahlman. After a futile search for a local owner, Stahlman sold the *Banner* to the Gannett newspaper chain for $14.1 million. "At the time, he thought Gannett was a good solid conservative organization," Mildred Stahlman said. Before long, Stahlman would get so upset with the way Gannett ran his old newspaper that he demanded that the publishers take his name and his father's name off the paper's masthead.

During Gannett's tenure as the owner of the *Banner*, there would be no more editorial crusades and no more front-page editorials. Most of the changes that Gannett made to the *Banner* were in the name of standardization and professionalism, done under new *Banner* publisher Wayne Sargent.

Prior to Gannett's purchase of the *Banner*, few stories appeared in either newspaper that companies did not want to see. "The business columns during those years were basically pieced together by press release," said Wayne Whitt, who worked for the morning newspaper from 1946 until 1989. "You did not get much business news out of the *Tennessean* or the *Banner*. If you wanted business news, you had to take the *Wall Street Journal*." One of the first notable changes at the *Banner* after Gannett's purchase of it was that it began doing business stories that were not necessarily straight from a press release.

Pete Bird, one of the first reporters to do non-press release business journalism in Nashville, said it wasn't easy because no one expected it. "In those days, business was about as lowly regarded a beat as obituaries," said Bird, who worked at the *Banner* from 1976 to 1981. "Everyone seemed kind of surprised half the time when I called." Because of the *Banner's* improved business coverage, Nashville's readers knew a lot more about the big business stories of the 1970s—such as the collapse of Genesco—than they knew about the big stories of the 1960s, such as the rise of Kentucky Fried Chicken.

Brinton said there were other things about Gannett's management style that were refreshing. "They never told us what to do editorially, not one time," said Brinton, who became the *Banner's* managing editor under Gannett's ownership. Brinton said it was easier to get money under Gannett than under Stahlman and easier to find good reporters because of Gannett's talent pool.

The same year Gannett bought the *Banner*, the *Nashville Tennessean* changed its name to the *Tennessean* in an attempt to broaden its audience to other parts of Middle Tennessee. During the next few years, there were signs that the *Tennessean* and *Banner* rivalry was beginning to fade. In 1976, the *Tennessean* published several stories by staff historian Hugh Walker to commemorate the

Banner's one hundredth anniversary. Only one of the stories talked much about Gannett, and that one contained only the most basic information about the national newspaper chain. "Is it GANNett or GannETT?" the story began.[11]

However, the relationship between Gannett and the *Tennessean* was awful during the 1970s. As the owner of the *Banner*, Gannett owned the city's smaller newspaper and the paper which could not, by contract, come out with a morning or a Sunday edition. The only real way for Gannett to make more money, therefore, was to put pressure on *Tennessean* publisher Amon Evans to do things their way. But Evans did not have any intention of doing what Gannett wanted him to. "Gannett was not satisfied with the profit margin, and this manifested itself in many ways," said Seigenthaler. "But Amon and his mother were perfectly happy with it.

"Eventually, things got so bad that Amon and Wayne Sargent had a showdown. After that, Amon would only communicate with Wayne through me." At that point, Seigenthaler became convinced that Gannett was either going to sell the *Banner* and withdraw from Nashville or find a way to take over the *Tennessean*.

By the late 1970s, Evans was dealing with some of the same issues that Stahlman had dealt with a decade earlier. After four decades of family ownership, the Evans family had a small fortune in the *Tennessean*. But it was all tied up in a non-liquid asset, and the family would be taxed heavily when it was officially passed from Amon's mother to himself. Amon, then married to his fifth wife, also had the added complication of alimony.

It was in this environment that Karl Eller, owner of a chain of newspapers called Combined Communications, approached Evans about buying the *Tennessean*. At first, Evans turned Eller down. "It was a flat, blunt turndown," Seigenthaler said. Eller did not give up, though. After his first rejection, Eller asked several people in town about Evans and found out that the *Tennessean* publisher had attended grade school with John Jay Hooker Jr. Eller then met with Hooker and hired him to try to broker the sale of the *Tennessean*.

What Evans and Seigenthaler did not know at the time was that someone had sent Eller. Prior to his first trip to Nashville, Eller had agreed to sell Combined Communications to Gannett. As a part of that sale, Eller promised Gannett CEO Al Neuharth that he would try to buy the *Tennessean* from Evans.

After the news about Combined Communications merger with Gannett became public, Eller came back to Evans and offered him $50 million for the paper. The offer was so high, Evans later admitted, that there was no way he could turn it down. Gannett's purchase of the *Tennessean* was announced on July 6, 1979. Years later, Neuharth gave a very brief summary of the transaction in his memoirs. "We got the big paper in town and Evans got wife number six," the Gannett CEO wrote.[12]

Under federal antitrust law, there was no legal way that Gannett could continue to own both Nashville daily newspapers. During the months after Gannett and Evans came to an agreement, Hooker found two investors willing to help him buy the *Banner* for $24 million. One was former Equitable Securities executive Brownlee Currey Jr. The other was a Franklin banker named Irby Simpkins. As Gannett and the *Banner's* future owners negotiated the deal, they also rewrote the newspaper's joint operating agreement, giving the *Tennessean* 70 percent of future profits.

At first, John Seigenthaler was hesitant to work for Gannett because he had previously been a critic of newspaper chains. But after Neuharth agreed to give Seigenthaler complete editorial control over the newspaper, plus a contract that carried him through the age of sixty-five, the *Tennessean* editor changed his mind.

Under Gannett's guidance, the *Tennessean* and *Banner* agreed in 1988 to a $75 million upgrade to their printing presses and enlargement of its building. In the late 1980s, the *Tennessean* showed that it still had teeth by fiercely opposing Bill Boner's mayoral administration. Seigenthaler remained at the *Tennessean* until 1991, when he retired and was replaced as editor by former *Tennessean* reporter Frank Sutherland.

Under Sutherland, the *Tennessean* put more emphasis on features, sports, business, and suburban coverage and less emphasis on political stories and coverage of the courts. The paper also became a strong ally of Mayor Phil Bredesen, supporting the Meharry-Hubbard merger, several tax breaks, and the building of the arena, NFL stadium, and downtown library during Bredesen's tenure. As was always the case during the twentieth century, the paper was not without its critics. "It competes too much with TV instead of concentrating on what a newspaper can do best," former *Tennessean* publisher Amon Evans said in 1999. "And I don't think the newspaper is a voice for change anymore." In 1980, the *Tennessean* had a daily circulation of 130,000 and Sunday circulation of 240,000. By the end of the century, daily circulation was over 170,000 and Sunday's topped 270,000.

The *Tennessean* had always regarded the *Banner* as its main rival, but competition was a more difficult concept for Nashville's morning newspaper to define in the 1990s. For one thing, people were more likely to get their news from television than from newspapers. For another, niche publications were taking a larger percentage of the market than before.

Starting in the late 1960s, Nashville had several generations of monthly glossy magazines, including *Nashville, Nashville!* and *Advantage*. These magazines typically lasted about five years, thriving under their original editorial staffs and dwindling under their successors. In 1985, investor Gary Dunham started a weekly tabloid publication in Nashville called *Business Journal*. About a year of losing money later, the *Memphis Business Journal* bought Dunham's publication and changed its name to *Nashville Business Journal*. Within a few years, *Nashville Business Journal* had built up a circulation of about seven thousand under the editorship of former *Banner* reporter Roger Shirley. In 1998, a Charlotte-based chain called American City Business Journals bought the Memphis and Nashville business journals.

In 1988, a newspaper advertising salesman named Albie Del Favero talked *Banner* reporter Bruce Dobie into helping him start a weekly newspaper. Like other so-called alternative weeklies in other U.S. cities, the newspaper that Del Favero envisioned would be free and contain movie and entertainment listings and a limited amount of news and commentary. After putting together a group of investors through former Commerce Union chief Ed Nelson's venture capital firm Nelson Capital, Del Favero and Dobie took over a shopping weekly called the *Nashville Scene*. It took several months of losing money to convert the *Scene* from a shopping weekly with a circulation of 104,000 to an alternative weekly with a circulation of 55,000. "Every so often, Albie would walk into my office, stand there in front of my desk, and look at me as if a brick had fallen on his head," Dobie wrote later. "'I just don't see how we're going to make it,' he would say. 'We only have about ten weeks to live.'"[13] However, the *Scene* grew so profitable that Del Favero and Dobie bought out the original investors in 1996.

John Jay Hooker Jr.'s stint as *Banner* publisher was short and colorful. One time, Hooker left a group of staffers waiting in his office for thirty minutes while he went out to give a new car a test drive. On another occasion, the *Banner* restaurant reviewer wrote a negative review of one of Hooker's favorite restaurants. Hooker got so angry that he stopped the presses and pulled the story.

Some *Banner* staffers couldn't stand Hooker; Brinton, for example, left the paper and went to work in television at WLAC-TV, Channel 5, because of disputes with Hooker. But other people who worked at the *Banner* at that time got a kick out of working for Hooker. "He was fun to work around," said Mike Pigott, who worked at the *Banner* from 1976 until 1988. "He and I had some knock-down drag-out fights, but I liked him and found him very entertaining to be around."

In January 1982, Currey and Simpkins bought out Hooker's share of the *Banner*. A few years later, former Chamber of Commerce official Eddie Jones was hired as editor of the *Banner*. During the next few years, the *Banner* maintained its status as Nashville's second-largest newspaper by frequently breaking news that the *Tennessean* did not have. But the paper's days of covering the business community critically were over. One story is typical of dozens of anecdotes at the *Banner* during the 1980s and 1990s; business reporter Sharon Curtis-Flair wrote a column in1994 about how silly it was that people who owned Saturn cars were paying to take part in the Saturn Homecoming. After Saturn's corporate office and several Saturn dealerships complained about the column, Jones brought Curtis-Flair into his office and ordered her to make it up to Saturn by writing a nice story about the company. Curtis-Flair ultimately quit over the incident.

As the *Banner's* circulation slid downward in the 1990s, there were constant rumors of its demise. Simpkins vehemently denied that he had any plans to shut down the *Banner*, going as far as telling staffers that he intended to pass on the newspaper to his children. But in February 1998, Simpkins announced that the *Banner's* owners and Gannett had decided to shut the afternoon paper down. Under the deal (the finances of which were not disclosed at the time), Simpkins and Currey were paid $58 million to cease publication, effectively releasing Gannett from the terms of the JOA. The *Banner* owners also agreed to donate the newspaper's archive to the Nashville public library.

CHAPTER 15

The Little General

etween 1969 and 1971, Nashville's attention—as far as restaurants were concerned—was focused on the departure of Kentucky Fried Chicken and the decline of Minnie Pearl's Fried Chicken. But during this period, three other restaurant chains started that would be based in Nashville much longer than KFC or Minnie's. One was a fish-and-chips place in Donelson called Mr. D's, owned by Big Boy franchisee Ray Danner and managed by a young man named Dave Wachtel III. Another was an unusual business—gas station, gift shop, and restaurant—located just off Interstate 40 in Lebanon. Its owner Dan Evins gave his new business the name Cracker Barrel Old Country Store. The third was a sit-down eatery near Vanderbilt called O'Charley's.

Some people drift from business to business because they can't find one at which they excel. In the 1950s, Ray Danner drifted from business to business because he couldn't find one he liked. Danner, whose father was a German immigrant, grew up in a one-room apartment located above his uncle's grocery store in Louisville. After a stint in the Army Air Corps during World War II (he spent two years at flight school but never actually went to the war), Danner went back to Kentucky and tried his hand at a series of small business ventures, all of which he said made a profit. First he bought and operated a small grocery store in Louisville. After he sold it, he built a bowling alley in Cynthiana, Kentucky. "In order to generate business, I went around town and organized leagues," Danner said. Then he built and operated a drive-in movie theater in Clarksville. Next, he moved back to Louisville and started a restaurant and bar.

Around 1955, Danner became intrigued by the success of drive-in restaurants, in particular a chain franchised out of California called Big Boy. Danner approached the Big Boy franchisee in Kentucky, who turned down his offer to buy part of it. Then, Danner went to see a Charleston, West Virginia, man named Alex Schoenbaum, who owned the Big Boy franchises in the entire Southeast and operated them under the name Shoney's Big Boy (Shoney's being a shortened and less ethnic version of Schoenbaum). After some persuasion, Schoenbaum sold Danner the rights to the Big Boy franchise for Tennessee. "At first, my idea was to build them in Clarksville, because that was where my drive-in had been," Danner said. "After I thought about it, I realized that Nashville was definitely the place to go."

In January 1959, Danner and a partner named James Craft opened Tennessee's first Shoney's Big Boy restaurant in a small building near the new Madison Square Shopping Center. Unlike most Big Boy units in that era, Danner and Craft's location including a sit-down restaurant in addition to drive-ins. It also featured a more upscale menu than most Big Boys.

Danner and Craft turned a profit immediately and built new units as quickly as they could finance them. Within four years, there were Shoney's Big Boy restaurants on Thompson Lane, Murfreesboro Road, Gallatin Road, Harding Road, Fourth Avenue, and in Donelson and Clarksville. In 1965, in the midst of all this growth, Craft left the partnership. "He told me I worked too hard," Danner said in 1999.

One reason Shoney's did well was that Nashville had very few restaurants. But it also grew because Danner knew how to run an impeccably clean restaurant where the service was prompt and the food tasted good.

Danner did not run his restaurant chain from a distance, either. Everyone who ever worked for Shoney's will tell you that they lived in fear of Danner's frequent surprise inspections. When Danner showed up, his first stop was usually the bathroom, which he insisted be spotless. If the bathrooms were dirty, he would find someone to clean it fast. If everyone was busy, he would clean it himself and have a talk with the manager later. "If I had to cook or wash dishes or bus tables or clean the shithouse then it wouldn't matter," Danner said. "We'd fix it first, then talk about what happened later."

Throughout most of his career, Sunday was when Danner traveled from restaurant to restaurant giving managers heart failure. In the 1970s, when Shoney's became a huge company and Danner could afford to travel on a private plane, he wouldn't even tell his pilot where they were going until he had started the engine, to make sure no one knew which restaurant he planned to visit. "My restaurants were good because you did not know when I was going to show up, and you did not want me not liking your restaurant," Danner said. "I was a mean little son of a bitch. I had all kinds of names: Thrush, Little General, you name it."

Like a sergeant at boot camp, Danner believed fear eventually bred pride. "Because of the fear, we developed better operations than most of our competitors," Danner said. "But if you made it through the fear portion, you would realize that your sales were great and your store was always clean and the next thing you know you were damn proud of what you did."

However, J. Mitchell Boyd, who managed the Shoney's restaurant on Fourth Avenue in the 1960s and became the company's chief executive in the 1980s, said Danner's style had a tendency to breed "masochistic" people. "Through the process of elimination over the years, Ray weeded out people who wouldn't take a slap on the face and say 'Boy I really needed that,'" Boyd said. "He had one of those fits with me one time, and I just laughed at him. Here I am a Vanderbilt graduate who had been a corpsman in the military. I just looked at him with amusement and followed him around and did what he said. But he never pulled one of those on me again."

In 1964, Danner's business got an unexpected boost in the form of a phone call from new Kentucky Fried Chicken chairman Jack Massey. Negotiations between KFC and the previous owner of the Louisville franchisee had broken down, and Massey needed someone with restaurant experience to take over KFC's operation in Louisville. "Massey said I had just been awarded the franchise for Louisville," Danner said. "I hadn't even asked for it, and so I said 'Jack, I don't want to do that!' And Jack said, 'Ray, it's already been decided. Now get up there and open some stores!' So I did."

As franchisee for Louisville, Danner picked several locations for KFC stores and sent some of his more promising Shoney's managers to run the operation. Eventually, Shoney's built twenty-two Kentucky Fried Chicken locations in Louisville that provided Danner's company with a constant stream of profits.

As Danner built Shoney's Big Boy units in Nashville and KFC stores in Louisville, he created an impressive infrastructure to support them. In order to build all these new restaurants, he put together a cost-effective construction team. In order to keep managers from having to buy food separately, he built a commissary on Elm Hill Pike that baked bread, shaped hamburger patties, mixed fish batter, and distributed everything a Shoney's restaurant needed except milk and produce.

By 1968, Danner's twenty restaurants grossed over $4 million, and investment bankers began telling him how much money he could raise if he took his company public. In 1969, J. C. Bradford sold stock in Danner Foods Inc., whose main assets included a dozen Shoney's Big Boy restaurants in Nashville and a dozen KFC outlets in Louisville.

The success of Danner Foods' IPO enabled the company to go ahead with several important moves. About the same time it went public, the company opened a fish-and-chips restaurant in Donelson called Mr. D's. "Long John Silver's was doing a lousy job, and about everything they sold we already had in Shoney's," Danner explained years later. The first Mr. D's store did quite well, in part because of a young restaurant manager named Dave Wachtel.

With the added capital provided by the initial public offering, the company began creating a Mr. D's chain and opened eight stores the first year. Danner's company thus jumped in against other companies trying to develop a fish-and-chips chain at that time, the most notable being KFC.

The more important move had to do with Schoenbaum, the West Virginia man to whom Danner's Big Boy restaurants had been sending franchise fees for ten years. Danner was building Big Boy restaurants so fast in Tennessee that he would soon run out of places to build them. Meanwhile, Schoenbaum owned the Big Boy franchise for ten southeastern states but was building new units so slowly that parts of the South had no Shoney's locations at all. Franchisee had become larger than franchiser.

After the public offering, Danner and Schoenbaum made a deal. Danner Foods paid Schoenbaum $1.75 million in cash and 290,000 shares of stock. In return, Danner Foods took possession of the fourteen restaurants owned by Schoenbaum, the one hundred or so franchise agreements that Schoenbaum had with other Big Boy franchises, and the right to build Shoney's Big Boy locations in ten more states.

With the announcement that Danner had bought out Schoenbaum, Shoney's stock nearly doubled in value. Danner then changed the name of his company to Shoney's Big Boy Enterprises. After executing a secondary offering of four hundred thousand shares in 1972, Danner turned loose his machine. Shoney's franchisees that lost money under Schoenbaum's regime changed their menus to target a more upscale audience and began to buy food from the Nashville commissary. Managers who just months earlier had not even heard of Ray Danner began to have nightmares about surprise inspections. A problem market in Atlanta was turned into one of the company's strongest markets under a franchisee named Sam Ingram. After Danner concluded that his firm was paying too much money for salad dressing and tartar sauce, it bought a Nashville condiment producer called Mike Rose Foods, which Shoney's used in tandem with its commissary.

For the next several years, Shoney's became one of the best Nashville-based stocks to own. Danner expanded his firm, but with other restaurant companies suffering the ill effects of premature growth, made certain it did not grow too fast. During the 1970s, Shoney's grew mostly from within, increasing the number of its restaurants by about 10 percent each year.

In 1972, Shoney's earned $2.7 million on revenue of $57 million. Nine years later—after thirty-six consecutive quarters of earnings increases—the company earned $14.8 million on revenue of $269 million. Unlike many other companies of the era, Shoney's balance sheet almost never produced surprises, a trend that ironically kept it from getting much press. "Shoney's earnings growth was so routine that nobody paid attention to it," said Hal Kennedy, who did public relations for the company in the 1970s.

One reason Shoney's did so well was that it wasn't afraid to try new things. After becoming convinced that drive-in service was more trouble than it was worth, the company began phasing it out in 1975. "I can't tell you how many times I had to chase teenagers out of the parking lot for not buying anything," said Danner. About the same time, the company began putting salad bars in all its restaurants. Customers loved the salad bar (a new idea at the time), but accountants liked it even more. As salad bars went in, Shoney's raised its prices by about 20 percent and cut back its wait staff by about 20 percent.

The other big success story was the fish-and-chips chain. In 1973, after five years of building Mr. D's into a chain of about thirty, the company hired an outside consultant who told Shoney's it could do better. "Our product wasn't being accepted up North, the building was pretty bad, and the name wasn't helping us," said Wachtel, head of Mr. D's in the early 1970s. The company changed the fish and shrimp recipes and hired an architect to come up with a maritime design. During the next three years the stores experienced comparable increases between 20 percent and 30 percent per year. Starting in 1974, Shoney's began actively franchising out Mr. D's locations for the first time. The next year, with 250 units in operation, Shoney's changed the name of Mr. D's to Captain D's.

Whenever Shoney's was written about in magazines, attention was always focused on Ray Danner's spot visits to his restaurants. Less attention was paid to the fact that Danner liked to promote from within and use money as a huge motivator. Shoney's executives had a low base pay but received generous bonuses of up to 20 percent of the increase in division profits.

One example of someone who had worked his way up at Shoney's was Wachtel, who had started as a busboy at the Madison Shoney's in 1959. Wachtel was so good at doing what Danner told him to do that he occasionally overdid it. "One time, Ray told me that he thought there was something wrong with the chickens we were serving in Louisville, and he thought that we needed to compare the chickens we were serving with chickens that we knew were barnyard chickens," Wachtel said in 1999. "So he told me to go get him five barnyard chickens."

Later that week, Wachtel walked into the Shoney's corporate office on Fourth Avenue with five live chickens in a burlap sack. "Dave, I want them dead and cleaned first!" Danner said to Wachtel, while other workers peered in the office and laughed about the odd noises coming from the sack.

During the 1970s, Wachtel was one of two individuals who emerged as potential successors to Danner. The other was Boyd, who started running Shoney's franchising division in 1971. In 1981, Danner promoted Wachtel to chief executive officer. Danner, who still owned about 16 percent of the company's stock, remained on the board in a close advisory position.

Wachtel did not waste time making major changes. First of all, he sent Boyd away to be a Shoney's franchisee in Virginia. He then sold the company's twenty-two Kentucky Fried Chicken stores to KFC parent Heublein for $5.7 million in stock. Shoney's then turned around and acquired Famous Recipe Fried Chicken, which had 220 franchised stores and no company-owned stores, for $2.2 million. The deal looked even better about a year later, when RJR Nabisco acquired Heublein, nearly doubling the value of Heublein's stock.

About the same time, Shoney's started the breakfast bar, an all-you-can-eat morning buffet that almost immediately became a part of southern culture. The way the breakfast bar came about is indicative of the bottom-up way in which Shoney's made changes at that time. Breakfast had historically been a weak spot for Shoney's. In 1981, Wachtel and Shoney's president Gary Spoleta challenged Atlanta franchisee Sam Ingram to come up with a way to change that. Ingram installed a buffet at one of his locations, and within weeks his restaurants were doing so well that Wachtel and Spoleta made it a company-wide program. "Breakfast doubled, and in some cases tripled," Wachtel said. "And instead of having four breakfast cooks back there, we only needed one or two."

Profits were up, and Wall Street seemed happy with Wachtel's style. But Danner wasn't. In August 1982, the Shoney's board fired Wachtel after only nine months as chief executive. The source of trouble, the company claimed, had to do with Wachtel's tendency to make big decisions without the board's consent. On one occasion, Wachtel surprised the board with the news that he had acquired the Nashville-area franchise for a fried chicken chain called Popeye's, a deal that dragged Shoney's into a lawsuit over franchise rights. "Dave would get excited about things and go do them without us really knowing," Danner said. "I was talking about controlled growth and Dave was more into getting it done right now."

Years later, Wachtel admitted he did not handle his relationship with Danner well. "I should have showed him a little more respect than I did, but I thought I knew more than he did," Wachtel said. "Had I managed that relationship different I probably never would have left. But had I never left I wouldn't have been as successful as I have. So it probably was a good thing I got fired."

With Wachtel gone, Danner stepped back in and served as CEO for three more years. And in 1985, Shoney's made a major announcement Wall Street loved. After twenty-seven years as a Big Boy franchisee, Shoney's paid Marriott $13 million to let it out of its franchise agreements. No longer could Shoney's use the ubiquitous Big Boy to advertise its restaurants. But as a result of the move, Shoney's was no longer tied down to the Southeast.

In March 1986, Danner resigned as CEO for the second time in five years, this time naming Boyd to succeed him. However, as had been the case with Wachtel, Danner did not retire but continued to come to work and exert power as chairman and lead shareholder. As part of Boyd's hiring, Shoney's took over a specialty restaurant chain called Pargo's that Boyd had started in Virginia.

Over the years, Shoney's had maintained a fairly conservative balance sheet, expanding consistently but deliberately while keeping debt to a minimum. But in 1988, Shoney's made a major change in this approach; its shareholders voted overwhelmingly to approve a major stock recapitalization and issue a one-time dividend of $20 per share. As was noted in the national press, the stock recap was an enormous payoff for Danner, who got a $140 million payment as a result. Nashville residents who had invested $1,000 in Danner Foods stock in 1968 now got a dividend check of more than $20,000 on top of their capital gain. But the transaction saddled Shoney's with $585 million in debt and forced the firm to scale back its expansion from about sixty to twenty new company-owned restaurants per year.

Years later, critics would say that the stock recap was the biggest mistake Shoney's ever made because it made it harder for the company to upgrade its restaurants. However, both Taylor Henry, chief financial officer at Shoney's at the time of the recap, and Boyd say it is wrong to blame Shoney's problems in the 1990s on the stock recap of 1988. "The recap was where it needed to be," Boyd said. "Ray needed to cash out." Both Henry and Boyd also point out that the company was way ahead in paying off its stock recap during the next four years. "Same store sales went way up the next year because of stock options that we made available as a part of the stock recap to everyone down to the level of store manager," Henry said.

About this time, major disagreements ensued between Boyd and the board, which Boyd says was then dominated by Danner, Dan Maddox Jr., and Wallace Rasmussen. With Shoney's same-store sales numbers falling behind competitors, Boyd thought the company needed to upgrade its restaurants. "We were falling way behind our remodeling schedule," Boyd said. "I was begging, pleading, and demanding the board to spend some money to keep the stores upgraded and keep them nice. But these guys grew up during the depression and debt was a serious, serious matter and they could not see themselves through that debt."

The other major disagreement between Boyd and the board had to do with a massive legal problem.

In May 1988, a married couple named Henry and Billie Elliott went to visit a Tallahassee, Florida, attorney named Tommy Warren. The Elliotts—who were white—told Warren that they had been fired as managers of a Captain D's restaurant in Marianna, Florida, because they refused to fire black employees simply because they were black. The Elliotts went on to say that what happened to them was by no means an isolated incident. They said that the policy of keeping black employees scarce and in low-profile positions at Captain D's came directly from the Shoney's home office in Nashville.

Warren got about a dozen witnesses (white and black) to verify the story about why the Elliotts were fired. After successfully soliciting financial help from the NAACP's Legal Defense Fund, Warren found a former Shoney's waitress in Montgomery named Sharon Johnson. Johnson, who was black, told Elliott that in 1985, her store manager asked her to hide in a bathroom during an inspection by the area manager, who had told his managers he wanted the number of black waitresses kept to a minimum.

A few months later, Warren found Terry Toney, who had been fired as manager of a Lee's Famous Recipe Chicken outlet in Nashville while that chain was owned by Shoney's. According to Toney's deposition, Danner himself told Toney to reduce the number of black employees at the store during a surprise inspection. A few weeks later, Danner returned, saw that Toney had ignored his order, and literally dragged him into the cooler. "I told you to get rid of the damn niggers weeks ago and you did not do it," Danner reportedly said. "Now get rid of the damn niggers or it's going to be your job."[1]

In April 1989, Warren filed suit in federal court in Pensacola on behalf of nine individuals who said they had been discriminated against by Shoney's. During the next few weeks, as the lawsuit became publicized, Warren got many more. By July, when he filed a motion for summary judgment, Warren had testimony from two dozen current and former white employees and about fifty current and former black employees. Their stories implicated people from every level of Shoney's management.

In the summer of 1989, Boyd hired Nashville attorney Jim Neal to assess Shoney's legal situation. After studying the case, Neal told Boyd that Shoney's would almost certainly lose the lawsuit and that the best thing for the company to do would be to settle out of court. Boyd asked Neal how much money it would take. Neal said around $30 million.

Boyd took Neal's recommendation to the next board meeting, but the board rejected Neal's advice. According to Boyd, Maddox criticized Neal's recommendation more strongly than any other board member. A few months later, Boyd was fired and replaced with former Arby's CEO Len Roberts.

Years later, Roberts told author Steve Watkins that when he accepted the job as Shoney's CEO, he had no idea how serious the discrimination lawsuit was. But once he took over, he spent enormous amounts of time trying to negotiate a settlement between the plaintiffs, the Shoney's board, and Danner, whom Roberts believed should pay a large portion of the settlement personally.

The case dragged on for over four years, mainly because it took the plaintiffs that long to make the Shoney's board (and Danner) realize how much it was going to pay. Perhaps the most damaging testimony came from Wachtel. The former Shoney's CEO said Danner's attitude toward African Americans was well-known within the company, and that it was more than just consumer-driven. "Ray Danner often voiced his support for the Ku Klux Klan," Wachtel told Warren in February 1992.[2] Wachtel also said Danner had talked to him about the idea of Shoney's possibly matching senior officials' contributions to the Klan.

Years later, Wachtel said he "did not have any choice" but to testify. "My choice was to be named a defendant or to tell them the truth, and I told them the truth." In a 1999 interview, Warren said he could not comment on whether Wachtel would have been in legal trouble had he not testified. But it was a matter of public record that the plaintiffs agreed not to sue Wachtel as a part of his agreement to testify.

Danner, however, said a lot of the testimony put forth in the case was not true. "The lawyers would coach these people before they'd go in for a depo[sition]," Danner said. Regarding Wachtel's testimony, Danner said, "I never had anything to do with the Klan. . . . I don't know where that would have come from. Maybe that's in his [Wachtel's] mind."

On November 3, 1992, Shoney's announced it would settle out of court with the plaintiffs. In one of the biggest settlements ever in a race discrimination suit, the company agreed to pay $105 million to workers or job applicants, so long as they could prove they were discriminated against (over twenty-one thousand people eventually received checks). The company also was ordered to pay $20 million in legal fees to the plaintiffs' attorneys. A few months later, Danner agreed to pay about $67 million of the settlement out of his own pocket.

During the next several years, Shoney's embarked on a massive affirmative action plan. By 1995, 22 percent of management was black. By 1996, Shoney's had made so many changes that the *Wall Street Journal* quoted Warren as saying, "This is the kind of turnaround that we like to see. . . . This is real. Black people know this is a company where they can get ahead."[3]

However, by the time Warren made his statement, Shoney's had fallen behind in the eyes of customers.

Historically, Shoney's had grown consistently but carefully because of Danner's concern that overzealous growth bred bad restaurants. In 1989, when Roberts took over, Shoney's owned about seven hundred restaurants and had franchised about eight hundred more. Almost immediately, Roberts announced an ambitious growth program called Project 500, which called for the construction of five hundred new restaurants per year by 1994.

Such a growth plan may have worked when Roberts was CEO at Arby's, but it did not work at Shoney's. After years of being told operations are far more important than new restaurants, franchisees were not about to change. "Len Roberts put an emphasis on franchising that no one—including myself—believed was possible," Taylor Henry said. "Before then, the company had never pushed franchising. The approach had always been to let the franchisees develop at their own pace." Not only did franchisees resist Roberts, many were beginning to have a dim view of the Shoney's board, which by this time did not have a single person who had ever run a Shoney's restaurant. Some franchisees were also becoming cynical about the fact that the corporate home office was telling them to open new stores only four years after it pulled back its own expansion plans in order to pay for the stock recap. The fact that Roberts spent far less time visiting Shoney's restaurants than his four predecessors did not help.

In order to meet Roberts's ambitious goals, Shoney's acquired thirty Chicago-area restaurants from Marriott Corp. and began converting them to Shoney's. However, those restaurants did not make a profit and would later be closed.

By early 1992, it had become obvious that Shoney's sales per restaurant were falling way behind competitors such as Cracker Barrel. At that point, Roberts did an about-face and announced that customer satisfaction, not growth, was now top priority. His new catch phrase was "Project 85," meaning that the goal was 85 percent customer satisfaction. Three months later, Shoney's changed its menu to include more pasta and vegetable dishes and told its waitresses to start using customer's names instead of numbers to keep track of people waiting to be seated. "We have become walking encyclopedias about what people like and don't like about our restaurants," Roberts said.[4] In December 1992, Roberts was fired and replaced with Henry.

Reenter Ray Danner. In March 1993, Danner made public his desire to sell his remaining 4.6 million shares back to the company. However, during the subsequent weeks, while his proposal was being mulled over by the board and by institutional shareholders, Shoney's stock slipped about three dollars. Danner called off the sale, resigned from the board, and told reporters he would never eat at Shoney's again.

By this time, a failed franchising push, a massive discrimination lawsuit, and a series of squabbles with the company's founder had taken their toll on Shoney's restaurants. In 1993 and 1994, Shoney's same store sales declined for the first time. After franchisees failed to jump headlong into a remodeling campaign, Henry and the board decided it was time for the company to re-focus. In August 1994, the Shoney's board hired the consulting firm McKinsey & Co. to come up with a plan to completely revamp the company.

Several months and $2 million later, McKinsey & Co. came back with its recommendation: sell every single division other than the Shoney's restaurants and the commissary. Henry disagreed with some of the recommendations and was able to convince the board to hold onto the ever-profitable Captain D's chain. But in a press conference a few days later, Henry announced that Shoney's would sell the Lee's Famous Recipe Chicken, Pargo's, Fifth Quarter, and Mike Rose Foods divisions. Henry also announced he would be leaving the company, as would Shoney's Inc. president Jim Arnett and Shoney's division president Jim Grout.

Years later, Henry said it was a mistake to go public with the announcement that such major changes were going to be made. "Announcing all this up front was a terrible move and sent chills up and down the spines of all our key people," he said. "For the first time in the history of the company, employees no longer trusted management." Henry also said that announcing the sales up front made negotiations to sell divisions all the more difficult, which is why Shoney's didn't find a buyer for Pargo's or Fifth Quarter.

Reenter Ray Danner. In March 1995, while the stock dropped below ten dollars a share, Danner made a public offer to come back as CEO. He said he would accept a salary of one dollar per year, plus stock options that could only be exercised after the stock price reached twenty dollars per share. Anticipating attacks because of his role in the racism lawsuit, Danner went as far as to say he would offer a seat on the board of directors to one of the plaintiffs in the 1989 lawsuit.

However, by now the Shoney's board no longer took Ray Danner seriously. It chose former Sonic chief executive Steve Lynn to be his successor. Lynn closed forty-one money-losing restaurants in 1996 and invested money in a new television advertising campaign starring Andy Griffith. But sales did not rebound, nor were they helped when an ABC television news show included the company in a report on unsanitary conditions in restaurants. Lynn closed another seventy-five stores in 1997. By January 1998, the stock fell below four dollars a share, less than a fourth of its value four years earlier.

Lynn was ousted in 1998 in a board coup by Ray Schoenbaum, the son of Shoney's cofounder Alex Schoenbaum. Schoenbaum installed Mike Bodnar as the company's new CEO. But with the stock price lagging and debt problems mounting, many analysts and investors were wondering if Bodnar would be Shoney's last CEO.

Just as the opening of Interstate 75 set into motion a series of events leading to the rise of Kentucky Fried Chicken, the opening of Interstate 40 led to the rise of Cracker Barrel.

In 1969, Dan Evins, a nephew of U.S. Representative Joe Evins, was a salesmen for Shell Oil's products in Wilson, Smith, and DeKalb Counties. When the new interstate opened, gas stations in that area were slow to open near it, which made him worry that drivers along the new freeway would be buying gas elsewhere.

Evins decided to open his own gas station at the intersection of Highway 109 and I-40, near Lebanon. To give travelers an additional motivation to stop, Evins built a restaurant and gift shop along with it. "I had just driven all the way to Atlanta, and I thought it was such a boring drive," Evins said in 1999. "You could stop at Stuckey's and get a peanut log or you could stop at a service station, and that was about it. My idea was to build a place that would add some interest, where you could take a break from the road, get some fuel, get something to eat, or just browse around. The atmosphere and the memorabilia and everything came out of that."

Evins had never run a restaurant or a gift shop before, nor had he ever decorated a business. "We went over and looked at the Old Country Store in Lynchburg and then just picked up things here and there," he said.

Evins's glorified gas station—called Cracker Barrel Old Country Store—opened in September 1969 and made a profit almost immediately. The next year, using the logic that what works on one freeway intersection will work on another, Evins began to build other restaurants with fellow Shell salesmen as business partners. Within five years, he had built a chain of ten gas stations/restaurants/gift shops, all of them on interstates.

The restaurants and gift shops did so well that before long, Evins began to wonder whether the gas pumps were doing any good. "It became difficult to associate petroleum products with good food," Evans said. During the gas shortage of 1974, Evins severed his ties with Shell and started building Cracker Barrel stores without gas stations. "We were a little nervous at first," Evins said. "But it wasn't long before we realized that it improved our business."

Besides timing and interstate locations, there were two other important parts of the Cracker Barrel formula. One was that the food tasted better and tasted more like home-cooked than most other chain restaurants, featuring items such as country ham, turnip greens, and homemade biscuits and gravy. The other was the atmosphere, perhaps best described as nostalgic country. While waiting to eat at a Cracker Barrel, customers could browse in a gift shop, sit in rocking chairs, or play checkers. "You might have a lady in a fur coat sitting next to a guy in overalls with muddy boots on," Evins said. "She's there because she thought it was quaint. He's there because he was hungry."

By 1981, Cracker Barrel had twenty-five units, all located along interstate highways in the South. At that point, with interest rates at record highs, it made a lot more sense to try to finance further expansion by selling stock to the public than to continue to borrow money from banks. J. C. Bradford handled the initial public offering.

There were two crucial differences between the corporate organization at Cracker Barrel and that at Shoney's. One was that Cracker Barrel did not franchise its concept. "We were afraid we'd lose the ability to capture the quality image that we wanted to develop," Evins said. Cracker Barrel also chose not to build a central commissary, but to contract out its food orders and have individual vendors make deliveries. "We were afraid it would divert our attention," Evins said. "We wanted to be restaurant people and not warehouse people." Cracker Barrel did, however, build a distribution center in Lebanon for its gift shops.

Even without franchising, Cracker Barrel's balance sheet grew fast. In 1987, the company had fifty-three stores and annual sales of about $100 million. Four years later, the number of stores and the amount of revenue doubled. More importantly, Cracker Barrel's same store sales increases far exceeded such industry rivals as Shoney's and Denny's.

Nevertheless, there was one interesting similarity between Cracker Barrel and Shoney's, and that is each company's well-publicized discrimination controversy. In January 1991, Cracker Barrel adopted a policy that said the company would no longer employ homosexuals. During the next few weeks, the company dismissed at least ten gay employees. Since there was no federal law that prohibited discrimination in hiring based on sexual preference, none of the dismissed employees could sue the company. But as word about the policy spread, Cracker Barrel came under intense criticism from gay rights and civil liberties organizations. Only a few weeks after the policy was instituted, Cracker Barrel issued a press release rescinding the policy. That statement, which described the original policy as "well-intentioned," made the criticism and publicity more intense.

Within months, after becoming convinced that the company was still refusing to hire homosexuals, gay rights groups began targeting Cracker Barrel, putting the small restaurant chain in the center of a national debate on gay rights. Protesters marched on several Cracker Barrel locations, chanting, "We're here! We're queer! Get used to it!"[5] New York City's retirement fund, which owned $6 million in Cracker Barrel stock, asked that the company further clarify its policy. When the company did not, New York City fund managers submitted a resolution to shareholders that the company adopt a nondiscriminatory policy. That resolution failed in November 1993.

Interestingly enough, Cracker Barrel's homosexual controversy did not hurt the company's bottom line. In 1991, otherwise a terrible year for business because of recession and the Persian Gulf War, Cracker Barrel's sales rose 33 percent and its profits rose 50 percent. "Nostalgia sells," a restaurant analyst told *Forbes*.[6]

For the rest of the 1990s, Cracker Barrel built between thirty and forty new stores per year. It continued to put them almost exclusively on interstate exits, although it did put a few in select tourist destinations such as Pigeon Forge, Tennessee, and Hilton Head, South Carolina. By 1998, the company had over 350 stores in almost all parts of the United States except the West Coast. At that point, it reorganized itself as a holding company called CBRL under a new chief operating officer named Ted McGruder.

By the time McGruder took over, however, there was beginning to be evidence that the Cracker Barrel restaurant concept was hitting a wall in terms of sales increases, forcing the company to look for a new concept. In 1998, CBRL bought the forty-unit Logan's Roadhouse chain—then under the leadership of CEO Ted Moats—and began experimenting with a new Italian and gourmet restaurant concept out of Florida called Carmine's. The glorified gas station had grown into a $1.1 billion company with seven hundred employees in Lebanon and forty-five thousand across the United States.

Dave Wachtel was only forty when the Shoney's board of directors fired him. With plenty of money, plenty of energy, and plenty of ego, he wasn't idle long. After raising money, Wachtel bought a half-interest in the Nashville franchise for Western Sizzlin and all of the Nashville franchise for a chain called Luther's Barbeque. But after building two sites, he realized Luther's wasn't bringing in the customers.

About that time, Nick Spiva and Nick Hill, the owners of a restaurant near Vanderbilt, approached Wachtel about buying their business. Wachtel hesitated at first. After all, the Twenty-first Avenue eatery, called O'Charley's, had lost $65,000 during the previous year on revenues of about $750,000. But since the lease was so cheap ($1,000 a month), Wachtel decided to give it a shot. For $65,000, Wachtel's business bought an option to buy the business, on the condition that the owners let him make a few changes.

Within weeks, Wachtel added some items to the menu, installed some new equipment, and put in a new accounting system (with the help of an accountant named Greg Burns). Before long, O'Charley's was making money. It was making so much money, in fact, that Wachtel decided to give up on barbecue and turn his Luther's sites into O'Charley's units. A couple of years later, when the chain was up to six locations in the Nashville area, Wachtel made two major changes to the concept. One was to make the decor more casual, putting in neon lighting fixtures, beer signs, and framed black and white photos on the walls. The other was to improve the food and come up with some new recipes.

O'Charley's grew fast in the late 1980s, going head to head with similar concepts such as T.G.I. Friday's and Applebee's. By July 1990, when the company went public, there were around thirty locations.

O'Charley's had a rocky road during its first five years of existence as a public company. About the same time as the IPO, O'Charley's restaurants began to have poor sales numbers because its menu prices were too high. O'Charley's was also hurt badly by the fact that many of its units were located near military bases and therefore had poor sales during the Persian Gulf War. After going public at nine dollars a share, O'Charley's missed its first quarter's earnings and the stock fell to three dollars.

After the war ended and the recession abated, O'Charley's began to report good sales numbers again, and the stock began to work its way back to its value at the IPO. But it was around then that a struggle ensued between Wachtel and the O'Charley's board.

At the root of the problem was the fact that Wachtel had several irons in the fire. In 1991, while O'Charley's was in the middle of its public offering, Wachtel and a group of investors started a new restaurant in Kentucky called Logan's Roadhouse (the same chain Cracker Barrel would buy seven years later). Some O'Charley's executives and board members (including Burns) saw this moonlighting as a conflict of interest. Nevertheless, after Logan's began to look promising,

Wachtel convinced O'Charley's to buy 20 percent interest in the budding chain.

Wachtel had a tougher time with the next major purchase he proposed to the board. In 1993, Wachtel suggested that O'Charley's buy Western Sizzlin out of bankruptcy. Wachtel, who owned half of the Nashville-area Western Sizzlin franchise and to whom Western Sizzlin owed money, told the board that many Western Sizzlin locations would be great Logan's Roadhouse and O'Charley's sites. "My vision was to have a company like Shoney's with four or five different concepts," Wachtel said. The board turned him down and told Wachtel that they wanted him to either divest from other restaurant chains and focus on O'Charley's or resign. He chose the latter. Wachtel later took over as CEO at Western Sizzlin but was ousted from that job in 1995. By 1998, he was involved in the management of three different restaurant concepts: a start-up Tex-Mex chain called Santa Fe Cantina, a catfish chain called Uncle Bud's, and an upscale eatery called the Merchants.

Wachtel was replaced by Burns, who had been adamantly opposed to the Western Sizzlin idea. The split-up was an emotional one for both Burns and Wachtel, much like the one ten years earlier between Danner and Wachtel. "Dave is a very smart man and a good restaurant promoter who has good conceptual ideas," Burns said in 1999. "But I don't think he knows how to execute. He did back in the Shoney's days, but the business has changed."

Like Shoney's and Cracker Barrel, O'Charley's had some controversy along the way. No sooner had Wachtel left than three former O'Charley's employees filed a racial discrimination lawsuit against the company. Burns and other company officials vehemently denied the charges, but the next year, attorneys for the plaintiffs won class-action status for the lawsuit.

Finally, in a board meeting in February 1996, Burns told the board that the company had to settle just to get the lawsuit behind it. "Operationally, we were having tremendous performance, but we were not getting any recognition in the marketplace," Burns said. "A lot of investors were telling us that we sounded good but that they did not want to invest until the lawsuit was over. And it was getting to the point where it might have cost us some key people."

O'Charley's agreed to settle for $6.2 million, despite the fact that Burns maintained that the company had done nothing wrong. "The whole thing was the legal system gone amok there truly had been an ongoing environment of racial discrimination, why wouldn't 50 or 60 percent of African Americans in the company participate instead of less than 25 percent?"

With the lawsuit behind it, O'Charley's settled into a long period of slow but consistent growth. By 1999, the company had about one hundred restaurants in eleven states and was beginning to explore new concepts.

As O'Charley's appeared to be finally turning the corner, the company hoped that it would one day become as good a stock to own as Shoney's had once been. But there was one big difference between the way O'Charley's was being run at the turn of the century and the way Shoney's had been run twenty-five years earlier, and that had to do with employee relations. "You don't have bodies lying around that you can fire right and left and intimidate anymore," Burns said in 1999. "The whole concept of employee-manager relations has changed in the last fifteen years and so has the availability of young people. There is so much competition for workers that if they come in the door and don't like the relationship that they have with you, they're gone. . . . People don't put up with crap anymore."

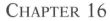

CHAPTER 16

None of Your Business

N ot all of Nashville's large employers were publicly owned. There were several companies that kept their stock in the family. Maybe it was because the president couldn't stand the idea of having to answer to analysts and newspaper reporters. Maybe it was because the company was in a business that was seasonal and therefore not conducive to public ownership. Or maybe it was because the family that owned the company had so much money that it did not need to raise capital through a stock offering.

Werthan

No one knows why Meier Werthan came to the United States or why he first went to Cincinnati. What we do know is that by 1868, Werthan was an active member of the Nashville Jewish community and an employee of a Confederate veteran named Sigmund Godhelp. Werthan and Godhelp became friends, business partners, and—after Werthan married Godhelp's sister-in-law—family.

In many ways, Godhelp & Co. of 155 South Market Street was typical of the businesses in the Jewish neighborhood of Lower Broad, drifting from one focus to another as it sought a market niche. Between 1870 and 1895, Godhelp & Co. is listed in various Nashville City Directories as a business that sold produce, then rags, then "feathers, wool, and ginseng," then secondhand furniture, then hides and furs, and finally just junk.

Meier Werthan may have been a small-time businessman, but his two sons Morris and Joe were better educated than he was and had high expectations. After Godhelp died in 1895, Morris and Joe went to work with their father, and the business became known as Werthan & Co. In 1901, Morris moved to St. Louis and started a second branch of the junk business. A decade later, the business changed its name to Werthan Bag & Burlap and began to specialize in the sale of new and secondhand bags.

Werthan Bag came of age between 1912 and 1920, in part because of the demand for sandbags during World War I. By the end of the war, Werthan was a full-fledged bag manufacturer that was giving North Nashville bag manufacturer Morgan & Hamilton Co. a run for its money. The business also thrived in St. Louis.

Meier Werthan died in 1922. Morris then moved his family back to Nashville and combined his business with his brother's.

By this time, the Werthan family was no longer regarded as lowly junk dealers. Joe Werthan was one of many other German-Americans such as Henry Neuhoff and Lee Loventhal who helped Ed Potter Jr. start the German-American Bank in 1916. Thanks to that affiliation, Werthan was able to obtain capital to purchase the old Marathon car factory building in 1922 and filled it with up-to-date bag-making equipment.

Werthan made two types of bags that were in great demand in a city that had flour mills, wholesale grocers, and fertilizer companies. Cotton bags were used for flour and sugar. Werthan's largest cotton bag customers were Colonial Milling, General Mills, Pillsbury, and Holly Sugar. Fertilizer and feed were usually sold in burlap bags that Werthan made out of material imported from India. Ralston Purina and the Fletch-Wilson Coffee Company were two of Werthan's largest burlap bag customers.

In 1928, Werthan Bag took a step that doubled its capacity and ensured a constant supply of good cotton. The company acquired Morgan & Hamilton and made major upgrades to its facility. Like many businesses of that era, it did so by issuing industrial revenue bonds underwritten by Caldwell & Co. The new Werthan-Morgan-Hamilton Co., as it was known for several years, had bag-making machines, a cotton mill, a bleachery, and a finishing plant. About the same time, Werthan established a branch plant in New Orleans that made burlap sacks for trade along the Mississippi River and in Cuba.

During the 1920s, Morris's two sons Bernard and Albert had come into the business—Bernard on the manufacturing side and Albert on the sales side. After Morris died in 1931, Bernard and Albert ran the business with their Uncle Joe.

When the Great Depression hit Nashville in 1931, Nashville companies were laying off employees. Meanwhile, Werthan Bag thrived. After all, most of the bags it produced were for selling in large quantities. During the depression, people were more likely to buy in large quantities because it was cheaper to do so.

There was another reason Werthan Bag did so well through the hard times of the depression. Consumer goods were hard to afford in the 1930s and hard to find in the 1940s. Because of this, housewives became adept at recycling cotton bags and making them into curtains, pillowcases, washcloths, and even clothes. The practice became so common that eventually Werthan invested in special equipment that made so-called "dress print bags." Put enough of the right bags together, and you could make an entire dress. "A housewife might come into a store and see a bag toward the bottom of the stack of bags that she needed and ask the merchant to move four of five bags so she could get to it," Albert Werthan said in 1998.

By 1930, Werthan Bag had over one thousand employees. The company dominated the North Nashville neighborhood that surrounded it so much that it actually had a whistle that blew at five A.M. to wake up workers who lived there.

Despite the labor unrest of the late 1930s (and the new wage and hour laws that followed it), Werthan Bag remained a cash cow. By 1935, the company was in such good financial condition that it retired all the debt that it had taken on in 1928. In addition to its usual commercial customers, World War II brought another huge demand for sandbags. Perhaps the best indicator of Werthan Bag's profitability is the fact that in 1947, the three highest salaried men in Tennessee (according to information released by the U.S. Treasury Department) were Joe, Bernard, and Albert Werthan.

What no one knew at the time was that the decline of the textile bag business was just around the corner. During World War II, the shortage of burlap and cotton led the bag industry to invest in new equipment that made multi-wall paper bags. Werthan reacted to this change in 1953 by spending over $1 million in paper-bag-making machines. But as major customers transitioned from cotton and burlap to paper, it became obvious that paper bags would not be nearly as profitable as burlap and cotton bags had been.

As the fourth generation took over Werthan Bag, the company had about twelve hundred employees and annual revenues of about $35 million. But with the domestic textile and bag business shrinking fast, the family realized that its asset would deteriorate fast if it did not branch into other industries. In 1968, Albert Werthan's son-in-law Herb Shayne, a Harvard Business School graduate with a marketing background, moved to Nashville to help the company diversify.

During the next fifteen years, Werthan Bag would branch off into three unrelated businesses while it continued to operate a shrinking bag business. The first and most successful was the 1971 purchase of a Nashville firm called Check Printers Inc., a business that had been started in 1960 by several former employees of McQuiddy Printing. As

The Werthan Bag plant, around 1950 (Tennessee State Library and Archives).

Herb Shayne considered buying Check Printers, which produced
checks for several large banks, many skeptics warned him that a
"check-less society" was just around the corner. After a Goldman
Sachs analyst told him that such talk was garbage, Shayne bought it.

There were two reasons that Werthan's investment in Check Printers
turned out to be, in Shayne's words, a "home run." One was because
check printing turned out to be a high-margin business with loyal
clients. The other was that Check Printers had astute on-site managers
who knew what they were doing. "One time, they told me that I wasn't
coming down there enough," Shayne said. "I told them that as long as
they met their budget that I would leave them alone." When his
managers told Shayne they needed to buy a new piece of equipment,
start a new product, or open a new plant, Shayne took their advice.

Eventually, Check Printers had 350 employees, two more plants in
Jacksonville and Winston-Salem, and had shifted from printing checks
to printing mortgage coupons. A fter Werthan sold Check Printers to a
group of New York investors called Greenwich Capital Partners in
1998, the family calculated that the investment had an annual
compounded growth rate, including dividends, of about 17 percent.

Werthan's second diversification basically broke even. Morris
Werthan, a cousin of Herb Shayne, bought a small auto parts business
and expanded it until it was a twenty-eight-unit chain in five states
called Honey's. Eventually, it became clear to Morris that he had to
either sell it or expand it nationally—a step that would have required
a public offering of stock. In 1982, the family sold the business.

Werthan's third major diversification—a passive investment in a
computer software firm called Synercom—proved to be a complete
bust that lost about $2 million. "It wasn't a bad idea," Shayne said.
"But it was a crap shoot and it did not work."

Meanwhile, some form of the bag business remained intact
through the end of the century. After the labor unrest of the 1930s,
Werthan's management was almost always successful at keeping
unions out of its factories. During the decades after World War II,
Werthan's workers rejected unions time and time again. "Every union
around tried to organize Werthan," said Nashville labor attorney Cecil
Branstetter. "Every time they did, the workers would get a ten-cent
wage increase, and the union went away."

In 1962, Werthan built a plastic bag plant just north of Lebanon
Pike that predominantly made bags for fertilizer. For a short time,
Werthan Bag made four kinds of bags—burlap, cotton, paper, and
plastic. But by the 1970s, the market for burlap and cotton bags was
vanishing fast. "One of the things I envy about people who start new
businesses is that they don't have this legacy of obsolescence,"
Werthan Bag president Bernard Werthan Jr. once told a reporter.[1] In
1974, Werthan shut down the textile mill that produced cotton bag

material, laying off 400 people in the process. "I cried," Werthan Jr. said years later. Four years later, the company closed its printing and finishing plant, which had about 250 workers.

As the twenty-first century neared, bag-making was nowhere near as labor-intensive and profitable as it had once been. But the Werthan Bag business—now called Werthan Packaging—still turned a profit decades after most of their competitors had moved on to something else. In 1998, Werthan still had about four hundred employees making about three million paper bags per week—mostly for pet food—out of the factory in North Nashville. "We're doing pretty well," Werthan Jr. said in 1998. "We've had some tough times in the last ten years, but we are pretty pleased with our prospects." Werthan was also proud of the fact that his son Tony was active in the business, raising the likelihood that the business would pass to its fifth generation of management.

Aladdin

The first big jolt that the Nashville economy received after World War II came in 1948, when the Mantle Lamp Co. announced it was building a factory in Nashville that made vacuum bottles (later known as thermoses). Mantle Lamp would soon thereafter change its name to Aladdin Industries and move its entire operation to Nashville. Because of this, the early history of the firm would almost be forgotten.

In 1905, before most Americans had electricity in their homes, a German inventor came up with an improvement to the kerosene mantle lamp. Three years later, a soap salesman in Iowa named Victor Johnson saw one and predicted that the lamp would soon be all the rage. Johnson switched from selling soap to selling imported lamps. After making and patenting a couple of improvements to the mantle lamp, he started a small factory to make them.

Johnson's lamp, which he called Aladdin, became the best-selling lamp in America by World War I. A few years later he developed a side business making insulated jugs and dishes.

Johnson died in 1943, leaving control of the company to his thirty-year-old son Victor Jr. By that time, Mantle Lamp's American operation consisted of a headquarters and a small electronics plant in Chicago and a lamp and vacuum bottle factory in Alexandria, Indiana (where natural gas had been discovered in the nineteenth century). Overseas, the company had extensive operations in England.

After taking over the family business, Johnson Jr. decided to expand the vacuum bottle side of the business, which he figured had a brighter future than kerosene lamps.

Fifty years later, Johnson said there were two main reasons that he chose Nashville. One was the city's central location and easy road and rail access. The other was the availability of the new natural gas line through Nashville that had just been installed by the Nashville Gas Co. City leaders steered Johnson to Murfreesboro Road because the army was selling over a thousand acres there that had previously been used as a classification center during the war.

Johnson would later deny that the cost of labor had anything to do with his decision to move the factory from Indiana to Tennessee. But it is worth pointing out that the Mantle Lamp factory in Indiana was unionized, and that—at first—the one in Nashville was not. One thing was for certain: Mantle Lamp's move south hurt Alexandria's economy. In 1949, Alexandria had about ten thousand employees. Fifty years later, it had half that amount.

One thing that did not have anything to do with Aladdin's move to Nashville was government help. Unlike many of the large companies that moved operations to the Nashville area later in the century such as Nissan, Columbia/HCA, and Dell Computer, Aladdin neither asked for nor received infrastructure help or tax breaks from the city, county, or state governments. "We received nothing from the city or county," Johnson said. "We even built our own sewer and water lines."

Not long after the company moved, Johnson would become an active business leader and one of the leading advocates of a Metropolitan government in Nashville. But when he first arrived in the city, Johnson viewed Nashville as sort of a hick town. "I remember looking out my office window every morning and seeing a woman walk out into her front yard with a bonnet on her head to get water out of the well in her front yard," Johnson said. "That was Nashville in 1949." Within a few years, the woman's property became the site of the American Bread Co.

Another thing Johnson remembered vividly fifty years after moving his company to Nashville was the stir it caused by having white and black employees working side by side. "At that time, there were certain jobs that were known to be jobs for black people by tradition, such as hard manual jobs and janitorial jobs. Before we even came down here, I received letters from certain people who were hoping that we would not change the historical pattern of having jobs for the white and jobs for the black. And I received letters from several people in the black community expressing hope that we would not continue the practice of having jobs for the white and jobs for the black. We put whites and blacks together side by side."

Johnson found other ways to upset the apple cart. Aladdin paid better and had better benefits than other large employers such as iron foundries and textile mills, which is why the company had over three thousand applications for its initial 180 jobs. "Aladdin was one of the first to have benefits," said Lillian Jenkins, who went to work for Aladdin in 1949 and was head of the company's human resource division half a century later. Rather than go with one of Nashville's large general contractors such as Foster & Creighton, Aladdin hired a relative unknown named Robert Mathews. And unlike most large employers, which affiliated themselves with a Nashville bank, law firm, and accounting firm, Aladdin kept its affiliation with a bank, law firm, and accounting firm in Chicago. "The business leadership in Nashville felt like Victor Johnson was an outsider and a maverick," said longtime *Tennessean* editor John Seigenthaler.

Many other business leaders in Nashville said Johnson stayed with professional organizations in Chicago in order to keep Aladdin's affairs as secret as possible. Johnson denied that was the case.

"We had a long relationship with Harris Trust that was so good that I could always call them up and tell them I wanted money and I would get it. And we had the outstanding law firm in the country in the field of patents and trademarks, which was our main area. I did not see why I should let parochialism make my decisions."

But perhaps the biggest way in which Aladdin changed the power structure in Nashville was in the area of organized labor. After the textile strikes of 1937, business executives in Nashville became even more adamantly opposed to unions than they had been before. But during World War II, unions gained an important foothold in Nashville with the coming of Avco. When the Mantle Lamp Co. first talked about the idea of coming to Nashville, Kerrigan Iron Works president Phillip Kerrigan Jr. reportedly said Nashville did not need employers such as Mantle Lamp because they would make it hard for existing companies to keep unions out.

Although Kerrigan was heavily criticized for his comments by other business leaders in Nashville, he was accurate to some degree. In 1952, Aladdin's Nashville employment shot up from two hundred to five hundred when the company moved its lamp manufacturing operation to Nashville. About that time, Aladdin's workers voted to join the United Steelworkers of America.

During the long contract negotiations that followed that vote, Aladdin's workers went on strike. The strike was especially significant because at one point, Chancellor William Wade tried to order truckers (represented by the Teamsters union) to cross picketing workers and transport products being made by Aladdin's replacement workers. The case went all the way to the U.S. Supreme Court, which ruled that the government could not order truckers to cross picket lines.

By the time Aladdin moved to Nashville, the growth side of its business was in vacuum bottles, many of which were sold inside metal lunch boxes. And in the 1950s and 1960s, Aladdin went head to head with the leader in the lunch box/vacuum bottle business, a Connecticut-based firm called American Thermos Co.

The first major salvo in this war took place in 1950, when Johnson and Aladdin sales chief Verne Church came up with the bright idea of decorating the side of the lunch box with a television character called Hopalong Cassidy. Church may have gotten the idea from the fact that Westinghouse had begun decorating plates and mugs with Disney characters in the 1950s. Nevertheless, in an era when lunch boxes came in three flavors (green, red, and blue), this was a major innovation.

In the fall of 1950, children across America took one look at the Hopalong Cassidy lunch kit and decided that they had to have it. "Next thing you know, we had an order from Sears & Roebuck for fifty thousand," Johnson said. American Thermos turned its nose up to the decorated lunch kit for three years, until it came out with one with Roy Rogers and Dale Evans on it. By the late 1950s, both Aladdin and American Thermos were coming out with several lunch kit lines every year in a high-stakes game of trying to predict what kids wanted. In 1963 alone, Aladdin came out with seven different lunch boxes: *The Jetsons*, *Bonanza*, *Yogi Bear*, *The Beverly Hillbillies*, *The Mickey Mouse Club*, *Junior Miss*, and *Shari Lewis*.

On the research and development front, Aladdin's victories were less apparent but just as effective. Prior to the construction of its Nashville factory, American Thermos made a better product than Aladdin, according to the July 1949 issue of *Consumers' Research Bulletin*. But in the 1950s, Aladdin came up with several innovations to the vacuum bottle. The most important was a rubber top that replaced the old cork ones. Later, Aladdin replaced the rubber top with a plastic one.

Perhaps the most important thing Aladdin did, however, was on the retail side. In the 1950s, most vacuum bottles were sold in variety stores and corner drugstores such as Kress and Woolworth's. When mass merchandisers such as K Mart began to emerge in the 1960s, Church—whose nickname was the "human dynamo"—began to cultivate those retail outlets.

By 1960, Aladdin's Nashville operation had revenues of $7 million and consisted of several divisions. The largest by far made vacuum bottles and lunch boxes. But the company also had a small lamp assembly factory and an electronics component called Aladdin Electronics.

One of the most interesting legal chapters in Aladdin history had to do with the use of the word "thermos." A predecessor of the American Thermos Co. had trademarked the word in 1907. But as the years went by, the word became commonly used to describe all vacuum bottles. In 1958, Aladdin began using the word "thermos" to describe some of its products, prompting a suit from American Thermos. In July 1962, a federal judge in New Haven, Connecticut,

decided in Aladdin's favor. The word thermos, like nylon, aspirin, and escalator, thus slipped into the public domain.

Aladdin workers pack Stanley thermoses, around 1970 (Aladdin Industries).

In 1965, Aladdin made the biggest acquisition in its history with the purchase of the Stanley division of Landers, Frary & Clark. The Nashville company thus added to its line a thermos brand used primarily by campers. Immediately after the purchase, Aladdin shut down the Stanley plant in Connecticut, laid off most of its workers, and built a new Stanley factory in Nashville.

Meanwhile, Aladdin's international division was also thriving. In the early 1960s, Aladdin opened a space heater factory in England and a parts plant in Brazil. Later, the company would open plants in Iran, Iraq, and Jordan.

Some of the best ideas come at the most absurd times. In 1966, a stewardess on a flight from Nashville to Chicago accidentally dropped several dinner trays. "It was awful," said John Bridges, who worked in Aladdin's research and development department. "Green beans, mashed potatoes, half-filled cups of coffee. It was just a disaster. The poor girl was just almost in tears."

Bridges began sketching a new serving tray that would stack better. When he got back to Nashville, he took the idea to a new level and began trying to come up with a way to keep hot food hotter and cold food colder.

Bridges approached his immediate supervisor in R&D, who told him to stick to thermoses. However, Bridges ignored his boss and started spending work time on insulated trays. A few weeks later,

Victor Johnson Jr. dropped in the R&D office after lunch. Bridges was worried at first, thinking he would get fired for disobeying his boss. "I did not know what to do, because I was clearly violating the chain of command," Bridges said in 1999. "But I figured that the president of the company had a right to know what I was doing. So I told him. And he put his arm around me and said, 'That's a good idea. Keep going, son.'"

By 1968, Aladdin had found two entities willing to give Bridges's insulated tray service a chance. One was Meharry-Hubbard Hospital, on whose board Johnson served. The other was Allegheny Airlines, the president of which Victor Johnson Jr. met at a Chamber of Commerce function in 1967. "My idea wasn't so much to make money off Allegheny, but to use the airline as a traveling trade show for the product," Johnson said.

As it turned out, hospitals were far more receptive to Aladdin's insulated trays than airlines were. One hospital became five, then twenty. By the end of 1970, over one hundred hospitals were serving their meals on Aladdin trays.

By this time, Johnson needed an insulated tray factory. Needing more real estate, he called Robert (Bobby) Mathews Jr., whose company had a long-standing relationship with Aladdin.

Johnson's call to Mathews came at an opportune time. Since taking over his father's company a few years earlier, Mathews had turned it from general contractor to general contractor/developer. "I thought if I had a big chunk of real estate and a company came to town and bought part of it, then I could build whatever they needed on that site for them," Mathews said. The idea had already worked once. Along with partner Hillsboro Enterprises, Mathews converted a farm into Metro Industrial Park, which had several large tenants including Kroger and United Parcel.

In 1969, while looking for a follow-up to the Metro Industrial Park, Mathews went to see some property that the Bush family was selling in North Nashville. After getting his car stuck in the mud, he pulled out his map and began imagining what could be done with the land. After becoming convinced that a dike would protect the land from future flooding, Mathews bought options on about six hundred acres. At the time, Mathews envisioned a heavy industrial park on the site.

When Johnson called Mathews and asked him about land for his new insulated tray factory, Mathews told him about his North Nashville development. Johnson was intrigued by the idea but thought it would be bad for the city to have heavy industry in the middle of town. After several months of studying the property, Mathews and Johnson decided to promote it as a mixed residential, commercial, industrial, and retail area called MetroCenter.

Ironically, Aladdin did not end up building its insulated tray factory in MetroCenter; it instead built it next to its thermos factory on Murfreesboro Road. But Aladdin became a codeveloper nonetheless, and was able to get Third National Bank and Prudential Securities to back the project. The partnership convinced Metro to support the plan by rerouting its plan for the Clarksville Highway, developing a golf course on a former dump adjacent to the project and building a cloverleaf interchange at I-265. By 1971, Mathews was building roads, sewer lines, and dikes on the property. The next year, he built a speculative office building on the site.

MetroCenter's master plan called for several kinds of development from retail to light commercial to heavy industrial. At first, the project showed signs of success and landed many commercial and industrial tenants such as IBM, Hewlett Packard, and the Service Merchandise distribution center. MetroCenter also managed to attract a hotel and convention center named for the Maxwell House Hotel that had burned in 1961.

However, Johnson's attempt to get the city to put a performing arts center on the site failed when the center ended up downtown. And in the late 1970s, MetroCenter did not fill up as quickly as it needed to in order to be a financial success. Mathews and Johnson disagreed about several things. Johnson, for example, wanted to build the infrastructure up front, while Mathews wanted to build it gradually (Johnson prevailed). Another sticking point for MetroCenter was that it took a lot longer to get the state to build a new Clarksville Highway bridge than Mathews and Johnson hoped. High interest rates, which dramatically increased the cost of new development, were also a huge hindrance. Mathews got out of the partnership in 1979, after which Johnson brought in Barry Oxford to run it under the business name Aladdin Resources.

In the early 1980s, competition from the Maryland Farms office park in Brentwood hurt MetroCenter. In 1988, Aladdin Resources developed a retail mall on the site called Fountain Square that failed miserably. "Maryland Farms sounded the death knell for MetroCenter as an office park," said Tony Martin, an executive with C. B. Commercial Real Estate Group in Nashville in the 1980s and 1990s. "Fountain Square Mall was more like the boat anchor that took it down." In 1989, Aladdin sold its interest in MetroCenter.

Years later, Mathews said he regretted not sticking to his original idea, which was to develop it as an industrial park. "MetroCenter could have succeeded," he said in 1999.

Johnson admitted that the investment had not worked out as well as he had originally thought. But he said that the project did an enormous amount to help the city's tax base. "Right now, MetroCenter is probably contributing over $6 million to the city's tax base," Johnson said. "Before, that land was probably contributing $4,000. Quaint as it might seem today, Aladdin perceived MetroCenter as being truly coupled with a significant public interest."

Throughout the 1970s and 1980s, Aladdin had around fifteen hundred Nashville employees. Lunch kits and thermoses were always a big seller, but insulated trays were the big growth area; over one thousand hospitals used the trays by 1978 and over three thousand by 1985.

Nevertheless, Aladdin stumbled along the way as it learned what it was good at and what it was not good at. In 1979, the company sold its electronics division. "When you are in the electronics business, a young man in a garage in L.A. could come up with a crazy idea that would obsolete you," Johnson said. Aladdin sold its kerosene heater business a couple of years later.

Over the years, many people in Nashville speculated that Aladdin was a good company to go public. But Johnson declined to sell stock because of the need public companies have to report consistently improving earnings. "If I had to worry each year about whether my earnings were going to be X percent more than the year before, I would start fudging a little bit," Johnson said. "If anything, I preferred to keep my profits as low as possible and invest in R&D."

Aladdin would have probably made an unpredictable public company because of the boom-or-bust nature of the lunch kit business. Since lunch kits had to be produced long before the season in which they were sold, Aladdin had to bet on which movie or television show would be a hit a year in advance. In addition to that investment, Aladdin also had to pay royalty fees for the use of the logos and characters' likenesses. In the 1950s and 1960s, Hollywood filmmakers charged a 5 percent royalty for lunch boxes. By the 1980s, that percent had gone up to 10 percent, and producers began charging six-figure up-front fees.

When Aladdin bet well, it got follow-up orders and needed more people. When it bet poorly, the company had to lay off workers. Poor sales of lunch boxes was one of the reasons Aladdin had layoffs in 1980, 1982, and 1984.

By 1985, it was time for Victor Johnson Jr. to retire. But unlike many other presidents of Nashville companies, he did not encourage his son to succeed him. "He wanted me to have my own career, and wasn't anxious to see me follow him in the business," said Victor (Torry) Johnson III, who later became Metro's district attorney. In 1985, Victor Johnson Jr. retired and announced that his successor would be Fred Meyer, who had previously worked as an Aladdin executive in the 1960s.

Meyer would remain as CEO for nine years. During his tenure, the company developed several lines of insulated cups and mugs, most of which were sold in convenience stores.

Nineteen ninety-three was one of the most successful years in Aladdin's history. Aladdin owned the rights to Hollywood's two biggest children's movies—*The Lion King* and *Power Rangers*. Demand was so great for Aladdin's lunch kits that retailers could hardly keep them on the shelves.

The next year was one of the worst in Aladdin's history. In 1994, Meyer retired and was replaced by Bob Garda. Less than a year later, Garda was fired and Aladdin laid off two hundred workers. Aladdin's board of directors then took the very unusual step of suing Garda for "mismanagement" during his tenure. Garda and Aladdin later settled out of court, but not before Aladdin had gone public in a nasty dispute with its former CEO.

After Garda's dismissal, Meyer came out of retirement. But no sooner had he done so than Aladdin bet on several poorly performing movies, including *Hercules* and *The Hunchback of Notre Dame*. In 1997, Aladdin got out of the lunch kit business, having decided that it was too risky. The next year, the company sold its insulated tray division.

Aladdin ended the twentieth century in two main businesses: producing Stanley thermoses and insulated cups. It also ended the century with new leadership in the person of Ari Chaney, a former General Electric executive hired by Aladdin in the spring of 1999.

Washington

Winston Churchill once described the Soviet Union as "a riddle wrapped within a mystery inside an enigma." Nashville's Washington Manufacturing could have also been described in this manner.

Washington had many things in common with Genesco. Like Genesco, Washington grew when apparel manufacturing migrated south in search of cheap labor. Like Genesco, Washington got a boost from World War II. Like Genesco, Washington was dominated by a man who inherited a small company from his father and expanded it to many times its original size. Like Genesco, Washington diversified wildly in the 1960s. And like Genesco, Washington had serious financial troubles in the 1970s.

However, unlike Genesco, Washington was a private company that grew by borrowing money rather than raising it through stock sales. Unlike Genesco, Washington hated publicity and was rarely profiled in newspapers or magazines. And unlike Genesco, Washington did not survive the 1980s.

The driving force behind the rise and fall of Washington Manufacturing was Guy Comer. In 1918, Guy Comer went to work for his dad Robert Comer's apparel company, started four years earlier under the name Dodd-Comer. Shortly thereafter, Robert Comer bought out his partner's half of the business. Since "Dodd-Comer" was abbreviated "D-C," the firm then changed its name to Washington Manufacturing.

Guy Comer became president of the company in 1932. By the mid-1930s Washington was one of the twenty largest apparel producers in the country, with two plants in Nashville (on Second Avenue and at Fifth and Charlotte), two in Cookeville, one in Glasgow, Kentucky, and one in Milan, Kentucky. The company produced overalls, work pants, and children's play suits.

In the summer of 1937, things got very ugly at Washington. In April, the Amalgamated Clothing Workers of America (ACWA) opened a Nashville office and began trying to organize textile workers at several plants, including Washington and Ingram Manufacturing. ACWA organizers later claimed that they were making progress at Washington's two factories when, on May 1, Comer closed his two Nashville factories and laid off six hundred workers. A few weeks later, when organizers tried to hand out leaflets outside the Cookeville factory, they were attacked and beaten by fifteen Washington employees.

As a result of the closure and the incident, Washington was accused of violating the Wagner Act, and Guy Comer was ordered to testify before the National Labor Relations Board. At that board hearing, several Washington workers testified that they had been warned by their bosses not to show up at any organizing meetings or do anything to encourage the union. One worker claimed that her foreman told her that by signing a union card she did "the worse thing you have ever done. It will put us all out of work."[2] Eventually, Washington reopened its Nashville plants. But Comer succeeded in keeping his factories union-free.

The 1940s were huge growth years for Washington Manufacturing. During the war, the federal government took over many Washington factories in order to make uniforms. As it did, Comer used money made from the contracts to buy new plants. "The government forced us into growing," Guy Comer's son T. W. (Wick) Comer said in 1999.

After World War II, Washington's product dominated the small-town apparel market and could be found in places such as Junior Department Stores, the Scottsville, Kentucky, chain started in 1945 by Cal Turner Sr. "We were a big customer of Mr. Guy Comer," said Cal Turner Jr., later the chief executive officer of Dollar General. "My dad had a quasi-father-son relationship with him."

Guy Comer was a religious man, a member of a Church of Christ, and a man who hated paying taxes. So it was not completely surprising when in 1946 he formed a foundation into which he began to pool his assets. However, Comer set up the foundation, which later became known as the Church of Christ Foundation, to function differently than many of the other large foundations that were created in Nashville in the twentieth century. According to the way Comer set it up, the Church of Christ Foundation owned a majority of the stock in Washington Manufacturing. As long as Comer lived, he controlled the foundation's board. But the arrangement made it inevitable that a power struggle would result from his death.

The apparel industry in the South did quite well in the 1950s and 1960s. Thanks in part to cheap labor, Washington Manufacturing was able to increase its market share and open new plants. By the mid-1960s, Washington had about fifteen manufacturing plants, most of which were in Kentucky and Tennessee. That number jumped to about twenty-five with the 1966 purchase of a St. Louis work shirt manufacturer called Ely & Walker, a transaction that made Washington the seventh largest apparel company in the United States. Major brand names produced by the company included Dee Cee brand work clothing, Deer Creek sportswear, and Happy Jack and Happy Jill children's clothes. Washington was also a leader in permanent press—clothing made of fibers that never needed ironing.

In 1968, Washington had nine sales offices, including New York, Chicago, and Los Angeles. But its primary market was family-owned stores in rural areas of the South and Midwest.

In the 1960s, Guy Comer began to diversify and invest in other types of businesses, including:

A wholesale dry goods operation called William R. Moore that provided merchandise to small-town variety and discount stores.

A small-town department store chain called Sullivan's that sold Washington-made clothes.

Nashville's Phillips & Buttorff Co., which Comer bought from fellow First American board member Douglas Binns. By the time Washington bought it in the 1960s, Phillips & Buttorff was in the business of making electric stoves.

Ford car dealerships in Gallatin, Clarksville, and Scottsville, Kentucky.

A Fire & Casualty Insurance Co. that primarily insured Washington's plants and retail stores.

A discount furniture store in Nashville's Cummins Station called Manufacturer's Warehouse Co.

By the late 1960s, Washington had over $250 million in revenue and close to ten thousand employees, making it one of the largest private companies in the United States. Despite its size, Washington Industries (as it became known in the 1960s) remained an entity that was little known in Nashville except among its employees. Washington had no outsiders on its board. And unlike the heads of other private companies, such as Victor Johnson Jr. and Bronson Ingram, Guy Comer was not active in either the Chamber of Commerce or civic clubs such as Rotary. "There is little that Guy Comer wanted said," said Hix Clark, who went to work as an executive with Washington in 1951 and stayed until 1984.

Guy Comer died in 1969. By that time, he had been replaced as president by his son Wick Comer.

It is easy to see why Washington Industries began to have serious financial problems in the 1970s. During his last years at the company, Guy Comer had borrowed about $50 million in order to make acquisitions. As interest rates climbed, the burden of that debt increased. Meanwhile, many of Washington's divisions were in industries that were changing fast, and in some cases becoming extinct. Small-town, locally owned apparel stores would become nonexistent with the emergence of Wal-Mart. Phillips & Buttorff was no longer in a profitable industry. Most importantly, apparel manufacturing was quickly moving overseas, which surprised Washington's management as much as it did Genesco's. "I did not see the apparel moving overseas thing," said Clark. "When I went to work for Washington, I thought that it would one day be as big as General Motors."

Washington's management structure did not help. After Guy Comer's death, the Church of Christ Foundation—the key members of which were Clark, attorney William Berry, and longtime Washington executives Paul Hargis and Meredith Shepherd—owned about 60 percent of Washington Industries stock. Meanwhile, Washington Industries president Wick Comer was neither a member of the board of the Church of Christ Foundation nor did he have any say about who those members were. Not surprisingly, conflict between Comer and the foundation ensued almost immediately. "It was twelve people against me from day one," Comer said.

Years later, when many of the key members of the foundation board were dead, it was hard to learn details about the struggle between Wick Comer and the board. Comer, however, claimed that he wanted to make dramatic changes to the company and to sell off some of its losing assets. "Our debt was so high that we were paying all of our gross products out in interest," Comer said.

In 1973, the fight between Comer and the foundation made it to Chancery Court. In the case, Comer asked the court to dismiss the trustees of the Church of Christ Foundation on the grounds that the foundation was running the for-profit Washington Industries rather than being a charity. The courtroom battle that followed had its share of melodrama: at one point, a forty-year employee of Washington named Robert Billingsley had a heart attack on the witness stand and died. In January 1975, Chancellor Frank Drowota III concluded the case by ordering the foundation's board to take on nine new trustees. But the ruling left the foundation still with control of the company. The next year, Comer resigned, leaving Hargis as the next president.

By this time, Washington's grip on the apparel business had slipped dramatically. When large discount stores such as K Mart and Wal-Mart began to take over the retail business in the rural South and Midwest, Washington did not cultivate those customers. "The market was disappearing," said Ben Kooch, who joined Washington as a sales representative in 1965 and eventually became the company's national sales manager. "You either had to step up to the Wal-Marts or you were going to be out of business. And we did not move."

When Washington's sales department made deals, the company's manufacturing side wasn't always on the same page. Kooch said unfulfilled orders became a major problem around 1970 and got worse from then on. "I booked a lot of back-to-school orders and the customers never received them," Kooch said. "There were times when we simply couldn't get the goods out, and that slowly developed into a major, major problem. . . . Salesmen would get nailed to the wall every time they walked into the store because of deliveries and orders that were unfulfilled."

As Washington deteriorated, Kooch said he saw very few signs that the company was trying to fix its problems. "I remember going to one meeting and saying that we needed to look at what Wrangler was doing, because they were just tearing up the market with their kid's line," Kooch said. "Mr. Shepherd said, 'We don't want to get into that.'"

In 1986, Nashville resident Van Hill and two other investors took over Washington's assets in a leveraged buyout. Hill began seeking buyers for Washington's assets with an eye toward taking part of the company public. He found it tougher than he first thought. In March 1988, Washington filed for Chapter 11 bankruptcy protection and immediately shut down several apparel plants, leaving about thirty-five hundred workers without paychecks for several weeks. During the next few months, the receiver sold the company's apparel plants and its many pieces of real estate. One of the more important pieces was the Second Avenue factory, sold to an out-of-town developer for conversion into offices.

By 1990, there was virtually nothing left of Washington Industries.

CHAPTER 17

A Nashville Dynasty

M artha Rivers was a disc jockey for station WCSC in Charleston, South Carolina. Listeners of her classical music radio show knew her by the pseudonym Elizabeth Crawford.

In February 1958, Rivers made a weekend trip to Nashville to visit a former Vassar classmate named Grace Ward. Before Rivers left Charleston, Ward told her friend that she already had two double dates planned. On Friday night, Martha would be accompanied by a young man who ran his father's chain of gas stations. His name was Bronson Ingram. On Saturday night, her date would be a young man who helped run his father's shoe company. His name was Franklin Jarman.

This was Martha's second date with Bronson, and this one went better than the first. As the date ended, the young man asked Miss Rivers what her plans were for Saturday night. "Well, that's all right," said Bronson, when he heard about Martha's scheduled date with Jarman. "I'll just call him and tell him that you'll be going out with me." Ingram did just that, elbowing out Jarman in an incident that was curiously symbolic of what would happen to the mens' business fortunes during the next few years.

Six months later, Bronson and Martha Ingram were married. Martha Rivers thus became a member of one of the South's wealthiest families.

The Ingram family first became wealthy in the 1850s, when a midwesterner named Orrin Henry Ingram became a leader in

314

Wisconsin's lumber industry. Later, Ingram was one of many landowners of that area who consolidated his assets into a company called Weyerhaeuser Timber Co.

In the 1920s, one of Orrin Ingram's grandsons, also named Orrin Henry (Hank) Ingram, married Hortense Bigelow, daughter of the president of the St. Paul Fire and Marine Insurance Co. A few years later, Hank Ingram came to Nashville to run a yarn factory that the family owned in Nashville. According to family legend, Hank Ingram got the carpet factory running better and went back to Minnesota. A few months later, he looked out his window during a midwinter snowstorm and said to his wife, "Only a damn fool or an eskimo would live here when you could live in Nashville. Let's move back." Hank subsequently returned to Nashville and renamed the factory Ingram Manufacturing. By the mid-1930s it had 550 workers and had two divisions: one that made yarn and another that made bathroom rugs.

The strike of 1937 convinced Hank Ingram that there were safer places to put his assets than manufacturing. After the strike ended, Ingram sold half ownership of the yarn factory to a man named Ernest Jones. Ingram Spinning, it then became known, remained in operation on Centennial Boulevard until around 1950. Hank Ingram sold the rug division to an employee named Ernest Moench, who moved it to a factory building near Fisk University. Tennessee Tufting, as it became known, remained in operation until the 1960s.

Hank Ingram had capital from both his and his wife's side of the family and decided to invest it in oil. In the late 1930s, oil companies were appearing all over the United States to meet the enormous new demand for fossil fuels in an era when many Americans were buying their first automobile. In 1938, Ingram and oil magnate Fred Koch bought one such business called the Wood River Oil and Refining Co. Like many oil businesses of that era, Wood River had a refinery (this one in St. Louis) and operated a barge fleet that moved gasoline up the Mississippi River.

Hank Ingram's partnership with Koch dissolved a few years later, when they sold Wood River to Sinclair Oil and Refining Co.[1] Hank Ingram then began putting together his own oil company. First, he ordered a small fleet of towboats and barges. He then built a network of terminals that eventually included Nashville, Louisville, St. Paul, Tampa, Mobile, New Orleans, and Sheffield, Alabama. "He [Hank Ingram] always liked boats, and he liked to build things," said Jimmy Granbery, who worked on the barge side of Ingram Oil & Refining Co. from 1947 to 1957. The firm used its fleet to tow petroleum products up and down the Mississippi, Cumberland, Ohio, and Illinois Rivers.

In 1953, Ingram built a $4 million refinery just south of New Orleans. Shortly thereafter, Ingram started a chain of gas stations. After building and acquiring about sixty, Ingram bought a chain of

O. H. (Hank) Ingram,
around 1950 (Orrin
Ingram).

stations called Transamerica Oil Co. (Taoco) from
Nashville resident Gilbert Dickey. "We were somewhat reluctant to get our own gas stations at first,
because we knew this was putting us in competition
with our customers," said Andrew Mizell III, who worked for Ingram
Oil & Refining from 1955 until 1962.[2] Years later, Nashville residents
still remembered the Ingram gas station in Belle Meade, which had a
unique futuristic design. "It looked like a flying nun's hat," Mizell said.

In the later 1950s, Hank Ingram moved the headquarters of the oil
company to New Orleans (although he refused to move there himself).
Ingram used the refinery to produce gasoline that was then trans-
ported via Ingram Barge to the company's network of terminals. From
there, the gasoline was taken by truck to the service stations and truck
stops, which numbered over two hundred by the late 1950s.

By this time, Hank Ingram's two sons were working in the business. Fredric (Fritz), the oldest, worked for a man named Jim O'Neil,
who ran the Ingram refinery. Bronson worked for Mizell, who ran the
gas stations.

Like many businessmen who start with a small operation and
eventually work their way into much bigger things, Bronson Ingram

later liked to reminisce about his days operating his father's chain of gas stations. According to one story, Bronson once drove up to a station on Sunday and found it unattended. The younger Ingram brother rolled up his sleeves and started pumping gas. During his years in the gas station business, Bronson also concluded that you made a lot more money from the sale of cigarettes and condoms than on the sale of fuel.

The oil business consolidated fast, making it tough for a medium-sized player like Ingram to compete. In the fall of 1961, Hank Ingram sold Ingram Products to Murphy Oil, the Arkansas firm that had a year earlier bought Nashville-based Spur Oil. During the next couple of years, Hank Ingram made several investments. He bought a Nashville firm called Cumberland River Sand & Gravel Co., which had a fleet of barges and a nice business dredging for sand and carrying it to various points in Kentucky and Tennessee. He negotiated the purchase of a Nashville-based barge line called Barrett, which hauled rock from a quarry in Kentucky to various Army Corps of Engineer projects along the Cumberland River. Ingram also started a fiberglass boat building business in Nashville called Superglass.

All this buying and selling would have been big news in Nashville had people known about it. But Hank Ingram rarely discussed his personal finances or sought attention. "Hank Ingram was a very, very private man," Mizell said. "No one knew anything about his finances—not even his closest friends. People knew he was rich, but not how rich." Hank Ingram did most of his banking in Chicago, St. Paul, and New Orleans and turned down several directorships with Nashville companies.

Hank Ingram's death of heart attack in April 1963 came as a complete shock to everyone. After a few months, the Ingram family decided to organize the family business under an umbrella organization called Ingram Corp. Ingram Corp., they decided, would keep its inland barge line, which continued to haul petroleum, rock, and sand. But the real business of Ingram Corp. would be the construction of oil-related facilities.

In retrospect, it is interesting that Fritz and Bronson decided to be partners. "Fritz and Bronson never did get along well, even as little boys," Mizell said. "I remember Hank Ingram saying to me many times, 'For God's sake Andy, let's see if there isn't some way in the world that we can get those boys to get along together a little better.'"

Fritz loved the high-stakes game of buying and selling businesses, and New Orleans fit his style perfectly. Bronson was more conservative. After the sale of Ingram Oil, Bronson moved his wife Martha and his two young sons back to Nashville. "We loved it in New Orleans, but you had to wait your turn to be taken into this club or that and to become prominent," Martha Ingram said in 1999. "Meanwhile, we were already established in Nashville, and it was a wonderful place to rear children." Bronson and Fritz also had two sisters who owned a large chunk of stock in the family business: Patricia (who later married Rodes Hart Jr.) and Alice (who later married Henry Hooker).

Ingram Corp.'s first venture into the pipeline construction business was through a small company called Marsh Services Inc., which Ingram bought from a Louisiana man named Nick Popich. During the late 1960s, Ingram Corp. laid pipeline along the floor of the Gulf of Mexico, connecting offshore oil rigs to refineries in Texas and Louisiana. Tony Martin, who spent a summer as an Ingram rigger, said having a job for that company at that time was quite a challenge. "I worked twelve hours a day, seven days a week," said Martin, who later became the head of C. B. Commercial Real Estate Group in Nashville. "They paid pretty well and gave me room and board. I saved a lot." Eventually, Ingram moved on to larger and more distant projects. By the mid-1960s, Ingram Contractors (as the construction division became known) was building oil platforms for Exxon off the coast of Australia.

In 1969, Ingram Corp. bought a pipeline construction company called Great Plains. That acquisition gave Ingram the size it needed to successfully bid on a portion of the Alaskan pipeline. About that time, Ingram announced its intention to go public. Those plans were dropped after a few months because the stock market was not conducive to public offerings at that time. A few months later, Ingram Corp. sold its offshore construction arm.

The riskiest venture in Ingram Corp.'s history was the development of a $300 million oil refinery near Baton Rouge. The refinery, cofinanced with John and Albert Kaneb of Boston, was highly leveraged and highly speculative. Its financial plan was based on federal incentives set up to encourage independent, U.S.-owned refiners. While the refinery was under construction, Congress got rid of the incentives, and for a few months it appeared as if the refinery would lose money. At the last moment, Marathon Oil stepped in and bought the refinery, saving the Ingrams and Kanebs from possible disaster.

Years later, Martha Ingram said she could remember many sleepless nights over the construction of the refinery. "It could have wiped us all out," she said. "After the venture, I remember saying to Bronson that I hope we would not bet the farm anymore."

Despite the close brush with disaster, high-stakes trading picked up speed. In the early 1970s, Ingram Corp. bought a small British oil transporter called Rowbotham. A couple of years later, it bought a British trading company called Tampimex Oil, which had an annual trading volume of about $700 million. Fritz Ingram would later say that the entire negotiating process for Tampimex only took six days.

Compared to the oil business, Bronson's entry into books seemed dull.

A few months after Hank Ingram's death, a former vice chancellor at Vanderbilt named Jack Stambaugh asked Bronson to help him acquire a textbook distributor called the Tennessee Book Company. Ingram pitched in half of the $250,000 needed for the purchase, mainly because Stambaugh had been a friend of his father's. A few years later, Stambaugh had to move to Arizona because his wife had contracted emphysema. Bronson bought out Stambaugh's half and complained about what his dad's friend had gotten him into. "What the hell am I going to do with this little book company?" he told Martha that night. "I don't know anything about the book business! I'm an oil man!"

Bronson Ingram's solution to the problem was the same one he would use again and again during the next twenty-five years: find the smartest person he could find to run his business and monitor that person closely. For Tennessee Book Co., that person in the early years was Harry Hoffman, a former FBI agent with a background in marketing. After Hoffman was named general manager, Ingram Book Co.—as it soon became known—grew through a combination of good fortune, innovation, and acquisition. In addition to being a textbook distributor, the Tennessee Book Co. also provided books for school and public libraries. One of the major initiatives of Lyndon Johnson's Great Society programs was to dramatically increase the amount of books in school and public libraries. In Tennessee, Ingram Book got the lion's share of that increase.

By 1970, the money for the Great Society had begun to dry up, and Ingram Book's fortunes appeared to be on the way down. At that point, Hoffman began using the company to service small, locally owned bookstores—most of which still bought books directly from publishers and had to wait as much as six weeks for titles. "In those days, if a bookstore got the book in a week or ten days, that was much better service than they had gotten by buying directly from the publishers," said Phil Pfeffer, who became president of Ingram Book in 1978. "The publishers were fairly good at getting new books out into the market, but when it came time to replenish, it took them anywhere from four weeks to two or three months."

During the next several years, Ingram Book introduced one innovation and service after another. First it was toll-free telephone ordering. Then came same-day shipments. Then came microfiche, which made the inventory list so small that it could be easily distributed. Next came on-line order entry for its distribution centers, which dramatically decreased wait time.

Ingram Book started with a large warehouse in Nashville and in 1975 built another near Baltimore. The next year, Ingram bought the

Raymar Book Company and its warehouse in California, giving the company national coverage for the first time. In only seven years, Ingram Book's inventory grew from five hundred titles to fifteen thousand titles. Between 1970 and 1976, revenue grew from $3 million to $70 million.

Ingram Book was doing business with thousands of bookstores all over the country, but it was still small potatoes in Fritz Ingram's mind. Around 1975, Bronson Ingram took Ingram Book president Harry Hoffman to make a presentation to an Ingram Corp. board meeting in New Orleans. When it came time for Hoffman to speak, Fritz turned to Bronson and said, "Is there anything you want to say about your little bookstore in Nashville? If not, we stand adjourned."

Hoffman returned to Nashville devastated. But both he and his successor Phil Pfeffer used the incident to motivate themselves. "Those became fighting words for us at Ingram Book," Pfeffer said. "We would tease around and refer to ourselves as the little bookstore in Nashville."

Despite the high-risk nature of Ingram Corp.'s oil operation and the steady expansion of its book distribution business, it was the barge business that put the two brothers in the national spotlight. As oil companies began to increasingly use pipelines, Ingram had to look for new uses for its barge fleet. In 1971, Ingram Barge was granted a $43 million contract to remove sewage sludge from Chicago. Four years later, a woman who had recently been fired from the sanitary district office told federal officials that Ingram executives had bribed Chicago officials to get the project.

A ten-month probe into Ingram Barge followed. Fritz and Bronson were indicted and tried in connection with the one hundred thousand dollar bribe allegations. In the case that followed, an Ingram executive named Joe Benton agreed to testify against the company. In the trial, it was revealed that Ingram Corp. had borrowed the alleged bribe money from Commerce Union Bank's international department. But according to Commerce Union officials, Ingram officials never told the bank what the money was going to be used for.

The case was reported in detail by the Nashville, Chicago, and New Orleans media. Fritz's attorney was Herbert Miller, who had previously been one of Richard Nixon's Watergate attorneys. Bronson's was Jim Neal, previously a Watergate prosecutor.

On November 8, 1977, Fritz Ingram was found guilty on twenty-nine counts and sentenced to four years in prison. Bronson Ingram was acquitted of all charges.

"It was a nightmare," Martha Ingram said. "Even when he was extricated, it was very bittersweet to see your brother convicted like that. The whole thing was something we never really discussed again. It was so traumatic. It was as bad as life can get."

Four months later, while Fritz appealed the conviction, the Ingram brothers divided the business. Fritz kept Ingram Corp., whose main assets were Tampimex and the pipeline business. Bronson took over the book distribution company and barge line, now called Ingram Industries.

Fritz spent sixteen months in federal prison at Florida's Eglin Air Force Base, after which President Carter commuted his sentence. Fritz then renounced his U.S. citizenship and became an Irish citizen. For the next several years, he maintained residences in London and Beverly Hills. He and his brother would have only minimal contact for the rest of their lives.

For a short time after his release from prison, Fritz's side of the business prospered. But in 1982, Ingram lost heavily by betting on oil futures. Two years later, after the collapse of the oil industry, Ingram Corp. defaulted on loans totaling $54 million. By 1986, Ingram Corp. was an empty shell.

Meanwhile, Bronson's side of the family business prospered. In 1978, Hoffman left Ingram Book and was replaced by Phil Pfeffer, who worked for Genesco before he came to Ingram as director of financial planning in 1976. Pfeffer constantly explored what items the company could distribute besides books. Videocassettes, which began appearing in the marketplace around 1980, were among the first products. "We got into the video business because we thought bookstores would become centers for education, entertainment, and information, regardless of media," Pfeffer said. "But as it turned out, most bookstores loved books and wanted to stay in books. As it turned out, video did not go over as a sale item, but as a rental item. . . . But the distribution requirements were very much the same for videos as they were for books." When video rental chains such as Blockbuster and Tower began to proliferate, Ingram was perfectly situated to be their distributor. In 1982, the firm organized its videocassette side into a separate division called Ingram Entertainment.

Meanwhile, Ingram's book distribution company continued to grow. In 1986, Ingram Book distributed 55 million general interest books and more than one hundred thousand titles. At that point, the company built a 204,000 square-foot headquarters facility in La Vergne, Tennessee. About that same time, Ingram Book proved that it was still on the cutting edge of its industry by introducing an on-line ordering system that allowed any clerk in the world to order books without ever having to pick up the phone. The on-line order system worked so well that by 1995, two-thirds of Ingram Book's orders came via computer.

By this time, the distribution side was doing so well that Bronson was beginning to diversify in more ways. In 1982, after American General took over National Life & Accident and announced its intention to sell National Life's country music assets such as the Opryland theme park and Opryland Hotel, Ingram thought he had a deal with American General CEO Harold Hook to buy those properties. Right when it appeared that Hook and Ingram were set to sign a letter of intent, Hook got a better offer from Ed Gaylord of Oklahoma City. Rather than tell him about his decision over the phone, Hook sent an investment banker to Nashville to tell Ingram about his decision. "Bronson was furious," said Phil Pfeffer, then president of the Ingram Book Co. "I thought he was going to literally throw this guy out of his office window."

However, Ingram's failure to buy Opryland was probably a blessing in disguise for his family's long-term financial future. In the early 1980s, the Ingram Distribution Group (as Ingram Book and Ingram Entertainment were then known) started a computer software distribution arm. During the next few years, the family would need every bit of capital it could get in order to keep up with the expanding computer distribution business. In 1985, Ingram bought two competing distributors: one called Software Distribution Services and another called Soft Team. A few months later, Ingram spent $6.7 million to buy 51 percent of a California-based software distributor called Micro D. A long battle between Ingram and Micro D management followed. Then, in 1989, Ingram bought the rest of the company's stock for $44 million. The Nashville company then merged Micro D with its own distribution system and took the entire company private.

Ingram Industries was now a wholesaling giant doing business with just about every book, video, and computer store in the country. Incredibly, the company had not sold any stock to the public along the way. "Bronson was very much opposed to going public," Pfeffer said. "He did not want to run a public company and be accountable to outside shareholders and report earnings on a quarterly basis." In the early 1990s, as millions of Americans invested in computers for the first time, Ingram Micro's revenues skyrocketed past Ingram's other divisions. One of the main reasons for this resurgence was Ingram Micro's chief executive officer Chip Lacy, who was so driven and talked so fast that he became known as the "Tasmanian Devil." By 1994, Ingram Micro's net sales were about $8 billion.

Since he always refused to be interviewed, the public knew little during Bronson's lifetime about his leadership style and philosophy of management. But according to Pfeffer, Bronson Ingram was not the kind of boss who would breathe down your neck all the time. "When he made you the president and CEO of one of his companies, you were in charge and you were accountable to the board of that company," Pfeffer said. "He would often refer to himself as a senior advisor." Pfeffer also said Ingram was always careful not to get involved in businesses that he did not understand. "Whenever people asked Bronson why he never got involved in other businesses, he would always say 'I got involved in the number of businesses that I thought I could become knowledgeable enough in to be an advisor.'"

Although Ingram served as Chamber of Commerce president in 1967 and was a long-standing Vanderbilt trustee, he was no socialite. "He did not really see the need for meeting a whole lot of new people," Martha Ingram said. "I used to tease Bronson and say that if it had not been for me, he would have only known Jake [Wallace] and Ed [Nelson] and no one else, because he was just content to be with his friends."

Martha was far more outgoing than her husband. Starting in 1974, she led the successful fund-raising campaign for a performing arts center in Nashville. After the campaign, Bronson told his wife that he wanted her to learn more about the business in case something ever happened to him. Before long, Martha Ingram was doing public relations for the company and sitting in on its board meetings.

Never has there been a better illustration of what money can't buy you. On December 1, 1994, Bronson Ingram, one of the wealthiest men in the United States, was diagnosed with cancer. Physicians started chemotherapy and radiation treatment a few days later. "At first, he and I both had this very positive attitude that we were going to lick this thing and we did not even allow a negative thought to creep in," said Martha Ingram. But when cancer reached his liver, Bronson realized that the treatment was pointless. In early spring, he took a few more trips with his family. "We even went to one last Masters, and he could hardly walk at that point," she said. On June 15, 1995, Bronson Ingram died.

Weeks after Bronson's funeral, Ingram Industries announced a major reorganization. Ingram Micro would be spun off in a public offering, with the rest of the company arranged in a way that would give each of Bronson's three sons a chance to run a part of the company. Youngest son David would take over Ingram Entertainment, which would be spun off as an independent private company. Meanwhile, Ingram Book and Ingram Barge would remain a part of Ingram Industries, under the presidency of John and Orrin, respectively.

A 1997 *Business Week* story later implied that the reorganization of the Ingram business empire was something Bronson would not have blessed. But Martha Ingram said she did not think that depiction was accurate. "One of the things he and I frequently talked about was how we would one day structure our businesses so that our children could excel while not being in conflict with one another," she said. "Years ago, it became obvious that Orrin loved the barge business,

John seemed quite taken with the book business, and David loved the video business."

Nonetheless, the public offering of Ingram Micro did not exactly come off without a hitch. After the IPO was announced but before it took place, the company announced that Lacy would resign from the company. The reason, as described by both Lacy and the Ingram board, was governance. "After Bronson's death, Chip basically did not want to answer to anybody," Martha Ingram said. About the same time, Pfeffer left Ingram to become president of Random House.

The Ingram Micro IPO took place in November 1996. Two years later, the Ingram family donated twenty million shares of Ingram Micro stock to Vanderbilt University. Worth $340 million at the time, it was the largest single private donation to a university in American history.

However, 1998 and 1999 were bad years for the Ingram family empire. As more Americans began buying their computers directly from manufacturers such as Dell and Gateway, they bypassed wholesalers such as Ingram Micro. During 1999, Ingram Micro's stock fell from about thirty-five dollars to ten dollars a share. Meanwhile, several large booksellers such as Barnes & Noble and Amazon.com began building their own distribution networks. By the end of the century, Bronson Ingram's children had their work cut out for them.

CHAPTER 18

Salvation & Controversy

W hen hundreds of thousands of World War II veterans came home, got married, and started having kids, they began taking their new families to church. That meant good news for the city known as the Protestant Vatican.

Between 1945 and 1960, Nashville's religious publishers tripled their business. By 1960, close to ten thousand Nashville residents worked for either a religious publisher or one of their vendors.

But funny things began to happen in the 1960s. The Civil Rights Movement and the Vietnam War shook the foundation of American society, a part of which was the church. As America changed, Nashville's religious publishers found themselves in the middle of interdenominational debates on the Scriptures and under attack for their roles in race relations. During the last three decades of the twentieth century, the United Methodists would struggle over their shrinking church rolls, while the Baptist Sunday School Board became engulfed in an increasingly bitter fight between moderates and conservatives.

The Methodists

The main reason that the northern and southern branches of the Methodist Church merged in 1939 was because there was no longer a major ideological reason to keep them apart. But another big reason was that the northern branch had serious financial problems. Rather than keep its publishing arm centralized over the years, the northern branch had regional offices—each with its own outdated printing operation—in New York, Chicago, Philadelphia, Cincinnati, and San Francisco. After the merger, it established the headquarters operation of the combined Methodist Publishing House in Nashville and took months to sift through hundreds of unpaid bills left by the former northern Methodist's Book Concern before it could even quantify the debt.

During World War II, a Methodist author named George Buttrick came up with the idea of a massive study Bible—complete with the King James Version, Revised Standard Version, and commentaries. No one had ever done anything like it before. After the war ended, the Methodist Publishing House moved ahead with the project.

The Interpreter's Bible took 124 writers and fifteen years. When volume one was released, *Time* magazine called it a landmark of biblical scholarship.[1] The book eventually became a necessity for every Methodist, Presbyterian, and Lutheran clergyman in the United States and was probably used to help write more sermons than any other Bible commentary in history. The twelve-volume Interpreter's Bible sold over three million copies, making it the best-selling book of all time for the Methodist Publishing House (other than hymnbooks).

The decision to name Lovick Pierce president of the Methodist Publishing House in 1946 spoke volumes about the way the organization worked. Pierce, a lifelong employee of the organization, had no college degree. But he was long on family connections. A street near what eventually became the Vanderbilt Hospital was named for his great-grandfather, Bishop Lovick Pierce.

Pierce's first twenty years as president were fat years for the Methodist Publishing House. Thanks to the 1939 merger with the northern branch of the Methodist Church, the publishing house had about twice as many customers in the 1940s as it had in the 1930s. After World War II, Sunday school attendance grew steadily with the baby boom. In addition to the Interpreter's Bible, the publishing entity came out with a four-volume Interpreter's Dictionary of the Bible in the early 1960s that also proved to be a best-seller by religious publishing standards.

Under Pierce's direction, the publishing house took several steps to meet its new, larger audience, including building a new home for its offices and printing plant at the corner of Eighth Avenue and Demonbreun. But Pierce took very few steps to centralize the new national publishing organization and instead maintained six regional centers across the country. This regional system would eventually prove to be very wasteful and unnecessary as modern distribution methods rendered regional shipping operations obsolete.

One of Pierce's most ambitious moves was to launch a slick, new Methodist magazine called *Together*, which was intended to bring

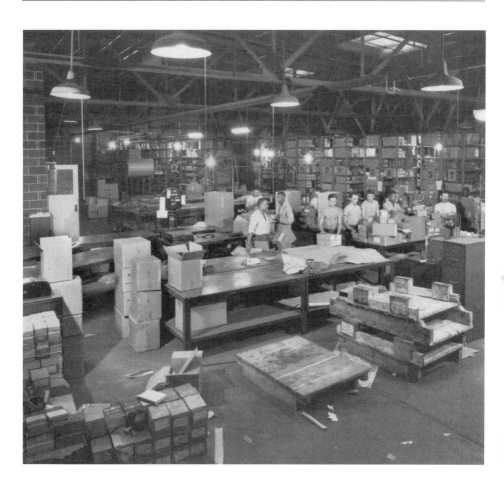

Methodist periodicals into the slick age of "eye-catching secular periodicals."[2] In its early years, *Together* featured the writing of everyone from Norman Vincent Peale to Carl Sandburg. *The Nation* sarcastically called it "the hottest thing in the publishing world since *Playboy* began its rise."[3]

Workers at the Methodist Publishing House, around 1950 (United Methodist Publishing House).

However, if *Together* was a literary achievement for the world of religious publishing, it was hardly an achievement in accounting. During its first four years of existence, *Together* lost over $2 million. Part of the problem had to do with distribution. In 1959, *Together* claimed a circulation of about a million copies. But when the home office in Nashville investigated how *Together's* office in Chicago was managing to lose so much money, it discovered that circulation was actually about 30 percent less than advertised. Because of careless record keeping, the magazine was, in hundreds of thousands of cases, mailing multiple copies to the same address.

Together also had to deal with the same restrictions on advertisements that had applied to *Christian Advocate* since the mid-1850s. "It wasn't just that we did not sell tobacco and liquor advertisements," said John Procter, vice president of publishing for the house in the 1960s. "Other types of advertisers such as automobile companies wouldn't advertise, either, because they did not consider us a complete product because of our ban on tobacco and liquor advertisements." Despite its financial problems, Pierce and the publishing board stuck with *Together* throughout the 1960s.

One project that was a financial success for the Methodist Publishing House was the 1965 hymnbook, which sold 2.2 million advance copies and over five million total copies. However, the hymnbook gave Methodist Publishing House officials its share of headaches. After years of working on its contents, and while copies were coming off the press, the publishing house became aware that a company called Manna Music Inc. claimed to own the copyright to the hymn "How Great Thou Art." After months of negotiations, Methodist officials came to the conclusion that Manna's case wouldn't hold up in court. But the house paid Manna Music twenty-five thousand dollars for the rights to the song anyway, to avoid the chance of Manna Music obtaining an injunction to delay the hymnbook's release.

Starting about 1963, Methodist ministers began loudly criticizing their own publishing arm for its failure to promote African Americans to executive positions. Publishing officials, led by Pierce, denied that racism was prevalent at the organization but admitted there were virtually no blacks in high positions. The controversy grew worse when the Methodist Church refused to join an ecumenical movement that was trying to end discrimination in employment by utilizing the power of the church dollar. In 1969, about 125 people marched in the publishing house parking lot. One of them was the Rev. James Lawson, the former Vanderbilt Divinity student who was expelled by the university for taking part in the sit-in movement in 1960. "I'm a Methodist through and through and I've never let any material not published here come into my church," Lawson said. "But I will unless the publishing house changes its practices."[4]

As a result of the criticism, the 1968 General Conference of the Methodist Church appointed a committee to study the policies and operations of the Methodist Publishing House. That report, issued a year later, concluded that the publishing house had a "defensive, 'closed door' management problem."[5] Although it did not find any overt pattern of wage discrimination, it recommended that the board select new leaders. A few weeks after the report was released, Pierce announced he would retire.

The publishing house's political problems were a contributing factor, but not the only cause, of another problem coming to the forefront about the same time. During Pierce's twenty-two-year tenure, the publishing concern's annual revenue rose from about $12 million to about $30 million. But in 1970, the United Methodist Publishing House—which had run a surplus every year since the Great Depression—ran a deficit of $400,000.

It was almost certainly because of this deficit that the board appointed John Procter to be the publishing house's new president. Procter, a self-described "bean-counter," started in the United Methodist Publishing House's accounting division in 1940 and worked his way up to the number two job at the organization because of his knack for finding ways to save money. "You wouldn't believe what some people were paying for paper clips before I came along," he said in 1998.

When Procter took over in 1970, the Methodist Publishing House had twenty-five hundred employees, five regional centers, a magazine that was losing $650,000 per year, a deficit-plagued chain of bookstores and—in his own words—"a lot of people who were not doing anything in the world." The house also had an enormous political problem because of its lack of African Americans in high positions.

Within five years, Procter had changed much of this. He eliminated three of the regional centers, plus a printing operation in Dayton, Ohio, that the publishing house had obtained in the 1970 merger with the Evangelical United Brethren Church, a small Methodist denomination, which resulted in the addition of "United" to the organization's corporate name. He closed *Together* magazine. He shut down some bookstores, renovated others, and built new ones, eventually turning the retail operation into a moneymaker. He named an African American, W. T. Handy, vice president of personnel and public relations.

Procter is not generally regarded as an innovator of new products, but he had at least one growth idea that was ignored. By the mid-1970s, for-profit companies such as Word and Thomas Nelson had carved out a niche in publishing books for conservative Christians, a reader the Methodist Publishing House historically ignored. Procter approached one of his editors and suggested that the organization either buy Word or form its own conservative imprint. "He became very upset about that suggestion," Procter said. "I let him talk me out of it, and frankly that was a mistake."

When Procter retired in 1983, the United Methodist Church was far more concerned about its declining rolls than anything else. Between 1965 and 1998, the population of America more than doubled. However, membership of the United Methodist Church actually declined from 10.7 million in 1965 to about 8.5 million in 1998. Methodist ministers agonized over the causes of this trend. Some of the more common reasons that were given would be pluralism, the growth of more conservative denominations, and the passing of the baby boom. But by the turn of the century, many ministers were acknowledging the fact that myriad social changes had altered the way many Americans viewed organized religion.

Because of this concern about shrinking church rolls, the publishing house board put a huge emphasis on new product development as they searched for Procter's replacement. In the end, the board chose Bob Feaster, an executive with a Massachusetts textbook company who knew almost nothing about the United Methodist Publishing House.

Feaster's first major move was to conduct an extensive marketing survey to study exactly who was reading the publishing house's material. "We found out that the people who read religious books are middle-aged women," Feaster later said. The house then formed a new popular imprint called *Dimensions for Living* that it targeted at what it considered to be its primary audience. A typical release was the book *Yes, Lord, I Have Sinned, But I Have Several Excellent Excuses* by a Houston minister named Jim Moore.

During Feaster's tenure, the publishing house also came out with three enormously successful products: an in-depth Bible study called *Disciple*, a revised version of *The Interpreter's Bible* called *The New Interpreter's Bible*, and a hymnbook. Much like its predecessor, *The New Interpreter's Bible* would be a massive undertaking, requiring a $10 million budget, almost one hundred writers, and eleven years. And although the twelve-volume set wasn't cheap ($504 by subscription), its initial sales were better than expected.

The selection process for the hymnbook produced one of the more entertaining controversies in the publishing house's history: the great debate about whether to include the now politically incorrect standard "Onward Christian Soldiers." In the end, "Onward Christian Soldiers" made it.

The 1989 announcement that the publishing house would close its printing plant, Parthenon Press, after 135 years of continuous operation was less amusing. Beginning in the 1960s, when printing became a more capital intensive and specialized industry, the house's printing press began to be a drag on the organization's balance sheet. In the 1970s, Procter called the Baptist Sunday School Board and asked it if it would consider buying 50 percent of Parthenon and operating it jointly. The Baptists were not interested. Eventually, it became obvious that the United Methodist Publishing House had to either invest huge amounts of money in new equipment—which it could not justify—or shut the press down.

The closure of Parthenon Press was not the largest layoff in United Methodist Publishing House history, but it was the largest as far as its Nashville operations were concerned. As a result, the move was strongly criticized by its 240 employees and by the local media. "After giving the most productive years of their lives to the company in the hopes of a secure and comfortable retirement, they [Parthenon Press employees] feel robbed, cheated and deceived," *Tennessean* columnist Jerry Thompson wrote.[6]

Ten years later, Feaster had not forgotten the coverage of the event or the media's failure to report the extent of the severance package offered to Parthenon Press employees. "I've never seen anything more unfair in my life than the way we got treated," Feaster later said. "Our consultant told us it was the richest severance package he had ever seen."

During Feaster's tenure, total sales by the publishing house rose from $60 to $100 million. However, when Feaster was replaced in 1996 by former Abingdon Press publisher Neil Alexander, the publishing house was due for another series of cutbacks and personnel reductions. This time, the problem was coming from customers that the United Methodist Publishing House had always taken for granted. With the advent of more consumer choices and better computer technology, Sunday school teachers in the United Methodist Church were increasingly turning away from the publishing house's literature. By 1998, Alexander estimated that only about 60 percent of the material being used in United Methodist Sunday schools was produced by the publishing house, down from about 90 percent a few years earlier. "Some teachers are buying their literature elsewhere, others are having the class read a book or something, and even others are writing their own and publishing it on a desktop computer," Alexander said.

Alexander focused his efforts on producing new types of Sunday school material and on drastically reducing the time it took to produce it. He also took several steps to reduce the organization's overhead and improve the publishing house's distribution system. One of the most important of these steps was to begin using Ingram Book as its chief distributor.

During his first four years as president, Alexander reduced total employment from about twelve hundred to eleven hundred through early retirement and layoffs. In 1998, the United Methodist Publishing House had about $110 million in revenue, about $45 million of which came from its numerous bookstores and the rest through direct orders.

Nevertheless, the publishing house continued with some losing projects it considered a part of its ministry. The two best examples of this were a Spanish language hymnal that lost about six hundred thousand dollars and a Korean hymnal that lost about five hundred thousand dollars.

The Southern Baptists

Even before James Sullivan became president of the Baptist Sunday School Board in 1953, he had already had some experience as a Nashville civic leader of sorts. Sullivan had previously been pastor of the influential Belmont Heights Baptist Church, a church that included Jack Massey and Cecil Branstetter among its members. In that position, Sullivan had played a pivotal role in the formation of Baptist Hospital.

During his very first week on his new job, Sullivan found out from his predecessor Thomas Holcomb that the Baptist Sunday School Board had some serious organizational problems. "He told me that it was up to me to reorganize the Sunday School Board," Sullivan said forty-five years later. "He told me that he was not an organization man, but a promotional man. He told me that the board hasn't followed processes enough to be efficient, and that we are eventually going to bog down."

If Sullivan did not know exactly what Holcomb meant at the time, he would soon find out. During Holcomb's tenure, the number of employees at the Sunday School Board tripled, but the organization had kept the same basic structure. Holcomb never believed in delegation; he sat at his desk and signed nine hundred paychecks every week. Meanwhile, the Sunday School Board's physical plant needed work. The board's shipping department was such a mess by the mid-1950s, trucks waited for hours to be loaded.

One of the first things Sullivan did was write a job description for every position, something that had never occurred to anyone to do before. Another thing he did was to try to better match people with the jobs that they had. "The tendency that I noticed was when a man was an excellent editor, they would often make him head of the department," Sullivan said. "But there is a big difference between working with a manuscript and working with a person."

Sullivan took over an organization that was in dire need of new investment in buildings. Sullivan built or renovated over fifty during his tenure, including many new bookstores. Perhaps the most important capital project began in 1959, when the board began replacing its outmoded home with a $4 million operations building that stretched for several hundred feet along the train gulch.

Sullivan's initiatives were timely. The Sunday School Board's revenue grew from $17 million in the mid-1950s to about $50 million two decades later. Under Sullivan's leadership, the Sunday School Board in the early 1960s surpassed the size of the Methodist Publishing House.

Although Sunday school material was by far the largest source of revenue for the Sunday School Board, the board also took major steps to upgrade its publishing arm. Prior to 1955, Broadman Press was known for little more than hymnals and sermon books. In 1956, Broadman took a major step forward by publishing religious fiction for the first time. Sullivan's openness toward new types of publishing would remain throughout his tenure. In 1975, Broadman published an autobiography of a Georgia governor (and a Baptist) named Jimmy Carter. After Carter became a serious presidential candidate, the book sold 650,000 copies.

During Sullivan's tenure, the board began work on the massive *Encyclopedia of Southern Baptists*, a work intended to help the denomination's self-awareness and understanding of its history. It also began to produce the *Broadman Bible Commentary*, a twelve-volume set meant to be the Baptist's answer to the Methodist's Interpreter's Bible.

Hymnbooks were still the biggest cash cows, and Broadman came out with two of them during the Sullivan years. And even though hymnbooks were of course a long, bureaucratic mire, they did not usually generate huge controversies among Baptists like they did else-where. "Some of the issues that the Methodists and Presbyterians found to be very troubling, we did not find troubling at all," said Jim Clark, head of Broadman Press in the 1960s. "We put 'Onward Christian Soldiers' in with no problem."

However, most of the Baptist Sunday School Board's publicity during Sullivan's tenure had little to do with corporate reorganization and everything to do with social change. Sullivan's predecessors were rarely called upon to comment on social issues, except to make the occasional speech against alcohol, gambling, or playing hooky from Sunday school. But during Sullivan's twenty-two years as head of the Sunday School Board, Americans were wrestling with changes in race relations, their view of their own country, and their view of religion. Despite Sullivan's desire that the Sunday School Board stay out of controversial issues, his organization kept getting in the middle of them again and again.

One of those issues was the debate over evolution versus creationism. In 1961, Broadman Press released five thousand copies of *The Message of Genesis* by Ralph Elliott, a professor of Old Testament at the Midwestern Baptist Theological Seminary in Kansas City. In the book, Elliott stressed that the story of the creation is best viewed from a theological point of view, not from a historical point of view. A year later, the Southern Baptist Convention met in San Francisco and called on the board to recall the book. The board refused to do so. But a few months later, Sullivan decided not to come out with a second edition of the book even though there were over one thousand back orders. Sullivan was then sharply criticized by liberal members of the denomination. One pastor equated the

In this photograph, taken around 1953, James Sullivan of the Baptist Sunday School Board (top left) is shown with Thomas Holcomb (bottom right). The other two people in the picture are William Francis Howell (pastor of the First Baptist Church in Nashville from 1921–1955) and long-time Baptist Sunday School Board secretary Ethel Allen (LifeWay Christian Resources).

decision not to do a second printing with "ecclesiastical thought control."[7]

A similar debate came up again in 1969, when the board released volume one of the twelve-volume *Broadman Bible Commentary*, covering Genesis and Exodus. The criticism revolved around the interpretation of the story of Abraham's offering to sacrifice his son. When the Southern Baptist Convention met in October 1969, it requested that the board withdraw the first volume from consideration and rewrite it "with due consideration of the conservative viewpoint." The board did just that, dismissing the authors and rewriting the first volume.

If Sullivan was criticized from within his church on the issue of creationism, his harshest criticism from outside the church came in the area of race. By the middle of the twentieth century, the Baptist Church was by far the largest institution in the South. Many southerners expected the top official in the Southern Baptist Convention's publishing arm to speak on the issue of race, especially after some southern governors began defying the 1954 Supreme Court case that rejected the old doctrine of "separate but equal" institutions. But Sullivan did not speak out against segregation. "While we never promoted integration per se, we always pushed for a Christian attitude toward all people," Sullivan wrote in 1974.[8] Leaders of the Southern Baptist Convention took much the same approach. Evangelist Billy Graham told ten thousand delegates at the Southern Baptist Convention of 1958 that the race issue should be handled at the local level—in other words, that the convention shouldn't take stances on the issue.

At one point, Sullivan's reticence on the race issue led National Baptist Publishing Board president T. B. Boyd Jr. to label Sullivan a racist, something the Southern Baptist never forgot. "They got the impression that I was a racist I guess because I was raised in Mississippi," Sullivan said. "They did not know that I watched some lynchings when I was a kid and made up my mind that I would rather be a victim in a lynching that a party to one."

The most widely publicized racial debate that the Sunday School Board ever created concerned the January-March issue of a routine Sunday school quarterly for fourteen- and fifteen-year-olds called *Becoming*. After printing 140,000 copies of the quarterlies in the fall of 1971, the Sunday School Board decided not to release them because of an article and a photograph that dealt with interracial issues. The photograph in question showed an African-American young man standing in a hallway while conversing with two white girls, both of whom were several feet away from him. But in the opinion of Sullivan and Sunday School Board director of church services Allen Comish, the material was "potentially inflammatory," since the black boy and white girls appeared almost side-by-side because of the way the photograph appeared between two magazine pages.[9]

Every copy of *Becoming* was subsequently destroyed. *Becoming* editor Frank Grayum resigned. Baptist state conventions in North Carolina and Maryland criticized the Sunday School Board's move.

When asked to describe Sullivan's successor Grady Cothen, most people used words like "reticent" and "shy." But during Cothen's nine-year tenure, the board took two of the largest financial steps in its history. Even though the Baptist Sunday School Board was one of the largest (if not the largest) distributors of Bibles in the United States, the organization couldn't publish its own Bibles because it did not have plates for the King James Version nor the rights to any of the more modern translations. Cothen and Jim Clark decided to change that. In 1979, the board paid $2.3 million to buy Holman & Co., a Bible publishing firm in New Jersey that was in financial duress. With the purchase of Holman, the Sunday School Board obtained plates and negatives for the King James Version, plus the right to print the Revised Standard Version and the New International Version. The board immediately started working on study Bibles and came out with the RSV Master Study Bible during Cothen's term.

Cothen's other major initiative was just as bold but less financially successful. In an era in which satellites and cable television were just beginning to make an impact on lifestyles, Cothen envisioned a network that would allow the board to communicate directly with its forty thousand churches. The project, known as the Baptist Television Network, eventually made it into several thousand Baptist churches.

However, the board could never figure out a way to generate any revenue through BTN. After an $18 million investment in BTN, Cothen's successor Lloyd Elder scrapped the program under the strong advice of other board officials.

Financially, Lloyd Elder's reign as president of the Sunday School Board had its bright points. In 1985, Broadman released a paperback version of the New Testament, called *Good News America: God Loves You*, which sold over 2.5 million copies. Later in his tenure, Broadman came out with the *NIV Disciple Study Bible* and a successful hymnal. The board also constructed the $16 million Centennial Tower, the largest structure ever built by a religious publishing house in Nashville.

But in many ways, Elder's reign was the most turbulent time in the history of the organization. There had always been a struggle in the Baptist Church between moderates and fundamentalists over whether someone had to believe the literal interpretation of the Bible in order to be a good Baptist. Starting around 1979, fundamentalists began to assert more power in the Southern Baptist Convention. By the time of Elder's presidency, the convention had become very critical of some of its long-standing institutions, especially seminaries and the Sunday School Board. "Keep in mind that of the thirty-nine thousand pastors in the convention, about eighteen thousand never attended seminary," said Dr. Bill Sherman, pastor of the Woodmont Baptist Church in Nashville from 1968 through 1997. "The battle in many ways has always been between the educated and the uneducated."

The struggle between moderates and fundamentalists was played out between the Sunday School Board's ninety-three trustees and Elder, a self-described conservative but not a fundamentalist. One controversy had to do with a Sunday school lesson based on the story of Job. Another had to do with whether board literature should publicize the fact that some Baptist churches were ordaining women as deacons and ministers, something to which fundamentalists were opposed.

Perhaps the most symbolic dispute had to do with the Sunday School Board's centennial history. In 1941 and again in 1966, the board commissioned and published a version of its history. As the publishing entity's hundredth anniversary approached, the board commissioned Leon McBeth, a professor at Southwestern Baptist Theological Seminary in Ft. Worth, Texas, to write a new history of the publishing entity.

When the manuscript was complete, several trustees read it and concluded that it made fundamentalist trustees look bad. After several heated meetings between Elder and the trustees, the board voted to not publish the book.

There were other incidents between Elder and the trustees that had nothing to do with ideology. The most notable was when Elder denied taping phone conversations with two of the trustees when he had in fact taped them. "Lloyd made some crucial errors," said Jim Clark, an executive at the Sunday School Board from 1971 until 1989.

Nevertheless, Elder's termination in January 1991 was viewed by many as a sign of just how powerful fundamentalists had become in the Baptist Church. "They had no reason to fire Lloyd Elder," said Sherman. "He was a gentleman, a Christian, morally capable, and they fired him because he was a moderate."

Elder was replaced by Jimmy Draper, previously pastor of the First Baptist Church of Euless, Texas. From the day of his ascendancy, Draper began making dramatic statements about the financial status of the Sunday School Board. In February 1991, he warned the board of trustees that the Sunday School Board was in danger of dying. Among the reasons for this were the fact that only four of the publisher's seventeen programs made a profit in 1990.

Elder and Clark would later say that some of Draper's early statements represented significant exaggeration of the board's true financial status. For one thing, the Sunday School Board recorded a surplus in both 1990 and 1991 in spite of both the recession and the construction of the Centennial Tower. Elder and Clark would also argue that many of the programs that Draper referred to were never set up to make money in the first place. "When Draper and those around him came to the conclusion that the board should eliminate those lines that are not profitable, that was a significant change in philosophy from the administrations that had come before them," Clark said. Among the programs that Draper was referring to were one that helped churches develop libraries, another that helped church leaders develop ideas for recreational programs, and a third that helped small churches devise architectural blueprints for new sanctuaries. Around two hundred people were either laid off or took early retirement in 1992 and 1993 when Draper axed several such programs.

Draper also took major steps to revamp the Sunday School Board's bookstore chain. He changed Broadman's focus from denominational books to evangelical books that were not necessarily Baptist-oriented. He also took major steps toward streamlining the huge bureaucracy of the publishing organization. "When we got here, it took three years and eighteen signatures to publish a book," Mike Arrington, Draper's director of corporate affairs, said in 1998. "Now it takes one year and three signatures."

In part because of the many one-time write-offs affiliated with so many changes, the board recorded a $2 million loss in 1993 and a $8.2 million loss in 1994. But the numbers began to improve the next year.

In 1997, the board reported a record surplus of $14 million on a budget that was nearing $300 million.

As the look and content of Sunday School Board literature began to shift to the right, many independent churches began to buy the board's products for the first time, which contributed to rising revenues. But as revenues climbed, some moderate and liberal Baptist churches began to feel alienated. About the same time Elder was fired, a group of moderate Baptist churches formed a new organization called the Baptist Fellowship. By 1998, about fifteen hundred Baptist churches were buying at least some of their literature from a Baptist publisher in St. Louis called Smyth & Helwys.

In 1997, the Sunday School Board's trustees voted to change the name of the 106-year-old organization to LifeWay Christian Resources. The Draper administration said that the move was long overdue because Sunday school material only accounted for about 25 percent of the organization's business. It also pointed out that the new name would help the organization sell its material to people who don't attend Baptist churches.

The National Baptists

When T. B. Boyd Jr. succeeded his father in 1959, the National Baptist Publishing Board (NBPB) was still the official publisher of the National Baptist Convention of America (a completely different organization from the National Baptist Convention U.S.A.). Like many new presidents of family-run companies, Boyd Jr. found himself having to discontinue a family tradition in order to put the family business on more solid financial ground. The *Nashville Globe* played an essential role in the Nashville black community during the first half of the twentieth century. But as mainstream newspapers such as the *Tennessean* began to write more about the African-American community, the *Globe's* loyal following began to ebb. By the time T. B. Boyd Jr. took over the organization, it had been losing money for several years. Boyd discontinued its publication.

In the 1960s, Boyd steered the NBPB to a mainstream course and kept the organization in the good graces of the thousands of National Baptist Convention of America churches that supported it. But Boyd also supported Dr. Martin Luther King Jr. and the Civil Rights Movement, going as far as to threaten to boycott paper companies not sympathetic to civil rights causes. In 1968, the NBPB also did something some conservative church leaders found offensive: depicting biblical characters with dark skin to help young people better identify with the Scriptures. The first time the literature went out with black characters, almost half of it came back. But eventually the churches grew more accustomed to it.

In 1967, the NBPB left its long-standing site north of the court-house and built a new plant on Centennial Boulevard. About that time, revenue topped $1 million for the first time.

Most members of the Boyd family had lived to old age, which is why T. B. Boyd Jr.'s death in 1979, at the age of sixty-two, came as a shock to his thirty-two-year-old son T. B. Boyd III. And though the oldest Boyd son had several brothers, his father had made it very clear that he wanted control of the organization to pass to his oldest son.

From a business perspective, T. B. Boyd III probably did more to reform the NPBP than any of his three successors. He reorganized it into five divisions, invested a lot of money in new equipment, and improved the appearance of the Sunday school literature. He made dramatic increases in the number of books being published by the organization. Most important, he oversaw the production of a new hymnbook, although the project was galvanized by a woman named Ruth Lomax Davis. Released in 1984, the *New National Baptist Hymnal* sold over six million copies and was bought by many churches from other black conventions. By 1998, the NBPB had about two hundred employees and close to $15 million in revenue.

However, T. B. Boyd III was unable to do something his father and great-uncle had done, and that was to maintain the publishing board's official affiliation with the National Baptist Convention of America. In 1988, the National Baptist Convention of America broke off official ties with the NBPB because its leaders were critical of the publishing board's financial autonomy. The event, almost identical to the split that had occurred in 1915, hurt the publishing board's business. But just as had happened in 1915, thousands of churches remained loyal to the Boyd family and formed a new convention called the National Missionary Baptist Convention. It continued to buy everything from literature to bulletins from the NBPB.

Meanwhile, Nashville's other African-American publishing organization—the Sunday School Board of the National Baptist Convention U.S.A.—also had a tendency to stay with the same leader for a long time. Spruce Street Baptist Church minister A. M. Townsend took charge of the publishing arm in 1921 and remained in that post until 1960. At his retirement, the National Baptist Convention U.S.A.'s publishing imprint was named Townsend Press.

An Alabama preacher named D. C. Washington was Townsend's official successor. But Washington knew little about the publishing arm and delegated most of his responsibilities to an accountant named Cecelia Adkins. Adkins would officially succeed Washington in 1975 and remain head of the National Baptist Convention U.S.A.'s Sunday School Board until 1996. For most of her career, Adkins

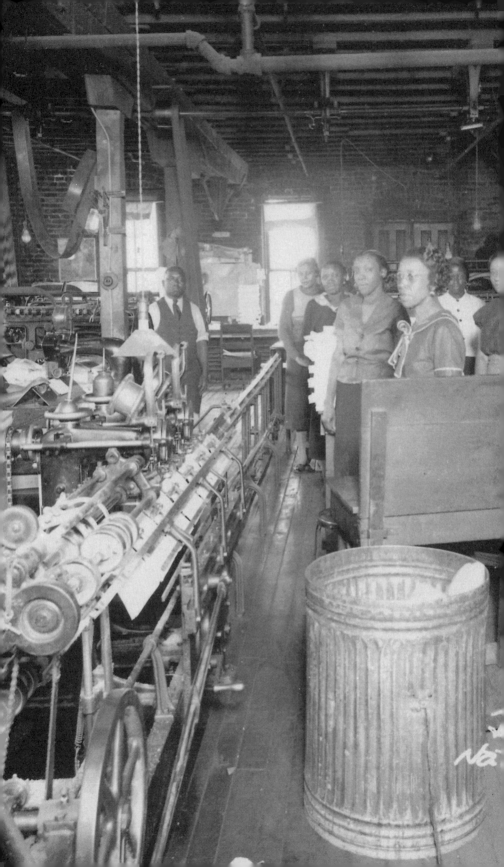

The book bindery department of the National Baptist Publishing Board, around 1930 (National Baptist Publishing Board).

would be the most prominent African-American female in a Nashville business community that was overwhelmingly white and male.

Adkins got her start through family connections: her father was one of A. M. Townsend's best friends. As a student at Fisk, Adkins chose to pursue a minor in business against the advice of her mother, who told her that "nice girls don't study business." One Sunday afternoon in 1942, Townsend was visiting Adkins's father when he noticed she had accounting papers strewn all over the room. Impressed that a young woman wanted to be an accountant, Townsend offered her a job at the publishing house.

Seven years after going to work there, Adkins had been promoted to head of the Sunday School Publishing Board's accounting department. After Washington took over the organization in 1960, he made a couple of small but unpopular changes to the Sunday school literature. "After that, he sort of left the business operations up to me," Adkins said.

When Adkins became executive director of the organization in 1975, she made one immediate change that got everyone's attention in the convention. Up to that point, all the material being produced by the Sunday School Publishing Board was black and white. The organization borrowed about five hundred thousand dollars for a color printer. "The first time we printed our literature in colors, the people couldn't believe it," Adkins said. "The churches were so shocked when they saw the material in color that we got a lot of additional customers." Another change that Adkins made was in the hiring of white staffers, something that hadn't been done in decades.

However, Adkins generally was regarded as a very conservative businesswoman, and perhaps the best example of this is the fact that the Sunday School Publishing Board never produced a successor to the old *Baptist Standard Hymnal.* "I do not think you ought to give up the old hymns," she said in 1998. "I think we are too quick to get rid of the old for the new and then when you get the new you don't like it and you have to go get something else." It was in part because of the Sunday School Publishing Board's reluctance to come out with a new hymnal that the National Baptist Publishing Board was so successful with its 1984 hymnal.

One of Adkins's most important skills was her ability to keep her organization running smoothly despite frequent controversy at the National Baptist Convention. Nonetheless, on at least two occasions convention politics would interfere with the Sunday School Publishing Board's bottom line.

Dr. Joseph Jackson of Chicago held the presidency of the National Baptist Convention from 1953 until 1982. In 1960, Jackson survived a serious challenge to his presidency from a group of young, upstart church leaders who thought Jackson was too powerful. These church leaders were so upset about the way Jackson had retained his position that they formed the Progressive National Baptist Convention. The Progressive Convention made its headquarters in Washington and received most of its literature from another religious publishing house.

After the Progressive Convention split off and became affiliated with the Civil Rights Movement, Jackson became a bitter critic of that movement and Dr. Martin Luther King Jr. Throughout the 1960s, Jackson accused civil rights leaders of being communists. He also frequently stated his opinion that civil disobedience was a sin. "Negroes should stop letting white folks fool them into believing the only way to win is through civil disobedience," Jackson said.[10] In 1972, Jackson went so far as to praise Richard Nixon and attack George McGovern in a speech before the National Baptist Convention. Although he was loudly booed, Jackson remained president for another ten years.

In 1982, Dr. Theodore Jemison of Baton Rouge, Louisiana—whose father preceded Jackson as head of the convention—succeeded Jackson. Jemison turned the convention on a more socially active course, restoring relations with many of the civil rights leaders Jackson had alienated. Jemison's pet project eventually became a new headquarters for the convention on Whites Creek Pike, a project for which he solicited the help of Sunday School Publishing Board director Cecelia Adkins.

When the Baptist World Center opened in June 1989, it was acclaimed as a major achievement for the National Baptist Convention. But almost immediately it became clear that the convention could not afford the payments on the $10 million structure.

Jemison retired in 1994 and was replaced by Rev. Henry Lyons of St. Petersburg, Florida. Because of the financial state of affairs he inherited, Lyons initiated many new fund-raising sources for the convention. The most creative of these was the convention's endorsment of a Canadian funeral home company as its official death care provider, a move that infuriated many African-American funeral home owners.

In 1997, serious questions about Lyons's personal life were raised when his wife set fire to a home that Lyons had purchased with another woman. As reporters dug into the affair, they uncovered many disturbing facts about Lyons's handling of the National Baptist Convention's money. Eventually, Lyons was convicted by Florida state and federal officials for racketeering and theft. In 1999, Lyons was sentenced to five years in prison. Although the Sunday School Board did not comment, the Lyons situation caused some National Baptist Convention churches to suspend payments to the convention and stop buying convention material.

Southwestern

There wasn't much to Southwestern Co. when Dortch Oldham began rebuilding its sales force in 1946. The company had five full-time employees and a summer sales force of around seven hundred students. And it had been years since it published a book.

In many ways, Southwestern had changed little in the way it did business in the previous fifty years. At the beginning of the summer, students paid their own way to come to Nashville for a week of training. They were sent all over the country and were in charge of coming up with their own living arrangements. They got 40 percent commission off every book they sold.

One thing had dramatically changed since Oldham had started selling books for Southwestern during the Great Depression, however. After World War II, Americans had plenty of money and nothing to spend it on, which made life wonderful for Southwestern's sales force. "After the war, it was so easy to sell that it was like taking candy from a baby," Oldham later said.

A generation before outsourcing became the corporate craze, Southwestern was the epitome of a streamlined firm. During the fall and winter, Oldham worked hard coming up with new book ideas—a very important part of the company since Southwestern only sold books that it published. If he was looking for a new children's Bible storybook, he would hire a couple of ministers to write it. If it was a history book of some kind, he'd find a professor. On other occasions, Southwestern would simply buy a book or a series of books already in existence, which is how the company acquired encyclopedias or dictionaries. The company would usually hire R. R. Donnelly and Sons in Chicago or Kingsport Press of Kingsport, Tennessee, to print books.

In 1959, the Henderson family sold Southwestern to Oldham for $150,000. By that time, Southwestern had an annual sales force of about three thousand students.

Years later, Oldham would say that the best part about Southwestern was getting to work with college students. Many of them would say that Oldham was like a father figure to them. Ralph Mosley, who went to work selling books for Southwestern in 1959, says Oldham once had a talk with him about his plans to go into the military.

"I told him that I wanted to enlist in the marines or the army because that would get me in and out quickest," Mosley said. "He said 'Son, if you go into the marines or the army, you go to the front line, and they shoot real bullets and they kill you. Do I make myself clear?'

"It was because of that conversation that I went into officer candidate school for the Navy."

During the 1960s, Oldham reorganized Southwestern in various sales divisions, many of which were headed by people whom Oldham had once recruited to sell for the company and who now owned stock in it. Spencer Hays was in charge of Bible libraries. Ted Welch, who first went to work for Southwestern as a student in 1953, was in charge of selling dictionaries.

In 1972, with Southwestern's full-time staff at two hundred and its sales force at over seven thousand, Oldham sold the company to Times Mirror, then looking for a way to diversify from newspapers. Some of Southwestern's minority shareholders were sad to see the company sold. But none had the capital to buy it.

The newly retired Oldham ran for governor in 1974, losing the Republican nomination to Lamar Alexander.

Times Mirror put Spencer Hays in charge of its new Southwestern division and moved it from downtown to a new site near I-65 in Franklin. A couple of years later, the division branched off into the area of cookbooks.

Times Mirror's ownership of Southwestern lasted about a decade. In 1982, in an attempt to focus its assets on newspapers and cable, the media conglomerate sold Southwestern for $24 million to a group of investors that included Hays, Mosley, and several other Southwestern executives. Some mortgaged their homes in order to take part in the transaction.

By 1999, Southwestern/Great American had about 250 share-holders and 700 full-time employees at its headquarters off Briley Parkway. Door-to-door bookselling (which no longer included Bibles) accounted for about one-fifth of its total revenue. Other sources included fund-raising (the division called Great American), a direct mail business, and a job placement business. Nevertheless, the Southwestern tradition of thousands of students coming to Nashville every May still remained.

Thomas Nelson

Nashville has rarely produced a Horatio Alger story quite like Sam Moore. Born in Beirut in 1930 under the name Salim Zaidy, he came to the United States on the advice of a missionary from Pennsylvania. In 1949, with six hundred dollars in savings, Zaidy enrolled in Columbia Bible College in South Carolina.

In order to pay his way through school, Zaidy took jobs washing dishes and pumping gas. Then, someone told him that he could earn a lot more money over the summer selling Bibles door-to-door for the International Book Company. Zaidy gave it a shot. After his first week of selling, Zaidy had encountered friendly people and unfriendly dogs but had only sold two books. "By Saturday night, I was in despair," he wrote years later. "What had I gotten myself into?"[11]

However, Zaidy stuck with it and actually saved $2,685 that first summer. The experience improved Zaidy's English and taught him how to converse with ordinary Americans. It also taught him how to turn a potentially negative situation into a positive one. At the end of his first summer, when he went to buy his first car, the dealer was suspicious of a foreigner with $1,700 in cash. By the end of the afternoon, Zaidy had not only convinced the car salesman of his integrity, but he had sold the dealer and his staff $600 worth of books.

Later, Zaidy changed his last name on a whim during his citizenship induction ceremony. Since the word "zaidy" means "more" in Moore's native language, his original intention was to spell his last name with one "O." But the court reporter made a mistake and misspelled the word, which is how Salim Zaidy's last name became Moore.

After graduating from the University of South Carolina, Sam Moore moved to Johnson City, Tennessee, and went to work for Chase Manhattan Bank. Not content with the amount of money he was making, Moore left the bank and started a firm called the National Book Company. Like International Book and Southwestern, National Book sent college students out every summer to sell books door-to-door. Since Nashville was a much better location for a religious book company than Johnson City, Moore put his office in Nashville and frequently drove back and forth.

National Book did well for a few years. But by this time, Sam Moore wanted to do more than just sell Bibles. In the early 1960s, Moore spent a lot of time hanging out at Kingsport Press. From the people at Kingsport, Moore learned a lot about the very specialized trade of printing Bibles (which is different than printing other books because the pages are so thin).

During all those summers selling door-to-door, Moore had learned plenty about what people wanted in their Bible. Now that he had his own company, Moore decided that he wanted to produce a Bible with maps, art, and an index targeted at the ordinary reader. But at that time, no one in Nashville—despite the city's long history of religious book publishing—had ever published Bibles. And everyone knew that the production and printing of such a book would be an extremely expensive task, perhaps best left to big northern publishers. "Nobody was in the Bible publishing business back then," Moore said in 1999. "When I came to Nashville and published Bibles, people laughed at me."

In 1961, Moore changed the name of his business to Royal Publishers and changed it from a sales company to a publisher. Since neither Equitable Securities nor J. C. Bradford & Co. would handle an underwriting less than five hundred thousand dollars, a little-known Nashville underwriting firm called Tennessee Securities handled the three hundred thousand dollar IPO. Many of the main investors in this offering were Moore's friends and connections in Johnson City, including grocer Carl Young, Johnson City Press owner Carl Jones, and banker Carl Raizen.

Moore recruited several scholars to work on his Bible project, the most important of whom was a professor at Columbia Theological Seminary named Dr. Mansford Gutzke. He hired Kingsport Press to do the printing. The *New Clarified Reference Bible* was released in 1964. Its sales doubled every year through 1968, when Royal Publishers sold $2.5 million worth of copies.

The astonishingly high sales of The New Clarified Reference Bible made Sam Moore realize just how lucrative a niche he had found. The Bible is the best-selling book in world history. But it is a massive and complex work written in numerous languages. Most people who read it need help to understand it, but their needs were not being met by traditional volumes that contained little more than text. The New Clarified Reference Bible was the first time Moore found a huge demand for a book that made the Scriptures more readable and accessible. It would not be the last.

Moore was so proud of his new Bible that he thought it made perfect sense to merge his company with Southwestern—thus giving his company a direct connection with Southwestern's army of young door-to-door salesmen while giving those salesmen something new to sell. Moore called Dortch Oldham sometime in the mid-1960s and suggested that the two merge. Oldham did not think it was such a good idea. "We were growing so fast that we had about all we could handle," Oldham said in 1999.

By the mid-1960s, Royal Publishers had begun to get the attention of big investors in Nashville, some of whom—including Fred Wright, Stirton Oman, John Jay Hooker Jr., and John Clay—bought large chunks of the company and became directors. The most important by far, according to Moore, was Jack Massey, who bought fifteen thousand shares in 1967 and sat on the company's board for the rest of his life.

In 1969, Moore's success attracted the attention of a British company called Thomas Nelson and Sons. As the original publisher of John Bunyan's *Pilgrim's Progress*, Nelson had a rich history dating back to 1798. But by the late 1960s, Nelson had fallen on hard times because of its failure to defend its exclusive right to the *Revised Standard Version* of the Bible. Nelson originally contacted Moore because the company wanted him to be president. But before he went to New York, Moore talked to Massey about the idea of buying Nelson instead. "If you can buy it and you need the money, don't worry about it, because we can come up with it," Massey told Moore.

Nelson's physical plant in Camden, New Jersey, and its books were a mess. But as the owner of three translations of the Bible, the company had enormous earning potential. Moore eventually negotiated a $2.64

million purchase of Nelson, something he financed mainly through a secondary offering on Royal Publishers.

After putting his two companies together and naming them both Thomas Nelson Inc., Moore set out to produce more versions of the Bible. The first was one targeted at people who are farsighted, something Moore knew was needed because of all the elderly people who read the Bible. "Today we would call this idea a 'no brainer,'" Moore later wrote. "But back then this was revolutionary within the industry."[12] The *Giant Print Bible* was also a best-seller.

In 1972, Nelson came out with another study Bible called The Open Bible, this one even more user-friendly than the *New Clarified Reference Bible*. With its helpful reference sections, its colorful maps, the Open Bible eventually sold over five million copies.

In 1973, Sam Moore's eleven-year-old son Joseph asked his father why Nelson did not produce a Bible he could understand. That question plagued Moore for months and reminded him of the way he had felt as a recent immigrant studying the Bible in 1950. "I remember one time when I ran across the word 'kine' in the Old Testament and I did not know what the word meant and couldn't find it in a dictionary," Moore said in 1999. "My professor told me the word meant cow. And I thought 'Now I've got a double-whammy! I get to learn the English to start with, and now I have to learn the King James English!'"

Shortly thereafter, Moore began putting together what eventually became known as the *New King James Version* of the Bible. The new translation was a massive undertaking involving a seventy-five-member group called the North American Overview Committee. By the time the translation was completed in 1982, the committee had decided to strike from the new translation words such as *thee* and *thou*, plus obsolete verb forms such as *lookest* and *cometh*. Eventually, the new translation sold over 30 million copies in all of its editions.

Moore's first major success in secular books came as a result of the American Bicentennial. In 1975, patriotism was unfashionable because of the Vietnam War and the Watergate scandal. Because of this, most New York publishers overlooked America's two hundredth birthday as a marketing opportunity for books. Not Nelson. In 1976, the Nashville publisher came out with *The Bicentennial Almanac*. During the next year, it sold six hundred thousand copies at $19.95 a copy and was the main reason that the company's revenues jumped from about $10 million to $16 million that year.

The success of the almanac convinced Moore to add a book division to his company, which quickly signed several well-known Christian authors such as Chuck Swindoll and Robert Schuller. One of the division's early successes was a Schuller book called *Tough Times Never Last, but Tough People Do!* which sold over four hundred thousand copies.

In 1982, Nelson made its first major acquisition under Moore's ownership by buying Dodd Mead, a publisher specializing in reference books, sports books, and the Agatha Christie mystery series. The next year, Nelson acquired the Interstate Book Manufacturing Company of Kansas City and invested millions in a new printing plant for the company.

However, the mid-1980s were bad years for Nelson. With the English pound falling to new levels, Nelson found it difficult to compete on a cost-by-cost basis with British Bible companies. Moore also found out the hard way that it is very difficult for a book publisher to make a profit with a printing company. With his company on the verge of bankruptcy, Nelson sold Interstate for a huge loss, then disposed of Dodd Mead.

With disaster averted, Nelson went back to a focus based on its retail markets. Starting about 1990, Nelson began producing more types of products for the Christian bookstores with which it already had accounts, such as photo albums and prayer journals. By 1992, Moore was back in an acquiring mode again. But this time, Nelson branched off into the Christian music business. With the $72 million acquisition of Word Inc. of Dallas, Texas, Nelson nearly doubled in size.

Wall Street loves what it perceives as "synergy" between two business entities, and so it loved the marriage between Nelson and Word. In February 1995, the *Wall Street Journal* painted a picture of Nelson as a firm perfectly positioned for the inevitable boom in Christian music popularity. "We like to think we're helping God," Moore was quoted as saying.[13] Nelson's secondary offering of 2.5 million shares five months later went remarkably well. By September, Nelson's stock reached an all-time high of $26.50 with the news that it bought a gift company called C. R. Gibson.

However, in October 1995, Nelson's stock fell from about $25 to $16 in only a few hours after the company announced earnings far below expectations. A few months later, Nelson made another such announcement that sent the stock back to the $12.50 range and led one analyst to compare Nelson to a baseball player who deserved to be sent back to the minor leagues. Just as it had ten years earlier, Nelson had a round of layoffs.

There were several reasons that Nelson had a weak fiscal 1996. The most important was that Christian books and Christian music are two completely different industries. Moore had plenty of experience coming up with books people wanted to buy but little experience in how to run a music club, how to deal with music retailers, and how to compete against media conglomerates. In November 1996, Nelson sold Word to Gaylord Entertainment Co. for $110 million. For the second time in ten years, Moore said he planned to refocus on the core business of Christian book publishing.

The Gideons

As big and important as all Nashville's religious publishing organizations were, none of them were as internationally famous as the Gideons. Ironically, none of them were as little-known in Nashville.

In 1899, three traveling salesmen named John Nicholson, Samuel Hill, and William Knights met in Janesville, Wisconsin, and formed an association as evangelical traveling salesmen. Pulling the word from the Old Testament, they called themselves the Gideons. A few years later, a pastor in Iowa suggested that since they spent most of their evenings in hotel rooms that they begin leaving Bibles there. The idea caught fire. Hotel rooms eventually led to jails, military bases, and schools.

The Gideons were based in Chicago until 1964, when the high cost of doing business in that city forced them to look elsewhere. After a systematic search, the Gideons chose Nashville because of the cost of living, availability of Christian employees, accessibility, and weather. "The Nashville religious publishing industry actually had nothing to do with the decision, although it was very supportive once we got here," said M. A. Henderson, who went to work for the Gideons in 1956 and eventually became the organization's executive director. The Gideons chose a site on Lebanon Road and hired a then-unknown architect named Earl Swensson to design a new headquarters.

After moving to Nashville, the Gideons continued to grow, with financial support coming from membership dues and offerings taken once a year at evangelical churches. The distribution of Bibles grew and grew until it hit staggering numbers. In 1987, the Gideons distributed 30 million Bibles in sixty languages. Ten years later—boosted by the collapse of the Iron Curtain—the numbers were up to 55 million Bibles and seventy-seven languages. Most of these Bibles were printed by Philadelphia's National Publishing Co.

By the end of the twentieth century, millions of Americans could identify the Gideons as the organization that places Bibles free of charge in hotel rooms. Nevertheless, the Gideons received very little publicity in Nashville for two reasons. One was because of its streamlined staff. When the Gideons moved to Nashville in 1964, the organization only had thirty full-time employees, a number that increased to about fifty-five by the turn of century. The other reason is that the Gideons did not seek headlines. "We shied away from publicity," Henderson said.

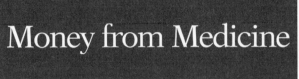

CHAPTER 19

Money from Medicine

I t started in the shadow of the Parthenon. In 1961, twenty-five Nashville physicians contributed $11,000 each and borrowed $1.2 million from the National Life & Accident Insurance Co. to build a nursing home next to Centennial Park. Four years later, the group recruited more investors and converted the nursing home to a hospital.

Parkview Hospital, as it became known, soon needed more capital improvements and more investors. By 1967, the number of physician-investors had grown to sixty-two. But by that time, many of them wanted to get their money out of the hospital because it was requiring increasing amounts of capital. The investors, led by a cardiologist named Thomas Frist, began talking about turning the hospital over to the Metropolitan Government of Davidson County.

Frist and hospital attorney Henry Hooker approached Mayor Beverly Briley about Metro buying the hospital for $5.2 million in municipal bonds. Briley went along with it. But the *Nashville Tennessean* editorialized against the transaction. "It is a tax dodge, legal under federal law, to benefit the current hospital owners," the paper claimed.[1] The deal fell apart, in part because of the newspaper's opposition.

During the next several months, Frist and Hooker discussed the idea with two more people. One was Jack Massey, an old friend of Frist's and the man who had successfully transformed Kentucky Fried Chicken from a one-man operation into a national chain. The other was Frist's son Tommy Jr., a flight surgeon in the Air Force stationed in Georgia who was about to get out of the service.

Three decades later, it is difficult to know exactly who came up with the idea of forming a hospital company and why. But it is easy to see what other companies and endeavors were influencing the four at the time. Massey was influenced by his success at KFC and in the surgical supply business. Hooker's thoughts were no doubt shaped by Minnie Pearl's Fried Chicken and Whale, both of which were riding high at the time. Frist Sr. had been a board member at St. Thomas and an investor in three hospitals. Frist Jr. was inspired by several companies. One was KFC. The second was Extendicare, a Louisville nursing home firm in which he owned stock. The third was Holiday Inn, whose founder Kemmons Wilson had a son in Frist Jr.'s fraternity at Vanderbilt. "I told Dad that we should do to hospitals what Kemmons Wilson had done with hotels," Frist Jr. said in 1999.

One Sunday in February 1968, the four men met and laid out rough plans for a hospital company. They came up with three basic parameters: that the company would own its hospitals and not franchise; that it would both acquire existing hospitals and build new ones; and that it would not own any nursing homes.

A few weeks later, Frist Sr. convinced his fellow owners to exchange their stock in Parkview for stock in this new company, called Hospital Corporation of America (HCA). "The vote was 64–1," said Dr. Robert McClellan, president of Parkview's board at the time. The only dissenter was Dr. Sumpter Anderson, an anesthesiologist who admitted to McClellan that he had never voted for anything in his life.

There were two reasons that Nashville in 1968 was a great time and place to start a chain of for-profit hospitals.

Historically, the great American medical institutions were in the Northeast, funded by prestigious universities, strong local governments, and an influential Catholic Church. When the South began to develop industrially, many parts of it did not have hospitals. Population centers such as Nashville and Atlanta eventually built them. But smaller communities could not afford to do so.

Because of this, many of the hospitals in the South were actually funded by physicians. Even though doctor-owned hospitals usually were not the best in the world, they served the needs of many people who did not live near big cities. But there was one major problem with them. As the cost of medical technology rose in the 1950s and 1960s, physician-owners had to take out more loans to get their hospitals updated. Soon, the hospitals were getting bigger and more expensive. Meanwhile, the physician owners were getting older and wondering whether they would ever reap any money from their investments.

The second reason was Medicare. In 1965, the federal government started the Medicare system to provide guaranteed health care for

elderly Americans. Within two years of Medicare's implementation, the amount of time elderly people spent in the hospital more than doubled, filling hospital beds and creating a demand for new hospitals.

Jack Massey, center, visits the New York Stock Exchange, 1968 (Barbara Massey Rogers).

When HCA was first discussed in the newspapers, the idea behind it seemed rather simple. At a time when equipment was becoming more expensive and medical care billing becoming more complicated, it made sense for hospitals to combine their operations. Not only could merged hospitals save money by sharing expensive equipment, they could also save by buying supplies and pharmaceuticals in bulk. Frist and his colleagues also said that their company would do well because privately owned operations were simply run better than government-owned ones.

HCA hit the ground running. Initially, the idea behind its acquisitions was to put together a chain of hospitals within one hundred miles of Nashville. HCA did this by two means. One was by using HCA stock to acquire physician-owned hospitals in small towns like Carthage, Smithville, and Lewisburg. Many physicians agreed to join HCA because people had faith in Frist Sr. as a colleague and Massey as a salesman. "Dad had great credentials as a practicing physician and Mr. Massey was up on a pedestal as a businessman," Frist Jr. said in 1999. "A lot of the doctors anticipated getting HCA stock and seeing it go on a ride like Kentucky Fried Chicken had done." However, not all of HCA's early acquisitions were physician-owned hospitals. One of the first hospitals that the company bought was a small not-for-profit hospital in Livingston, Tennessee.

Meanwhile, HCA built new hospitals in places like Chattanooga; Macon, Georgia; and Albany, Georgia. One of the new hospitals was a $1.5 million, one-hundred-bed facility in Donelson that had been originally planned as a physician-owned hospital like Parkview. As HCA opened new hospitals, it tried to staff them with administrators who were familiar with the market. Clayton McWhorter, the head of HCA's new hospital in Albany, Georgia, had previously been head pharmacist at another hospital there. "One of the reasons HCA was interested in me is that I had a knowledge-base of that community," McWhorter said.

HCA had eleven hospitals, about half of them under construction, when the New York investment banking firm Goodbody & Co. took the company public on March 4, 1969. The stock started at $18 on that day and shot up to $42. Physicians who had agreed to sell their hospitals to HCA for $10 a share only months earlier were wealthy overnight. Those fortunate enough to have been on the inside track thanked their lucky stars and began to keep their eyes open for similar companies. Those physicians who missed out began talking about getting in on the next hospital company.

They wouldn't have long to wait. Within months of HCA's appearance, two other hospital companies appeared on Nashville's horizon. Two former Parkview physician owners named Irwin Eskind and Herbert Schulman were so impressed with HCA that they figured another company could do just as well. After convincing Eskind's brother Richard and Schulman's brother-in-law Baron Coleman to start the company with them, the four men named their company Hospital Affiliates International (HAI). "If we had known enough at the time, we would have known that we couldn't do it," Irwin Eskind said years later. "We started out with the American Hospital Association book and a telephone. It was amazing the things that we could learn and find out over the telephone."

Before HCA went public, HAI had signed deals to buy a handful of hospitals. The first acquisition was the toughest. HAI was in the process of finalizing a deal with a Houston hospital called Spring

Branch when a hospital official asked how many other hospitals HAI owned. When HAI said Spring Branch would be the first, the hospital official said he wanted his facility to be the second. "We had to hustle and get a first," Irwin Eskind said. "But we found it before too long."

The third hospital company was General Care Corp. General Care started as a nursing home company headed by former University of Kentucky basketball player Joel Gordon and financed by Holiday Inn franchisee Marvin Friedman. But after it went public at twelve dollars a share, the government lowered nursing home reimbursement rates and the stock fell to two dollars a share. At that point, many of the doctors who had made a killing off their investment in Parkview/HCA approached Gordon and Friedman and talked them into changing General Care to a hospital company. With the new investment, General Care built a hospital called Westside almost across the street from Parkview.

Why were hospitals so willing to be acquired? One reason was that many physicians who owned hospitals all over the South and West were looking for a way to cash out. "Once we got past the first couple, the hospitals started jumping on board like people jumping on a lifeboat at sea," said Irwin Eskind. John Neff, the chief financial officer at HCA during its early years, put it a different way: "Doctors had dollar signs in their eyes."

After the initial wave of acquisitions took place, something else began fueling the process: the Medicare reimbursement system. In its early years, Medicare's system of reimbursement was a simple one and in retrospect a naive one. A patient goes to the hospital. A doctor diagnoses his condition and treats him. The hospital sends the government the bill for its cost plus a fee. The government reimbursed the hospital. Few questions were asked.

Medicare's payment system—known as "cost-plus"—created incentives for charging more. After all, if a hospital claimed that something cost $100, Medicare might send them $110. If a hospital claimed that something cost $120, the government might send them $132.

With Medicare's payment system in place, it did not take accountants long to come up with ways to finance the purchase of a hospital on the Medicare payments that you were guaranteed once you got it. "Under the cost-plus reimbursement system, it was difficult to lose money," said Larry Coleman, who ran a health care venture capital fund in the 1980s. "It led to a huge proliferation of facilities. I wish I had been in the hospital-buying business back then."

Nashville wasn't the only place for-profit hospital companies were appearing. Besides HCA, two large hospital companies were Philadelphia-based American Medicorp and Louisville-based Humana. Humana had started at Extendicare, the nursing home company in which Frist Jr. had owned stock. According to a story repeated many times, Extendicare cofounder Wendell Cherry decided to get into the hospital business after Massey told him about HCA at a Kentucky Fried Chicken board meeting.

One thing all these hospital companies had in common was that they were harshly criticized. In February 1970, the Antitrust and Monopoly Subcommittee of the U.S. Senate's Judiciary Committee heard testimony from for-profit hospital companies and their critics. One of those critics was Vanderbilt Medical Center director Joe Greathouse, who charged that for-profit chains did not provide a full range of services. Another was John Gadd of Lee Memorial Hospital in Ft. Myers, Florida, who charged companies like HCA with "skimming off high-paying patients while dumping indigent patients on general institutions." Massey did not appreciate the criticism, telling the subcommittee that "we do not see anything wrong with tax-paying hospitals earning a fair return on investment." And in a reference to the many companies whose products were being used at the Vietnam War, Massey added that "other companies make profits in building automobiles and bombs that kill."[2]

Bad blood between Vanderbilt and HCA remained for a long time. In an interview before his death in 1990, Jack Massey stated with some satisfaction that in HCA's early years, "Vanderbilt spent many dollars to try to get us out of business."[3] In 1988, when Nashville surgeon and Vanderbilt staff member Jeff Pennington told Vanderbilt Medical Center director Roscoe Robinson he was going to work for HCA, Robinson told Pennington he couldn't believe it. "He told me he was extremely disappointed," Pennington said. "I could almost see tears welling up. He felt that I was doing the wrong thing and an immoral sort of thing. . . . He had a real concern that Vanderbilt doctors who practiced at both institutions would send the charity care to Vanderbilt and the paying patients to HCA."

In later years, Baptist Hospital would also become a harsh critic of for-profit health care. But that was not the case in the early years, mainly because Baptist president Gene Kidd—a close friend of Massey's—very nearly became a cofounder of HCA.

In March 1970, former Aetna Life Insurance president John Hill became HCA's president. During his term, Hill had three main lieutenants: operations man Bob Brooks, finance man Neff, and development man Tommy Frist Jr. Since most of the work in those days was acquiring and building new hospitals, Frist Jr. was especially busy. "I'd be in the office until lunch and then get in my little airplane and fly a few hundred miles away to meet with doctors for hours on end," said Frist Jr., a private pilot. "And then I'd be back in Nashville at one or two in the morning."

One of the biggest challenges HCA faced was borrowing money. "No one wanted to lend money to a for-profit hospital because no one had heard of a for-profit hospital," Neff said. "Many of the board members of the big banks and big insurance companies out East were also members of big hospital boards who had given lots of money to hospitals. Their memories of hospital financing was going out and begging people to put money in hospitals."

Nevertheless, HCA succeeded in raising money, thanks to Massey's stature and Hill's experience as former president of an insurance company. Rather than try to finance each construction project one by one, HCA directed its efforts toward borrowing a chunk of money from a consortium of banks. After securing participation from First American, Third National, and Commerce Union, Massey, Hill, and Neff went to see officials at the First National City Bank of New York. When it looked as if the bank was going to turn the group down, Massey made a speech. "You don't have any relationship with anyone in the hospital field or in the medical field," Massey told the group of bankers. "Don't you want to be the first one in it? Don't you want to lead out and get the business of this company as it grows?"[4] A few weeks later, in July 1970, City Bank agreed to be the lead bank in a $30 million consortium.

HCA followed that loan up by getting $27 million from a group of eight insurance companies in 1972 and $35 million from a bank consortium in 1974. But the 1974 loan did not come without another challenge. After HCA officials thought that they had the $35 million loan settled, First American changed its mind and decided not to take part in the financing. "It was a near disaster," Neff said. Massey called his old friend, Third National Bank chairman Sam Fleming. Fleming spent a day calling banks around the country. By the end of the day, he found other banks to help finance the deal. It took years for First American to patch things up with HCA.

These loans, in tandem with several secondary stock offerings in the 1970s, gave HCA the money to grow quickly. Soon, HCA was buying larger hospitals in bigger markets such as Roanoke, Virginia; Richmond, Virginia; and De Kalb, Illinois. Although most were physician-owned, about a third were previously not-for-profit hospitals. HCA occasionally even built new hospitals in places like Frankfort, Kentucky, and Aiken, South Carolina, that replaced existing not-for-profit hospitals. By 1975, HCA had seventy hospitals, some of which were overseas.

Since HCA was the largest of Nashville's three hospital companies, and the only one that would remain until the 1980s, people often overlooked HAI and General Care. But it is important to remember that Nashville's "other" hospital companies came up with many innovations in their attempts to compete with HCA.

By the time HAI went public, the stock market was in a general decline, and HAI's public offering did not go as well as HCA's. HAI also did not have the backing of a business magnate such as Jack Massey. Because of these factors, HAI never had anywhere close to HCA's equity base. "HCA could buy and build high quality hospitals in the best locations, particularly fast-growing suburban locations," said HAI executive Richard Ragsdale. "When we bought hospitals, they were generally under-performing hospitals that we could buy cheap and then turn around. And HAI tended to build in smaller markets and build smaller hospitals than HCA."

HAI's lack of equity forced its president, John Anderson, to get creative. In 1971, HAI started managing not-for-profit hospitals on a fee basis, a practice almost unheard of at the time. "When we stared managing non-profit hospitals, it was thought of as a shady thing for a non-profit to do," Ragsdale said. But HAI soon found there were many not-for-profit hospitals not interested in being acquired that were interested in farming out their management.

HAI was the only Nashville company in the hospital management business for several years. But in 1976, HCA started managing hospitals for a fee, hiring former HAI executive Joe Hutts to help them get into the business.

HAI's lack of money also forced it to get creative in the area of cost sharing. At one point, HAI bought a CT machine for its six Houston hospitals and mounted it to a trailer which it took from hospital to hospital. "We thought it made more sense than putting six of them in six hospitals," Irwin Eskind said. The mobile CT worked for a while. But eventually, HAI bought one for all its hospitals.

In 1977, INA Corp., a Philadelphia-based insurance company, bought HAI for $75 million. At the time, HAI's executives in Nashville thought the purchase would put INA on at least an equal footing with HCA. "Part of what we saw as the benefit of the INA deal was that we would finally have the capital to compete with HCA," Ragsdale said. However, not much changed at HAI after the merger with INA. Eventually, it became clear that INA hadn't bought the Nashville hospital company to expand it, but to use it to divert into other areas of health care.

General Care, which was much smaller than HCA and HAI, also started a practice that would later be copied by future hospital companies. When General Care entered a market to build a new hospital, it announced over the physician grapevine that it was soliciting investments of up to fifteen thousand dollars from doctors. Once enough physician money was lined up to pay for 20 percent of the cost of the new facility, General Care would finance the rest and start construction.

Although no one could ever prove it, many critics of for-profit health care claimed General Care did this only to encourage doctors to refer patients to their hospitals. And at the time, officials at HCA and HAI agreed with those critics. "I felt that doctors should not own hospitals," said Frist Jr. "I felt that it was a conflict."

However, Gordon said turning local doctors into the primary shareholders of a hospital made good management sense. "Physicians are the best source of information about what is needed in the health care system, how it best should be operated, how to attract the best people and what type of equipment to buy," Gordon said. "I have never seen a physician who used a hospital because he had an ownership position. He used it because it had the type of service he wanted."

As it turned out, General Care's physician venture strategy would be used by other hospital companies—most notably Columbia—in the 1980s. But the conflict-of-interest arguments against such deals would come up again and again.

General Care was a profitable company but did not grow very fast because it did not acquire existing hospitals like HCA and HAI. "In retrospect, that was a big mistake," Gordon said. It was not the only mistake General Care made. In 1975, the company started a fast food restaurant chain called Judy's. Judy's performed reasonably well at first, until Wendy's sued it, claiming it was a copycat franchise. "It was an interesting experience that I don't need again," Gordon said of the Judy's venture.

The growth of HCA, HAI, and General Care caused reverberations through Nashville's economy. Hospital companies needed investment bankers to sell their stock, banks to loan them money, lawyers to take care of all their paperwork, and general contractors to build their hospitals. The companies that happened to be involved in HCA's and HAI's early deals often became regular business partners through fortuitous means.

The two best examples of this phenomenon were Rodgers Construction and Gresham & Smith. In 1968, a young general contractor named Joe Rodgers was thrilled when a friend gave him a ticket and a place to stay at the Master's golf tournament in Georgia. When he got to Augusta, Rodgers found that one of his housemates for the stay was Dr. Thomas Frist Sr. "He looked one hundred years old even then and I was nice to him," Rodgers said years later. "As we walked through the golf course, he told me about this dream they had of building a chain of hospitals." A few weeks after the tournament, Frist called Rodgers and asked him if he would be interested in building a hospital in Erin, Tennessee. That project led to another, then another, and then another.

Between 1968 and 1979, Rodgers Construction built over two hundred HCA hospitals. Rodgers said he never forgot the loyalty Dr. Frist Sr. showed him, nor the importance that Frist placed on aesthetics. "Dr. Frist believed that the surroundings and that the beauty of the hospitals was very important to the recovery of the patient. Back then a lot of hospitals had vinyl tile floors and gray on the walls and exposed pipes—they were terrible! But he wanted his to be pretty."[5]

An architect named Batey Gresham had the good fortune to be one of Frist Sr.'s patients in the mid-1960s. In early 1968, Frist called Gresham to congratulate him when his small firm, Gresham & Smith, was selected to design a high-rise residential facility in Atlanta. At that point, Frist asked him if he had any interest in designing hospitals. A few months later, Gresham & Smith designed HCA's first three hospitals (identical to each other) in Macon, Albany, and Chattanooga. "Early on it was pretty interesting," Gresham said in 1999. "I remember one time, Joe Rodgers asked them how they would be able to pay us. Frist said 'I guess we'll just pay you out of the treasury.' The treasury meant Jack Massey's pocket."

Eventually, Gresham & Smith designed about 150 HCA hospitals, providing the architectural firm with enough business to grow from less than ten people to fifty by the mid-1970s. At that point, Gresham & Smith began to diversify, designing several office buildings on West End Avenue, the City Center Building downtown, and the airport terminal. By the late 1990s, Gresham & Smith had almost five hundred employees in Nashville and two hundred in seven other cities, making it one of the largest architectural and engineering firms in the South. Gresham said there was no way the company would have ever grown so large without HCA. "Today, there is no way that a hospital company could go public with an architect that had never built hospitals before," Gresham said in 1999. "But back then it never occurred to Dr. Frist that it would never come out well."

When John Neff resigned as HCA's president in 1978, Tommy Frist Jr. thought it was his turn to run the show. However, the HCA board (under the recommendation of Jack Massey) brought in Don MacNaughton to be chairman and CEO and made Frist Jr. president and COO. MacNaughton made many changes, one of the most notable being that he began bidding out contracts to vendors that the company hadn't used before (to the dismay of Rodgers Construction and Gresham & Smith). Nevertheless, Frist Jr. had become more powerful at the company by this time, mainly because both his father and Massey had gone into semi-retirement. And it was under the younger Frist's strong influence that HCA went into acquisition mode. In 1980, HCA bought General Care for $78 million, bringing HCA's total number of owned hospitals to seventy-five. A year later, HCA bought HAI for $650 million, leaving Hospital Corp. with 197 owned and 163 managed hospitals.

The purchase of HAI by HCA might seem logical in retrospect, but in fact it took HAI's employees completely by surprise. "We had competed with HCA for so long for acquisitions and contracts and deals that it was just a shock," Ragsdale said. "We were out to beat them and vice versa." One of the reasons that the merger was so unexpected is that it was not long in the works. "We put that together in less than a week and a half," Frist Jr. said.

Nevertheless, the consolidation of Nashville's three hospital companies was for Ragsdale and many others the greatest event of their professional lives. Too young to retire, many of HAI's and General Care's executives took their stock gains and started new companies.

HealthAmerica. One of the most important Nashvillians of the late–twentieth century came to Nashville because HCA hired his wife. In 1975, HCA hired Andrea Conte to run its international nursing department. After she and her husband Phil Bredesen moved here, Bredesen landed a job with HAI selling management contracts. In 1980, Bredesen approached Richard Eskind about helping him start an HMO. Eskind, Irwin Eskind, Herbert Schulman, and Baron Coleman—the same four people who had financed HAI's start in 1969—became initial investors in Bredesen's new business, called Healthplans. In the early 1980s, when Wall Street was looking favorably on managed care companies, Healthplans grew fast and acquired thirteen other HMOs to become the second largest for-profit HMO in the United States. Not everyone in Nashville's health care industry was cheering. "For most hospital companies, HMOs were their worst nightmare," Bredesen said. "There were a lot of people who were doing spin-offs in the hospital business. But I was the guy who had gone in with the enemy." Healthplans later changed its name to HealthAmerica and was acquired by Maxicare in 1986. At that point, Bredesen became one of the initial investors in another start-up HMO called Coventry Corp.

Republic. After HCA took over HAI, Ragsdale got together with Anderson and former HAI executive Charles Miller and started a new hospital company in Dallas called Republic Health Corp. With only two hospitals in its possession, Republic came up with enough equity in 1982 to buy eighteen hospitals from HCA for $215 million. During the next two years, Republic grew faster than anyone could possibly have predicted, raising $400 million in equity and bond offerings in 1983 and 1984. One of the main reasons it raised so much money was the enormous energy of its securities lawyer, a then-unknown Dallas attorney named Rick Scott.

Surgical Care Affiliates. In 1982, HCA executive Andrew Miller and former General Care executive Joel Gordon formed Surgical Care Affiliates with seed capital from the venture capital firm Massey-Burch.

The idea behind SCA was that technological advances would begin to shift the emphasis from inpatient to outpatient care. "Back then, a lot of things that used to take a three- or four-day hospital stay were beginning to be done on an outpatient basis," Gordon said in 1999. "They had improved anesthesia. They had come out with arthroscopic technology. Gall bladders used to take a week in the hospital and now they were doing a gall bladder operation in one day." SCA acquired surgery centers and started building new ones in large cities. As Gordon had done at General Care, he built new surgery centers with help from physician investors. In January 1984, SCA went public and raised about $15 million. As Gordon had hoped, the company was quite profitable because surgery centers had much lower overhead than hospitals.

CHAPTER 20

Profits, Prisons, & Parking Spaces

One of the more curious things about Nashville's large companies in the twentieth century is how many of them were affiliated with one leader, such as Genesco with Maxey Jarman, Washington Industries with Guy Comer, Shoney's with Ray Danner, and Aladdin with Victor Johnson Jr. Service Merchandise, which grew under the energy of Ray Zimmerman and collapsed after his departure, also falls under this category. As the twentieth century ended, Dollar General, Corrections Corporation of America, and Central Parking were hoping to avoid a similar fate.

Service Merchandise

The story of Service Merchandise parallels the story of Shoney's. Both companies were built by a workaholic entrepreneur whose first name was Ray. Both companies made their stockholders very happy in the 1970s. Both executed stock recapitalizations in the late 1980s that gave their shareholders a one-time payoff and saddled the company with debt. Both had a hard time dealing with competition in the 1980s and 1990s. Both had trouble finding successors to the men who had built the companies. Both hobbled into the twenty-first century.

Ray Zimmerman's life changed in 1960. At a time when he and his father Harry were operating a dry goods warehouse in Nashville called Service Wholesale Co., Zimmerman read an article in a trade publication about a new retail concept called a catalog showroom. Showrooms, the article said, were usually located in parts of town away from the nice department stores. A showroom could stock up to five thousand items in a small store because it only displayed one sample of each item. When the customer wanted an item, it was retrieved from a back room. Since there was no need to restock shelves and no need for sales personnel in a showroom, the overhead cost of a showroom was less than that of a traditional department store. Because of this, a showroom could sell items such as gifts, appliances, and electronics below the price of traditional retailers. Finally, showrooms made extensive use of catalogs as advertising tools.

Harry and Ray Zimmerman drove to Minneapolis to visit Modern Merchandising, the nation's most successful showroom at that time. They were so impressed by the volume of traffic at the store that they came back to Nashville, leased a building on Lower Broadway, printed a catalog, and opened a catalog showroom called Service Merchandise. The next month, November 1960, Service Merchandise had five times more sales than Harry and Ray Zimmerman ever had in the wholesale business. Service was doing so well, in fact, that the Zimmermans were in Louisville looking for a site for a second store before the end of the year. No sooner had the Zimmermans opened that store than they began looking for other sites—rapid expansion being driven by a fear that if they did not move fast, someone else would claim their territory. During the 1960s, Service Merchandise stores opened in Chicago, Memphis, Atlanta, Chattanooga, Cincinnati, and Huntsville. By 1970, sales were $16 million.

The catalog showroom business was fairly straightforward, but there were several keys to running it profitably. One was keeping enough items in stock so that the store never ran out. Another was to use most of the merchandise as a "loss leader" to generate traffic but to make money off of the sale of jewelry.

Perhaps the most important part of Service Merchandise was Ray Zimmerman, who was practically running the company by the mid-1960s even though he did not assume its presidency from his father until 1973. "Raymond Zimmerman worked twenty hours a day, seven days a week, fifty-two weeks a year," said Floyd Dean, head of real estate for Service in the 1980s. "He did not mess around. He did not vacation. He was always working. He has energy and enthusiasm and he is also the brightest, quickest mind of anyone I have ever met." Zimmerman was also known to quickly get rid of people who either argued with him or did not produce results to his satisfaction. "We were ruthless and people knew it," Zimmerman once said.[1]

In November 1971, Ray Zimmerman took his company public. Service Merchandise's 210,000 public shares rose from $14 to $22 the first day. Six months later, it sold for $56 per share.

During the 1970s and 1980s, Service Merchandise stock did so well that the company was able to build about ten stores per year and buy up many of its competitors in other parts of the country. Service's first big acquisition was in 1974, when the company acquired Malone & Hyde's eight showrooms in Arkansas and Missouri. Four years later, Service bought Value House, a New Jersey-based chain of twenty in the Northeast. By 1979, Service Merchandise had one hundred stores and six distribution centers. The company was also mailing its catalog to more than two million households.

Service Merchandise hit the $1 billion mark in 1982. But Zimmerman was worried. For one thing, the rise of Wal-Mart was making many people believe that catalog showrooms were about to go the way of the dinosaur. "Running the very best catalog showroom in town might be a little bit like running the very best buggy whip factory in town," *Forbes* said.[2] Zimmerman also wanted to expand the company into other retail concepts that were less seasonal, since catalog showrooms made almost all their money at Christmas. In the early and mid-1980s, Service Merchandise made several attempts at diversification that failed. They were a toy store chain simply called The Toy Store, a chain of mall jewelry stores, and a mall lingerie store.

Service Merchandise's biggest diversification failure took place in the area of home improvement warehouses. In 1984, Zimmerman was so impressed with a chain of three stores in Atlanta called Home Depot that he tried to buy it. After negotiations broke down, Zimmerman took a vacation to Florida and drove by a Home Depot clone in Boca Vista called Mr. How. Zimmerman bought the store that afternoon.

Zimmerman knew the success of Service Merchandise had a lot to do with rapid expansion. His impression of the home improvement warehouse concept made him think the same thing was about to happen in that industry. Because of this, Zimmerman put Mr. How on an ambitious growth plan, expanding the chain from one store to thirty-eight in less than two years and moving into markets as far apart as Chicago and Tampa. However, Mr. How grew faster than its management and distribution system could handle.

About the same time, Service Merchandise bought the H. J. Wilson catalog showroom chain, which had eighty-seven stores and was strong in Texas and Florida. That acquisition turned out to be troublesome when Service had trouble converting Wilson stores to Service Merchandise stores.

In 1986, Zimmerman decided to abandon his attempt at a home improvement warehouse, selling many Mr. How sites to Home Depot and giving that Atlanta company an inexpensive inroad into several new markets. That year, Service Merchandise took a $47 million loss. Its stock, which had sold for $27 in 1983, fell to less than $4.

Service Merchandise bounced back in 1987 and reported a profit of $30 million that year, mainly by focusing on its core operation. The turnaround was so dramatic that there were rumors that Service would be taken over in a leveraged buyout, which helped the company's stock climb back up to the $20 range.

In 1988, Zimmerman watched closely while Shoney's chairman Ray Danner pocketed over $100 million in a one-time stock recapitalization. The next year, Service Merchandise voted to do something similar, giving its shareholders a one-time $10 per share dividend and giving Zimmerman and his family about $40 million. At the time, chirpy analysts ensured the public that it was a wise move and something that the company could easily afford. But the $975 million stock recap saddled the company with enormous debt, something it had very little of before that time. After the stock recap, Service Merchandise stock plummeted back to the $5 range.

In the 1990s, virtually everything went wrong at Service Merchandise. No sooner was the stock recap completed than the company came under investigation by the Internal Revenue Service for operating an illegal slush fund. As a result of that case, Service executive Howard Levy—who was once Zimmerman's brother-in-law—pleaded guilty to a charge of defrauding the government and was sentenced to house arrest. Despite prosecutors' attempts to link Zimmerman to the case, Service's CEO was never charged.

In the 1990s, Service Merchandise never found a way to duplicate the double digit earnings that it had experienced in the previous three decades. After disappointing sales in 1991, the company tried to increase profitability by reducing prices in 1992 and then by a major advertising blitz in 1993, but both failed to help the company's bottom line. Meanwhile, the company failed at several diversification attempts—the most notable of which was a Toys "R" Us clone called Kids Central.

In November 1994, Service hired former Saks Fifth Avenue executive Gary Witkin to be president and heir apparent to Zimmerman. Witkin made it clear that his intention was to make radical changes at the company. During the mid-1990s, Witkin revamped a lot of Service Merchandise locations and experimented with the idea of taking toys and electronics out of the stores. He raised prices on many items in order to increase profitability. He even tried to merge Service Merchandise with Pier One, convinced that the showroom concept was completely outmoded.

Little of what Witkin tried worked. In the midst of a booming national economy, store sales fell three percent in 1995 and two percent in 1996. In March 1997, the company closed sixty stores and laid off twenty-two hundred workers nationwide. "This is all about pruning," Witkin said.[3]

In 1997, same-store sales continued to fall and the company lost $92 million. In desperation, Service closed fifty-three stores, replaced its large catalog with six small ones, and shifted the merchandise mix to include high-margin furniture and fashion items. Both of those moves only made things worse. In 1998, same-store sales declined nine percent and the company lost $110 million.

In January 1999, Witkin resigned after a five-year tenure as one of the most unsuccessful CEOs in Nashville history. A few weeks later, Service filed for Chapter 11 bankruptcy protection and creditor Citicorp installed Bettina Whyte as interim CEO. White closed 134 of the company's 347 stores and fired 150 people at company headquarters in Brentwood.

In April, Whyte was replaced by former Service CEO Sam Cusano. During the summer of 1999, Cusano shifted Service's mix back to hard goods and reprinted the Service Merchandise catalog. Then, after what the company described as an "encouraging" Christmas 1999, Service laid off 5,200 workers and announced it would be leasing about half its store space to other retailers. As the company began the twenty-first century, its continued existence seemed uncertain.

Dollar General

Dollar General had been around for decades when it moved its headquarters to Nashville in 1989. But like the Fourth and First National Bank, the Nashville Trust Co., and Cheek-Neal Coffee Co., Dollar General traced its roots to a man who once sold goods for a Nashville-based wholesaler. Luther Turner was a drummer for Nashville's Neely, Harwell & Co. In 1939, Turner amassed enough money to start his own business in Scottsville, Kentucky, called J. L. Turner & Son Wholesale Notions and Hosiery.

Dry goods wholesaling declined after World War II, forcing J. L. Turner's son Cal (who effectively ran the business by that time) to shift from wholesale to retail. In the late 1940s, the family business was called Junior Department Stores and sold middle-level apparel— much of which came from Nashville's Washington Manufacturing Co. By the mid-1950s there were thirty-five Junior Department Stores in Kentucky and Tennessee.

Like all successful merchants, Cal Turner Sr. studied the competition closely for ways to improve the revenue of his operation. One of the things that intrigued Turner in the 1950s was the way department stores in Louisville and Nashville would occasionally have monthly promotions called Dollar Days, where all items were priced at the nearest even dollar. Around 1955, Turner gathered his senior management team together and told them he was thinking about starting a store that sold everything in stock for only one dollar. "He knew it would simplify accounting and simplify checking the customer out," said his son Cal Turner Jr., a high school student at the time. "But more importantly, he thought that the customers' mind would get reprogrammed not to item and price as much, that they would just get excited about the fact that you could buy one of these and two of these and four of those." Turner Sr. told his management staff that he knew that the "Dollar Stores" would have to sell some items at below cost. "But he knew if he had to sell one thing below cost that he could make it up somewhere else, maybe on cheap ceramics from Japan that he had bought for four dollars a dozen."

Some of Turner Sr.'s colleagues thought he had lost his mind, but they went along with the idea and the company opened its first Dollar General store in Springfield, Kentucky, in 1955. That store did quite well, but it was the Dollar General store that opened in Memphis the next year that really made Turner realize he had hit the jackpot. "The Memphis store had sales of over a million dollars during its first ten months," Turner Jr. said. "My dad said 'wow' and so did a lot of other people." Soon the success of the Memphis Dollar General store had created imitators all over the South, such as Main Dollar of Memphis, Top Dollar of Jasper, Alabama, and Bill's Dollar Store in Columbia, Mississippi.

Turner converted his Junior Department Stores to Dollar General stores and began expanding the chain. In 1962, by which time the company had gotten away from the "everything for $1 concept" and simply become a discount retailer, Dollar General had about one hundred stores and close to $15 million in revenue. At that point, Turner began working with Bear Stearns of New York to take the company public. After the stock market slumped, Bear Stearns advised Turner to wait—which is why Dollar General did not go public until 1968.

Cal Turner Jr. originally had no intention of going into the family business. After graduating from Vanderbilt and doing a three-year stint as a naval officer, Cal Jr. started to become a minister. But the family pastor advised Turner against it. "He told me that we have far too many ministers who are not called," Turner Jr. said in 1999. "He told me that if there is anything else I could do that I should do that." In 1965, Turner went to work for his dad's company. Years later, he said he had no regrets. "I've had more of an impact on people in this business than I ever would have had from the pulpit," he said.[4]

Turner worked alongside his father through Dollar General's initial public offering and the growth that followed it. Most of his attention was directed at keeping the company as efficient as possible, executing such corporate directives as the company's insistence that its stores turn a profit after only two months in operation. In 1977, Turner Jr.'s father named him president of the company. By that time, Dollar General had close to seven hundred stores and $200 million in revenue and had begun to make large acquisitions. The first large one was the 1983 takeover of the St. Louis-based P. N. Hirsch Stores, which added 280 sites to the chain. The second was Miami-based Eagle Family Discount Stores, a chain of about two hundred stores.

The Eagle acquisition was a disaster, since it turned out to be far less profitable than Turner first thought. While Dollar General was

trying to recover from the acquisition, many analysts and investors began to speculate that the company would not survive the decade. It was at this point that Turner realized that his company had serious merchandising problems. "Instead of buying things and putting them in the store because we had the opportunity to do so, we needed to define core merchandise and do whatever it took to be in stock every day," said Turner. After considerable study, Dollar General decided that its core merchandise consisted of consumables such as home cleaning products, basic housewares, basic apparel, and toilet paper. "The consumption needs of low income people are not a mystery," Turner said. In addition to revamping his company's merchandise mix, Turner also cut the company's advertising budget to nearly zero.

Cal Turner Jr., circa 1980 (Dollar General Corp.).

Turner also made a lot of personnel changes, replacing about two hundred of his top three hundred executives. No one was exempt, not even Cal's brother and chief operating officer Steve Turner. "We could not go along with the sibling rivalry, the big brother/little brother CEO/COO situation," Cal Turner said. Years later, Steve Turner said he held no grudge against his brother. "There was not a lot of acrimony," the younger Turner said. "You just couldn't have two leaders."[5]

About this time, Cal Turner soon found himself with another tough decision that went against a close family member. As early as 1977, the company realized that it had become tough to recruit executives because the firm was based in tiny Scottsville, Kentucky. In 1988, Turner—against the wishes of his father—decided to move the headquarters to Nashville. "My dad hated it," Turner said. "But being just across the state line, we had always sort of been a Nashville company anyway."

In 1989, with the nation mired in recession, Dollar General's stores began a remarkable streak of success. When Wal-Mart expanded its sixty-thousand-square-foot stores into one hundred thousand-square-foot superstores far away from many communities, Dollar General's six thousand-square-foot stores in the middle of town did quite well because of location. "Many of our customers can't get to Wal-Mart," Turner said.

In the 1990s, while most other retailers were reporting same-store sales increases in the range of zero to five percent, Dollar General's were going up between fifteen percent and twenty percent. By 1999, Dollar General had about $3.5 billion in revenue and thirty-nine hundred stores—all of which were located in either small towns or in urban areas with low income demographics. During the decade, its stock had increased in value to ten times its value of a decade earlier, making it one of the best performing stocks in America. Through it all, Turner maintained a theme of values at his company that had several direct impacts on his stores; Dollar General, for example, did not sell cigarettes despite the fact that the company knew it could make money off the sales.

Dollar General also made two major contributions to Nashville's landscape during the last decade of the century. In 1993, the company opened a store and training center in South Nashville's Sam Levy housing project. That store, built in partnership with Nashville's Metro government—served as a prototype for three others that helped welfare recipients develop job skills. Four years later, Dollar General announced that it was building a new corporate headquarters building near Rivergate Mall.

If there was one area of concern for Dollar General, that was succession. Twice in the decade, high ranking officials resigned from the company—first, chief financial officer Kent Garner in 1995 and then president Bruce Krysiak in 1997.

Nevertheless, Dollar General entered the twenty-first century as Nashville's most successful public company. "There is no way we will run out of markets anytime soon," Turner said. "In the twenty-four states in which we currently operate, there are another twenty-five hundred potential store sites. That leaves the other states."

Corrections Corporation of America

Everyone who has ever started a business has experienced that moment of desperation, when it looks as if the venture on which they have risked everything will fail miserably. For Tom Beasley, that moment came on New Year's Eve 1983, when he drove around

Houston, Texas, in search of a motel to buy.

"I stopped at every one I could find," Beasley said years later. "I drove all day, stopped, and had a late dinner, and then drove almost all night. I was getting pretty despondent. Finally, at about three o'clock in the morning, I found a small place called the Olympic Motel. The Chinese girl behind the counter there went and got her father or grandfather, and we started negotiating."

The path that led Beasley on his mad search for a hotel purchase had started over three years earlier when, as the chairman of the Tennessee Republican Party, he attended a cocktail party for U.S. Senator Howard Baker. On that day, the *Tennessean* published a front-page story about overcrowded state prisons, which led several people at the event to talk about what could be done to fix the state's troubled Corrections Department. "They'll never solve that problem until they figure out a way to get the private sector involved," Beasley heard someone say.

Beasley spent the next several months talking about the idea of a private prison company. Private prisons were not anything new; in fact the United States had hundreds of privately run prisons before virtually all of them were taken over by the government in the 1950s. But by the early 1980s, many state governments—including Tennessee—stopped devoting money and attention to running prisons. Beasley, an independent minded, conservative army veteran, believed the private sector could do just about anything more efficiently than the government.

Eventually, Beasley began talking up his idea, which he began referring to as Corrections Corporation of America. Many of his acquaintances—including the man who had made the comment at the cocktail party—told him his idea probably wouldn't work. But he found five important people who thought it would. Two of them—Doctor Crants and Sam Bartholomew Jr.—were former West Point graduates and Vietnam War veterans. A third was former Virginia Corrections Commissioner Don Hutto, who agreed to move to Nashville to run the operations side of the company. A fourth was John Neff, formerly president of HCA and by that time the state commerce and insurance commissioner.

As is the case with many start-ups, connections and luck were a big part of it. Neff put Beasley in touch with the venture capital firm Massey-Burch, whose president Lucius Burch III loved the idea. "We had already been studying the idea of a business that would do in prisons exactly what HCA had done in the hospital business," Burch said. After only one meeting, Massey-Burch agreed to raise half a million dollars for the company in exchange for a 50 percent ownership position.

With Hutto's experience, Beasley's enthusiasm, and Crants's mastery of numbers, CCA started the long, uphill climb of building a revenue base. "Crants and Beasley were a great team," said Bartholomew, one of the founding partners of the law firm Stokes & Bartholomew. "Beasley was the ultimate salesman. Crants is an academic type. It was kind of like Captain Kirk and Spock." One of CCA's first contracts was a workhouse in Hamilton County, a facility featured in a *60 Minutes* television segment. "The *60 Minutes* thing was fabulous," Beasley said. "We used it as a marketing piece until they made us quit."

Things seemed to be going very well when Beasley negotiated the company's first contract with the federal government—this one to operate an immigration detention facility in Houston. However, when the construction project fell behind schedule, it looked as if CCA might not be able to open on schedule. Hutto suggested the idea of using a motel, which is why Tom Beasley was driving around Houston looking to buy one.

Sometime around noon on January 1, 1984, Beasley convinced the owner of Houston's Olympic Motel to lease him his facility. Nine days later, when the federal government transferred two hundred illegal aliens to CCA, the Nashville company housed them in a small hotel surrounded by a new fence. "They were no problem," Beasley said.

By this time, CCA had some proof of what Beasley and Crants had been saying from the beginning about private prisons being quicker to build and cheaper to operate than their public counterparts. In May 1984, *Newsweek* reported that some private prisons were operating at 30 percent below the cost of their public counterparts.

The next year, CCA landed a contract in Panama City, Florida, to operate its first real jail. On the flight back to Nashville, Beasley felt so confident that he came up with an ambitious plan: to make a bid to take over the entire Tennessee prison system. "Our original plan was that we would not do any business in Tennessee," Beasley said. "But we got so excited after we landed the Panama City jail, so we thought we could do it." CCA's plan was aided by the fact that the state's prison system had been neglected by Gov. Lamar Alexander—so much so that a federal judge had ordered the state to begin releasing inmates.

A few months later, CCA called a press conference and announced its desire to take over the Tennessee prison system. At a press conference attended by CCA investor Jack Massey, the company said it would pay the state a $100 million franchise fee and invest $150 million to upgrade the Tennessee system in exchange for a long-term deal to run it.

Beasley, Hutto, and Crants spent much of the next six months lobbying the legislature hard to pass some sort of prison privatization bill, but failed miserably. "It was an outrageous proposal," Beasley admitted years later. "The problem was that we were not big enough for anyone to take us seriously." CCA's case wasn't helped by the fact that both Alexander's wife Honey and then-House Speaker Ned McWherter owned CCA stock that they had bought at private offering. Rather than privatize the Tennessee system, the legislature built several new state-run prisons.

CCA's failure to win any of Tennessee's prison system disappointed Beasley, Crants, and Hutto, but they felt better about everything after a successful public offering in October 1986. CCA then set its sights on other states. Georgia was one of the first, but a year-long effort to get part of the state prison system there yielded little. But in 1987, Beasley spent four months in Austin, Texas, successfully lobbying the legislature there to pass a bill authorizing four privately run 450-bed prisons. "That was big," Beasley said. "Texas doing it was a big statement to the rest of the world." Eventually, CCA got to build two of those prisons (the other two going to Wackenhut Corrections Corp. of Florida).

During the next couple of years, CCA got major prison contracts in New Mexico, Louisiana, Oklahoma, and Texas, plus a contract to build and run a jail for the metropolitan government of Nashville. In 1990, the company—by now under the presidency of Crants—turned a profit for the first time. The next year, Tennessee Gov. Ned McWherter had the idea of building two identical prisons and letting a private company run one and the state run the other. Through this program, CCA built its first state prison in Tennessee, the South Central Correctional Facility.

McWherter's plan would later produce an in-depth study comparing the cost of CCA's Tennessee prison to the similar one operated by state employees. According to the study—which would be brought up frequently during for-profit prison debates for the rest of the decade—there was negligible difference in the cost of the CCA prison and the state-run prison. But CCA officials dismissed the study. "That study was bogus," Beasley said. "It doesn't correctly account for their costs and it layers in a lot of their overhead into our costs."

After a financial slump in 1991, CCA bounced back and had its most successful years. During the first six months of 1994, CCA's stock nearly doubled, in part because investors perceived that the company would benefit from proposed legislation that would increase prison sentences. The company also benefited from a streak of positive media coverage. In a CCA profile that ran in the *New York Times*, a prisoner rights' activist in Texas was quoted as saying: "At Corrections Corporation prisons you don't have the atmosphere of impending violence that you have in a state prison. If Corrections Corporation ran more prisons, I am sure you'd see an increase in savings and a decrease in violence."[6]

By 1996, CCA had over twenty-eight thousand inmates and fifty-nine facilities. But the company still wanted to operate more of

Tennessee's prison system. In April 1997, word leaked out that CCA had been having secret talks with state legislators about taking over the entire Tennessee prison system. The proposal created a furor—in part because it was sponsored by Lt. Gov. John Wilder, lobbied by Betty Anderson (wife of House Speaker Jimmy Naifeh), and supported by Gov. Don Sundquist. But opponents of the bill, which included the Tennessee State Employee Association and the state's largest newspapers, eventually won out. Much like it had in 1985, CCA's attempt to get a large chunk of its home state business failed miserably.

After that, things only got worse for the nation's largest for-profit prison company. In late 1997, CCA split into two different firms. One, which continued under the name CCA, had its operational contracts. The other, called Prison Realty Corp., owned the company's real estate. Based on the stock's performance, investors liked the arrangement. However, no sooner had people gotten used to it than the operational side of CCA was taken private and folded into Prison Realty. Wall Street hated that move and hated it even more when Prison Realty missed several consecutive earnings goals.

Central Parking Corporation

The last large public company to emerge in twentieth-century Nashville had a curious tie with the most important company in Nashville at the beginning of the twentieth century.

In the early 1950s, Nashville, Chattanooga & St. Louis Railroad assistant comptroller Monroe Carell Sr. had to find a new way to make a living when his employer was merged with the Louisville & Nashville. At that point, Carell and another former N. C. & St. Louis executive named Roy Dennis bought some land from their former employer and went into the business of operating those parcels as parking lots. The company, called Central Parking, did business in Nashville and Atlanta.

About ten years later, Carell and Dennis turned their small company over to their respective sons: Bob Dennis, who lived in Atlanta, and Monroe Carell Jr., a Vanderbilt graduate who previously worked as an engineer for a rural electrical cooperative in Shelbyville. "I had no idea what I was really getting into and I had no idea of the size of the company," Carell Jr. said years later. "If I had known how small it was, I wouldn't have ever done it."

After a few weeks of studying the books, Monroe Carell Jr. concluded that he had to expand the company in order to save it. He also decided that the best place to acquire contracts was in new cities, and he chose St. Louis as the first of those markets. For almost a year, Carell practically lived in St. Louis. "The St. Louis Cardinals won the World Series that year, and I remember flagging cars before all the games," Carell Jr. said. His work was rewarded with almost a dozen parking contracts.

During the next few years, Central Parking entered several other markets, including Kansas City, Denver, and Charlotte (the company generally avoided the Northeast because the business was far more competitive there). Virtually all of the growth in this period was by acquiring the parking contracts for new buildings in downtown areas.

In the 1970s, Carell Jr. shed two of his co-owners: Bob Dennis, who took the Atlanta contracts with him when he left the partnership, and Monroe Carell Sr., who did not always see eye-to-eye with his son. "My father and I had some disputes early on," Carell Jr. said. "I had an agreement to buy the company and we had some disputes about him honoring that agreement."

By 1980, Central Parking had become a major player in a few U.S. markets. But it never would have emerged as an important company had it not been for changes that Carell Jr. made to its operation during the next decade. Prior to about 1986, virtually all of the contracts in the parking business were made on a fee basis, which meant that Central Parking simply got a percentage of the revenue that it brought in and had very little at risk. "Parking was not looked upon as a profit center," Carell said. "It was amenity, analogous to elevators." The event that signaled a change in the industry was the real estate recession of the late 1980s, which brought downtown construction to a halt and made Carell realize that his company could not grow by getting newly built garages anymore. About the same time, owners of many large downtown buildings began bidding out their parking contracts rather than simply hiring a company to do it on a fee basis. Central Parking thus got the need and the opportunity to take business away from its competitors.

The parking business had always been dominated by small, independent operators, many of whom had never thought hard about how to squeeze more profit out of their operation. Carell developed two strategies to outdo the competition. One was to hire ambitious college graduates, train them very well, promote them when they exceed, and pay them well. The other was to apply many of the principals of engineering that Carell learned at Vanderbilt into the business of running a parking operation.

Eventually, Central Parking's executives would be able to immediately drive through a parking garage or lot and estimate its revenues to within 10 percent. They would be able to come up with many ways to take over an existing property and increase its profit by doing everything from redrawing the parking lines to keeping it open longer hours to acquiring other corporate customers to use it. They would study the difference between the economic benefit of "all-day" users and the benefit of "transit" users. They also learned various tricks of

the business, such as the fact that it costs a lot more to reserve a desig-
nated space for a particular user than it does to simply reserve them
a place somewhere in the garage.

Starting in the mid-1980s, Central Parking worked circles around
the competition and took over facilities all over the U.S. By 1992,
Central had over one thousand locations and annual revenue of about
$45 million. It had also started a successful international operation
that ran the parking at London's Heathrow Airport.

At that point, another aspect of the parking business began to
change as large property owners began asking their parking vendors
to take care of upgrades to their parking facilities. As one of the
largest parking companies in the United States, Central Parking was
better prepared to make these kinds of commitments than most of its
competitors. But Carell thought that the company still needed more
capital to be able to take on these types of contracts, which is the main
reason the company went public in October 1995. Central Parking's
stock price more than tripled during its first year.

In 1996 and 1997, Central Parking took advantage of its buying
power by expanding through dozens of minor acquisitions and several
major ones. The first large merger was the $80 million takeover of
New Jersey-based Square Industries, which increased Central's
annual revenue by 45 percent, gave it a major foothold in New York,
and made it the nation's largest parking company. The second was the
$206 million acquisition of Kinney Systems Holding of New York,
doubling Central's presence in the Northeast. The third, and the
largest, was the $500 million purchase of Allright Parking of Houston.
After each major and minor acquisition, Carell rarely kept the old
company's previous management in place. "If you are making an
acquisition and you are depending on the people who you are buying
the company from to run it afterwards, forget it," Carell said.

By 1999, Central Parking had seventeen thousand employees and
controlled 1.6 million parking spaces around the world, in places as
diverse as Atlanta's Turner Field and Kuala Lumpur, Malaysia's eighty-
eight-story City Centre complex. The company dominated the parking
business in cities as large as St. Louis, Charlotte, and Seattle (and of
course, Nashville). Revenues topped $800 million, making the
company more than three times the size of the next largest parking
company and giving it about a fourth of the nation's commercial
parking business.

Throughout this period of astounding growth, there were three
aspects of Central Parking's culture that made it unique in Nashville.
One was the company's tireless work ethic and its intolerance for
employees who could not cope with it, particularly middle-level
managers who did not acquire new properties for the company. "We
indicate what we expect of our employees," Carell said. "If they don't

accomplish it, we have to make a change. If you want a company that sends you home at 4:30 in the afternoon and pays you twenty-five thousand dollars a year, this isn't the place to be." Another was a minimal corporate staff; in an era when many of Nashville's CEOs hid from the press, Carell took all of his media calls personally and saw no reason to hire a public relations specialist. A third aspect was corporate frugality. At the turn of the century, Carell still used a desk made from a kit. Central Parking executives were still required to share hotel rooms when on road trips. And perhaps there was no better example of Central Parking's corporate frugality than the fact that in 1996—when almost every other Nashville company (profitable or otherwise) committed to spend six figures per year to buy a luxury box for Nashville's new NFL team—Central Parking did no such thing. "I have regional offices in several other major cities," Carell explained. "If I buy a luxury box here, I have to buy one there."

As a buyer and seller of worn-out properties in downtown areas, Central Parking came under frequent criticism for tearing down old buildings. In Nashville, Central tore down several structures along Church Street during the 1990s, as the once-proud shopping district transitioned to other uses. "We are the buyer of last resort," Carell said. "If there is any possible way to use a building as a meaningful part of society, then it carries more value than we can pay for it." In 1996, Central Parking's plans to tear down the old Harvey's Department Store Building on Church Street came under such criticism that Carell agreed to hold the building for six months and sell it to another user at the same price his company had paid for it. After no buyer emerged, the building came down.

Central Parking was so dominant in its field by the late 1990s that there appeared to be only two possible threats to its continued growth. The first was antitrust problems, which first came up when the U.S. Justice Department ordered Central to divest seventy-four of its properties from the Allright takeover in March 1999. The second was Carell's eventual retirement. And although Carell admitted that there was nothing he could do about the first problem, he said he was doing everything he could to ensure a smooth and profitable transition to his chosen successor, Central Parking president Jim Bond. "My family still owns 50 percent of the company," Carell said. "All my work can go down the tubes if my successor doesn't do well."

CHAPTER 21

Detroit South

I n some ways Nissan's plant in Smyrna and Saturn's facility in Spring Hill couldn't have been more different. When Nissan came to Tennessee in the early 1980s, the company kept the United Auto Workers out. The Saturn plant, on the other hand, was a union facility from its inception. When Nissan opened, it hired thousands of residents from Middle Tennessee, almost none of whom had ever worked in an auto plant before. When the Saturn plant opened ten years later, its entire workforce consisted of people who had been either laid off or transferred from other General Motors divisions around the country.

From the start, Nissan planned to build the same kind of vehicles in Tennessee that it was building at other facilities in the world. From the start, General Motors planned to build a kind of vehicle at its Saturn plant that was different than any it had ever built before.

When Nissan's trucks first came off the line in Smyrna, the company's biggest challenge was convincing people that they were as good as others produced by its parent company. When Saturn's cars came off the line in Spring Hill, the company's biggest challenge was convincing people that they were good in spite of its parent company.

The first president of Nissan's Tennessee plant was Marvin Runyon, who promoted a sense of openness at his company that would remain long after his departure. Saturn went through three presidents during its first ten years. All would maintain a low profile in Tennessee and a level of secrecy in their plants that would frustrate reporters.

However, Nissan and Saturn came to Tennessee for the same reason. During the late 1970s, American consumers began buying Japanese-made automobiles and trucks at a rate no one had ever predicted. By 1980, sales of American-made cars were in such a slump that two hundred thousand U.S. auto workers were out of work. This buying wave caused two changes. One is that it caused a wave of protectionist feelings in the United States that indirectly led to Nissan's Tennessee plant. The other is that it forced General Motors to go through a lot of soul searching, a process that eventually led to Saturn.

Smyrna's Nissan plant was in many ways a milestone for the Nashville area. But it is important to place it properly in history. It was not the first foreign-owned car plant in the United States (Volkswagen had a plant near Pittsburgh). It was not Tennessee's first large car plant (Ford had a plant in Memphis that it built in the mid-1920s and closed in 1948). It was not the first large employer in Middle Tennessee to be owned by the Japanese (Toshiba was already in Lebanon). In fact, it wasn't even Middle Tennessee's first car plant, if you consider the Marathon factory that was open in Nashville for a short time in the early twentieth century.

Nissan was, however, the first foreign-owned car plant in the South. It was also one of the most significant jolts the Middle Tennessee economy had ever received, comparable to the construction of the DuPont rayon factory in the 1920s and the arrival of the Vultee aircraft factory in the 1940s.

Starting in the late 1970s, executives of Detroit's big three auto companies began asking Congress to raise tariffs on imported vehicles, claiming they could not compete with a country with labor costs as low as Japan's. The Carter administration heard Detroit's cries and began putting pressure on Japanese car companies to transfer some of their manufacturing operations to the United States. "If something isn't done, you will find during this election year a great swell of protectionist legislation," U.S. Ambassador to Japan Mike Mansfield told the Japan Press Club.[1]

American officials were asking for car (rather than truck) plants, which is why they were especially happy with Honda's decision to build a plant in Marysville, Ohio. But Nissan—then the second largest foreign seller of vehicles to the United States behind Toyota—had serious concerns about the ability of American workers to meet their quality standards. In April 1980, Nissan announced that it too would build a plant in the United States. But Nissan made it clear that the plant would produce passenger trucks (trucks being simpler to make than cars). Initially, Nissan said the facility would cost $300 million and produce 120,000 trucks per year. Nissan did not say where the plant would be located. But the *Wall Street Journal* hinted it would be in the Midwest.

What the national media did not know at the time was that Nissan was also looking in the South. Back in July 1979, Nissan officials and representatives of the Nashville-area Chamber of Commerce began looking at sites in places like Cockrill Bend, Mt. Juliet, and Smyrna. Nissan specified that the site had to be three hundred acres, near an interstate, and flat.

Since no one at the Nashville Chamber spoke Japanese or was familiar with Japanese customs, it wasn't easy. "We would get up early and go all day," said Fred Harris, one of the chamber officials involved in selecting a site. "Then we would go out to dinner and have fourteen drinks and then we would sit down and review what we had done all day. . . . The hours were so long, I almost had to get divorced." The process went on for months, during which time not a single reporter found out about it. "Restaurateurs are pretty good at keeping secrets," Harris said.

After a few months, Nissan and Chamber officials homed in on a farm near Smyrna that was owned by a retired schoolteacher named Maymee Cantrell. But there was only one problem: Cantrell did not want to sell. In desperation, state and Chamber officials asked Gov. Lamar Alexander to intercede. Alexander paid a visit to Cantrell at her home in Waverly. Over a slice of key lime pie, Cantrell agreed to sign an option to sell her property. "When they parted, the governor had promised to help find a new dairy farm for Mrs. Cantrell and her tenant," an account of the meeting said.[2]

Despite these efforts, Nissan was still leaning toward Ohio. But that would change with the company's June 1980 decision to hire Runyon as the head of its North American division. Runyon had worked for Ford for thirty-seven years, starting as an assembly line worker and working his way up to general foreman to trouble shooter to plant construction manager to plant manager to regional manager. By the time he left Ford, Runyon had worked at virtually every assembly plant in its system and become its vice president of body and assembly, with over 200,000 people working for him. But Runyon was looking for a new challenge, and he was looking for a new place to live. "I retired from Ford because I had lived in Michigan for eleven years," Runyon said in 1999. "My wife was sick. She hated the place, and I wasn't real thrilled with it."

During his many interviews with Nissan, Runyon had made two things clear. One was that he would only work for Nissan if they allowed him to run the plant autonomously. The other was that he would only work for Nissan if they allowed him to build the plant in the South. "When I heard that they were considering a site in Ohio, I told them that I was no longer a candidate for the job," Runyon said. "They said 'well, it is southern Ohio.' And I said, 'there is no southern Ohio—it is all north!' A few weeks later, they called me back and told me that Ohio was out, and that they wanted me for the job."

Runyon narrowed the site selection to three places: one in Smyrna and two near Atlanta. His bosses at Nissan preferred the Georgia sites because of the presence of a Ford plant near Atlanta and because of Georgia's proximity to the Atlantic Ocean. Runyon preferred Tennessee. One reason was that a preliminary study showed that the Tennessee site would save Nissan $12 million a year in transportation costs because of proximity to customers. The other reason was that the Ford plant in Georgia was unionized, and Runyon did not want his plant to be unionized. "They had unions in Japan and they thought this plant should be organized," he said. "But I told them it wasn't going to be. I had seen non-union operation and union operations and in my opinion the only reason you have unions is because of poor management."

Runyon said that one factor that did not enter into the decision-making process was the presence of automotive-related industries in the Nashville area. By 1980, Middle Tennessee had a Ford Glass Plant (built in 1956) and a Firestone plant (built in 1972). But neither of those facilities entered into consideration, Runyon said.

As Nissan considered sites in Tennessee and Georgia, the company had discussions with the state, county, and local governments it would impact. Eventually, Nissan received assurances that if it came to Smyrna the state of Tennessee would connect the site to Interstate 24 with a four-lane road. The state also gave Nissan about $7 million in assistance to train its workers. "The rules put out by Lamar were that we would help build the infrastructure and help train workers, but we would not pay to do anything on site," Harris said. "The logic that we used was that if we built a road then no matter what happened we would still have the road, and that if we trained people then we would still have the people." Nissan also worked out a deal with the city of Smyrna whereby its property taxes were replaced by a payment in lieu of taxes that increased with time. The total government package—estimated by Harris to be about $30 million— was criticized at the time but dwarfed by government tax breaks that would come in later years.

In October 1980, Nissan announced it had chosen Smyrna, Tennessee, as the site for a 3.5-million-square-foot truck assembly plant. Its initial cost was to be $300 million and its initial employment about twenty-two hundred (numbers that jumped to $500 million and thirty-one hundred within a few months).

Within weeks of the announcement, word had begun to leak out that Runyon intended to keep the United Autoworkers out of his plant. This speculation became louder after Nissan chose Daniel Construction of Greenville, South Carolina—a non-union contractor—to build the plant.

Nissan's groundbreaking on February 3, 1981, will not go down as one of those Chamber of Commerce moments for Middle Tennessee. With national media looking on, an estimated one to two thousand union protesters picketed the ceremony, many of them shouting phrases such as "Go Home Japs." After several short speeches, Alexander was supposed to drive a Nissan truck equipped with a snowplow a few hundred feet. Since the truck was surrounded by hostile union members and covered with pro-union bumpers stickers, Runyon got in the driver's seat instead, a nervous moment for the Nissan executive since he had never driven a Japanese truck before. Since the vehicle's tires had been slashed, he could only move it a few feet. "I wanted to dig a hole and crawl into it," said Douglas Henry Jr., the state senator who attended the ceremony.[3]

Organized labor succeeded in its attempt to disrupt Nissan's groundbreaking. But during the days following the groundbreaking, newspaper editorials and legislators blasted organized labor for its part in the demonstration. "There could have been other ways to handle it," said Jim Neeley, who had just been elected president of the Tennessee Labor Council at the time. "We should have not . . . the labor movement should have not been as belligerent as they were on that occasion." The protests hurt organized labor's reputation with

Protesters surround a truck while Nissan's Marvin Runyon tries to drive it at the Nissan groundbreaking, February 1981 (Tennessee Photographic Services).

the future Nissan workers it was trying to recruit in the first place. In fact, the groundbreaking created such a public relations problem for Neeley that Alexander gloated about it in a private meeting with the labor leader. "After this was all over with, we had a meeting out at the residence with Lamar," Neeley said. "He told me 'I had an opportunity to kick your ass, and I took advantage of it.'"

Nissan's Marvin Runyon, Gov. Lamar Alexander, Nissan's Masataka Okuma, and Nissan's Kaichi Kanao at the Nissan groundbreaking, February 1981. Sen. Douglas Henry Jr. can be seen in the background between Runyon and Alexander (Tennessee Photographic Services).

The development of Nissan's Smyrna plant proved to be a case study in cultural compromise. Between announcement and production were dozens of examples of how Japanese culture differed from that of the South. Early plant blueprints showed a dormitory on the property. "I asked what it was, and they told me that it was a dormitory for the workers," Runyon said. "I said 'we don't have dormitories here.' They said 'Well the workers have to stay somewhere.'"

According to Runyon, one of the keys to the success of the Nissan plant was the company's willingness to allow Americans to manage it. "When it came to how to run the plant and where to buy parts, I had total autonomy—much more than I had at Ford," Runyon said. "At Ford, the plant manager is only responsible for the labor—all the parts are bought by someone else and shipped in. With Nissan, I was responsible for buying parts, and I was authorized to switch suppliers if I wanted to." Runyon was also completely authorized to hire whomever he wanted. Among his first hires were several engineers and managers from Ford, including one named Jerry Benefield.

As a committee of American and Japanese Nissan officials came up with the plant's operating strategy, it took on several aspects similar to a Japanese company. The way it was set up, Tennessee's Nissan plant had only five levels of management between the president and an assembly line worker—compared to up to twenty at American car plants. Much like factories in Japan, Tennessee's Nissan plant required its workers to cross-train in order to keep a few workers from having to do all the hard jobs. "If a section had one job that was especially tough, we would divide it up so that maybe four workers would do [it] over an eight-hour shift," Runyon said. "At Ford, you did the same job every day." Much like factories in Japan, each section had a ten-minute meeting at the beginning of each shift where the supervisor went over what had to be done that day and who was going to do it. "At Ford, you just walked up to the assembly line and started working," Runyon said. The Nissan plant also did not contain separate eating places for executive and rank-and-file workers, something the plant's head of quality control, Shuichi Yoshida, was very insistent about.

However, Nissan's Smyrna plant did not adopt every aspect of Japanese work culture. "There are a lot of things about the Japanese system that won't work here," said Benefield. "In Japan, young people make less than old people. People with children make more than people without children. Women make less than men. Women can't work at the plant and can't work at night." Benefield also insisted that the Nissan plant in Smyrna take employee participation a step further than Nissan's plants in Japan. "In Japan, participative management is more of a tactic to involve the low-level workers but often the important decisions are made at the very top of the company and they are pretty autocratically applied. We tried to take it a step further and involve our employees in some of the more important decisions such as corporate policy and philosophy."

Nissan received over one hundred thousand applications during the two years after it announced it was coming to Tennessee. The company hired about two thousand of those applicants in 1982 and 1983, most of them Tennessee residents who had never worked in an automobile factory before. During the months preceding the plant opening, several hundred of those workers went to Japan for training.

When the Nissan plant first went into production in June 1983, about three-fourths of its parts had been imported from Japan and brought in by train from the West Coast. During the next fifteen years, Nissan would bring so many suppliers to Middle Tennessee and southern Kentucky that only thirty percent of the parts were being imported by 1999.

The first big local supplier was the Ford Glass Plant, which in 1982 began making glass for the Nissan vehicles. Eventually, other large suppliers included Calsonic in Shelbyville (heaters, radiators, and air conditioners), Yoruzu in Morrison (steel stampings and metal parts), Kantus in Lewisburg (gauges), Vintec in Murfreesboro (seats), M-Tek in Manchester (door panels), and A. G. Simpson in Dickson (stampings and metal parts).

Nissan's executives in Japan had been very honest in their concern about whether an American plant could make vehicles that met their quality standards. When trucks began rolling off the assembly line in the summer of 1983, they brought ten of them to Japan and inspected them closely. The executives were impressed—so impressed that in May 1984, the company announced it would invest another $200 million and hire seventeen hundred people to mass-produce a sedan called the Sentra. "I had always believed that if given the chance that Americans could make cars that were up to Japanese quality," said Benefield, who was promoted to president when Runyon retired in 1988. "We proved we were right."

The strategy on which Runyon had organized the plant faced a major challenge within a year of Benefield's taking over. In May 1989, the UAW obtained signatures from 30 percent of Nissan's employees and forced a vote on whether plant workers should organize. For two months, about thirty UAW workers handed out leaflets, made speeches to workers, and did everything they could to draw publicity to what they said was a mistreated workforce and unsafe workplace. Pro-union workers inside the plant wore t-shirts that said "Vote Yes for a Safer Workplace" or "Unite! The 13 colonies did it!" Nevertheless, the offensive did not work. On July 27, 1989, Nissan's workers voted 1,622 to 711 against the UAW, handing the national union one of the most decisive defeats in its history. There would be no more attempts to organize the Nissan plant for the rest of the century. In 1999, when asked if there was any chance that his plant would organize, Benefield responded "No chance. Not while I'm president and not when anyone else is president."

During the 1990s, Nissan continued to invest money in the Tennessee facility, producing a new vehicle called the Altima and building a new engine plant in Decherd, Tennessee. However, Nissan's corporate financial health declined in the latter part of the decade, partly due to a recession in Japan. In 1998, decreasing demand for small cars forced Nissan's Tennessee plant to make major changes to its production line—replacing the Sentra sedan and the 200SX coupe with the Xterra sport utility vehicle and four-door Frontier pickup truck. In 1998, the facility produced about 300,000 vehicles, a number that had declined from a peak of 450,000 in the early 1990s.

In the 1960s, the American effort to put a man on the moon went by the code name Saturn. Two decades later, General Motors gave the same name to their attempt to make a small car that could compete with the imports. "Without the Saturn project, we don't stand a chance against the Japanese," said GM chairman Roger Smith.[4]

Smith had grandiose ideas for Saturn. In 1983, two years before Tennessee was chosen as Saturn's home, General Motors came up with the basic parameters for the vehicle it wanted. The vehicle would be ten inches shorter than the Chevrolet Cavalier, have an aluminum engine, and get forty-five miles per gallon of gas in the city. GM had also made it clear that it wanted to dramatically reduce the number of man-hours required to build the car while still improving quality.

However, GM knew that none of these plans would have worked without cooperation from the United Auto Workers, which represented employees at virtually every GM facility in the United States. In 1983, GM first mentioned the Saturn project to Don Ephlin, director of the UAW's GM department. When GM told Ephlin that they envisioned a six-member planning group for the Saturn project, Ephlin suggested they make the number much higher. The group ended up having ninety-nine members—about half of them UAW members who worked for GM and about half of them GM executives.

For several months, GM's "Group of 99" toured car plants around the country, visited suppliers and dealers, met with management experts of various kinds, and mapped out a strategy for the company. Eventually, its members became very excited about the potential of their project. "The emotions, the tears, the whatever it took to really create a team and a culture and a commitment—I could never fully describe it," said Neil De Koker, a member of the Group of 99 who later became Saturn's director of business systems.[5] Although the grand plan put forward by the Group of 99 was later described by Ephlin as "kind of utopian," it did have several important conclusions. One of those was the recommendation that Saturn be a wholly owned subsidiary of GM but be completely different than the rest of the company. Another was that Saturn have a separate labor/management agreement that would theoretically do away with the confrontational relationship between the two.

Although GM started openly discussing the Saturn project in 1983, the company did not announce that Saturn would be a separate organization built from the ground up until January 8, 1985. At that press conference, Smith said GM would invest five billion dollars in the Saturn project, making it the largest one-time investment in American history. Smith said Saturn would break ground within a year and be producing a car by 1989. The GM chairman said he did not know where the Saturn plant would be located, but only said it would be located somewhere in the United States besides Detroit.

As GM turned its attention to site selection, the company found that it did not need to do much but answer its phone. The state of Ohio sent eighty-three possible sites to GM and convinced two hundred thousand school children to write letters asking for the plant. Illinois promised a $50 million recreational and child care center for GM employees.

In the spring of 1985, several governors went on the Phil Donahue show to talk about why their states were ideal for Saturn. Tennessee Gov. Lamar Alexander was not one of them. But at the exact moment the Donahue show was being taped, an emissary of Alexander's was having a three-hour meeting in Detroit with several key members of the General Motor's site selection team. That emissary was Bill Long, Tennessee's Commissioner of Economic and Community Development.

In many ways, Long was completely unqualified to recruit General Motors to Tennessee. He had not been involved in the state's recruitment of Nissan a few years earlier. He knew very little about the car industry. In fact, the former Marine Corps colonel had never even worked in the private sector. But Long, who had once lost a congressional race to a twenty-eight-year-old named Albert Gore Jr., worked hard, and did things by the book. Unlike his counterparts in other states, Long did not pull any publicity stunts. But he kept in continuous touch with the GM site selection team. After making his first presentation to the GM people, Long promised he would not become a nuisance but said he would call them every time there was new information that might be relevant to the site selection process. Long also promised them that every time GM asked for new information, it would be delivered by hand, something that eventually set Tennessee apart from every other state that was trying to land Saturn. "I have always believed that if you take the right information to the right people at the right time and deliver it in person it gets there immediately," Long said.

During the first six months of 1985, twenty-six governors flew to Detroit to ask for the plant, including Arkansas's Bill Clinton, Alabama's George Wallace, and New York's Mario Cuomo. Alexander did not make such a trip. The only time Alexander met with GM officials was in February 1985, when U.S. Senator Howard Baker arranged a meeting between Alexander and Roger Smith at the Peabody Hotel in Memphis. After state officials presented information to Smith about Tennessee's central location and low taxes, Alexander then took the floor and made a reference to Nissan. "Lamar told Roger Smith that if you are going to compete with the Japanese, then you should get on a level playing field with them—that is, unless you think that the other team has better coaches," Long said. "I will always believe that this was the turning point. I am sure that Lamar got Roger Smith's attention with that statement."

While all this was going on, representatives of GM and the UAW sat down and worked out a labor agreement. The deal had dozens of significant aspects, including the fact that the union would allow Saturn more autonomy in cross-training its worker than at other GM plants. But from the state of Tennessee's perspective, the most important aspect of the deal was one that involved hiring: according to the agreement, Saturn would not hire any production workers who were not already members of the UAW. In other words, Saturn would not hire locals.

In early May, GM official Ed Dilworth visited Nashville attorney Jim Neal and asked him if he could recommend someone to help him secure options on a site for the Saturn plant. Neal sent him to Maclin Davis Jr. and Lawrence Dortch of the law firm Waller Lansden Dortch and Davis.

During the next several weeks, Waller Lansden attorneys worked long hours securing options on about three thousand acres in Maury County, just outside of Spring Hill (a site that happened to be close to Dortch's boyhood home). They did so in constant fear that word would leak out, causing a property owner to hold out in order to get more money from General Motors.

A few days before all the options had been signed, rumors that Spring Hill had been chosen for the site reached the ears of *Tennessean* reporter James Pratt. "I made a beeline to the Maury County Courthouse, and the clerks there helped me find what I was looking for," Pratt said. Pratt's story that GM was optioning a site near Spring Hill broke on July 9.

Immediately after the UAW and GM signed the Saturn labor contract, UAW officials told Detroit newspapers that they were almost certain that the plant was going to be built in Tennessee. With that news, out-of-state buyers from as far away as New York began buying up land around the Spring Hill site. "There are a significant number of strange people riding around in cars with out-of-state license plates on them," said one real estate agent.[6] The next day, U.S. Senators Al Gore and Jim Sasser infuriated Alexander by announcing that the Saturn plant was almost certainly going to Tennessee.

On Tuesday, July 30, 1985, General Motors announced it would break ground near Spring Hill within six months for the Saturn plant. At that time, GM said that the plant would cost $5 billion, employ six thousand people, and produce up to five hundred thousand cars per year. The UAW said it hoped that the Saturn plant would help it organize the nearby Nissan plant.

National coverage of the Saturn announcement focused not so much on Nashville but on tiny Spring Hill, whose previous claim to fame was that it was the home of Peter Jenkins, the author of a best-selling book called *A Walk Across America*. Several newspapers ran photographs of grizzled old men in bib overalls, grinning and holding copies of newspapers that announced the Saturn decision. A few days later, Alexander ran full-page advertisements in several national publications, including the *Wall Street Journal*, boasting about Tennessee's achievement.

During the entire site selection process, one aspect that hadn't been discussed at great length was what the state of Tennessee was willing to do for GM regarding infrastructure and tax breaks. That negotiating process began in early July 1985, when Long, Dilworth, and Columbia, Tennessee, banker Waymon Hickman sat down and began negotiations. "We never offered General Motors a single thing before they made their decision—not a nickel's worth," Long said. "After the announcement, I had a talk with Lamar and got a general idea of what we would do and wouldn't do. A few days later, Ed Dilworth and I sat down and he had about an eight-page list of things that they wanted. I was terrified. They wanted everything from playgrounds to schools to roads to training. And he'd just go down the list and I'd say 'yes' or 'no' or 'hell, no.' And he'd just say okay." Eventually, Tennessee did many of the same things for Saturn that it did for Nissan—including building a four-lane road connecting the plant to Interstate 65 and arranging for the plant to pay a graduating "in lieu of tax" fee to Maury County rather than pay property taxes.

GM never went public with a complete explanation as to why it chose its site. But according to several people who were involved in the process, GM originally chose to put its plant near Lexington, Kentucky. After Lexington officials declined GM's request to have a large tract of land discreetly rezoned, the car manufacturer changed its mind, went back to the drawing board, and homed in on three places: Nashville, Knoxville, and Huntsville, Alabama. Knoxville was later eliminated because it did not have a large, flat site. Huntsville was eliminated because it had relatively poor interstate access.

During the following year, GM's financial situation worsened, causing the company to rethink many aspects of the Saturn project. By late 1986, GM decided to reduce the number of cars initially produced at Spring Hill from 500,000 to 250,000 and to reduce the initial employment from six thousand to thirty-five hundred. GM also decided to rely more on outside suppliers than originally planned and to buy a substantial number of parts from overseas locations. All of the above allowed GM to reduce Saturn's original budget from about $5 billion to about half that.

The GM executive who presided over the development and opening of the Saturn plant was actually its third president. Saturn's first president, Joe Sanchez, died only twenty days after his appointment in January 1985. Its second president, Bill Hoglund, stayed only through the site selection process. When Richard ("Skip") Lafauve was promoted from head of the Buick/Oldsmobile/Cadillac division to Saturn president in February 1986, Saturn was still months from breaking ground.

While the Saturn plant was being developed, Lafauve and his colleagues had several barriers to overcome. One was the perception—very prevalent in 1986 and early 1987—that Saturn might never be built at all. Another was that its unusual labor-management agreement would either be rejected by the UAW or watered down to mean very little. A third difficulty was the resentment that many people at GM felt about Saturn. "There were executives who wanted money for other projects who were being told that they couldn't have it who did not like the idea of putting $2.5 billion off to the side in a newfangled idea about union management," Lafauve said. "Chevrolet was very resentful, as a matter of fact." Perhaps the biggest challenge faced by Lafauve and his colleagues was the perception that the largest industrial relocation in American history would prove to be a money-burning experiment that would never make a profit, a GM diversion that would go down in history as the "Vega" of the 1990s.

One thing Saturn built from scratch was its dealership strategy. GM's original "Group of 99" concluded that the American public had a low view of car dealers. Because of this, Saturn decided to have fewer dealers, discourage competition among dealers, and encourage them to emphasize customer satisfaction. Saturn also directed its dealers to adopt a "no-haggle" pricing system.

Another aspect of Saturn that was unique was the advertising strategy. Rather than use GM's normal ad agencies in the Midwest, GM hired a San Francisco agency that had little experience in the car industry. That agency, which had produced the commercials for Ronald Reagan's 1980 political campaign, produced a video called "Spring in Spring Hill" for Saturn's vendors. The video went over so well that Lafauve considered using it as the centerpiece of Saturn's advertisement campaign. But he was concerned that Spring Hill natives, some of whom were upset about Saturn's policy of not hiring locals, would think that the video exploited them. "We had a showing and invited all the local folks to come in and see it with the idea that if they felt we were exploiting them that they could make suggestions that would make them more comfortable or simply veto it." Lafauve said. "They gave it a standing ovation."

At that meeting, Lafauve fielded a question from a local about why the company wasn't hiring locals. After talking about GM's national problems, an elderly lady rose and addressed the crowd. "I'll never forget it," Lafauve said. "She said 'Let's face it: this is a very difficult time for a new company to get started. And you gotta understand: these people ain't gonna live forever. Our children are going to have jobs at Saturn and that's what is really important.' And that just changed the whole tune about local hiring. It was her philosophy of the long term that really built the relationship that we had with the people in Spring Hill."

The first few months of the Saturn plant's operation were alarming, if not nearly disastrous. Saturn was supposed to start sending cars to dealers in quantity in October. But as cars began coming off the assembly line, Saturn's quality control inspectors kept sending them back because of problems such as doors that wouldn't shut all the way and cars that had excessive vibrations. "We started with a brand new product, a brand new engine, a new casting process, and the union-management arrangement," said Lafauve. "Everything we did was from scratch. We also made up our mind that we were not going to send out cars that did not meet high standards." Because of quality problems, Saturn only produced twenty-two hundred cars during its first four months of operations. "I'm sure we've lost some sales," because of the shortage of cars, a Saturn dealer in Arizona told the *Wall Street Journal*.[7]

No sooner did Saturn begin to get the doors to shut and the cars to stop vibrating when another problem turned up. For some strange reason, Saturn owners all over the country began having problems with their cars' coolant systems. Saturn engineers worked around the clock, checking the pumps and then the seals. Finally, they realized that the problem had nothing to do with the cars themselves, but with the fact that Saturn had received a large shipment of anti-freeze that somehow got mixed with highly toxic water. "The toxic water was eating up the whole cooling system," Lafauve said.

Had the problem been less serious, Saturn might have simply replaced the part. But since it was virtually impossible to replace and guarantee every coolant system, a Saturn team met and decided instead to replace all 1,836 cars. "We thought that was the end of the company," said Lafauve. "I mean, who would buy a car from a company that couldn't put a car together right and had to replace the whole car?"

Incredibly, Saturn's decision to recall all those cars probably paid off in the end. In late 1991, the Saturn plant finally began churning out cars in quantity, and Saturn cars began to get high marks for quality. In May 1992, Saturn produced twenty thousand vehicles per month—twice what it had produced six months earlier. Demand was so great that many people were waiting thirty days for their car.

Despite increased sales, Saturn was still far from profitable. In May, Lafauve called a meeting of Saturn team leaders to say that the company was nowhere near making a profit because of overtime costs and bottlenecks. He told them that in order to make a profit they had to reduce the cost of manufacturing every single car by more than fifteen hundred dollars. During the next few months, Saturn took major steps to reduce cost, such as reducing overtime, cutting back on advertising, and raising the price it was charging dealers by about one hundred dollars per car. By the fall, Saturn had made dramatic reductions in its cost side. But its sales had declined considerably, something many dealers attributed to the reduction in advertising.

In January 1994, Lafauve called a press conference and announced that Saturn had turned a profit during the previous year. When pressed for details, Lafauve admitted that in this case "profit" was calculated on operating expenses and not when the cost of GM's $2.5 billion in developing costs were taken into account. Nevertheless, Lafauve said it was still fair to call Saturn profitable, and he claimed that the subsidiary's performance justified the bonuses that he was giving to his eight thousand employees. Lafauve also announced that Saturn would be having an event called a "Homecoming" the following July, when all Saturn owners would be invited to Spring Hill. "The idea for Homecoming came out of our marketing department and was based upon the idea of the annual reunion of Harley Davidson owners," Lafauve said. Saturn expected about fifteen thousand people to come to its first Homecoming. About thirty thousand came.

By the middle of 1994, GM knew it would not make money off its massive investment in Saturn unless it either expanded the plant or added a new Saturn division. Since demand for small cars had decreased by this time, the company decided in 1995 to build a new midsize Saturn vehicle. But GM decided to build the new vehicle at an old GM facility in Wilmington, Delaware, rather than build it in Tennessee. And GM also decided not to duplicate the unusual union-labor agreement at the second Saturn plant but rather to go with the traditional GM labor agreement. "The customer will see through it," said Mike Bennett, president of the UAW office in Spring Hill. "It won't be a Saturn."[8] Shortly after this announcement was made, Lafauve was promoted within GM and replaced by Don Hudler.

During the latter part of the 1990s, the sales of Saturn's vehicles gradually declined, a factor that many attributed to the declining popularity of the small car market as a whole. From a peak production of 314,000 vehicles in 1996, Saturn fell to 244,000 vehicles two years later. And in the summer of 1998, Saturn's seventy-two hundred workers voted overwhelmingly to authorize a strike because of several issues, including GM's long-term plans to build more Saturn components in places other than Spring Hill. In last-minute negotiations, GM agreed to build a sport-utility vehicle in Spring Hill, which would add between seven hundred and one thousand jobs to the facility. However, critics speculated that Saturn had waited too long to start building sport-utility vehicles, sales of which had begun increasing a decade earlier. By the time Cynthia Trudell was named president of Saturn in March 1999, national publications described the GM subsidiary as struggling. Nonetheless, Trudell said she thought Saturn had a bright future, so long as its parent company continues to expand its product line. "I think Saturn has only begun," she said. "Once we expand the product line and carefully manage the change, it's going to be neat to look back at Saturn ten years from now."[9]

CHAPTER 22

Doo-Wah-Ditty City

Despite the fact that the Grand Ole Opry lured hundreds of thousands of visitors to the city every year in the 1930s and 1940s, Nashville residents remained ambivalent about country music. In the 1930s, the Chamber of Commerce produced brochures featuring photographs of all the large hotels downtown, plus pictures of the Parthenon, the state capitol, Fort Nashborough, the War Memorial Building, and Sulphur Dell baseball park. A book of Nashville postcards printed in the 1940s and a series of maps printed by Jersey Farms Dairies in the 1950s features a similar list of sites. But none of the literature printed before the 1950s mentions the Ryman Auditorium or the Grand Ole Opry. "Among some of the people in Nashville there seemed to be a feeling about the music business that said, 'If you don't feed it, it will go away,'" said Buddy Killen, who in 1951 moved to Nashville from Florence, Alabama, to play bass for a country singer named Autry Inman.[1]

A lot of that changed in the 1960s. With the establishment of music publishing companies and studios, country music evolved from a weekly show into a respectable industry. After country music rebounded in the early 1960s, many affluent people realized that country music was big business, and many Nashville residents began to respect it more.

In 1961, the Country Music Association approached Nashville's largest banks and told them about its dream for a Country Music Hall of Fame and Museum. It took years for plans to begin to materialize, but by 1966, the country music industry had raised $400,000 toward

War Memorial Building, one of Nashville's spacious convention auditoriums located in the heart of the hotel district

COME TO NASHVILLE

For a successful and enjoyable convention make it Nashville, "The Ideal Convention City of the South." Its central location means transportation economy and convenience to delegates assuring larger attendance.

Nashville is only 232 miles from the exact center of population of the United States and approximately one-half of the entire population of the Nation is within an overnight trip.

Excellent hotels, good restaurants, convention auditoriums seating up to five thousand, a moderate climate with an average annual temperature of 59.4, a network of trunkline railways, airlines and perfect highways all contribute to making Nashville an ideal convention city.

Six modern golf courses open twelve months in the year, Southeastern Conference football, Southern League baseball, and many other sporting attractions are available to visitors.

Among the scenic and historical points of interest in easy driving distance of Nashville are: Great Smoky Mountains National Park and Norris Dam near Knoxville, Lookout and Signal Mountains and Chickamauga Park near Chattanooga, Wilson and Wheeler Dams in northern Alabama, Birthplace of Abraham Lincoln, "My Old Kentucky Home" and Mammoth Cave in southern Kentucky.

Rich in romance and historical interest, nestling in the bluegrass region near the foothills of the Cumberlands, Nashville offers your delegates varied opportunities for relaxation and the enjoyment of genuine Southern hospitality.

For Information Address
CONVENTION BUREAU
Chamber of Commerce
Nashville, Tenn.

the project and a committee headed by First American president Andrew Benedict had raised $350,000. As the money was being raised, the city of Nashville agreed to donate land for the Hall of Fame near the area where music-related businesses had been migrating since about 1955. After the Hall of Fame opened in 1967, it became one of Nashville's top tourist attractions and a boost to the city's hotels and restaurants.

Page from a 1930s Nashville Chamber of Commerce brochure.

About the same time, a change in the law gave Nashville's tourism industry another boost. Before the 1960s, Tennessee's cities and towns could have liquor and beer stores and allow bars to sell beer, but they could not authorize the sale of mixed drinks of any kind. In 1967, the legislature changed the law, allowing Tennessee's four largest cities to authorize mixed drink sales if they voted to do so by referendum.

Within days of the state law change, supporters of liquor by the drink in Nashville gathered enough signatures to authorize a referendum on the issue. The debate raged through the summer of 1967. Many churches and temperance groups spoke out against the proposal, saying it would result in increased drinking, alcoholism, and drunken driving. The Nashville Chamber of Commerce actively supported liquor by the drink, claiming its passage would help Nashville lure better hotels and restaurants and saying that the old policy actually encouraged inebriation. "Young people would go out and instead of being able to buy a drink they had to buy a bottle," said real estate developer Nelson Andrews, one of the Chamber's leaders at that time. "Since they had a bottle, they had to kill it because they did not have anything to do with it." Proponents of the measure, which also included the *Tennessean*, pointed out that the existing bans on mixed drink sales actually helped businesses that not only offered illegal drinks but also illegal gambling at places such as Al Alessio's Automobile Business Club in Bordeaux.

After Memphis voters rejected a liquor by the drink proposal in August, it seemed Nashville's referendum would also fail. But on September 28, 1967, the matter passed in Nashville by a vote of about forty-seven thousand to thirty-seven thousand.

The success of the Country Music Hall of Fame proved once and for all that country music could be turned into tourism dollars. The passage of liquor by the drink meant that Nashville could, theoretically at least, become a big convention destination. Although no one knew it at the time, both of these events set up the biggest development in the history of Nashville's tourism industry.

By the 1960s, there was an uneasy alliance between National Life & Accident parent NLT and country music. NLT suffered its share of embarrassing moments because of its affiliation with the Grand Ole Opry, such as the time Ernest Tubb shot a gun in the company's lobby. By the 1960s, the Ryman Auditorium, home to the Grand Ole Opry, was a firetrap and its structure was deteriorating. It also had no dressing facilities, inadequate bathrooms, and no air-conditioning. "People were having heat prostration," said longtime NLT executive Walter Robinson Jr. "The actresses would say that it was the only theater in the country where your lipstick rolled down your lips it was so hot in there. It got to be an impossible place to play." In an era before historic preservation became a powerful force, the Ryman was also often ridiculed as an entertainment venue. "[The] Ryman is big and it's ugly," *Broadcasting* magazine declared, without attribution, in 1963.[2]

NLT could have done a major renovation to the Ryman. But there was another reason the company wanted to move the Grand Ole Opry. By the 1960s, the area around the Ryman had many businesses NLT executives thought were detrimental to country music's image, not to mention theirs. Honky-tonks such as Tootsie's Orchid Lounge were one thing. Gin houses, adult bookstores, and hotels that rented by the hour were another. "People were getting shot across the street and cars were getting broken into," said E. W. (Bud) Wendell, Opry manager in the 1960s. "When all those people would stand in line around the block, every itinerant preacher, beggar, hooker, and shoe shine boy in Nashville was bothering them. It was an embarrassment and a potential huge liability. . . . Meanwhile, the city paid no attention to it. We were not looked on as a big plus at that time."

Many of NLT's executives thought it was time to sell the Ryman and the Grand Ole Opry and get out of country music once and for all. Others argued that the country music business was worth staying in.

It was in the middle of this debate that Johnny Cash taped a series of shows at the Ryman for ABC-TV. The series, which debuted on June 7, 1969, featured guests such as Bob Dylan, Linda Ronstadt, Mahalia Jackson, and the Who. "Those shows were great," said Waylon Jennings, who had shared an apartment with Cash only a few years earlier. "He brought a lot of people on those shows and proved that all music is relative." The shows were so widely acclaimed that they swayed the argument, then underway at the top echelon at NLT, about what to do with the Ryman and the Opry. "The comfort level we got out of those shows led NLT to decide to move the Opry rather than sell it," Wendell said.

Once NLT had made the decision to stay in the country music business, the company began working on plans for a new home for the Opry that would have first-rate television production capabilities. After what had happened to the neighborhood surrounding the Grand Ole Opry, NLT decided to put the new structure outside of downtown. "We wanted to buy enough land so that we would never be surrounded again," said NLT executive C. A. (Neil) Craig II.

However, the decision to move the Opry led to concern about whether people would still come to see it. The discussion about how to draw people to the new Opry House evolved into a theme park called Opryland. WSM president Irving Waugh—who said he came up with the idea—said the concept was based on something he saw on a visit to Houston. "When I saw what they had done around the

Astrodome, with a ride-oriented park and hotels, it made me wonder,"
Waugh said. "In Houston, the Astrodome was the centerpiece to that
theme park. In Anaheim, the castle was the centerpiece to Disneyland.
And in Nashville, the Opry House was going to be our centerpiece."[3]

Under Waugh's plan, Opryland would be organized on the
different types of music that had influenced country music. Part of the
park would be called the New Orleans area and would have jazz
music. Another part of the park would have sort of an Appalachian
feel and feature bluegrass music. The park would also have rides, but
not as many as other amusement parks. "I was never a ride enthusiast," Waugh said. "I wanted the park to have a certain number of
rides, but I wanted a mix rather than a ride-oriented park." With the
Opry House and a theme park going in, it made logical sense to also
put a hotel on the site.

Years earlier, the National Life board would have almost certainly
rejected the idea of a theme park and hotel. But National Life was
now NLT, a holding company looking for ways to diversify. "Because
of some peculiar personality things that existed at that time, it was
possible to do it," Waugh said.

In September 1969, NLT announced it would spend $16 million to
build the Opryland U.S.A. theme park, a new Grand Ole Opry House,
and a 150-room hotel called the Oprytowne Inn. The company said it
was considering nine possible sites—two of those being parcels the
company had bought in Williamson and Cheatham Counties. Two
weeks later, after Mayor Beverly Briley lobbied for the theme park to
be in Davidson County, NLT said it had chosen four hundred acres
adjacent to a four-lane road, then under construction, that later took
the name Briley Parkway. The company asked the city to build an
interchange leading to the theme park (which the city built). But it did
not ask the city for any tax breaks.

NLT hired a national theme park planner named Mike Downs to
run Opryland during its construction phase. Under the plans by
California architect named Randy Dewell, Opryland was laid out and
ground was broken on July 1, 1970. The theme park opened on May 27,
1972—by which time its areas had been given clever names such as a
fifties area called "Doo Wah Ditty City." Admission cost $5.25 for
adults, $3.50 for children. Opryland exceeded even the most opti-
mistic projections. Almost 1.5 million people attended the park in
1972, a number that increased to almost two million by 1975.

NLT delayed the construction of its hotel because of the gas
shortage of the early 1970s. By the time the company was ready to
move ahead with its development, Wendell had been promoted from
Opry manager to head of the theme park and hotel. Unfamiliar with
the hotel business, Wendell hired an executive with the Century Plaza
Hotel in Los Angeles named Jack Vaughn to run the Oprytowne Inn.

Vaughn and new marketing director Mike Dimond sold Wendell on the idea of turning the inn into a convention hotel. "They convinced me that the convention business is more stable than the motel business and that the convention business is a more profitable business," Wendell said. Wendell and Waugh went to NLT chief executive Bill Weaver Jr. with a proposal to build a one-thousand-room convention hotel called the Opryland Hotel and Convention Center. NLT instead chose to build a six-hundred-room convention hotel with enough public space to easily be expanded. Nashville architect Earl Swensson designed the hotel, which was built by Nashville contractor Hall Hardaway Jr.

By the time the Opryland Hotel and Convention Center opened in November 1977, bookings were way above expectations. The new Opry House was also a hit and was frequently booked for television variety shows for entertainers such as Perry Como and Carol Burnett.

The Opryland complex did so well, in fact, that it even bred other hotels and other tourist attractions. According to numbers provided by the Nashville Convention and Visitors Bureau, Nashville had about five thousand hotel rooms when the Opryland complex opened in the spring of 1972. That number increased to over nine thousand before the Opryland Hotel even opened five and a half years later.

Many of the city's new hotel rooms were clustered in several tourist areas. While the hotel was still under construction, a Nashville businessman named John A. Hobbs partnered with Louis McRedmond, Dan Rudy, and Fred Rudy and developed a 114-room hotel called the Fiddler's Inn across the street from the Opryland Hotel site. The Fiddler's Inn did so well that Hobbs doubled its size within a year. Eventually, Hobbs added three more hotels, a putt-putt golf course, a wax museum, a car museum, and a country music club called the Nashville Palace.

The Nashville community was obviously excited about Opryland. But some people were not so excited about another part of NLT's plans. On January 14, 1973, Weaver stated NLT's intention to tear down the Ryman and use its bricks, stained glass windows, and pews to build a new chapel at Opryland. "After all, it began as a house of worship, and what could be more fitting than to see that it has another life as a house of worship?" Weaver wrote in a letter to the *Tennessean*.

NLT officials insisted they had only one reason to raze the Ryman—that being economic. Since buying it in 1963 for $207,000, hardly anyone besides the Opry had used it. That being the case, the company felt it would be just an empty shell after the Opry moved. On the other hand, if it were torn down, the land could be used for parking or a new building.

But after NLT announced its plans for the Ryman, many in Nashville accused the company of having another motive: to ensure the Opryland complex succeeded and that country music fans accepted the Opry in its new home. Tearing down the Ryman, after all, would make it clear there was no turning back.

NLT badly underestimated how sentimental Nashville had gotten about the Ryman, particularly about the building's role in the development of country music. During the next several months, preservationist groups such as the Tennessee Historical Sites Foundation and Historic Nashville Inc. held public meetings and organized a movement to save the structure. The groups were so effective that the Metro Council passed a resolution asking NLT to save it.

Needing some professional backing, NLT brought in Jo Mielziner, an authority on theater and stage designs from New York, to give them a third-party opinion about the Ryman's historical value. Mielziner told NLT what it wanted to hear. "To preserve and reconstruct this building on the grounds that it was an important example of Nashville's architectural past would be an act of total disregard for this city's very rare and well-known gems," Mielziner wrote. "The sad truth is that in a period when fine craftsmen, particularly stone masons, were easily obtainable, the Ryman is and was in its heyday full of bad workmanship."[4]

A few weeks later, a *New York Times* story ridiculed NLT's plans. "The final indignity is that National Life intends to use the bricks and some of the artifacts from the bulldozed Ryman to build—we kid you not—'The Little Church of Opryland' in the new amusement park," said a *Times* article, which was reprinted in the *Tennessean*. "That probably takes first prize for misuse of a landmark and the total misunderstanding of the principles of preservation."[5]

Since the last thing NLT wanted was public controversy, the company postponed its plans to tear down the Ryman until after the Opry was moved. On March 9, 1974, the Grand Ole Opry was performed at the Ryman Auditorium for the last time. Reporters from around the country attended the show, all looking for proof that the performers were sad about leaving the old building behind. But except for a few tears shed by Minnie Pearl, most of the performers said they were glad to be leaving the old building behind. "I'm not sentimental," Louis "Grandpa" Jones said. "No, no. Not when they're a-betterin' the deal."

But by then, historic preservationists had gathered so much momentum that President Nixon, who made an appearance at the Opry in 1973, expressed his hope that the Ryman would be saved. After that, NLT never publicly announced any plans to tear it down.

The saving of the Ryman had a galvanizing effect on the preservationist movement in Nashville. Organizations like Historic Nashville

Inc. would go on to play a vital role in the transformation of Second Avenue and Lower Broadway into a tourist attraction with a historic flavor. However, the experience did not turn NLT's leaders into preservationists. A few years later, the company tore down the five-story building that had been its headquarters for nearly half a century. The birthplace of WSM and the Grand Ole Opry was razed to make way for an underground parking garage and plaza.

Opryland was mostly insulated from the series of events that led to American General's hostile takeover of NLT. But NLT's last-minute attempts to avoid being a takeover target had one major impact on its country music assets. In 1980, NLT chairman Rusty Wagner told his fellow executives that the company desperately needed to find a way to boost the company's stock. After that meeting, WSM came up with the idea of a cable network called The Nashville Network (TNN). When the WSM staff proposed the cable network to the NLT board, they projected that the network would require a $60 million initial investment. NLT agreed to do it. "Surprised the fire out of us," Wendell said. "It was a huge, huge hit for National Life to invest that kind of money." One reason NLT went along with the plan to start TNN was that Wendell had arranged a partnership with Westinghouse Electric Corp. under which the Pittsburgh company agreed to do marketing for TNN in exchange for a percentage ownership in the network.

NLT would not last long enough to see TNN become the success Wagner hoped it would be. But by 1980, the Nashville insurance firm had seen the Opryland Hotel and Convention Center exceed even the most optimistic projections. Because of this, NLT announced a major addition to the Opryland Hotel in 1981, expanding it from about six hundred to about eleven hundred rooms.

Only months after American General took over NLT, Wendell gave American General CEO Harold Hook a tour of the Opryland complex. "After that tour, I told my guys that he was going to sell us real quick," Wendell said. "He was very concerned about the liability from the rides at Opryland." Wendell was heavily involved in making presentations regarding the Opryland complex to several prospective buyers that included a group of NLT executives, Bronson Ingram, Disney, and Anheuser-Busch. In the end, Opryland was sold to Ed Gaylord, an Oklahoma City newspaper and television station owner who also owned the *Hee Haw* show. Gaylord bought the Opryland U.S.A. theme park, the Opryland Hotel and Convention Center, the Grand Ole Opry, and WSM for $400 million.

Wendell soon found that Gaylord took the concept of hands-off management to a new level. "I worked for him for fourteen years and I never got a letter, never got a memo," Wendell said. "I don't think we talked once a month. He believes in putting his confidence in people and letting them run the business." Wendell said that virtually every capital improvement made at the Opryland complex, such as a new ride at the theme park, started as a recommendation by him and his staff. "I can't think of any recommendation that we made to him [Gaylord] that he ever turned down," Wendell said.

Gaylord never had reason to doubt the wisdom of his investment. During the 1980s, the Opryland Hotel and Convention Center continued to astound the hotel industry with occupancy rates far in excess of industry averages. TNN turned the corner in the mid-1980s and became one of the most widely exposed cable networks in the United States. Meanwhile, Opryland had 2.5 million visitors by 1985 and was ranked as one of the top fifteen theme parks by attendance in America.

It is almost impossible to overstate the importance of Opryland U.S.A. in Nashville during the late twentieth century. Thanks to Opryland, Nashville had something that other southern cities did not have. The theme park also had a lot to do with Nashville developing an image as a friendly and clean place, something that Birmingham, Memphis, and Chattanooga could not say. Opryland's visitors came back again and again and had the time of their lives, riding roller coasters such as the "Wabash Cannonball" and attending shows such as "I Hear America Singing." Thousands of young people worked their first jobs at Opryland, driving a train, putting tourists on a log flume, or singing in a show. "When I came from high school, I only knew people from my high school," said Ashland City native Velvet Hunter, who worked in the Opryland parking lot for three consecutive summers in the 1980s. "When I went to Opryland, I met so many people my age from all over Nashville."

Back in 1880, Nashville celebrated its centennial with an exposition at the corner of Eighth and Broadway. As the city's bicentennial approached, many civic leaders wanted to do something just as memorable. In 1977, Mayor Richard Fulton appointed an eleven-member steering committee, chaired by *Tennessean* owner Amon Carter Evans, to make plans for Nashville's two hundredth anniversary. A couple of years later, the committee came out with a plan that called for a convention center, seventeen thousand-seat arena, and fifty thousand-seat stadium in the Sulphur Dell area north of the state capitol.

Fulton knew the committee's recommendations were way too ambitious. He eventually focused on a convention center for two reasons: one, because studies had shown that conventions had more of an economic impact on a downtown than sports teams, and two, because the city did not have a major league sports team and did not appear likely to get one anytime soon. But not everyone liked the idea of putting the convention center on the Sulphur Dell site. Some members of the business community, notably Jack Massey and developer Ted Welch, wanted to put it in the train gulch area west of downtown. Eventually, under the strong influence of Fulton's son Richard L. Fulton (then the director of development for the Metropolitan Development and Housing Authority), the mayor decided to put it at the corner of Fifth and Broadway.

Mayor Fulton did not want to raise property taxes, so he had to get very creative to fund a $40 million convention center. First, he convinced the state legislature to raise Nashville's hotel-motel tax from three to four cents and to designate two of the four cents to build and operate the convention center. This was not easy and was made all the more difficult by the fact that Opryland, fearing competition, openly lobbied against it.

The next part of the project was to convince a convention-level hotel to come to the site. Eventually, Chattanooga developer Franklin Haney came up with a deal to put a twenty-five-story Stouffer hotel adjacent to the convention center. To help Haney put the deal together, the city exempted the hotel site from sales tax and got a $9.1 million Urban Development Action Grant from the federal government.[6]

Finally, the Fulton administration wiped out a block of Sixth Avenue and made major improvements to Commerce Street, which had been only three lanes wide before. In order to get the federal and state governments to fund the Commerce Street improvements, the city took the very unusual step of having Broadway's designation as Highway 70 moved one block north to Commerce. After Commerce Street had been improved, the Highway 70 designation was moved back to Broadway.

The Downtown Convention Center opened in January 1987. By that time, the Opryland Hotel and Convention Center had begun an expansion that, with two thousand rooms, made it one of the largest convention hotels in the country. With so much convention space coming on line at the same time, some people were concerned that Nashville had overbuilt its convention facilities. But by 1993, both facilities were practically booked year round.

The tourism industry appeared to be solid in Nashville by the middle of the 1980s. But there were developments elsewhere that would eventually have a dramatic effect on Opryland and on the tourism industry.

In 1967, a music theater opened in the small Ozark Mountain tourist town Branson, Missouri. For several years, Presley's Mountain Music Theatre was the only one in the area. But in the 1980s, several well-known country music stars—all of whom were past their prime as hit makers—began moving to Branson and building theaters of their own. Eventually, they included Roy Clark, Mel Tillis, Ray Stevens, Boxcar Willie, and more than a dozen others (although the most successful Branson theater featured a fiddle player from Japan named Shoji Tabuchi). "It's more like Vegas used to be years and years before they became a convention center," said Andy Williams, who built a theater in Branson in 1992.[7]

Publicity about Branson hit a peak in 1991. By that time, there was no question that many people were going to Branson to find something that they couldn't get in Nashville—frequently scheduled, live entertainment featuring stars with whom they were familiar.

The second item of interest took place in the Smoky Mountain town of Pigeon Forge. In May 1986, country music entertainer and actress Dolly Parton purchased part ownership of a theme park called Silver Dollar City and renamed it for herself. At first, Dollywood's main claim to fame was that it was the butt of more jokes than any other tourist attraction in America. But as Dollywood's owners invested heavily in new rides and as Parton became heavily involved in its marketing, Dollywood became a financial success. By 1992, when Dollywood's attendance broke the two million mark, it had long since advanced as major competition for Opryland.

The third development in the tourism industry took place in several parts of the United States. There was a time when Americans had to go to Nevada or Atlantic City to gamble legally. But during the decades after World War II, Americans became more enthusiastic about games of chance. By the early 1990s, all eight states that bordered Tennessee had some sort of legalized gambling, from a lottery in Kentucky to casinos on the Cherokee Indian Reservation in North Carolina to horse racing in Hot Springs, Arkansas. However, Tennessee refused to legalize a lottery and did not allow communities to have casinos.

In 1989, the Mississippi legislature authorized riverboat gambling on the Mississippi River. Within a few years, large gambling companies had opened huge casinos on landlocked barges in Tunica County, a rural area thirty-five miles south of Memphis that had previously been the poorest county in Mississippi. By the middle of the decade, Tunica had over a dozen casinos and even more hotels. A vast majority of the two million people who visited Tunica each year by the mid-1990s were Tennessee residents.

Gaylord, which became a public company in 1991, responded to all the competition with a series of new attractions. The first big step came in March 1993, when the company announced it would spend $8 million to bring the Ryman Auditorium up to codes and convert it to a facility that could house big-name concerts again. As a part of the renovation, Gaylord added a large wing to the Ryman and installed air-conditioning in the building.

At almost the same time, the company announced that it was building an enormous dance complex on Second Avenue called the Wildhorse Saloon. "We were interested in a downtown TV production location, and line dancing was huge," said Wendell. In order to facilitate traffic between Opryland and Gaylord's downtown properties, the company also started a water taxi service along the Cumberland River.

With Nashville's new downtown arena already under construction, the renovation of the Ryman and construction of the Wildhorse signaled a new era for downtown Nashville. Downtown had been a place frequented by tourists in the 1940s and 1950s. But after much of it deteriorated and the Grand Ole Opry left downtown, tourists generally stayed in parts of town like Opryland or the area surrounding Music Row. The opening of the Downtown Convention Center in 1987 was the first major event that drew visitors back to the city's core. Within months of Gaylord's 1993 announcements, corporate-owned businesses catering to tourists migrated to Second Avenue and Lower Broadway, driving property values up and forcing out many existing tenants. Within two years, the historic neighborhood had a Hard Rock Cafe, Planet Hollywood, several boot stores, a couple of fast food restaurants, and a laser tag complex. Meanwhile, small locally owned businesses such as the Phillips & Quarles Hardware Store and a small gift shop called the Nature's Gallery were told to get out. "There's no question that Hard Rock and Wildhorse have increased my business," said Nature's Gallery owner Rick Ritter, upon learning that his business had to move. "They've increased it to the point where I'm out of business."[8]

Within weeks of the Ryman and Wildhorse announcements, Gaylord announced two more initiatives to boost their business and draw more people to Nashville. One—in what was obviously a response to Branson—was a summer-long series of 730 concerts called Nashville on Stage featuring big-name stars such as George Jones, Alabama, and the Oak Ridge Boys. The second was a $175 million expansion to the Opryland Hotel and Convention Center—the largest construction project in Nashville history. Along with the hotel expansion, Gaylord asked Nashville mayor Phil Bredesen for a tax break. In the deal that was eventually approved by Metro Council, Opryland had its property taxes reduced by $2.2 million per year for ten years and its hotel-motel taxes reduced by about $2 million per year. The city also agreed not to expand the Downtown Convention Center for a period of ten years.

Between 1993 and 1995, Gaylord was coming out with so many projects that there was beginning to be anticipation that the company would soon get into the professional sports business. Much of this speculation came from Gaylord's 1993 hiring of Richard Evans as chief operating officer. From the moment he got to Nashville, Evans—previously an executive with New York's Madison Square Garden—was heavily involved in the development of Nashville's downtown arena and the ultimately successful attempt to bring professional sports to Nashville. "When it came to recruiting big-league sports, Dick Evans brought a big-city mentality to a medium-sized city," said Peter Heidenreich, head of the arena construction project. "Dick Evans was introducing Nashvillians to people that they had never thought about meeting before, such as [NHL president] Gary Betman. To his credit, the big leagues found out where we were and Nashville became a potential site."

Evans and Gaylord were also vocal about their intent to manage the downtown arena. Since Gaylord was an entertainment company that owned a cable network, many people speculated that Gaylord might be interested in owning a large percentage of a hockey or basketball team and televising them on TNN. In fact, Gaylord was never seriously interested in owning a hockey team, according to Wendell. "I picked up the rumble that we wanted to be the owners of hockey and I told Dick that was not going to happen," Wendell said. "My concept was that if hockey was going to come that we should be a player, but I wanted lot of people in Nashville to have a piece of that team. I was more interested in hockey being owned by twenty companies in Nashville and we being one of them."

Opryland began booking its new hotel rooms while they were still under construction, making the hotel's fourth expansion a success before it was even completed. Thanks to all the new attractions downtown and the expansion at the Opryland Hotel, Nashville's tourism numbers went up in 1995 and 1996, giving the city a sense of community spirit that aided Mayor Phil Bredesen's crusade to lure the Houston Oilers to town. But despite the increase in visitors, all was not well at Gaylord Entertainment. First of all, Nashville on Stage flopped miserably, losing over $8 million during its first year. "The main reason it did not work is that it was in a theme park setting, and very few entertainers like those kind of venues," said Mike Dimond, who was in charge of Opryland's marketing at the time. Attendance at the Opryland U.S.A. theme park also began to decline. By 1994, Nashville's theme park had slipped to twenty-sixth nationally in attendance. And although Nashville residents were inclined to blame the attendance figure on admission prices (which were nearing thirty dollars for adults), Opryland's ticket prices were very much in line with those at competing theme parks.

One reason Opryland's attendance was slumping was that people coming to Nashville were spending more time visiting other places, such as all the restaurants and shops on Second Avenue. But there was more to it than that; Gaylord had not installed new rides at the park as fast as other theme parks such as Six Flags over Georgia. "In the industry it is generally believed that you have to add a big thing at least every two years," said Tom Powell, a columnist for the trade publication *Amusement Business*. "Opryland hasn't done that."[9]

The most obvious sign that something was amiss was in September 1996, when Gaylord fired Richard Evans, a move that surprised analysts and left the company without a clear line of succession. "Dick's style just did not fit our style and he resigned," Wendell said. "Dick really wanted and hoped that he was going to succeed me, and when he felt that wasn't going to happen then I think he felt that he would go onto other areas." Wendell said Evans was also very disappointed that Gaylord did not become more heavily involved in professional sports.

Wendell retired about the same time and was replaced by former chief financial officer Terry London. Almost immediately, rumors began to circulate that Gaylord intended to do something very different with the theme park, such as sell it or lease it to an operator such as Time-Warner. Fueling the rumors was speculation on Wall Street that Gaylord intended to sell his entire company to a firm such as Westinghouse, Disney, or Seagram. When asked about the rumors, Gaylord consistently dismissed them as nonsense.

Gaylord made more changes in 1996 and 1997 than the company had made in the fifteen years prior.

The first major announcement came in November 1996, when Gaylord bought Word, a Christian music label, from Thomas Nelson, Inc. for $110 million. Analysts who had been expecting Gaylord to either sell out or invest money in more hotels and more cable programming scratched their heads.

The next announcement came in February 1997, when Gaylord revealed that it had agreed to sell TNN and CMT to Westinghouse/CBS for $1.5 billion. The agreement did not come as a shock to anyone, since Westinghouse already owned part of TNN and was one of several companies that had expressed an interest in buying the rest of the cable networks. Nevertheless, it was a dramatic step for Gaylord and the end of the era of local ownership for the city's only two cable networks.

Gaylord made the most dramatic and surprising announcement a few months later. In October 1997, the company announced it would be closing the Opryland theme park, thus doing away with Nashville's top tourist attraction. In its place, Gaylord said it would build a huge shopping and entertainment complex called Opry Mills. Under the terms of the deal, national mall developer Mills Corp.

agreed to basically fund the $400 million shopping complex. But Gaylord would own about a third of it once it was completed.

Many Nashville residents were stunned by Gaylord's decision to close Opryland and replace it with a mall. At the time of the announcement, company spokesmen said that because of slumping attendance the theme park was not nearly as profitable as it once had been. They also said that there was no economic connection between the marginally successful theme park and the highly successful hotel and convention center next door to it.

However, it is interesting to note that no one was more surprised by Gaylord's decision to close the theme park than Wendell, who had retired as Gaylord CEO only months before the announcement. "I was just as surprised to read it in the paper as everybody else," said Wendell, adding that during his reign as CEO there were no discussions of any kind with the Mills Corp. Wendell said the theme park was not extraordinarily profitable in terms of its capital value, but said he never thought of it as something that could be separated from the company's other assets. "Based on what I would perceive the value of the park, it was not an outstanding return if you just stood it on its own," Wendell said. "But how do you stand the park on its own when you know that it also draws people that stay at the hotel, that go to the park, that ride the *General Jackson* (showboat), or go to the other areas that we had?"

Mike Dimond, who left Gaylord to run his own marketing company about the time the company closed the theme park, predicted in 1999 that the Mills project would be successful. He also said that the decision to close the theme park is best understood as a decision that a public company made regarding cash flow. "The analysts would have killed them if they had stayed in the theme park business," he said.

Dimond said there was no question that the closure of Opryland had hurt Nashville. But he said the park was having a hard time competing against other theme parks because the company had not invested enough money in it over the years. "The theme park got to be tired by the last few years," Dimond said. "As someone who had the responsibility of marketing the Opryland theme park, it was very difficult to compete with the Six Flags and the Disneys and the Universals. At Six Flags, they can move a ride around from one park to the other and an old ride can be a new ride again and again. And at Disney, they put in $90 million rides every three years. How do you compete with $90 million rides every three years?" Dimond also said Gaylord had missed an opportunity by not building a water park along the way.

Whether the decision to close the Opryland theme park was a wise one for Gaylord was not immediately clear. But there was no question that the loss of Nashville's largest attraction was a crushing blow to Nashville's tourism business. The industry was further hindered by the April 1998 tornado and by the fact that interstate construction was so prevalent that year that the American Automobile Association (AAA) was routing people away from the city. By the turn of the century, most of the tourist-related businesses near Opryland were reporting revenue drops of about a third. Business was hurting even more on Music Row, where most tourist attractions closed down. In the fall of 1998, Gaylord CEO Terry London actually apologized to a crowd of tourism industry workers for the impact that Opryland's closure had on Nashville. But he said he still did not regret his company's decision to close the theme park.

CHAPTER 23

Dueling Developers

N ashville wasn't the only American city with a real estate boom
and bust in the 1980s. For many parts of the United States,
overbuilding was rooted in two changes made during the early
years of the Reagan administration. One was the decision to allow
savings and loan associations to expand from residential real estate into
other areas, such as commercial real estate and commercial lending.
Another was the Economic Recovery Act of 1981, which dramatically
increased the tax benefits of owning commercial real estate.

One factor made what took place in Nashville in the 1980s
extreme, however. That was the general perception that Nashville was
going to become the "next Atlanta" thanks to Middle Tennessee's
bustling car industry (Nissan and Saturn) and to the 1985 announcement that Nashville would become one of American Airlines' hubs.
Both of these developments came at a time when developers had
begun running out of projects in Texas and Oklahoma due to the
decline in the oil industry. "Things started going downhill about 1982,
and by 1986, oil prices hit rock bottom, Houston was floundering, and
Dallas was dead," said Jim Loyd, who at that time worked for a
Houston developer called Murphree. "You couldn't do new deals and
if you can't do new deals developers starve. Nashville was a booming
economy in great contrast."

The developers came and brought plenty of capital with them. By
1988 there were half a dozen new office buildings on West End
Avenue and three large ones downtown. But by the time they had
opened, everything had changed. Developers had built too much too

fast. Saturn had shrunk to half of its proposed size, arrived late, and had far less impact on the real estate community in Nashville than had been predicted. Nashville lost three locally based financial institutions to mergers—Third National Bank, Commerce Union Bank, and Nashville City Bank. Finally, the Tax Reform Act of 1986 dramatically and adversely changed the tax benefits of real estate investments, sending the book value of real estate plummeting and Savings and Loan Associations (S&Ls) and property management companies scrambling for cover.

When the glut came, people who had been riding high one minute were facing bankruptcy the next. "I was about as low as I could get emotionally," said Criswell Freeman, the former president of a property management company called Freeman Properties who later became a psychologist. "One day I was a big real estate executive making a lot of money and the next day I was sitting in a downtown mental health facility making six dollars an hour counseling somebody."

David Emery's wild ride started with a wonderful opportunity. In the late 1960s, Emery landed a job with R. A. McDowell, a Nashville-based road contractor who had a side business buying and developing properties at interstate exits. "Bob McDowell was a visionary and he was one of the first people to realize what the interstate meant," Emery said in 1999. "Working for him was a great experience. One day I had to deal with rural farmers whose land I was trying to buy and the next day I was dealing with a national chain of gas stations that wanted to build there."

In 1973, Emery helped develop his first building, the Rokeby high-rise condominiums on Harding Road. It was the first of many projects involving lender Third National Bank, and Emery's first experience with a project that did not do as well as planned. "We eventually got the loan paid off, but not as quickly as the bank had first hoped," Emery said.

Emery then had a stroke of luck that would change his life. One of Emery's fellow tenants in his home office building was a fast-growing architectural firm called Gresham & Smith, which was busy designing hospitals for Hospital Corporation of America. Around 1976, Batey Gresham asked Emery if he would find a place for a new office building that Gresham & Smith would help occupy.

"I told him that I thought the place to be was on a direct line between the central business district and the part of town where the wealthiest people lived," Emery said. "I knew that was the most expensive site. But I always thought if a site is cheap, there is a reason it is cheap. And I always thought that if you are going to be in the real estate business, you should find the most expensive site and buy it or you shouldn't be in the business to begin with."

Emery lined up the site, located at 3310 West End Avenue, and put together a deal wherein Gresham & Smith would design the seven-story building and agree to lease two stories of it once it was completed. The rest of the space was then leased to a small insurance company and a few other tenants (one of whom was a young entrepreneur named Phil Bredesen). Emery also arranged for Third National to loan money for the construction of the project. The building, which went by the simple name 3310, came off without a hitch.

Emery then moved on to do two similar projects in the same area. The first was a seven-story building at 3401 West End Avenue, partially occupied by Shearson Lehman Brothers and American Express. The second was a twelve-story building at 3322 West End Avenue, partially occupied by Bredesen's company, HealthAmerica. Third National made loans for the construction of both projects.

By this time, Emery wanted to do a big downtown project. The only problem was that he wasn't the only developer who did.

By 1980, Third National Bank had outgrown its building at Fourth Avenue and Church Street and needed more space. Nashville developer Bobby Mathews Jr. was one of the first people to approach the bank with the idea of building a high-rise office building next door to the bank at Fifth and Church. However, before Mathews or the bank secured the parcels needed for the building, one of the local newspapers published a story about plans for the building. By the time Third National began looking at specific financial and architectural proposals from various developers, it was common knowledge in Nashville that they intended to acquire all the property on the site. "We spoke with the mayor [Richard H. Fulton] and were assured by the city and the council that this wasn't going to be a problem and that we would be able to obtain the property through eminent domain," said Charles Kane, then the CEO of Third National.

Third National considered simply letting Mathews develop the building for them. But it also took other bids, one of which came from Houston developer Murphree. Murphree proposed to build a twenty-three-story office building, name it for the bank, ensure long-term financing from Equitable Life Insurance Co., and give 25 percent of the ownership of the building to Third National—all in exchange for Third National's commitment to lease one hundred thousand square feet. "The best deal for Third National Bank by far was through Murphree," Kane said.

Third National considered and rejected several other bids. One of those was from Emery, who did not have a track record of building high-rise office buildings and did not have the backing of a large entity like Equitable. Emery did, however, have something Murphree did not have. After hearing about Third National's plans for a new building, Emery had assembled the proposed site through options on five of the six property owners and an agreement to purchase land from the sixth. (The sixth was John Noel, who owned two parcels at 424 and 426 Church Street that were leased to Petway-Reavis men's clothier.) Years later, Emery said he actually offered to sell control of those parcels to the bank after they rejected his offer to develop the building. But the bank turned him down, convinced they would be able to acquire the land through other means.

Mathews and Emery both moved onto other projects. A few years earlier, Mathews had been involved with Ohio's Edward DeBartolo Sr. in the attempted development of a mall near Maryland Farms. In the early 1980s, DeBartolo told Mathews he was interested in building an office tower in downtown Nashville. Mathews steered DeBartolo to a site at Fourth and Commerce, where his father had owned land for decades and where he had bought additional parcels since his divestiture from the MetroCenter project a couple of years earlier.

DeBartolo was so prominent in national business circles that he had little trouble lining up construction financing with Mellon Bank of Pittsburgh and in helping to line up Aetna Life Insurance Co. and IBM as tenants. After the twenty-three-story building broke ground in 1983, Mathews negotiated the structure's most important lease with Nashville City Bank.

Emery, meanwhile, moved his plans to the corner of Sixth and Union and began putting together a deal to build a high-rise in which the lead tenant would be First Tennessee Bank and the lender would be Urban Properties of Chicago.

The issue of whether to allow Third National to take property through condemnation eventually intensified into one of the most emotionally charged political debates in Nashville business history. Interestingly enough, the only reason the debate took place was that the Fifth and Church site had not been included in an Urban Renewal "redevelopment zone" that would have authorized the city to condemn the land on the bank's behalf without council action (as had been the case with the First American Center a few years earlier). Had Third National picked a site in another part of downtown, or had the bank had the site included in a "redevelopment district" years earlier, the bank would have had no trouble getting the property.

After being selected for the Third National Tower, Murphree sent representative Jim Loyd to Nashville. Loyd had many jobs to do, from coming up with an architectural design for the tower to lining up tenants. But his first job was to get the land. To that end, he bought options on five of the six parcels on the footprint. Since David Emery wouldn't sell him the Petway-Reavis parcel, Loyd began the process of asking Metro Council to condemn the land on behalf of the bank.

The bill authorizing the condemnation passed quietly on first and second readings in December 1982. But by the time the third reading came up, it had stirred deep feelings among Nashville citizens, some of whom were still angry about the amount of property the federal government took during interstate construction and the local government took during Urban Renewal. In an interesting twist, the *Tennessean* sided with Third National—claiming the bank needed the property in the name of progress—while the *Banner* sided with Emery—saying the city had no right to take property away from a local developer in order to sell it to one from Houston.

During the debate, many people in Nashville perceived that Emery was trying to hold out against the bank to ensure that his building at Sixth and Union went up first or to simply get back at Third National for not letting him develop its building. Years later, Emery said that was simply not the case. "I never intended to hold out against the bank, but the bank never gave me a way out," said Emery. "My position before they filed for condemnation was that I would sell them the parcel if they had asked to buy it. But I wasn't going to sell it to them as long as they were trying to take it from me by force."

In January 1983, the council rejected the bill on third reading. Years later, Loyd said he still couldn't believe it. "It is unheard of for something to fail on third reading," Loyd said. But Richard L. Fulton, then head of development for the Metropolitan Development and Housing Authority, said there was also opposition to the bill because they thought it gave the bank too much power. "It is hard to believe this now because of how much land was condemned during Mayor Bredesen's administration with no opposition," Fulton said in 1999. "But condemnation was still a very controversial thing back then because of the Convention Center and because of what Vanderbilt had done to the neighborhood adjacent to it in the 1970s."

Nonetheless, Murphree wasn't about to let the vote keep them from building a $68 million office building. After the bill failed, Loyd told the architect to redesign the building around the Petway-Reavis parcel. The building was thus changed from being centered on the footprint to one backed up on the north half of the parcel. A few months later, Rodgers Construction broke ground on the new Third National Tower, the construction of which was backed by City Corp. Rodgers Construction had to take great care during excavation not to damage the Petway-Reavis store adjacent to it.

In 1984, Emery sold the Petway-Reavis property to Joe Rodgers, who immediately flipped it to Third National. Third National paid

$900,000 for the piece of property Emery had paid $450,000 for three years earlier. By the time the bank got the property, construction of the office tower was so far along that it was too late to go back to its original design.

Emery then moved on to his site at Sixth and Union. Back in 1985, Emery thought he had a deal lined up where Urban Properties out of Chicago would finance a building there, and the Bank of Tennessee would occupy its first three floors. But in 1986, Urban backed out of the project and sold the land to Morgan Stanley. About a year later, after Morgan Stanley had decided not to get involved after all, Emery flew to Texas and convinced financier Robert Bass to back a building on the site called City Center. Incredibly, Emery broke ground in 1986 with only 20 percent of the building pre-leased.

Between 1986 and 1989, competition over tenants was fierce between Loyd's Third National Tower and Emery's City Center Building. Eventually, Loyd lined up law firm Farris Warfield and Kanady and accounting firm Touche Ross & Co. Emery landed law firms Waller Lansden Dortch and Davis, Trabue Sturdivant & DeWitt, and accounting firm Pete Marwick. One of the most competitive deals was the fight over the Cumberland Club, which eventually decided to relocate from the First American Center to the City Center.

By this time, Nashville had a real estate glut that was affecting virtually every commercial and residential project in the city.

Much like the boom of the early 1980s, the bust of the late 1980s came about because of events that were both national and local. The most significant national event was the Tax Reform Act of 1986, which severely restricted investors' ability to deduct depreciation for syndication investments. "The laws that encouraged syndications never made any economic sense, and I could see that doing away with those laws would have a profound impact on the real estate business," said Tony Martin, head of C. B. Commercial's real estate operation in Nashville in the 1990s.

The Tax Act of 1986 brought real estate values down overnight. It would not have had nearly as severe an impact on the marketplace had it not been for the fact that the bill did not "grandfather in" existing properties. "We thought it would be all right because we had all the properties with the tax shelters on them," said Nelson Andrews, president of the Nashville property management company Brookside Properties. "Little did we know that the law would be retroactive."

The wildly optimistic predictions about Nashville's growth had also not taken into account the possibility that the city would lose several locally owned financial institutions. In the early 1980s, the Tennessee legislature passed a reciprocal bank agreement that allowed cross-state banking between Tennessee and a handful of other southeastern banks. Third National, foreseeing massive consolidation, began looking for someone to merge with. "We knew changes were coming, and we wanted to pick a partner with the same philosophy we had," said Kane, who by that time had become Third National's chairman. Third National commissioned a study that identified Wachovia Bank of Charlotte and SunTrust Bank of Atlanta as its two best matches. On September 1986, Third National announced a $775 million merger with SunTrust, an institution that had been created in an earlier union between Sun Bank of Orlando and Trust Company of Georgia. Unlike many bank mergers that came in later years, the Third National-SunTrust merger did not precede a massive personnel reduction. In fact, virtually all of the executives at Third National moved on to top jobs at SunTrust.

The following year, Jack Massey and Calvin Houghland sold Nashville City Bank to Dominion Bank of Virginia, and Commerce Union was acquired by Sovran Bank of Norfolk, Virginia. "I thought that consolidation would benefit some of the early players," said Denny Bottorff, the CEO of Commerce Union during that merger.

SunTrust would continue to have a corporate presence in Nashville through the end of the century. The same could not be said of Sovran, which was almost immediately eclipsed by two mergers that took place after its purchase of Commerce Union. In 1989, Sovran merged with Citizens & Southern Bank, a century-old institution that had played a major role in the development of Atlanta in the twentieth century. Under the merger deal, Bottorff became the president of the new bank. C&S Sovran, as it was called, had two corporate offices: one in Norfolk and the other in Atlanta.

However, C&S Sovran was not long for this world. In 1989 and 1990, the bank had massive real estate problems in its portfolio (especially in the suburban Washington, D.C., area) and problems with its merger. "Mergers of equals are difficult to do," Bottorff said years later. "We were trying to put together C&S Sovran in the midst of a declining economy and in the midst of this real estate downturn. We needed increased focus, and a merger of equals by definition has less focus because everything has to be done by committee. So I felt like the best thing to do was sell the bank." In 1991, Charlotte-based North Carolina National Bank (NCNB) took over C&S Sovran. As the merger was being negotiated, NCNB chief executive officer Hugh McColl Jr. decided to name the combined institution NationsBank.

Amid the complicated series of mergers, there was constant speculation that First American would be taken over. Rumors to that effect became especially loud when First American announced in early 1990 that it had lost $45 million due to bad real estate loans, that it was firing chief executive officer Ken Roberts, and that it was laying off 380 people. However, despite the existence of many suitors, First American did not become a division of another bank in the early 1990s. In 1992, First American replaced Roberts with former Commerce Union CEO Denny Bottorff.

The loss of Third National, Commerce Union, and Nashville City Bank had a sobering effect on Nashville's commercial real estate market. "The loss of the financial institutions changed the whole dynamics of building occupancies downtown," Martin said. "When the banks became non-resident, they began to make personnel reductions and they ceased growing. Meanwhile, all the law firms and accounting firms which had thrived on them ceased to grow and even began to shrink."

The bank mergers of the late 1980s also created the opportunity for new locally-owned banks. In 1989, a group of business and political leaders including Monroe Carell Jr., Leon Moore, Perry Moskovitz, and Richard H. Fulton helped form a new institution called The Bank of Nashville. Former Nashville City Bank executive Richard Chambers became TBON's first president, and the Life & Casualty Tower became its first home. "Third National, Commerce Union, and City Bank had all been acquired," said Mack Linebaugh Jr., a former First American executive who replaced Chambers in 1992. "They saw an opportunity for another locally-owned bank."

A few years after the formation of TBON, several employees with the Nashville division of Birmingham-based SouthTrust Bank saw a similar opportunity. In 1994, SouthTrust's Rick Hart became president of Nashville-based Capital Bank & Trust, a bank which made the unusual step of putting its headquarters outside of downtown on West End Avenue. "We are mainly a small business bank, and small business owners do not like to go downtown," Hart explained. Among its early directors were Garth Brook's manager Bob Doyle, Baptist Hospital physician Newton Lovvorn Jr., and Dale Insulation president Albert Dale III.

By the late 1980s, Nashville simply had too much office space, due in part to the development of several suburban projects described below.

Vanderbilt Plaza. In the 1940s, Jack Massey and Dr. Thomas Frist bought several parcels of land at the northwest corner of West End and Twenty-first Avenues that were for two decades the home of Massey's surgical supply business and Frist's office. Starting in the mid-1970s, Massey began talking about putting a hotel there. The project got off the ground around 1981, when it was put in the hands of developers Joe Rodgers, Jim Caden, and Chip Christianson. By that time, Massey and Frist's parcels were combined with a few others, one of which had once contained the governor's mansion.[1]

In 1982, the trio (doing business as CRC Holdings) announced plans to build a $40 million hotel and office building on the site. After Massey and Frist each put in $5 million investments, CRC solicited investments at $20,000 increments from about 140 prominent Nashville residents—many of whom were physicians who had previously made money through their ownership of HCA stock. Largely due to Massey's prominence, Mellon Bank of Pittsburgh agreed to be the construction lender.

Because of key tenants such as Dean Witter and Earl Swensson Associates, Vanderbilt Plaza's office side was about two-thirds occupied when it opened in 1984. But the Vanderbilt Plaza Hotel found it very hard to get its occupancy and room rates as high as had been projected. "I remember having to rent rooms for up to 50 percent less than what we thought we would have gotten," Caden said. In November 1986, the organization that owned Vanderbilt Plaza filed bankruptcy. Two years later, the bankruptcy court turned it over to mortgagee Traveler's Insurance, which later sold the hotel and office building to Loews. In the end, Vanderbilt Plaza's owners got about 10 percent of the money back that they had invested.

Maryland Farms. Back in the 1950s and 1960s, it might have seemed unusual for Life & Casualty Insurance Co. executive Truman Ward to commute all the way from downtown Nashville to Maryland Farms, his horse farm south of the Davidson County line. However, after Interstate 65 opened, real estate agents began to view Ward's 390-acre property as a prime site for future development.

In 1970, Ward signed an option to sell his property to a group of investors led by Jack Massey for $3.1 million. Over the next few years, Massey-Ward Investments, as it was called, developed the property piecemeal into commercial and office space. Whenever a new piece was developed, a new partnership consisting of various individuals (Massey, John Neff, Clarence Edmonds, Ken Larish, and William Ogilvie) would buy the land from the Ward family, borrow money from a bank, and build a new project. A new business entity was formed with each new piece, which meant that the Maryland Farms development was actually dozens of individual real estate ventures.

Office users began filling up Maryland Farms in the early 1980s. As the project became more successful, some of its investors began leveraging parts of it to finance other real estate ventures.

When the real estate market collapsed in 1989, some of the side ventures started by some of these investors failed. In 1990 and 1991, many of those investors declared personal bankruptcy. Control of the

Maryland Farms project eventually transferred to the estate of Jack Massey.

Palmer Plaza. In 1985, Nashville developer Alex Palmer obtained backing from Metropolitan Life Insurance Co. to build an eighteen-story speculative office building at 1801 West End Avenue, once the site of a Lincoln-Mercury dealership owned by Palmer's father. Before the building was completed, Palmer Plaza landed a huge tenant in the form of Equicor, a joint venture between HCA and Equitable Life Insurance Co. Since Equicor occupied twelve stories, the lease single-handedly ensured the success of the project.

CIGNA HealthCare eventually acquired Equicor. Palmer kept the building and went on to develop other office buildings at Burton Hills and Maryland Farms.

One American Center. One of the many developers that came to Nashville from Texas and Oklahoma was Lincoln Properties. In 1984, Murfreesboro developer Tommy Smith got them interested in putting an office building at the northwest corner of West End and Thirty-first Avenues—a site then occupied by a small apartment building. The next year, Lincoln representative Pat Emery (no relation to developer David Emery) announced the twelve-story, $27 million project called One American Center. Like many of Lincoln's projects in the Southwest, One American Center's main investors lived in Texas and Oklahoma. At the time of its groundbreaking, Emery had only signed one major lease, American Retirement Corporation.

Things were equally tough downtown. In 1989, Mathews sold his part ownership in the building he had developed at Fourth and Commerce (now known as the Dominion Tower) to his partner DeBartolo. At that time, Mathews said the building was about 75 percent occupied (a number below what was projected but still high enough to keep the building in the black). However, the building's occupancy decreased during the next few years, as DeBartolo's national empire ran into financial trouble and his clout with national clients slipped. In 1996, the building was no longer making enough money to pay its bank note and the Teachers Annuity Association took possession of it.

Third National Financial Center opened in 1986 with about 65 percent occupancy and then "hit a brick wall" as far as landing tenants, in the words of developer Jim Loyd. The merger between Third National and SunTrust did not help. "Third National's expansion requirements came to a screeching halt because a lot of what they needed expansion room for was going to get consolidated in a function in Atlanta," Loyd said. "Instead of picking up a floor every two or three years, which was their initial thinking, they wouldn't take

any more space in the building because they did not need it." The
SunTrust-Third National merger also affected their affiliated law firm
(Farris Warfield and Kanady) and accounting firm (Touche Ross &
Co.), which both also rented space in the building. Eventually,
building co-owners Equitable Life and Third National wrote off major
losses on the project.

As the real estate market collapsed, several related Nashville businesses went down with it. One was Freeman Properties, which had
started as a property management company and increased its ownership portfolio when limited partnerships became the rage in the
1980s. "We had gone fifteen or twenty years where we had never lost
a piece of property and never lost money on a deal," said Freeman
president Criswell Freeman. "Then, after the 1986 tax act, our portfolio lost a lot of value overnight, and by 1990 we couldn't even pay
the overhead anymore."

Many developers found themselves completely unprepared for the
real estate crash. Jerry Ezell started his life as a sharecropper's son in
Louisiana. By the 1980s, Ezell borrowed enough money to control
more than $600 million in real estate projects in ten states. Some of
them were office buildings, but others were retail. In the late 1980s,
some of Ezell's retail properties were not making enough money to
pay their bank notes. When federal regulators began coming down
hard on banks and S&Ls for their liberal lending practices, Ezell's
projects—such as the Stones River Mall in Murfreesboro—were cut
off in mid-construction. By 1990, financial institutions were fore-
closing on Ezell's assets. While Ezell was recovering from a heart
attack in January 1991, Dominion Bank foreclosed on his home. A few
months later, Ezell filed bankruptcy, citing $120 million in debts.
Barry Dotson, Ezell's partner in several of his retail ventures, also
declared bankruptcy.

The largest business to go under was in the savings and loan
industry. When the federal government lifted many of the restrictions
on S&Ls, several such businesses became major players in the real
estate underwriting business in Nashville. After the real estate market
collapsed, the federal government's Office of Thrift Supervision came
down hard on several S&Ls, whose balance sheets were more vulnerable to fluctuations in real estate prices than large banks.

In the late 1980s, regulators began focusing on Nashville's
Metropolitan Federal Savings & Loan, which had backed many of the
projects put together by Freeman Properties. In late 1990, regulators
began ordering Met Fed to mark down the book value of many pieces
of real estate. In one case, Met Fed had priced a large chunk of land
across Interstate 65 from CoolSprings Galleria as if it would be

developed within four years. Regulators looked at the land, said it would not be developed for at least ten years, and marked the land down to less than half what Met Fed said it was worth.[2] Each time Met Fed marked down an asset, the number of tangible assets in its portfolio slipped a little further, from five percent to three percent and then to below two percent.

On April 19, 1991, forty agents from the federal government's Resolution Trust Corp. division told Met Fed president Ted Moats that they had declared his business insolvent. "They gave me forty-five minutes to pack my things and leave the building," said Moats, who later became chairman of Logan's Roadhouse. At the time, Met Fed had over 250 employees—all of whom lost their jobs—and $1.2 billion in assets—all of which were eventually sold to other buyers.

People in the real estate industry who did survive barely did so. Brookside Properties had gotten its start in the 1970s, when the company bought an entire neighborhood of duplexes off White Bridge Road, converted them to single-family units, and sold them at a profit. By the mid-1980s, Brookside had put together similar deals all over the Southeast. But the 1986 tax law sent the value of some of Brookside's assets plummeting, the largest of which was a complex of more than three hundred duplexes in Tampa, Florida. "Brookside survived, and that was all it was for a good while was survival," said Brookside president Nelson Andrews. "That was all it was—people like me working seven days a week and umpteen hours a day just to survive."

By the time the 1980s were over, the only people in the Nashville real estate community who were doing well were the ones who were lucky enough to have missed it. Nashville developer Joe Rodgers was the American ambassador to France from 1985 until 1989. "It is not as if I was any smarter than Nelson Andrews and Bobby Mathews or anyone," Rodgers said. "It was just that I was in France. If I had been here I would have been doing just what the others were doing, which was overbuilding."

The 1980s were so rough for Nashville business that they left one of the greatest capitalists in American history scratching his head.

Jack Massey rarely stood still. Even while he was launching HCA, Massey started an investment firm called Massey Investment Corp. Then, in 1971, Massey and a group of investors formed an equipment leasing business called Volunteer Capital (VCC) and merged it with a languishing Tennessee-based mutual fund called Volunteer Fund. VCC, run by Massey colleague Earl Beasley Jr., did well at first. But it got hurt by the credit crunch of 1974 and started looking for new opportunities. A few years after former KFC franchisee Dave

Thomas started a hamburger chain called Wendy's, Volunteer Capital became Wendy's largest franchisee.

VCC made a successful transformation from equipment leasing company to owner and operator of Wendy's restaurants in California, Louisiana, South Carolina, and Massachusetts. But in the late 1970s, Massey decided to get back in the chicken business, convinced that KFC parent Heublein was neglecting its business and letting its restaurants decline. In 1979, VCC bought a chain of fast food chicken restaurants called Granny's. Granny's soon became Mrs. Winner's, and Volunteer Capital became Winners Corp. Beasley and Massey later had a falling out of sorts, and Massey hired Buck Hussung to take over Volunteer Capital.

Meanwhile, Massey Investment became a significant entity in its own right. In the early 1970s, Massey Investment became a paid consultant to several companies that went public, the most notable being Danner Foods (later Shoney's) and Wendy's International. In 1981, Massey Investment evolved into a venture capital firm named Massey-Burch Investment Group Inc. with Lucius Burch III as its president and co-owner. It provided seed money to help start other companies in exchange for fees and equity in those start-ups. During the next several years, Massey-Burch helped start several successful companies, including Surgical Care Affiliates, Corrections Corporation of America, ComData, and PhyCor. "Back when we first started, the venture capital world was very unorganized," said Burch. "Eventually, we played a major role in the formation of many, many different firms."

On August 8, 1984, Winners Corp. made it to the New York Stock Exchange (NYSE), making Jack Massey the first individual in American history to take three unrelated companies to the Big Board. "I see lots of men in Florida who ran big companies and are now retired," Massey told a reporter about this time. "They soon get sick, or something happens to them, after they quit. I couldn't do that. Working is my life."[3]

Winners Corp. grew fast in the early 1980s—jumping from 62 locations in 1982 to 184 in 1984. But after the wave of expansion came a wave of bad earnings reports. Winners made several mistakes, the main one being inadequate penetration in individual markets to justify the advertising needed to bring in customers. The company lost $3.6 million in 1985 and about $2 million per year for each of the next three years. Winners Corp. stock, which sold for over $13 in 1984, dropped to about $3 two years later. No one was more upset by the company's performance than its founder. "Jack Massey for the last two years has been in and out of the hospital and has admittedly neglected the company," Massey told *Forbes*, referring to himself in the third person.[4] It was not really a matter of neglect. Competition for the fast food dollar was simply a lot tougher than it had been for Kentucky Fried Chicken twenty years earlier.

In 1989, Hussung's successor Lonnie Stout II sold the Mrs. Winners business for $30 million to RTM Inc., a private entity based in Atlanta. Stout would eventually sell the Wendy's business to Wendy's International and transform Winners Corp. to a chain of upscale eateries called J. Alexander's.

The difficulties of Winners Corp. and the bankruptcy of Vanderbilt Plaza were painful episodes for Jack Massey. But he never let defeat get him down or force him into retirement. In addition to Winners Corp., Massey remained active with his venture capital company and continued to be an active board member for Thomas Nelson Inc. In 1986, he gave $1.2 million to Belmont University for the establishment of a business school of "national reputation." Two years later, Massey called the groundbreaking ceremony for the Massey Graduate School of Business "the highlight of my life."[5] Eventually, Massey and his charitable foundation would give over $25 million to the university.

Like many older men, Massey never tired of having people listen to him. And like many other Nashville residents, he was frustrated by the course of business events of the late 1980s. In late 1989, Massey invited reporter Bruce Dobie to his house in Belle Meade. "We have a lot of problems," said Massey, by this time confined to a wheelchair because of back pain. "We're not growing. We're losing business. We think we're growing but we're not. We used to have a different kind of business than what we have now. What we have now is branch offices, whereas we used to have headquarters here. We still have some, but not like we did have, and not like we should have. Charlotte, North Carolina, is taking them all. We need to find out what Charlotte is doing."[6] Massey died a few weeks later at the age of eighty-five.

CHAPTER 24

Outlaws & Marketing Majors

By the mid-1960s, country music had grown from a division of National Life & Accident Insurance Co. to an industry in its own right. But the world of country music was still a very small place. There were so few backup musicians in Nashville that the same ones seemed to pop up on every record. There were so few studios that almost every hit was recorded in either Chet Atkins's or Owen Bradley's studio. And even though several national record labels had a presence in Nashville, each used Tennessee as a recording outpost and did not allow its people there to do other things such as market the music, pick the singles, and come up with the album cover.

Because of this, Nashville's record labels and music publishers had tiny staffs and little turnover. In the 1960s, the Nashville division of Mercury Records was basically a two-man business run by Shelby Singleton and Jerry Kennedy. RCA was a three-person operation run by Atkins, a studio engineer, and a secretary. Tree Music Publishing's entire staff consisted of Buddy Killen, Jerry Crutchfield, and a secretary.

Nevertheless, the country music industry produced huge quantities of albums during the 1960s. In an era in which artists might come out with three albums per year, a single country label might release forty per year. Part of the reason that the industry was so prolific was that it did not cost very much to produce an album. "When I got here, you could get four songs recorded in the studio for less than a thousand dollars," said Kennedy, who came to Nashville to work for Mercury in 1963. Another reason that country music produced so many artists and so many albums is that in those days, national record labels rarely interfered with their Nashville divisions when it came to the recording process. "The home office never said that this is the kind of artist that you can sign or that you can't sign this guy," Kennedy said. "I never had to fill out proposals or go through a lot of bureaucracy. They trusted us. We could sign as many artists as we liked and we could record as many albums as we had songs for."

Eventually, the cost of putting out an album would skyrocket, raising the number of albums that had to be sold to several times its previous level. "There was once a time when if we sold 150,000 units, we were so happy that we got drunk," said Joe Talbot III, a one-time backup musician for Hank Snow who later started a record pressing company. "Now, if you don't sell 500,000 units, you will lose your record deal." The other factor that drove overhead costs was the fact that labels became larger employers, hiring everyone from publicists to marketing people to graphic artists. "I did not really notice the change taking place, because I was so damn busy putting out albums," Kennedy said. "All I remember is that at some point, we looked up and there were an awful lot of people who I did not know."

Nineteen sixty-eight was a milestone year for Nashville business. Genesco peaked at sixty-five thousand employees. Minnie Pearl's Fried Chicken stock soared. National Life and Third National formed a conglomerate called NLT. Hospital Corporation of America was formed.

Nineteen sixty-eight was also the year country music made a breakthrough. On November 20, 1968, the CMA Awards were televised for the first time. The broadcast was sponsored by Kraft Foods, hosted by Roy Rogers and Dale Evans, and filmed at the Ryman Auditorium.

The year 1968 may also be viewed as the year that country music began to go through a change, as a new generation of country stars began to eclipse the ones that had dominated the charts in the 1950s and early 1960s. Many of these "new" country stars made more money, had a larger audience, and got more attention from the mainstream press than early country stars dared dream of.

Perhaps the most important of the country stars to emerge in the late 1960s came from the Memphis record label that had only a few years earlier produced Elvis Presley. Johnny Cash grew up in Arkansas during the Great Depression and picked cotton just like everyone else in his family. After graduating from high school, Cash did a stint on an assembly line in Michigan and another as an enlisted man in the Air Force before moving back to Memphis and trying his hand in music. Within months, Cash's deep, somber voice got the attention of Sam Phillips at Sun Records. A few years later, Cash recorded a smash hit called "I Walk the Line," which won him a considerable following outside of country's traditional audience. Soon thereafter, Cash—like Presley—got too expensive for Phillips and signed a deal with Columbia.

Cash was a commercial success mainly because of his unique style and his somber ballads. The peak of his fame came in the late 1960s, when he seemed to single-handedly personify country music's answer to the social upheaval going on elsewhere in America. In July 1969, the *New York Times* described Cash as

> the first grim and gutsy pusher of social causes—he has broken the mold of Nashville Grand Ole Opry-type country-western and is pounding out his own folk form, trying to entertain while moving away from the rackety, say-nothing song types that have prevented many people from taking his field seriously.[1]

By that time, Cash was playing to sold-out audiences in places like Detroit and Los Angeles. He was also starring in his own television variety show and was the first country star to draw a seven-figure salary.

Cash was huge for Columbia, but by the late 1960s another CBS division in Nashville called Epic Records was also making a lot of money. The main reason for Epic's success was not so much because of an artist but because of a producer named Billy Sherrill. Like Decca's Owen Bradley and RCA's Chet Atkins, Sherrill had a strong influence on the music he produced. And despite the fact that he paid almost no attention to country music before he came to Nashville in 1962, Sherrill soon developed a knack for picking music country fans loved. Among the artists who had extraordinary success with music produced by Sherrill and Epic were Tammy Wynette, George Jones, and Barbara Mandrell.

Another one of Epic's biggest commercial successes was Charlie Rich, who had one of the most erratic careers in country music history. After he signed with Epic in 1967, Rich changed from a blues and jazz stylist to smooth country balladeer. In 1974, after the success of several albums including *Behind Closed Doors*, Rich was named Entertainer of the Year by the CMA. However, Rich showed up drunk at the 1975 CMA Awards and—in one of the strangest moments in country music history—set fire to the envelope as he announced John Denver's selection as his successor. "That absolutely cost him his career," said Rick Blackburn, an executive with CBS at the time. "I have never seen anyone go from the height of his career to being gone so fast."

As it turns out, Rich's stunt was a watershed for Nashville's country music industry. By the mid-1970s, the smooth Nashville

Sound had run its course. Nothing demonstrated that fact better than the ascent of Denver—a Colorado singer and acoustic guitar player whose simple songs about life and nature appealed to everyone from hippies to middle-class Americans. It was time for many changes on Music Row—changes in the type of product, the image, the personalities, and the business side of the industry. Perhaps no two artists exemplified this change more than Willie Nelson and Waylon Jennings.

Long before he became a star, Willie Nelson was one of country music's most successful songwriters. Hugh Nelson, as he was once called, wrote Patsy Cline's "Crazy" and Faron Young's "Hello Walls" in addition to dozens of other hits. But Nelson's commercial career stagnated throughout the 1960s, mainly because Nelson's voice and style did not mix well with the heavily produced Nashville Sound in vogue at the time. By 1972, after producing fifteen albums for RCA, Nelson quit country music and moved to Austin, Texas, to become a pig farmer. A few months later, Nelson started playing live music again. In those shows, Nelson developed a new kind of sound—a sound influenced by everything from cowboy music to black blues to gospel to rock. "Unlike the syrupy Nashville studio sound, Nelson's was a road band sound, a gritty, live performance sound," a *New York Times* profile said.[2] Inspired by his new success, Nelson signed a new contract with Atlantic Records, then trying to get a foothold in country music.

Nelson did not really take off until 1975, when Atlantic sold his contract and an album called *Red Headed Stranger* to Nelson's new label, Columbia. "When we bought *Red Headed Stranger*, we thought it was a demo at first, it was so rough and simple," said then-Columbia executive Rick Blackburn. "But Willie told us that none of it needed to be re-taped. He told us that the only thing that album needed was to be out. And he was right." Despite the fact that *Red Headed Stranger* only cost twenty thousand dollars to produce, it sold over five hundred thousand copies.

For the rest of the decade, Nelson reigned as the undisputed king of country music. Unlike most of the big stars that had preceded him, he had the authority to take his music where he wanted. "When we brought him in, Willie was very much in charge of his product," said Blackburn. "My role with Willie was to listen to him and say 'You're right. Of course.'"

Like Nelson, Jennings had a long road to stardom. In 1965, RCA executive Bobby Bare caught Jennings's act at a Phoenix club and immediately signed the former Buddy Holly band member to his label. But despite critical acclaim (not to mention his role in a 1966 B-rate movie called *Nashville Rebel*) Jennings's career did not take off. By the time Johnny Cash became a superstar in 1968, his old roommate

Waylon Jennings, circa 1980 (Metro Nashville Archives).

Jennings had become disillusioned with a music industry that he thought did not allow room for originality. After several failed attempts to turn him into a Nashville Sound artist, Jennings decided he couldn't stand the heavily produced product in vogue in 1960s country music. "I wanted a live sound," Jennings said.

Jennings also had problems with other aspects of the corporate-dominated culture of country music. He did not appreciate the fact that RCA required him to record in their studios with backup musicians and with producers it chose. "Some of those producers were ridiculous and did not understand me at all," he said.

Jennings decided to take a stand against his label in 1973. According to his contract, RCA would only release material recorded in the studio it owned.

But one night, Jennings went into an independent studio owned by Tompall Glaser and recorded an album called *This Time*. "It was a big violation of my contract," Jennings later admitted. But after a heated argument with RCA executive Jerry Bradley, the label backed down and decided to release Jennings's album anyway.

After RCA released *This Time* in 1974, word leaked out about RCA's decision to allow Jennings to break his contract. During the next few years, other artists began to ask for the same right. It wasn't long before Nashville's record labels were getting out of the studio business.

Despite his landmark stance against RCA, Jennings still wasn't selling as many albums as Bradley thought he could. At that point, Bradley had the idea of putting out an album comprising music by Jennings along with Willie Nelson, Glaser, and Jessi Colter (Jennings's wife and a country singer). "I knew it would cost the company zero, because we owned master recordings from Willie and Jessi from when both were with RCA," Bradley said. Bradley thought it would be a great idea to make the album look like an old "Wanted!" poster. "I got the idea from the old *Time-Life* books on the Old West," Bradley said. Within months of its release, *Wanted! The Outlaws* became the first platinum-selling album in country music history.

Meanwhile, the changes taking place inside Music Row's office buildings were also dramatic. In the early 1970s, the business of country music was still being done much the same way it had been done in the late 1950s. The people who worked for country music labels were responsible for producing records but not for other aspects of the business, such as coming up with album covers and promoting the artists. "In the old days, producers such as my dad [Owen Bradley] and Chet Atkins did not have to make business decisions," said Bradley. "They would find the song, work with the artist, record the songs, and send their masters to New York. Then they would go play golf. New York would do everything else for them."

This arrangement slowly began to change as Nashville's first generation of record label executives (RCA's Chet Atkins, MCA/Decca's Owen Bradley, Epic's Billy Sherrill) began to turn over control to the next generation. The changes happened first at RCA. By the early 1970s, Jerry Bradley was tired of the way New York kept producing album covers that he thought were patronizing. "I remember one time they sent me one down with a barn, cows, a fence, and a hill on it," Bradley said. "I took an ink pen and put little dots on it and sent it back up there. They called me and said 'What in the world are the dots?' I said 'That's the cow shit that you left out.'"

The first time RCA let its Nashville office create an album cover was in 1973, when the label released an album by Johnny Russell called *Rednecks, White Socks and Blue Ribbon Beer*. Shortly thereafter, RCA began giving Bradley more power, letting him hire a promotion man and a sales manager. "The key was Mel Elbermann, who was then head of RCA," Bradley said. "At a time when other record labels down here were getting no authority, Mel encouraged me to make business decisions."

Elbermann also wanted RCA's Nashville division to become more autonomous in other ways, which is why he sent a young executive named Joe Galante to work with Bradley. At first, the decision to send Galante to Nashville seemed strange. "I grew up on Cream and the Rolling Stones," Galante said. "Being from New York and being sent to the South in the 1970s was not an opportunity. It was a sentence." Galante felt even worse when he met his new boss, Jerry Bradley. "I remember that at first, Jerry's attitude was 'what the hell do I need a Yankee down here for?'"

However, Bradley soon found that Galante—a marketing and accounting major in college—knew how to run a business. In 1976,

RCA promoted Galante to head its country music division. After three years in New York and two years cultivating connections among trade reporters and radio stations, Galante hit the ground running. "I knew every single way to affect a record and to move it up the charts, and I came up with plan after plan to get our songs on top of the charts," Galante said. "Other labels just sent a record out and let it be. I came up with a promotional attack to get all the stations to play a record the same day. I came up with the idea to send out colored vinyl singles, so our singles stood out from all the rest and so disc jockeys could find ours in the stack.

"Once we started doing this type of thing, people started asking 'what would RCA do next?' At that point, we were really promoting and getting the radio stations' attention."

By the late 1970s, Columbia and MCA had also beefed up their Nashville divisions and were allowing them to make more decisions. Like RCA, they also put executives in place who had more experience in the business side of music—Rick Blackburn at Columbia and Bruce Hinton at MCA.

As Nashville's record labels came under the control of people with connections in other types of music, national labels began to encourage Nashville to experiment with the product's threshold. Before long, the emphasis on Music Row shifted from producing country music to producing music that "crossed over" to the pop charts.

One of the first big crossover artists was Capitol's Glen Campbell, a former session guitarist in Los Angeles who had a string of hits in the late 1960s and early 1970s on both the country and pop charts. Campbell also was one of the first country singers to break into television, with a variety show in 1968 and a costarring role in the 1972 John Wayne movie *True Grit*.

The next big crossover success story was Willie Nelson, who constantly experimented with other kinds of music in his own attempt to keep himself from stagnating. "Willie was always very concerned that he not fall into a rut and be predictable," Columbia's Rick Blackburn said. "He was likely to walk in with a jazz record or something." In 1978, Nelson came out with an album of remade pop songs called *Stardust* that eventually sold over four million copies. The next year, he appeared in the Robert Redford movie *The Electric Horseman*.

No label had as many crossover successes as RCA, including Ronnie Milsap, Jerry Reed, Dolly Parton, and Sylvia. Years later, RCA's Joe Galante maintained that aggressive marketing had everything to do with the success of these acts. "I knew as many of the pop stations as I knew the country stations. It was about developing a system whereby we knew what to do. I knew which stations to go after and which of my promotion guys could get it done."

In 1980, RCA was looking for a country group to put up against MCA's Oak Ridge Boys and Mercury/Polygram's Statler Brothers. "I put the word out that we were looking for a band," Bradley said. Within days, Bradley and Galante had heard about a group from Fort Payne, Alabama, that had already recorded an album with a tiny independent label. RCA bought the album rights for twenty-five thousand dollars and signed the group, called Alabama. Alabama's music appealed to country fans, but in some ways the music sounded more like 1970s rock than country acts of the past. Within months, sales of Alabama's first album were eclipsing the Oak Ridge Boys and Statler Brothers. During the next two decades, Alabama sold sixty million units.

Perhaps the greatest crossover artist of the late 1970s and early 1980s was Kenny Rogers, who switched labels repeatedly. Rogers released eighteen albums between 1976 and 1984, all of which sold at least five hundred thousand copies. He also had two of his songs, "The Gambler" and "Coward of the County," turned into movies.

While country music was breaking new ground in the area of crossover, technology and creativity were changing other aspects of the industry as well. By the late 1970s, the business of recording and mixing a country song had come a long way since the days when country artists could record a song in its final version in an hour or so. Studio engineers were beginning to piece together the final version of a song based on parts of several different takes, creating the possibility that a song heard on the radio might actually be a compilation of several different recordings.

One of the best examples of this phenomenon was the 1979 Barbara Mandrell hit "I Was Country When Country Wasn't Cool." Mandrell recorded the song in a California studio with no bass player. Producer Tom Collins took the recording back to Nashville, added the sound of a bass to the song and the sound of a live audience to it. But there was still something missing. "I thought it would be really good if we could get a great singer to come on at the end and do sort of a duet," Collins said. Mandrell asked George Jones, who recorded his part of the song by himself in a Nashville studio. "I Was Country When Country Wasn't Cool" became a smash country hit, in spite of the fact that it did not have a country melody. Almost everyone who heard the record was under the impression that Mandrell and Jones recorded it together with a complete band in front of a live audience.

Because of the crossover acts, country music went through a period of immense popularity from about 1977 until 1982. The period, aided by the ascent of a country music fan named Jimmy Carter to the presidency, left its mark not just in music but also in television, film, and fashion. Country stars like Barbara Mandrell and Dolly Parton appeared in many televised variety shows. Kenny Rogers and Willie

Nelson made their way to the big screen. Waylon Jennings became the host of a television show about two fast-driving rednecks called the *Dukes of Hazzard*. And like many other people who discovered Hollywood, the country artists who successfully got a piece of the crossover couldn't get over how profitable it could be. "I wish I could find another one of those things," Jennings said in 1999, referring to his *Dukes of Hazzard* involvement. "You almost had to back up a truck to get your money because it was so easy." No single production symbolized the boom better than a 1980 movie called *Urban Cowboy*, a film that had hundreds of bars across the country investing money in mechanical bulls.

By 1982, however, something bad began to happen to country music. One major country artist after another—from Dolly Parton to Barbara Mandrell to Kenny Rogers—had abandoned the music that they had started with and become a pop singer/television personality. However, audiences were not embracing the new acts being put forward by the country labels. They were, however, very excited about what they were hearing from other types of music; Michael Jackson's 1982 album *Thriller* sold over twenty million copies, and Bruce Springsteen's 1984 album *Born in the U.S.A.* sold over ten million. By the early 1980s, country music was in a slump.

At the nadir of country music's popularity, Nashville had two acts that were worth getting excited about. The first was a mother and daughter team called the Judds that successfully auditioned in Joe Galante's office at RCA in March 1983 and became the most successful duo in country music history. The second was Ricky Skaggs, whose bluegrass sound is credited with helping to bring country music back to its roots.

The story behind Ricky Skaggs's rise to fame says much about the nature of Nashville's music business. Before he was a solo artist, Skaggs played backup for Emmylou Harris. In 1982, Capitol Records executive Lynn Shults heard some of Skaggs's music and wanted to sign him, but his label bosses nixed the idea because Skaggs was a bluegrass singer in the age of the crossover. Not wanting to let Skaggs down, Shults called Columbia's Rick Blackburn and told him about Skaggs. Blackburn, who grew up in a family where several of his relatives played bluegrass music, obtained a Skaggs tape and loved it. A few weeks later, Blackburn and Skaggs met at Nashville's Irelands Restaurant, where they worked out a deal on a napkin.

The person often credited with signaling the "comeback" of country music got his start as a cook at the Nashville Palace Nightclub near Opryland. In the early 1980s, Randy Traywick and his wife worked at the Palace while trying to sell Traywick's independently recorded album. In 1985, Warner Brothers signed Traywick and changed his stage name to Travis. The next year, Randy Travis's

Storms of Life album became the first country album to go multi-platinum. "When *Storms of Life* came out in 1986, country music was still wallowing in the post-*Urban Cowboy* recession, chasing elusive crossover dreams," one publication later said. "Travis brought the music back to its basics."[3]

Two of the other dominant country acts of the late 1980s came from the same label. In 1980, at the peak of country music's "crossover" mania, MCA signed a Texan named George Strait, whose music was classified as traditional country and whose trademark was a big black cowboy hat. Throughout the decade, Strait released ten albums, all of which went either gold or platinum. Then, in 1984, MCA signed a former Mercury artist named Reba McEntire. McEntire's career, which had only been marginally successful to that point, took off. Her string of fourteen consecutive number-one songs made her the first dominant female solo artist in country music in more than a decade.

There was nothing in the background of an Oklahoma boy at all to suggest that he would one day become a country music star, let alone the biggest country music star of all time.

Troyal Garth Brooks grew up in a typical American neighborhood in a suburb of Oklahoma City. Like just about every American boy who grew up in the 1970s, Brooks listened to music by Elton John, Journey, and Kansas and dreamed of playing professional sports. Like many of the boys he grew up with, Brooks attended Oklahoma State University, eventually earning a partial track scholarship.

After graduating with a degree in marketing, Brooks started playing clubs. In 1985, he drove to Nashville, proudly presented a demo tape to an executive at ASCAP and was turned down flat. Two years of club-playing later, Brooks was back in Nashville, this time with his wife Sandy. After making ends meet by working in a western boot store, Brooks played some of his music for a different ASCAP executive named Bob Doyle. Doyle was so excited that he immediately quit his job and formed a publishing company that bought Brooks's music. He also lined up former MTV executive Pam Lewis to comanage Brooks's affairs.

Doyle thought for sure that one of Nashville's major record labels would sign Brooks, but at first none did. Then, in May 1988, Capitol's Lynn Shults saw Brooks play at the Bluebird Café and became a believer. "His vocal performance and the magnetism of his personality connected with the people who did not even know who Garth Brooks was," Shults said years later. "What went through the mind was that I had just seen somebody who was as good—if not better than—anyone I had ever seen."[4] Shults brought Brooks to the attention of Capitol's Nashville head man Jim Fogelsong, who immediately signed the singer. Less than a year later, Capitol released Brooks's self-titled first album. After two of the album's singles—"If Tomorrow Never Comes" and "The Dance" hit number one, the sales of Brooks's first album went triple platinum and became the best-selling country album of the 1980s.

Brooks went back to the studio in the summer of 1990 and taped the album *No Fences*. That fall, when the time came to release it, Jimmy Bowen (who had replaced Jim Fogelsong as the head of Capitol Records in Nashville) engineered a marketing stunt not atypical of ones he often pulled during his controversial music career. Rather than release it to all radio stations simultaneously, Bowen released it early to a station in Oklahoma City. The controversy that the move generated contributed to the publicity surrounding *No Fences*, which sold seven hundred thousand copies during its first ten days. "I want to thank God," Brooks said when he received CMA's Horizon Award a few months later. "He's done a hell of a lot for me."

Brooks had already begun to show an instinctual ability to generate publicity through controversy that would repeatedly help his records sell. In April 1991, Liberty (the new name for Capitol Records that year) released the video for his song "The Thunder Rolls." The video depicted a wife-beating, adulterous husband who is murdered by his wife. For two days, Gaylord's CMT network aired the video six times a day. But on the third day, CMT announced it would no longer be airing it. Rather than hurt the sales of *No Fences*, CMT's move had just the opposite effect. "The episode quickly turned into the best thing yet to happen to Garth Brooks's career," one author said.[5]

By this time, *No Fences* was well on its way to becoming the best-selling country album of all time. Liberty and Brooks struck again while the iron was hot, releasing *Ropin' the Wind* in the fall of 1991. *Ropin' the Wind* immediately became the first album to ever debut at number one on the pop and country charts and then remained atop the country chart for almost a year. In January 1992, Brooks did a prime-time special on NBC that had higher ratings than an ABC special on Michael Jackson. During the next few months, Brooks appeared on the cover of *Time, People,* and *Forbes.* By late summer, he had become so huge that Liberty Records made the unprecedented move of charging one dollar more for his album *The Chase* than it had been charging for all other releases (a move Brooks criticized).

One thing that distinguished Garth Brooks from previous country artists was his concerts. Historically, country music fans had become accustomed to seeing stars stand motionless behind a microphone for two hours. But when it came to live performances, Brooks took a page from the rock bands that he had listened to in the 1970s—climbing onto speakers, hanging from cables, and even smashing guitars. "Garth's act incorporated what he had seen growing up," Brooks's agent Tony Conway once said. "He used to see Queen and figured there was no reason he couldn't do those kinds of theatrics in country."[6] Brooks did so much moving during his concerts that his headset microphone became one of his trademarks (along with a huge black cowboy hat and tight jeans).

There is no question that Garth Brooks did more to draw attention to country music than any artist in decades. There is also no question that Brooks became caught up in his own success. For one thing, Brooks began threatening to retire starting in 1992. For another, he began to make social and political statements on television and in magazine articles, such as the time he announced that his sister was gay on national television without asking her permission. Brooks also began to act as if he thought that his celebrity status translated to political power, such as the time he tried to arrange a meeting with President Clinton to discuss world peace. Perhaps the strangest example of Brooks's behavior came in 1994. That year, he was selected as the Favorite Artist of the Year at the American Music Awards. Brooks walked to the podium, announced that he did not agree with the judges, and left the trophy on the stage.

Brooks was so huge that he became the first country artist to effectively bring a major record label to its knees. In 1991, Brooks became increasingly at odds with Bowen over the terms of his contract with Liberty. After Brooks became frustrated with Bowen, he went over Bowen's head to Capitol executive James Fifield in London. In January 1993, the deal was finalized. Although terms were never disclosed, it apparently gave Brooks ownership of his recordings and somewhere around 50 percent of the net profit from his music, giving him close to three dollars for every album sold. Incredibly, the terms of the contract were retroactive to the first day of his contract with Capitol, which gave Brooks a lump sum of close to $90 million from records he had already sold.

Despite how much money everyone made off Garth Brooks's success, there were two very well-publicized personal disputes that came out of it. One was between Bob Doyle and Pam Lewis, who ended up having to get a chancery judge to decide how much money each made from managing Brooks's career. The other was between Brooks and Bowen. After Brooks's record sales began to slip in 1993 and 1994, he became increasingly critical of Bowen and finally started a personal campaign within his label to get Bowen fired.

Liberty's corporate bosses did not have to decide whether to go with Bowen or Brooks. In the summer of 1994, Bowen was diagnosed with lymphoma and retired.

There were many theories about the immense popularity of country music in the early 1990s. One of the most credible was that country music filled the void of rock music, which had been supplanted by rap music. "Country music is all about everyday life and everyday experience," a *Forbes* reporter wrote. "Rapper Ice Cube writes about burning down Korean grocery stores. [Rap group] The Geto Boys talk about a horrifically violent rape."[7] Some Americans went as far as to partially blame rap music lyrics for the Los Angeles riots of April 1992, which took place as Garth Brooks's popularity was hitting its peak.

By the 1990s, the definition of country music had been widened to include many songs that would have never been considered country in previous years. Wynonna Judd's first solo album, released in early 1992, was acclaimed by critics and became the best-selling studio album by a female in country music history. But as one country music author pointed out: "Strictly speaking, the album wasn't very country—there was no fiddle or pedal steel on any of the cuts."[8]

Whatever the cause, the boom in Nashville's music industry was very real. According to numbers provided by the Recording Industry Association of America, country music's share of the music dollar rose from 7.3 percent in 1989 to 17.4 percent in 1992. The country music boom of the early 1990s had ramifications all over the national economic spectrum. "Discos are being converted into country bars," *Nation's Business* reported in March 1993. "Shoe stores have moved cowboy boots to prime positions in their display cases. Nouvelle cuisine is giving way to country cooking." Nowhere was the boom more important than in Nashville. By 1992, the number of record labels on Music Row began to multiply, and the city went through an increase in tourist traffic that was affiliated with its status as the home of country music. Country music got so big, in fact, that some investors began betting on the idea that Christian music—which had been loosely affiliated with Nashville—would also go through a boom period. Such speculation led to two major transactions: Thomas Nelson's 1992 purchase of Word Records and BMG's 1995 purchase of Reunion Records.

The popularity of the music being made in Nashville tapered off after 1996. The industry retrenched, as many of the small, independent labels and corporate start-up labels started in the first part of the decade closed (the most notable being A&M and MCA's Decca division). But by the middle of 1997, it was clear that the downside of this boom would be nothing like the one that followed the *Urban Cowboy* boom of the early 1980s. Although the sale of Garth Brooks's albums declined as the decade passed, several other acts filled the void, including Mercury's Shania Twain, Arista's Brooks & Dunn, and Curb's Lee Ann Rimes.

Nevertheless, the industry had its critics. Some raised concern that the definition of country music was being stretched so far that the music being made in Nashville wasn't country anymore, setting the industry up for another "boom and bust" cycle that followed the crossover mania of the late 1970s. Others raised concern that in the era of videos, country music was more about visuals than it was about music. "We used to have hits with people and the public never knew what they looked like," Chet Atkins told one author. "They just liked the songs. They bought the songs. But now they put some guy or girl that they think's handsome and good-looking. . . . And [they] all sound alike. But they look great."[9] Other Music Row old-timers were more abrupt, especially after Twain's music rose to the top of the charts by the overt use of sex as a marketing tool. "That Shania Twain oughta be dancing down here at Déjà Vu," said Joe Talbot III, referring to a local stip joint.

By the mid-1990s, most Nashville residents had come to accept country music as a part of the city's economic and cultural landscape. Nonetheless, there was still the occasional burst of frustration from residents over Nashville's image being tied to country music—the most famous of which came from Mayor Phil Bredesen. In November 1995, Bredesen made a disparaging remark about Nashville's "hayseed" image in the *Wall Street Journal*. A few days later, he explained that comment to a *Tennessean* reporter. "Country music is great and everything," Bredesen said. "But saying Nashville is about nothing more than country music is like saying that New York is about nothing more than getting mugged."[10] Since Bredesen criticized Vanderbilt in the same interview, Vanderbilt chancellor Joe Wyatt came to the defense of the music industry the next day, mentioning a Nashville bluegrass club called the Station Inn. "I consider myself sort of a hayseed," said Wyatt. "I know who George Jones is, and I know who Willie Nelson is, and I know where the Station Inn is, and I am comfortable with those settings." Nashville's country music industry, which started when a Vanderbilt graduate named Humphrey Bate sang on WSM, thus ended the century being defended by a Vanderbilt chancellor.

CHAPTER 25

King Rick

Hospital Corporation of American CEO Tommy Frist Jr. sat in his office and simmered. The night before, he had received a phone call from HCA board member Irving Shapiro, formerly the chairman of DuPont. Shapiro told Frist that a group of three men in Texas was putting together a $4 billion bid to buy HCA.

There was no way Frist would even consider the offer, he had told his fellow executives that morning. After all, the three men probably did not have the financing. The investment bankers would never go along with it. And there was no way he was going to sell his father's company.

Several aspects of the deal bothered Frist. One was the fact that banks and insurance companies were willing to step forward and loan these men enough money to pull off this stunt. Another was the way he had been contacted.

But perhaps the biggest vexation was that he hardly knew anything about the three men. He had at least heard of two of them— former Hospital Affiliates International executives Richard Ragsdale and Charlie Miller. But he had never even heard of the third—a Dallas attorney named Rick Scott. And in that regard, Frist was not alone. "There are a lot of skeptics who wonder who the hell these people are," a Dean Witter analyst was quoted as saying that day.[1]

The 1980s were bad years for hospital companies.

First of all, Congress did something critics of Medicare had been calling for it to do for fifteen years. In 1983, Congress threw out the cost-plus system of reimbursement and replaced it with a system called "Diagnosis Related Groups" (DRGs). Under cost-plus, the government had reimbursed a hospital based on what the hospital charged for treatment. Under the new DRG system, the government would only reimburse a hospital a fixed amount for a certain disease. If, for example, an elderly patient were diagnosed with appendicitis, and if the government's reimbursement for appendicitis was five hundred dollars, the hospital had to find a way to treat the patient for less than five hundred dollars if it wanted to make money. Since Medicare accounted for between 30 percent to 40 percent of hospital bills, the DRG system immediately had a major impact on hospitals' bottom lines.

The second change to the industry was more gradual. By the early 1980s, employers began putting pressure on insurers to stop raising employee health care rates. Health maintenance organizations (HMOs), which had incentives to keep private health care costs to a minimum, became a factor by the mid-1980s. They were especially important in urban areas, where HMOs could play one hospital against another in order to contain costs. Between 1983 and 1994, HMO membership in the United States grew from 12.5 million to about 50 million.

The third element hospital companies had to deal with was a product of technology and the renewed emphasis on cost control by HMOs and the DRG system. Now that it was possible to conduct routine operations outside of hospitals, outpatient surgery centers began popping up everywhere. No company benefited more from this trend than Nashville's Surgical Care Affiliates. "When we got in the business, only about 10 percent of surgery was done outpatient," said Surgical Care founder Joel Gordon. "By 1994, over 60 percent of surgery was done on an outpatient basis."

All of the above three factors hurt hospital companies such as HCA. In October 1985, three years after being named CEO and a month after being named chairman, Tommy Frist Jr. told analysts that his company would have flat earnings during the next year. The truth ended up being a lot worse; during the fourth quarter of 1986, HCA lost $42 million.

Poor earnings among hospital companies forced new strategies that did not always pay off. With so much more emphasis on cost control, analysts began to predict that vertical integration would soon take over the health care industry. "The feeling at that time was that there would be a huge consolidation in health care and that the country would end up with about six major health services companies, all providing a broad spectrum of health care," said Ragsdale.

With the idea of becoming one of these major health service companies, HCA announced a plan to merge with international hospital supply firm American Hospital Supply on April 1, 1985. On one level, the merger made sense as a way for HCA to cut costs and become a company with many services. "In the back of my mind, my strategy was that I wanted us to become the General Electric of health care," Frist Jr. said. "American Hospital Supply was going to be the first piece, and the second might have been something like Pfizer." But as the merger was scrutinized in the industry and on Wall Street, it backfired. Many of AHS's customers were competitors of HCAs and had no intention of buying their supplies from HCA. After large not-for-profit purchasing groups threatened to pull their business, another large hospital supply firm called Baxter Travenol came in with another offer to merge with AHS. Baxter prevailed.

The trend toward vertical integration also led hospital companies to get into health insurance. Louisville-based Humana led the way, launching an HMO in 1983. HCA followed two years later when it bought several HMOs and operated them as a joint venture with Equitable Life Insurance called Equicor. For a short while, it looked as though hospital companies and insurance companies might blend well. But it turned out that hospital companies and insurers did not mix because it put firms like HCA and Humana at odds with their own hospitals and the physicians that contracted with those hospitals. "It turned out to be a good financial move but not a good strategic move," said Joe Hutts, then HCA's official in charge of its health insurance operation. "As HCA got into it, they did not want to put their full weight behind that much managed care strategy."

HCA eventually sold its insurance business to Cigna. Humana stayed in the insurance business until 1991. At that point, Humana split its company in half, with Humana remaining in the insurance business and a new company called Galen taking over its hospitals.

By 1987, slumping earnings and failed attempts to diversify made HCA seem like a floundering giant in need of direction. It was then that Ragsdale, Miller, and Scott made their failed bid to buy HCA for $47 a share. "One of the reasons we made the bid was that we had heard rumors from a couple of sources that Tommy might be interested in retiring and doing other things," Ragsdale said years later. "One of the major mistakes we made was to pay attention to rumors." Frist rejected the bid outright and the trio withdrew it a couple of weeks later. Nonetheless, the fact that the offer even took place made Frist realize he needed to do something dramatic to rejuvenate HCA.

Frist's solution was to shrink his company. In the summer of 1987, HCA reduced the size of its corporate staff by about 25 percent by eliminating several levels of management between the top of the company and its hospitals. A few months later, the company spun off 104 of its poorer performing hospitals into a separate company called HealthTrust, headed by HCA president and chief operating officer

Clayton McWhorter. That left HCA a much smaller and, Frist hoped, more profitable machine.

However, if Frist was hoping that the HealthTrust spin-off would be enough to get institutional investors more excited about his stock, he was wrong. HCA's stock price had peaked at about forty-eight dollars a share in the summer of 1985 and again in the summer of 1987. But even after HCA spun off HealthTrust, HCA's stock still hovered in the thirty-five-dollar range through most of 1988.

Frist's next announcement took Wall Street by complete surprise. In September 1988, Frist announced that he was planning a leveraged buyout of the company's stock at forty-seven dollars a share. "It was both defensive and offensive," Frist said. "It was offensive in that I knew we had to do radical restructuring to the company, and it is easier to take those hits when you are a private company. . . . It was defensive in the sense that the marketplace was not enamored with the hospital industry. With the junk bond situation being what it was then, I was worried that someone might come in like Ragsdale and them and take us over." At first, many analysts were skeptical that Frist could do it. Two months later, after a legal challenge from some disgruntled shareholders, Frist executed the LBO with the backing of Morgan Guaranty Trust Co. In March 1989, HCA became a private company.

When HCA spun off 104 poorly performing hospitals into a new company called HealthTrust, new HealthTrust CEO Clayton McWhorter knew what Wall Street was saying. "Back then, a lot of people in the marketplace thought rural hospitals were going to become a thing of the past," said McWhorter. "The general feeling was that all the technology was going to go to the larger markets and that small hospitals were going to become first aid stations."

During the next few years, HealthTrust defied the odds and turned its mix of underperforming hospitals into a profitable machine. One of the important steps in this process was selling twenty-two of its hospitals to reduce debt. But the most important was to focus on the unique needs of rural hospitals. "Our focus was survival," McWhorter said. "There was no question that we had a gun to our heads. I preached that every day. I kept saying that we had a bunch of dogs, but that we were going to make a bunch of pedigree greyhounds out of them."

One of the most important people in this turnaround was Charlie Martin, a former General Care and HCA executive and the president at HealthTrust from 1987 and 1991. The temperamental, detail-oriented, and hard-charging Martin made an interesting contrast with the more relaxed and less confrontational McWhorter. Not everyone got along with Martin or the way he did business; in the first eighteen months of HealthTrust's existence, 60 percent of its hospital CEOs were either fired or resigned. Years later, Martin said financial goals were reached not by doing anything huge but by paying attention to "about a gazillion little individually insignificant things that in the aggregate got a good result."

HealthTrust did not stay a private company for long, nor was it ever meant to. "We acted like a public company from day one," McWhorter said. "I stayed in touch with the analysts that followed the hospital industry, knowing that when it came time to go public that they would know everything that there was to know about this company." In 1991, McWhorter's work paid dividends when HealthTrust had a successful public offering.

Meanwhile, things got turned around at HCA. For two years, Frist cut costs and streamlined the focus of his company. During 1989 and 1990, the privately held HCA took several steps to reduce debt. First, it spun off its 150 hospital management contracts into a new company called Quorum. It sold its Australian hospitals for $83 million. In 1990, the company sold most of its stake in HealthTrust for $600 million.

Then, in February 1992, Frist and the institutions that had helped him pull off the LBO three years earlier sold 34 million shares of stock, asking more than eight times what they had paid for the stock less than two and a half years earlier. "The only reason we went public again was that the banks had invested a lot of money in it and wanted to liquidate," Frist said. Nevertheless, no individual profited more from the offering than Frist, who pocketed $127 million from stock options.

By this time, another wave of Nashville health care companies had cropped up and become major industry players.

OrNda. In September 1991, Martin left HealthTrust to be CEO at Republic, the Dallas-based hospital chain cofounded by HAI alumnus Richard Ragsdale a few years earlier. Martin soon changed almost everything about the company, including its name (OrNda), its hometown (Nashville), and its assets (selling its surgery centers and labs). Martin also dismantled the company's physician ventures at a time when many other companies were getting into the physician venture business. "In an era when physicians increasingly had less discretion over where patients went, it made no sense," Martin said. "It seemed to me that there were better ways to link with the physicians than selling one hundred guys a little tiny piece of the hospital." In 1994, OrNda more than doubled in size by linking with Dallas-based American Healthcare Management and California-based Summit Health.

Quorum. Quorum acquired a competitor called Hospital Management Professionals in 1992 and the next year got into the hospital-ownership business with the purchase of ten hospitals owned by Charter Medical Corp. Quorum became a public company in 1994. Five years later, Quorum had revenues of about $1.5 billion, owned twenty-one hospitals, and managed about three hundred others. Of all its vital statistics, Quorum CEO Jim Dalton boasted the most about Quorum's 92 percent contract renewal rate.

American HomePatient. Like HCA and SCA, the idea behind American HomePatient was to put together a chain of existing businesses. In this case, the industries were nursing homes and home health companies that provide and service medical equipment for use in private residences, such as oxygen systems, hospital beds, and wheelchairs. American HomePatient was founded in 1984 by Ed Wissing, an Atlanta businessman who had previously been an executive for a home health company called Glasrock Home Care. The company moved to Nashville two years later when several HCA executives invested money in the company. Like HCA, American HomePatient went private in 1989 and went public again in 1992. In 1994, it spun off its nursing home business into another Nashville-based firm called Advocat. By the end of the century, American HomePatient was a $400 million company with about 170 Nashville employees. But like the rest of the home care industry, American HomePatient was in a slump because the federal government was cutting back on Medicare reimbursement rates.

PhyCor. In the mid-1980s, HCA executive Joe Hutts began talking about a company that would put physician practices together into a national organization of multispecialty clinics. When Hutts approached the venture capital firm of Massey-Burch, he was delighted to learn that Lucius Burch III—whose father and grandfather were physicians—had been studying the idea of putting together a national organization of single-specialty eye care clinics. "His model was better," Burch said years later. "We cut a deal with Joe Hutts to create that company in one afternoon." PhyCor was organized in 1988. Eventually, the company ended up with two branches: one that acquired practices and another that organized physicians into managed care networks.

In the midst of health care's mergers, acquisitions, and spin-offs, one recurring story in the industry was the controversy sometimes caused when a for-profit company such as HCA and HealthTrust acquired a not-for-profit hospital. It may have been easier for Nashville residents to understand these controversies better after November 1993.

Back in 1961, one of the early Parkview physician-investors was a surgeon named Jeff Pennington. After Parkview opened, Pennington tried to get many of his fellow investors to pool their money and start a similar facility in East Nashville. When that venture failed, Pennington started a fund-raising drive that eventually raised about $1.5 million in pledges (only half of which was actually later collected). Some of those donations came from business owners and wealthy Nashville residents such as homebuilder Clay Gaines, Genesco executive Nobel Caudill, and Werthan Bag executive Bernard Werthan. However, much of it also came from working-class East Nashville residents who gave $250 each.

Pennington then secured a $2 million grant from the federal government and over $2 million in revenue bonds backed by Third National Bank. In 1964, the community of Madison broke ground on Memorial Hospital. Under Memorial's charter, similar to that of other not-for-profits of that era, the hospital was governed by a board of directors that could sell the hospital if it chose. But Pennington, who resigned from the board shortly after the hospital opened and was replaced by *Tennessean* publisher Amon Carter Evans, said no one even considered that possibility in 1965.

A quarter of a century later, the 314-bed Memorial Hospital had become a full-scale tertiary hospital with $70 million in annual revenue. In addition to having a full-service emergency room, the hospital had a cancer treatment center and open-heart surgery capability. Memorial also had a staff of about one thousand people, two hundred of whom were physicians.

However, Memorial chief executive officer J. D. Elliott was worried. The same factors that hurt hospital companies in the late 1980s—Medicare reimbursement rates and technological advances that moved more treatment to outpatient centers—were beginning to adversely impact his hospital's bottom line. In a city with more beds per capita than the national average, Elliott knew competition for patients was tough and getting tougher. As more companies began turning to managed care for their health insurance, Elliott knew Memorial had a problem that other Nashville hospitals like Baptist and St. Thomas did not have: a location far away from most of the city's large employers. "We had always thought of ourselves as a premier hospital with excellent physicians and excellent services," Elliott said in 1999. "But we were concerned about whether we could continue to do this." Memorial Hospital did not lose money in either 1992 or 1993. But Elliott said that the gap was definitely closing.

Elliott may have also been affected by the consensus in the media that hospitals located in crowded markets were in for a major shake-up. The October 23, 1993, issue of *The Economist* contained an article that profiled Nashville as a typical American city with several hospitals that were in major trouble because of managed care. "The city, with a population of 500,000, has no fewer than ten general hospitals," the article said. "Scarcely three of those ten may survive the 1990s," it added, without attribution.

Elliott's first idea was to merge Memorial with a larger not-for-profit hospital. But years later, he said he couldn't find any interested parties. "With Nashville being as over-bedded as it was, they [other not-for-profit hospitals] were concerned about filling their own beds," Elliott said. There was, however, a for-profit entity interested in Memorial: HealthTrust, which already owned ten small hospitals within ninety minutes' drive of Nashville and wanted a hub for its regional network.

Meanwhile, Jeff Pennington was far removed from the day-to-day operation of Memorial. During the years since his involvement in starting Memorial, Pennington had operated his surgery practice on the west side of Nashville, done a short stint with HCA, and then gone to work as an administrator at Meharry-Hubbard Hospital. But over the years, Memorial's doctors continued to tell him about how things were going at the hospital. And in 1993, doctors began to report that things were not going well.

"They did not think the hospital was doing anything to prepare for managed care," Pennington said. "Several of them wanted to get together and start an independent practice association so they would have some protection from the onslaught of managed care. But the doctors couldn't get the administration to respond."

Pennington was in the process of calling board members to find out why nothing was being done on November 5, 1993. That day, the *Tennessean* ran a story that said HealthTrust had signed an agreement to buy Memorial. During the next few weeks, Pennington became one of the harshest critics of the Memorial-HealthTrust deal. But there were others, some of whom remembered giving money to the hospital decades earlier. A pharmacist in Inglewood who had donated one thousand dollars to the hospital in 1963 said "it wasn't their [the Memorial board's] money. They have no right to sell it."[2]

One aspect of the agreement between HealthTrust and Memorial that was heavily criticized was its secrecy. It would be months before the news was released that HealthTrust had agreed to pay $108 million for the hospital and that most of that money would fund a new foundation.

Perhaps no group of people was as upset with the deal as some of Memorial's doctors. A few days after the sale was announced, a group of about sixty physicians filed an injunction to have the sale blocked. That injunction went all the way to the state attorney general, who eventually ruled that there was no legal basis on which to block the hospital's sale.

In 1999, Pennington said he still thought East Nashville and Madison would have been better off with a public hospital than with a private one. "Whenever a for-profit company buys a hospital, they have to make more money than the hospital was making before to pay the cost of buying it," said Pennington. "They do this by not giving as much charity care and by charging more. They are very good at raising rates."

Elliott said he could not address the issue of charity care or rates since he was no longer affiliated with the hospital (Elliott left the health care industry to head the Memorial Foundation in 1996). But he said that the foundation—which donated about $23 million to not-for-profit organizations during its first four years of existence—had and would continue to do far more for the community than the hospital could have done. Elliott also said he did not think that either he or the board could have handled the sale of the hospital any better. "I don't think we could have arranged an effective sale if we had gone out on the front end and said that we were going to sell the hospital," Elliott said. "A lot of the people who were opposed to it then are very positive about it now."

Elliott said people were even more positive about the sale when they found out that Columbia/HCA (which merged with HealthTrust in 1995) planned to build a new $100 million hospital at the intersection of I-24 and I-65 to replace Memorial. "The new hospital would have never been built had the board not sold the old hospital," Elliott said.

Despite Nashville's dominance of the for-profit health care world, the superstar of the industry in 1992 and 1993 did not even live in Music City, at least not yet. That person was Rick Scott, a member of the trio that failed in its attempt to take over HCA back in 1987.

Not long after the failed takeover, Texas investor and HCA board member Richard Rainwater was looking for someone to help him start a hospital company. Miller and Ragsdale suggested the thirty-four-year-old Scott, who had impressed them with the work he did while Republic Health Care's attorney in 1985 and 1986. "He has enormous energy," Ragsdale later said of Scott. "We would be working all night long, and at four in the morning he was as fresh as he was at eight at night. I was about ready to collapse, and he was having at it." After Rainwater and Scott formed a partnership, Scott showed the same work ethic and persistence that he had shown when he was Republic's attorney. In November 1987, he wrote one thousand letters to people who might be interested in selling their hospital to his new company, which he called Columbia. He got one thousand rejections. "I tried everything," Scott said. "I called everybody. I flew all over the place."[3]

Scott did not give up, and in July 1988, Columbia borrowed $65 million from Citicorp and bought two El Paso, Texas, hospitals from

HealthTrust. During the next few months, Scott made the El Paso hospitals work by demonstrating three "hallmarks" of his management style, as defined by the authors of a 1995 book called *The For-Profit Healthcare Revolution*. One was to sell up to 40 percent of the ownership of its hospitals to local physicians—a practice that Nashville's General Care had actually initiated in the 1970s. The second was the practice of buying crosstown hospitals and shutting them down in order to make one profitable. The third was to not enter a market unless the company had an eye toward dominating it and becoming the leading player for managed care companies in that area.

Columbia grew quickly during its first five years but was little noticed in the industry because it was a relatively small company. But in June 1993, Columbia burst onto the national map with its purchase of Louisville's Galen Health Care (the seventy-four hospitals previously owned by Humana). After the Galen acquisition, Columbia moved its headquarters to Louisville.

After the Galen acquisition was announced, many of the investors and analysts in the healthcare industry began to compare the second largest hospital company (Columbia) with the largest (HCA). And the conclusion that many drew was that there was little comparison between Scott and Frist. Scott had come out of nowhere and gone from last place to second place among hospital companies in only five years. He was so aggressive that he needed little sleep; so cost-conscious that he clipped coupons; so desperate to buy hospitals that he once got his brother (a high school vice principal in North Kansas City, Missouri) to talk to the mayor there about helping Columbia buy a hospital in that market. Scott's philosophy of growth was summarized by a paperweight on his desk that read, "If you are not the lead dog, the view never changes."

Frist's company, on the other hand, had gone from owning 376 hospitals in 1983 to 96 in 1993. Frist had turned down the chance to acquire Galen before Columbia had done so. Most important of all, Frist couldn't find the energy to imitate the brash young healthcare magnate out of Louisville. "I remember our people saying that we could do what Columbia was doing, that we could go on the acquisition trail and we could put together these networks," Frist said in 1999. "And I remember thinking 'Do I really want to get into this? Do I really want to get into a ten-year project and rebuild my management team?'"

There was, therefore, a sense of inevitability in the air on October 2, 1993, when Hospital Corporation of America announced it had agreed to be acquired by Columbia for $5.7 billion in stock. During the announcement, Frist said that it was a friendly merger that he had initiated after reading President Clinton's blueprint for healthcare reform a few weeks earlier. He also made it sound as if he and other

HCA executives had a lot to learn from Columbia and Rick Scott. "We're going to reposition this company not only to survive, but to prosper," Frist said that day.[4]

At the time, Scott and Frist told reporters that they had not decided whether Columbia/HCA's headquarters would be in Louisville or Nashville. But within weeks, Scott began hinting that he would have to have tax breaks before the company would come to Nashville. In November, Columbia/HCA officials began to talk to Mayor Phil Bredesen about how much of a tax break Nashville's government could give the company. But those talks came to a sudden halt in early December when the *Louisville Courier-Journal* reported that Bredesen was planning to offer Columbia a $38-million-a-year incentive package. Bredesen denied that the offer had taken place, and he suspected that Scott was trying to use him. "I don't want to simply be used as a foil to get something out of Kentucky for them," Bredesen said. "As to whether there is an offer, absolutely not."[5]

During the next few months, Scott's relationship with the state of Kentucky and the city of Louisville deteriorated. Several Louisville officials harshly criticized Scott for breaking plans to build a new Columbia headquarters building in that city's downtown. Scott, meanwhile, criticized the state of Kentucky and the city of Louisville for not doing enough to keep his company's headquarters.

In early 1994, HealthTrust CEO Clayton McWhorter began testing the waters in a run for the Democratic nomination for governor. About that same time, his company began having preliminary discussions with two possible suitors: Columbia/HCA and Tenet Healthcare of Santa Barbara, California.

McWhorter dropped out of the governor's race in May. But when he returned to the day-to-day activities of running HealthTrust, he discovered that he had almost lost his job in what he later described as a "palace revolt" by several of his top executives. There was no media coverage of the HealthTrust's internal rebellion, the split it caused in the company's board, or the reasons for it. But several of McWhorter's lieutenants did not want the company to become a part of Columbia. "They thought I was in Tommy Frist's pocket," McWhorter said, adding that "there was no question that I was upset about the way it was handled and what they did and how they did it."

In secret negotiations lasting several months, Columbia/HCA and Tenet bid back and forth over HealthTrust. In September 1994, Tenet appeared to be the final victor when its bid for HealthTrust was reported in the *Wall Street Journal*. But at the last minute, Scott and Frist called McWhorter and upped Columbia/HCA's offer. In October, the sale of HealthTrust to Columbia/HCA for $3.6 billion in stock and the assumption of about $1.8 billion in debt was announced.

By this time, Bredesen thought there was a real chance that Nashville would lose its status as the capital of the for-profit health-care world. In November and December 1994, Bredesen worked out state and local tax breaks for Columbia/HCA worth $2.6 million per year for ten years. On January 10, 1995, the Nashville mayor called a press conference in which he, Scott, Frist, and McWhorter announced that Columbia/HCA's new headquarters would be in Nashville. The *Tennessean* could hardly restrain its enthusiasm, greeting readers with the front-page headline "Silicon Valley of Health Care." The *Louisville Courier-Journal* did not try to hold back its disgust. In the *Courier-Journal's* most bitter editorial cartoon, Rick Scott was depicted as having just had sex with a prostitute (representing the city of Louisville and the state of Kentucky). On his way out the door, Scott left the woman a ten dollar bill.

The city of Nashville and the state of Tennessee obviously gave Columbia/HCA tax breaks out of fear that the company wouldn't come without them. But in a 1999 interview, Frist said that the decision to headquarter Columbia/HCA in Nashville was made when Columbia merged with HCA in October 1993. "Behind the scenes, it was always planned to have the company here," Frist said. "There wasn't any question. I had that understanding with Rainwater and Rick Scott, but they did not know that in Louisville. And we had to have an event to give us an excuse, and the HealthTrust thing was the event. . . . Nashville is too important to me, and it is where the company should be anyway."

McWhorter's story of Columbia/HCA's move back to Nashville is different. McWhorter said Columbia/HCA was not planning to move its headquarters to Nashville until it merged with HealthTrust in the fall of 1994. "One of the conditions that I put on the merger with Columbia/HCA is that the headquarters had to come back to Nashville and that I would make every effort to get tax incentives," McWhorter said.

Nashville has never had a company as big and powerful as Columbia/HCA was between 1994 and 1997. The firm grew to have $20 billion in revenue and almost 200,000 employees. As the fast-growing leader in the burgeoning for-profit healthcare sector, Columbia/HCA became one of the most closely followed firms in the country. By 1996, the Nashville architecture and engineering firm of Gresham, Smith, and Partners had 350 employees, about seventy of whom worked on Columbia-related projects. The Nashville office of Bovis Inc. was managing over ten construction projects for Columbia per year. In 1996 alone, Columbia booked more than forty-two thousand flights leaving from or arriving in Nashville, making it by far the largest single corporate user of the airport in Nashville history.

However, as Columbia/HCA acquired all that revenue, all those employees, all those hospitals, and all that power, it acquired something else—a reputation as one of America's most arrogant companies.

One of the most obvious indicators of this trend was the amount of national press Columbia/HCA was getting. On July 12, 1994, the *Wall Street Journal* ran a front-page story detailing the manner in which Columbia had put together a network of hospitals in west Florida. "In places such as Florida, Columbia has employed big money, tough tactics and relentless pressure to become the state's single largest provider of healthcare," the story stated. The story described Columbia's pursuit of physician investors and its willingness to use political pressure to make acquisitions. "They (Columbia executives) are slowly decimating the ability of the not-for-profits and the public hospitals to stay competitive," a Florida healthcare official was quoted as saying. A few months later, a *Journal* story about Columbia pointed out that, "Many of the nation's 4,569 not-for-profit hospitals are becoming acquisition targets, as investor-owned hospital chains look for new ways to expand."[6]

Of course, much of what newspapers were reporting was not new. For-profit hospitals had been taking over not-for-profit hospitals since

1969, when HCA bought several community-owned hospitals during its first year. Likewise, physicians had owned hospitals since early in the twentieth century, and for-profit hospital companies had organized physician ventures since General Care started doing it in 1970. But in the mid-1990s, for the first time, a hospital company was big enough and powerful enough to pose a threat to large not-for-profit hospitals in the North.

In June 1995, the Massachusetts attorney general announced that he would hold a hearing to review Columbia's announced merger with a teaching hospital system there. A year later, a Michigan judge ruled that Columbia's proposed acquisition of a non-profit hospital in Lansing violated state law that prohibited assets of charitable entities being mingled with for-profit concerns. In September 1996, Columbia University even sued the Nashville company for poaching its venerable name.

Columbia's biggest controversy took place in the Midwest. In April 1996, the Nashville company announced it would acquire Blue Cross & Blue Shield of Ohio for $300 million. Many Wall Street analysts were puzzled by the deal, since several mergers between hospital companies and insurers had failed in the 1980s. Some Columbia board members were just as confused. "I never understood that [the Blue Cross deal], never got a good explanation, and never was in favor of it," said McWhorter, then the chairman of Columbia/HCA's board. But industry insiders said the deal was a power play to help Columbia break into Ohio markets that had previously shut them out, most notably Cleveland.

The proposed merger between Columbia/HCA and Blue Cross of Ohio was heavily criticized by consumer groups and state insurance regulators. Some warned that Columbia would become far too powerful if it started taking over not-for-profit insurers. Others argued that Ohio Blue Cross's assets (including $233 million in surplus reserves) had been accumulated at the expense of taxpayers. As details of the deal came out, it came under fire for another reason: several of Blue Cross Ohio's individual board members stood to pocket a total of $17 million in so-called "non-compete" fees as a part of the transaction. In the fall of 1996, that aspect of the proposed deal was the focus of a segment by the CBS television show *60 Minutes*.

Columbia/HCA obviously wasn't thrilled about the nature of all this media coverage, but the company wasn't exactly trying to maintain a low profile. Historically, HCA had downplayed their brand name and left advertising up to individual hospitals and markets. In the fall of 1996, Columbia/HCA launched a $100 million advertising and branding campaign meant to familiarize America with the company's name. The cornerstone of the campaign was a series of prime-time television commercials in which a man walked up to strangers and talked about Columbia/HCA.

As Columbia became more and more involved in controversy, many Nashville residents wondered whether Tommy Frist Jr. still had anything to do with the way his company was being run. In a 1999 interview, Frist said that the answer was no. Frist said after Columbia merged with HCA in the fall of 1993, he had virtually no authority. "During the year that I was chairman, I was chairman in name only and would just convene the meeting and turn it over to Rick Scott."

Frist said it was clear to him that by 1995 Scott was making several huge mistakes, the biggest of which was growing too fast and not taking time to build an infrastructure. But he said there were other cultural problems, from working his executives too hard to angering reporters. "He'd work people eighteen hours a day, and if they did not show up the next day he figured someone else would be lined up," Frist said. "He treated people as commodities. . . . It was an in-your-face attitude towards everybody. He was saying 'if you don't join me, I'll run you into the ground and I'll beat you.'"

Frist said he tried to get Scott's attention in 1996 and early 1997, to no avail. Between October 1996 and July 1997, Frist said that he and Scott had "maybe five minutes of conversation. . . . It got so bad that I would wave to him through my office window and he wouldn't even wave back." After federal agents raided Columbia/HCA's El Paso, Texas, hospitals in March 1997, Frist said he wrote Scott a letter telling him that the company was heading for trouble, recommending ten or eleven courses of action. "I told him to unwind the joint ventures, quit the silly branding campaign. . . . But he just wouldn't listen."

The account from former HealthTrust CEO Clayton McWhorter, who succeeded Frist as Columbia/HCA chairman in 1995, is similar to Frist's. "I did not feel comfortable saying a lot at the board meetings, but I had a lot of one-on-one talks with Rick," McWhorter said. In April 1997, McWhorter and Scott had a long conversation in which the former HealthTrust CEO advised Scott to resign. "I told him that in building this big company that he had pissed off the attorney generals in every state in which we are doing business, that he had pissed off the media, that he had pissed off the competition, and that he had pissed off the government," McWhorter said. But at a Columbia/HCA board meeting only weeks after that conversation, Scott made no mention of it.

No one who worked at Columbia/HCA will ever forget July 16, 1997. Hundreds of investigators from the U.S. Justice Department descended on nineteen Columbia hospitals and offices in six states, including the company's headquarters in Nashville. Their instructions to Columbia workers they encountered: Stop what you are doing. Get away from the filing cabinet. Do not touch that computer.

By the end of the week, it had become apparent that the investigation into Columbia/HCA was the largest investigation of a healthcare company in the history of the U.S. Justice Department. It involved four hundred government investigators and hundreds of truckloads of paperwork, and it represented several years of work.

What was in many ways almost as remarkable as the investigation itself was the national media's coverage of it. The *Wall Street Journal* and *New York Times*, which almost ignored the emergence of hospital companies in the 1970s and early 1980s, devoted dozens of reporters to the Columbia/HCA story. Through April and May of 1997, hardly a day went by without a story about a "revelation" from the Columbia/HCA investigation. Many of the stories claimed federal investigators were convinced that they had found systemic fraud at Columbia/HCA's Medicare filings. They also said that the investigators had also found problems in the way Columbia/HCA did everything from physician ventures to home health. However, virtually none of the stories cited a source from within the U.S. Justice Department, whose official position was not to comment on the investigation.

In the wake of the investigation, changes took place quickly at Columbia/HCA. In August, the board met and fired Rick Scott and Columbia chief operating officer David Vandewater, replacing them with Tommy Frist Jr. and Jack Bovender respectively. During the next few weeks, Frist fired dozens of middle-level executives at Columbia offices all over the country. Frist also began criticizing Scott publicly.

In 1998 and 1999, with the federal investigation hanging over their heads, Frist and Bovender made several changes at Columbia. The nearly one thousand physician ventures that the company had were dismantled one by one. Over half of the members of the Columbia board were replaced. And in a move that reminded people of what Frist had done at HCA ten years earlier, Columbia spun off two new hospital companies—a chain of thirty-seven called Triad and a chain of twenty-five called LifePoint.

By the fall of 1999, there were beginning to be signs that Columbia/HCA was about to emerge from its two-year legal quagmire, as federal officials began to confirm that they were in discussions with the Nashville company about a financial settlement. But as the twentieth century ended, the investigation into Columbia and the new federal reimbursement rules that accompanied it cast a shadow across the entire for-profit healthcare industry.

CONCLUSION

No book about Nashville's business community in the twentieth century would be complete without a mention of the extraordinary tenure of Mayor Phil Bredesen. The Nashville economy was so bad in 1990 that it was hard to imagine the city recovering anytime soon. But for most of the last decade of the twentieth century, just about every major sector of Nashville's economy did well. For-profit healthcare was hot, causing a wave of new start-ups and a trend of consolidation that led to the creation of Columbia/HCA. Country music became more popular than ever, thanks in part to the overwhelming success of Garth Brooks. Nashville grew as a tourism and convention destination. And although several of Nashville's older public companies struggled (such as Shoney's and Service Merchandise), several seemed to take their place (such as Dollar General and Central Parking).

The power of the mayor's office in Nashville seemed to ascend with the rise in Nashville's economy. Bredesen, a New Jersey native, Harvard graduate, and former healthcare executive, was elected in 1991. Thanks in part to the city's general dissatisfaction with his predecessor, Bill Boner, Bredesen put together a broad constituency of supporters including business leaders, neighborhood activists, the media, and African-American leaders. Bredesen took on one major project after another during his two terms as Nashville mayor and succeeded at almost every one. His first mission was to close down the aging and inefficient Metro General Hospital and move its functions to Hubbard Hospital, a step that practically saved Hubbard from bankruptcy. His next move was to build a seventeen thousand-seat arena across the street from the Downtown Convention Center. Although the arena cost far more than originally planned (it started as the $100 million arena and rose to the $170 million arena), its development was one of the reasons Lower Broadway and Second Avenue went through a major renaissance as a tourist destination. The arena also led the NHL to put an expansion team in Nashville. Bredesen, a Democrat, lost the governor's race to Don Sundquist during the Republican landslide of 1994. But within two months of his defeat, Bredesen regained his momentum with the deal to bring Columbia/HCA's headquarters back from Louisville.

The Columbia/HCA tax break—worth about $26 million from Metro coffers—was one of several tax breaks negotiated during Bredesen's two terms. Bredesen negotiated more tax breaks than all his predecessors combined, including deals for Gaylord Entertainment, Thomas Nelson, Ingram Book, Dollar General, and in his last major act as mayor, a sales tax "rebate" for Dell Computer worth five hundred dollars per year per Dell employee. By the end of Bredesen's tenure, it was hard to imagine a large company moving its headquarters to Nashville or building a new building in Nashville without significant tax help of some kind. But members of his administration claimed that they gave out few tax breaks compared to other cities. "If you go back several decades, Nashville didn't put together these kinds of deals because no city put together these kinds of deals," said Lady Jackson, head of Bredesen's Office of Economic Development through most of his tenure. "Today, if you want a company to relocate to your area, you have to consider abatements."

Despite Bredesen's efforts, the last few years of the century seemed more alarming than invigorating for Nashville. The first bad news was the U.S. Justice Department raids on Columbia/HCA in July 1997. Those raids and the Medicare reimbursement cuts that followed them signaled a major slowdown in the for-profit healthcare industry. The next was the October 1997 announcement by Gaylord that it would close the Opryland U.S.A. theme park, a move that deflated Nashville's tourism industry.

The biggest blow took place in May 1999, when AmSouth Bank of Birmingham took over First American, creating an institution with $42 billion in assets and doing away with Nashville's last large locally owned bank in the process. Unlike the Third National–SunTrust merger thirteen years earlier, there was no pretense of an equal "partnership" between the two banks. In the weeks after the AmSouth–First American merger, AmSouth announced it would be laying off about a thousand First American employees in Nashville. A few weeks later, AmSouth announced that former First American CEO Denny Bottorff, who had negotiated the merger of the two institutions, would be receiving $1.25 million per year for the rest of his life in severance pay. The largest white-collar layoff in Nashville history was thus accompanied by the largest golden parachute in Nashville history.

The AmSouth–First American merger, and the massive layoff that followed, put an end to the days when Nashville could claim to be a center of banking. As the twenty-first century began, Nashville's largest two banks were The Bank of Nashville ($250 million in assets) and Capital Bank & Trust ($120 million). "It is a sad, sad day for Nashville," Jimmy Bradford Jr. said, reflecting on the AmSouth purchase of First American.

At the end of his tenure in 1999, Bredesen said he hoped he would be remembered for his $330 million public school upgrade and his $75 million library improvement package. But the most controversial project he ever undertook was putting together a deal to bring a professional football team to Nashville.

From 1987 to 1995, the Houston Oilers unsuccessfully lobbied the city of Houston and the state of Texas to get a new football stadium. Finally, Oilers owner K. S. "Bud" Adams told team executive vice president Mike McClure to look for a new home city. In part because of the success of the Carolina Panthers in North Carolina, McClure decided Nashville would be a good place—not just because of the immediate market but also because of fans in Memphis, Knoxville, and Huntsville, Alabama. In June, McClure called Butch Spyridon of the Nashville Convention and Visitors Bureau. Spyridon put McClure in touch with Byron Trauger, a Nashville attorney and friend of Bredesen who had actually campaigned for Bredesen opponent Betty Nixon in the 1991 mayor's race.

Talks between the Bredesen administration and the Oilers remained secret for several weeks, during which time Bredesen was reelected on a platform of doing more for Nashville's neighborhoods. By the time the media discovered the Oilers were interested in Nashville, Bredesen and Trauger were well on the way to putting the deal together. A few days after the election, they convinced Adams to sign an agreement to limit his negotiating to Nashville, which was important because of a fear that the Oilers might have been using Nashville to get concessions out of Houston.

In October, Bredesen presented a plan to the Metro Council under which the stadium could be built and the Oilers given a $35 million "relocation" fee. In one of the most creative financial packages ever put together by a Nashville mayor, Bredesen said that the stadium could be funded through advanced season ticket sales, diverting one-fourth of the city's four-cent hotel/motel tax, pledging all sales tax revenues collected at the stadium site to the project, and using $4 million per year that was then going to a Metro Water Department reserve.

During the following months, over forty thousand Nashville residents paid between $250 and $4,500 for personal seat licenses (PSLs), which gave holders the "right" to buy season tickets. A committee headed by attorney Sam Bartholomew Jr. sold over one hundred luxury boxes for between $50,000 and $250,000 per year—money which went to the team and not to the stadium. Although many of the companies that bought luxury boxes were thriving at the time, some—such as Baptist Hospital, Thomas Nelson, and Fruit of the Loom—were either losing money or laying off employees. Meanwhile, the Nashville media was practically unanimous in its enthusiasm for Bredesen's plan. The week PSLs went on the market, the *Tennessean* published an entire section promoting their sale.

The Oilers deal seemed to be going swimmingly, but Bredesen made a major mistake by dismissing opposition in the community. In October 1995, the mayor's allies in the council squashed a motion that would have called for a citywide vote on the Oilers issue. During the next few weeks, several of those councilmen, including Eric Crafton of West Meade and Lawrence Hart of Inglewood, started a petition drive to force such a referendum. Despite the fact that the petition drive was almost ignored by the local media, it succeeded in delivering over forty-three thousand signatures and forcing a referendum. During the weeks leading up to the stadium vote, people opposed to the stadium proposal pointed out that the city had more pressing needs, especially in the public school system. They also argued—and rightfully so as it turned out—that Bredesen would seek a property tax increase as soon as money for the Oilers had been secured. Meanwhile, proponents of the stadium said it would improve the city's entertainment offerings and help the city recruit large businesses. They pointed out that the stadium would clear a long-neglected industrial sector of Nashville and provide Tennessee State University with a new place to play football games. Proponents also had something opponents didn't have: enough money to pay for billboards, television commercials, and even pep rallies.

Through the debate, stadium advocates also maintained that an NFL team would be a plus for Nashville's image and that it would help the city in its quest to keep pace with cities like Atlanta and Charlotte. That argument was eerily similar to one that had been raised many times in Nashville before. Back in 1900, Nashville's business leaders were saying their city wasn't growing fast enough, that it needed to shake its image as a bastion of the Old South, and that it wasn't doing enough to keep up with other southern cities like Atlanta and Birmingham. In 1996, many were arguing that Nashville wasn't growing fast enough, that it needed to shake its image as Music City U.S.A., and that it wasn't doing enough to keep up with other southern cities like Atlanta and Charlotte.

On May 5, 1996, in a record turnout, 59 percent of Davidson County voters chose to move ahead with the stadium. Under Bredesen's original plan, Nashville's NFL stadium would have been completed in time for the 1998 season. But the referendum delayed construction. While the Oilers waited for their new facility, they played for one year in the Liberty Bowl in Memphis and one year at Vanderbilt stadium. Attendance was poor at both sites. The team didn't help its case by committing one public relations blunder after another. At one point, Adams reneged on his promise to change the team's name. At another, the team admitted that it had no intention of spending any money on advertising until the new stadium was ready.

On August 27, 1999, sixty-seven thousand people packed into a brand new stadium in downtown Nashville. It was an exciting moment for Nashville, the night that put an end to Nashville's four-year wait for its new facility and its new team. It was also a strange night for the Nashville business community, still reeling from two pieces of business news. The first was Dell Computer's announcement that it would build a new manufacturing facility in Nashville in exchange for the city's decision to give it the largest tax break in its history. The second was AmSouth's announcement that it would fire over a thousand people who had previously worked at Nashville's largest bank. Adding to the strange atmosphere was the fact that under First American's agreement to sponsor the NFL team prior to being taken over by AmSouth, the First American logo was still plastered on the scoreboard at the new stadium and that every Titans first down was described as a "First American First Down" by the play-by-play announcers on the radio.

The Tennessee Titans, as the Oilers had been rechristened during the off-season, wasted no time in giving the crowd something to cheer about. On the game's first play, backup quarterback Neal O'Donnell completed a bomb to receiver Yancey Thigpen—addressing what had been one of the team's main weaknesses of a year earlier in the lack of a deep passing threat. Even though it was only an exhibition game, those in attendance were loud and boisterous, described by a television announcer as "the most enthusiastic crowd I have ever seen at a pre-season game."

In a way, that was almost a shame. It was such a historic night in Nashville that there was no telling how many ghosts were out. Had it been quieter, the sixty-seven thousand people might have been able to make out another noise echoing off the banks of the Cumberland River—the sound of hundreds of people building warships and barges at that precise site years earlier. Had it been darker in the stadium, the fans might have been able to make out the outline of a shoe factory that once stood in the stadium parking lot. Had they looked closely at that factory, they might have seen two men, a father and son team named Jarman, working feverishly inside that plant to come up with a plan to make a dress shoe that sold for less than $5. Had the football fans looked the other direction, they might have seen the outline of a house long since burned to the ground in the East Nashville fire of 1916. And had they looked closely at that house, they might have seen a man named Joel Cheek staying up late at night mixing coffee beans in his attempt to come up with the perfect combination. Down Woodland, at the crossroads that eventually became known as Five Points, they might have heard a headstrong entrepreneur named Horace Greeley Hill as he climbed down from a streetcar, directing his lieutenants to have a new store opened at that location by Monday. And across the river, below the giant buildings that dominated Nashville's skyline, they would have seen all sorts of people: hot-shot brokers walking around with cigars in their mouths and stock certificates in their coat pockets; insurance salesmen paying calls on everyone from the wealthy to the working class; flamboyant lawyers explaining their plan to start a national fried chicken enterprise; and pharmacists plotting ways to turn their small businesses into full-blown surgical supply companies.

Chapter 1

1. *Nashville Tennessean* magazine, June 6, 1937.
2. *Chattanooga News*, April 19, 1900.
3. *Nashville Banner*, November 10, 1904.
4. Waller, *Nashville in the 1890s*, 262.
5. Jack Knox, *Riverman* (Nashville: Abingdon Press, 1971), 18–19.
6. *Nashville Banner*, April 6, 1907.
7. Louis Brownlow, *A Passion for Politics* (University of Chicago, 1955), 181–82.
8. *Automobile Quarterly*, Winter 1993.

Chapter 2

1. James Penn Pilkington, *The United Methodist Publishing House: A History* (Nashville: Cokesbury Press, 1968), 320–21.
2. *Christian Advocate*, April 25, 1861.
3. Paul Conkin, *Gone with the Ivy* (Knoxville: University of Tennessee Press, 1985), 17.
4. J. M. Frost, *Sunday School Board: History and Work* (Nashville: Broadman Press, 1914), 21.
5. Ibid., 82.
6. Walter Shurden, *The Sunday School Board: Ninety Years of Service.* (Nashville: Broadman Press, 1981), 57.
7. Ibid., 57.
8. *Nashville American*, January 4, 1901.
9. Ibid.
10. *Nashville Tennessean* magazine, June 6, 1937.

Chapter 3

1. Arch Trawick's memoirs.
2. Trawick.

3. Ibid.

4. *Nashville Banner*, January 6, 1899. After an exhaustive search, I concluded that this was probably Hill's first newspaper ad.

5. *Nashville Globe*, October 4, 18, and 25, 1907.

6. Horace Wade, *Opportunity* magazine (unknown date and issue; copy provided courtesy of Joel Cheek's grandson Joel Cheek).

7. *Nashville Banner*, October 17, 1898.

8. *Nashville Banner*, January 10, 1903.

9. It should be pointed out that in a 1939 letter to General Foods Corp., Joel Cheek's son Robert Cheek said his father had been present when Roosevelt drank his cup of coffee at The Hermitage and that the president did, in fact, say it was "good to the last drop." It is hard to believe, however, that Joel Cheek would have been in a better place to hear what Roosevelt said than the reporters.

10. *Ladies Home Journal*, June 1922.

11. *Saturday Evening Post*, January 5, 1946.

12. *Printers Ink*, September 22, 1927.

13. *Nashville Banner*, April 6 and May 4, 1915.

14. Nancy Rubin, *American Empress: The Life and Times of Marjorie Merriweather Post* (New York: Villard Books, 1995), 137.

15. *Nashville Banner*, April 22, 1910.

16. *New Republic*, April 4, 1928.

17. *Nashville Tennessean*, April 5, 1968.

18. *Circle*, a Belmont University publication, Winter 1999.

19. *Nation's Business*, September 1969.

20. *Tennessean*, July 29, 1994.

Chapter 4

1. *Nashville Banner*, November 2, 1901.

2. Excerpts from a speech by Jesse Wills at the National Life Pearl Jubilee in 1932.

3. *Nashville Banner*, December 27, 1901.

4. Era Irene Emmons, *The Thrift Family: The Story of the Life & Casualty Insurance Co.* (Nashville: Life & Casualty Co., 1943), 23–24.

5. *Our Shield*, 1922.

6. *Mirror*, n.d.

7. R. Carlyle Buley, *The American Life Convention: A Study in the History of Life Insurance* (New York: Appleton-Century-Crotis, 1953), 111–12.

8. A devout Church of Christ member, Johnson moved to the campus of David Lipscomb College after she retired and donated almost all her money to the college. "Granny" Johnson, as she eventually became known, lived until 1959.

9. *Our Shield*, October 24, 1922.

10. *Our Shield*, September 22, 1925.

11. *Nashville Tennessean* magazine, August 17, 1952.

12. *Our Shield*, December 1925.

13. *Our Shield*, April 20, 1925.

14. Ibid.

15. Ibid.

16. *Nashville Banner*, May 9, 1926.

17. *Nashville Banner*, May 23, 1926.

18. *Nashville Tennessean* magazine, August 15, 1937.

19. *Nashville Tennessean*, March 11, 1928.

Chapter 5
1. Wilbur Creighton, *Building of Nashville* (Nashville: Wilbur Creighton, 1969), 165.
2. James E. Caldwell, *Recollections of a Life Time* (Nashville: Baird-Ward, 1923), 220.
3. Unpublished history of Citizen's Bank, provided courtesy of Citizen's Bank.
4. James R. Kellam Jr., *Bootstraps: A History of Commerce Union Bank* (Nashville: Commerce Union, 1967), 32.
5. *Nashville Tennessean* magazine, October 27, 1963.
6. *Time*, June 8, 1931.
7. John Berry McFerrin, *Caldwell and Company: A Southern Financial Empire* (Nashville: Vanderbilt University Press, 1969), 33.
8. Jesse Hill Ford, *Mister Potter and His Bank* (Commerce Union Bank, 1977), 38–39.
9. McFerrin, 261.
10. Ibid., 133.
11. The account of the conversation between Davis and Delano is according to Andrew Benedict.
12. *Nashville Tennessean* magazine, October 27, 1963.
13. *Nashville Tennessean*, November 5, 1930.
14. *Nashville Tennessean*, November 13, 1930.
15. *Nashville Tennessean* magazine, October 20, 1963.
16. McFerrin, 191.
17. *Nashville Tennessean* magazine, October 20, 1963.
18. *Time*, March 13, 1933.
19. *Nashville Tennessean*, March 15, 1933.

Chapter 6
1. Wilbur Creighton Sr., *Toil and Turmoil* (unpublished manuscript, written about 1950), 4.
2. Ibid., 137.
3. *NABRICO News* (company newsletter), January 1958, 2.
4. *Nashville Tennessean*, July 4, 1943.
5. Hardaway Construction of Columbus is unrelated to the Nashville construction company also named Hardaway that was formed years later.
6. Creighton Sr., 146.
7. *Tennessean*, December 17, 1973.

Chapter 7
1. *Old Hickory, Tennessee*, a brochure produced by the Nashville Industrial Corp. (undated).
2. *Nashville Banner*, July 23, 1923.
3. *New York Times*, April 9, 1924.
4. *Nashville Tennessean*, December 3, 1939.
5. Creed Black, *Parsonage to Publisher: The Life of Silliman Evans, 1894–1955* (unpublished manuscript, written about 1956), 158.
6. *Business Week*, November 3, 1956.

Chapter 8
1. Albert Cunniff, "Muscle Behind the Music: The Life and Times of Jim Denny," in the *Journal of Country Music*, vol. 9, nos. 1, 2, 3.

2. Ibid.

3. Charles K. Wolfe, *Tennessee Strings: The Story of Country Music in Tennessee* (Knoxville: University of Tennessee Press), 75.

4. "A Handshake and a Promise," a twenty-fifth anniversary publication produced by Acuff-Rose in 1968.

5. Chet Atkins with Bill Neely, *Country Gentleman* (Chicago: Henry Regnery Co, 1974), 172.

6. "A Handshake and a Promise."

7. *Broadcasting*, January 28, 1963.

8. Atkins, 123.

9. Country Music Foundation, *Pickers, Slickers, Cheatin' Hearts & Superstars: Country: The Music and the Musicians* (New York: Abbeville Press, 1988), 93–94.

10. Buddy Killen with Tom Carter, *By the Seat of My Pants: My Life in Country Music* (New York: Simon & Schuster, 1993), 127.

11. *Nashville Tennessean*, March 3, 1963.

12. A couple of years later, Holly and his band were touring the Midwest when Holly decided to book a charter flight to get them to Minnesota. Jennings was origi- nally supposed to be on that flight—which crashed and killed everyone on board—but gave up his seat at the last minute to make way for a fellow band member.

13. Country Music Foundation, 455.

14. Ibid, 407.

Chapter 9

1. *New York Times*, May 14, 1967.

2. *Manufacturer's Record*, June 1949.

3. *Wall Street Journal*, July 20, 1949.

4. *Nashville Banner*, May 20, 1977.

5. *Business Week*, August 7, 1971.

Chapter 10

1. Jim Cheek Jr. is a grandson of Cheek-Neal Coffee founder Joel Cheek.

2. *Nashville American*, February 6, 1898.

3. *Nashville Banner*, November 14, 1930.

4. *American Business*, May 1947.

5. *Sales Management*, February 1, 1940.

6. *Sales Management*, May 1, 1939.

7. Ibid.

8. Amelia Whitsitt Edwards, *Growing up in Edgefield* (Nashville: Amelia Whitsitt Edwards, 1998), 90.

9. *The Magazine of Wall Street*, June 27, 1953, 411.

10. *Business Week*, July 7, 1951, 116–17.

11. *Nashville Banner*, December 17, 1958.

12. *Nashville Tennessean*, June 18, 1965.

13. *New York Times*, August 5, 1956.

14. *Tennessean*, October 16, 1994.

15. *New York Times*, September 8, 1968.

16. *Nashville Banner*, February 19, 1970.

17. *New York Times*, March 11, 1973.

18. *Wall Street Journal*, September 17, 1970.

19. *Business Week*, July 7, 1975.

20. *Nashville Banner*, August 13, 1973.

21. *Business Week*, July 7, 1975.

Chapter 11

1. James R. Kellam Jr., *Bootstraps: A History of Commerce Union Bank* (Nashville: Commerce Union, 1967), 44.

2. "Advantage Interviews Sam Fleming," *Advantage* magazine, July 1979.

3. *Journal of Country Music*, vol. 11, no. 2.

4. *New York Times*, January 6, 1969.

5. Third National leased its old building to J. C. Bradford & Co. Years after Bradford left, the building was converted into a Courtyard by Marriott Hotel.

6. Between 1972 and 1974, Commerce Union's holding company was called Tennessee Valley Bancorp.

Chapter 12

1. "The Untold Story," an unpublished NLT history, 3.

2. Burton died in 1966. His widow left the Nine Hills property to David Lipscomb, which sold it to be converted into a residential and commercial complex called Burton Hills. Burton left over a hundred descendants, the most famous of whom is a great-granddaughter named Amy Grant.

3. *Nashville Tennessean*, April 27, 1969.

4. *Nashville Tennessean*, November 7, 1956.

5. Much more detail about the Opryland concept and its significance to Nashville is included in chapter 23.

6. *Business Week*, May 9, 1983.

7. *Nashville Banner*, November 24, 1981.

8. *Wall Street Journal*, April 29, 1982.

9. *Nashville Banner*, May 20, 1982.

10. *Wall Street Journal*, May 26, 1982.

Chapter 13

1. Unpublished manuscript on the life of Jack Massey (copy of which was obtained from Barbara Massey Rogers), 25.

2. "Living Legends," a 1989 video tape featuring an interview with Jack Massey.

3. "Interview with Dr. Lawrence Jackson," video, [1985?].

4. *New Yorker*, February 14, 1970, 40.

5. *Nashville Tennessean*, January 27, 1964.

6. *New Yorker*, February 14, 1970, 40.

7. *Nashville* magazine, April 1969.

8. *Nashville Tennessean*, May 2, 1968.

9. *Fortune*, October 1968.

10. *Nashville* magazine, November 1968.

11. *Nashville Tennessean*, August 21, 1969.

12. *Business Week*, February 28, 1970.

13. *Fortune*, March 1970.

14. *Nashville Banner*, September 14, 1970.

15. *Wall Street Journal*, September 4, 1970.

16. *Business Week*, September 14, 1970.

Chapter 14

1. Tom Flake, "Nashville Banner" (historical essay on file at Nashville public library's Nashville Room).

2. *Nashville Banner*, March 18, 1903.

3. *Nashville Tennessean*, April 26, 1908.

4. *Nashville Globe*, April 12, 1907.

5. Creed Black, *Parsonage to Publisher: The Life of Silliman Evans, 1894–1955* (unpublished manuscript, written about 1956), 39.

6. Black, 112.

7. *Nashville Tennessean*, January 22, 1941.

8. Black, 163.

9. *U.S. News and World Report*, February 24, 1956.

10. *Nashville Banner*, May 3, 1976.

11. *Tennessean*, April 7, 1976. Two decades later, Hugh Walker's son Henry Walker became a critic of the *Tennessean* through a column in the *Nashville Scene*.

12. Al Neuharth, *Confessions of an SOB* (New York: Doubleday, 1989), 191.

13. *Nashville Scene*, June 24, 1999.

Chapter 15

1. Steve Watkins, *The Black O: Racism and Redemption in an American Corporate Empire* (Athens, Georgia: University of Georgia Press, 1997), 109.

2. Ibid., 174.

3. *Wall Street Journal*, April 6, 1996.

4. *Tennessean*, October 19, 1982.

5. *New York Times*, April 9, 1992.

6. *Forbes*, April 27, 1992.

Chapter 16

1. *Tennessean*, January 6, 1985.

2. *Nashville Tennessean*, June 24, 1937.

Chapter 17

1. Koch remained in the oil business. In 1999, Koch Industries was the second-largest privately held company in the United States.

2. Life & Casualty Insurance Co. founder Andrew Mizell Burton was named after Andrew Mizell III's grandfather, a grocery wholesaler in Nashville at the turn of the century.

Chapter 18

1. *Time*, October 22, 1951.

2. Walter Newton Vernon Jr., *The United Methodist Publishing House: A History From 1870 to 1988* (Nashville: Abingdon Press, 1989), 432.

3. *The Nation*, January 19, 1957.

4. *Nashville Tennessean*, April 12, 1969.

5. Vernon, 468.

6. *Tennessean*, November 20, 1989.

7. *Nashville Tennessean*, July 15, 1962.

8. James L. Sullivan, *God Is My Record* (Nashville: Broadman Press, 1974), 90.

9. *Nashville Tennessean*, November 6, 1971.

10. *Nashville Tennessean*, September 7, 1968.

11. Sam Moore, *American by Choice* (Nelson, 1998), 51.

12. Ibid, 125.

13. *Wall Street Journal*, February 6, 1995.

Chapter 19

1. *Nashville Tennessean*, August 21, 1967.
2. *New York Times*, February 26, 1970; *Business Week*, May 30, 1970.
3. "Living Legends," a 1989 video featuring an interview with Jack Massey.
4. Ibid.
5. In the 1980s, Rodgers became National Finance chairman of the Republican Party and later the American ambassador to France. Incredibly, he was the third of four consecutive Republican Party Finance chairman to be from Nashville. Others included David K. (Pat) Wilson, Ted Welch, and Mike Curb.

Chapter 20

1. *Nashville Banner*, August 30, 1978.
2. *Forbes*, May 4, 1987.
3. *Wall Street Journal*, March 28, 1997.
4. *Fortune*, July 6, 1998.
5. *Tennessean*, August 27, 1995.
6. *New York Times*, August 14, 1994.

Chapter 21

1. *Wall Street Journal*, January 29, 1980.
2. "Nissan in Tennessee," by Nissan Motor Manufacturing Corp. (1983), 28.
3. *Nashville Banner*, February, 5, 1981.
4. *Wall Street Journal*, May 14, 1984.
5. Joe Sherman, *In the Rings of Saturn* (New York: Oxford University Press, 1994), 82.
6. *Nashville Banner*, July 25, 1985.
7. *Wall Street Journal*, December 4, 1990.
8. *Wall Street Journal*, July 27, 1995.
9. *Tennessean*, March 5, 1999.

Chapter 22

1. Buddy Killen with Tom Carter, *By the Seat of My Pants* (New York: Simon & Schuster, 1993), 61.
2. *Broadcasting*, January 28, 1963.
3. National Life executives Walter Robinson Jr. and Neil Craig II also credit Waugh with coming up with the idea for Opryland. But two other National Life employees claimed Opryland was their idea. One was one-time WSM president Jack DeWitt. The other was Elmer Alley, longtime program director at WSMV-TV.
4. *Tennessean*, April 22, 1973.
5. *Tennessean*, May 13, 1973.
6. Under the terms of the UDAG grant, the hotel eventually began contributing to a fund that, according to federal regulations, should have been used to spend money to help people who live in Nashville's "pocket of poverty." In 1994, about five hundred thousand dollars of that money was used to build a water taxi dock at Riverfront Park for Gaylord Entertainment Co.
7. *Nashville Banner*, July 6, 1992.
8. *Tennessean*, October 15, 1994.
9. *Tennessean*, May 5, 1996.

Chapter 23
1. The former governor's mansion on West End Avenue was torn down in 1979 to make way for a Popeye's fast food restaurant.
2. As it turns out, Met Fed was more accurate about when the Cool Springs land would be developed. By 1995, that property contained several large retailers, including a Home Depot.
3. *Forbes*, September 24, 1984.
4. *Forbes*, December 15, 1986.
5. *Tennessean*, February 16, 1990.
6. *Nashville Scene*, February 22, 1990.

Chapter 24
1. *New York Times* magazine, July 21, 1969.
2. *New York Times* magazine, March 26, 1978.
3. Brian Mansfield and Stephen Thomas Erlewine, Randy Travis Profile in *All-Music Guide*.
4. Bruce Feiler, *Dreaming Out Loud: Garth Brooks, Wynonna Judd, Wade Hayes, and the Changing Face of Nashville* (New York: Avon Books, 1998), 110.
5. Feiler, 185.
6. *Forbes*, March 2, 1992.
7. *Ibid.*
8. Feiler, 209.
9. Dan Daley, *Nashville's Unwritten Rules: Inside the Business of Country Music* (New York: Overlook Press, 1999), 58.
10. *Tennessean*, November 29, 1995.

Chapter 25
1. *Wall Street Journal*, April 13, 1987.
2. *Nashville Banner*, November 12, 1993.
3. Sandy Lutz and E. Preston Gee, *The For-Profit Health Care Revolution: The Growing Impact of Investor-Owned Health Systems* (Chicago: Irwin Professional Publishing, 1995), 79.
4. *Wall Street Journal*, October 5, 1993.
5. *Tennessean*, December 9, 1993.
6. *Wall Street Journal*, October 11, 1994.

I conducted more than 160 interviews for the book between July 1998 and August 1999. About half of them were done via telephone and the other half in person. Everyone was given the opportunity to speak "off the record," which meant that the tape recorder was off for that part of the interview. I ensured everyone I interviewed that anything said "off the record" would not be presented in the book in a way that would be traceable. Cassette tapes of the interviews will eventually become the property of the Massey School of Business at Belmont University.

There were several sources that were consulted so many times that I would have to cite them for almost every single chapter and instead I will cite them here. The first two were Don Doyle's two-part series on Nashville history, published as *Nashville in the New South* (Knoxville: University of Tennessee Press, 1985) and *Nashville Since the 1920s* (Knoxville: University of Tennessee Press, 1985). I probably consulted Doyle's book on twenty of my twenty-five chapters.

Another source was the annual city directories, which I regarded as the definitive authority on when people moved to Nashville, where they lived, and where their businesses were located.

A fourth source was the *Moody's Directory of Financial Companies*, from which I pulled financial data on various companies.

Chapter 1

Interviews:
David Carlton, Wilbur Creighton Jr., Robert Dale, Don Doyle, Sam Fleming, Jack May, David Rollins, Lem Stevens Jr., Barry Walker.

Nashville's appearance and self-image:
Nashville Banner: April 19 and 21, 1900; Sept. 7, 1900; Nov. 10 and 11, 1904; Dec. 6 and 23, 1904; March 28, 1908.
Tennessean: June 6, 1937; Oct. 11, 1964.
Waller, William. *Nashville in the 1890s*. Nashville: Vanderbilt University Press, 1970.
————. *Nashville: 1900-1910*. Nashville: Vanderbilt University Press, 1972.

The state of manufacturing in turn-of-the-century Nashville:
Nashville Banner, Sept. 15, 1895; Sept. 16, 1895; March 10, 1902; April 6, 1907; July 23, 1923; April 6, 1924; Nov. 15, 1930; Dec. 5, 1930.
Tennessean, Jan. 19, 1908.

L&N railroad:
"A Pictorial History of the Louisville and Nashville Railroad." (Pamphlet produced by L&N in the 1970s.)
Nashville Banner: April 10, 1901.
Crew, H. W. *History of Nashville, Tennessee*. Nashville: Publishing House of the M.E. Church, 1890.
Klein, Maury. *History of the L&N Railroad*. New York: Macmillan, 1972.
Manufacturer's Record, June 1947.

Flour milling:
Dawson, Clarence. "History of the Flour Milling Industry of Nashville." A master's thesis at George Peabody School for Teachers (1931).
Rogers, Glenn. "Localization of a Few Select Industries in Nashville." A master's thesis at George Peabody School for Teachers (1932).

Iron foundries:
Gray & Dudley's twelve hundred page catalog.
Gray & Dudley prospectus, 1937.
Lewis, W. David. *Sloss Furnaces and the Rise of the Birmingham District*. Tuscaloosa, Ala.: University of Alabama Press, 1994.
Manufacturer's Record, Oct. 1955.

Rafts on the river:
Douglas, Byrd. *Steamboatin' on the Cumberland*. Nashville: Tennessee Book Company, 1961.
Knox, Jack. *Riverman*. Abingdon Press, 1971.

Martha White:
Nashville Banner: March 29, 1954; Jan. 16, 1988.
Nashville magazine: April 1968.
Tennessean: April 8, 1956, Feb. 27, 1965; July 1, 1968; Aug. 1, 1975.

Gerst:
Nashville Tennessean: March 11, 1933.

Marathon Motor Works:
Automobile Quarterly, Winter 1993.

Chapters 2 and 18

Interviews:
John Ambrose, Mike Arrington, David Bailey Sr., Ed Benson, T. B. Boyd III, Chris
    Chamberlain, James Clark, Lloyd Elder, Bob Feaster, Frank Gulley, Bobby
    Lovett, Robert McNeely, David McQuiddy Jr., Reavis Mitchell, Sam Moore,
    Ralph Mosley, Dortch Oldham, Ron Pitkin, John Procter, Bill Sherman, Chip
    Smith, James Sullivan, James Thomas, Ray Waddle, Ted Welch.

The United Methodist Publishing House:
Conkin, Paul. *Gone with the Ivy*. Knoxville: University of Tennessee Press, 1985.
Pilkington, James Penn. *The United Methodist Publishing House: A History*. Nashville:
    United Methodist Publishing House, 1968.
Nashville Banner: Sept. 7, 1951; Sept. 19, 1961; Oct. 30, 1974; Oct. 29, 1975; Dec. 20,
    1985; May 13, 1988; Jan. 31, 1989.
Tennessean: Sept. 14, 1945; June 19, 1948; Sept. 15, 1950; Sept. 13, 1951; Oct. 1, 1957;
    June 28, 1959; July 21, 1959; Aug. 20, 1959; Oct. 6, 1962; July 11, 1963; July 13,
    1966; April 27, 1968; May 1, 1968; April 12, 1969; Feb. 5, 1970; March 30, 1973;
    Oct. 19, 1980; Nov. 2, 1980; Sept. 8, 1983; July 10, 1985; Oct. 31, 1985; April 17,
    1988; Oct. 27, 1988; March 2, 1989; Nov. 20, 1989; April 29, 1990; June 21, 1990;
    Sept. 25, 1991; Feb. 2, 1992; Dec. 18, 1994; April 25, 1996; Feb. 9, 1997.
Vernon, Walter Newton, Jr. *The United Methodist Publishing House: A History*,
    Volume II. Nashville: United Methodist Publishing House, 1989.

The Baptist Sunday School Board:
Baker, Robert A. *The Story of the Sunday School Board*. Nashville: Broadman Press,
    1966.
Burroughs, P. E. *Fifty Fruitful Years: 1891–1941*. Nashville: Broadman Press, 1946.
Frost, J. M. *Sunday School Board: History and Work*. Nashville: Broadman Press, 1914.
Nashville Banner: July 13, 1923; Feb. 1, 1962; Jan. 26, 1966; Dec. 12, 1969; Aug. 14,
    1970; May 20, 1993.
Shurden, Walter. *The Sunday School Board: Ninety Years of Service*. Nashville:
    Broadman Press, 1981.
New York Times: Aug. 12, 1979; March 30, 1981; Oct. 9, 1988.
Tennessean: Dec. 13, 1939; May 11, 1941; June 11, 1942; June 3, 1947; Jan. 23, 1949;
    July 1, 1951; April 12, 1956; Dec. 5, 1957; Jan. 29, 1958; May 13, 1958; July 15,
    1962; Aug. 9, 1968; Aug. 23, 1970; Oct. 30, 1971; Nov. 6, 1971; Nov. 13, 1971; Nov.
    26, 1971; Dec. 31, 1971; Feb. 2, 1972; Jan. 12, 1991; Jan. 18, 1991; Feb. 9, 1991;
    March 10, 1991; June 3, 1991; Aug. 31, 1992; Aug. 19, 1993; Feb. 14, 1995; June 11,
    1998; June 20, 1998.

The National Baptist Publishing Board:
Lovett, Bobby. *A Black Man's Dream: The First One Hundred Years*. Mega Corporation,
    1993.
Nashville Banner: Sept. 5, 1968; Nov. 7, 1968.
Tennessean: Nov. 21, 1988.

The National Baptist Convention's Sunday School Publishing Board:
Nashville Banner: Jan. 22, 1958; Sept. 7, 8, 9, 17, 1960; April 19, 1962; May 16, 1963;
    Aug. 27, 1965; May 8, 1970; Jan. 24, 1985; June 20, 1989; Jan. 24, 1990; Feb. 19,
    1992.

Tennessean: Nov. 8, 1957; Sept. 11, 1961; May 17, 1963; July 4, 1965; Sept. 6, 7, 1968; Sept. 9, 1972; Sept. 8, 1973; May 7, 1983; Jan. 24, 1988; Feb. 25, 1989; June 18, 1989; Dec. 6, 1990; Feb. 19, 1992; March 10, 1992; Sept. 9, 1993; Jan. 19, 1995; Feb. 26, 1995.

Thomas Nelson:
Moore, Sam. *American by Choice*. Nashville: Thomas Nelson, 1998.
Tennessean: March 10, 1996, April 18, 1996, Sept. 22, 1996, Nov. 22, 1996.
Wall Street Journal: Feb. 6, 1995.

Nashville's printing industry:
Advantage: Sept. 1979.
American: Jan. 4, 1901.
Crabb, Alfred L. *Nashville: Personality of a City*. New York: Bobbs-Merrill, 1960.
Egerton, John. *Nashville: Faces of Two Centuries*. Nashville: PlusMedia Inc., 1979.
Kaser, David. *A Directory of the Book and Printing Industries of Ante-bellum Nashville*. New York: New York Public Library, 1966.
Morrison, Andrew. *Nashville: Engelhardt's Series of American Cities*. St. Louis & Nashville, 1892.
Nashville Banner: April 18, 1900.
Nashville!: Aug. 1973.
Publisher's Weekly: Nov. 15, 1976.

Chapter 3

Interviews:
Wentworth Caldwell, James Cheek Jr., John Cheek Jr., Will T. Cheek Jr., John Hardcastle, Jane Hill Head, Peggy Grow, Bill Troutt.

H. G. Hill:
American: Oct. 20 and 23, 1907.
H. G. Hill Co.: *100 Family Recipes Celebrating Our 100th Anniversary*. Nashville: H. G. Hill Co., 1996.
Nashville Banner: Dec. 17, 1898; Jan. 6, 1899; Feb. 23 and 24, 1899; Jan. 3 and 9, 1902; March 7 and 28, 1902; April 1, 1902; April 3, 1907; Oct. 25, 1907; April 8 and 22, 1910; July 15, 1923; Nov. 4, 1960; Sept. 13, 1962; Sept. 13, 1963; Feb. 12, 1975; June 17, 1987.
Tennessean: April 17, 1910; Nov. 13, 1945; June 4, 1950; July 19, 1956; Aug. 2, 1957; July 4, 1962; Feb. 27, 1966; Jan. 18, 1969; Feb. 11, 1975; Sept. 26, 1993; July 29, 1994.
Trawick, Arch. Papers on file at State Library and Archives.
Waterways Journal: Jan. 11, 1958.

Cheek-Neal:
American: Oct. 20 and 23, 1907.
Editor & Publisher: Dec. 21, 1935.
Nashville Banner: Oct. 17, 1898; July 17, 1899; June 4, 1901; Oct. 5, 1901; Nov. 9 and 25, 1901; Jan. 4, 1902; March 29, 1902; Jan. 10, 1903; March 14 and 30, 1903; May 13, 1905; Dec. 29, 1906; Oct. 22, 25 and 26, 1907; Feb. 10, 1915; March 24, 1915; Nov. 5, 1930.
Newsweek: Jan. 8, 1962.
New York Times: July 28, 1928.

Printers' Ink: Sept. 22, 1927; Oct. 11, 1928; Feb. 2, 1933.

Rubin, Nancy. *American Empress: The Life and Times of Marjorie Merriweather Post.* New York: Villard Books, 1995.

Tennessean: Nov. 11, 1928.

Tennessee Historic Quarterly: Fall 1967.

Lay's:

Lay's prospectus, June 1956.

Nation's Business: Sept. 1969.

Tennessean: April 5, 1968.

Chain stores in general:

Barron's: Aug. 20, 1928.

Nation: Nov. 28, 1928.

New Republic: April 4, 1928.

Printers' Ink: July 6, 1922.

Chapters 4 and 12

Interviews:

J. C. Bradford Jr., Nelson Burton, C. A. Craig II, Guilford Dudley Jr., Sam Fleming, Douglas Henry Jr., Sydney Keeble Jr., Robins Ledyard, George McIntosh, Jack Nuismer Jr., J. Bradbury Reed, Walter Robinson Jr., Bill Tyne, Bob Walker, Irving Waugh, E. W. (Bud) Wendell, Ridley Wills II.

National Life & Accident:

Business Week: May 9, 1983.

Nashville Banner: Oct. 18, 1901; Nov. 2, 1901; Dec. 27, 1901; Jan. 19, 1908; May 9, 16 and 23, 1926; Oct. 22, 1965; April 23, 24, and 25, 1973; Feb. 20 and 21, 1974; March 16, 1974; Dec. 8, 1976; Aug. 2 and 3, 1978; Oct. 3, 6 and 26, 1978; Dec. 5 and 7, 1978; Jan. 9, 1979; Feb. 20 and 27, 1979; March 5, 1979; May 23 and 30, 1979; June 4, 1979; June 25, 1979; Sept. 13, 1979; Sept. 3, 1980; May 14, 1981; June 14, 1981; Nov. 24, 1981; May 20, 1982; June 2, 16, 25, and 29, 1982; July 1, 2, and 5, 1982; Sept. 29 and 30, 1982; Jan. 19, 1983; Feb. 24, 1983; July 29, 1983; Aug. 16, 1983; Jan. 28, 1984; Jan. 10, 1985; April 2 and 19, 1990; May 12, 1993.

New York Times: Jan. 6, 1969; Feb. 9, 1969; March 25, 1969; Nov. 5, 1969.

Our Shield, National Life & Accident newsletter.

Stamper, Wallace. *The National Life Story*. Nashville: New York: Appleton-Century-Crofts, 1968.

Tennessean: Feb. 5 and 19, 1928; March 11, 1928; Aug. 19, 1928; Nov. 11, 1928; Aug. 15, 1937; Aug. 17, 1952; Nov. 7, 8 and 30 1956; Dec. 9, 16, 23 and 30, 1956; Jan. 13, 20, 23, 25, and 27, 1957; Feb. 3 and 24, 1957; April 30, 1957; May 8, 1957; June 19, 1957; May 8, 1962; Oct. 23, 1965; Sept. 24 and 25, 1968; Oct. 19, 1968; Nov. 21, 1968; Dec. 31, 1968; Sept. 28, 1969; Oct. 13, 1969; Nov. 21, 1969; Jan. 5, 1970; July 2, 1970; Dec. 12, 1970; March 13, 1971; March 16, 1972; May 21, 1972; Sept. 30, 1972; Jan. 14, 1973, March 4, 1973; April 22, 23, 24, 25, and 28, 1973; May 13, 1973; March 11 and 13, 1974; Dec. 9, 1976; Oct. 7, 1978; Dec. 5, 1978; Feb. 24, 1980; March 12, 1980; May 23, 1980; Dec. 5, 1980; May 20, 1982; June 3, 5, 17, and 24, 1982; July 4 and 5, 1982; Sept. 14, 1982; March 22, 1984; Dec. 13, 1984; March 23 and 24, 1985; Feb. 18, 1982; May 3 and 14, 1990; Sept. 20, 1990; Dec. 7 and 9, 1990.

Wall Street Journal: Nov. 24, 1969; Sept. 1 and 22, 1981; April 19, 28, and 29, 1982; May 16 and 20, 1982; June 3, 8, 17, 24, and 30, 1982; July 6 and 7, 1982; Jan. 31, 1983; March 14, 1983.

Wills, Jesse. Speech made at National Life's Pearl Jubilee in 1932 (copy of which held by Ridley Wills II).

Life & Casualty:
Mirror (L&C newsletter).
Nashville Banner: Sept. 14, 1955; April 19, 1969; May 12, 1989.
New York Times: Feb. 7, 1960; June 21, 1969.
Emmons, Era Irene. *The Thrift Family: The Story of the Life & Casualty Insurance Co.*, 1943.
Tennessean: May 17 and 18, 1958; Sept. 6, 1958; March 27, 1960; April 3, 1960; Feb. 11, 1962; Sept. 27, 1966; Dec. 2, 1967; April 27, 1969; May 1, 1969; Sept. 15, 1995.
Wall Street Journal: March 10, 1955; Aug. 5, 1955; May 27, 1958.

The nature of industrial insurance:
Buley, R. Carlyle. *The American Life Convention: A Study in the History of Life Insurance*. New York: Appleton-Century-Crotis, 1953.
Stalson, J. Owen. *Marketing Life Insurance: Its History in America*. Cambridge, Mass.: Harvard University Press, 1942.
Institute of Life Insurance. *Life Insurance Fact Book* (annual publication). New York.

Warren Buffett's strategy:
Hagstrom, Robert. *The Warren Buffett Way: Investment Strategies of the World's Greatest Investor*. New York: Wiley & Sons, 1994.

Chapters 5 and 11

Interviews:
James Bass Jr., Andrew Benedict, J. C. Bradford Jr., Brownlee Currey Jr., Bill Farris, Sam Fleming, Gus Haliburton, John Hardcastle, Virginia Lyle, Reavis Mitchell, Edward G. Nelson, William Nelson, Aaron Shelton, David K. (Pat) Wilson.

Written sources:
American: Dec. 14, 1891; Jan. 2, 1909.
Business Week: Nov. 26, 1930.
Caldwell, James E. *Recollections from a Lifetime*. Nashville: Baird-Ward, 1923.
Creighton, Wilbur. *Building of Nashville*. Nashville, 1969.
Ford, Jesse Hill. *Mister Potter and His Bank*. Commerce Union Bank, 1977.
Kellam, James R. Jr. *Bootstraps: A History of Commerce Union Bank (1916–66)*. Nashville: Commerce Union, 1967.
Lovett, Bobby. *The African-American History of Nashville, Tennessee: 1780–1930*. Fayetteville, Arkansas: University of Arkansas Press, 1999.
Manufacturer's Record, Aug. 8, 1929.
McFerrin, John Berry. *Caldwell and Company: A Southern Financial Empire*. Nashville: Vanderbilt University Press, 1939.
Nashville Banner: July 28 and 31, 1935.
Nashville magazine: July 1978.
New York Times: Nov. 6, 1930; Nov. 11, 1930; Nov. 15, 1930; Nov. 20, 1930; Dec. 5, 1930; Dec. 6, 1930.

Tennessean: July 3, 1927; March 1–31, 1933; Nov. 26, 1939; Dec. 3, 6, and 16, 1939; Sept. 16, 1956; Oct. 20 and 27, 1963; Nov. 3, 1963.

Tidwell, Mary Louise Lea. *Luke Lea of Tennessee*. Bowling Green, Ohio: Bowling Green State University Popular Press, 1993.

Time: Nov. 17, 1930; Nov. 24, 1930; Dec. 1, 1930; June 8, 1931.

Time: March 13, 1933.

Wetternau, C. H. "A History of First American." (Unpublished manuscript.)

Chapter 6

Interviews:
Wilbur Creighton Jr., Wilbur Creighton III, Robert C. Mathews Jr., A. J. Dyer III, Jerry Metz, Howard Pruett, Herbert Morris, T. Ray Jackson, Neal Langdon.

Foster-Creighton:
Creighton, Wilbur Jr. *A Paragraph from Nashville's History: The Foster-Creighton Story*, 1974.

The Foster-Creighton Record Since 1885, a complete list of company projects.

Creighton, Wilbur. *Toil and Turmoil*. (Unpublished manuscript.)

Tennessean: July 21, 1984.

Nashville Bridge:
King, Adeline: *The Life of A. J. Dyer*. (Unpublished manuscript.)

NABRICO newsletters from May 1952 and Jan. 1958.

Nashville Banner: July 26, 1951; May 4, 1953; Dec. 24, 1957; Nov. 30, 1967; Sept. 2, 1969; Aug. 1, 1972; March 8, 1973; Dec. 17, 1973; Jan. 30, 1974; Jan. 23, 1979; Oct. 13, 1981; Sept. 30, 1982; April 30, 1983; April 4, 1986; Sept. 15, 1989.

Tennessean: March 25, 1941; April 3, 1941; March 6, 1942; May 22 and 23, 1942; June 10, 1943; July 4, 1943; Feb. 20, 1944; June 18, 1944; Dec. 8, 1944; Aug. 14, 1946; July 13, 1947; July 27, 1948; Sept. 26, 1950; July 3, 1951; Oct. 3, 1954; Dec. 24, 1957; June 3, 1960; July 14, 1961; Dec. 11, 1961; March 4, 1962; Nov. 15 and 29, 1962; May 28, 1963; March 5, 1964; Nov. 19, 1964; Dec. 3, 1964; June 6, 1965; Oct. 20, 1966; May 10, 1969; Nov. 11, 1969; Dec. 17, 1973; Jan. 7, 1975; Aug. 23, 1975; Sept. 17, 1975; March 22, 1981; Sept. 30, 1982; May 7, 1983; March 21, 1984; April 4, 1984; Sept. 19, 1988.

Waterways Journal: Jan. 11, 1958.

Chapter 7

Interviews:
John Brandon, Wilbur Creighton Jr., Richard Elliott, Paul Hall, Julian Kottler, Earl Swensson, Jim Fyke, Maria Tootle.

DuPont:
Business Week: Oct. 5, 1962.

Fortune: Oct. 1950; Dec. 1962; Nov. 1964.

Hall, Paul. "DuPont: Reflections of the Past." (Unpublished collection.)

Nashville Banner: July 13, 14, 15, 18, 19, 21, and 23, 1923; April 8, 9, 10, and 11, 1924.

Nashville magazine: Jan. 1963.

New York Times: Feb. 3 and 5, 1918; April 19, 1920; April 15, 1922; Aug. 8, 1922; Sept. 27, 1922; July 26 and 29, 1923; Aug. 17, 1923; Feb. 12 and 24, 1924; April 9, 11, 12, and 13, 1924.
Rayon Yarn (DuPont Old Hickory Newsletter).
Tennessean: Dec. 3, 1939.

Vultee/Avco:
Barron's: Jan. 11, 1945.
Business Week: Nov. 3, 1956; Aug. 22, 1964.
Forbes: April 2, 1979.
Fortune: March 1940; Feb. 1957.
Manufacturer's Record: July 1940; Nov. 1940; July 1947.
Nashville Banner: July 21, 1951; Aug. 14, 1951; Aug. 26, 1953; March 1 and 31, 1956; Oct. 30, 1956; April 11, 1957; July 2, 1960; Jan. 13, 1961; Sept. 18, 1961; Jan. 25, 1962; Dec. 19, 1962; Oct. 18, 1968; March 16, 1973; Oct. 13, 1976; July 5, 1977; Jan. 20, 1982; June 9, 1983; March 8, 1984; Dec. 3, 1984; July 19, 1985; Aug. 13, 1986; Dec. 26, 1986; May 23, 1987; Oct. 15, 1987; Jan. 29, 1988; May 12, 1988; Aug. 16, 1988; Dec. 14, 1988; Sept. 13, 1989.
Nashville magazine: April 1963.
New York Times: Oct. 6, 1939.
Tennessean: Oct, 6, 1939; Dec. 3, 1939; May 4, 1941; Jan. 6, 1951; July 21, 1951; April 17, 1952; June 22, 1952; Jan. 6, 1954; April 18, 1954; March 28, 1956; Oct. 30, 1956; April 4, 1957; April 3, 1959; Nov. 15, 1960; Dec. 21, 1962; Aug. 23, 1963; July 23, 1963; July 30, 1964; Oct. 1, 1965; April 16, 1966; Jan. 8, 1967; Sept. 2, 1968; March 14, 1969; Jan. 10, 1971; April 20, 1971; July 24, 1980; Oct. 1, 1981; Jan. 21, 1982; April 3, 1982; Feb. 15, 1984; June 10, 1984; June 4, 1986; July 24, 1986; Sept. 26, 1986; March 25, 1987; May 13, 1988; Sept. 22, 1988; Oct. 3, 1989.

Chapters 8 and 24

Many of the topics covered in this book had never been researched in great detail. This was not the case with country music. I am indebted to several country music historians/authors who preceded me such as Ronnie Pugh, Albert Cunniff, Charles Wolfe, Don Cusic, Robert Oermann, and Bill Malone.

Interviews:
Rick Blackburn, Harold Bradley, Jerry Bradley, Tom Collins, C. A. Craig II, Don Cusic, Joe Galante, John Hardcastle, Waylon Jennings, Jerry Kennedy, Buddy Killen, Ken Nelson, Jim Ed Norman, Frances Preston, Aaron Shelton, Joe Talbot III, Irving Waugh, E. W. (Bud) Wendell.

Written sources:
Atkins, Chet and Bill Neely. *Country Gentleman*. Chicago: Henry Regnery Co., 1974.
Broadcasting: Jan. 28, 1963.
Business Week: March 19, 1966.
Country Music Foundation. *Country: The Music and Musicians*. New York: Abbeville Press, 1988.
Daley, Dan. *Nashville's Unwritten Rules: Inside the Business of Country Music*. New York: Overlook Press, 1999.
Economist: March 11, 1978.
Feiler, Bruce. *Dreaming Out Loud: Garth Brooks, Wynonna Judd, Wade Hayes and the Changing Face of Nashville*. New York: Avon Books, 1998.

Forbes: March 2, 1992.
Journal of Country Music: Vol. XI, nos. 1, 2, 3.
Killen, Buddy and Tom Carter. *By the Seat of My Pants: My Life in Country Music*. New York: Simon & Schuster, 1993.
Los Angeles Times: May 1, 1992; Aug. 26, 1992.
Malone, Bill. *Country Music U.S.A.* Austin, Texas: University of Texas Press, 1985.
Nation's Business: March 1993.
Newsweek: April 4, 1966; June 18, 1973.
New York Times: Sept. 21, 1969; May 26, 1978.
Rolling Stone: April 16, 1992.
Wolfe, Charles K. *A Good-Natured Riot: The Birth of the Grand Ole Opry*. Nashville: Country Music Foundation and Vanderbilt University Press, 1999.
Tennessean magazine: March 28, 1948; March 3, 1963.
Time: May 5, 1974; Sept. 18, 1978.

Chapter 9

Interviews:
J. C. Bradford Jr., Fred Bryan, Brownlee Currey Jr., Ray Danner, Sam Fleming, Gus Haliburton, Ronnie Scott, Robert Stamps, Charles Trabue Jr.

Equitable Securities:
Manufacturer's Record: July 1949 (article), plus ads in virtually every issue from about 1945 to 1960.
Nashville magazine: Feb. 1957; July 1968.
New York Times: May 14, 1967; Nov. 10, 1967.
Tennessean: May 4, 1941; April 26, 1945; Feb. 21, 1952; March 2, 1952; Nov. 10 and 23, 1967.
Wall Street Journal: July 20, 1949; March 17, 1955; Nov. 16, 1956; Jan. 18, 1957; Feb. 26, 1963; Nov. 10, 1967.

J. C. Bradford:
Business Week: Aug. 7, 1971.
Nashville Banner: June 4, 1963; Jan. 18, 1966; Oct. 17, 1966; Nov. 12, 1969; March 29, 1971; May 20, 1977; July 16, 1979; Jan. 22, 1980; April 14, 1980; March 12, 1981; Oct. 14, 1983; April 1, 1986.
Tennessean: Oct. 11, 1961; Sept. 7, 1962; Feb. 27, 1965; Dec. 23, 1965; Jan. 8, 1967.

Chapter 10

Interviews:
Elizabeth Barrett, James Cheek Jr., Sam Fleming, James Fowlkes, John Gifford, Dick Hanselmann, Robert Hilton, Franklin Jarman, Robert Hilton, Peter Mangione, Andrew Mizell III, Nell Massey, Joe Russell, Geraldine Stutz, Bill Wills, David K. (Pat) Wilson, Bill Wire II, DeVaughn Woods.
Written Sources:
American Business: April and May 1947.
Barron's: Dec. 27, 1948; May 15, 1950.
Business Week: July 7, 1951; Feb. 25, 1956; June 15, 1957; Jan. 21, 1961; March 10, 1973.

Forbes: Oct. 15, 1970.

Jarman, W. Maxey. *A Businessman Looks at the Bible*. New York: Fleming Revell Co., 1965.

Magazine of Wall Street: June 27, 1953.

Marsten, Richard. *The Spiked Heel*. New York: Fawcett Publications, 1957.

Nashville Banner: April 24, 1924; Nov. 14, 1930; Nov. 28, 1930; May 27, 1950; Feb. 13, 1951; Aug. 3, 1951; Oct. 2, 1953; March 29, 1955; Feb. 17, 1956; Dec. 15 and 17, 1958; Feb. 5, 1960; Sept. 19, 1959; Dec. 19, 1959; June 30, 1960; Oct. 27, 1961; Oct. 4, 1963; Oct. 17, 1968; Feb. 12, 1969; May 9, 1972; Dec. 1, 2, and 4, 1972; Feb. 28, 1973; March 20, 1973; June 20 and 21, 1973; Aug. 13 and 31, 1973; March 28, 1975; June 30, 1975; May 12, 1976; Jan. 4, 5, and 19, 1977; March 23, 1977; April 11 and 15, 1977; Aug. 9 and 10, 1977; Sept. 1, 1977; Oct. 9 and 20, 1978; Dec. 5, 1978; June 11, 1980; Sept. 9 and 25, 1980; Oct. 14 and 27, 1980; Dec. 4, 1980; Feb. 12, 1981; March 16, 1981; May 25, 1981; June 24, 1981; Aug. 25, 1982; Sept. 8, 1983; Oct. 27, 1983; Oct. 11, 1984; April 2, 1986; June 13, 1986; May 19, 1987; Jan. 20, 1990; May 22, 1992.

New York Times: Feb. 18, 1956; Aug 5, 1956; April 16, 1966; Sept. 8, 1968; Nov. 28, 1971; Dec. 5, 1972; Feb. 28, 1973; March 11, 1973; Jan. 3 and 4, 1977.

Sales Management: May 1, 1939; Feb. 1, 1940.

Tennessean: Nov. 18, 1928; Aug. 23, 1938; Feb. 16 and 17, 1939; April 16, 1944; July 30, 1944; Nov. 6, 1945; April 19, 1948; Aug. 12, 1953; Dec. 15, 1953; Feb. 20, 1955; March 30, 1955; May 19, 1955; Sept. 22, 1955; Feb. 17 and 18, 1956; July 19, 1956; Nov. 2, 1957; Dec. 12, 16, 18, and 21, 1958; Feb. 6, 1959; March 31, 1961; Sept. 29, 1961; Oct. 26, 1961; May 12, 1963; Feb. 4, 1964; Aug. 18, 1964; April 20, 1965; June 18, 1965; Aug. 22, 1965; Jan. 17, 1968; Aug. 18 and 28, 1968; May 8, 9, and 11, 1972; Aug. 25, 1972; Oct. 5, 1972; Dec. 4 and 5, 1972; Feb. 28, 1973; Sept. 5, 1973; Dec. 4, 1973; Jan. 13, 1974; Feb. 27, 1974; Nov. 21, 1974; Jan. 4, 5, 9, and 17, 1977; Nov. 17, 1977; June 2, 1978; March 20, 1980; Sept. 9, 1980; Aug. 23, 1984; Nov. 14 and 24, 1985; March 1, 1986; April 4, 1986; July 13, 1986; Aug. 5, 1986; March 28, 1990; Dec. 18, 1990; Sept. 4, 1991.

Wall Street Journal: Jan. 21, 1955; Aug. 10, 1955; July 7, 1975; April 11, 1977; April 3, 1978.

Whitsitt, Amelia Parker and Amelia Whitsitt Edwards. *Growing Up in Edgefield*. Nashville: Amelia Whitsitt Edwards, 1998.

Chapter 13

Interviews:

John Y. Brown Jr., J. C. Bradford Jr., Edward G. Nelson, Guilford Dudley Jr., Richard L. Fulton, Richard H. Fulton, Jim Neal, Bill Willis Jr., John Seigenthaler, Larry Brinton, Thomas Wiseman Jr., Martha Ingram, Marvin Hopper, Hunter Woods, Omega Sattler, Alyne Massey, Barbara Massey Rogers, Dr. Jeff Pennington, Dr. James Sullivan, Ben Betty, Ray Danner, and Dave Wachtel. I was also aided by videotapes on file at Belmont University that quote Thomas Frist Sr., Lawrence Jackson, and Jack Massey.

Kentucky Fried Chicken:

Business Week: June 24, 1967; June 27, 1970.

Nashville Banner: March 6, 1964; March 24, 1969.

Nation's Business: Feb. 1973.

New York Times: June 9, 1968; Jan. 8, 1969; Jan. 17, 1969; April 11, 1969; March 24, 1970.

New Yorker: Feb. 14, 1970.

Tennessean: Dec. 27, 1962; Jan. 27, 1964; Jan. 12, 1965; June 2, 1966; July 21, 1966; Aug. 3, 1966; Nov. 9, 1966; Nov. 18, 1966; Dec. 11, 1966; Jan. 8, 1967; Feb. 1, 1967; May 9, 1967; June 18, 1967; Nov. 15, 1967.

Wall Street Journal: March 18, 1966; April 12, 1968; Oct. 15, 1968; Oct. 24, 1968; Aug. 7, 1969; Aug. 8, 1969; Jan. 21, 1970; Feb. 26, 1970; April 3, 1970.

Minnie Pearl/Whale:

Barron's: Aug. 10, 1970.

Business Week: Feb. 28, 1970; Sept. 19, 1970.

Forbes: June 15, 1968.

Fortune: Oct. 1968, March 1970.

Nashville: Nov. 1968, April 1969.

Nashville Banner: Aug. 1 and 19, 1967; Aug. 13, 1968; March 28, 1969; Nov. 5, 1969; Jan. 29, 1970; Feb. 17, 18, and 19, 1970; March 2 and 4, 1970; July 20 and 23, 1970; Aug. 4, 5, and 17, 1970; Sept. 8, 9, 10, 11, 14, 15, 17, and 21, 1970; Oct. 8, 23, 1970; Oct. 7, 1971; Dec. 23, 1971; April 11, 1973; June 2, 1973; Aug. 21, 1973; Aug. 31, 1973; Jan. 11, 1974; April 9, 1975; July 25, 1978; Aug. 24, 1978; Sept. 26, 1978.

New York Times: Jan. 27, 1970.

Tennessean: June 18, 1967; Aug. 25 and 31, 1967; Oct. 14 and 17, 1967; Dec. 31, 1967; March 5 and 12, 1968; April 17, 1968; May 2 and 30, 1968; June 2 and 11, 1968; July 28 and 31, 1968; Aug. 3, 4, and 14, 1968; Sept. 1, 1968; Nov. 17 and 19, 1968; Jan 22, 1969, Feb. 14, 1969; Aug. 21, 1969; Sept. 18, 1969; Nov. 5, 1969; Dec. 18, 1969; July 26 and 28, 1970; Sept. 10, 1970.

Wall Street Journal: Jan 14, 1969; May 22, 1969; Aug. 22, 1969; Sept. 19, 1969; Dec. 24, 1969; Jan. 26, 1970; March 11 and 16, 1970; Aug. 4, 1970; Sept. 4, 1970; Nov. 9 and 11, 1970; Dec. 23, 1970.

Chapter 14

Interviews:

Pete Bird, T. B. Boyd III, J. C. Bradford Jr., Larry Brinton, Brownlee Currey Jr., Larry Daughtrey, Albie Del Favero, Amon Carter Evans, Sharon Curtis-Flair, Bill Hance, Bill Kovach, Mike Pigott, Roger Shirley, John Seigenthaler, Irby Simpkins, Dr. Mildred Stahlman, Wayne Whitt.

Written sources:

Black, Creed. *Parsonage to Publisher: The Life of Silliman Evans, 1894–1955.* (Unpublished manuscript.)

Flake, Tom. "Nashville Banner." (Essay on file at Nashville Room of Metro Public Library.)

Fontenay, Charles. "Nashville Tennessean." (Essay on file at Nashville Room of Metro Public Library.)

Haynes, B. F. *Sketch of My Life.* Louisville: Pentecostal Publishing Co., 1921.

Nashville Banner: Oct. 26, 1901; March 18, 1903; Nov. 2, 1930; Aug. 12, 13, and 14, 1930; Feb. 28, 1956; April 19, 1967; April 8, 1976; May 2, 1976; May 3, 1976; July 6, 1979.

Nashville Globe: April 12, 1907.

Nashville Scene: June 24, 1999.

Neuharth, Al. *Confessions of an SOB*. New York: Doubleday, 1989.
Tennessean: Jan. 26, 1908; April 26, 1908; Aug. 13, 1930; July 6, 1979.
Tidwell, Mary Louise Lea. *Luke Lea of Tennessee*. Bowling Green, Ohio: Bowling Green State University Popular Press, 1993.
Waller, William. *Nashville from 1900 to 1910*. Nashville: Vanderbilt University Press, 1972.

Two further notes about chapter 14: This is a partial list of sources. Many articles that are cited in other chapters (such as the ones about Minnie Pearl's Fried Chicken) also influenced the tone of chapter 14. Also, the author wrote for the *Tennessean*.

Chapter 15

Interviews:
J. Mitchell Boyd, J. C. Bradford Jr., Greg Burns, Ray Danner, Dan Evins, Taylor Henry, Ted Moats, Jim Neal, Dave Wachtel, Tommy Warren, Steve Watkins, Craig Weichmann.

Shoney's/Captain D's:
Business Week: April 15, 1985; Dec. 25, 1989; Oct. 8, 1990.
Forbes: July 19, 1982; Aug. 2, 1993.
Nashville Banner: Sept. 5, 1960; Feb. 21, 1963; Jan. 20, 1967; June 23, 1969; Oct. 29, 1969; Jan. 17, 1970; Feb. 24, 1970; July 3 and 8, 1970: Jan. 1 and 20, 1971; Feb. 1, 1971; Oct. 19, 1972; Nov. 4, 1972; Dec. 4, 1972; May 19, 1978; March 8, 1979.
Tennessean: Jan. 1, 1959; Jan. 20, 1969; Aug. 15 and 25, 1969; Jan. 11, 1970; Jan. 10, 1971; March 1, 1970; Jan. 4, 1973; June 10, 1992; Oct. 19, 1992; Dec. 18, 1992; Jan. 7, 1993; July 1, 1993; Oct. 29, 1993; Nov. 5, 1993; Dec. 23, 1993; Aug. 19, 1994; Sept. 2 and 9, 1994; Jan. 17, 1995; July 11, 1997; Sept. 20, 1997; March 29, 1998; April 3, 1998; Oct. 21, 1998; Dec. 22, 1998; Jan. 26, 1999.
Wall Street Journal: May 31, 1974; Feb. 20, 1986; June 24, 1988; Sept. 26, 1991; June 3, 1992; Nov. 4, 1992; Dec. 18 and 21, 1992; Jan. 26, 1993; March 10, 1993; July 1, 1993; Jan. 17, 1995; March 31, 1995; April 10, 1995; April 16, 1996; June 17 and 24, 1997.

Cracker Barrel:
Forbes: April 27, 1992.
Nashville Banner: Jan. 1, 1980; July 16, 1981; Sept. 2, 1983; March 17, 1987.
New York Times: Feb. 28, 1991; March 20, 1991; April 9, 1992; Nov. 25, 1992; Oct. 19, 1993; Nov. 24, 1993.
Tennessean: Oct. 23, 1978; Aug. 21, 1983.
Wall Street Journal: Feb. 28, 1991; Feb. 2, 1992; Jan. 26, 1993; Nov. 3, 1993; July 10, 1995.

O'Charley's:
Nashville Banner: March 23, 1971; Feb. 24, 1987; Nov. 6, 1989.
Restaurant Business: Sept. 15, 1998.
Tennessean: March 24, 1988; Oct. 24, 1989; Oct. 30, 1998.

Chapter 16

Interviews:
John Bridges, Cecil Branstetter, Larry Brinton, Hix Clark, Wick Comer, Wilbur Creighton Jr., Maclin Davis Jr., Nancy Draper, Victor Johnson Jr., Victor (Tory)

Johnson III, Lillian Jenkins, Ben Kooch, Robert C. Mathews Jr., Herb Shayne, Jon Shayne, John Seigenthaler, Cal Turner Jr., Albert Werthan, Bernard Werthan Jr.

Werthan:
Advantage: March 1983.
Nashville Banner: Oct. 16, 1970; Nov. 29, 1979; May 20, 1982; May 26, 1986; Jan. 17, 1990; Nov. 4, 1992.
Package Printing: Sept. 1978.
Saco-Lowell Bulletin: Jan. 1955.
Tennessean: June 13, 1949; Feb. 10, 1950; Nov. 4, 1966; Aug. 29, 1968; July 9, 1971; Dec. 24, 1974; May 17, 1982; Jan. 6, 1985; Jan. 13, 1990; July 1, 1990; Feb. 16, 1994.

Aladdin:
Business Week: Dec. 11, 1954.
Consumer's Research Bulletin: July 1949.
Courter, J. W. *Aladdin: The Magic Name in Lamps.* (Self-published article in 1997.)
Detroit Free Press: Nov. 23, 1997.
Nashville!: March 1979.
Nashville Banner: June 25 and 30, 1947; Jan. 11, 1966; May 30, 1980; Aug. 21, 1980; Oct. 1, 1982; July 22, 1983; Aug. 2, 1983; July 26, 1985.
Nashville magazine: Aug. 1963.
Tennessean: May 8, 1947; June 30, 1947; May 5, 1949; June 25, 1952; July 6, 1955; Aug. 23, 1960; Nov. 18, 1960; July 6, 1962; May 25, 1965; Feb. 12, 1967; Oct. 31, 1968; Oct. 11, 1970; Nov. 1, 1970; Dec. 19, 1971; June 28, 1974; Sept. 17, 1976; Sept. 16, 1979; Oct. 20, 1979; May 10, 1981; July 17, 1983; Aug. 3, 1983; April 26, 1985; July 10, 1985; April 6, 1986; July 23, 1989; Oct. 4, 1989; July 7, 1991; March 27, 1992; April 26, 1992; Nov. 11, 1992; Sept. 12, 1993.

Washington:
Nashville Banner: May 13, 1961; Aug. 9, 1973; Oct. 23, 24, 25, 29, and 31, 1973; Nov. 1, 1973; Nov. 12, 1986; March 1, 2, 21, 1988.
Tennessean: June 2, 3, 4, 5, 6, 11, 12, 14, 19, 20, 22, 23, 26, 27, and 28, 1937; July 1, 2, 8, and 12, 1937; Aug. 1, 1937; Aug. 14, 1960; May 16, 1965; Aug. 23, 1965; Dec. 16, 1965; April 27, 1966; Oct. 20, 1969; Feb. 23 and 24, 1973; April 14, 1973; Jan. 9, 1974; Oct. 25, 1973; Jan. 1, 1975; Oct. 1, 1986; March 2 and 6, 1988; May 1, 1988; June 25, 1988; Aug. 25, 1988; Sept. 25, 1988.

Chapter 17

Interviews:
John M. Donnelly Jr., Jim Granberry Jr., Martha Ingram, Tony Martin, Andy Mizell, Ernest Moench Jr., Edward G. Nelson, Phil Pfeffer, Jake Wallace, J. C. Ward Jr.

Written sources:
Business Week: Aug. 9, 1976; Sept. 29, 1997.
Electronic News: Jan. 13, 1986; Jan. 16 and 23, 1989; March 13, 1989.
Forbes: Nov. 1, 1976; Nov. 8, 1993.
Fortune: Sept. 29, 1997.
Nashville Banner: Jan. 30, 1953; April 26, 1963; June 11, 1963; June 14, 1974.

Publisher's Weekly: Aug. 23, 1976; Oct. 25, 1976; Nov. 15, 1976; April 11, 1980; Feb. 5, 1982; May 21, 1982; Feb. 7, 1986; Dec. 5, 1986; July 10, 1987; April 28, 1989; April 6, 1990; Aug. 2, 1991; Nov. 8 and 29, 1991; April 19 and 26, 1993; May 24, 1993; June 14, 1993; Sept. 6, 1993; Nov. 8, 1993; Dec. 6, 1993.

Tennessean: March 24, 1960; Dec. 9, 1962; April 27, 1963; Oct. 17, 1969; June 16, 1995; Sept. 24, 1997.

Wall Street Journal: Oct. 20, 1958; Jan. 27, 1970; March 2, 1970; June 15 and 17, 1970; Nov. 18, 1971; July 11, 1973; Sept. 19, 1973; Oct. 8, 1973; May 31, 1974; June 6, 1974; July 8, 1974; Feb. 20, 1975; June 29, 1976; Nov. 9 and 15, 1977; Dec. 15, 1977.

Chapters 19 and 25

Interviews:
Julie Bell, Phil Bredesen, Larry Coleman, Jim Dalton, Ames Davis, J. D. Elliott, Irwin Eskind, William Ewers, Joel Gordon, Batey Gresham, David A. Fox, Thomas Frist Jr., Joe Hutts, Paula Lovell, Charlie Martin, Robert McClellan, Clayton McWhorter, John Neff, Josh Nemzoff, Jeff Pennington, Richard Ragsdale, Joe Rodgers. I also used tapes of interviews done in the 1980s with Thomas Frist Sr., Lawrence Jackson, and Jack Massey.

Written sources:
Business Week: May 30, 1970.
Forbes: Oct. 15, 1970; Nov. 15, 1976.
Lutz, Sandy and E. Preston Gee. *The For-Profit Health Care Revolution: The Growing Impact of Investor-Owned Health Systems*. Chicago: Irwin Professional Publishing, 1995.
Nashville Banner: Oct. 18, 1968; Nov. 29, 1968; July 25, 1969; Aug. 3, 1969; Nov. 11, 1969; Jan. 13, 1970; June 4, 1970; Aug. 7, 1970; Sept. 5, 1973; Oct. 9, 1973; Aug. 15, 1978; June 7, 1979; April 20 and 21, 1981; Nov. 12 and 15, 1993; Dec. 9, 1993.
New York Times: Feb. 26, 1970.
Tennessean: Dec. 18, 1961; Oct. 3, 1965; Aug. 15, 16, and 21, 1967; May 19, 1968; June 25, 1968; Dec. 12, 1968; June 18, 1969; Oct. 23, 1970; March 5, 1971; Aug. 6, 1971; Aug. 15, 1981; Oct. 5, 1993; Oct. 7, 1993; Oct. 10, 1993; Oct. 17, 1993; Nov. 5, 11, 13, 14, 19, and 23, 1993; Dec. 3 and 9, 1993; Dec. 11, 1993; Feb. 11, 1994; March 4, 1994; Sept. 13, 1994; Jan. 10, 1995; Jan. 12, 1995; Sept. 4, 1997.
Wall Street Journal: March 5, 1969; July 15, 1970; Feb. 24, 1971; Jan. 5, 1972; July 21, 1976; March 11, 1983; Nov. 23, 1984; Oct. 10, 1985; April 10, 1987; April 13, 1987; Nov. 17, 1987; Sept. 16, 1988; Jan. 16, 1992; March 24, 1993; Oct. 5, 1993; July 12, 1994; Oct. 5, 1994; Oct. 11, 1994; May 24, 1995; June 26, 1995; May 1, 1996; June 18, 1996; July 30, 1996; Sept. 9, 1996; March 24, 1997; virtually every day from July 17–Oct 31, 1997.

Chapter 20

Interviews:
Sam Bartholomew Jr., Tom Beasley, Monroe Carell Jr., Floyd Dean, Cal Turner Jr.

Service Merchandise:
Nashville Banner: June 8, 1977; Aug. 25 and 30, 1978; Oct. 25, 1979; June 6, 1980; June 19, 1981; Feb. 9, 1988; July 12, 1989; Sept. 13, 1989; Jan. 11 and 12, 1990; Oct. 9, 1991; Jan 17, 1992.

Tennessean: April 27, 1972; Dec. 6, 1984; Jan. 26, 1988; May 26, 1988; Sept. 11 and 20, 1988; March 29, 1989; May 8 and 10, 1989; July 7, 1989; Dec. 25, 1990; Dec. 31, 1991; March 12, 1992; April 18, 1992; June 19, 1992; July 8 and 9, 1992; Jan. 6 and 27, 1993; Jan. 27, 1994; June 20, 1994.

Dollar General:
Discount Store News: May 24, 1999.
Fortune: July 6, 1998.
Tennessean: Aug. 27, 1995.
Wall Street Journal: March 20, 1998.

Corrections Corporation of America:
Nashville Banner: Aug. 2, 1984; Sept. 12, 1985; Oct. 24, 1985; Oct. 8, 1990.
Newsweek: May 7, 1984.
New York Times: Feb. 18, 1985; Aug. 14, 1994.
Tennessean: May 29, 1983; Sept. 15, 1985; Nov. 12 and 24, 1985; Oct. 3, 1986; July 11, 1994; Dec. 11, 1996; March 31, 1998.

Central Parking:
Investor's Daily Business: Sept. 24, 1996.
Tennessean: May 27, 1996; Dec. 10, 1996; Nov. 25, 1998; July 15, 1999.

Chapter 21

Interviews:
Jerry Benefield, Maclin Davis Jr., Bruce Dobie, Fred Harris, Richard "Skip" Lafauve, Bill Long, James Pratt, Marvin Runyon.

Nissan:
Nashville Banner: July 16 and 30, 1980; Sept. 18, 19, 20, and 23, 1980; Feb. 3, 4, and 5, 1981.
Tennessean: April 17 and 18, 1980; Sept. 19, 21, 29, and 30, 1980; Feb. 1, 1981.
Wall Street Journal: Jan. 24 and 29, 1980; Feb. 19 and 28, 1980; April 7, 10, and 16, 1980; May 16, 1980; June 13, 1980; Sept. 19, 1980; Oct. 30 and 31, 1980; April 15, 1981; Aug. 4, 1981; Sept. 14, 1981; Jan. 14, 1982; March 1, 1982; Feb. 24, 1983; March 23, 1983; Feb. 2, 1984; May 14, 1984; Dec. 13, 1984; May 22, 1989; June 15, 1989; July 25 and 28, 1989.

Saturn:
Nashville Banner: July 10, 18, 25, 26, 27, 29, 30, and 31, 1985; Aug. 2, 5, 6, 7, and 8, 1985; Dec. 19, 1985.
Sherman, Joe. *In the Rings of Saturn*. New York: Oxford University Press, 1994.
Tennessean: July 9, 10, 14, 1985; Dec. 22 and 29, 1985; Sept. 5, 9, and 10, 1998; Oct. 7 and 15, 1998; Feb. 4 and 26, 1999; March 5, 1999; April 1, 1999; May 1995; Aug. 7, 1996; Aug. 25, 1998; Dec. 15, 1998.
Wall Street Journal: May 14, 1984; Nov. 29, 1984; Jan. 9, 10, 11, and 28, 1985; March 22, 1985; June 6, 1985; July 25, 29, and 30, 1985; Aug. 2 and 5, 1985; June 3 and 6, 1986; Aug. 7, 1986; Sept. 19, 1986; Oct. 30, 1986; Nov. 6 and 25, 1986; July 9 and 31, 1990; Nov. 1, 1990; Dec. 4, 1990; May 24, 1991; Oct. 11, 1991; Nov. 11, 1991; June 16, 1993; Aug. 11 and 12, 1993; Dec. 16, 1993; Jan. 6, 1994; Feb. 18, 1994; March 18, 1994; April 26, 1994; June 17, 1994; April 18, 1995; July 26 and 27, 1999; June 5, 12, and 18, 1999; July 9, 1999; Aug. 6 and 19, 1999.

Chapter 22

Interviews:
Tom Adkinson, Nelson Andrews, Phil Bredesen, Terry Clements, C. A. (Neil) Craig, Mike Dimond, Richard L. Fulton, John Hobbs, Velvet Hunter, Martha Ingram, Waylon Jennings, Buddy Killen, Paula Lovell, Phil Pfeffer, Frances Preston, Walter Robinson Jr., Irving Waugh, Earl W. (Bud) Wendell, David K. (Pat) Wilson.

Written sources:
Nashville Banner: April 27, 1966; April 1, 1967; Oct. 13, 1969; Jan. 2 and 3, 1994; June 21, 1994; Oct. 7, 1994.
Newsweek: Nov. 13, 1954.
Tennessean: June 20, 1937; Feb. 15, 1966; Jan. 8, 1967; May 3, 1967; June 23, 1967; Aug. 9, 22, 27, and 30, 1967; Sept. 15, 18, 28, and 29, 1967; Sept. 28, 1969; May 21, 1972; June 11, 1989; Feb. 10, 1991; Dec. 17, 1991; May 30, 1994; May 5, 1996.

Chapter 23

Interviews:
Nelson Andrews, Lucius Burch III, Jim Caden, Bruce Dobie, Townes Duncan, David Emery, Pat Emery, Criswell Freeman, Richard L. Fulton, Charles Kane, Jim Loyd, Tony Martin, Robert C. Mathews Jr., Ted Moats, Alex Palmer, J. Bradbury Reed, Joe Rodgers, Barbara Massey Rogers.

Written sources:
Atlanta Journal-Constitution: Sept. 7, 1986.
Business Week: Sept. 20, 1976.
Forbes: Sept. 24, 1984; Dec. 15, 1986.
Nashville Banner: Sept. 2 and 10, 1986.
Nashville Scene: Feb. 22, 1990.
Tennessean: Sept. 4, 5, and 28, 1986; Feb. 16, 1990; May 6, 1990; Aug. 22, 1990; April 20, 21, 22, 23, 25, and 28, 1991; Sept. 10, 1991; Oct. 16, 1991.
Wall Street Journal: Feb. 7, 1989; Aug. 15 and 21, 1989.

Conclusion

Interviews:
J. C. Bradford Jr., Phil Bredesen, Eric Crafton, Lady Jackson, Butch Spyridon, Byron Trauger.

The author had firsthand knowledge of most of the events described in the conclusion resulting from his work as a reporter for the *Tennessean* from 1993 to 1998. However, parts of the account of the Oilers negotiations with Nashville came from the February 29, 1996, issue of the *Nashville Scene*.

Buntin, Dan, 4
Buntin, Thomas, 270
Bunyan, John, 347
Burch, Lucius, III, 371, 422, 443
Burkesville, Ky., 44
Burnett, Carol, 399
Burns, Greg, 292–93
Burton, Andrew Mizell (A. M.), 68–70, 74, 76, 80, 82, 165, 216–18, **221**
Burton, J. Booker, 69
Burton, Nelson, 69
Burton Hills, 419
Bush, William G., 16
Bush Brick Company, 17, 127
Business Journal, 276
Business Week, 137, 166, 182, 190–91, 227, 255, 257, 266, 323
Butler, Candler, 182
Buttorff, Henry, 1, 10, 17, 86, 114, **2**
Buttrick, George, 326

C&S Sovran, 416
Caden, Jim, 418
Cadillac, 390
Cain, John, 97
Cain-Sloan, 199, 163
Caldwell, Ashley, 63
Caldwell, Frances Hill (Mrs. Wentworth Sr.), 97
Caldwell, James E., 5, 84–87, 91, 97, 104, 110–11, 194, **85**
Caldwell, Rogers, 56, 91–94, 96–97, 100–102, 104–7, 217, 248
Caldwell, Wentworth, Jr., 40, 54, 62–64
Caldwell, Wentworth, Sr., 97
Caldwell and Co., 56, 91–94, 96–97, 100–102, 104–6, 108, 157–58, 208, 266, 296, **93, 95**
Caldwell and Company: A Southern Financial Empire, 94
Caldwell & Company Building, 112, 209
California-Western States Life Insurance Co., 226–27
Calsonic, 385
Camden, N.J., 347
Camel Caravan, 140
Cammack, Bill, 158, 162–63
Campbell, Glen, 430
Campbell, Stewart, 206

Camp Campbell, 118
Camp Forrest, 118
Canal Bank and Trust Co., 106
Candler, Warren, 23
Cannon, Newton, 201
Cannon, Sarah. *See* Minnie Pearl
Cantrell, Maymee, 380
Capital Bank & Trust, 457
Capital Blend coffee, 45
Capital City Bank, 210
Capitol Hill Redevelopment Plan, 115, 223
Capitol Mall Redevelopment Area, 176
Capitol Records, 146, 154–55, 430, 432–35
Captain D's, 166, 282, 285, 288
Carell, Monroe, Jr., 374–77, 417
Carell, Monroe, Sr., 374–75
Carlucci, Frank, 139
Carolina Panthers, 457
Carmack, Edward, 262–63
Carmichael, Stokely, 272
Carmine's, 291
Carnegie Hall, 155
Carrollton, Ga., 173
Carter, Amon, 269
Carter, DeWitt, 96
Carter, Jimmy, 139, 259, 321, 333, 379, 431
Carter, Joel, 169
Carter County, 120
Carter Sisters, 148
Carthage, Tenn., 168, 191, 354
Cash, Johnny, 397, 425–27
Cason, Albert, 257
Cassidy, Hopalong, 304
Castalian Springs, Tenn., 68–69, 76
Castalian Springs Barn Dance Orchestra, 76
Castle Recording Laboratory, 145–46, 151, 202
Castner-Knott, 107, 199, 263
Caudill, Noble, 172–73, 444
C. B. Commercial Real Estate Group, 307, 318, 415
CBRL, 291
CBS records, 426
CBS-TV, 451

Cedarwood publishing, 149, 151, 153–54
Celina, Tenn., 12
Centennial Boulevard, 190, 315, 339
Centennial Club, 4
Centennial Company, 8
Centennial Tower, 336–37
Centennial Hospital, 11
Centennial Park, 215, 217, 351
Centerville, Tenn., 168, 192
Central Bank & Trust, 96, 102, 105–6
Central Baptist Association of Texas, 29
Central Parking, 167, 363, 374–77, 455
Century Plaza Hotel, 398
Chamber of Commerce Office Building, 73
Chamberlain, David, 193
Chambers, John, 258
Chambers, Richard, 417
Chaney, Ari, 309
Chapel Hill, Tenn., 174
Charles, Ray, 155
Charleston, S.C., 2, 165, 314
Charleston, Va., 26
Charleston, W. Va., 279
Charlotte, N. C., 113, 120, 159, 375–76, 416, 423, 458
Charlotte Avenue, 30, 62, 88, 223, 310
Charlotte Pike, 11, 112, 188, 254
Charter Medical Corp., 443
Charter Oil Company, 226
Chase & Sanborn, 51
Chase Manhattan Bank, 161, 346
Chase National Bank, 161
Chattanooga, Tenn., 6, 18, 29, 54, 58, 66–67, 113, 158, 160, 165, 180, 190, 210, 239, 354, 360, 364, 402–3
Chattanooga News, the, 3
Chattanooga Times, 105
Cheatham County, 223, 398
Cheatham Place, 112
Check Printers Inc., 297, 300
Cheek, Christopher Tompkins (C. T.), 44, 49

Cheek, Frank, 51
Cheek, Jim, 51
Cheek, Jim, Jr., 169, 178
Cheek, Joel Owsley, 5, 44–47, 49, 51–52, 56–57, 460
Cheek, Leon, 51
Cheek, Leslie, 49, 52, 54
Cheek, Newman, 56
Cheek, Robert, 51, 56
Cheek, Will, Sr., 52
Cheek, Will T., Jr., 52–53
Cheek & Norton, 45
Cheek-Neal Coffee Co., 39, 47–49, 51–52, 89, 220, 367, **50**
Chemical Bank, 158
Cherokee Indian Reservation, 404
Cherokee Life, 214
Cherokee Photo Finishers, 165
Cherry, Wendell, 356
Cherry Street, 4
Chestnut Street, 15, 146
Chevrolet, 390
Chicago Exposition of 1893, 7–8
Chicago, Ill., 6–7, 12, 18, 35, 51, 76, 92, 111, 135, 140, 145–46, 154, 198, 301, 303, 305, 311, 317, 320, 326–27, 344, 364–65, 413, 415
Chicago Tribune, 101
Christian Advocate, the, 4, 25, 328
Christian-Moerlein Brewers, 16
Christianson, Chip, 418
Christie, Agatha, 349
Church, Verne, 303
Church of Christ Foundation, 311–13
Church Street, 3, 27, 37, 42, 44, 46, 73, 86, 97, 146, 196, 198, 202, 215, 235, 237, 239, 267, 377, 412–13
Churchill, Winston, 309
Cincinnati, Ohio, 6, 12, 15–16, 20, 39, 54, 58, 69, 180, 295, 326, 364
CIGNA HealthCare, 419, 440
Citicorp, 367, 446
Citizens & Southern Bank, 416
Citizens Bank, 264
Citizen's Bank & Trust, 104
Citizen's Fidelity Bank & Trust, 211
Citizen's Savings Bank & Trust, 88–89

490

492

495

496